90 0508199 1

WITHDRAWN
FROM
UNIVERSITY OF PLYMOUTH
LIBRARY SERVICES

Charles Seale-Hayne Library
University of Plymouth
(01752) 588 588
LibraryandITenquiries@plymouth.ac.uk

PERSPECTIVES ON HUMAN MEMORY AND COGNITIVE AGING: ESSAYS IN HONOUR OF FERGUS CRAIK

PERSPECTIVES ON HUMAN MEMORY AND COGNITIVE AGING:

Essays in Honour of Fergus Craik

edited by
Moshe Naveh-Benjamin
Ben-Gurion University of the Negev
Morris Moscovitch
University of Toronto
Henry L. Roediger, III
Washington University in St. Louis

USA	Publishing Office:	PSCYHOLOGY PRESS *A member of the Taylor & Francis Group* 29 West 35th Street New York, NY 10001 Tel: (212) 216-7800 Fax: (212) 564-7854
	Distribution Center:	PSYCHOLOGY PRESS *A member of the Taylor & Francis Group* 7625 Empire Drive Florence, KY 41042 Tel: 1-800-634-7064 Fax: 1-800-248-4724
UK		PSYCHOLOGY PRESS *A member of the Taylor & Francis Group* 27 Church Road Hove E. Sussex, BN3 2FA Tel: +44 (0) 1273 207411 Fax: +44 (0) 1273 205612

PERSPECTIVES ON HUMAN MEMORY AND COGNITIVE AGING: Essays in Honour of Fergus Craik

Copyright © 2001 Psychology Press. All rights reserved. Printed in the United States of America. Except as permitted under the United States Copyright Act of 1976, no part of this publication may be reproduced or distributed in any form or by any means, or stored in a database or retrieval system, without prior written permission of the publisher.

1 2 3 4 5 6 7 8 9 0

Printed by Edwards Brothers, Ann Arbor, MI, 2001.
Cover design by Nancy Abbott
Color illustration: "Reverend Robert Walker Skating at Duddingston Loch" by Sir Henry Raeburn. Owned by the National Gallery of Scotland.

A CIP catalog record for this book is available from the British Library.
∞ The paper in this publication meets the requirements of the ANSI Standard Z39.48-1984 (Permanence of Paper).

Library of Congress Cataloging-in-Publication Data

Perspectives on human memory and cognitive aging : essays in honour of Fergus Craik /
[edited] by Moshe Naveh-Benjamin, Morris Moscovitch, and Henry Roediger.
    p. cm.
   Includes bibliographical references and index.
    ISBN 1-84169-040-6 (alk. paper) ✓
    1. Cognition—Age factors. 2. Memory—Age factors. 3. Aging—Psychological
aspects. I. Craik, Fergus I. M. II. Naveh-Benjamin, Moshe. III. Moscovitch, Morris,
1945- IV. Roediger, Henry L.

BF724.55.C63 P475 2001
153.1'2—dc21

2001048285

ISBN: 1-84169-040-6 (case)

CONTENTS

UNIVERSITY OF PLYMOUTH

Item No. 9005081991

Date 1 3 MAY 2002 Z

Class No. 153.12 PER

Cont. No.

PLYMOUTH LIBRARY

Preface   IX
List of Contributors   XI
Fergus Craik: A Biographical Sketch   XVI

PART I. LEVELS OF PROCESSING AND MEMORY THEORY

Chapter 1   Part I Introduction: Levels of Processing   3
             Michael J. Watkins

Chapter 2   Does Memory Encoding Exist?   6
             Endel Tulving

Chapter 3   Levels of Processing: Some Unanswered Questions   28
             Henry L. Roediger, III and David A. Gallo

Chapter 4   Levels of Processing: Validating the Concept   48
             Boris M. Velichkovsky

Chapter 5   Involuntary Levels-of-Processing Effects in Perceptual
             and Conceptual Priming   71
             John M. Gardiner, Alan Richardson-Klavehn, Cristina Ramponi,
             and Barbara M. Brooks

Chapter 6   Text Processing: Memory Representations Mediate
             Fluent Reading   83
             Betty Ann Levy

Chapter 7   Commentary: Levels of Processing and Memory Theory   99
             Robert S. Lockhart

PART II. WORKING MEMORY AND ATTENTION

Chapter **8**   **Part II Introduction: Encoding, Retrieving, and Aging**   105
Michael T. Turvey

a. WORKING MEMORY

Chapter **9**   **Levels of Working Memory**   111
Alan D. Baddeley

Chapter **10**   **Deconstructing Retrieval Mode**   124
Tim Shallice

Chapter **11**   **Levels of Processing in Selective Attention and Inhibition: Age Differences and Similarities**   135
Joan M. McDowd

Chapter **12**   **Working Memory and Aging**   148
Denise C. Park and Trey Hedden

Chapter **13**   **Commentary: Working Memory, Long-Term Memory, and the Effects of Aging**   161
Meredyth Daneman

b. ATTENTION AT ENCODING AND RETRIEVAL

Chapter **14**   **Working-With-Memory and Cognitive Resources: A Component-Process Account of Divided Attention and Memory**   171
Morris Moscovitch, Myra Fernandes, and Angela Troyer

Chapter **15**   **The Effects of Divided Attention on Encoding Processes: Underlying Mechanisms**   193
Moshe Naveh-Benjamin

Chapter **16**   **The Attentional Demands and Attentional Control of Encoding and Retrieval**   208
Nicole D. Anderson

Chapter **17**   **Commentary: Dividing Attention to Study the Resource Demands of Memory Processes**   226
Colin M. MacLeod

PART III. AGE-RELATED CHANGES IN MEMORY AND COGNITION

Chapter **18**   **Part III Introduction: Toward a Taxonomy of Research
on Memory and Aging**   237
Aaron S. Benjamin

Chapter **19**   **Forms of Bias: Age-Related Differences in Memory
and Cognition**   240
Larry L. Jacoby, Elizabeth J. Marsh, and Patrick O. Dolan

Chapter **20**   **Aging, Cognition, and Health**   253
Lars-Göran Nilsson and Hedvig Söderlund

Chapter **21**   **Source Memory, Aging, and the Frontal Lobes**   265
Elizabeth L. Glisky

Chapter **22**   **The Broader Context of Craik's Self-Initiated
Processing Hypothesis**   277
Timothy A. Salthouse

Chapter **23**   **Inhibitory Control, Environmental Support,
and Self-Initiated Processing in Aging**   286
Lynn Hasher, Simon T. Tonev, Cindy Lustig, and Rose T. Zacks

Chapter **24**   **Sensation, Cognition, and Levels of Processing in Aging**   298
Bruce A. Schneider

Chapter **25**   **Commentary: Some Observations on the Self-Initiated
Processing Hypothesis**   315
Leah L. Light

PART IV. NEUROSCIENCE PERSPECTIVES ON MEMORY AND AGING

Chapter **26**   **Part IV Introduction: How the Study of Brain Function Is
Influenced by the Function of Craik's Brain**   323
Anthony Randal McIntosh

Chapter **27**   **Age-Related Changes in the Functional Neuroanatomy
of Memory**   325
Cheryl L. Grady

Chapter **28**   **Aging: Not an Escarpment, but Many Different Slopes**   334
Donald T. Stuss and Malcolm A. Binns

Chapter **29**   **Episodic Memory Impairment in Schizophrenia:
A View from Cognitive Psychopathology**   348
*Pierre Vidailhet, Bruce K. Christensen, Jean-Marie Danion,
and Shitij Kapur*

Chapter **30**   **Memory Distortion and Aging**   362
Wilma Koutstaal and Daniel L. Schacter

Chapter **31**   **Commentary: Levels of Neuroprocessing**   384
Gordon Winocur

Author Index   393

Subject Index   411

Figure 16.1   425

Figure 27.1   426

PREFACE

This volume evolved from a conference held at the University of Toronto in May 2000 in honor of Fergus Craik's retirement from the University of Toronto.

In light of Gus Craik's important contributions to the study of memory and of cognitive aging, we felt that a high-level scientific meeting, where theoretical perspectives and empirical findings related to Craik's scientific contributions could be presented and discussed in both formal and informal settings, would be an appropriate way to celebrate the occasion. While working with others on organizing the event, we realized the extent of Gus Craik's social network and friendships. When we approached others regarding this idea, the response was overwhelmingly positive. One example of this is the program for the conference: Of the 31 people who were invited, all readily agreed to participate and no one declined the invitation. Many of these people came from afar: Alan Baddeley, Tim Shallice, and John Gardiner from England; Lars-Goran Nilsson from Sweden; and Boris Velichkovsky from Germany. Others came from different places in the United States and Canada. The two-day meeting proved very successful and the presentations were interesting and provocative. Each session was attended by 75–150 people, among whom were Craik's colleagues, friends, research associates, students, and former students.

During his 35-year career, Craik's significant theoretical and empirical research has led to his recognition as one of the world's leaders in human memory and cognitive aging research. His conceptual analysis and empirical findings have greatly contributed to the psychological study of memory and have also had a strong impact on the related fields of neuropsychology, gerontology, and education. A biographical sketch follows this preface.

The organization of this book is based largely on the sessions of the conference. The goal of this volume is to reflect on the past and to evaluate the current status of the various issues that have been of interest to Craik throughout his career. Another, no less important goal, is to discuss future directions of concepts and ideas related to human memory and cognitive aging.

The book is divided into four parts. Part I includes chapters related to memory theory and the levels-of-processing framework. The second part addresses issues related to working memory and attention. Parts III and IV are devoted to issues of cognitive aging, with Part IV also incorporating neuroscience perspectives. Each part is introduced by the moderator of the corresponding conference session and concludes with a discussant's chapter. Terry Picton moderated a session but could not contribute a chapter; Aaron Benjamin replaced him and wrote the introductory chapter to Part III.

We would like to thank all the people who helped make this symposium a reality, in particular, Pat Bennett, Bob Lockhart, Allison Sekuler, Ian Spence, Jennie Sawula, and Linda Mamelak of the Psychology Department at the University of Toronto, as well as Jill Kester, Alan Castel, Carol Okamoto, and Aaron Benjamin from the Craik lab. Thanks also go to the Department of Psychology, the Connaught Committee, and the Faculty of Arts and Science at the University of Toronto, and to the Rotman Research Institute and Psychology Press, who generously supported the conference.

We believe that this collection of essays is a fitting tribute to Fergus Craik. It represents the cutting edge of research and thinking on some of the most fundamental issues in human memory and cognitive aging. This collection also represents the esteem and high regard in which his colleagues, peers, and students hold Gus, and we present this volume to him with appreciation and affection.

Moshe Naveh-Benjamin
Ben-Gurion University of the Negev

Morris Moscovitch
University of Toronto

Henry L. Roediger, III
Washington University in St. Louis

CONTRIBUTORS

Participants in the meeting in honor of Fergus Craik.

Nicole D. Anderson
Princess Margaret Hospital, University Health Network
Toronto, Ontario, Canada

Alan D. Baddeley
Department of Experimental Psychology
University of Bristol
Bristol, England

Aaron S. Benjamin
Department of Psychology, University of Illinois, Urbana
Champaign, Illinois, USA

Malcolm A. Binns
Rotman Research Institute, Baycrest Centre for Geriatric Care
University of Toronto
Toronto, Ontario, Canada

Barbara M. Brooks
University of East London
London, England

Bruce K. Christensen
Centre for Addiction and Mental Health and
University of Toronto
Toronto, Ontario, Canada

Meredyth Daneman
Department of Psychology, Erindale College
University of Toronto at Mississauga
Toronto, Ontario, Canada

Jean-Marie Danion
Fédération de Psychiatrie, Hôpital Civil
and Unité INSERM 405
Strasbourg, France

Patrick O. Dolan
Department of Psychology, Washington University in St. Louis
St. Louis, Missouri, USA

Myra Fernandes
Department of Psychology, University of Toronto
Toronto, Ontario, Canada

David A. Gallo
Department of Psychology, Washington University in St. Louis
St. Louis, Missouri, USA

John M. Gardiner
School of Cognitive & Computing Sciences, University of Sussex
Brighton, England

Elizabeth L. Glisky
Department of Psychology, University of Arizona
Tucson, Arizona, USA

Cheryl L. Grady
Rotman Research Institute, Baycrest Centre for Geriatric Care
Toronto, Ontario, Canada

Lynn Hasher
Department of Psychology, University of Toronto
Toronto, Ontario, Canada

Trey Hedden
Department of Psychology, University of Michigan
Ann Arbor, Michigan, USA

Larry L. Jacoby
Department of Psychology, Washington University in St. Louis
St. Louis, Missouri, USA

Shitij Kapur
Centre for Addiction and Mental Health
Toronto, Ontario, Canada

Wilma Koutstaal
Department of Psychology
University of Reading
Reading, England

Betty Ann Levy
Department of Psychology, McMaster University
Hamilton, Ontario, Canada

Leah L. Light
Department of Psychology, Pitzer College
Claremont, California, USA

Robert S. Lockhart
Department of Psychology, University of Toronto
Toronto, Ontario, Canada

Cindy Lustig
Department of Experimental Psychology, Duke University
Durham, North Carolina, USA

Colin M. MacLeod
Division of Life Sciences, University of Toronto at Scarborough
Scarborough, Ontario, Canada

Elizabeth J. Marsh
Department of Psychology, Washington University in St. Louis
St. Louis, Missouri, USA

Joan M. McDowd
OT Education, Kansas University Medical Center
Kansas City, Kansas, USA

Anthony Randal McIntosh
Rotman Research Institute, Baycrest Centre for Geriatric Care
Department of Psychology, University of Toronto
Toronto, Ontario, Canada

Morris Moscovitch
Department of Psychology, University of Toronto
Toronto, Ontario, Canada

Moshe Naveh-Benjamin
Department of Behavioral Sciences
Ben-Gurion University of the Negev
Beer-Sheva, Israel

Lars-Göran Nilsson
Department of Psychology, Stockholm University
Stockholm, Sweden

Denise C. Park
Department of Psychology, University of Michigan
Ann Arbor, Michigan, USA

Cristina Ramponi
MRC Cognition and Brain Sciences Unit
Cambridge, England

Alan Richardson-Klavehn
Goldsmiths College, University of London
London, England

Henry L. Roediger, III
Department of Psychology, Washington University in St. Louis
St. Louis, Missouri, USA

Timothy A. Salthouse
Department of Psychology, University of Virginia
Charlottesville, Virginia, USA

Daniel L. Schacter
Department of Psychology, Harvard University
Cambridge, Massachusetts, USA

Bruce A. Schneider
Department of Psychology, Erindale College
University of Toronto at Mississauga
Toronto, Ontario, Canada

Tim Shallice
Institute of Cognitive Neuroscience, University College London
London, England

Hedvig Söderlund
Department of Psychology, Stockholm University
Stockholm, Sweden

Donald T. Stuss
Rotman Research Institute, Baycrest Centre for Geriatric Care
Toronto, Ontario, Canada

Simon T. Tonev
Department of Experimental Psychology, Duke University
Durham, North Carolina, USA

Angela Troyer
Rotman Research Institute, Baycrest Centre for Geriatric Care
and Department of Psychology, University of Toronto
Toronto, Ontario, Canada

Endel Tulving
Rotman Research Institute, Baycrest Centre for Geriatric Care
Department of Psychology, University of Toronto
Toronto, Ontario, Canada

Michael T. Turvey
Center for the Ecological Study of Perception and Action
Department of Psychology, University of Connecticut - Storrs
Storrs, Connecticut, USA

Boris M. Velichkovsky
Department of Psychology, Dresden University of Technology
Dresden, Germany

Pierre Vidailhet
Fédération de Psychiatrie, Hôpital Civil
Strasbourg, France

Michael J. Watkins
Department of Psychology, Rice University
Houston, Texas, USA

Gordon Winocur
Rotman Research Institute, Baycrest Centre for Geriatric Care
Toronto, Ontario, Canada

Rose T. Zacks
Department of Psychology, Michigan State University
East Lansing, Michigan, USA

FERGUS CRAIK:
A BIOGRAPHICAL SKETCH

Fergus Craik was born in Edinburgh, Scotland on April 17, 1935. He spent the first year and a half of his life there, mostly romping nude in the Botanical Gardens, if the photographic record is to be believed, and then moved with his parents to Lockerbie, a small market town in the southwest of Scotland, where his father was appointed manager of the local Bank of Scotland.

Craik spent a very happy childhood in Lockerbie, attending Lockerbie Academy and roaming the woods, fields, and streams of the surrounding countryside. His parents were ambitious for him and so sent him to an excellent high school in Edinburgh (George Watson's Boys' College) at the age of 12. His best subjects there were English, physics, and biological sciences, so a career in medicine seemed to be a reasonable option. He was accepted as a medical student at the University of Edinburgh, but his experience in the medical school was not a happy one. He enjoyed studying physiology and was intrigued by neurology and psychiatry, but found the catalogues of relations in anatomy boring and hard to master. He also found that he rather disliked the company of sick people—not a good sign in a potential physician! So, to everyone's relief, he switched to the study of psychology and found that much more congenial.

Craik was introduced to experimental psychology in his final year at the university, when he carried out his undergraduate thesis project on the effect of rate of information processing on time perception. The experiment was inspired by reading George Miller's paper, "The Magical Number 7, Plus or Minus 2," and in it several groups of subjects made absolute perceptual judgments of varying complexity and then later judged how long they had been engaged on the task. The results showed a nice function relating rate of processing to subjectively experienced duration. In addition, the experiment conveyed an unexpected benefit: It was apparently acceptable to approach young women in the common room and ask if they would participate in a psychology experiment. Craik tested 120 participants in the study, possibly the largest scale study of his career! But he did the right thing and married one of them, his wife Anne.

The Edinburgh Department of Psychology also introduced Craik to some exciting ideas in theoretical psychology. Professor James Drever was head of department, and he ran a seminar group that read and discussed the work of Hebb, Bindra, Gibson, and the ethologists. Ian Hunter taught a course on memory and learning, which also interested Craik, although he was more captured by theoretical notions in the areas of attention and perception.

After graduating from Edinburgh in 1960, Craik accepted a position at the Medical Research Council's unit for research into aspects of the aging process. This MRC unit was attached to the Department of Psychology at the University of Liverpool and was directed by Dr. Alastair Heron. The research group was in some ways the successor to Alan Welford's experimental group in Cambridge, although the work in Liverpool was oriented more to the solution of occupational aspects of aging. Craik's project was to study age-related changes in confidence and decision making, first using Rotter's level of aspiration theory and then using the framework of signal detection theory. This series of experiments, directed first by Alastair Heron and then by Dennis Bromley, became the core of Craik's Ph.D. dissertation at the University of Liverpool. He obtained the degree in 1965.

One advantage of being in the MRC system of research units was the easy access to other MRC research groups. The main group of interest to Craik was Donald Broadbent's Applied Research Unit at Cambridge, so he made several trips to Cambridge while at Liverpool, spending time with such leaders of British experimental psychology as Broadbent and Conrad and also with the bright and creative younger set: Alan Baddeley, John Morton, and Pat Rabbitt. These trips and interactions swung Craik's scientific interests strongly over to the emerging cognitive psychology of information processing, attention, and short-term memory.

Liverpool was a lively place in the early 1960s. The Beatles had left town by then, but there were many other groups playing in the Cavern and elsewhere. Craik's own musical tastes ran more to small group jazz, and he played electric guitar in a would-be-Jim-Hallish sort of way with the university jazz band. He also rose through the ranks to the giddy heights of being president of the Inter-University Jazz Federation—his first taste of administration and public office! But day-to-day life in Liverpool was more about analyzing the most recent experiment, conferring with colleagues such as Norman Wetherick, Ann Davies, and Terry Rick, having a pint in one of the many warm and cheerful pubs, and settling into married life with Anne and their first child Lindsay, born in 1963.

Craik was appointed to his first faculty position in 1965. The post was a lectureship at Birkbeck College, part of the University of London, and he was there from 1965 until 1971. Birkbeck specialized in part-time evening students who worked during the day and were older than the typical university undergraduate. There was great demand for places in psychology in the London area, so those accepted were very bright and highly motivated. At first, this made teaching rather daunting, but Craik adjusted to the new level and enjoyed his teaching and research into problems of attention and short-term memory. Peter Venables was the research professor at Birkbeck, and his work on the neurophysiology of schizophrenia had a big effect on Craik's thinking. Clearly, normal aging is not the same as mild schizophrenia, but there are parallels in the processing deficits and in the methods used to study them. There was a good deal of interaction with neighboring colleges and hospitals too, and Craik had his first exposure to theories and findings in neuropsychology through many conversations with Tim Shallice and Elizabeth Warrington. Craik was extremely fortunate in his graduate students at Birkbeck. The four people he supervised—Vernon Gregg, Kim Kirsner, Michael Watkins, and John Gardiner—all subsequently made their mark as top-class researchers and scholars.

Life in London in the 1960s was fast-paced and exciting. Teaching and research work at Birkbeck College was stimulating but also quite stressful at times, so Craik was glad to return each evening to the new family home in Richmond. Weekends provided the opportunity for walks by the river and in the park, socializing with friends, visits to local pubs, and outings with Lindsay and, now, Neil, born in 1965.

In 1967, Craik was invited to a NATO-sponsored meeting on memory held in Cambridge. The meeting was organized in part by Donald Broadbent and also involved such international figures as Arthur Melton, Donald Norman, and Endel Tulving. The conference lasted 2 weeks and afforded exciting insights into current theories and methods in the study of memory. Craik was eager to spend a year at a North American university and was very pleased when Tulving offered him an opportunity at the University of Toronto in 1968–1969. At that time, memory research at the University of Toronto centered on the work of Endel Tulving, Bennet Murdock, and their students, who held a weekly seminar on memory under the awe-inspiring rubric of the "Ebbinghaus Empire." The graduate students and postdocs were a lively lot, and Craik benefited greatly from talks with Bob Lockhart, Steve Madigan, Betty Ann Levy, and many others. The Craik family returned to London at the end of the year, but both research and family life had been pleasant in Toronto, so they moved back to Toronto on a more permanent basis in 1971.

Craik took up the position of associate professor of psychology at the Erindale Campus of the University of Toronto in the fall of 1971 and was in the Department of Psychology, first at Erindale and later on the St. George Campus, until he retired from the university in June 2000. His first few years in Toronto were dominated by the development of the levels-of-processing framework for memory research. Anne Treisman had developed a theory of attention in the 1960s that involved levels of perceptual analysis running from pure sensory levels to later lexical and semantic levels. It seemed to Craik that memory encoding could be seen as the products of these various analyses, that *memory* and *attention* are thus intimately intertwined, and that the later "deeper" analyses would yield encoded representations that were longer lasting. On returning to Toronto in 1971, he was delighted to find that his friend Bob Lockhart was thinking along very similar lines, so they decided to join forces to write an article that had been invited by Endel Tulving, who was editor of the *Journal of Verbal Learning* at that time. The Craik–Lockhart article on levels of processing appeared in December 1972 and owes much to the editorial suggestions of Tulving, who subsequently collaborated with Craik on a series of related experimental tests of the "levels" ideas. The resulting empirical paper was published in 1975.

The next 10 years were productive ones for the Craik lab at Erindale. The young Larry Jacoby visited for a year, and his creative theorizing had a major impact on Craik's thinking. The views of Morris Moscovitch at Erindale and Paul Kolers at the downtown campus were other major influences. The lab (referred to as "The

LMR" for obscure reasons) was lively both scientifically and socially, with lab discussions often ending up in one of the local pubs. Jan Rabinowitz, Betty Glisky, Leslie Cake, and Gigi Tiedemann were among the personnel at that time. Craik's interests also turned back to aging research; he contributed the chapter on memory to the first edition of the Birren and Schaie *Handbook*, and this return to the literature on aging suggested a number of experiments that were subsequently carried out in collaboration with Mark Byrd, Joan McDowd, and others. The Erindale lab also attracted a number of outstanding postdoctoral fellows, including Ronald Fisher, Eileen Simon, Brian Ackerman, Mary Gick, and Robin Morris. These and other visitors provided stimulating company and were the source of new ideas and new research directions.

Like any involved researcher, Craik served on the editorial boards of several journals over the years. From 1980–1984, he edited the *Journal of Verbal Learning and Verbal Behavior*—JVLVB in the popular parlance. He half expected that his editorship would encourage a wave of articles on aging, but the numbers for his 4-year tenure were zero, zero, one, and two—a trend perhaps?! He also spent 2 separate years at Stanford around this time: 1977–1978 as a visitor in the psychology department, and 1982–1983 at the Center for Advanced Studies in the Behavioral Sciences. These changes of scene were challenging and stimulating intellectually, and Craik's ideas for theories and experiments benefited accordingly.

Back in Toronto, Craik served a term as chair of the Psychology department from 1985–1990. Although some of his predecessors had found this position unrewarding, Craik quite enjoyed the wheeling and dealing aspects of being a departmental chair, but he was happy to get back to research and teaching when his term was up. He remained on the downtown (St. George) campus after his chairmanship, despite feeling guilty about leaving the very congenial Erindale group. Ebbinghaus Empire meetings continued to be the highlight of the research week, with droll comments from Norm Slamecka ("the funniest man in verbal learning") often providing the backdrop to excellent talks by local residents and such regular visitors as Roddy Roediger and Lars-Göran Nilsson. Visitors from overseas were especially welcome, as they brought new perspectives and assumptions to enrich and challenge Craik's thinking. Boris Velichkovsky from Germany, Timo Mäntylä from Sweden, Erlijn Dirkx from Switzerland, and Lily Service from Finland were among this group.

Two very significant events in the 1990s were the advent of functional neuroimaging and the creation of the Rotman Research Institute. The University of Toronto acquired a PET scanner in 1992, and Craik collaborated with Shitij Kapur, Endel Tulving, Cheryl Grady, and Randy McIntosh, among others, in some exciting studies relating memory encoding and retrieval to functional brain states. This new line of work was greatly facilitated by the founding of the Rotman Research Institute at the Baycrest Centre for Geriatric Care in north Toronto. Under the directorship of Donald Stuss, the Rotman Institute's mission is to study cognitive processes as they occur in normal and abnormal aging and as consequences of brain damage. Craik was involved in the early planning of the Institute, participated in its activities throughout the 1990s, and is now based there, pursuing his various research lines in memory, attention, and cognitive aging. Much of this recent work has been done in fruitful collaboration with Moshe Naveh-Benjamin, one of the editors of the present volume.

Craik is keenly aware that many of his ideas for theories and experiments have arisen through interactions with his students, postdocs, and colleagues. He has been extremely fortunate in the scientific and personal contexts provided by Liverpool, London, and Toronto, and is grateful to all his friends and colleagues in these and other settings. He is also more than grateful to his family for putting up with him over the years. His wife Anne is owed a special debt of gratitude, as are his children Lindsay and Neil. They now have children of their own, who regard their grandpa with a mixture of affection and tolerant amusement.

Craik is a fellow of the Royal Society of Canada and a fellow of the Canadian and American Psychological Associations. The Canadian Psychological Association honored him by conferring on him their Distinguished Contribution to Psychology as a Science Award in 1987 and by appointing him honorary president of the Association in 1997. He is also a fellow of the Society of Experimental Psychologists and was presented with the William James Fellow Award in 1993 by the American Psychological Society. He was awarded a Killam Research Fellowship in 1982 and a Guggenheim Fellowship the same year. Craik held the Glassman Chair in Neuropsychology at the University of Toronto and Baycrest Centre from 1996–2000 and was appointed to the rank of University Professor in 1997. Finally, he was extremely pleased to be the first recipient of the Hebb Award, from the Canadian Society for Brain, Behaviour, and Cognitive Science in 1998 and to receive the Killam Prize for Science in 2000.

Fergus Craik's Ph.D. Students and Postdoctoral Fellows

Ph.D. Students

1970	Vernon Gregg (London)	1983	Elizabeth Glisky (Toronto)
1971	Kim Kirsner (London)	1986	Joan McDowd (Toronto)
1972	John Gardiner (London)	1990	Raymond Shaw (Toronto)
1975	Michael Watkins (London)	1991	Daniel Read (Toronto)
1975	Michael Anderson (Toronto)	1993	Randy Sollenberger (Toronto)
1977	David Ostry (Toronto)	1994	Michael Gemar (Toronto)
1981	Jean Newman (Toronto)	1996	Karen Li (Toronto)
1981	Mark Byrd (Toronto)	1997	Nicole Anderson (Toronto)
1983	Shelley Parlow (Toronto)	2000	Scott Brown (Toronto)

Postdoctoral Fellows

1974–1975	Deborah MacMillan	1990	Timo Mäntylä
1975–1978	Ronald Fisher	1990–1991	Elisabet Service
1977–1978	Eileen Simon	1990–1995	Elizabeth Bosman
1978–1979	Brian Ackerman	1990–1994	Carolyn Szostak
1978–1980	Jan Rabinowitz	1990–1992	Gail Eskes
1979–1980	Leslie Cake	1993–1995	Marko Jelicic
1983–1985	Mary Gick	1995	Pierre Foisy
1984–1987	Robin Morris	1995–1998	Jennifer Mangels
1986–1987	Hareo Yamaguchi	1996–1999	Robert West
1986–1987	Joan McDowd	1997–1998	Tetsuya Iidaka
1988–1989	Erlijn Dirkx	1998–2001	Aaron Benjamin

LEVELS OF PROCESSING
AND MEMORY THEORY

Michael J. Watkins

Part I Introduction:
Levels of Processing

A little more than three decades ago, a singular young researcher joined his students at lunch and mentioned that he had been thinking. His students harkened at once, for Fergus Craik is a modest man, not given to bluster. Craik reached for a scrap of paper and drew a horizontal line, from which dropped two vertical lines, one short and one long.

"What's that, Gus?"

"It seems to me," said he, "that memory for something depends on how deeply the something is processed or analyzed."

"That's it, Gus?"

"Well, that's the essence of it . . . "

The notion was at once bemusing and appealing. The drawing seemed too insubstantial and too wobbly to compete with the solid boxes-and-arrows drawings that were the hallmark of the dazzling new information processing era. Yet, it depicted an idea that was both simple and plausible.

The mixed reactions of Craik's students foreshadowed those of the wider world, as is aptly attested in the five chapters that follow. In the first two of these chapters, the levels-of-processing proposal is subjected to such weighty arguments and so many recalcitrant findings that the reader might be forgiven for assuming the proposal to be now perfectly dead. But even in a field not known for swift and certain demise, this proposal has an unusual penchant for resurrection, and sure enough, with the next three chapters it is back in fine fettle, shaping the conduct of research and the digestion of its fruits.

Why do some argue so passionately for fundamentally revising the levels-of-processing proposal or even consigning it to history while others continue to embrace it? Part of the answer may lie in a general disinclination to see the proposal as itself submitting to different levels of analysis. From the start, the authors gave it a metatheoretical status on the premise that it is not a theory but a framework (Craik & Lockhart, 1972; see also Robert Lockhart's discussion in chapter 7), but not everyone has accepted the validity of this premise. Perhaps it should be regarded as half valid. Thus, the notion that memory is a byproduct of perceptual-cognitive analyses constitutes a general perspective on memory or an approach to its study, and *framework* serves well enough for this purpose. But the notion that these analyses have an inherent depth that determines memory durability is a *theory* by almost any definition.

The first two chapters of this tribute address a fundamental limitation of the first, or metatheoretical, component: If an event of time 1 is recalled at time 2, then the levels-of-processing proposal addresses only time 1 and so cannot depict the complete memory process. In particular, it is silent on any effect involving type of test. As Lockhart notes in chapter 7, Craik and Lockhart (1972) willingly conceded this limitation from the start. And yet, to this day, it troubles certain prominent memory theorists. In chapter 2, Endel Tulving exhorts Craik to extend his consideration at least a little way beyond time 1, and in chapter 3 Henry Roediger and David Gallo argue that consideration should be extended all the way to time 2. At play here is the abiding convention that times 1 and 2 frame a unitary mechanism, their temporal disparity being bridged by a memory "trace." From this perspective, an account of memory confined to time 1 is no more complete than an account of the telephone system confined to the mouthpiece. The reader may do well to keep in mind, however, that, absent grander pretensions, an account of a telephone mouthpiece may, of itself, be entirely valid and potentially useful.

Tulving marshals evidence for dissociating the perceptual and cognitive encoding addressed by the levels-of-processing proposal from subsequent encoding that is assumed to occur in trace formation, and he affectionately castigates Craik for neglecting the latter. And it is no defense, Tulving adds, that some of the evidence he offers comes from beyond the realm of psychology, for cognitive psychology can no longer be pursued in isolation from the brain sciences. Here Tulving is unquestionably tapping into conventional wisdom and, having acceded to this wisdom, Craik may indeed appear vulnerable to the charge of leaving the trace underburdened in his conception of memory. One possible response to this difficulty would be to retreat to a radically functional position whereby recall and its manifestations in various memory tests at time 2 are a function of analyses that occurred at time 1, with the idea of an intervening memory trace inaccessible to psychological enquiry being rejected as the subject of natural science rather than of psychology. A more likely response is that the levels-of-processing proposal was never intended to explain all memory findings.

Roediger and Gallo focus on the showcase paradigm for levels-of-processing research, in which the effects on memory are compared for items subjected to two or more tasks designed to restrict processing to different depths. Specifically, they review several findings that collectively, if not individually, seriously undermine or even disconfirm a strict reading of the levels-of-processing proposal, both as metatheory and as theory. But taken literally, the proposal was a nonstarter. For example, that orienting tasks do not always constrain processing to the designated level is clearly demonstrated by the venerable Stroop effect, wherein the meaning of a word may affect the naming of the color in which it is written. Perhaps the moral of Roediger and Gallo's review, then, is merely that the proposal should not be taken literally; certainly, this moral has been studiously respected by the authors. Nevertheless, the levels-of-processing proposal has surely increased the significance of noncompliant findings, and to this extent, at least, it has infiltrated our collective wisdom.

Such infiltration is transparent in the remaining three chapters of Part I. Boris Velichkovsky argues that the levels-of-processing concept may turn out to be just the psychological aspect of a grander dynamic system that also includes the activity and evolution of eye and brain. John Gardiner, Alan Richardson-Klavehn, Cristina Ramponi, and Barbara Brooks show that, contrary to conventional wisdom, an effect of processing level may extend to incidental, or involuntary, remembering. And Betty Ann Levy argues from research on the acquisition of reading fluency, and specifically on the conditions under which the reading of a text is facilitated by a specific prior reading, for the relation between processing and memory being, not one way, but reciprocal.

The chapters in Part I increment a Craik and Lockhart (1972) citation count that is, as Roediger and Gallo document, astonishing by any measure. And, as Lockhart predicts, its core proposal will continue to color our thinking—even as it draws sustenance from would-be obituaries—for many years to come.

Reference

Craik, F. I. M., & Lockhart, R. S. (1972). Levels of processing: A framework for memory research. *Journal of Verbal Learning and Verbal Behavior, 11,* 671–684.

Endel Tulving

Does Memory Encoding Exist?

Does memory encoding exist? What a silly question—of course it does! The whole world's literature on memory is full of papers and books on encoding, or phenomena involving encoding, and surely one cannot write about something that does not exist, at least not in science. Or can one?

At one time physicists wrote at great length about the aether, chemists about phlogiston, and biologists about élan vital, and everything that was said about these things turned out to be wrong, because they did not exist. While pursuing their interests, scientists did find out many things about their subject matter that became not only useful but true, but the fact remains that it is quite possible for scientists to think, talk, and write about nonexistent entities. Is encoding one of them?

There are two basic kinds of existences in the world: physical and mental. Many very clever people, from Descartes to the great thinkers of our own age, have written a great deal about the nature of the relation between the physical and the mental. Physical existences include things such as galaxies, stars, planets, oceans, pebbles on the seashore, tortoises, and worms, and the molecules and atoms that they are made of. Mental ones consist in emergent creations of an unbelievable physical thing, the brain: percepts, images, feelings, ideas, beliefs and the like, and their equivalents in nonhuman animals.

Whether or not encoding exists in the physical world is as yet unknown, but encoding certainly exists as a thought in the minds of many people. Encoding is a concept. In the science of memory, we have a very large number of concepts. We use them continually and are utterly dependent on their existence. We have linguistic, or sometimes mathematical, labels for them, *terms* as these labels are called, very much in the same way that we have symbolic labels for things that do exist as tangible physical entities. We create concepts and terms, describe and define and explain them, have faith in them, defend them against nonbelievers, and measure the progress in the understanding of our subject matter by evaluating the usefulness and validity of our terms and concepts.

Now, encoding may exist as a concept, but the bigger question is whether encoding also exists in the world, outside some individuals' imaginations. Is it a real part of something that happens even if there are no sentient beings who think about it? A falling tree in the woods makes no sound if there is no living soul around to hear it—sound is the product of an appropriately endowed nervous system—but it does produce compressions of the air regardless of the presence of witnesses.

It is appropriate to raise the question about the existence of encoding in the present context because our friend and colleague, Fergus Craik, whose brilliant scientific career this volume is meant to celebrate, has repeatedly expressed doubts about such existence. Others may use the term designating the concept, but he does not believe it corresponds to anything in reality. Encoding is, our friend implies, memory science's élan vital, a thought in the minds of some thinkers, but it does not exist in reality. What does exist is perception, different kinds of perception at that, and the term *encoding* is mistakenly applied to some of these kinds.

Is our friend right? If so, it follows that those others who believe in encoding must be wrong. The question of who is right and who wrong is obviously of some interest, because we cannot expect to get very far in our pursuits of the truth about memory unless we solve the encoding problem first. I am not suggesting that the encoding problem is the only hurdle to be crossed before progress in our understanding of memory can occur, but I am suggesting it is among the very basic ones.

The issue before us, then, is this: Is there something in nature that corresponds to the idea that (many) students of memory have and that they designate as encoding and that is different from *perception*? Tackling the issue also means asking how we can find out. How do we go about establishing the existence of something that is invisible, inaudible, and intangible, and how do we determine its "basic" difference from another such? And, most germane to the occasion, is there a way of persuading Gus Craik to accept encoding as a part of reality?

This essay consists of five parts:

1. A brief history of the science of memory, the concept of encoding, and Gus's place in it.
2. *Byproduct theory* of trace formation: What is it and why is it postulated?
3. GAPS (general abstract processing system): Summary of the opposing view. What is it, how does it differ from the byproduct theory, and why is it postulated?
4. Functional neuroimaging and the *novelty encoding hypothesis*: Fleshing out the encoding's skeleton.
5. These four main sections are followed by a concluding statement.

☐   A Brief History of the Science of Memory

As this is a historic occasion, let us begin by placing our friend's thoughts about encoding into some kind of a historical perspective. The following thumbnail sketch of the history of the psychological science of memory, borrowed from Tulving (1993), is extremely brief and undoubtedly biased, but it serves the current purpose. For a fuller and more objective view, see Bower (2000).

The short history of the study of human memory can be divided into four successive stages, each stage bringing in innovations not known in the preceding one. The stages are shown in Table 2.1. The first one began in antiquity and ended in 1885. In that year, the second stage was launched by the publication of Herman Ebbinghaus's *Über das Gedächtnis* (Ebbinghaus, 1885). It lasted some 75 years, to around 1960. During that time the field came to be dominated by English-speaking scientists, especially in America. Problems of memory were pursued by experimental psychologists under the general rubric of *verbal learning*. Most of the research activity had to do with precise measurement of basic phenomena of learning and forgetting of lists of verbal materials under tightly controlled experimental conditions. The central theoretical concepts were *association* and its single property, *strength*. Theories consisted of attempts to explain observed facts in terms of

TABLE 2.1. Four successive stages of the science of memory

Metaphysics	From the early Greeks on
Verbal learning	After 1885
Information processing	After circa 1960
Cognitive neuroscience	After circa 1980

acquisition, retention, and transfer of, interference with, and mediation by associations. In America, the dissenting voice of Frederic Bartlett (1932) from across the Atlantic was not heard.

In the years around 1960, the associative verbal-learning framework saw a rival emerging in the form of the *information processing* paradigm. A much wider variety of problems, issues, approaches, methods, and theoretical interpretations was adopted. Paired-associate and serial learning were largely abandoned in favor of free and cued recall, as well as recognition and various kinds of *memory judgments*, such as recency and frequency. To-be-learned lists that had served as units of experimental and theoretical analysis were replaced by to-be-remembered (TBR) single items, and single-trial memory studies became popular. Associations among single items were studied under the rubric of *organization*. Later, the TBR items came to be thought of as TBR *events*. Experimental studies of short-term memory led to a theoretical distinction between primary (short-term) and secondary (long-term) memory. Experimental findings were interpreted in terms of processes such as encoding, decision, storage, and retrieval. The distinction between storage and retrieval became a significant experimental and theoretical concern. Influential concepts such as levels of processing, encoding specificity, and encoding/retrieval interactions emerged during this stage, as did *context* and *context effects*. Connections were established between the previously isolated disciplines of cognitive psychology and neuropsychology.

The concept of encoding found its way into the verbal learning and memory literature through the back door, so to speak. James Deese, as well as some other participants at a verbal learning conference organized by Charles Cofer in 1959 (Cofer, 1961), used the term encoding in the sense of *response integration*. The field was still under a strong Ebbinghausian influence, and the use of nonsense syllables as learning materials was widespread. Such materials, according to then-prevailing views, had to be "integrated" or "unitized" before they could enter into associative relations, and Deese used the term encoding to refer to this process. One of his original proposals was that encoding was an all or none feature of verbal units and did not covary with other features of words, such as their frequency of occurrence in natural language. A low-frequency word such as "giraffe" was as well encoded as a high-frequency word such as "dog." These were novel ideas in 1959, and vigorously debated at the conference.

Deese's encoding, in its intended meaning, did not make it into the permanent literature. However, it did influence the thinking of Arthur Melton (1963), who, at the next Cofer conference 2 years later (Cofer & Musgrave, 1963), used the concept in discussing the recently discovered phenomena of short-term memory (Brown, 1958; Peterson & Peterson, 1959). The distinction between perceptual traces, associated with "immediate" memory, and memory traces, associated with "delayed" memory, was under discussion. Melton accepted the new reality of short- and long-term memory, but rejected any notion of a sharp discontinuity between them: "I suspect that there is no fundamental dichotomy between perceptual traces and memory traces, but rather a continuum of *rates of encoding* sensory information into memory traces based on previous experience and the compatibility of the experience with such previous experience" (p. 359).

Melton's "encoding sensory information into memory traces" was a harbinger of things to come in at least two senses. First, *memory trace* was a new concept, meant to take the place that had been occupied by *strengthened associations*. Second, it introduced the concept of encoding in the sense in which it has become an inseparable part of the memory world today. The new ideas spread quickly. By 1972, the concept of encoding was so well ensconced on the verbal learning and memory scene that Arthur Melton and Edwin Martin saw a need to edit a book on the topic entitled *Coding Processes in Human Memory* (Melton & Martin, 1972). In his chapter in that book, Gordon Bower called encoding "the truly central concept in modern theories of memory" (Bower, 1972, p. 85).

The current era of research, beginning some time around 1980, could be labelled the *cognitive neuroscience of memory*, although not every student of memory would accept this designation. It is characterized by further expansion and liberalization of methods, techniques, and choices of questions and problems that had been introduced under the banner of information processing. Like the previous shifts, it did not replace the reigning practices. It was not a Kuhnian paradigm shift—the science of memory is still waiting for its first paradigm—but rather an expansion of the domain, initially methodologically and conceptually, and eventually in terms of fact and theory. Among the central concepts of the era so far have been *priming, implicit memory, multiple memory systems, and functional neuroimaging*. There has been a steadily growing convergence between cognitive psychology and neuropsychology, interest has deepened in the study of memory processes in memory-impaired patients, more attention is being paid to autobiographical memory in real life and to its development over the life-span, theoretically motivated and precisely controlled psychopharmacological studies of memory have begun to appear on the scene, mathematical and computational modelling of memory processes has become increasingly sophisticated, and functional neuroimaging approaches to the study of memory are gradually overcoming their initial teething problems and beginning to generate large amounts of data. What was once the private sandbox of psychology has become the playing field of a larger collection of brain sciences. The unprecedented flourish in research on human memory was paralleled by increasingly vigorous investigations of learning and memory in nonhuman animals at the levels of behavior, neuroanatomy, and neurobiology. Today the multidisciplinary study of memory has taken off and is proceeding with abandon.

Gus Craik discovered memory as a possible scientific love object near the middle of the information processing epoch, safely outside the era of the (not terribly exciting) research on paired-associate learning and transfer. Like all of us, his approach to memory was shaped by a myriad of unfathomable forces. But three basic background factors, shared by many at the time, seem to have played a dominant role in shaping his thinking.

First, psychology was an autonomous scientific discipline that did not have to learn from any other and was best kept from the possibly corrupting influences of other disciplines, such as neuropsychology or physiology. Every graduate student of experimental psychology at the time knew that there was nothing useful that one could learn from physiology and that smart experimentalists stayed away from brain-damaged amnesic patients, because we had problems enough with more-or-less normal sophomores and their minds and did not need any extra troubles.

Second, the greatest virtue of any scientific idea or theory was its parsimony. The ultimate psychological bliss would be a single-factor theory of the whole mind, or at most a two-factor theory. Any kind of admitted complication was an anathema, possibly a sign of mental weakness on the part of the thinker. Because of psychology's isolationist independence, few people had heard of Einstein's dictum that the scientist's duty is to simplify nature as much as possible but not more. As we had not heard of it, everybody was playing Procrustes with a vengeance.

Third, and more specifically with respect to his chosen field, our friend, at a safe distance from the American preoccupation with Ebbinghaus's legacy and closer to where Bartlett had reflected on perceiving and remembering, had learned to think of memory in terms of what we know about it from everyday observations in real life. One of the most obvious things about real-life memory is that remembering occurs naturally and effortlessly. School learning aside, people walk through life and remember what happened to them without making any special attempt to commit any life experiences to memory. They perceive, they comprehend, they think, and then they remember, if not everything then at least many things. It is easy to imagine, then, that memory is an automatic byproduct of such perceiving, thinkings, and understandings. No special learning, or acquisition, or impressing-on-the-mind process is needed. Indeed, memory as a special, separate faculty of the mind is not needed. Memory is delayed perception of internal representations of earlier perceived stimuli.

☐ Byproduct Theory of Trace Formation

The famous levels-of-processing (LOP) paper by Craik and Lockhart (1972) presented a framework for the study of memory. A framework is like a theory, except it is usually broader than a theory and may be more vague. A framework in psychology is not unlike Thomas Kuhn's *paradigm* in mature sciences. A major difference is that a framework lacks the universal or near-universal acceptance by the practitioners in the field that a paradigm enjoys. The purpose of a framework, such as LOP, is to provide guidance for thinking about phenomena within its purview and to suggest ideas for research of a kind that would not be undertaken in the absence of the framework. History shows that LOP triumphed on both of these counts.

A major message of the LOP paper was "that the memory trace can be understood as a byproduct of perceptual analysis and that trace persistence is a positive function of the depth to which the stimulus has been analyzed" (Craik & Lockhart, 1972, p. 671).

Further: "Retention is a function of depth, and various factors, such as the amount of attention devoted to a stimulus, its compatibility with the analyzing structures, and the processing time available, will determine the depth to which it is processed" (Craik & Lockhart, 1972, p. 676).

The most important consequences of the framework are spelled out in the concluding comments of the paper: "If the memory trace is viewed as a byproduct of perceptual analysis, an important goal for future research will be to specify the memorial consequences of various types of perceptual operations" (Craik & Lockhart, 1972, p. 676).

Note the presence here of several basic concepts: memory trace, perceptual analysis, and depth of processing. And note the central idea that "*the memory trace can be understood as a byproduct of perceptual analysis.*" No explicit mention of encoding, anywhere, because it is not needed. Perceptual analysis automatically produces the memory trace. Perceived items can be analyzed shallowly, or deeply, as well as at levels between the two extremes, and the resultant trace has a strength, or *persistence*, that reflects the level of processing.

Gus Craik had, at the time of writing the LOP paper, already conducted some preliminary experiments (Craik, 1973) of the kind that later were published in a longer report (Craik & Tulving, 1975) on the effects on recall and recognition of experimentally manipulated *orienting tasks*. Others had experimented with orienting tasks (Postman & Adams, 1956; Saltzman, 1956). In the absence of an appropriate framework for thinking about the data, however, the findings, historically speaking, amounted to nothing. More influential were earlier studies on the effects of orienting tasks done by Jenkins and his students

(Hyde & Jenkins, 1969; Johnston & Jenkins, 1971) that paved the way for the LOP steam-roller. The results of all these studies vividly illustrated the previously unknown and unimagined power of the orienting tasks. Perhaps even more important was their demonstration that the intention to learn, a sine qua non of learning in the Ebbinghausian tradition and one of the mainstays in verbal learning (McGeoch & Irion, 1952), was largely if not entirely irrelevant for subsequent recall or recognition. It was the realization of that fact, shown by both the Jenkins and the LOP experiments, that turned the verbal learning world, as it operated at the time, upside down.

Craik and Lockhart (1972) did not, of course, deny the existence of a hypothetical process whose product was the memory trace. In that respect, they were securely in the camp of the information processing orientation that had recently arrived on the scene (Tulving & Madigan, 1970). What they were arguing against, however, was a special, dedicated, critical process that transcended perception, or *perceptual analysis*, and that represented a property of the faculty or mental ability of memory. Indeed, our friend went so far as to deny the existence of any such special faculty. In an important paper (Craik, 1983) in which he reviewed the fate of the LOP ideas in their first 10 years, he wrote:

> In any event, the central idea is that memory is not a separate faculty in any sense, but is a reflection of processing carried out primarily for the purposes of perception and comprehension, with certain types of processing (typically, richer, more elaborate, and more meaningful encodings) being associated with higher levels of retention. (p. 343)

For other observers of the memory scene, this kind of thinking was getting serious. Here was a statement whose implications went far beyond the earlier claims. For a card-carrying information processor it may have been possible to live without encoding, by simply assuming that Craik's perceptual analysis was simply a different term for the same concept that others labelled encoding. But the denial of the status of a separate faculty to the most important part of the human mind was bordering on treason! We were told, in essence, that not only is there no encoding, and no need whatsoever to postulate it, there was no such thing as memory! What we think is memory is nothing more nor less than a byproduct of perception. Among other things, if our friend was right, then those of us who thought we had spent our lifetimes (or good chunks of it) in studying memory had to change our self-concepts and ruefully admit that we had done no such thing. In reality, we had been doing nothing more than dabbling with byproducts of perception!

Was this kind of seditious thinking just a matter of Gus's romantic indiscretion? Evidence shows that while he may have shown ambivalence on the issue—one can, if one tries hard, detect signs of wavering now and then—the fact is that as late as 1999 he lovingly quoted the earlier lines:

> In our 1972 paper Lockhart and I stressed that the "levels" we were talking about were not "levels of memory" but rather levels of general cognitive processing, running from early data-driven sensory analysis to later conceptually-driven analysis of meaning and implication. By this view there is no self-contained "memory module": rather, memory is a byproduct of the general processes of perception and comprehension. Attention and memory are intimately linked in this model, since it is attentional processes that largely determine how deeply a stimulus is processed." (Craik, 1999, p. 101)

At this point he could have informed the reader that these views were those he (and Lockhart) held in 1972, that in the meantime the world had changed, and that his early romantic views no longer seemed reasonable. But there was no such renunciation. The flames of early loves burn, if not forever, then at least for a very long, long time.

If Gus Craik were completely alone in his views, we might try to solve the problem by simply ignoring him whenever he departs from the party line. But he is not. To pick an example not entirely at random: Gus's friend and colleague Boris Velichkovsky has recently expressed enthusiastic agreement with Craik and Lockhart's position that "memory performance is a byproduct of perceptual-cognitive processing" (Velichkovsky, 1999, p. 203). And the mutinous sentiments are spreading to the younger generation, some of whom seem to have embraced the "parsimony-at-any-cost" vision of science. For example, Randy Buckner and colleagues, who are well known for their work in functional imaging of memory, approvingly mention the byproduct theory of trace formation, although they may have developed the concept independently of Craik and Lockhart (Buckner, Kelley, & Peterson, 1999). In the context of our present discussion, and to remind our friend, however, the important point is that functional neuroimaging data, too, point to the existence of special, postperceptual, memory-related encoding processes.

In the present context, too, it is worth noting that Gus Craik's one-time student, Michael Watkins, has gone on record arguing against not just encoding, but all other postulated, "reified" happenings in the mind, including memory traces (Watkins, 2001). Children, in their rebellion against the parents, frequently take the road of greatly exaggerating what they perceive as parental shortcomings. Craik would not accept any special memory-related process at the input side, such as encoding, but otherwise has always adhered to the standard cognitive-psychology line on memory. Watkins goes further and would banish from the psychological science of memory every term that hints at any kind of contents of the black box of the mind. For him, the mind ("consciousness," he would say) is the object of study of psychology, and because psychology is a sovereign science, and not other natural sciences' handmaiden, phenomena of memory are to be described independently of anything that is not mind and not psychology. The worst thing that students of memory can do is to try to explain their findings in terms of hypothetical constructs or neural correlates, because these things are not part of psychology (Watkins, 2001).

We will return to the byproduct theory, to see whether it has any merit, later in the chapter. Next, however, let us consider an alternative to it.

☐ General Abstract Processing System: GAPS

Some time ago I described "a conceptual framework for the study and understanding of episodic memory" (Tulving, 1983, p. 129) that I called the general abstract processing system, or GAPS for short. Its purpose was to help to integrate the diverse research findings, suggest theoretical interpretations of the data, and relate the laboratory work on memory to remembering as experienced by people in real life.

Some people think GAPS was "Tulving's theory," but it was neither mine nor a theory. It was my way of summarizing the broad features of the experimental doings and theoretical thinkings of the practitioners in the information processing approach to memory.

The GAPS framework of 1983 held that an act of memory begins with encoding processes and ends with the use, or retrieval, of the encoded information. In total it consisted of 13 conceptual components, or elements: four observables, four hypothetical processes, and five hypothetical states. One of the central elements was encoding, defined as the process that converts an event into an engram, or memory trace. The other central concepts were engram, ecphory, and ecphoric information. Encoding was defined as the process that converts the event-information (provided by perception or thought) into an engram (memory trace); ecphory is the process that combines the information in the engram and the retrieval cue into ecphoric information. Ecphoric information determines recollective experience, the end product of an act of cognitive memory. Encoding and engram are the principal components of storage of information in memory; ecphory and ecphoric information are the principal components of retrieval of the stored information.

Note that the sequentially cumulative organization of the elements of (episodic) memory in GAPS is meant to parallel the same kind of organization in real-life memory situations, in which any given process necessarily reflects or depends on something that has happened earlier. Encoding depends on the perceived event and the cognitive environment, the original engram depends on the event and its encoding, and so on through the totality of an act of remembering, ending up, for cognitively important purposes, with conscious recollection of the event that depends on everything that has preceded it in the given sequence.

At any rate, whereas in the byproduct theory memory traces result from perceptual analysis, in GAPS they result from the encoding process. The question, then, is whether there is a difference, other than semantic, between the two hypotheses, and if so, exactly wherein it lies.

The difficulty in answering this question lies in the fact that both theories are highly similar in that both do postulate a hypothetical (not directly observable) process that begins with the act of perception and ends with the formation of the memory trace. They just name the process differently: perceptual analysis versus encoding. Is that all there is to it?

One can, of course, try to differentiate the two ideas by pointing to specific empirical facts and say, "explain this in terms of your ideas," or even better, "tell me again how you can explain this without invoking my ideas," and watch the opponent tumble. This procedure sounds useful in principle—what is more noble than adjudicating scientific disputes by facts?—but it does not work in practice, as all veteran scientists know.

One difference between the ideas of perceptual analysis and encoding is that the latter postulates the existence of a process that is more than, or transcends, "mere" perceptual analysis. That is, perceptual analysis may be necessary for trace formation, but it is not sufficient. Trace formation requires something like an act of perception (the perceived object or event, of course, could be either external or internal), plus something else that follows it or is superimposed on it, namely encoding. Perception, or perceptual analysis, of an event may result in trace formation (when it leads to encoding), but it need not (when it does not).

We will now turn to some examples of phenomena of memory that would be difficult to make sense of without postulating some process like encoding that intervenes between the act of perception of an item or an event and the formation of the trace of that item or event. Needless to say, many more such examples could be given, otherwise the concept of encoding would not be as widely used as it actually is. For the purposes of the exercise that follows, we ignore the retrieval side of memory processes, although retrieval processes are at least as important, if not more so, than encoding processes (Roediger & McDermott, 2000). Here we are concerned with the issue of trace formation and the roles that perception (comprehension, attention) alone versus perception (comprehension, attention) plus encoding play in it.

☐ Empirical Difficulties for the Byproduct Theory?

Interrupted Encoding

I reported a study some time ago that I suggested demonstrated *retrograde amnesia* in normal healthy university students (Tulving, 1969). (Replications and extensions of the study have been described by Schulz, 1971 and Guynn & Roediger, 1995.) Subjects studied lists of 15 items. Experimental lists consisted of 14 familiar words and 1 name of a famous person (such as Freud, Churchill, or Beethoven). Control lists contained familiar words only, and no 'high-priority events' occurred. A large number of these two kinds of lists were presented in haphazard order. Subjects were tested for immediate free recall after each list. They had been instructed to be on the lookout for the names of famous persons. Whenever one occurred in a list, it was to be produced first in recall, before any other words.

The results in the condition in which the high-priority event appeared in the middle of the list, in serial position 8, are shown in Figure 2.1. The level of recall of the high-priority event was, as expected, very high. But the interesting finding was that the presentation and recall of the high-priority event was associated with rather low recall of the one or two words that had immediately preceded the high-priority event in the presentation sequence. I used the somewhat whimsical appellation of retrograde amnesia to describe this outcome: A highly conspicuous and memorable event seems to have suppressed the memory for events immediately preceding it.

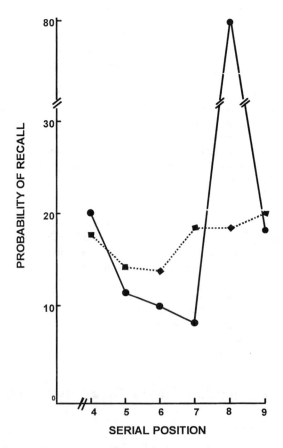

FIGURE 2.1. Probability of recall of words as a function of serial position in a single-trial free-recall task in which a high-priority event (e.g., the name of a famous person) occurred in serial position 8. (Data reported by Tulving, 1969.)

An additional finding was that the results as described were obtained only with very fast rates of presentations of the words, namely .5 seconds or 1 second per word. When the rate of presentation was slowed to 2 seconds per word, the effect disappeared (Tulving, 1969).

How are we to interpret, or make sense of, these miniature retrograde amnesia effects. The interpretation offered at the time still seems viable: Some kind of an encoding or consolidation-like process occurs for each perceived (read) item. When the presentation rate is slow, these processes run their normal course, and, together with other processes of the kind specified in GAPS, determine the item's subsequent recall (and recognition, as in Schultz's study). With the fast presentation rate, however, the encoding processes for successive items overlap: Processing of one item is not yet completed when the next item is presented. When a high-priority event occurs, it is immediately recognized as such, and the relevant processing resources (a nice Craikian term!) are withdrawn from items "on line," and devoted to the encoding of the high-priority event. In other words, the onset of the high-priority item prematurely terminates the encoding of the immediately preceding item and therefore impairs its trace formation.

Can one argue that the retrograde amnesia results from inadequate perception of items? The fact that the effect disappeared with slower rates of presentation, which was also observed by Guynn and Roediger (1995), could mean that the subjects needed more time than 1 second per word for the words' full perception and comprehension. One can, of course, come up with this kind of an explanation, especially if one is really desperate, but I do not think that Gus would take this low road.

Remembering Events That Never Happened

Consider another difference between the byproduct and encoding theories. If perceptual analysis of an object or an event determines the trace of the object or event, it is easy enough to see how forgetting occurs, or even distortions in what is being remembered. But it would be more difficult to see how it is ever possible for anyone to remember an event that never happened and therefore could not have been originally perceived, because a nonperceived event could not have any byproduct; that is, it would leave no trace in the memory system. If retrieval, even of events that never happened, requires a trace, absence of the trace would make retrieval impossible. Thus it looks as if the byproduct theory could not say anything very useful about those aspects of *constructive memory* that consist in memory distortions, memory illusions, and false memories, on which a rich literature is now available, ably reviewed by Roediger and McDermott (2000). The problem again is that trace formation is too rigidly tied to perception.

The GAPS scheme is different. Perception plays an important role in trace formation, of course, but there is more to trace formation than just perception and comprehension of what is being perceived at input. At retrieval, the relevant trace information must be available, otherwise retrieval could not occur, as it could not occur in the absence of relevant retrieval cues. But the trace information need not have been originally perceived, just encoded as a part of the study task. Thus it is that GAPS even allows remembering something that never happened (Tulving, 1983, p. 183). In the early 1980s, psychologists were not greatly interested in false remembering, but the mere existence of errors such as false alarms in recognition and intrusions in recall made it necessary to postulate retrieval of originally nonperceived items.

Could one argue that perception and, especially, comprehension of lists like those that are used these days to demonstrate false remembering in the Deese–Roediger–McDermott (DRM) paradigm (Roediger & McDermott, 1995) are broad enough concepts to include the kinds of inferential processes that probably underlie remembering of events that never happened in the DRM paradigm and comparable situations? Of course one could. Psychology is a flexible science. The question is how far one is willing to extend the definition of "perception and comprehension," and why the extension is preferable to the idea of postperceptual encoding.

Anterograde Amnesia

Direct evidence against the byproduct theory is provided by brain damaged patients with anterograde amnesia (Mayes, 2000; Squire, 1992). The brain damage that causes amnesia may involve different structures and pathways: medial temporal lobe and diencephalic, as well as other limbic-system regions (Markowitsch, 2000). In anterograde amnesia—a pathological impairment in the ability to remember ongoing happenings and to learn new information—perception occurs, but there is no memory byproduct. Why not? What is missing in the amnesic brain that is present in the normal one? It would be difficult to argue that what is missing is perception, or perceptual analysis, or comprehension, because typical amnesic patients have no problems in these spheres. Indeed, the clinical definition of amnesia is two-pronged: It specifies what is impaired (ability to remember ongoing experiences and to acquire new knowledge) and what is preserved (general intelligence, perceptual and conceptual abilities, language, reasoning, and even short-term memory). Neurological patients with memory impairments who also have other mental deficits are classified as demented, not as amnesic (Hodges, 2000).

Many students of amnesia today accept the idea that anterograde amnesia can be attributed to a faulty process of encoding information into long-term memory, that is, long-term memory trace formation (Milner, 1966; Squire, 1992). To the extent that this is so, we can think of anterograde amnesia as evidence that it is not faulty perception that is responsible for the failure of the establishment of memory traces.

Psychopharmacology of Encoding

Our final example, although it does not exhaust the reservoir of possible examples, is provided by experiments on the effects of various amnestic drugs, such as benzodiazepines (BZs), on memory performance. In these experiments, subjects study lists of words, have no difficulty perceiving and comprehending the words, but subsequently show serious impairment in explicit retrieval of the words. These kinds of effects suggest that the drugs adversely affect some necessary postperceptual processing. Is it encoding? Or perhaps retrieval?

In a typical study of the kind that helps us to identify the source of the amnestic effects of the BZ drugs, subjects study two lists of words. Between the two study periods they are administered either the drug or a placebo. Then they are tested on two occasions: (a) while still under the influence of the drug, and (b) when the drug effects have worn off. The results of such studies show that (a) administering the drug before the learning of the list (severely) reduces recall performance, both in the same state (tested under the influence) and in the different state (tested sober), and (b) administering the test while the subjects are under the influence of the drug does not reduce the performance in comparison with the placebo condition. Conclusion: The drug's amnestic influence operates through its effect on some part of the encoding process. (For reviews, see Curran, 1991; Ghoneim & Mewaldt, 1990; Polster, 1993.)

Thus, here we have another case where it would be difficult to argue that trace formation is a byproduct of perceptual analysis. BZ drugs have little deleterious influence on perception, working memory, or retrieval of previously acquired long-term information, but do impair encoding, the process that converts the perceived information into the memory trace.

We have considered four examples: Interrupted processing reduces memory after perception, perfectly normal people remember events they did not perceive, brain-damaged people do not remember things they do perceive, and amnestic drugs knock out encoding of perceived items while leaving retrieval intact. How would a byproduct theorist deal with such apparently troublesome facts?

Gus Craik has not said anything about interrupted processing, or false memory, or drug effects on encoding. But he did briefly discuss the problem of anterograde amnesia. In the abstract of a paper based on a talk he gave at The Royal Society discussion meeting on memory he wrote:

> It is argued that memory is largely a function of depth and elaboration of the initial encoding, and that the memory deficits found in elderly people and under conditions of divided attention reflect impaired comprehension of the material. On the other hand, amnesic patients exhibit adequate comprehension yet poor memory, suggesting that some physiological process of consolidation may also be involved in normal learning and remembering. (Craik, 1983, p. 341)

And in the text of the paper, he wrote:

> Most cases of clinical amnesia are not well described by the present account, since these patients show at least adequate comprehension yet extremely poor subsequent recollection. (Craik, 1983, p. 356)

How did our friend deal with the trouble? Three devices are possible. Perhaps what manifests itself as amnesia is rooted in a deficit of conscious recollection. Perhaps it is rapid forgetting. And if neither, it may be a function of the breakdown of some physiological process, such as consolidation, but if so, it still leaves the psychological theory intact! In 1983 most of us psychologists did not pay much attention to physiology.

Regrettably, there is little support for the first of these two possible escape routes. Although Warrington and Weiskrantz (1970, 1974) did consider the idea that anterograde amnesia is a condition in which encoding is intact and retrieval is impaired, they themselves (Warrington & Weiskrantz, 1978) renounced the theory because it was not supported by data. Since no other champions of the retrieval theory of amnesia have emerged, Brenda Milner's (1966) original idea still holds: Amnesics such as HM show the horrendous memory deficit because of their inability to encode the information appropriately. (In the terminology of that time: They cannot get the information from the short-term memory store into the long-term store, according to the then-prevailing "modal models" [Murdock, 1967].)

The idea of amnesia as rapid forgetting would save the appearance of the byproduct theory, because it would mean that the requisite trace information was formed correctly, as a consequence of perception, but then lost. The obstacle here, however, is that there is little or no evidence for rapid forgetting in amnesia. Indeed, the evidence generated by studies directly designed to examine the issue shows that once amnesics have acquired the material to the same level as their controls, the subsequent forgetting is usually indistinguishable for the two populations. In one dramatic case, Freed and colleagues (Freed, Corkin, & Cohen, 1987) equated HM's initial learning of pictures of natural scenes with the initial level of acquisition of the same pictures by normal controls, by the simple device of allowing HM much more time to study the pictures, and then measured the retention performance over intervals extending to 1 week. The results showed that HM's retention performance was equivalent to that of the controls throughout the retention interval.

The last attempt by our friend to avoid facing the full consequences of anterograde amnesia for the byproduct theory, namely a firm separation between psychology and physiology, took the following form. In discussing the implications of anterograde amnesia for his theory, Gus Craik, acting in form as a real scientist, readily admitted that:

> Some "consolidation" process is necessary to "fix" in a permanently accessible fashion the changes in neural circuitry induced by the original event. . . . (Craik, 1983, p. 356)

But then he immediately continued:

> The evidence supporting consolidation is still incomplete, but there seems to be no reason in principle that a psychological account of remembering in terms of depth and elaboration of processing during initial perception and comprehension could not coexist with a more clearly physiological process of altering the underlying neural mechanism in some permanent fashion. (Craik, 1983, p. 356)

This was in 1983. Psychology and physiology were in separate domains, and it was natural for psychologists to ignore physiology then. All of us in experimental psychology did so. The "ignore the brain" stratagem may have worked back then, especially when the Zeitgeist of psychology allowed us to ignore physiological findings about memory, but it would be a less admired way to save a psychological theory today, because today physiology, under the cloak of functional neuroimaging, has become highly relevant to what we do as students of memory.

Functional Brain Measures of Encoding

Everyone knows today that techniques of functional neuroimaging, positron emission tomography (PET), and functional magnetic resonance imaging (fMRI) can be used to localize cognitive function in the brain. Not everyone in cognitive psychology cares much about such localization, because knowledge of neuroanatomical sites that are involved does not help much with cognitive problems and cognitive theories. What difference does it make if, say, encoding is associated with neural activity in the left or right prefrontal cortex, or the frontal operculum, or the cerebellum, or some combination of these or many other areas?

Perhaps localization does not matter much, indeed. But functional neuroimaging does much more than just provide information on where in the brain "something happens." Among other things, it has contributed enormously to making consciousness, the central psychological "problem," scientifically respectable. It can also illuminate purely theoretical problems and help to settle them. With respect to the issue under scrutiny in this paper, functional neuroimaging research has turned out to be invaluable.

Let us go back to one of the basic premises of the present discussion. Everyone, including our friend Gus Craik, accepts the fact that encoding exists as an idea in many theorist's minds. It is a genuine part of the mental world, or World 2 as conceptualized by Popper and Eccles (1977). The uncertainty, and the ensuing debate, has to do with the question of whether encoding as a process "exists" or occurs in the world outside scientists' thought— the physical world, or Popper and Eccles's World 1? If so, is it possible to get evidence for such existence that is more direct than mere inferences from observed behavior? We know, of course, that we will never be able to get direct sensory evidence, because encoding processes are no more visible or tangible than entities such as seeing and feeling. Hence the question, Can we get *more direct* evidence than that suggested by observed behavior? The answer is yes, and such more direct evidence is provided by looking at what the brain does when some information is encoded into memory.

The original evidence of brain activity correlated with encoding did not have to wait until the advent of PET and fMRI. The very first time that the encoding process was identified at the level of brain activity was the event-related potentials (ERPs) experiment reported by Sanquist, Rohrbaugh, Syndulko, and Lindsley (1980). These investigators recorded ERP signals (scalp-recorded EEG voltage changes time-locked to stimulus events) in an explicit recognition experiment and found systematic differences between encoding of words that were subsequently recognized and encoding of those that were not. Since then, many others have replicated and extended these results (see Rugg, 1995, for review).

Although ERPs provide fine information about temporal changes in neural activity, their spatial resolution is poor. From the point of view of localization, better evidence is provided by the findings from functional neuroimaging studies, and especially from those using the event-related fMRI technique (Buckner et al., 1996; Dale & Buckner, 1997). This technique, like ERPs, allows the experimenter to sort individual stimulus events (at study, or at test, or both) into categories according to their behavioral or cognitive fate, on the basis of any one of a variety of criteria, such as "recognized," "highly confidently recognized," "not recognized," "correctly rejected," or even "recognized but not remembered," and then examine the neural signatures of such categories, averaged over all stimulus events in the category.

The first event-related fMRI study of encoding, designed to compare the neural signatures of encoding of items that were subsequently remembered versus those that were subsequently forgotten, was reported by Wagner et al. (1998). In this study, subjects made abstract or concrete judgments about successively presented words that later appeared in a yes/no recognition test in which confidence ratings were also taken. Brewer, Zhao, Glover, and Gabrieli (1998) conducted a similar study, but used pictures (indoor and outdoor scenes) and examined only selected brain slices, whereas Wagner et al. (1998) looked at the whole brain. Wagner et al. (1998) found that neural activity *at encoding*, in specific brain regions, specifically left prefrontal and temporal cortices, was higher for studied words that were subsequently confidently recognized than for studied words that were not recognized. The activity at study in these regions, therefore, can be said to predict what happens to the studied items in the recognition test.

These studies thus have provided neural evidence of the existence of processes at the time of study that (a) determine the subsequent retrievability of the studied items and (b) are differentiated at the level of brain activity in specific cortical and subcortical regions. Does such different neural activity reflect differences in perception or differences in encoding? The data from a single experiment never answers broad questions of this sort, because a single experiment cannot control or manipulate all possibly relevant variables. But it seems more reasonable to attribute the differences to (postperceptual) encoding rather than to perception, for at least two reasons. First, there was no behavioral or cognitive evidence of any differences in perception or comprehension of the subsequently remembered and not remembered words. Second, and more important—perhaps even more interesting, in that it shows how 'localization of function' might turn out to be relevant even to purely cognitive issues, after all—was the finding that at least some of the regions of the brain in which the neural differences between remembered and nonremembered items were observed, such as the left prefrontal cortex, are better known as regions related to memory than to perception. Neuropsychological studies have shown that damage to frontal lobes can impair memory performance (for a review, see Wheeler, Stuss, & Tulving, 1995), yet few studies have shown that such damage impairs perception or comprehension. Functional neuroimaging studies, too, have consistently implicated the prefrontal cortex in memory processes, including encoding, but not in perception or comprehension (for an extensive review of relevant neuroimaging findings, see Cabeza & Nyberg, 2000).

Although the initial results of this kind of research, showing that circumscribed regional brain activity at study "predicts" the subsequent memorial fate of TBR items, seem to be more amenable to the interpretation in terms of encoding (that is, perception plus something else) than perception (and comprehension) alone, as in our other examples, they do not force an encoding interpretation. Nor do they totally exclude a perceptual byproduct kind of interpretation. The main significance of these results lies in the direction to which they point by way of future research. They imply that it should be possible to systematically control and manipulate relevant perceptual and attentional variables, as well as variables related to different aspects of postperceptual encoding processes, and observe the consequences of such manipulations at retrieval.

☐ Novelty Encoding Hypothesis

We have just seen how functional neuroimaging data can illuminate one of the most difficult problems that memory theorists have faced from the earliest days of memory research: What determines which particular items from a studied lot are and which ones are not remembered? The answer is that, partly at least, the memorial fate of an item depends on how it is dealt with by the brain at encoding—on its neural processing. But why are different items processed differently in the brain?

Many properties of items, verbal or otherwise, are known to be correlated with their memorability. Textbooks of learning and memory discuss them routinely. Here, in the last section of this chapter, let us consider an item variable whose effect on memorability is less well known. The variable is the item's novelty or familiarity to the rememberer (or just novelty, for easier reference). The story of novelty fits well into the present context, because it dissociates, in a sense, perception and memory: When a particular item is presented repeatedly, its perception is facilitated while its subsequent retrieval, at least in the recognition test, is reduced. Such a state of affairs has obvious implications for the byproduct theory and its rivals.

The relevant data come from experiments in which all properties of TBR items are held constant except one: situation-specific novelty. The general procedures are as follows: (a) Subjects are exposed to some stimulus items in the "prefamiliarization" phase to produce "familiar" items. Such prefamiliarization may take different forms, and items may be presented once or more times. (b) The subjects are then given a list of items to study for a subsequent memory test. The study list consists of both familiar items, as defined, and novel items of the same general class—items that the subjects have not encountered in the experiment. (c) They are then tested for their memory for the study list items. Typically this test is one of recognition. If so, in the recognition test there are both novel and familiar studied items, and novel and familiar distractors—items not encountered in the study list.

The typical results from experiments of this kind is that novel items are recognized more readily than familiar items. A summary of data from 13 different conditions in six different experiments is given in Table 1. These data come from experiments by Kinsbourne and George (1974), Tulving and Kroll (1995), Habib (2000), and Kormi-Nouri, Nilsson, and Ohta (2000). Stimulus items in all six experiments were single words, but otherwise the experiments differed with respect to details of the procedure. Thus, for example, Kinsbourne and George (1974) used both high and low background frequency words presented visually; Habib (2000) did the experiment in both the visual and auditory modality, and also varied the encoding task (deep versus shallow processing, as in a typical LOP study); Kormi-Nouri et al. (2000) prefamiliarized their subjects with the TBR materials, in different experiments, in three different kinds of subject-performed-tasks procedures,

TABLE 2.2. Hit rates and false alarm rates in recognition of novel and familiar items from 13 experimental conditions in 4 experiments. See text for details.

Experiment	Condition		Hits		FAs	
			Nov	Fam	Nov	Fam
Kinsbourne	Hi F		.64	.54	.36	.46
	Lo F		.80	.70	.20	.30
Tulving			.77	.67	.21	.47
Kormi–Nouri	Exp 1	V	.71	.58	.15	.26
		N	.84	.76	.10	.23
	Exp 2	V	.75	.57	.16	.23
		N	.88	.77	.09	.19
	Exp 3	V	.78	.70	.09	.21
		N	.88	.81	.04	.13
Habib	Vis	D	.91	.85	.04	.07
		S	.65	.59	.08	.13
	Aud	D	.90	.90	.03	.09
		S	.80	.70	.10	.14
Average			.79	.70	.13	.22

Notes: Hi F = high-frequency words; Lo F = low-frequency words; V = verbs; N = nouns; Vis = visually presented; Aud = auditorily presented; D = deep encoding; S = shallow encoding.

and measured recognition for both verbs and nouns that had occurred in the verbal descriptions of tasks performed (Nilsson, 2000).

In Table 2.2, hit rates (proportions of studied items that are correctly recognized) and false alarm rates (proportions of distractors that are incorrectly identified as studied items) are presented for each of the 13 conditions. The data are remarkably stable. Almost without exception, hit rates are higher for novel than familiar items, and false alarms are higher for familiar than novel items. The overall measure of goodness of recognition, the difference between hit rates and false alarm rates calculated over the means listed in Table 2.2 (and ignoring the differences in the numbers of individual observations that went into the means) is sizable: .66 for novel items and .48 for familiar items. In this kind of experiment at least, people find it easier to remember novel information than familiar information.

How could these kinds of data be interpreted in terms of the byproduct theory? The perception and comprehension of repeated items is presumably facilitated by repetition. Such facilitation is well known and has been thoroughly studied under the label of priming (Roediger & McDermott, 1993; Schacter, 1987; Tulving & Schacter, 1990). Yet they are less well recognized as items presented in a particular study list. Why? Why should a readily perceived event produce a less viable memory trace? I submit that the answer is not obvious.

It turns out that the answer is not obvious even if we postulate encoding as a postperceptual process that converts the perceived information into the memory trace. At the time when GAPS was proposed (Tulving, 1983), students of memory knew little about the effect of situational novelty on recognition. The fact that infrequent words are more readily identified as old in memory experiments than are frequent words was, of course, a well-known fact even then (Gregg, 1976), but this is a fact about a correlation between two variables, and correlations are usually open to a myriad of explanations. The importance of the single experiment that had demonstrated a causal effect of novelty on recognition memory (Kinsbourne & George, 1974) was not appreciated.

However, the encoding theory seems easier to revise in light of the facts regarding novelty than the byproduct theory does. It requires the postulation of an early stage of the encoding process that has to do with the assessment of novelty of incoming or on-line information. If the information is novel, it is transmitted for further encoding. If not, it is not further processed. Thus, instead of the perception–encoding sequence of processes in GAPS, we assume a perception–novelty-assessment–encoding sequence in the revised GAPS. (Note that because novelty assessment necessarily requires a comparison of incoming information with information already available in the memory store, the novelty-assessment process involves retrieval of some kind. If so, the revision of GAPS is a bit more complex than just the insertion of another process. But this is another story, to be told some other day.)

The idea that the brain assesses incoming information for its novelty or familiarity makes good sense, because it provides a simple, but I believe convincing, answer to a question frequently asked of and by students of memory: Are all the experiences that a person has stored in memory? Despite the fact that, logically speaking, the question cannot be answered (at least not negatively) by the methods of science, the problem has been repeatedly discussed (e.g., Loftus & Loftus, 1980). Although it is logically impossible to disprove the possibility of all perception becoming potentially retrievable from long-term memory, rational reflection, aided by what we know about biological evolution, suggests that the answer to the question is highly likely to be negative. It is, of course, clearly advantageous to a creature to have all kinds of knowledge available for use "on line," and generally it may also be true that the more such knowledge there is, the better off the creature is in surviving long enough to make more of its kind. The problem is that long-term storage of everything that ever happened requires enormous storage capacity and is very costly. The brain does have enormous capacity, but probably not enough to record, in detail, an individual's lifetime experiences and all the inferences that can be drawn from them (Dudai, 1997). Another problem with the idea of storing everything is that it is dumb, because it would mean storing loads and loads of information that is already available in the long-term store. One thing we know about nature is that it is not dumb.

One possible alternative is that everything is indeed stored in long-term memory, but then, from time to time—perhaps when the owner of the memory store is asleep—in order to alleviate the storage problem, the "contents" of the store are purged of redundant information or information that has not been used for some time. This idea, however, looks like a nonstarter. It reminds one of Rube Goldberg rather than nature: It is horrendously and unnecessarily complicated. There exists a much simpler solution. It is called *novelty assessment.*

The idea, also discussed under the rubric of *novelty detection,* is this: All incoming (perceptual and on-line) information is filtered through novelty assessment circuits of the brain and is selected for long-term encoding depending upon its novelty/familiarity status. The idea has been called the *novelty encoding hypothesis* (Tulving, Markowitsch, Kapur, Habib, & Houle, 1994). It holds that the (neural) novelty assessment mechanism is a component of the (neural) encoding process. This means, among other things, that the encoding process is not unitary, as it was assumed to be in GAPS in 1983, but consists of at least two sets of concatenated subprocesses. The first is novelty assessment, and the second involves higher level encoding operations. The end product of the concatenation is the engram or memory trace. Thus, on-line information, including that provided by the sensory and perceptual systems, is transmitted for higher level encoding depending upon its novelty: novel information receives preferential treatment over familiar information. Completely redundant information of a perceived and comprehended stimulus event is screened out from further processing, is not encoded, and hence leaves no long-term trace, a state of affairs that I alluded to earlier when I talked about the difference between "mere" perceptual analysis and encoding.

Although the concept of novelty is not simple—there are presumably many different kinds and forms of novelty—the idea of novelty encoding as a basic component of the encoding process itself is. At Toronto, we stumbled onto it when we started doing PET studies of memory (Tulving et al., 1994; Tulving, Markowitsch, Craik, Habib, & Houle, 1996), but similar ideas had been discussed earlier by other researchers and modellers (e.g., Knight, 1984; Kohonen, Oja, & Lehtio (1989); Metcalfe (1993); Siddle, Packer, Donchin, & Fabiani (1991); and Sokolov (1963); among others).

Several other functional neuroimaging studies have identified brain regions that are more active for novel than familiar information of various kinds: scenes (Constable et al., 2000; Stern et al., 1996), words (Saykin et al., 1999), or both scenes and words (Kirchhoff, Wagner, Maril, and Stern, 2000). These regions include the hippocampal formation in the medial temporal lobes, long known to be critically involved in memory processes (Milner, 1966; Squire, 1992), as well as other regions in the extended limbic system of which the hippocampal formation is a part (Tulving et al., 1996). Still other functional imaging studies have reported and focused on similar novelty regions in the left inferior prefrontal cortex but interpreted the data in terms of the concept of priming rather than novelty detection or novelty assessment (Buckner, Koustaal, Schacter, & Rosen, 2000; Demb et al., 1995; Koutstaal et al., 2000; Wagner, Desmond, Demb, Glover, & Gabrieli, 1997; for a review of these studies see Habib, 2001).

The point, then, is this: Functional neuroimaging data suggest that the brain can respond differentially to novel as compared with familiar information. Why should it do so? One possibility is that such novelty detection is a part of the brain process that controls the encoding of information into long-term memory: Perceived information that is already available in the memory store is less likely to be encoded (converted into long-term traces) than information that is not yet available. The data summarized in Table 2.2 reflect this novelty encoding hypothesis, although there are many other "purely psychological" facts that do likewise and that can also be interpreted in terms of the evolved properties of the brain (Tulving et al., 1996).

☐ Conclusion

I began by praising Gus Craik as a brilliant explorer of the human mind, one who has fundamentally changed the way we think about memory, but also noting that he may have been wrong on one issue: the role of encoding in memory. "Craik's error" consisted in the idea that memory traces are a byproduct of perceptual processing of stimuli, and that it is not necessary to postulate the existence of an additional, separate, memory-related process of encoding.

This essay presents some reasons for believing that the concept of encoding corresponds to something in the physical or biological world. First, there are experimental findings that cannot readily be (or can only awkwardly be) explained without invoking processes that are "switched on" after perception and that, when they run their full course, produce a memory trace. Second, there are clinical observations of intelligent but brain-damaged amnesic patients, who perceive the world around them normally but who cannot remember later on what they perceived. Third, there are findings showing that certain psychoactive drugs, such as benzodiazepines, selectively impair the long-term encoding process while leaving perception, working memory, and even long-term retrieval intact. Fourth, there are functional brain imaging findings of encoding-related brain activity in brain regions not known for their involvement in perceptual processes. Finally, there is the question, Why should nature have evolved organisms that store in their long-term memory everything that they perceive? The answer here is that it has not. Organisms, including human beings, selectively encode and store incoming information on the basis of its novelty or familiarity. The strong form of this novelty encoding hypothesis holds that only nonredundant information is encoded and stored.

The evidence thus converges on a dissociation between perception and encoding. Some events are indeed perceived and encoded, or not perceived and therefore not encoded, as the byproduct theory would hold. Other events are perceived but not encoded, as in the case of anterograde amnesia. Or they are not perceived but nevertheless remembered, as in the case of false memory. Or their memorability may be inversely related to their perceivability, as in the case of novelty/familiarity of the TBR information. These and other similar dissociations are difficult to account for in terms of a single underlying process, and therefore pose problems for the byproduct theory. A theory that postulates perception and encoding as separate but related processes can make better sense of the facts.

Where does all this leave our friend and his encoding-less theorizing? In the long run, of course, it does not matter. Science as a self-correcting enterprise has a habit of proving all ideas that scientists have about what they observe wrong. It is only a question of time before both the byproduct theory and the GAPS framework, even if revised, become hopelessly inadequate. Moreover, even now it is not clear that the byproduct theory is wrong and the encoding theory right, or at least more so. When it comes to ontological problems (Does X exist even though we do not see it and cannot touch it?), there can be no decisive experiments producing incontrovertible data. There can be only decisive beliefs about controvertible data.

Therefore, the discussion here leaves our friend and esteemed colleague in the happy position of an exceptionally successful scientist who has the satisfaction of knowing that he was instrumental in bringing into our world one of the most influential systematic conceptual frameworks within which problems of memory can be raised and investigated and within which many findings can be accommodated and integrated. If the LOP framework does not cover *everything* about memory under the sun, and if there are aspects of memory to which it does not pertain, it simply means that LOP is like any other theory or framework: a part of the normal world of science. So be it.

☐ Acknowledgments

Preparation of this chapter was supported by an endowment by Anne and Max Tanenbaum in support of research in cognitive neuroscience and by a grant from the Natural Sciences and Engineering Research Council of Canada.

☐ References

Bartlett, F. C. (1932). *Remembering: A study in experimental and social psychology.* Cambridge, England: Cambridge University Press.
Bower, G. H. (1972). Stimulus-sampling theory of encoding variability. In A. W. Melton & E. Martin

(Eds.), *Coding processes in human memory* (pp. 85–124). Washington, DC: V. H. Winston & Sons.

Bower, G. H. (2000). A brief history of memory research. In E. Tulving & F. I. M. Craik (Eds.), *The Oxford handbook of memory* (pp. 3–32). New York: Oxford University Press.

Brewer, J. B., Zhao, Z., Glover, G. H., & Gabrieli, J. D. E. (1998). Making memories: Brain activity that predicts whether visual experiences will be remembered or forgotten. *Science, 281,* 1185–1187.

Brown, J. (1958). Some tests of the decay theory of immediate memory. *Quarterly Journal of Experimental Psychology, 10,* 12–21.

Buckner, R. L., Bandettini, P. A., O'Craven, K. M., Savoy, R. L., Petersen, S. E., Raichle, M. E., & Rosen, B. R. (1996). Detection of cortical activation during averaged single trials of a cognitive task using functional magnetic resonance imaging. *Proceedings of the National Academy of Science USA, 93,* 14878–14883.

Buckner, R. L., Kelley, W. H., & Peterson, S. E. (1999). Frontal cortex contributes to human memory formation. *Nature Neuroscience, 2,* 311–314.

Buckner, R. L., Koutstaal, W., Schacter, D. L., & Rosen, B. R. (2000). Functional MRI evidence for a role of frontal and inferior temporal cortex in amodal components of priming. *Brain, 123,* 620–640.

Cabeza, R., & Nyberg, L. (2000). Imaging cognition II: An empirical review of 275 PET and FMRI studies. *Journal of Cognitive Neuroscience, 12,* 1–47.

Cofer, C. N. (Ed.) (1961). *Verbal learning and verbal behavior.* New York: McGraw-Hill.

Cofer, C. N., & Musgrave, B. S. (Eds.). (1963). *Verbal behavior and learning.* New York: McGraw-Hill.

Constable, R. T., Carpentier, A., Pugh, K., Westerveld, M., Oszunar, Y., & Spencer, D. D. (2000). Investigation of the human hippocampal formation using a randomized event-related paradigm and z-shimmed functional MRI. *Neuroimage, 12,* 55–62.

Craik, F. I. M. (1973). A 'Levels of Analysis' view of memory. In P. Pliner, L. Krames, & T. M. Alloway (Eds.), *Communication and affect: Language and thought.* New York: Academic Press.

Craik, F. I. M. (1983). On the transfer of information from temporary to permanent memory. *Philosophical Transactions of the Royal Society of London, B302,* 341–359.

Craik, F. I. M. (1999). Levels of encoding and retrieval. In B. H. Challis & B. M. Velichkovsky (Eds.), *Stratification in cognition and consciousness* (pp. 97–101) Amsterdam: John Benjamins.

Craik, F. I. M., & Lockhart, R. S. (1972). Levels of processing: A framework for memory research. *Journal of Verbal Learning and Verbal Behavior, 11,* 671–684.

Craik, F. I. M., & Tulving, E. (1975). Depth of processing and the retention of words in episodic memory. *Journal of Experimental Psychology: General, 104,* 268–294.

Curran, H. V. (1991). Benzodiazepines, memory and mood: A review. *Psychopharmacology, 105,* 1–8.

Dale, A. M., & Buckner, R. L. (1997). Selective averaging of rapidly presented individual trials using fMRI. *Human Brain Mapping, 5,* 329–340.

Demb, J. B., Desmond, J. E., Wagner, A. D., Vaidya, C. J., Glover, G. H., & Gabrieli, J. D. E. (1995). Semantic encoding and retrieval in the left inferior prefrontal cortex: A functional MRI study of task difficulty and process specificity. *Journal of Neuroscience, 15,* 5870–5878.

Dudai, Y. (1997). How big is human memory, or on being just useful enough. *Learning & Memory, 3,* 341–365.

Ebbinghaus, H. (1885). *Über das Gedächtnis.* Leipzig: Duncker & Humblot.

Freed, D. M., Corkin, S., & Cohen, N. J. (1987). Forgetting in H. M.: A second look. *Neuropsychologia, 25,* 461–471.

Ghoneim, M. M., & Mewaldt, S. P. (1990) Benzodiazepines and human memory: A review. *Anesthesiology, 72,* 926–938.

Gregg, V. (1976). Word frequency, recognition and recall. In J. Brown (Ed.), *Recall and recognition* (pp. 183–216). London: Wiley.

Guynn, M. J., & Roediger, H. L. (1995). High priority event instructions affect implicit and explicit memory tests. *Psychological Research–Psychologische Forschung, 57,* 192–202.

Habib, R. (2001). On the relation between conceptual priming, neural priming, and novelty assessment. *Scandinavian Journal of Psychology, 42,* 187–195.

Habib, R. (2000). *Human novelty assessment systems: Positron emission tomography evidence.* Unpublished doctoral dissertation. University of Toronto.

Hodges, J. R. (2000). Memory in the dementias. In E. Tulving & F. I. M. Craik (Eds.), *The Oxford handbook of memory* (pp. 441–459). New York: Oxford University Press.

Hyde, T. S., & Jenkins, J. J. (1969). Differential effects of incidental tasks on the organization of recall of a list of highly associated words. *Journal of Experimental Psychology, 82,* 472–481.

Johnston, J. D., & Jenkins, J. J. (1971). Two more incidental tasks that differentially affect associative clustering in recall. *Journal of Experimental Psychology, 89,* 92–95.

Kinsbourne, M., & George, J. (1974). The mechanism of the word-frequency effect on recognition memory. *Journal of Verbal Learning and Verbal Behavior, 13,* 63–69.

Kirchhoff, B. A., Wagner, A. D., Maril, A., & Stern, C. E. (2000). Prefrontal-temporal circuitry for episodic encoding and subsequent memory. *Journal of Neuroscience, 20,* 6173–6180.

Knight, R. T. (1984). Decreased response to novel stimuli after prefrontal lesions in man. *Electroencephalography and Clinical Neurophysiology, 59,* 9–20.

Kohonen, T., Oja, E., & Lehtio, P. (1989). Storage and processing of information in distributed associative memory systems. In G. E. Hinton & J. A. Anderson (Eds.), *Parallel models of associative memory* (pp. 129–167). Hillsdale, NJ: Erlbaum.

Kormi-Nouri, R., Nilsson, L.-G., & Ohta, N. (2000, July). *The novelty effect: Support for the novelty/ encoding hypothesis.* Paper presented at the XXVII International Congress of Psychology. Stockholm, Sweden.

Koutstaal, W., Wagner, A. D., Rotte, M., Maril, A., Buckner, R. L., & Schacter, D. L. (2000). Perceptual specificity in visual object priming: Functional magnetic resonance evidence for a laterality difference in fusiform cortex. *Neuropsychologia, 39,* 184–199.

Loftus, E. F., & Loftus, G. R. (1980). On the permanence of stored information in the human brain. *American Psychologist, 35,* 409–420.

Markowitsch, H. J. (2000). Neuroanatomy of memory. In E. Tulving & F. I. M. Craik (Eds.), *The Oxford handbook of memory* (pp. 465–484). New York: Oxford University Press.

Mayes, A. R. (2000). Selective memory disorders. In E. Tulving & F. I. M. Craik (Eds.), *The Oxford handbook of memory* (pp. 427–440). New York: Oxford University Press.

McGeoch, J. A., & Irion, A. L. (1952). *The psychology of human learning.* New York: Longmans, Green.

Melton, A. W. (1963). Discussion of Professor Deese's paper. In C. N. Cofer & B. S. Musgrave (Eds.), *Verbal behavior and learning* (pp. 355–361). New York: McGraw-Hill.

Melton, A. W., & Martin, E. (Eds.). (1972). *Coding processes in human memory.* Washington, DC: V. H. Winston & Sons.

Metcalfe, J. (1993). Novelty monitoring, metacognition, and control in a composite holographic associative recall model: Implications for Korsakoff amnesia. *Psychological Review, 100,* 3–22.

Milner, B. (1966). Amnesia following operation on the temporal lobes. In C. W. M. Whitty & O. L. Zangwill (Eds.), *Amnesia* (pp. 109–133). London: Butterworth.

Murdock, B. B., Jr. (1967). Recent developments in short-term memory. *British Journal of Psychology, 58,* 421–433.

Nilsson, L.-G. (2000). Remembering actions and words. In E. Tulving & F. I. M. Craik (Eds.), *The Oxford handbook of memory* (pp. 137–148). New York: Oxford University Press.

Peterson, L. R., & Peterson, M. J. (1959). Short-term retention of individual verbal items. *Journal of Experimental Psychology, 58,* 193–198.

Polster, M. R. (1993) Drug-induced amnesia: implications for cognitive neuropsychological investigations of memory. *Psychological Bulletin, 114,* 477–493.

Popper, K. R., & Eccles, J. C. (1977). *The self and its brain.* Berlin: Springer International.

Postman, L., & Adams, P. A. (1956). Studies in incidental learning IV. The interaction of orienting tasks and stimulus materials. *Journal of Experimental Psychology, 51,* 329–333.

Roediger, H. L., & McDermott, K. B. (1993). Implicit memory in normal human subjects. In H. Spinnler & F. Boller (Eds.), *Handbook of neuropsychology* (pp. 63–131). Amsterdam: Elsevier.

Roediger, H. L., & McDermott, K. B. (1995). Creating false memories: Remembering words not presented in lists. *Journal of Experimental Psychology: Learning, Memory, and Cognition, 21,* 803–814.

Roediger, H. L., & McDermott, K. B. (2000). Distortions of memory. In E. Tulving & F. I. M. Craik (Eds.), *The Oxford handbook of memory* (pp. 149–162). New York: Oxford University Press.

Rugg, M. D. (1995). Event-related potential studies of human memory. In M. S. Gazzaniga (Ed.), *The cognitive neurosciences* (pp. 789–801). Cambridge, MA: MIT Press.

Saltzman, I. J. (1956). Comparisons of incidental and intentional learning with different orienting tasks. *American Journal of Psychology, 69,* 274–277.

Sanquist, T. F., Rohrbaugh, J. W., Syndulko, K., & Lindsley, D. B. (1980). Electrocortical signs of levels of processing: Perceptual analysis and recognition memory. *Psychophysiology, 17,* 568–576.

Saykin, A. J., Johnson, S. C., Flashman, L. A., McAllister, T. W., Sparling, M., Darcey, T. M., Moritz, C. H., Guerin, S. J., Weaver, J., & Mamourian, A. (1999). Functional differentiation of medial temporal and frontal regions involved in processing novel and familiar words: An fMRI study. *Brain, 122,* 1963–1971.

Schacter, D. L. (1987). Implicit memory: History and current status. *Journal of Experimental Psychology: Learning, Memory, and Cognition, 13,* 501–518.

Schulz, L. S. (1971). Effects of high-priority events on recall and recognition of other events. *Journal of Verbal Learning and Verbal Behavior, 10,* 322–330.

Siddle, D. A. T., Packer, J. S., Donchin, E., & Fabiani, M. (1991). Mnemonic information processing. In J. R. Jennings & M. G. H. Coles (Eds), *Handbook of cognitive psychophysiology: Central and autonomic nervous system approaches* (pp. 449–510). Chichester, England: Wiley.

Sokolov, E. N. (1963). Higher nervous functions: The orienting reflex. *Annual Review of Physiology, 25,* 545–580.

Squire, L. R. (1992). Memory and the hippocampus: A synthesis from findings with rats, monkeys, and humans. *Psychological Review, 99,* 195–231.

Stern, C. E., Corkin, S., Gonzalez, R. G., Guimaraes, A. R., Baker, J. R., Jennings, P. J., Carr, C. A., Sugiura, R. M., Vedantham, V., & Rosen, B. R. (1996). The hippocampal formation participates in novel picture encoding: Evidence from functional magnetic resonance imaging. *Proceedings of the National Academy of Science USA, 93,* 8660–8665.

Tulving, E. (1969). Retrograde amnesia in free recall. *Science, 164,* 88–90.

Tulving, E. (1983). *Elements of episodic memory.* Oxford, England: Clarendon Press.

Tulving, E. (1993). Human memory. In P. Andersen, O. Hvalby, O. Paulsen, & B. Hökfelt (Eds.), *Memory concepts - 1993: Basic and clinical aspects* (pp. 27–45). Amsterdam: Elsevier.

Tulving, E., & Kroll, N. E. A. (1995). Novelty assessment in the brain and long-term memory encoding. *Psychonomic Bulletin and Review, 2,* 387–390.

Tulving, E., & Madigan, S. A. (1970). Memory and verbal learning. *Annual Review of Psychology, 21,* 437–484.

Tulving, E., Markowitsch, H. J., Craik, F. I. M., Habib, R., & Houle, S. (1996). Novelty and familiarity activations in PET studies of memory encoding and retrieval. *Cerebral Cortex, 6,* 71–79.

Tulving, E., Markowitsch, H. J., Kapur, S., Habib, R., & Houle, S. (1994). Novelty encoding networks in the human brain: Positron emission tomography data. *Neuroreport, 5,* 2525–2528.

Tulving, E., & Schacter, D. L. (1990). Priming and human memory systems. *Science, 247,* 301–306.

Velichkovsky, B. M. (1999). From levels of processing to stratification of cognition. In B. H. Challis & B. M. Velichkovsky (Eds.), *Stratification in cognition and consciousness* (pp. 203–226). Amsterdam: John Benjamins.

Wagner, A. D., Desmond, J. E., Demb, J. B., Glover, G. H., & Gabrieli, J. D. E. (1997). Semantic repetition priming for verbal and pictorial knowledge: A functional MRI study of left inferior prefrontal cortex. *Journal of Cognitive Neuroscience, 9,* 714–726.

Wagner, A. D., Schacter, D. L., Rotte, M., Koutstaal, W., Maril, A., Dale, A. M., Rosen, B. R., & Buckner, R. L. (1998). Verbal memory encoding: Brain activity predicts subsequent remembering and forgetting. *Science, 281,* 1188–1191.

Warrington, E. K., & Weiskrantz, L. (1970). Amnesic syndrome: Consolidation or retrieval? *Nature, 228,* 628–630.

Warrington, E. K., and Weiskrantz, L. (1974). The effect of prior learning on subsequent retention in amnesic patients. *Neuropsychologia, 12,* 419–428.

Warrington, E. K., & Weiskrantz, L. (1978). Further analysis of the prior learning effect in amnesic patients. *Neuropsychologia, 16,* 169–177.

Watkins, M.J. (2001). The modality effect and the gentle law of speech ascendancy: Protesting the tyranny of reified memory. In H. L. Roediger, J. S. Nairne, I. Neath, & A. M. Suprenant (Eds.), *The nature of remembering: Essays in honor of Robert G. Crowder.* Washington, DC: American Psychological Association.

Wheeler, M., Stuss, D. T., & Tulving, E. (1995). Frontal lobes and memory impairment. *Journal of the International Neuropsychological Society, 1,* 525–536.

Henry L. Roediger, III
David A. Gallo

Levels of Processing:
Some Unanswered Questions

In 1960 Tresselt and Mayzner published an interesting experiment that showed large effects of an independent variable on recall. They gave three groups of subjects 100 words such as "career" and "monopoly" and asked each group to perform a task as they examined each word. One group was told to cross out vowels in each word, a second group was told to copy the words over, and a third group was asked to rate the words on a 7-point scale as to how much they belonged to the concept of "economic." (This rating task made sense in the context of the words selected.) Presentation of the words occurred under incidental learning instructions, so the 10-minute free recall test that occurred later came as a surprise to subjects.

Tresselt and Mayzner's (1960) results are shown in Figure 3.1. Recall was much greater following the "economic" rating task relative to the other two tasks. Recall was also somewhat greater after copying words than after crossing out vowels. The experiment was carefully conducted and there is no reason to doubt the results. However, reading the authors' interpretation of the results some 40 years after publication strikes contemporary researchers as somewhat odd. The economic judgment task improved recall, according to the authors, because it increased "the number of differential responses evoked by these words" relative to the other two conditions, an idea owing to Postman (e.g., Postman, Adams, & Phillips, 1955). Differential responses? No one uses these terms today in the study of human memory.

☐ Levels of Processing

Nowadays researchers attempting to explain results like those in Figure 3.1 would resort to quite different language to account for this striking pattern. We can thank Fergus Craik and Robert Lockhart (1972) for introducing the levels-of-processing framework that provides such explanatory power. Their paper (see also Craik, 1973) proposed that

> trace persistence is a function of depth of analysis, with deeper levels of analysis associated with more elaborate, longer lasting, and stronger traces. Since the organism is normally concerned only with the extraction of meaning from the stimuli, it is advantageous to store the

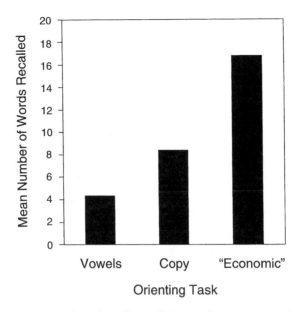

FIGURE 3.1. Mean number of words recalled in each orienting condition of Tresselt and Mayzner (1960).

products of such deep analyses, but there is usually no need to store the products of preliminary analyses. (p. 675)

In the original levels-of-processing framework, "depth of analysis" referred to basic perceptual processes that ranged from quite superficial (seeing patterns of lines and curves in
a visual stimulus such as a word) through intermediate representations (phonemic, based
on sound) to the deepest level of semantics or meaning. Depth of processing referred to
perception, with memory as a byproduct of perceptual analysis but not (usually) as an end
in itself (see Tulving, chapter 2 this volume, for examination of this last idea).

Craik and Lockhart (1972) showed that much of the extant literature could be interpreted by this straightforward but powerful idea of depth of processing. Their paper is
one of the most influential papers in the history of cognitive psychology and, indeed,
probably one of the most cited papers in all of psychology. Figure 3.2 shows cumulative
citations to this paper over the last 30 or so years compared to two other very influential
works published the same year (Tulving's [1972] chapter announcing the distinction between episodic and semantic memory and Anderson & Bower's [1972] associative theory
of recognition and retrieval processes in free recall). Although all three papers had great
impact, like few other papers in the field, Craik and Lockhart's contribution has far out-
paced the others in terms of cumulative citations. In fact, we can find no other paper in
the past 30 years that has been as influential (and perhaps only Miller's [1956] famous
paper rivals it over a longer period, at least within the cognitive psychology of human
memory).

Craik and Tulving (1975) developed a paradigm that helped to make the levels-of-processing ideas more concrete and provided the notion that three distinct levels of processing could be distinguished, at least for verbal materials. In considering single words, one
can perform a visual analysis of the letters, a phonemic analysis of the word's sound, or a

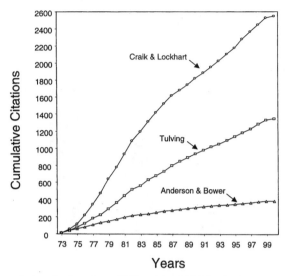

FIGURE 3.2. Cumulative citations from 1973 to May 2000 for Anderson and Bower (1972), Craik and Lockhart (1972), and Tulving (1972).

semantic analysis of its meaning, as shown in Figure 3.3. The paradigm that Craik and Tulving provided, illustrated on the right side of that figure, was designed to effect a particular level of processing by asking subjects questions that would direct attention to a particular level. So, a question about the word's letters would provide a (shallow) visual analysis, one about sound would lead to a phonemic analysis, and a question about a word's category or other meaningful qualities would provoke a semantic (deep) level of processing. The question was assumed to provoke an analysis at the appropriate level and

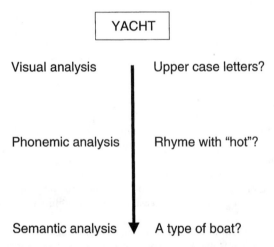

FIGURE 3.3. The standard levels-of-processing framework. During encoding, a word (e.g., "yacht") can be analyzed at several levels (left), with the final level of analysis specified by the type of orienting question (right). Levels of analysis proceed in a more or less linear fashion, with analysis at one level dependent upon completed analyses at shallower levels.

perhaps the levels assumed to occur prior to the critical level. So, for example, a phonemic level of analysis would require analysis of visual features and sound, but not meaning.

In a series of 10 experiments, Craik and Tulving (1975) produced beautiful results showing that free recall and recognition increased directly with the level of processing (as defined by the type of orienting task) accorded words during study. In their first few experiments, they used incidental learning instructions, curtailed the amount of time subjects had to examine words following the question, and meticulously measured time to answer questions (see also Craik, 1973). The assumption seems to have been that these factors were critical in obtaining the levels-of-processing effect. However, in later experiments Craik and Tulving abandoned these methodological strictures and still obtained elegant data. The results shown in Figure 3.4 come from Experiment 9b of their series, in which intentional learning instructions and a 6 s presentation rate were used and the subjects were 12 students in an undergraduate class. Sixty words were studied and students answered yes/no questions about each (case, rhyme, and category), with the answer being "yes" and "no" equally often. The recognition test consisted of the 60 studied words spread amidst 120 lures, with the students instructed to circle exactly 60 words. Despite the relaxed experimental conditions, the data in Figure 3.4 show a dramatic levels of processing effect, which interacted with the yes/no responses during encoding. The "levels" effect was larger for items to which "yes" was the correct answer during the study phase; further, words to which "yes" was the answer were recognized better than those for which "no" was the answer, except for the judgments of case. Of course, in some sense it is no surprise that these effects occurred under slow rates of presentation and intentional learning, because Jenkins and his colleagues had previously shown that type of instruction and time on the task had little effect in similar tasks (Hyde & Jenkins, 1969; Walsh & Jenkins, 1973).

These basic findings were repeated several times in the Craik and Tulving (1975) series of experiments and have been observed in dozens, maybe hundreds, of experiments in

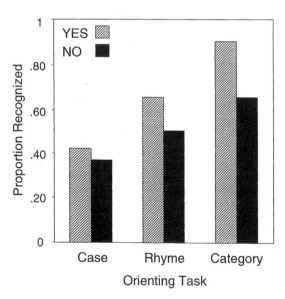

FIGURE 3.4. Mean proportion of words recognized as a function of orienting task and type of question (i.e., "yes" or "no" response) in Craik and Tulving (1975, Experiment 9b).

the past quarter century. Lockhart and Craik (1990) summarized much of the evidence surrounding these phenomena a decade ago and the volume has increased considerably since then. If a researcher today produces data like those of Tresselt and Mayzner (1960) shown in Figure 3.1, we know what to say to explain them: levels of processing is the answer. We would say that the crossing out of vowels involves visual (graphemic) analysis, that the copying of words may involve phonemic/lexical analysis, and that rating the relatedness of a word to the concept of "economic" requires a semantic analysis. No one seems to doubt this answer, and the levels-of-processing framework is mentioned favorably in every textbook (although sometimes qualified as incomplete in certain ways).

But is levels of processing really the answer to why orienting tasks affect performance on memory tests? The purpose of the remainder of this chapter is to raise some unanswered questions about data that arose from research within the levels of processing framework. None of the points should be particularly new, but they may seem new in the current context because the field seems to have collectively forgotten or ignored them.

☐ Unanswered Questions

If the unquestioned answer to the question of "Why do different orienting tasks strongly affect memory performance?" is "levels of processing," then the purpose of the remainder of the chapter is to ask the unanswered question of "Why does anyone believe this statement?" By 1980 we knew it wasn't true. Now, for readers familiar with the experimental psychology literature of the 1970s, the previous sentence may serve as a retrieval cue to call to mind many papers critical of the levels of processing framework in the 1970s. In fact, it was heavily criticized by a large number of people in papers and chapters: Anderson and Reder (1979), Baddeley (1978), Eysenck (1978), Kolers (1979), Morris, Bransford, and Franks (1977), D. L. Nelson (1979), T. O. Nelson (1977), and Tulving (1979), among other people, all voiced strong criticism. Many of these commentators raised cogent points (but see Lockhart & Craik, 1978, 1990, for replies to some of them). One often-voiced criticism had to do with the alleged circularity of the approach, which never worried many of us (see Lockhart, chapter 7 this volume, for discussion), or proposed alternative accounts of the data. However, the basic "levels-of-processing data" themselves were rarely called into question.

We do not want to renew the basic criticisms in the papers above. We instead want to resurrect another set of issues raised by data that were a direct product of the levels of processing approach and therefore seem to be inherently problematic. The data we have in mind are contained mostly in other papers and chapters: Craik and Tulving (1975), Lockhart, Craik, and Jacoby (1976), Moscovitch and Craik (1976), Craik (1977), Fisher and Craik (1977), Chow, Currie, and Craik (1978), and Jacoby, Craik, and Begg (1979). The astute reader will note that the common name here is the honoree of this volume: Fergus I. M. Craik. The mark of a great scientist is to test one's own theory as vigorously as one's critics do. We believe Craik did this in the 1970s.

In the remainder of this chapter, we consider some central aspects of the problematic data produced by Craik and his colleagues that provided challenges to the levels of processing approach. These challenges have never been entirely answered (although Lockhart & Craik, 1978, 1990 addressed some points). To presage, the conclusion we reach is that the original levels of processing approach, taken literally, is undercut by these data from the 1970s and 1980s. We consider six fundamental problems for the levels-of-processing approach, mostly ones introduced by Craik himself.

Question 1. Why does the nature of answers to questions so greatly affect recall and recognition, when they do not affect levels of processing in the task?

This problem appears in full force in Figure 3.4. Answering either "yes" or "no" about the word "yacht" to the question, "Is it a type of boat?" requires subjects to access the meaning of the word. Yet recognition is much greater following "yes" answers than following "no" answers. In general, the levels-of-processing effect is greater for questions to which the answer is "yes" in the typical Craik and Tulving (1975) paradigm. There is no ready explanation within Craik and Lockhart's (1972) theory, but the idea added later was that "richness" or "elaborateness" of encoding was the factor that mattered. Craik and Tulving (Experiments 6 and 7) provided tests of this new idea that were ultimately supporting. They argued that questions answered "yes" generally provided for a more congruous encoding than questions answered "no," and this congruity led to richer, more elaborate encodings that could be used more effectively on the test.

Moscovitch and Craik (1976) manipulated orienting tasks at study and the congruity between encoding and retrieval by providing the questions used at study as retrieval cues during the test. They showed that whether the standard levels of processing effect occurs depends on the nature of retrieval conditions (see also Fisher & Craik, 1977), and they concluded that "other factors may be as important as levels of processing in determining memory performance" (p. 455). In particular, the answer to an orienting question ("yes" or "no"), whether the test employed free or cued recall, and whether cues were unique to a word or shared among words all greatly affected performance. However, the question that these results (and many others) raise is, If all these other factors are important in determining recall and recognition, is the idea of levels of processing needed at all? Can the data be subsumed under another theory? Moscovitch and Craik argued that levels of processing ideas are still needed. We consider this issue more fully in Question 6, after discussing some other issues.

Question 2. Why do levels-of-processing effects occur under intentional learning conditions?

The early experiments by Craik (1973) and Craik and Tulving (1975) generally employed incidental learning conditions and brief tachistoscopic presentation of the words that were to be processed. The assumption was that intentional learning instructions promote meaningful processing, and therefore attempts to induce only shallow levels of processing might be undone by intentional instructions. Keep in mind that depth refers to the level of basic perceptual processing of a word, which can presumably be accomplished in a fraction of a second even by a slow reader, so fast presentation and incidental instructions were thought to be critical to the effect. Yet the general finding is that type of learning instructions does not have much effect on the standard levels-of-processing effect, and this conclusion has been generally accepted.

Consider the experiment of Hyde and Jenkins (1969), who had seven independent groups of subjects engage in free recall of 24-word lists. Their design crossed three types of orienting tasks (checking words for e's, quickly estimating the number of letters, or rating words for their pleasantness on a 7-point scale) with intentional and incidental learning instructions. A seventh group was given standard intentional learning instructions with no orienting task. Within the levels-of-processing framework, pleasantness rating is a deep task, and the other two (involving surface features of the words) are shallow tasks.

TABLE 3.1. Mean percent recalled as a function of learning instruction and orienting task in Hyde and Jenkins (1969).

Orienting task	Mean recall
Incidental learning	
Check e's	39%
Estimate letters	41%
Pleasantness rating	68%
Intentional learning	
Check e's	43%
Estimate letters	53%
Pleasantness rating	69%
No task	67%

Hyde and Jenkins's (1969) results are shown in Table 3.1, and indeed, pleasantness rating produced greater recall than did the other two tasks. Further, the intentional learning condition with no orienting task produced about the same level of recall as did the pleasantness rating conditions (whether intentional or incidental). This outcome seems to indicate that an instruction to learn material is tantamount to a deep level of processing manipulation (so long as one is a bit cavalier in accepting the null hypothesis).

But this outcome raises a puzzle: When subjects are given so-called shallow orienting tasks under intentional learning instructions, why doesn't recall increase dramatically? The improvement was negligible in the case of checking e's and modest in the case of estimating letters (see Table 3.1). Why didn't recall approach that of the other intentional conditions when subjects knew they had to learn and remember the material? Was it that subjects did not have enough time? Time seems an unlikely candidate, as Hyde and Jenkins (1969) permitted subjects 2 s/item and, in a second experiment, 4 s/item.

Craik and Tulving (1975, Experiment 4) replicated a strong effect of orienting task under intentional learning conditions. They pointed out that the outcome was at odds with the original notion of levels of processing because

> surely under intentional learning conditions the subject would analyze and perceive the name and meaning of the target word with all three types of question. In this case equal retention should ensue (by the Craik and Lockhart formulation), but Experiment 4 showed that large differences in recall were still found. (p. 279)

Craik and Tulving endorsed the concept of degrees of stimulus elaboration as more appropriate to explain the effects of orienting tasks on recall and recognition than the original levels of processing ideas.

Chow, Currie, and Craik (1978) created conditions that would seem to have produced benefits from intentional learning, if it were possible to do so, following shallow orienting tasks. They used the standard Craik and Tulving (1975) paradigm with intentional learning instructions, but with very slow presentation rates (6 or 12 s/word). For the critical conditions, subjects received special instructions. With one set of instructions the subjects were given intentional learning conditions and a short lecture on the levels of processing effect, with the advice given that after completing the orienting task, it would help their memory if they generated an adjective for each word. With another set, the special task given was to decide whether a word would fit into a sentence frame that was provided. The authors expected that the levels of processing effect would be eliminated under these instructions, because all subjects would process items to a deep level. However, the effect was eliminated only when subjects were given the explicit sentence frame and asked if the word would fit into it, not when they had to generate adjectives. Postman and Kruesi (1977) also showed that intentional learning instructions can benefit performance with shallow encoding tasks, but the levels-of-processing effect remains strong in all experiments with intentional encoding.

It is difficult to understand why intentional learning instructions, with large amounts of study time, do not eliminate (or at least greatly attenuate) the effect of orienting tasks on recall and recognition if the original framework emphasizing perceptual levels of processing is valid. Yet, unless subjects are specifically given a second orienting task that demands semantic processing, the levels effect remains under intentional conditions with slow presentation rates. Does the shallow orienting task short-circuit or curtail subjects' ability to engage voluntarily in meaningful processing? Does the shallow orienting task create some inhibitory process that semantic processing cannot overcome? Whatever the answer, Craik and Tulving's (1975) point seems correct: These results surely pose a problem for the original version of the levels-of-processing framework, one that has never been solved.

Question 3. Why can't the levels-of-processing effect be eliminated by reversing the usual procedure during encoding?

The standard paradigm for studying the effect of orienting tasks is to give people the orienting task ("Does the word contain an e?") first and then give them the stimulus to be judged (hedgehog). The idea is to arrest processing at the prescribed level or (in this case) at a visual level of analysis. However, suppose this usual procedure is reversed and the word is given to the subject for several seconds before the question is given. If intentional learning instructions are used, then according to the Craik and Lockhart (1972) formulation, the levels-of-processing effect should disappear. Surely subjects would process the word to a deep, semantic level before the question is even presented and two seconds would be ample time to do so.

As far as we can tell, this sort of experiment has rarely been tried, because it makes little sense from the levels of processing perspective. However, Craik (1977) directly compared these two ways to manipulate the orienting task, with the procedure outlined in Figure 3.5, under both intentional and incidental learning conditions (Moeser, 1983, also employed the "reversed" paradigm, but only with incidental instructions). In the standard paradigm, subjects received the question and then the word; in the reversed paradigm, subjects saw the word for 2 s and then, after a full 5 s delay, received the question. Surely meaning would have been extracted from the word after 7 s of study under intentional learning conditions. Nonetheless, as can be seen in Figure 3.6, Craik (1977) still observed a very strong effect of orienting tasks under these "reversed" conditions, although the effect was not as great as when the question was given before the word. As Craik (1977, p. 689) noted, it is "mystifying" that these conditions (intentional learning for 7 s with the word given before the question) did not have a greater impact on performance in the shallow conditions and eliminate the levels-of-processing effect.

The problem posed in this section is essentially the same as in the preceding point: Even when subjects are given ample time and conditions designed to encourage meaningful processing, the effect of orienting tasks—the "levels-of-processing effect"—still occurs. This outcome leads to the conclusion that the original levels-of-processing framework is wrong and that other principles must be brought to bear to explain these phenomena, as Craik and Tulving (1975) and Craik (1977) concluded many years ago.

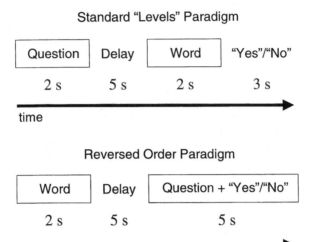

FIGURE 3.5. Representative trials for each of the two methodologies employed by Craik (1977, Experiment II). In the standard paradigm, the orienting question precedes the word, whereas in the reversed paradigm the word precedes the question.

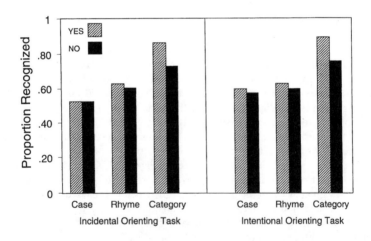

FIGURE 3.6. Mean proportion of words recognized in each learning condition of the reversed order paradigm (i.e., word presented before orienting question), as estimated from Figure 2 of Craik (1977). Performance within each orienting task is presented separately for "yes" and "no" responses to the orienting question.

Question 4. Why do variations within a particular level of processing affect memory performance?

Most experiments in the levels-of-processing tradition manipulate orienting tasks designed to effect distinct levels of processing, much as Craik and Tulving (1975) did. Following Craik and Tulving's lead, many researchers attempted to induce all three levels shown in Figure 3.3 by choosing tasks that require graphemic (visual), phonemic (acoustic), and semantic (meaningful) analyses. Many other researchers contented themselves with two levels of processing, one deep (meaningful) and the other shallow (graphemic or phonemic). The data produced nearly always supported the general levels-of-processing framework, with greater recall or recognition for semantically coded words. However, it is rare that an investigator manipulates the type of orienting task within one domain, visual, phonemics, or semantic. Can recall be similarly affected when orienting tasks are manipulated within one domain (all involving one type or level of processing) as when they are manipulated across domains?

Data from a study by Packman and Battig (1978) indicate that the answer is yes. Packman and Battig gave subjects 50 words under one of seven orienting tasks, manipulated between subjects, and then gave a surprise free recall test after a brief delay. All seven orienting tasks were designed to force a deep level of processing. The full set of data are complex, but consider the results from just three conditions shown in Figure 3.7. The data appear orderly and apparently show a nice levels-of-processing effect. However, all three orienting tasks (rating words for meaningfulness, concreteness, or pleasantness) required meaningful processing. Indeed, the task showing the lowest level of recall of these three was the one that required ratings of meaning! If variations of tasks within one putative level of processing can mimic effects typically obtained between levels of processing, then

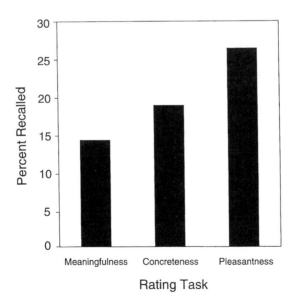

FIGURE 3.7. Mean percent of words recalled in three orienting conditions of Packman and Battig (1978).

we can again question whether the levels-of-processing framework provides a satisfactory explanation of the results from manipulating orienting tasks. Seamon and Virostek (1978) reported rather similar data to those of Packman and Battig, but few other reports exist in which this experimental tactic has been used (see also Challis, Velichkovsky, & Craik, 1996; Hyde & Jenkins, 1973; and Mathews, 1977).

Question 5. If levels-of-processing theory were correct, how could subjects free recall items after orienting tasks that require shallow levels of processing?

Most experiments varying orienting tasks have measured recognition. Recognition memory is usually greater than chance, even after shallow levels of processing (checking for e's or making case judgments). Of course, in recognition memory, researchers have proposed that correct decisions can be made on the basis of familiarity or perceptual fluency (e.g., Mandler, 1980; Jacoby & Dallas, 1981), and these qualities may be supported by traces left from shallow levels of processing. However, the original "levels" framework proposed levels of perceptual analysis. If processing of a word were arrested at graphemic or phonological levels, how could they be recalled minutes or hours later? If all one knew was that a word was in upper case letters or that it had a particular sound, how could the correct word be reconstructed? It could not, of course, yet subjects show reasonable levels of free recall even after shallow orienting tasks.

Roediger, Payne, Gillespie, and Lean (1982) conducted a relevant experiment. Subjects performed a standard set of orienting tasks during the encoding phase of the experiment (graphemic, phonemic, semantic) in a typical Craik–Tulving type of experiment. They studied 60 words under intentional learning conditions, with questions directing attention to one of the three "levels" for 20 words. After list presentation, subjects were distracted by another task for 1 minute to clear short-term memory. Then they were given instructions to recall as many items as possible from the list. A novel feature of the experiment was that two different conditions were employed during testing. All subjects were tested under free recall conditions, but one group was given three 7-minute tests on the words. That is, they recalled as many words as possible for 7 minutes, then their recall sheets were removed and they were given another sheet with instructions to recall as many list items as possible (both ones previously recalled and any new ones that came to mind) for another 7 minutes. Then the procedure was repeated a third time. (The purpose of the experiment was to examine hypermnesia, the recovery of additional information over repeated tests.) A second group of subjects was given one long (21-minute) test, with short breaks after 7 and 14 minutes, during which they were exhorted to continue trying as a control for total time spent in recall. For both groups, subjects drew a line under the last word recalled after each minute, so measures of cumulative recall could be obtained.

The results are shown in Figure 3.8, where solid lines and filled symbols represent the cumulative recall functions for subjects taking three tests and the broken lines and open symbols represent recall of subjects taking one long test. This variable did not affect performance much, replicating prior research by Roediger and Thorpe (1978). Of more interest in the present context is the effect of the orienting task, where the standard levels of processing effect clearly emerged. Further, the recovery of items processed to superficial levels continued to increase over the 21-minute period, which raises the issue noted above: If words were *only* processed to graphemic or phonemic levels, how would they be recalled from long-term memory at all? And how would items that were not semantically coded be recovered over these long intervals? Many researchers assume that free recall is

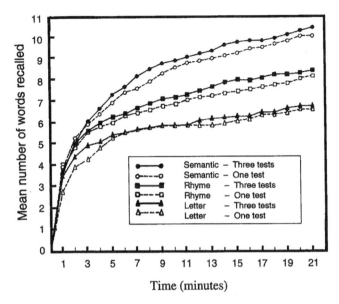

FIGURE 3.8. Cumulative recall curves for sets of items studied under each of the three orienting questions in Roediger et al. (1982). Solid lines and black symbols represent data from the group that received three 7-minute tests, whereas dashed lines and white symbols represent data from the group that received one 21-minute test.

largely driven by semantic or conceptual factors (e.g., Roediger, Weldon, & Challis, 1989); if so, then only words accorded a deep, semantic processing should be recalled.

An alternative idea that would account for the results in Figure 8 and in other free recall experiments is as follows. Perhaps the manipulation of orienting tasks in the standard Craik–Tulving type of encoding experiment does not "arrest" analysis at different levels in the perceptual system. Perhaps all orienting tasks encourage or discourage semantic analysis of words to varying degrees. A task such as pleasantness rating focuses attention on meaning, whereas tasks such as checking for e's or making a case judgment or a rhyme judgment focus attention on dimensions other than meaning. However, for free recall, what matters most is meaningful processing, perhaps because meaning is the most salient dimension upon which words can be differentiated. If we assume that all items recalled during a free recall test were processed for meaning, then the items successfully recalled following graphemic and phonemic encoding were also processed for meaning and not just for graphemic or phonemic features (see Cermak, Schnorr, Buschke, & Atkinson, 1970). Shallow orienting tasks may then be understood in part as divided attention tasks in which subjects' attention is partially diverted from their meaningful analysis of the words.

These statements above echo ideas voiced by Postman and Kruesi (1977) in reflecting on their own experimental results (see also Arbuckle & Katz, 1976). Postman and Kruesi (1977) noted:

> It may be well to remember that subjects come to the experiment with a lifelong habit of processing English words semantically. It may be a basic error to assume that instructions to attend to a nonsemantic property effectively shunt out this disposition. Rather, the imposition of a nonsemantic task may interfere to a greater or lesser degree with a persisting tendency to process words semantically. . . . If one took seriously the assumption that subjects given a

nonsemantic task no longer engage in semantic processing, one is left with no apparent explanation of why subjects recall as much as they do [following nonsemantic orienting tasks]. (p. 368).

This is just the problem we are raising with reference to the Roediger et al. (1982) data displayed in Figure 3.8, but of course the problem exists in any set of free recall data showing substantial recall (and meaningful clustering of related words) following shallow orienting tasks (e.g., Hyde & Jenkins, 1969). Once again, the challenge proposed by Postman and Kruesi and here has never been successfully answered and offers another reason for doubting the strict (perceptual) levels-of-processing formulation. Other types of tests besides free recall provide another significant challenge, under the rubric of transfer-appropriate processing.

Question 6. Why do orienting tasks affect various tests differently?

The original levels of processing framework represented a relatively pure encoding or trace-dependent (Tulving, 1974) theory of memory. Encoding activities lead to different types of memory traces, these traces support different levels of memory performance and persist differentially over time (Craik & Lockhart, 1972). The implicit assumption was that retrieval processes did not much matter, and neither did the type of test, although Craik and Lockhart (p. 678) did briefly consider such matters. Perhaps the primary empirical problem challenging the original levels of processing formulation in the past 30 or so years has to do with the interaction of encoding and testing conditions. There are several interrelated concerns.

First, in the basic Craik–Tulving variety levels-of-processing experiment, the distinctiveness of the question and the level of processing that the question promotes are confounded. In explaining the fact that positive answers to questions lead to better retention than do negative answers, Craik and Tulving (1975) proposed that the question may serve as a cue during the test, and that "yes" answers produce more congruous encodings than do "no" answers. In addition, the types of questions provide differentially distinctive cues across types of encoding. In asking about the case of words, there are usually only two (upper and lower); in asking about rhymes, the word endings are often somewhat similar across words. However, in asking whether a word belongs to a category or fits into a sentence, the possibilities for dimensions of meaning are many. Moscovitch and Craik (1976) examined the cueing power of questions in three experiments that manipulated type of orienting task and other factors. They concluded that the provision of retrieval cues, the distinctiveness of retrieval cues, and the compatibility of cues with encoded traces all powerfully affected recall, although they thought the concept of levels of processing was necessary to explain their results, too.

Later researchers argued that the concept of levels of processing was superfluous and that notions of transfer-appropriate processing (Morris et al., 1977) or encoding specificity (Tulving, 1979) were the only concepts necessary to explain memory performance in paradigms that manipulate orienting task. The basic type of experiment used as evidence for this proposition was performed by several sets of researchers at roughly the same time: Fisher and Craik (1977); Jacoby (1975); McDaniel, Friedman, and Bourne (1978); and Morris et al. (see also Bransford, Franks, Morris, & Stein, 1979). (The papers focused on somewhat different issues among themselves.) We will present data reported by Morris et al. as illustrative of the main point, but Fisher and Craik (1977) reported rather similar experiments.

Morris et al. (1977, Experiment 1) manipulated the encoding task during study by having subjects read words in sentence frames that were designed to effect either phonemic or semantic encodings. For example, the word "eagle" appeared with a sentence frame such as "_____ rhymes with legal" or "_____ is a large bird" to instantiate the two types of encoding. Subjects responded "yes" or "no" to each item, although for present purposes we will consider only the results from items that were given "yes" responses. Subjects' memories were tested under two different types of retrieval conditions, both employing recognition tests. On a standard yes/no recognition test, subjects were given a series of words that had been studied mixed in with new (nonstudied) words, and their task was to judge each word as studied ("yes") or not ("no"). In this test subjects were assumed to consult the meaning of the words in making their judgments. Other subjects were given a rhyme recognition test in which they also received a long series of test words, none of which had actually been studied. However, half the words on the test rhymed with words that had been studied and subjects were now instructed to say "yes" if the test word (e.g., "beagle") rhymed with a studied word and "no" if it did not.

The experiment represents a 2 × 2 manipulation of encoding and retrieval conditions, as illustrated in Table 3.2. The standard (semantic) recognition test shows the usual levels of processing effect, with recognition following a semantic orienting task (84% hits) much better than performance following the phonemic orienting task (63%). However, on the novel rhyme recognition test, the hit rate was greater following phonemic encoding (49%) than following semantic encoding (33%), a reversal of the typical levels-of-processing effect. Morris et al. (1977) argued that there are no encoding tasks that are inherently deep (or good) for memory. Rather, how well encoded experiences are expressed on tests reflects the appropriateness of the conditions of transfer between study and test (see also Kolers & Roediger, 1984).

This transfer-appropriate processing framework incorporates the levels-of-processing approach as a special case: Semantic processing of words does produce better performance than phonemic or graphemic processing, but only on tests that require access to semantic information. Although most explicit memory tests do rely on conceptual or semantic processing, the rhyme recognition test does not. Fisher and Craik (1977) obtained no levels-of-processing effect on a rhyme-cued recall test and Jacoby (1975) and McDaniel et al. (1978) reported similar results. Certain types of graphemic recall and recognition tests show equal or greater retention following graphemic than semantic processing (e.g., Blaxton, 1989; Stein, 1978).

TABLE 3.2. Transfer-appropriate processing. Encoding conditions emphasized phonemic or semantic dimensions of words. Retrieval conditions required predominant use of one dimension or the other, creating a strong interaction. From Morris, Bransford, and Franks (1977, Experiment 1).

| | | Retrieval condition | |
		Semantic	Rhyme
Encoding condition	Semantic	.84	.33
	Rhyme	.63	.49

Of course, as Lockhart and Craik (1990, p. 101) noted, even when study and test processes are appropriately matched on episodic memory tests, the greatest recall and recognition tends to occur with semantic tasks. For instance, from Table 3.2 it can be seen that, even though the typical "levels" effect was reversed on the rhyme test, performance was still greater with semantic study and semantic test (.84) than with rhyme study and rhyme test (.49). When verbal materials are used, it seems unlikely that any combination of low-level encoding tasks combined with a compatible retrieval task will give as great recall and recognition as do standard semantic encoding and semantic retrieval tests. Therefore, Craik and Lockhart's (1972) emphasis on meaning, especially for verbal materials, as promoting excellent memory performance is well taken (but see Tulving, 1979, for a contrary view).

Although these findings of superiority of semantic encoding and test conditions can be taken as supporting the notion of "levels" of encoding, we feel that this conclusion may be limited. Rather, to us, such an effect serves as a reminder that the to-be-learned materials in almost all levels-of-processing experiments are words. As alluded to earlier, the usual purpose of words in language is to convey semantic information. Given this fact, it is not too surprising that episodic memory for words, qua words, is optimal with an orienting task that does not deflect from the mind's usual way of processing these materials (i.e., semantically) and with a test that is sensitive to meaningful processing (see also Jenkins, 1974, pp. 17–18; Kolers, 1979, pp. 382–384, for related views). In this restricted sense, the levels-of-processing framework is upheld, but again more as a special case of transfer-appropriate processing that applies to memory for words on meaning-based tests. Nonetheless, because meaning is obviously a critical (maybe even the critical) feature in mental representation in most circumstances with verbal materials, the levels-of-processing framework correctly emphasizes this key aspect of mental life, in our opinion.

A case can be made, however, that the underlying dimension promoting good retention is a matter of expertise, not levels of processing (see Bransford et al., 1979). Human adults are expert in using language and in extracting meaning from spoken and written words. If researchers turn their attention to the myriad other types of human activities—baseball hitters' expertise in remembering the kinds of pitches and the pitching patterns of hundreds of pitchers, or ornithologists' memory for the coloration patterns of birds, and on and on endlessly—then the relevant dimension that permits excellent encoding and retrieval might be conceived more broadly as the expertise of the individual for the stimulus vocabulary of their subject matter. Virtually all adult humans are expert in language, hence its use as the lingua franca of memory experiments, but if we broaden consideration to other domains, then meaning may not be the critical feature (Bransford et al., 1979; Kolers & Roediger, 1984).

The problem of generalizability across domains, even within the sphere of language, is also highlighted by the fact that the levels-of-processing effect disappears on perceptual implicit memory tests, as was first shown by Jacoby and Dallas (1981). They conducted a Craik–Tulving type of encoding experiment and measured priming on a word identification test in which subjects were given brief glimpses of words (30 ms or so of exposure time) and tried to guess the identity of the flashed words. Jacoby and Dallas (1981) obtained priming from prior encoding (i.e., subjects identified previously studied words at higher levels than words that had not been studied), but the type of orienting task (graphemic, phonemic, or semantic) did not affect priming on the word identification test. Similar results have been obtained with other perceptual implicit memory tests. Levels of processing generally produces little or no effect on priming on tests such as word stem or word fragment completion in which subjects identify words from their first few letters (ele_____) or from a fragmented form (e _ e _ h _ _t) (e.g., Graf & Mandler, 1984; Roediger,

Weldon, Stadler, & Riegler, 1992). Priming on such tests seems to depend on accessing a perceptual record of experience (Kirsner & Dunn, 1985) or access to a lexical representation (Weldon, 1991), and manipulation of types of orienting task appears not to alter the basic perceptual record or lexical activation. The implication is that even the shallowest graphemic levels of processing (case judgments, checking for e's) seems to permit such processing that is needed to support priming on perceptual implicit memory tests. If graphemic processing arrested perception at a very early level (e.g., access of only visual features, but not of word forms), as postulated by the original levels-of-processing framework, then no priming might be expected to occur from the shallowest levels of processing.

In the wisdom of hindsight, the effect of orienting tasks (the "levels-of-processing effect") that seemed so powerful on certain tests does not have wide generalizability. Many tests (especially certain implicit tests) that validly assess retention show no levels of processing effect. This outcome fits with ideas about transfer-appropriate processing, but not with the original levels-of-processing framework. As noted above, the levels-of-processing framework that emphasizes meaning as a key element of mental representations is important, but has the unfortunate consequence of de-emphasizing other dimensions that in the right circumstances are themselves critical to memory performance (Kolers & Roediger, 1984). In fairness, the original levels-of-processing framework was designed to account for performance on what are today called explicit memory tests and one could say that implicit tests lie outside the boundary conditions of the framework. This is true, but the bulk of this chapter has pointed out problems even in the domain of explicit tests, and, of course, the levels-of-processing effect is not obtained on certain explicit tests (rhyme recognition, rhyme cued recall, recognition of graphemic differences; Fisher & Craik, 1977; Jacoby, 1975; McDaniel et al., 1978; Morris, et al., 1977; Stein, 1978). The transfer-appropriate processing framework provides a superior account of most of the findings problematic for the levels-of-processing framework, but in fairness some puzzles pointed out earlier in this chapter and elsewhere (e.g., McDermott & Roediger, 1996) do not fit well within that framework, either.

☐ Conclusions

The original levels-of-processing framework proposed that items could be processed to various levels of perceptual analysis and that this idea was helpful in understanding many effects in the psychology of memory. In particular, orienting tasks were thought to arrest processing at various levels of perceptual analysis (graphemic, phonemic, and semantic for verbal materials) and retention was said to be a function of the depth of perceptual analysis. The literal version of this theory was recognized as inadequate to handle the data, if not downright wrong, almost as soon as it was proposed. Even in the 1972 paper, Craik and Lockhart wrote that "'spread' of encoding might be a more accurate description" than levels of processing [for various reasons] but that "the term 'depth' will be retained as it conveys the flavor of our argument" (p. 676). In later papers, Craik and his colleagues distanced themselves even further from the strict levels-of-processing ideas, preferring other descriptors to capture encoding differences, such as elaboration, spread, distinctiveness, richness, and the like (e.g., Craik & Tulving, 1975; Lockhart, Craik, & Jacoby, 1976; Moscovitch & Craik, 1976). However, none of these terms or ideas has been specified well in the intervening years and none has received general agreement in the field as a replacement for the terms "depth" or "levels" of processing, which still reigns supreme.

Few of the points made in this chapter are really new or original. In fact, Craik and Lockhart and their collaborators made most of them in the 1970s, so a chapter like this one could have been written in 1980. We have known since at least then that the levels-of-processing framework—the original version that emphasizes strict levels of perceptual processing—is just wrong. Curiously, it was originally criticized as being circular and untestable by several commentators (e.g., Baddeley, 1978; Eysenck, 1978; and T. O. Nelson, 1977), but Craik and his collaborators provided many telling observations that called the framework into question. Their research conducted on the so-called levels-of-processing paradigm (as embodied in, say, the Craik and Tulving, 1975, experiments) undercuts rather than supports the levels-of-processing framework for the reasons given above and for others (e.g., D. L. Nelson, 1979). Hence the paradigm is misnamed and might be called (more neutrally) the Craik–Tulving paradigm. Today the term *levels of processing* is used more generically by the field, to emphasize the fact that different types of processing of words during encoding provide various levels of memory performance (albeit depending on the test used to assess retention).

The strict levels-of- (perceptual) processing framework may be wrong, but in our opinion the contributions from this approach still represent one of the most valuable developments in the psychology of memory in the 115-year history of its empirical study. Craik and Lockhart's (1972) paper deserves all of its fame, for many reasons. First, it challenged the existing conception of memory as composed of various stores. This has always been the received wisdom about memory—people are thought to search through various stores to locate memories (Roediger, 1980). Second, it began a new way of thinking about remembering, not as static traces in the head, but rather as actions and activities. The critical focus was on processing. Processing approaches to remembering, as embodied in the work of Kolers (1979) and others, still have not been satisfactorily developed, but to the extent that processing approaches have developed at all, the credit goes to Craik and Lockhart for blazing the trail. Third, the levels-of-processing framework has been fruitful and generative, providing a powerful set of experimental techniques for exploring the phenomena of memory. The manipulation of various orienting tasks predated the 1972 paper by many years and was used as an experimental technique sporadically, to address various issues. However, since the 1972 paper, the manipulation of orienting tasks has taken center stage and represents one of the most frequently used techniques in the experimental study of memory.

In sum, the levels-of-processing framework has been of unsurpassed value in the psychology of memory. The purpose of this chapter is to point out that the original framework emphasizing levels of perceptual processing cannot explain the basic levels of processing effect (or the effect of orienting tasks on recall and recognition). The field has ignored this conclusion, despite the fact that Craik and Tulving (1975) and many others pointed it out in no uncertain terms a quarter of a century ago. We may hope that in the next 30 years, unlike the last 30, researchers and theorists will attempt to correct this situation and come to grips with these phenomena both theoretically and empirically.

☐ Acknowledgments

We thank Fergus Craik, Morris Moscovitch, Robert Lockhart, Endel Tulving, and Michael Watkins for their helpful comments on an earlier draft of this chapter. The writing of this chapter was supported by a contract from the Office of Technical Services of the U.S. Government awarded to the first author.

☐ References

Anderson, J. R., & Bower, G. H. (1972). Recognition and retrieval processes in free recall. *Psychological Review, 79,* 97–123.

Anderson, J. R., & Reder, L. M. (1979). An elaborative processing explanation of levels of processing. In L. S. Cermak & F. I. M. Craik (Eds.), *Levels of processing in human memory* (pp. 385–403). Hillsdale, NJ: Erlbaum.

Arbuckle, T. Y., & Katz, W. A. (1976). Structure of memory traces following semantic and nonsemantic orienting tasks in incidental learning. *Journal of Experimental Psychology: Human Learning and Memory, 2,* 362–369.

Baddeley, A. D. (1978). The trouble with levels: A reexamination of Craik and Lockhart's framework for memory research. *Psychological Review, 85,* 139–152.

Blaxton, T. A. (1989). Investigating dissociations among memory measures: Support for a transfer-appropriate processing framework. *Journal of Experimental Psychology: Learning, Memory and Cognition, 15,* 657–668.

Bransford, J. D., Franks, J. J., Morris, C. D., & Stein, B. S. (1979). Some general constraints on learning and memory research. In L. S. Cermak & F. I. M. Craik (Eds.), *Levels of processing in human memory* (pp. 331–354). Hillsdale, NJ: Erlbaum.

Cermak, G., Schnorr, J, Buschke, H., & Atkinson, R. C. (1970). Recognition memory as influenced by differential attention to semantic and acoustic properties of words. *Psychonomic Science, 19,* 79–81.

Challis, B.H., Velichkovsky, B. M., & Craik, F.I.M. (1996). Levels-of-processing effects on a variety of memory tasks: New findings and theoretical implications. *Consciousness and Cognition, 5,* 142–164.

Chow, P. C. P., Currie, J. L., & Craik, F. I. M. (1978). Intentional learning and retention of words following various orienting tasks. *Bulletin of the Psychonomic Society, 12,* 109–112.

Craik, F. I. M. (1973). A "levels of analysis" view of memory. In P. Pliner, L. Krames, & T. M. Alloway (Eds.), *Communication and affect: Language and thought* (pp. 45–65). New York: Academic Press.

Craik, F. I. M. (1977). Depth of processing in recall and recognition. In S. Dornic & P. M. A. Rabbitt (Eds.), *Attention and performance VI* (pp. 679–697). Hillsdale, NJ: Erlbaum.

Craik, F. I. M., & Lockhart, R. S. (1972). Levels of processing: A framework for memory research. *Journal of Verbal Learning and Verbal Behavior, 11,* 671–684.

Craik, F. I. M., & Tulving, E. (1975). Depth of processing and the retention of words in episodic memory. *Journal of Experimental Psychology: General, 104,* 268–294.

Eysenck, M. W. (1978). Levels of processing: A critique. *British Journal of Psychology, 69,* 157–169.

Fisher, R. P., & Craik, F. I. M. (1977). Interaction between encoding and retrieval operations in cued recall. *Journal of Experimental Psychology: Human Learning and Memory, 3,* 701–711.

Graf, P., & Mandler, G. (1984). Activation makes words more accessible, but not necessarily more retrievable. *Journal of Verbal Learning and Verbal Behavior, 23,* 553–568.

Hyde, T. S., & Jenkins, J. J. (1969). Differential effects of incidental tasks on the organization of recall of a list of highly associated words. *Journal of Experimental Psychology, 82,* 472–481.

Hyde, T. S., & Jenkins, J. J. (1973). Recall for words as a function of semantic, graphic, and syntactic orienting tasks. *Journal of Verbal Learning and Verbal Behavior, 12,* 471–480.

Jacoby, L. L. (1975). Physical features vs. meaning: A difference in decay? *Memory & Cognition, 3,* 247–251.

Jacoby, L. L., Craik, F. I. M., & Begg, I. (1979). Effects of decision difficulty on recognition and recall. *Journal of Verbal Learning and Verbal Behavior, 18,* 585–600.

Jacoby, L. L., & Dallas, M. (1981). On the relationship between autobiographical memory and perceptual learning. *Journal of Experimental Psychology: General, 110,* 306–340.

Jenkins, J. J. (1974). Can we have a meaningful theory of memory? In R. L. Solso (Ed.), *Theories in cognitive psychology: The Loyola symposium* (pp. 1–20). Potomac, MD: Erlbaum.

Kirsner, K., & Dunn, J. C. (1985). The perceptual record: A common factor in repetition priming and attribute retention. In M. I. Posner & O. S. M. Martin (Eds.), *Mechanisms of attention: Attention and performance, XI.* Hillsdale, NJ: Erlbaum.

Kolers, P. A. (1979). A pattern-analyzing basis of recognition. In L. S. Cermak & F. I. M. Craik (Eds.), *Levels of processing in human memory* (pp. 363–384). Hillsdale, NJ: Erlbaum.

Kolers, P. A., & Roediger, H. L., III. (1984). Procedures of mind. *Journal of Verbal Learning and Verbal Behavior, 23,* 425–449.

Lockhart, R. S., & Craik, F. I. M. (1978). Levels of processing: A reply to Eysenck. *British Journal of Psychology, 69,* 171–175.

Lockhart, R. S., & Craik, F. I. M. (1990). Levels of processing: A retrospective commentary on a framework for memory research. *Canadian Journal of Psychology, 44,* 87–112.

Lockhart, R. S., Craik, F. I. M., & Jacoby, L. L. (1976). Depth of processing, recognition, and recall. In J. Brown (Ed.), *Recall and recognition* (pp. 75–102). London: Academic Press.

Mandler, G. (1980). Recognizing: The judgment of previous occurrence. *Psychological Review, 87,* 252–271.

Mathews, R.C. (1977). Semantic judgments as encoding operations: The effects of attention to particular semantic categories on the usefulness of interitem relations in recall. *Journal of Experimental Psychology: Human Learning and Memory, 3,* 160–173.

McDaniel, M. A., Friedman, A., & Bourne, L. E. (1978). Remembering the levels of information in words. *Memory & Cognition, 6,* 156–164.

McDermott, K. B., & Roediger, H. L. (1996). Exact and conceptual repetition dissociate conceptual memory tests: Problems for transfer appropriate processing theory. *Canadian Journal of Experimental Psychology, 50,* 57–71.

Miller, G. A. (1956). The magical number seven, plus or minus two: Some limits on our capacity for processing information. *Psychological Review, 63,* 81–97.

Moeser, S. D. (1983). Levels of processing: Qualitative differences or task-demand differences? *Memory & Cognition, 11,* 316–323.

Morris, C. D., Bransford, J. D., & Franks, J. J. (1977). Levels of processing versus transfer appropriate processing. *Journal of Verbal Learning and Verbal Behavior, 16,* 519–533.

Moscovitch, M., & Craik, F. I. M. (1976). Depth of processing, retrieval cues, and uniqueness of encoding as factors in recall. *Journal of Verbal Learning and Verbal Behavior, 15,* 447–458.

Nelson, D. L. (1979). Remembering pictures and words: Appearance, significance, and name. In L. S. Cermak & F. I. M. Craik (Eds.), *Levels of processing in human memory,* (pp. 45–76). Hillsdale, NJ: Erlbaum.

Nelson, T. O. (1977). Repetition and depth of processing. *Journal of Verbal Learning and Verbal Behavior, 16,* 151–171.

Packman, J. L., & Battig, W. F. (1978). Effects of different kinds of semantic processing on memory for words. *Memory & Cognition, 6,* 502–508.

Postman, L., Adams, P. A., & Phillips, L. W. (1955). Studies in incidental learning. II. The effects of association value and of the method of testing. *Journal of Experimental Psychology, 49,* 1–10.

Postman, L., & Kruesi, E. (1977). The influence of orienting tasks on the encoding and recall of words. *Journal of Verbal Learning and Verbal Behavior, 16,* 353–369.

Roediger, H. L., III. (1980). Memory metaphors in cognitive psychology. *Memory & Cognition, 8,* 231–246.

Roediger, H. L., III, Payne, D. G., Gillespie, G. L., & Lean, D. S. (1982). Hypermnesia as determined by level of recall. *Journal of Verbal Learning and Verbal Behavior, 21,* 635–655.

Roediger, H. L., III, & Thorpe, L. A. (1978). The role of recall time in producing hypermnesia. *Memory & Cognition, 6,* 296–305.

Roediger, H. L., III, Weldon, M. S., & Challis, B. H. (1989). Explaining dissociations between implicit and explicit measures of retention: A processing account. In H. L. Roediger & F. I. M. Craik (Eds.), *Varieties of memory and consciousness: Essays in honour of Endel Tulving* (pp. 3–41). Hillsdale, NJ: Erlbaum.

Roediger, H. L., III, Weldon, M. S., Stadler, M. L., & Riegler, G. L. (1992). Direct comparison of two implicit memory tests: Word fragment and word stem completion. *Journal of Experimental Psychology: Learning, Memory, & Cognition, 18,* 1251–1269.

Seamon, J. G., & Virostek, S. (1978). Memory performance and subject-defined depth of processing. *Memory & Cognition, 6,* 283–287.

Stein, B. S. (1978). Depth of processing reexamined: The effects of precision of encoding and test appropriateness. *Journal of Verbal Learning and Verbal Behavior, 17,* 165–174.

Tresselt, M. E., & Mayzner, M. S. (1960). A study of incidental learning. *The Journal of Psychology, 50,* 339–347.

Tulving, E. (1972). Episodic and semantic memory. In E. Tulving & W. Donaldson (Eds.), *Organization and memory.* New York: Academic Press.

Tulving, E. (1974). Cue-dependent forgetting. *American Scientist, 62,* 74–82.

Tulving, E. (1979). Relation between encoding specificity and levels of processing. In L. S. Cermak & F. I. M. Craik (Eds.), *Levels-of-processing in human memory* (pp. 405–428). Hillsdale, NJ: Erlbaum.

Walsh, D. A., & Jenkins, J. J. (1973). Effects of orienting tasks on free recall in incidental learning: "Difficulty," "effort," and "process" explanations. *Journal of Verbal Learning and Verbal Behavior, 12,* 481–488.

Weldon, M. S. (1991). Mechanisms underlying priming on perceptual tests. *Journal of Experimental Psychology: Learning, Memory, & Cognition, 17,* 526–541.

CHAPTER Boris M. Velichkovsky

Levels of Processing: Validating the Concept

The history of science is full of examples of mutual misunderstanding among scientists belonging to different schools of thought or adhering to different scientific paradigms. Roediger and Gallo, in the previous chapter of this Festschrift, provide a nice illustration: What is generally known today as the levels-of-processing (LOP) effect, had been in the early 1960s attributed to "number of differential responses." Two (cognitive) memory experts from the late 20th century simply cannot accept an interpretation proposed by (neobehaviorist) experts of the middle of the century. The cognitive approach to memory experienced several paradigmatic switches itself. During its first decades, it was dominated by the computer metaphor and, ipso facto, by the multistore models of memory. Craik and Lockhart (1972) strongly contributed to the abandonment of these early structural models. The dominating idea of cognitive research of the last 20 years has been, and still is, that of domain-specific processing which led in its extreme formulation to the hypothesis of modularity of mind (Fodor, 1983). In the psychology of memory, one often speaks today about different memory subsystems and about local, domain-specific effects such as transfer-appropriate processing.

Against this background, Craik and Lockhart's approach enjoys an ongoing popularity but it also attracts as much criticism as in the times of the decline of the multistore models. What are the reasons for the attacks from a second generation of opponents? In my opinion, Fergus Craik and Robert Lockhart contributed to a scientific paradigm that is different both from the computer metaphor of the 1960s and from the modern phrenology of domain-specific models. Their sympathy obviously is with the idea of a hierarchical organization of everyday activities whereby the products of early (or shallow) sensory analyses can be used as the input to later (or deeper) semantic analyses (see, e.g., Lockhart & Craik, 1990, p. 88). The purpose of this chapter is to make explicit this general approach aimed at a *stratification*, i.e., at a reconstruction of hierarchical evolutionary mechanisms of cognition, first, with respect to some of its theoretical roots, and second, with respect to new empirical data.

☐ Personal Reminiscences

At the beginning of the 1970s, I received my diploma in psychology from Moscow State University and became a research assistant with Alexander Luria and Alexei N. Leont'ev. The scientific and personal atmosphere within the group was cosmopolitan and inspiring. Visitors such as Bruner, Piaget, Pribram, and (Don) Norman attended seminars, and new experimental results as well as recent papers in international journals were intensively discussed. However, there was a problem with the journals because they were always delayed by at least 10–12 months. The rumors were that the KGB read them all! Apparently, Craik and Lockhart's (1972) article had been judged to be not as subversive as some of their fellow colleagues would consider it. After the release of the issue, one of my friends discovered the paper "on the levels of memory," and we reviewed it at the Luria seminar. The impression was twofold. First, it was noted that the emphasis was on considering memory as a supportive function *within* the general context of goal-directed activities. For Craik and Lockhart, these activities had not only a quantitative (after the principle of "processing, more processing, even more processing") but also a qualitative dimension, the latter reflected in the discussion of different levels such as sensory or semantic encoding.

Another general impression was that this framework looked rather familiar, at least in the context of Russian activity psychology, which concentrated around Leont'ev and Luria. In particular, the founder of modern biomechanics and one of the protagonists of the ecological approach, Nikolai Bernstein, published in 1947 (reprinted, 1990) the book On the Construction of Movements, which described in detail four levels of neurophysiological mechanisms, levels A to D, involved in the coordination of human movements.[1] While Bernstein's emphasis was on the sensorimotor processes and not on cognition, he mentioned in the book the possibility of "one or two higher levels of symbolic coordinations" which are decoupled from necessary behavioral manifestations and selectively connected with associative areas of the cortex and with the frontal lobes. To show the sophistication of this approach, I offer in Appendix A a translation of some of the introductory pages of this remarkable book (from 1947, remember) relevant to the LOP discussion.

Under the influence of research on the physiology of activity (Bernstein, 1966) and the psychology of activity (Leont'ev, 1978), it is no wonder that much of memory research had to do with incidental learning. A. A. Smirnov (1966) investigated several involuntary memory effects as they related to the goals of everyday actions, and P. I. Zinchenko (1961) developed a method of memory analysis that closely resembled that of levels of processing: He used three types of encoding, directed to the perceptual features of material, its meaning, or self-initiated production of the material.

This case of parallel development is more than a historical curiosity, it shows that there may be deep reasons for a reoccurrence of similar ideas in seemingly different scientific conditions. Elsewhere, I have discussed other important contributions to the stratification paradigm starting with the works of John Hughlings-Jackson and Paul MacLean (see Velichkovsky, 1990, 1994). It may be useful to spell out the emerging architecture once again in order to make it clear what segments of the hierarchical brain mechanisms are associated with the typical encoding manipulations.

---

[1] Unfortunately, the theory is virtually unknown in the West. Bernstein died in 1966. His main oeuvre was forbidden in the Soviet Union (because of his critique of the official, Pavlov's doctrine) and reprinted for the first time in 1990. A popular version of Bernstein's theory was translated into English only a few years ago, see Bernstein (1996).

☐ Levels of Processing 2000 (+/– 50 Years)

As many as six global levels of organization can be differentiated if one takes into account, on the one hand, Bernstein's work on the construction of movements and, on the other hand, recent progress in the studies of metacognition and higher forms of consciousness (Leont'ev, 1978; Wheeler, Stuss, & Tulving, 1997; Velichkovsky, 1990).

The first group is built up by the primarily sensorimotor mechanisms clearly identified by Bernstein (1947/1990).

Level A: Paleokinetic Regulations. Bernstein also called this level the "rubro-spinal" level, having in mind the lowest structures of the spinal cord and brain stem regulating the tonus, paleovestibular reflexes, and basic defensive responses. The awareness of functioning is reduced to Head's (1920) prothopatic sensitivity, so diffuse and lacking in local signs that even the term "sensation" seems to be too intellectual.

Level B: Synergies. Due to the involvement of new neurological structures—the "thalamo-pallidar system," according to Bernstein—the regulation of an organism's movements as a whole is now possible; it becomes a "locomotory machine." The specializations of this level are rhythmic and cyclic patterns of motion underlying all forms of locomotion. Possibilities of awareness are limited to proprio- and tangoreceptoric sensations.

Level C: Spatial Field. A new spiral of evolution adds exteroception with the striatum and primary stimulotopically organized areas of the cortex as the control instances. This opens outer space and makes possible one-time extemporaneous goal-directed motions in the near environment. The corresponding subjective experience is that of a stable voluminous surrounding filled with localized but only globally sketched objects.

Level D: Object Actions. This next round of evolution leads to the building of secondary areas of neocortex that permit detailed form perception and object-adjusted manipulations. Individualized objects affording some but not other actions come to be the focus of attention. Formation and tuning of higher order sensorimotor and perceptual skills is supported by a huge memory of the procedural type. Phenomenal experience is the perceptive image.

The second group of mechanisms consists of two levels anticipated by Bernstein as higher levels of symbolic coordinations.

Level E: Conceptual Structures. Supramodal associative cortices provide the highest integration of various modalities supporting the ability to identify objects and events as members of generic classes. Development of language and human culture fosters this ability and virtually leads to formation of powerful declarative-procedural mechanisms of symbolic representation of the world. Common consciousness is the dominating mode of awareness at this level.

Level F: Metacognitive Coordinations. In advanced stages, changes in conceptual structures result not only from accretion of experience but also from experimentation with ontological parameters of knowledge. Necessary support for this "personal view of the world" is provided by those parts of the executive areas of neocortex that show excessive growth in anthropogenesis, notably by the right prefrontal regions. Coordinations of this last level make possible personal and interpersonal reference, reflective consciousness (Tulving's "autonoetic consciousness"), and productive imagination.

There can be an abundance of domain-specific effects, even apparently modular components, in this type of architecture. Furthermore, most of these levels work simultaneously by providing their specific competences and resources to the task solution. What makes a difference to the modular theories is that these contributions are not all equivalent by virtue of their being embedded in a kind of *gradient* of larger order evolutionary mechanisms, so that *systematic asymmetries* in relations of local, domain-specific effects should be expected.

In this conceptualization, memory mechanisms are in the service of, and are part of, global, hierarchically organized complexes of activities that can be related (though very approximately) to different forms of processing, from sensory and sensorimotor to semantic and metacognitive. The usual LOP manipulations can be identified with processes involving mainly levels D and E. Some of the results could be different if, for instance, two levels of perceptual processing, i.e., levels C and D, would be taken for contrasting encoding manipulations—I would expect an obvious LOP effect even with the perceptual indirect (implicit) memory tests.

The memory tests also have different "functional anatomies," especially with respect to their stratification according to the vertical dimension of processing. The *leading* level (see Appendix A) of all the direct (explicit) tests, whether they are called "perceptual" or "conceptual" ones, usually is the same: level F. It is not surprising, therefore, that one mostly finds a right prefrontal activation (the "retrieval volition" component; see, e.g., Gardiner, Richardson-Klavehn, Ramponi, & Brooks, chapter 5 of this volume) with this group of memory tasks. They are, however, different in their *background* coordinations (Appendix A), so that, for instance, recognition and free recall, both conceptual explicit tests, differ, first, in their use of level E facilities and, second, in the involvement of level D (and level C) with only recognition and not free recall.

As to indirect (implicit) memory tests, their levels of composition are defined by the content of the nonmemory "carrier" tasks. The leading levels of these tasks are D and E (if subjects do not discover that their memory is tested—discovery would immediately involve level F's coordinations and change the test to the explicit one).[2] As a result, the list of levels involved in the solution of the implicit memory tasks is usually shorter and the projection of their mechanisms on the vertical dimension of mental processing is *narrower* than in the case of explicit tasks. But this is already taking us to a discussion of the applicability and extension of the LOP approach. Putting aside the thousands of experimental replications, let us now concentrate on the few objections to this approach to memory research.

☐ Troubles With Levels—but of What Kind?

Not all of the objections and questions can be considered in detail here. Because some of them were addressed some time ago (Lockhart & Craik, 1990), I will select only the most serious ones. In particular, theoretical criticism concentrated on a circularity in the definition of levels: One initially took memory performance as the criterion of level or depth of processing and, later on, found the confirmation of this criterion in the data about memory performance (Baddeley, 1978; Eysenck, 1978). This situation has changed in recent years, even in the view of critically minded colleagues (see e.g., Eysenck & Keane, 2000, pp. 166–167). The remainder of the chapter will be devoted mostly to a review of the currently existing independent evidence.

---

[2] A theoretically important task for the future is the development of an indirect (implicit) test of memory with F as the leading level.

Another objection to the LOP approach was that it neglected the relationship between type of encoding and memory test. This consideration led to concepts such as transfer-appropriate processing and encoding specificity (the two are basically the same; see Roediger & Gallo, chapter 33 of this volume, for the major references). According to this variant of domain-specific thinking, there is no inherent continuum of higher to lower levels, but several, perhaps many, qualitatively different forms of processing that are parallel and, in a sense, equivalent. With respect to memory performance, the prediction was that even "shallow" encodings could demonstrate better retention than "deep" ones if the specific memory test initiated retrieval processes similar to (e.g., in terms of overlap between component mental operations) the processes that had been involved at the encoding stage. Indeed, there have been several demonstrations of trends in this direction (e.g., Morris, Bransford, & Franks, 1977), but even with an appropriate "shallow" test, the amount of memory performance seems to be lower than after an appropriate "deep" test such as free recall or recognition (R. P. Fisher & Craik, 1977). In other words, empirically, some types of encoding ("shallow") never yield excellent recognition or free recall with any retrieval cues, however "specific" or "appropriate."[3] I shall return to this particular problem in discussing experiments specially designed to compare between interactions of encoding and retrieval conditions.

A further complication (Roediger & Gallo, chapter 3 of this volume) was first addressed by Craik and Tulving in 1975. They showed that in positive trials the manipulation of encoding is more effective than in negative ones. This is why the notion of different "elaborations of the traces" was postulated. However, for Craik and Tulving, elaboration was only an additional mechanism. Indeed, in all of their experiments and subsequent experiments, there has also been a clear LOP effect in "no" trials.

In my opinion, there is no need to question the initial interpretation, at least on this occasion. Perception and cognition are hardly conceivable without their interaction with material or, broadly speaking, with situation. In psychology at large, notions such as Gibson's affordances or Aufforderungen in Gestalt theory are well known. They testify to the fact that different situations offer different support for their processing and comprehension. In "yes" trials, these affordances are richer than in negative ones, *and that is all*. The discussion shows that with respect to encoding, as in the case of retrieval, one should probably differentiate between "encoding intention" (attitude toward encoding material at some level that is developed after the task instruction is understood and accepted) and "encoding realization" (the same, but in interaction with material). In the following, I shall demonstrate how level of processing, as the task-attitude independent of the material (LOP1), and elaboration, as the task in its interaction with material (LOP2), could be differentiated on the basis of independent variables, such as parameters of eye movements.

Empirical data deviating from the expectations of the LOP approach in its initial form have been found particularly often with the broad introduction of implicit or indirect tests of memory. As a rule, these tests demonstrate little if any influence of encoding manipulations on the corresponding (perceptual) priming measures (Roediger, Weldon, Stadler, & Riegler, 1992). Even when post-hoc meta-analytic studies (Challis & Brodbeck, 1992) were able to show a tendency to stronger (perceptual) priming with semantic encoding, this effect was weak and less systematic than in direct memory measures. The most parsimonious explanation for the residual influence of levels manipulation is that of explicit

---

[3] Before the standing proposal to replace LOP terminology with the notion of transfer-appropriate processing can be seriously considered, one must solve one additional theoretical problem: "Appropriateness" seems to be circularly defined.

awareness in some subjects in some experiments of the proper goal of implicit tests (Stadler & Roediger, 1997). However, recent data cast doubt on this simple answer (Gardiner, Richardson-Klavehn, Ramponi, & Brooks, chapter 5 of this volume), so the differential influence of the LOP manipulations on explicit and implicit tests is one of the questions discussed in this chapter.

Of course, the levels concept has other, real research problems. The emphasis of the approach is on perceptual and cognitive processes, but these processes have seldom been discussed in detail (see Treisman, 1979). The distinction between physical, semantic, and, sometimes, phonological processing is not very sophisticated in view of data existing outside the psychology of memory. For instance, processes directed to the perceptual features of material could be rather different, and they may even be divided into further levels and domains, as, for instance, in the classical distinction between localization and identification or between ambient and focal vision (Bridgeman, 1999; Trevarthen, 1969; Velichkovsky, 1982). This distinction is similar to the one made by Bernstein (1947/1990) and Jeannerod (1981) in the investigation of motor control, and it is reflected in the contrasting levels C and D in our general model.

Self-referential encoding is another challenge, as it can have an even larger memory effect than semantic encoding (e.g., Bower & Gilligan, 1979; Miall, 1986). The growing evidence for metacognitive processing lends itself to an integration with the concept of levels, particularly with respect to this controversial issue (see Lockhart & Craik, 1990; Velichkovsky, 1994). Is it a genuinely new level or only an elaboration of the old? More for theoretical than empirical reasons, I included it as a separate level F in the general hierarchical model. The question could be empirically answered by contrasting neurophysiological mechanisms with semantic and self-referential encoding, or with, as this distinction was called in the Russian activity psychology (Leont'ev, 1978), representations of *meaning* and *personal sense*. Unfortunately, until recently, LOP effects have been interpreted with a functional bias, i.e., not as effects involving different neurophysiological structures.

In the following, I want to discuss the reasons why such a vague notion as "depth of processing" works so effectively. My method will be a comparison of several recent investigations that seem to demonstrate new evidence for multilevel effects in three different domains of research: eye-movement studies, brain imaging, and multivariate memory experiments.

☐ Searching for Independent Measures I: Levels and Eye Movements

The behavior of the human eye consists of a common "output" of several hierarchically related mechanisms. This claim is necessarily true in view of facts about the neuroanatomy of eye movement control, which is spread across at least four different levels of the brain's organization, from midbrain and basal ganglia to parietal and frontal cortex (e.g., Kennard, 1989). The new aspect of psychological discussions is that this organization is manifested in the temporal and spatial parameters of eye movements during the solution of perceptual and cognitive tasks (Deubel, 1999; Velichkovsky, 1995).

Some parameters of eye movements are under selective control of such hierarchical mechanisms. This is illustrated by results from investigation of visual search (Pomplun, 1998). The solution of this and similar tasks can be divided into two phases. During the first phase, which is connected with search operations per se, fixation duration is about 180 to 250 ms and it is mainly a function of spatial density of objects, independent of their identity. Dwell time (i.e., overall time spent in a particular area) depends in addition on the objects identifying features such as form or color. During the second, shorter phase, which is one of generation of a hypothesis, its testing, and a response, the average fixation duration rises to 500 ms or more. Obviously, this final phase of visual search can be attributed to some higher level of cognitive processing, which culminates in a conscious decision.

In a quite different setting, we found a similar increase in proportion of very long fixations as a function of task (Velichkovsky, 1995). The experiments investigated the natural human ability to take into account information about another person's gaze direction in communication and problem solving. Our task consisted of a cooperative solution of a puzzle. An intention to support verbal instruction by the gaze leads to a significant rise in the proportion of very long fixations (around 500 ms and more). These long fixations could be used in a communicative role, obviously as a source of referential (deictic) information.

On the basis of these results, one can expect that higher levels of encoding, i.e., those emphasizing processes that are predicated to be metacognitive, communicative, or involved in a conscious decision, may be correlated with a higher proportion of longer fixations.[4] There have been no studies of eye movements in the LOP tradition, though such studies are a prerequisite for any detailed analysis of visual encoding processes. What goes on, for instance, when people try to count visually presented words depending on their physical or semantic features? We have recently attempted to answer this and related questions in experiments with visual presentation of verbal material (Velichkovsky, 1999).

In one of the experiments, subjects had to study short biographical sketches, counting either all the words, or all the adjectives, or all the adjectives that had a self-referential value for them. These three instructions led to the expected LOP effect, i.e., to an increase in the number of words reproduced in a later free recall test. As to the eye-movement data, they were, at first sight, rather disappointing from the point of view of the working hypothesis. The longest mean fixation time was with counting words (275 ms), followed by the self-referential (213 ms) and the categorization (199 ms) conditions. One possible explanation could be that these differences reflect a different involvement of covert counting operations: When we are trying to count similar objects in a homogeneous array by sight, our eyes play the role of an index finger—they continue to fixate an object until a corresponding inner-speech enumeration is finished (Gippenreiter, Romanov, & Smirnov, 1969). Indeed, in a control experiment, when subjects counted not words, but similarly placed uniform grey bars, the result was an even more prolonged average fixation time (320 ms), obviously because staring at pieces became the only means to correct enumeration.

There were however, some parameters of eye movements that changed depending on the direction of encoding effects on memory performance. The first parameter was the positive skewness of fixation time distributions: It was least for counting words, more for counting adjectives, and most for counting self-referential adjectives, as shown in Figure 4.1a (the main effect is highly significant: $F_{(3,17)} = 5.62$, $p < 0.01$). In other words, "deeper" encodings lead to an increase *in proportion* of relatively long fixations, despite the shift in the average fixation duration caused by the counting operations. The second parameter was the number of fixations or a correlated parameter of dwell time spent in a word area.

---

[4] This thesis needs further specification. If the higher cognitive levels are, as they seem to be, resource sensitive, then a *concurrent* metacognitive task (e.g., a phone conversation during driving) can selectively remove longer fixations, actually with respective consequences for the depth of visual processing (see Velichkovsky, Dornhoefer, Pannasch, & Unema, 2000).

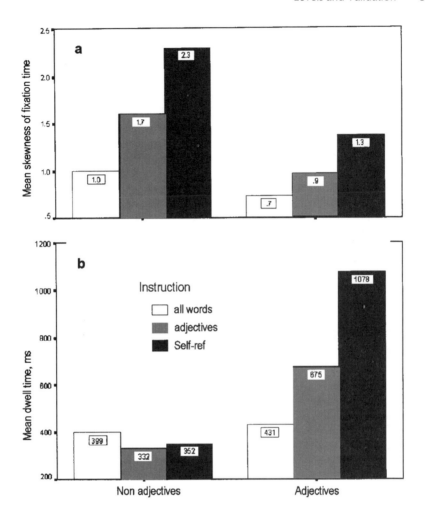

FIGURE 4.1. Skewness of fixation time distributions (a) and mean dwell times (b) depending on encoding instruction for nontarget and target words (after Velichkovsky, 1999).

(Figure 4.1b). Dwell time also monotonically increased with the LOP manipulations, but interestingly this happened for the adjectives only, i.e., for those encounters of the eye with words that supported *elaborative processing*. The tendencies are confirmed by highly significant main effect of LOP and its interaction with the type of material ($F_{(3,17)}$ = 13.66, p < 0.001 and $F_{(2,16)}$ = 47.29, p < 0.001, respectively).

It seems, therefore, that eye movement data are of obvious value in memory research. Moreover, they illustrate the distinction between two interpretations of the LOP concepts which I labeled LOP1 and LOP2 earlier in the chapter. LOP1 denotes the task set or attitude induced by instruction and present even in the absence of the appropriate material. Thus, the skewness of fixation time distributions changes depending on encoding conditions but in approximately the same way for positive and negative encounters of the eye with words (an analogue of "yes" and "no" trials in the experiments with a sequential presentation of information). Dwell time seems to be a measure of elaboration, or *encoding realization* (i.e., LOP2) because it strongly interacts with the relevance of the material (cf. Craik & Tulving, 1975).

☐ Searching for Independent Measures II: Levels and Brain Activity

In response to critical remarks on circularity in the definition of levels, there have been a number of attempts to find independent measures or correlates of LOP effects in psychophysiological data, such as event-related potentials (Naumann, 1985; Sanquist, Rohrbaugh, Syndulko, & Lindsley, 1980) and cardiovascular reactions (Vincent, Craik, & Furedy, 1993). Particularly compelling are recent studies of memory encoding and retrieval using methods of brain imaging.

In one of the first such studies, Blaxton and her colleagues (1996) conducted a positron emission tomography (PET) scan analysis of regional cerebral blood flow in four memory tests. Memory tests represented two theoretically important dimensions: perceptual versus conceptual processing and implicit versus explicit testing. Larger topographical changes were found between perceptual and conceptual tasks. Memory effects for perceptual fragment completion tests (both implicit and explicit) were localized in posterior regions, including the occipital cortex with some slight right-side asymmetry. In contrast, the analysis of conceptual tests of semantic-cued recall and word association revealed metabolic changes in the medial and superior temporal cortex, as well as in the left frontal cortex. Of course, these neuroanatomical differences have been found with respect to localization of retrieval processes, so it is interesting to compare them with results of encoding studies.

Gabrieli et al. (1996) used functional magnetic resonance imaging (fMRI) to compare perceptual and semantic encodings of visually presented words. They discovered a greater activation of the left inferior prefrontal cortex for semantic encoding. It is thus possible that the level I have designated "conceptual structures" (level E) has connections with the left frontal regions and perhaps with the temporal lobes of the cortex.[5]

One of our investigations of encoding has been based on a psychophysiological method known as evoked coherences analysis of EEG. A cheaper and faster alternative to PET scan (Velichkovsky, Klemm, Dettmar, & Volke, 1996). In a series of LOP experiments, we investigated a reproduction of visually and acoustically presented words in dependence on three encoding conditions: perceptive, semantic, and metacognitive (self-referential). Although the database of EEG analysis is completely different from that of PET scan or fMRI, the loci of global incoherence[6] in perceptual and semantic orienting tasks were found in approximately the same regions where Blaxton et al. (1996) discovered changes in metabolism for the corresponding memory tests. In the perceptual (form-oriented) encoding of visually presented words, the major incoherences are localized in the occipital

---

[5] Gardiner, Richardson-Klavehn, Ramponi, and Brooks (chapter 5 of this volume) report right prefrontal and parietal activation in a combined electroencephalography (EEG) and magnetoence phalography (MEG) study of a word-stem completion task. This suggests the involvement of two levels: F as the leading level and D as the major background structure. The selection of level D for this type of task may be connected with its rich assortment of pattern-recognition procedures.

[6] In this method of EEG analysis, global incoherence is the nearest analogue to metabolic activation from brain imaging studies. An incoherence of the EEG between some region and the rest of the cortex, separately evaluated for different bands of the spectrum, can testify to its involvement in particularly intensive processing.

and right occipitotemporal area. In semantic encoding, they expand to the more anteriorly located region, particularly including the bilateral temporal and left frontal areas (cf. similar data from another investigation of neuroanatomical correlates of LOP effects by Kapur et al,, 1994). In the third condition, self-referential encoding, even more anteriorly located regions within the frontal and right prefrontal lobes are involved.

The trend from the left anterior localization in semantic encoding to a predominantly *right prefrontal* activation (especially Brodmann's areas 9, 10, and 45) in self-referential encoding has been confirmed in a recent PET study comparing loci of self-referential encoding with those of other-referential and phonological processing (Craik et al., 1999).

This overall picture contradicts some attempts to attribute encoding exclusively to the left prefrontal lobes and (episodic) retrieval to the right prefrontal lobes (Tulving, 1998; Tulving, Kapur, Craik, Moscovitch, & Houle, 1994)—an exciting idea from the modularity of mind perspective, perhaps, but also one for which I can hardly see any evolutionary justification. At the same time, the described neuroanatomical changes are not at all astonishing from the point of view of neuropsychology (Goldberg, 1991; Luria, 1966) and neurophysiology (Christoff & Gabrieli, 2000; Mishkin, Suzuki, Gardian, & Vargha-Khadem, 1999). Theoretically important, in my opinion, are not the changes per se, but their direction. The posterior–anterior gradient corresponds to the main direction of evolutionary growth of the cortex (e.g., Deacon, 1996). In other words, these data suggest that a functional interpretation of LOP effects does not go far enough and should be revisited, perhaps, along with this simple principle: The deeper (or higher) a particular "level of processing" is, the more massive is the involvement of *phylogenetically recent* brain mechanisms in the task's solution.

This correspondence of functional and structural mechanisms is of course only a heuristic rule; our knowledge of brain functional evolution is still too fragmentary. However, the rule may work in several other cases. Let me show this with one additional example.

Until now, I have discussed the posterior–anterior gradient. There are several other lines of evolutionary development of the brain, for instance, one reflecting differences between subcortical and cortical mechanisms (for such analysis of motor control, see Bernstein, 1947/1990, 1996). One of the peculiarities of the human cortex is a relatively strongly developed right prefrontal lobe (Holloway & De la Coste-Lareymondie, 1982). The role of these structures in autobiographical and episodic remembering is well established (Cimino, Verfaillie, Bowers, & Heilmann, 1991; Gardiner, Richardson-Klavehn, Ramponi, & Brooks, chapter 5 of this volume; Tulving et al., 1994). However, the role is not limited to higher forms or aspects of memory. The same regions seem to be involved in the pragmatics of speech communication, understanding of fresh metaphors, irony, and humor, as well as self-awareness and the aspects of reflective social behavior known as manifestations of the "theory of mind" (Bihle, Brownell, Powelson, & Gardner, 1986; Shammi & Stuss, 1999; Velichkovsky, 1994; Wheeler et al., 1997). This list goes well beyond the span of memory phenomena approaching the "metacognitive coordinations," or level F in the above classification.

☐ Studying Memory With a Better Design

One methical drawback of most contemporary studies of memory is still the 2 × 2 experimental design. The problem with experiments using this design is that their results are of very limited use. They may be suitable only for rather rudimentary theoretical considerations such as dichotomous distinctions or the search for double dissociations or for "in principle" interactions of encoding and retrieval tasks.

FIGURE 4.2. Three hypothetical functions of memory performance depending on encoding conditions (see text for details).

Figure 4.2 shows three hypothetical functions of performance in a memory task in dependence on encoding conditions, arranged according to the hypothetical "vertical" dimension of depth. Though extremely simplified (for a more professional analysis, see Challis, Velichkovsky, & Craik, 1996, Table 1), these cases cannot be differentiated by the typical variation of two encoding conditions. Unfortunately, all three cases are meaningful and have different theoretical implications. The case of the nonmonotonic function (a) is one which is problematic for the LOP approach as it demonstrates strong domain specificity, or even modularity of the respective encoding–retrieval coupling. The next case, that of the one-step or "flat" LOP function (b), combines predictions of the basic approaches. On the one hand, there is a difference in efficiency between shallow and deep encoding, on the other hand, when one of the encoding conditions improves memory performance, this contribution seems to be preserved in all the higher levels of processing—an interesting example of the "modular voice" within a hierarchy. Finally, the last function (c) is what all "believers in the hierarchical order" would expect. However, this case is ambiguous. One possibility (let me call it the replacement model) is that the gradient-like function is produced by a consecutive involvement of new, more powerful mechanisms that demonstrate their performance without interaction with lower level structures. Another alternative is that of *vertical integration* (the integration model): Memory performance at some "deep" level of processing integrates contributions from some previous levels also.

Blaxton (1989) was the first to investigate a large group of memory tests under the same experimental conditions. She found that there are no essential differences between explicit and implicit tests if one other dimension is taken into account, namely, the emphasis on perceptual versus conceptual (semantic) processing. One aspect of her study, the difference in behavior between perceptual implicit tests and conceptual implicit tests, has been confirmed in several later experiments (e.g., Hamann, 1990; Tulving & Schacter, 1990). Though these results seem to be relevant to the present discussion, Blaxton used only two encoding conditions. If it would be possible in the same experiment to vary, systematically and over a broad range, both encoding conditions and memory tests, then one could decide among different theoretical models with greater certainty than before.

With this goal in mind, Challis et al. (1996) analyzed the effects of five different encoding conditions (plus one control condition) of visually presented lists of words on 13 memory tests (see also Velichkovsky, 1999). The memory tests were selected according to major theoretical points of view, such as perceptual versus conceptual and implicit versus explicit. Given this large matrix of encoding and retrieval conditions, several predictions are possible. From the strong domain-specific or modular view, one would expect several more-or-less equivalent clusters of interaction between encoding and retrieval in memory performance. That is, performance would be equally high when encoding and retrieval processing matched, and equally low elsewhere. From the LOP view, one would expect the clusters of interaction to be asymmetric through the creation of something like a gradient from weak to strong and perhaps to even stronger memory effects.

Our data, shown in Figure 4.3, were quite compelling in relation to these predictions. To see the trends clearly, one should, first, re-order incidental encoding conditions into

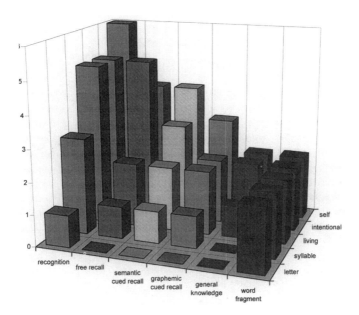

FIGURE 4.3. The number of statistically significant deviations from baseline (least significance differences, LSDs) in six memory tasks depending on five encoding conditions (after Challis et al., 1996).

the following sequence: perceptual (counting of letters deviating in form), phonological (counting of syllables), semantic (categorizing as a living thing), and metacognitive (evaluation of personal sense) processing. Second, explicit and implicit memory tests must be considered separately. It is in the first group of four explicit memory tasks (recognition, free recall, semantically and graphemically cued recall) where resulting interactions demonstrate a systematic, gradient-like growth—the perfect LOP effect—across at least most of the higher order encoding conditions.

Thus, when memory tests are explicit, performance functions are that of the type (c) from Figure 4.2, but in implicit tests they rather resemble the case (b). Indeed, priming functions in this last group of tests, which were word fragment completion and general knowledge tests, look different: They are much flatter, or there seems to be no effect at all. Some systematicity can, however, be discovered with respect to the point in the row of encoding conditions where variation in encoding starts to influence memory performance. In a general knowledge test, this starting point is the semantic encoding. In a word fragment completion test, priming is present in all encoding conditions. One can argue, in the spirit of a mixture of hierarchical and modular ideas, that the crucial influence is already present at the stage of perceptual encoding (our level D), and it is included in all further, higher level encodings as well.

Empirically, the more traditional case of intentional encoding finds its place somewhere between semantic and metacognitive conditions. It is quite amazing that in all but one case, incidental metacognitive processing leads to better memory performance tham even the intentional encoding. The only deviation is found in the free-recall task.[7] This small,

---

[7] This was actually the *only* nonmonotonic deviation from flat, one-step, and gradient-like memory effects in the array of 65 (!) comparisons of encoding and retrieval in this study (Challis et al., 1996).

albeit significant, deviation from the overall gradient-like picture can be attributed to the fact that intentional instructions invoke organizational strategies of particular benefit for free recall (Brown, 1979). Intentional encoding is, however, plastic and corresponds to the actually expected test. To emphasize this small effect as the case for the transfer-appropriate principle would mean simply not seeing the forest behind *one tree*.

This pattern of results is compatible with the hierarchical view of underlying mechanisms and supports the broad idea of multiple levels of processing. A dichotomous interpretation of our data would be that incidental encoding conditions provide a variable amount of semantic information for later retrieval, which increases from perceptual to metacognitive encoding. The notion that encoding semantic information can be more or less elaborated (Craik & Tulving, 1975) is well accepted, but it is not immediately clear why syllable encoding should involve more semantic activity than counting letters, or why judgment of personal relevance should recruit more semantic associations than semantic categorization itself.

An unqualified attribution of LOP effects to semantic processing alone (i.e., to a contribution of level E) is dubious in light of several other aspects of the data. For instance, free recall and recognition benefit from study conditions in different ways. Whereas it might be argued that free recall utilizes conceptual information to a greater degree, it is recognition that shows a stronger increase in performance as a function of the LOP manipulation. As I argued in discussion of the general hierarchical model, recognition has a more extended projection to the multilevel ladder: from C to F, in contrast to E and F in the case of free recall. It might be the contribution of level D that additionally raises the recognition function *across all the encoding conditions*. In fact, recognition performance deviates from baseline even after perceptual encoding, although this study condition involves little if any semantic processing.

There is another aspect of this type of analysis. In all explicit tests in Figure 4.3, one can see approximately the same rate of growth, i.e., memory performance with the highest (or "deepest") metacognitive processing is dependent on the number of all previous encoding conditions, which demonstrate LOP effects. This is a clear feature of the integration and not replacement model in the relationship of underlying mechanisms. Why, then, are there no similar signs of integration across several encoding conditions in implicit tasks? Perhaps implicit retrieval tasks address very narrowly tuned mechanisms in terms of our multilevel model, for instance, only level D or E, so that there is simply no basis for such a vertical integration. If the typical patterns of flat or one-step-like LOP functions found with implicit tests are connected with activation of relatively narrow segments of the hierarchical cognitive ladder, then it might be possible to produce similar results *even with explicit tasks* when their retrieval criteria are highly restrictive, narrowing down mechanisms involved to a single level of processing.

One of our experiments (Challis et al., 1996, Experiment 3) provides some support for this interpretation of data from explicit and implicit memory tests. After studying lists of words under the same five encoding conditions, subjects were presented with the test material, which consisted of the new words, 50% of which were graphemically similar and 50% semantically similar to those previously shown. In three parallel groups of subjects, the tasks were to find words similar to previously presented words either graphemically or phonologically or semantically. Although these tasks were explicit, the results presented in Figure 4.4 demonstrate the whole set of flat and one-step LOP functions that in all previous studies were typical of implicit tests. Again, it is the encoding condition where memory performance starts to deviate from baseline which shows a relation to underlying hierarchical architecture; this starting point shifts for graphemic, phonological, and semantic similarity tests to correspondingly higher levels of encoding.

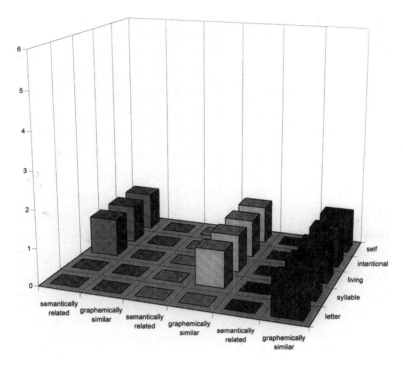

FIGURE 4.4. The number of significant deviations from baseline (least significance differences) in three new explicit memory tasks depending on five encoding conditions (after Challis et al., 1996).

Thus, the degree of integration among the levels seems to be dependent on the type of task. A feature of intentionally pursued tasks, of which explicit memory tests are one type, is usually a high degree of *vertical integration*, so that evidence from several levels are accumulated. There are no signs of this integration in implicit tests where responsibility is taken over, without much interference "from above," by narrowly tuned mechanisms, which can be themselves localized even at a relatively low level of the hierarchy. In view of such flexibility, the notion "heterarchy" (Turvey, Shaw, & Mace, 1978) may be more appropriate for describing the underlying functional architecture. Another implication of the results is a further challenge of the orthodox modularity. From the modular point of view, input systems are automatic and "cognitively impenetrable" (Pylyshyn, 1984); it seems, however, that perception can by quite accessible, up to retrieval of graphemic similarity experience, if the task conveys to perceptual mechanisms the status of the *leading level*.

In general, our results demonstrate that in its initial area (psychological investigation of memory), the LOP approach can produce data that are surprisingly consistent, indeed to a degree that is rare in psychological research. This consistency is a strong argument against reducing levels effects to some idiosyncratic domain-specific phenomena.

☐ Bridging Physiology and Everyday Behavior

Being close to the end of this overview, I want to stress exactly this point: the concept of levels presupposes some consistency of effects across different modalities, domains and modes of processing. In a period of history dominated by the search for double dissocia-tions and, presumably, isolated modular mechanisms, this multilevel paradigm plays an integrative function. In its systemic role, the LOP approach can be supported by some new experimental results that I will now describe.

An exciting chapter of evolutionary psychobiology is the analysis of behavioral effects of a sudden change of situation, for instance, when certain butterflies display their color-ful wing patterns to *psychologically immobilize* and escape a predator (Schlenoff, 1985). In a series of experiments we (Pannasch, Dornhoefer, Unema, & Velichkovsky, 2001; Unema & Velichkovsky, 2000) investigated some influences of such changes on eye movements, perception, and memory in human beings.

The starting point for us was the *distractor effect*, a phasic "freezing" of visual fixation (i.e., a delay of the next saccade) in the case of a sudden visual event (Findlay & Walker, 1999). It is currently explained as an oculomotor reflex involving structures of superior colliculus (Reingold & Stampe, 2000). This is the lowest level circuit (corresponding to level A) for eye movement responses. The remarkably short latency of this effect of only 100 ms, the fastest known behavioral responses of the human organism, leaves no alterna-tive to the proposed subcortical origin. However, we found that the distractor effect can also be produced, during exploration of visual scenes and in simulated driving, by acous-tic stimulation whereby the response time is obtained that is the same or even faster than with visual cues. In addition, we demonstrated a new *relevance effect*: the rise in duration of the subsequent fixation when a change is of relevance to the activity of the subject, for instance, when the subject should brake. This second effect could be observed at longer latencies of 300 to 400 ms.

Two lessons can be learned from these data. First, observation of behavior (via high-resolution eye-tracking) seems to demonstrate information processing stages in approxi-mately the same way as event-related potentials reveal them. The fast oculomotor responses to changes in stimulation, manifested in the distractor effect, are similar to the early N100 component of event-related potentials (ERPs). Although this may be a numerical coinci-dence, our relevance effect corresponds to other known aspects of ERPs, namely, that semantic and metacognitive variables usually influence relatively late components P300, P3b, and N400 (Kutas & King, 1996, Simons & Perlstein, 1997). The second lesson is that, though these effects clearly belong to the realm of "input systems" (cf. Fodor, 1983), they are not strictly modular and domain-specific, but rather intermodal and hierarchically organized. This similarity across domains, particularly the presence of the vertical dimen-sion, makes the phenomenon interesting for the LOP approach. In fact, our recent results testify that relevance leads to a better reproduction of information even if critical events are produced in close temporal vicinity to other changes, saccades, or blinks (Dornhoefer, Pannasch, Unema, & Velichkovsky, 2001).

There are other related eye movement phenomena. There is growing evidence that vi-sual fixations, depending on their durations, can be controlled by different hierarchically related mechanisms. Some fixations have an extremely short duration of about 100 ms or shorter (Velichkovsky, Sprenger, & Unema, 1997). They can be produced by the same fast biological mechanism that is responsible for the distractor effect and for other, mostly inhibitory, manifestations of orienting and startle reactions (Sokolov, 1963). A rather dif-ferent, partially reciprocal, type of behavior can be observed in the case of longest fixa-tions of 500 to 1000 ms. First, they are underrepresented during changes and in the begin-ning of presentation of new visual information. Second, their proportion steadily grows to the end of every period of presentation that can be treated as a sign of an expectation of change. All in all, there can be three to four functionally specific groups of fixations, ac-cording to their duration, in a seemingly unified distribution (Velichkovsky, 1999).

The investigation of free visual exploration of dynamic scenes and pictures, which is not restricted to the abrupt repetitive trials, is a challenge for experimental psychology. Picture processing is particularly problematic for the LOP approach because complex non-verbal material seldom demonstrates clear-cut encoding effects (Lockhart & Craik, 1990).[8] An approach to a differentiation of several levels in picture processing may rely on one of the first distinctions in the field, that between ambient and focal vision introduced by Colin Trevarthen (1968). This insightful distinction is largely forgotten today due to later proposals stressing cortical localization of spatial vision in humans. The situation has begun to change again recently, with increasing acceptance of the role of subcortical mechanisms, particularly the striatum. The distinction between ambient and focal processing seems to be consistent with our general levels model: It divides, on the one hand, level C and, on the other hand, level D and higher symbolic mechanisms.

In order to operationalize this distinction it is useful to consider the relationships between duration of fixation and amplitude of the next saccade (Dornhoefer, Pannasch, Velichkovsky, & Unema, 2000). Some fixations are followed by saccades that are twice as large as the radius of the fovea (>4°). This means that these saccades cannot be oriented by any detailed or "focal" visual representation of objects. Interestingly, corresponding fixations have a relatively short duration from 120 to 250 ms. If the spatial distributions of these and longer fixations over the surface of a picture are computed separately and applied as filters to process the picture itself (see, e.g., Velichkovsky, Pomplun, & Rieser, 1996), one gets the representations shown in Figure 4.5b and 4.5c. These representations can be called *ambient* and, respectively, *focal views* of the picture. It is important for the LOP approach that the surface covered by the ambient (or "shallow") fixations not only is much larger than in their focal counterparts, but remains relatively constant with different encoding instructions. On the contrary, spatial distribution of the focal (or "deep") fixations seems to be rather sensitive to the processing instruction, i.e. it is clearly task-dependent. This is why the method of *attentional landscapes filtering* seems to provide us with a reconstruction of subjective perspectives, which different hierarchical levels have on the same situation at the same time.

The analysis of optomotor behavior complements traditional memory research and brain imaging experiments by giving a more microgenetic and interactive view of the dynamics of processing. Data on eye movements provide strong evidence on some additional, earlier level of processing, preceding that of "physical" (level D) encoding from the classical LOP studies. Its function can be the detection of changes in stimulation and initiating of startle and orienting responses. The extraordinary speed and other features (Velichkovsky, 1999) speak for a deep subcortical localization of corresponding mechanisms, somewhere on the top of Bernstein's level A (Fischer & Weber, 1993; Reingold & Stampe, 2000). Other early forms of processing, revealed by several methods, including eye tracking experiments, can be associated with level C of our basic model, i.e., with a global spatial ("ambient") localization of sensory events.

All these aspects of cognitive organization seem to support the idea of a permanent interplay between several processing levels. Within the predominantly cortical levels, from D to conceptual structures E and metacognitive coordinations F, data on the gradient-like effects of encoding manipulations in memory tasks are paralleled by the shifts in duration

---

[8] Several explanations of this particular result are possible: (a) shallow instructions may not prevent a deeper, semantic processing of pictures (Boucart, Lorenceau, & Humphreys, 1995); (b) the shallow processing itself may be in this case very elaborated (Velichkovsky, 1982); (c) pictures—a Gibsonian interpretation—are representations of the world, i.e., every processing of a picture is in a sense semantic processing.

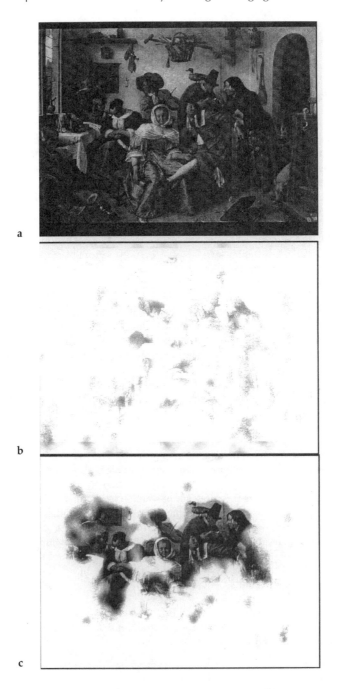

FIGURE 4.5. "The twisted world" by Jan Steen (1663): (a) copy of the original; (b) ambient (or shallow) view; (c) focal (or deep) view (after Dornhoefer et al., 2000).

of visual fixations. The simplest explanation of the increase in proportion of longer fixations in line with cognitive requirements is, of course, an increase in inhibitory control of motor functions with the progressive involvement of frontal brain mechanisms. In any case, we have here an example of a psychological concept—levels of processing—fulfilling its basic role by bridging the gap between continuous everyday activity and internal physiological machinery.

☐ Conclusions

It is impossible to validate (or invalidate) a concept or a scientific paradigm in a single chapter. A weak criterion for the validity for a concept is its consistent role in stimulating expanding research. A strong criterion is its ability to help us discover new relationships between hitherto separated domains of research and to evolve in the light of new data. In terms of both the weak and the strong criteria, the general hierarchical paradigm, in its LOP variant, has done well over the past 30 years. It has the potential for doing even better in the future.

But what can this future be? In discussing this paper with us, Michael Turvey stressed the necessity of a profound methodological change in the very style of doing cognitive psychology. According to this view of the current situation, a test of ecological validity may be too stringent for most of our textbook knowledge. However, levels ideas may survive even the eminent collapse of the present-day psychological science with its experimental methodology of factorial design, repetitive trials, and manipulation of encoding. If, under the influence of functional brain imaging and sophisticated on-line analysis of behavior, the dominating framework for research in memory and cognition becomes the dynamic system theory (in this point, I incline to agree with Turvey's remarks), then levels concept could still play a crucial role, e.g. in differentiating the leading and background coordination of the system and in explaining the evolutionary roots of its subcomponents. My best guess is that this will happen along the lines suggested by two outstanding scholars, Nikolai A. Bernstein and Fergus I. M. Craik.

☐ Acknowledgment

I wish to thank Bruce Bridgeman, Fergus Craik, John Gardiner, Anna Leonova, Robert Lockhart, and Henry Roediger for discussion of this chapter and my colleagues Pieter Unema, Beata Bauer, Sascha Dornhoefer, Sebastian Pannasch, and Hans-Juergen Volke for participation in research. Experiments described in the chapter were supported by DFG, the Konrad Lorenz Foundation, and BMW AG.

☐ References

Baddeley, A. D. (1978). The trouble with levels: A re-examination of Craik and Lockhart's framework for memory research. *Psychological Review, 85*, 139–152.

Bernstein, N. A. (1947). *O postrojenii dvizhenij [On the construction of movements]*. Moscow: Medgiz. (Reprinted in *Physiologia dvizhenij i activnost*, Moscow: Nauka, 1990).

Bernstein, N. A. (1967). *The coordination and regulation of movements*. Oxford, England: Pergamon.

Bernstein, N. A. (1996). *Dexterity and its development*. Mahwah, NJ: Erlbaum.

Bihle, A. M., Brownell, H. H., Powelson, J. A., & Gardner, H. (1986). Comprehension of humorous and nonhumorous materials by left and right brain damaged patients. *Brain and Cognition, 5,* 399–411.

Blaxton, T. A. (1989). Investigating dissociations among memory measures. *Journal of Experimental Psychology: Learning, Memory, and Cognition, 15,* 657–668.

Blaxton, T. A , Bookheimer, S. Y., Zefiro, Th. A., Figlozzi, C. M., Gaillard, W. D., & Theodore, W. H. (1996). Functional mapping of human memory using PET: Comparisons of conceptual and perceptual tests. *Canadian Journal of Experimental Psychology, 50(1),* 42–56.

Boucart, M., Lorenceau, J., & Humphreys, G. W. (1995). Automatic access to object identities. *Journal of Experimental Psychology: Human Perception and Performance, 21,* 584–601.

Bower, H., & Gilligan, S. G. (1979). Remembering information related to one's self. *Journal of Research in Personality, 13,* 420–432.

Bridgeman, B. (1999). Vertical modularity in the visual system. In B.H. Challis & B.M. Velichkovsky (Eds.), *Stratification in cognition and consciousness* (pp. 19–41). Amsterdam: John Benjamins.

Brown, A. L. (1979). Theories of memory and the problem of development. In L. A. Cermak & F.I.M. Craik (Eds.), *Levels of processing in human memory.* Hillsdale, NJ: Erlbaum.

Cimino, C. R., Verfaillie, M., Bowers, D., & Heilmann, K. M. (1991). Autobiographical memory: Influence of right hemisphere damage on emotionality and specificity. *Brain and Cognition, 15,* 106–118.

Challis, B. H., & Brodbeck, D. R. (1992). Level of processing affects priming in word fragment completion. *Journal of Experimental Psychology: Learning, Memory and Cognition, 18,* 595–607.

Challis, B. H., Velichkovsky, B. M., & Craik, F. I. M. (1996). Levels-of-processing effects on a variety of memory tasks: New findings and theoretical implications. *Consciousness & Cognition, 5(1/2),* 142–164.

Christoff, K., & Gabrieli, J. D. E. (2000). The frontopolar cortex and human cognition: Evidence for a rostrocadual hierarchical organization within the human prefrontal cortex. *Psychobiology, 28(2),* 168–186.

Craik, F. I. M., & Lockhart, R. (1972). Levels of processing: A framework for memory research. *Journal of Verbal Learning and Verbal Behaviour, 11,* 671–684.

Craik, F. I. M., Moroz, T. M., Moscovitch, M., Stuss, D. T., Vinokur, G., Tulving, E., & Kapur, S. (1999). In search of the Self: A positron emisson tomography study. *Psychological Science, 10(1),* 26–34.

Craik, F. I. M., & Tulving, E. (1975). Depth of processing and the retention of words in episodic memory. *Journal of Experimental Psychology: General, 104,* 268–294.

Deacon, T. W. (1996). Prefrontal cortex and symbolic learning: Why a brain capable of language evolved only once. In B. M. Velichkovsky & D. M. Rumbaugh (Eds.), *Communicating meaning: The evolution and development of language.* Mahwah, NJ: Erlbaum.

Deubel, H. (1999). Separate mechanisms for the adaptive control of reactive, volitional, and memory-guided saccadic eye movements. In D. Gopher & A. Koriat (Eds.), *Attention and performance XVII* (pp. 697–722). Cambridge, MA: MIT Press.

Dornhoefer, S., Joos, M., Pannasch, S., Rothert, A., Unema, P., & Velichkovsky, B. M. (2001). Blanks, blinks and saccades: How blind we really are for relevant visual events. In J. Hyönä, D. Munoz, W. Heide, & R. Radach (Eds.), *The brain's eyes: Neurobiological and clinical aspects of oculomotor research.* Oxford, UK: Elsevier.

Dornhoefer, S., Pannasch, S., Velichkovsky, B. M., & Unema, P. (2000). "Attentional landscapes" and phasic changes of fixation duration in picture perception. *Perception, 29*(Suppl.), 11–12.

Eysenck, M. W. (1978). Verbal remembering. In B. M. Ross (Ed.), *Psychology survey. No.1.* London: Allen & Unwin.

Eysenck, M. W., & Keane, M. T. (2000). *Cognitive psychology* (4th ed.). Hove, England: Psychology Press.

Findlay, J. M., & Walker, R. (1999). A model of saccadic generation based on parallel processing and competitive inhibition. *Behavioral and Brain Sciences, 22,* 661–674.

Fischer, B., & Weber, H. (1993). Express saccades and visual attention. *Behavioral and Brain Sciences, 16,* 553–610.

Fisher, R. P., & Craik, F. I. M. (1977). The interaction between encoding and retrieval operations in cued recall. *Journal of Experimental Psychology: Human Learning and Memory, 3,* 153–171.

Fodor, J. A. S. (1983). *The modularity of mind.* Cambridge, MA: MIT Press.

Gabrieli, J. D. E., Desmond, J. E., Demb, J. B., Wagner, A. D., Stone, M. V., Vaidya, C. J., & Glover, G. H. (1996). Functional magnetic resonance imaging of semantic memory processes in the frontal lobes. *Psychological Science, 7,* 278–283.

Gippenreiter, J. B., Romanov, V. J., & Smirnov, S. D. (1969). On the movements of hand and eye in the process of counting test object's elements. *Psychological Investigations, No.1.* Moscow: Moscow University Press.

Goldberg, E. (1991). Higher cortical functions in humans: The gradiental approach. In E. Goldberg (Ed.), *Contemporary neuropsychology and legacy of Luria.* Hillsdale, NJ: Erlbaum.

Hamann, S. B. (1990). Level-of-processing effects in conceptually driven implicit tasks. *Journal of Experimental Psychology: Learning, Memory and Cognition, 16,* 970–977.

Head, H. (1920). *Studies in neurology.* Oxford: Oxford University Press.

Holloway, R. L., & De la Coste-Lareymondie, M. (1982). Brain endocast asymmetry in pongids and hominids. *American Journal of Physical Anthropology, 58,* 108–116.

Jeannerod, M. (1981). Intersegmental coordination during reaching at natural visual objects. In J. Long & A. Baddeley (Eds.), *Attention and performance IX* (pp. 153–172). Hillsdale, NJ: Erlbaum.

Kapur, S., Craik, F. I. M., Tulving, E., Wilson, A. A., Houle, S., & Brown, G. M. (1994). Neuroanatomical correlates of encoding in episodic memory: Levels of processing effect. *Proceedings of the National Academy of Sciences, USA, 91,* 2008–2011.

Kennard, C. (1989). Hierarchical aspects of eye movement disorders. In C. Kennard & M. Swash (Eds.), *Hierarchies in neurology: A reappraisal of a Jacksonian concept.* London: Springer-Verlag.

Kutas, M., & King, J. W. (1996). The potentials for basic sentence processing: Differentiating integrative processes. In I. Toshio & J. L. McClelland (Eds.), *Attention and performance XVI.* Cambridge, MA: MIT Press.

Leont'ev, A. N. (1978). *Activity, consciousness, and personality.* Englewood Cliffs, NJ: Prentice-Hall.

Lockhart, R., & Craik, F. I. M. (1990). Levels of processing: A retrospective commentary on a framework for memory research. *Canadian Journal of Psychology, 44,* 87–112.

Luria, A. R. (1966). *Higher cortical functions in man.* London: Tavistock.

Miall, D. S. (1986). Emotion and the Self: The context of remembering. *British Journal of Psychology, 77,* 389–397.

Mishkin, M., Suzuki, W. A., Gardian, D. G., & Vargha-Khadem, F. (1999). Hierarchical organization of cognitive memory. In N. Burgess, K. J. Jeffrey & J. O'Keefe (Eds.), *The hyppocampal and parietal foundations of spatial cognition.* Oxford, England: Oxford University Press.

Morris, C. D. Bransford, J. D., & Franks, J. J. (1977). Levels of processing versus transfer appropriate processing. *Journal of Verbal Learning and Verbal Behavior, 16,* 519–533.

Naumann, E. (1985). *Ereigniskorrelierte Potentiale und Gedächtnis [Event-related potentials and memory].* Frankfurt, Germany: Lang.

Pannasch, S., Dornhoefer, S., Unema, P., & Velichkovsky, B. M. (2001). The omnipresent prolongation of visual fixations: Saccades are inhibited by changes in situation or subject's activity. *Vision Research.* In press.

Pomplun. M. (1998). *Analysis and models of comparative visual search.* Aacher, Germany: Cuvilier.

Pylyshyn, Z. W. (1984). *Computation and cognition.* Cambridge, MA: MIT Press.

Reingold, E., & Stampe, D. (2000). Saccadic inhibition and gaze contingent research paradigms. In A. Kennedy, R. Raddach, D. Heller, & J. Pynte (Eds.), *Reading as a perceptual process.* Amsterdam: Elsevier.

Roediger, H. L., Weldon, M. S., Stadler, M. L., & Riegler, G. L. (1992). Direct comparison of two implicit memory tests. *Journal of Experimental Psychology: Learning, Memory and Cognition, 18,* 1251–1269.

Sanquist, T. F., Rohrbaugh, J. W., Syndulko, K., & Lindsley, D. B. (1980). Electrocortical signs of levels of processing: Perceptual analysis and recognition memory. *Psychophysiology, 17,* 568–576.

Schlenoff, D. H. (1985). The startle responses of blue jays to *Catocala* (Lepidoptera: Noctuidae) prey models. *Animal Behavior, 33,* 1057–1067.

Shammi, P., & Stuss, D. T. (1999). Humor appreciation: A role of the right frontal lobe. *Brain, 122,* 657–666.

Simons, R. F., & Perlstein, W. M. (1997). A tale of two reflexes: An ERP analysis of prepulse inhibition and orienting. In P. Lang, R. F. Simons & M. T. Balaban (Eds.), *Attention and orienting: Sensory and motivational processes*. Mahwah, NJ: Erlbaum.

Smirnov, A. A. (1966). *Problemy psikhologii pamjati [Problems in psychology of memory]*. Moscow: Pedagogika.

Sokolov, E. N. (1963). *Perception and the conditioned reflex*. Oxford, England: Pergamon.

Stadler, M. A., & Roediger, H. L. (1997). The question of awareness in research on implicit learning. In M. A. Stadler & P. A. Frensch (Eds.), *Handbook of implicit learning*. London: Sage.

Treisman, A. (1979). The psychological reality of levels of processing. In L. A. Cermak & F. I. M. Craik (Eds.), *Levels of processing in human memory*. Hillsdale, NJ: Erlbaum.

Trevarthen, C. (1969). Two visual systems in primates. *Psychologische Forschung, 31*, 321–337.

Tulving, E. (1998). Brain/mind correlates of human memory. In M. Sabourin, F. I. M. Craik, & M. Robert (Eds.), *Advances in psychological sciences. Vol. 2*. Hove, England: Psychology Press.

Tulving, E., Kapur, S., Craik, F. I. M., Moscovitch, M., & Houle, S. (1994). Hemispheric encoding/ retrieval asymmetry in episodic memory. *Proceedings of the National Academy of Sciences, USA, 91*, 2016–2020.

Tulving, E., & Schacter, D. L. (1990). Priming and human memory systems. *Science, 247*, 301–305.

Turvey, M. T., Shaw, R. E., & Mace, W. (1978). Issues in the theory of action. In J. Requin (Ed.), *Attention and performance VII*. Hillsdale, NJ: Erlbaum.

Unema, P., & Velichkovsky, B. M. (2000). *Processing stages are revealed by dynamics of visual fixations: Distractor versus relevance effects*. Paper presented to the 41st Annual Meeting of the Psychonomic Society, New Orleans.

Velichkovsky, B. M. (1982). Visual cognition and its spatial-temporal context. In F. Klix, J. Hoffmann, & E. Van der Meer (Eds.), *Cognitive research in psychology*. Amsterdam: North Holland.

Velichkovsky, B. M. (1990). The vertical dimension of mental functioning. *Psychological Research, 52*, 282–289.

Velichkovsky, B. M. (1994). The levels endeavour in psychology and cognitive science. In P. Bertelson, P. Eelen, & G. d'Ydewalle (Eds.), *International perspectives in psychological sciences: Leading themes*. Hove, England: Erlbaum.

Velichkovsky, B. M. (1995). Communicating attention: Gaze position transfer in cooperative problem solving. *Pragmatics and Cognition, 3(2)*, 199–222.

Velichkovsky, B. M. (1999). From levels of processing to stratification of cognition. In B. H. Challis & B. M. Velichkovsky (Eds.), *Stratification in cognition and consciousness*. Amsterdam: John Benjamins.

Velichkovsky, B. M., Dornhoefer, S., Pannasch, S., & Unema, P. (2000). Visual fixations and level of attentional processing. In A. Duhowski (Ed.), *Eye tracking research and applications*. Palm Beach Gardens, FL: ACM Press.

Velichkovsky, B. M., Klemm, T., Dettmar P., & Volke, H.-J. (1996). Evoked coherence of EEG II: Communication of brain areas and depth of processing. *Zeitschrift für EEG-EMG, 27*, 111–119.

Velichkovsky, B. M., Pomplun, M., & Rieser, H. (1996). Attention and communication. In W. H. Zangemeister, S., Stiel, & C. Freksa (Eds.), *Visual attention and cognition*. Amsterdam: Elsevier.

Velichkovsky, B. M., Sprenger, A., & Unema, P. (1997). Towards gaze-mediated interaction: Collecting solutions of the "Midas touch problem". In S. Howard, J. Hammond, & G. Lindgaard (Eds.), *Human-computer interaction*, London: Chapman & Hall.

Vincent, A., Craik, F. I. M., & Furedy, J. J. (1993). Sensitivity of heart rate and T-wave amplitude to effort and processing level in a memory task. *Journal of Psychophysiology, 7(3)*, 202–208.

Wheeler, M. A., Stuss, D. T., & Tulving, E. (1997). Toward a theory of episodic memory: The frontal lobes and autonoetic consciousness. *Psychological Bulletin, 121*, 331–354.

Zinchenko, P. I. (1961). *Neproizvolnoje zapominanije [Incidental remembering]*. Moscow: Pedagogika.

☐ Appendix A

The following excerpt is from Bernstein (1947/1990, pp. 40–43), translated by M. Mirsky and B. M. Velichkovsky.

Thus, coordination of movements consists, in its precise definition, in overcoming the excessive degrees of freedom of the moving organ, i.e., in turning the latter into a controllable system. The solution to this problem is based on the principle of sensory corrections, which are provided jointly by a variety of afferentation systems and executed within the basic structural formula of a reflex circle. We define the construction of a given movement as a composition of those afferentational ensembles that participate in coordinating this movement, in carrying out the corrections required, and in providing the adequate recodings for the effector impulses, as well as the totality of systemic interactions between these components.

Sensory corrections are executed by the already *whole syntheses* whose complexity increases progressively from the bottom to the top [of the hierarchy—M.M. and B.V]. The syntheses are built from a great variety of sensory signals, which have undergone a deep integration. These syntheses, or sensory fields, are exactly what we call *levels of construction* of movements. *Each motor task finds for itself, depending upon its contents or meaningful structure, a certain level (in other words, a certain sensory synthesis) which, by the features and the composition of afferentations forming it, as well as by the principle of their synthetic integration, is the most adequate for the solution of this task.* This level is defined as the leading one for a given movement in regard to carrying out the most significant, decisive sensory corrections and to performing the recodings needed for it.

The best way to clarify the concept of the various leading, or key, levels of construction is to compare some examples of movements similar in their external shaping but drastically different in their level composition.

A person is capable of executing a circular arm and/or hand movement in a number of situations that are extraordinarily different: A. Often, when an outstanding virtuoso pianist performs a so-called vibrato, i.e., repeats the same note or octave at a frequency of 6 or 8 cycles per second, the trajectories of points on a moving wrist or forearm are forming small circles (or ovals): B. It is possible to draw a circle in the moving one's arm during a gymnastic exercise or a choreographic performance: C. One can trace, with a pencil, a circle drawn in advance or etched on a piece of paper (C1) or a copy a circle (C2) placed in front of one: D. A circular movement can be executed in the process of making a stitch with a needle, or untying a knot. E. Proving a geometric theorem, one can draw on a blackboard a circle as one of the components of the drawing used to show the proof.

Every one of these movements is a circle or something more or less similar, but nevertheless, in all the above examples, their origins, their central nervous "roots," the levels of their construction are substantially different, as will be shown below. In all the versions mentioned above, we encounter both differences in the mechanics of movement, of its external, spatial-dynamic pattern, and—which is even more important—deep differences in the mechanisms of coordination determining these movements. It is completely evident, first, that each of these circular movements is related to *different afferentations*.

Type A circles are formed involuntarily, brought about by a *proprioceptive reflex*, which is more or less unconscious. A circle of the gymnastic-dancing type (B) is also executed mainly on the basis of proprioceptive corrections, this time . . . mostly consciously realized and revealing already the prevalence of the joint-space over the muscle-force components of proprio-afferentations. The drawing of a circle that is traced (C1) or copied (C2) is led by visual control, more direct and primitive, in the former case, and carried out by a very complex synthesized afferentational "visual-spatial field" system in the latter. In the case D, the leading afferentational system is the representation of *an object,* its apperception, connected with knowledge of its shape and functional significance. This knowledge results in *an action* or series of actions aimed at a purposeful manipulation with the object. Finally, in the case E, of a circle drawn on a blackboard by the math lecturer, the central moment is the semi-convential or symbolic representation of its relations to other elements of a mathematical drawing, rather than the reproduction of its geometrical shape . . . Distortion of the correct circular shape will not disturb the original idea of the math lecturer, nor will it initiate any corrective impulses in his or her motorics. . . . All these movements (from A through E) are circles, in regards to their muscle-joint schemes, but their *construction,* as performed by the central nervous system, is executed at different levels for each of the mentioned versions.

There is no movement (perhaps with extremely rare exceptions) that is served by one and only one leading level of construction in all its coordinating details. Indeed, at the beginning stages of forming a new individual motor skill, almost all corrections are executed, in a surrogate mode, by the initiating leading level, but soon the situation changes. Every single technical part and detail of the complex movement sooner or later finds for itself such a level, *among the lower levels*, whose afferentations are the most adequate for this detail by the features of sensory corrections they provide. Thus, gradually, resulting from a sequence of switchings and step-by-step changes, a complex multilevel construction is being formed, headed by the *leading level* adequate for the *meaningful structure* of the motor act and providing only those very basic corrections that are decisive with respect to the sense of a movement. Under its guidance, a number of *background levels* participate in the further execution of a movement, subserving such background or technical details of the movement as tone, innervation and denervation, reciprocal inhibition, and complex synergies. *It is the process of switching the technical components of controlling the movement to the lower, background levels that is usually called automatization.*

In any movement, regardless of the absolute "height" of its level, *only the leading levels* as well as only those corrections that are executed at this very level are *consciously available*. For example, if the current motor act is tying a knot, which is performed at the level D, its technical components from the level of the spatial field (C), as a rule, do not reach the threshold of consciousness. However, if the next movement is a stretch or a smile, which occurs at the level B, this movement is consciously realized despite being of a level absolutely lower in the hierarchy than C. It does not mean, of course, that the degree of conscious apprehension should be the same for each leading level. To the contrary, *both the extent of conscious apprehension and the degree of volitional control increase when moving through the levels in the bottom-up fashion.*

Switching of the technical component from the leading level to one of the lower, background levels, in accordance with the above, results in such a component leaving the field of consciousness, and it is exactly this process that deserves the name *automatization.* The advantages of automatization are completely evident, for it results in freeing the consciousness from secondary technical material, enabling it to concentrate on the very significant and crucial facets of the movement that are, as a rule, a potent source of a variety of "unpredictables" requiring quick and adequate switchings. The process of a temporary or total decay of automatization, opposite to the one described, is called *deautomatization.*

The following excerpt is from Bernstein (1947/1990, pp. 112–113), translated by M. Mirsky and B. M. Velichkovsky.

It may be reasonable for our further analysis to introduce two notions: the notion of *meaningful structure* of an action and that of its *motor composition.* Meaningful structure of a motor act is defined by the content of the task raised, and in its turn, it defines the sensory or sensory-cognitive synthesis that is adequate to the task and can uphold the solution. In other words, the sensory-cognitive synthesis co-attuned with the task is the leading level of construction. Motor composition of an action is furthermore the result of a confrontation (as it were, a substitution of parameters in some general equation) between requirements of the task and the situation in the first line, the motor options being in possession of the organism for its solution. Motor composition includes many components such as the listing of sequential elements of a chain (if we are dealing with a chain action), the definition of motor procedures, supporting these elements, and the collection of the simultaneous background coordinations necessary for a fluent realization of a complex movement. Motor composition is also defined by the situation—by biomechanical design of levers and kinematic chains of the body, by innervational resources, by the inventory of sensory corrections, and, finally, by the tools that may be applied for the needed action. Thus, motor composition is a function of not only the task but also the task solver. Let us illustrate this by the same task of a fast relocation in space. A human will solve it by sprinting (or, for instance, by riding a bicycle), a horse by galloping, a bird by flight, etc.

John M. Gardiner
Alan Richardson-Klavehn
Cristina Ramponi
Barbara M. Brooks

Involuntary Levels-of-Processing Effects in Perceptual and Conceptual Priming

It is, for example, of great interest and a challenge to a comprehensive theory
of memory that some forms of implicit memory are unaffected by different
orienting tasks, even though the tasks vary over a wide range of levels of
processing.

—Lockhart and Craik, 1990

Level of processing has a profound impact not only on memory performance but also on what people are aware of when executing that performance. A deeper level of processing increases subjective experiences of *remembering* without affecting subjective experiences of *knowing* (Gardiner, 1988; Gardiner, Java, & Richardson-Klavehn, 1996). Thus level of processing affects autonoetic consciousness, the hallmark of an episodic memory system, and not noetic consciousness, the hallmark of a semantic memory system (Tulving, 1983, 1985).

Subjective experiences of remembering and of knowing are two ways in which people become aware of memory. Such awareness of memory has been dissociated empirically from *retrieval volition*, which refers to awareness of voluntary (intended) or involuntary (unintended) retrieval of study-list items (see Richardson-Klavehn, Clarke, & Gardiner, 1999; Richardson-Klavehn & Gardiner, 1995, 1996; Richardson-Klavehn, Gardiner, & Java, 1994, 1996). In this chapter, we are concerned with another way in which level of processing relates to what people are aware of, namely, its relation to retrieval volition.

This relation has been of considerable theoretical importance in comparing performance between intentional (or direct or explicit) and incidental (or indirect or implicit) memory tasks. The presence of levels-of-processing effects has been taken to indicate the subjective intention to retrieve items from the study list. The absence of levels-of-processing effects has been taken to indicate the absence of any subjective intention to retrieve items from the study list. These assumptions were formalized in the retrieval intentionality criterion proposed by Schacter, Bowers, and Booker (1989). Meeting this criterion requires the use of identical test items in both intentional and incidental tasks, so that the tasks differ only in retrieval instructions, together with a manipulation check that entails some independent variable known to affect voluntary retrieval. Level of processing was an obvious choice for such a variable. Early evidence was that it did not influence priming in incidental perceptual tests such as word-stem completion (e.g., Graf & Mandler, 1984), suggesting that priming was involuntary. According to the retrieval intentionality criterion, therefore, if incidental test performance does show levels-of-processing effects, then the test is presumed to be "contaminated" by deliberate attempts to retrieve studied words.

The absence of a levels-of-processing effect, in and of itself, cannot, of course, be taken to mean there was no deliberate attempt to retrieve studied words. Quite soon after Craik and Lockhart (1972) introduced levels of processing as a framework for memory research, it was discovered that even in intentional tests, levels-of-processing effects do not occur invariably. Whether or not they occur depends on retrieval cues and retrieval operations. Fergus Craik himself was among the first to demonstrate this point empirically. Fisher and Craik (1977) showed that with rhyming cues in cued recall, the difference between semantic and rhyme encoding was minimal. In the same year, Morris, Bransford, and Franks (1977) showed that levels-of-processing effects can even be reversed in intentional tests. With a rhyme recognition test they showed that rhyme encoding was superior to semantic encoding. That result was instrumental in the formulation of the transfer-appropriate-processing view, which was subsequently extended to explain dissociations between intentional and incidental tests (see Roediger, Weldon, and Challis, 1989). Thus to argue that incidental test performance is not contaminated by deliberate attempts to retrieve studied words, it is necessary to have additional evidence, such as that provided when the retrieval intentionality criterion is satisfied. Both the presence and absence of levels-of-processing effects have to be demonstrated in the respective tests.

This use of level of processing as an objective marker for retrieval volition has recently become more problematic. First, significant levels-of-processing effects have been found in meta-analyses of priming in incidental perceptual tests (Brown & Mitchell, 1994; Challis & Brodbeck, 1992) as well as in some individual experiments (e.g., Toth, Reingold, & Jacoby, 1994). Second, in incidental conceptual tests, significant levels-of-processing effects have often been found in individual experiments, as might be expected if only because a deeper level of processing involves more conceptual processing (e.g., Blaxton, 1989; Srinivas & Roediger, 1990). The combined effect of these developments seems to limit the usefulness of levels of processing in connection with the retrieval intentionality criterion.

Our main contention in this chapter is to argue that levels of processing still has a useful role to play in this respect. Levels-of-processing effects in incidental tests do not necessarily imply deliberate attempts to retrieve study-list items. Such effects may occur for other reasons, under conditions in which it is possible to discount a voluntary contamination hypothesis. Moreover, it is possible that those levels-of-processing effects could occur in conjunction with the absence of levels-of-processing effects under other conditions where such effects would be expected if people were trying to retrieve studied items. If so, then the retrieval intentionality criterion could still be met.

In the next part of the chapter we describe two illustrations of involuntary levels-of-processing effects. The first is in the perceptual test of word-stem completion. The second is in the conceptual test of word association. We then discuss the issue in relation to conceptual priming in a little more detail. In the latter part of the chapter, we describe some converging evidence and conclude with some broader comments on the need to make the distinction that we do between awareness of retrieval volition and awareness of memory.

☐ Involuntary Lexical Effects in Word-Stem Completion

One alternative reason that has been suggested for finding levels-of-processing effects in incidental perceptual tests has to do with the nature of the encoding task. Some low-level tasks, such as counting the enclosed spaces within the letters of studied words, could be accomplished without much processing of the word as a whole. People could perform that encoding task without much lexical processing. If lexical processing is necessary for full priming to occur and if (on only some proportion of occasions) lexical processing is curtailed in this task, then this would result in a deficit in priming compared with that obtained following other levels-of-processing tasks (see, e.g., Challis & Brodbeck, 1992; Roediger & McDermott, 1993).

This lexical processing hypothesis was put to the test by Richardson-Klavehn and Gardiner (1998). Our first experiment included several test conditions other than those we describe here, where we focus on two tests, an incidental test of word-stem completion and a corresponding intentional test of word-stem cued recall. There were three levels-of-processing tasks at study. A graphemic task involved counting the enclosed spaces within the letters of the words. A phonemic task involved counting the syllables in the words. And a semantic task involved rating the words' pleasantness. The study lists were 48 words long and the encoding tasks were blocked. The long list length and blocked encoding tasks were designed to maximize the chances of discovering a significant priming deficit in the graphemic task, a necessary precondition for testing the lexical processing hypothesis. In the test lists, the word-stem cues were randomized with respect to level of processing in order to prevent participants from being able to identify the level of processing from the cue and hence selectively vary their retrieval strategy between particular conditions.

The results from those two tests are summarized in the upper half of Table 5.1. There was clearly a strong levels-of-processing effect in the intentional test. But there was also a levels-of-processing effect in the incidental test, though the effect there was not quite the same. There was a priming deficit for the letters task, with no difference between priming for the syllables and meaning tasks. Most studies in the literature have tended to use only two levels-of-processing tasks (though see Challis, Velichkovsky, & Craik, 1996, and Velichkovsky, chapter 4 of this volume, for a notable exception). Had we only used the

TABLE 5.1. Proportions of Responses from Richardson–Klavehn and Gardiner (1998, Experiments 1 & 2).

Experiment 1, level of processing				
Test	Letters	Syllables	Meaning	Unstudied
Intentional	.10	.32	.57	.04
Incidental	.41	.51	.50	.29

Experiment 2 (incidental tests), level of processing				
Study Condition	Letters	Syllables	Meaning	Unstudied
Standard	.37	.47	.46	.28
Lexical Decision	.48	.45	.47	.27

letters and meaning tasks, the outcome would have been parallel effects in intentional and incidental tests and it would not have been possible to discount voluntary contamination of priming. Had we only used the syllables and meaning tasks, the outcome would have been a dissociation of effects that would satisfy the retrieval intentionality criterion. Thus the addition of the third level of processing considerably increased theoretical resolution because it allowed the data to reveal both parallel and dissociative effects of level of processing in conjunction. We can infer that studied words were retrieved involuntarily in the incidental test because had they been retrieved with the intention of so doing, priming would have also been much greater for the meaning task than for the syllables task.

Those results are consistent with the lexical processing hypothesis but do not directly confirm it. In a second experiment, Richardson-Klavehn and Gardiner (1998) tested the hypothesis more directly by comparing incidental test performance following two sets of study conditions. Both sets of study conditions involved the same levels-of-processing tasks as before and one of them essentially replicated the previous procedure. To the other set of study conditions a lexical decision task was added. Some nonwords were interspersed throughout the study list (with corresponding filler words in the other condition), and prior to carrying out the levels-of-processing task for each item, people in this group had to make a lexical decision. Because the nonwords were pronounceable, the letters and syllables tasks could also be applied to them. But instead of the pleasantness of meaning task, for nonwords the corresponding task was to rate the pleasantness of their sound.

If the priming deficit responsible for the involuntary levels-of-processing effect in the incidental test is attributable to reduced lexical processing, then the addition of the lexical decision task should eliminate that deficit. Equally important, the addition of the lexical decision task should have no impact upon priming for the other two levels of processing. The results are summarized in the lower half of Table 5.1. Clearly, these predictions were confirmed.

Thus our conclusion is that levels-of-processing effects may occur in perceptual priming even when study-list items are retrieved involuntarily and that one reason for those effects is reduced lexical processing. This does not, of course, imply that levels-of-processing effects in incidental tests do not occur for other reasons too, including voluntary contamination, under other circumstances. Nor does it imply that levels-of-processing effects will necessarily occur because of reduced lexical processing whenever a similar graphemic task is used (cf. Roediger, Weldon, Stadler, & Riegler, 1992). Other factors may be important, including whether or not the graphemic task is blocked, since blocking the task is more likely to encourage reduced lexical processing.

☐ Involuntary Elaborative Effects in Word Association

In accord with transfer-appropriate processing, just as perceptual priming benefits from the extent to which similar perceptual processing is engaged at both study and test (see, e.g., Richardson-Klavehn & Gardiner, 1996), conceptual priming benefits from the extent to which similar conceptual processing is engaged at study and test (see, e.g., Cabeza, 1994). If only for that reason, level of processing might be expected to have pervasive effects in conceptual priming. According to the retrieval intentionality criterion, the presence of such effects could indicate that conceptual priming is rather generally contaminated by voluntary retrieval of study-list items. Or it could indicate that level of processing is not an appropriate choice of variable in applying the criterion to conceptual tests.

However, there is some evidence, particularly in word association tests, that under certain circumstances levels-of-processing effects may be absent from conceptual priming. If so, then at least under those circumstances level of processing may still have a useful role to play in distinguishing voluntary from involuntary retrieval of studied items, even in conceptual tests.

Schacter and McGlynn (1989) found that incidental tests involving word pairs that were strongly associated (e.g., table–chair) did not show levels-of-processing effects, though associatively unrelated word pairs (e.g., table–key) did. In intentional tests, both kinds of word pairs showed levels-of-processing effects. The implication is that, unlike priming for the more weakly associated words, priming for the more strongly associated (or "unit-ized") word pairs cannot benefit from conceptual elaboration at study. But for reasons that remain unclear, other studies have yielded conflicting results. Vaidya et al. (1997) found similar results to those of Schacter and McGlynn (1989), whereas Weldon and Coyote (1996) found significant levels-of-processing effects in incidental word association even with strongly related paired associates.

There are similarly conflicting results with respect to the question of whether or not, like perceptual priming, conceptual priming tends to be preserved in old adults (cf. Java, 1996, with Jelicic, Craik, & Moscovitch, 1996). Since performance in old adults is im-paired in intentional tests, evidence that their conceptual priming is impaired is entirely consistent with the voluntary contamination hypothesis. Thus, both with respect to lev-els-of-processing effects and with respect to effects of normal aging in conceptual priming the situation is far from clear.

Ramponi (2001; Ramponi, Richardson-Klavehn, & Gardiner, 1999) carried out an ex-periment designed to provide some clarification. Strongly and weakly related paired asso-ciates were encoded in four different levels-of-processing tasks by young and old adults, whose performance was then compared in intentional and incidental word association tests. The strongly related associates (e.g., king–queen) had an average baseline associa-tion of 61%. The weakly related associates (e.g., guard–soldier) had an average baseline association of 12%. The four levels-of-processing tasks included similar letters, syllables, and meaning tasks to those used by Richardson-Klavehn and Gardiner (1998), together with a fourth imagery task. Participants had to decide (a) which of the two words in each pair had more letters that extended above the main body of the word, or (b) which of the two words had more syllables, or (c) which of the two words had the more pleasant mean-ing, or (d) which of the two words was easier to place in an interactive image. Long study lists of 112 words were divided into 28 paired associates for each level of processing, 14 strongly and 14 weakly related ones. The levels-of-processing tasks were blocked and as-sociative strength was randomised within each block. The test list consisted of 168 word association cues, where associative strength was again randomized, and the materials were rotated across all other experimental conditions.

If incidental test performance reflects voluntary contamination, then there should be parallel effects of level of processing and of age in incidental and intentional tests. Previ-ous findings, however, suggest that associative strength may be critical to whether there are parallel effects or dissociative effects in intentional and incidental tests. There may be parallel effects for weakly related paired associates together with dissociative effects for strongly related paired associates. If so, the retrieval intentionality criterion would be met and it could be inferred that in the incidental test, studied words were retrieved involun-tarily.

The results are summarized in Table 5.2. There were indeed both parallel and dissocia-tive effects in the two tests. The dissociative effects occurred with the strongly related associates. With these associates there were large effects of level of processing and of age in the intentional test. Both these effects were essentially absent in the incidental test. Table 5.2 shows those data highlighted in bold. For the effects of level of processing, the

TABLE 5.2. Proportions of responses from Ramponi (2001).

Intentional test, level of processing

Items	Group	Letters	Syllables	Meaning	Imagery	Unstudied
Strong	Young	.15	**.31**	**.84**	**.80**	.02
	Old	.06	**.15**	**.66**	**.61**	.02
Weak	Young	.05	.11	.65	.59	.00
	Old	.02	.03	.37	.32	.02

Incidental test, level of processing

Items	Group	Letters	Syllables	Meaning	Imagery	Unstudied
Strong	Young	.64	**.73**	**.76**	**.78**	.60
	Old	.66	**.67**	**.72**	**.74**	.59
Weak	Young	.16	.20	.41	.38	.12
	Old	.15	.16	.30	.27	.12

dissociation is most striking in comparing the syllables task with the meaning and imagery tasks. In contrast, the data for the corresponding conditions with weakly related word pairs showed parallel effects of level of processing and of age in both intentional and incidental tests.

These results indicate that studied words were retrieved involuntarily in the incidental test. To argue otherwise, one would have to assume that both young and old adults can discriminate between randomly ordered strong and weak associate cues during incidental tests and selectively attempt deliberate retrieval of studied associates for the former and not for the latter.

We briefly mention two other findings in Table 5.2. First, performance was generally lower following the letters task compared with the syllables task, as had been found by Richardson-Klavehn and Gardiner (1998). This levels-of-processing effect is presumably related to reduced lexical processing here too. Second, performance following the imagery task was generally rather similar to performance following the meaning task, though it had been hoped that this task would lead to increased performance, especially in the intentional test.

The main conclusion from this study is that involuntary levels-of-processing effects may also occur in conceptual priming, reflecting, perhaps, both lexical and conceptual processes. In particular, it seems that conceptual priming for the weakly but not for the strongly related associations in this word association task is sensitive to the effects of elaborative encoding and of age. This elaborative processing hypothesis, however, is not confirmed as directly as was the lexical processing hypothesis (Richardson-Klavehn & Gardiner, 1998) and so leaves several questions unanswered.

One question concerns the importance of associative strength as such, rather than the extent to which the paired associates form some single, unitized, representation (Schacter & McGlynn, 1989). Previous studies have not discriminated between these possibilities because the associates used have typically comprised a mix of some that seem unitized, and others that did not. In a further study, Ramponi (2001) held associative strength constant, at the weak level of about 20% according to normative data. She selected two groups of these associates, those that seemed unitized (e.g., hand–lotion, coat–hanger) and those that did not (e.g., gate–fence, scarf–neck). Using just the syllables and meaning encoding tasks, she then compared intentional with incidental test performance in a group of young adults. In the intentional test, there were large levels-of-processing effects for both unitized and nonunitized paired associates. In the incidental test, there was no levels-of-processing effect for the unitized paired associates, but there was an effect for the nonunitized paired associates. That outcome shows that dissociative effects of level of processing may occur even with weakly related associates, as defined normatively, depending on whether those associates form a single, unitized conceptual representation.

These findings imply that it should be possible to find other paradigms in which levels-of-processing effects are absent from conceptual priming, provided unitized representations are involved. One new paradigm that achieves this goal was introduced by Brooks, Gardiner, Kaminska, and Beavis (2001). The paradigm involves the names of famous people (e.g., Christopher Columbus, Charles Dickens, Bette Midler, and Ronald Reagan). At study, participants are shown only the surnames of these people. At test, participants are shown only the forenames of these people. Compared with our word association test, this famous names paradigm has the advantage of eliminating any perceptual overlap between what is seen at study and what is seen at test. Importantly, while the surnames of the famous people are unique, they all have relatively common forenames. Thus, in the incidental test in which participants are instructed to generate the first surname that comes to mind, alternative responses were possible. In their second experiment, Brooks et al. had groups of young and old adults study lists of 20 famous surnames, 10 for each of two levels-of-processing tasks. In one task, participants rated the readability of the names. In the other task, they rated the familiarity of the person. These tasks were blocked.

The results are summarized in Table 5.3. There were clearly large effects of level of processing and of age in the intentional test. Neither of these effects occurred in the incidental test. This outcome complements the results obtained by Ramponi (2001). It further confirms that, at least with strongly unitized representations, it is possible to use levels-of-processing manipulations to satisfy the retrieval intentionality criterion, even in conceptual tests. This famous names paradigm also extends previous research because in this paradigm the relationship between the word pairs is entirely arbitrary; it is devoid of semantic content (though this suggests that priming in this paradigm is perhaps rather more "lexical" than conceptual).

To sum up this part of the chapter. It has become apparent that levels-of-processing effects in incidental tests may occur for a variety of reasons of which voluntary contamination is only one. As we have illustrated, these reasons may include reduced lexical processing, in either perceptual or conceptual priming, and increased elaborative processing, at least in conceptual priming. The occurrence of such effects does not invalidate the use

TABLE 5.3. Proportions of responses from Brooks et al. (2001, Experiment 2).

Intentional test, level of processing			
Group	**Readability**	**Familiarity**	**Unstudied**
Young	.41	.73	.04
Old	.27	.46	.01

Incidental test, level of processing			
Group	**Readability**	**Familiarity**	**Unstudied**
Young	.42	.46	.23
Old	.44	.47	.26

of levels-of-processing manipulations to infer retrieval volition. To infer involuntary retrieval, it is necessary to show that these levels-of-processing effects occur in conjunction with the absence of other levels-of-processing effects where voluntary retrieval would lead one to expect them. To permit this kind of theoretical resolution, it is necessary to have several, rather than just two, levels-of-processing tasks.

☐ Converging Evidence

The conclusions that we have argued are supported by other sources of converging evidence that we have not yet mentioned. This evidence primarily consists of response latency measures, subjective reports, and results from "inclusion" tests as introduced (though not for the same purpose) by Jacoby, Toth, and Yonelinas (1993). Here, too, we select just a few illustrations.

Richardson-Klavehn and Gardiner (1998) measured response latencies in their intentional and incidental tests and compared them with response latencies in a control group of subjects who did not have a study list but who were instructed to complete the stems with the first words that came to mind. The mean seconds per test item were 4.9 in the intentional group, 2.5 in the incidental group, and 3.0 in the control group. Compared with the control group these latencies were significantly longer in the intentional group, and significantly shorter in the incidental group. Such differences increase confidence in the conclusion that the intentional and incidental tests involved different retrieval strategies.

Subjective reports of retrieval strategy elicited after the tests have also sometimes been obtained to provide further confirmation that peoples' awareness of their retrieval volition differed in the two tests. For example, in the Brooks et al. (2001) experiment, participants in incidental tests were told that they were likely to retrieve studied surnames, but nonetheless their goal was to retrieve the first name that came to mind. And participants subsequently reported trying to do just that, whereas participants in the intentional group reported trying to retrieve the studied surnames.

It seems highly unlikely that incidental test participants in the Brooks et al. (2001) experiment were any more unaware of which surnames they had studied than were the intentional test participants. In terms of their awareness of memory, as distinct from their awareness of retrieval volition, the two groups are unlikely to have differed much. In some other studies, there is direct evidence to this effect. For example, in another experiment by Ramponi (2001), she showed that in recognition tests following incidental word association tests participants recognized nearly all studied associates.

The implication is that involuntary as well as voluntary retrieval of studied words may occur under circumstances in which people are perfectly well aware which of their responses were from the study list. This suggests that conceptual tests could provide ideal paradigms for investigating involuntary compared with voluntary retrieval independent of any differences in awareness of memory for the items involved.

It has sometimes been objected that the retrieval intentionality criterion entails a response bias (or baseline) confound in that responses to all test items are required in incidental tests but only to some test items in intentional tests (see, e.g., Reingold & Toth, 1996). There is no doubt that this is so. The question is whether it matters. A further source of converging evidence comes from the use of inclusion tests in which participants are instructed to respond with studied items if they can, but if they cannot, to respond with the first item that comes to mind. The effect of this instruction is usually to equate baseline performance, and therefore response bias, in inclusion and in incidental tests. If response bias is critical, then the outcomes from these two tests should be similar. If response bias is essentially irrelevant, then the outcome from inclusion tests should be similar to the outcome from intentional tests. Both in word-stem completion tests (Richardson-Klavehn & Gardiner, 1996, 1998) and in word association tests (Ramponi, 2001; Ramponi et al., 1999) we have found similar levels-of-processing effects in inclusion and in intentional tests and no levels-of-processing effects in incidental tests, even when baseline performance in inclusion tests was indistinguishable from baseline performance in incidental tests.

☐ Broader Implications

Not all theories recognize the need to make the distinction that we do between awareness of whether studied items are retrieved with that purpose in mind or with some other purpose in mind, and awareness of whether the items were studied or not, regardless of how they were retrieved. This is perhaps largely because many influential theories closely identify conscious control with autonoetic awareness (or remembering) and hence with the episodic memory system. For example, in introducing the concept of retrieval mode, Tulving (1983, p. 46) stated: "Access to, or actualization of, information in the episodic system tends to be deliberate and usually requires conscious effort, whereas in the semantic system it tends to be automatic." This view is reflected more strongly by Lepage, Ghaffer, Nyberg, and Tulving (2000, p. 506), who claimed that an episodic retrieval mode "is a pivotal necessary condition for remembering past events."

Remembering is strongly identified with deliberate conscious effort in some process models too, such as the model underlying the process dissociation procedure, which aims to separate effortful (or voluntary) processes from automatic (or involuntary) processes. In this approach, recollection, the process that gives rise to remembering, is assumed to be effortful (see, e.g., Jacoby, 1991). In our view, approaches that equate remembering with effortful, voluntary retrieval are misplaced and can give rise to misleading conclusions, such as greatly overestimating the extent to which priming in incidental tests is contaminated by voluntary retrieval of study-list items (see, e.g., Richardson-Klavehn & Gardiner, 1996).

The view that past events are also remembered involuntarily, when there is no conscious effort to do so, would be appreciably strengthened by evidence of dissociations between brain processes underlying retrieval volition and brain processes underlying memory awareness. A study by Richardson-Klavehn et al. (2000) provides such evidence. This was a word-stem completion study in which, once again, level of processing served as the manipulation check in comparing intentional with incidental test performance. During both tests subjects had to monitor each completion for study-list membership (as in Richardson-Klavehn & Gardiner, 1995, 1996) and electromagnetic brain activity was recorded with both electroencephalography (EEG) and magnetoencephalography (MEG).

In EEG, intentional compared with incidental test instructions led to a sustained (1000–3000 ms) shift in activity with a right-frontal focus. This effect was similar for stems corresponding to both studied and unstudied words. So it reflects retrieval volition rather than awareness of memory for the study list. In contrast, studied compared with unstudied items led to a similar late-positive-component (LPC) at 500–1000 ms, maximal over the parietal region, in both intentional and incidental tests. This LPC effect is thought to reflect remembering, so the similarity of the effect in each test suggests a similar awareness of memory. Thus the effects of retrieval instructions, reflecting retrieval volition, were dissociated both temporally and topographically from the effects of study, reflecting awareness of memory. In MEG, however, retrieval instructions did lead to some topographic differences in the LPC effect, suggesting that awareness of memory may also be modulated by retrieval volition.

☐ Summary

We have argued that levels-of-processing effects may occur involuntarily in both perceptual and conceptual incidental tests. Those effects do not necessarily undermine the usefulness of level-of-processing manipulations for inferring retrieval volition according to the retrieval intentionality criterion. We have also argued that it is necessary to distinguish retrieval volition from awareness of memory. Conceptual priming may reflect involuntary retrieval of study-list items even though nearly all responses from the study list are remembered as such. There is also evidence for the distinction between retrieval volition and awareness of memory from electromagnetic measures of brain activity.

☐ Acknowledgment

Grant 000236225 from the Economic and Social Research Council to the first two authors supported much of the research reviewed in this chapter, and we are grateful for that support.

☐ References

Blaxton, T. A. (1989). Investigating dissociations among memory measures: Support for a transfer appropriate processing framework. *Journal of Experimental Psychology: Learning, Memory, and Cognition, 15*, 657–668.

Brooks, B. M., Gardiner, J. M., Kaminska, Z., & Beavis, Z. (2001). Implicit versus explicit retrieval of surnames of famous people: Dissociative effects of levels of processing and age. *Journal of Memory and Language, 44*, 118–130.

Brown, A. S., & Mitchell, D. B. (1994). A reevaluation of semantic versus nonsemantic processing in implicit memory. *Memory & Cognition, 22*, 533–541.

Cabeza, R. (1994). A dissociation between two implicit conceptual tests supports the distinction between types of conceptual processing. *Psychonomic Bulletin & Review, 1*, 505–508.

Challis, B. H., & Brodbeck, D. R. (1992). Level of processing affects priming in word fragment completion. *Journal of Experimental Psychology: Learning, Memory, and Cognition, 18*, 595–607.

Challis, B. H., Velichkovsky, B. M., & Craik, F. I. M. (1996). Levels-of-processing effects on a variety of memory tasks: New findings and theoretical implications. *Consciousness and Cognition, 5*, 142–164.

Craik, F. I. M., & Lockhart, R. S. (1972). Levels of processing: A framework for memory research. *Journal of Verbal Learning and Verbal Behavior, 11*, 671–684.

Fisher, R. P., & Craik, F. I. M. (1977). The interaction between encoding and retrieval operations in cued recall. *Journal of Experimental Psychology: Human Learning and Memory, 3*, 701–711.

Gardiner, J. M. (1988). Functional aspects of recollective experience. *Memory & Cognition, 16*, 309–313.

Gardiner, J. M., Java, R. I., & Richardson-Klavehn, A. (1996). How level of processing really influences awareness in recognition memory. *Canadian Journal of Experimental Psychology, 50*, 114–122.

Graf, P., & Mandler, G. (1984). Activation makes words more accessible, but not necessarily more retrievable. *Journal of Verbal Learning and Verbal Behavior, 23*, 553–568.

Jacoby, L. L. (1991). A process dissociation framework: Separating automatic from intentional uses of memory. *Journal of Memory and Language, 30*, 513–541.

Jacoby, L. L., Toth, J. P., & Yonelinas, A. P. (1993). Separating conscious and unconscious influences of memory: Measuring recollection. *Journal of Experimental Psychology: General, 122,* 139–154.

Java, R. I. (1996). Effects of age on state of awareness following implicit and explicit word association tasks. *Psychology and Aging, 11,* 108–111.

Jelicic, M., Craik, F. I. M., & Moscovitch, M. (1996). Effects of aging on different explicit and implicit word-association tasks. *European Journal of Cognitive Psychology, 8,* 225–234.

Lepage, M., Ghaffer, O., Nyberg, L., & Tulving, E. (2000). Prefrontal cortex and episodic retrieval mode. *Proceedings of the National Academy of Sciences, 97,* 506–511.

Lockhart, R. S., & Craik, F. I. M. (1990). Levels of processing: A retrospective commentary on a framework for memory research. *Canadian Journal of Psychology, 44,* 87–112.

Morris, C. D., Bransford, J. D., & Franks, J. J. (1977). Levels of processing versus transfer appropriate processing. *Journal of Verbal Learning and Verbal Behavior, 16,* 519–533.

Ramponi, C. (2001). *Effects of conceptual processing on recognition and conceptual implicit memory.* Unpublished Ph.D. dissertation, City University, London.

Ramponi, C., Richardson-Klavehn, A., & Gardiner, J. M. (1999, November). *Intact involuntary retrieval of conceptual information in old adults depends on associative strength and depth of processing.* Paper presented a the Annual Meeting of the Psychonomic Society, Los Angeles.

Reingold, E. M., & Toth, J. P. (1996). Process dissociations versus task dissociations: A controversy in progress. In G. F.Underwood (Ed.), *Implicit cognition* (pp. 159–202). Oxford, England: Oxford University Press.

Richardson-Klavehn, A., Clarke, A. J. B., & Gardiner, J. M. (1999). Conjoint dissociations reveal involuntary "perceptual" priming from generating at study. *Consciousness and Cognition, 8,* 271–284.

Richardson-Klavehn, A., Düzel, E., Schott, B., Heinrich, J. Hagner, T., Gardiner, J. M., & Heinze, H.-J. (2000, April). *Electromagnetic brain activity during incidental and intentional retrieval shows dissociation of retrieval mode from retrieval success.* Paper presented at the Annual Meeting of the Cognitive Neuroscience Society, San Francisco.

Richardson-Klavehn, A., & Gardiner, J. M. (1995). Retrieval volition and memorial awareness in stem completion: An empirical analysis. *Psychological Research, 57,* 166–178.

Richardson-Klavehn, A., & Gardiner, J. M. (1996). Cross-modality priming in stem completion reflects conscious memory, but not voluntary memory. *Psychonomic Bulletin & Review, 3,* 238–244.

Richardson-Klavehn, A., & Gardiner, J. M. (1998). Depth-of-processing effects on priming in stem completion: Tests of the voluntary contamination, conceptual processing, and lexical processing hypotheses. *Journal of Experimental Psychology: Learning, Memory, and Cognition, 24,* 593–609.

Richardson-Klavehn, A., Gardiner, J.M., & Java, R.I. (1994). Involuntary conscious memory and the method of opposition. *Memory, 2,* 1-29.

Richardson-Klavehn, A., Gardiner, J. M., & Java, R. I. (1996). Memory: Task dissociations, process dissociations, and dissociations of consciousness. In G. F.Underwood (Ed.), *Implicit cognition* (pp. 85–155). Oxford, England: Oxford University Press.

Roediger, H. L., & McDermott, K. B. (1993). Implicit memory in normal human subjects. In H. Spinnler, & F. Boller (Eds.), *Handbook of neuropyschology* (pp. 63–131). Amsterdam: Elsevier.

Roediger, H. L., Weldon, M. S., & Challis, B. H. (1989). Explaining dissociations between implicit and explicit measures of retention: A processing account. In H. L. Roediger & F. I. M. Craik (Eds.), *Varieties of memory and consciousness: Essays in honour of Endel Tulving* (pp. 3–41). Hillsdale, NJ: Erlbaum.

Roediger, H. L., Weldon, M. S., Stadler, M. L., & Riegler, G. L. (1992). Direct comparison of two implicit memory tests: Word fragment and word stem completion. *Journal of Experimental Psychology: Learning, Memory, and Cognition, 18,* 1251–1269.

Schacter, D. L., Bowers, J., & Booker, J. (1989). Intention, awareness, and implicit memory: The retrieval intentionality criterion. In S. Lewandowsky, J. C. Dunn, & K. Kirsner (Eds.), *Implicit memory* (pp. 47–65). Hillsdale, NJ: Erlbaum.

Schacter, D. L., & McGlynn, S. M. (1989). Implicit memory: Effects of elaboration depend on unitization. *American Journal of Psychology, 102,* 151–181.

Srinivas, K., & Roediger, H. L. (1990). Classifying implicit memory tests: Category association and anagram solution. *Journal of Memory and Language, 29,* 389–412.

Toth, J. P., Reingold, E. M., & Jacoby, L. L. (1994). Toward a redefinition of implicit memory: Process dissociations following elaborative processing and self-generation. *Journal of Experimental Psychology: Learning, Memory, and Cognition, 20,* 290–303.

Tulving, E. (1983). *Elements of episodic memory.* New York: Oxford University Press.

Tulving, E. (1985). Memory and consciousness. *Canadian Psychology, 26,* 1–12.

Vaidya, C. J., Gabrieli, J. D. E., Keane, M. M., Monti, L. A., Gutierrez-Rivas, H., & Zarella, M. M. (1997). Evidence for multiple mechanisms of conceptual priming on implicit memory tests. *Journal of Experimental Psychology: Learning, Memory, and Cognition, 23,* 1324–1343.

Weldon, M. S., & Coyote, K. C. (1996). Failure to find the picture superiority effect in implicit conceptual memory tests. *Journal of Experimental Psychology: Learning, Memory, and Cognition, 22,* 670–686.

CHAPTER

Betty Ann Levy

Text Processing: Memory Representations Mediate Fluent Reading

The classic work of Craik and Lockhart (1972) led cognitive psychologists to focus on the relationship between the initial processing that occurred during perception or acquisition, and the later memory for those learned materials. They argued that memory is a product of the type of processing that occurred during perception or acquisition. This reorientation to the importance of early processing in determining memory has had a profound influence on memory research over the past three decades. The work to be described in this chapter focuses on the "flip-side" of the processing–memory relationship. It shows the importance of *memory* in determining the ease of *processing*. That is, while Craik and Lockhart emphasized the importance of processing for memory, I will emphasize the importance of memory for processing. This flip-side or reciprocal relationship appears to be particularly important in understanding the development of *skilled* performance, in contrast to initial learning. The skill domain of particular interest in this paper is the development of reading skill or reading fluency.

☐ Text Rereading Benefits

When an adult, or even a beginning reader, repeatedly reads the same passage, reading rate and comprehension improve with each repetition (e.g., Levy, 1993; Levy, Nicholls, & Kohen, 1993; Rashotte & Torgeson, 1985; Samuels, 1979). That is, reading fluency improves with practice. The question is, What remains in memory following each reading encounter that improves reading fluency on the next encounter? Or, how does memory from a prior reading influence processing on a later occasion? Although the *repetition effect* in both word recognition and text processing has been clearly established (e.g., Carr, Brown, & Charalambous, 1989; Levy & Kirsner, 1989; Raney & Rayner, 1995; see also Tenpenny, 1995, for a review of the word repetition literature), the underlying mecha-

This paper was supported by an operating grant from the Natural Sciences and Engineering Research Council of Canada. We thank Sara Graydon for writing the experimental materials.

nisms that mediate this reprocessing benefit have been the cause of considerable debate. In text processing, the debate centers on the role played by word or lexical representations, versus that played by linguistic and text structure representations, in mediating the text rereading advantage. Carr et al. (1989) asked subjects to read aloud either short paragraphs or word sets constructed by scrambling the words of a paragraph (word salads). The subjects then reread either the coherent or the word salad form of the passage. Carr et al. reported that the second reading was always faster than the first reading. Interestingly, the transfer benefit was of the same magnitude whether the paragraph form (coherent vs. word salad) matched on the two occasions or not. This led Carr et al. to conclude that the rereading benefit was at the single word or lexical level, because changing the higher order linguistic context did not influence the magnitude of the transfer benefit. They also varied the features of the printed words (typescript, handwriting) read on the two occasions. Again, mismatches in print features caused no loss in the transfer benefit. This finding led Carr et al. to argue that the lexical representations were abstract because they bore no perceptual signatures of the encoding event.

However, Oliphant (1983) reported that when words were reprocessed in a lexical decision task, there was a repetition benefit if the words had been previously read in a lexical decision task, consistent with earlier literature showing word repetition or priming benefits. However, there was no repetition benefit if the first reading of the words had been in a text context (in the instructions or in a questionnaire), followed by later reprocessing in a lexical decision task. These findings suggested that processing context *is* represented in memory and this higher order contextual representation affects the reprocessing advantage for single words from a text. That is, the context in which words are processed on each encounter determines the magnitude of the repetition advantage. Similar modulating influences on the magnitude of the rereading advantage, due to contextual differences on the two processing occasions, were reported by Levy and Kirsner (1989) and by MacLeod (1989).

In a systematic exploration of text-level influences on the rereading benefit, Levy and Burns (1990) reported three experiments that were similar in design to those of Carr et al. (1989), except that the "scrambled texts" varied in the linguistic level of the scrambling. That is, subjects read scrambled or coherent texts on the first occasion and then reread the same or the opposite form. Levy and Burn's texts were much longer than those used by Carr et al., so as to enhance the text processing aspects of the task. They also used silent reading and instructions to read for meaning, along with passage recall after each reading, in order to promote text-level processing. Table 6.1 shows the basic savings across the two readings (in seconds), when the texts were scrambled at different linguistic levels during the first reading. As the table shows, when the text macrostructure differed on the two readings (caused by scrambling the paragraphs versus leaving the paragraphs properly ordered), there was no loss in the magnitude of the rereading advantage for normal versus scrambled conditions (Experiment1). However, when sentences were randomly ordered, so as to violate all of the passage logic, there was a loss in the magnitude of the rereading benefit for the scrambled compared to the normal conditions (Experiment 2). The rereading benefit was entirely lost when the first reading was of a word salad, prior to reading the intact text (Experiment 3), thus failing to replicate the Carr et al. results. This failure of replication occurred even when reading was oral (Experiment 4), as in the Carr et al. study, so this procedural difference did not explain the discrepancy. Levy and Burns also reported modality specificity in their transfer benefits, inconsistent with the featural nonspecificity of transfer in the Carr et al. work. Clearly, the findings of Levy and Burns were not consistent with those of Carr et al. and they suggested the involvement of linguistic and text-level representations in mediating the text rereading advantage. Levy and

TABLE 6.1. Reprocessing advantage (in seconds) for normal texts, when the first or original reading was of either a normal or scrambled version. Adapted from Levy and Burns (1990) for the four experiments with scrambling manipulations at different linguistic levels.

	Version on first-second readings	
	Normal-normal	Scrambled-normal
Experiment		
1	15.87	17.65
2	15.39	8.81
3	15.44	4.31
4	10.20	0.15

Burns argued that text representations are episodic in nature, and that the episodic representation was holistic, with the words bonded to the text structure. Transfer across readings could not cross linguistic levels in their view (i.e., single words to text or text to single words).

The opposing findings and theorizing of Carr and his colleagues and Levy and her colleagues led to a closer examination of the task differences that might explain these discrepancies. Carlson, Alejano, and Carr (1991) proposed that the 'focus of attention' during reading determined whether the resulting memorial representations would be abstract and at the lexical level or episodic, with words bonded to their text context. They supported this view by showing that when readers were told to read and reread texts in a word-by-word fashion, making no attempt to relate words, then rereading transfer was insensitive to differences beyond the single word level, as Carr et al. (1989) had found. However, when these same texts were read twice under instructions to process for meaning, following Levy and Kirsner (1989), then transfer appeared to be episodic in nature. Thus, the focus on wording versus message processing appeared to alter the memory resulting from reading.

The nature of the memory formed when attention is focused on different linguistic levels, in turn, influences the transfer benefits that can be observed during subsequent processing. This focus-of-attention hypothesis received some support from studies of individual differences. Faulkner and Levy (1994) examined transfer from reading scrambled words to reading text (following the design of Levy & Burns, 1990) for good and poor readers in elementary grades. Like adults, good readers showed no transfer from word reading to text processing; however, poor readers benefited in text reading from practice with words in scrambled displays (see also Levy, Abello, & Lysynchuk, 1997; Bourassa, Levy, Dowin, & Casey, 1998). These finding suggest that poor readers may be forced to focus their attention at the word-level even during text reading, because of the difficulty they experience in decoding print. This focus of attention, as shown by Carlson et al. (1991), leads to word-level representations that can mediate transfer even when the words are later reprocessed in another context. Further studies indicated that when the text was difficult for the reader's skill level, then word-level transfer was observed, even for adult readers (Faulkner & Levy, 1999). We argued that difficult texts force a reader to use a word-by-word processing strategy, thus weakening the meaning processing of the passage. When this happens, transfer reflects word-level representations rather than meaning-centered episodic representations. We also suggested that meaning-centered episodic transfer is important in fluent or skilled reading, while word-centered transfer is seen when reading is less fluent, as in poor readers or when reading difficult texts.

It has become clear, then, from research over the past decade that repetition effects can be mediated at different linguistic levels. The question is how these different levels of memorial representations combine to determine text processing fluency. Simply describing conditions that produce word or text-level transfer is unsatisfying without a text processing model that provides logic for these conditions. Unfortunately, the literature on text processing and the literature on repetition or rereading effects have developed quite independently. Recently, however, some connections have been drawn.

☐ Text Processing Models and Text Rereading Benefits

To further explore the role played by word-level versus text-level processes in reading, Levy, Barnes, and Martin (1993) examined transfer across readings of a passage when slight variations in form occurred between the readings. They reported that reading and then rereading passages that were line-by-line paraphrases of each other led to no loss in the rereading benefit, if the paraphrases contained only syntactic variations (e.g., passive to active transformations), with very few lexical items changed. However, if the line-by-line paraphrases were formed by changing a lot of the words (synonym substitutions), then there was still reliable transfer but the magnitude of the advantage decreased. For both types of paraphrases the message remained intact, so the reprocessing loss due to lexical changes suggested that lexical information was part of the "transfer surface." We credited the loss in transfer to word-specific or lexical sources, and the reliable transfer across synonyms to conceptual sources. Thus, in these experiments, word-specific and nonspecific meaning-based transfer cooccurred.

In order to explore further the specificity of transfer effects, Levy, Barnes, and Martin (1993) studied transfer across passages that were *related* in meaning or wording but were *different* texts. They used three conditions. In the related condition, participants first read a passage from a novel and then read a passage that was the continuation of the first passage. Thus there was continuation, not repetition, of message, but also overlap in wording as occurs naturally in novels. Thus, in this related condition, there was meaning continuation and shared words between the first and the transfer passages. In another condition, the second passage was the same as that used in the related condition, but the first passage read was on a totally different topic; however, the two different texts had the *same* number of shared words as in the related condition. In this *word overlap* condition, then, the two texts had repeated wording but the words were experienced in semantically unrelated contexts. Finally, in a control condition the two passages were semantically unrelated, and they shared no content words. Levy, Barnes, and Martin (1993) found that the second passage was read faster in the related than in the control condition, but the word-overlap condition was slower than the control condition. That is, when there was no semantic relationship between the two reading episodes, then there was no repetition advantage when words had been read previously. Only when the passages were semantically related was there a processing advantage for the second text. These findings supported the notion that texts are represented in a meaning-based episodic form, where word representations are bonded to that context. Simple word overlap in different contexts would not support a repetition benefit. However, once the episode is recruited through overlap in meaning, then word repetition plays a role in the transfer benefit, as illustrated also by the paraphrase studies.

Levy et al. (1995) reported seven experiments that replicated and extended the across-text transfer reported by Levy, Barnes, and Martin (1993). They separated word overlap and meaning overlap in the related condition but included an additional related-synonym condition, where synonyms were substituted for many of the words that overlapped in the two passages. This new condition had shared meaning between the two passages, as in the related condition, but there were few shared words. The results indicated that even when the related texts had little overlap in content words, there was still transfer across passages, so that the second text was read faster than in the unrelated control condition. Levy, Barnes, and Martin suggested that this meaning-based transfer could be explained by ease of integrating new information into memorial text representations that shared meaning. They related the text integration notions of Kintsch and his colleagues (Kintsch, 1991) to the meaning-based facilitation across related texts. This integration notion is not the same as the use of abstract schemas. The text representations described by Kintsch were formed from the semantic propositions of specific texts, with no particular relation to general knowledge about the topic. Consequently, these memory representations were very specific to the reading episode. This notion, then, might provide a text processing model for the *episodic transfer* view espoused by Levy and Burns (1990).

Recent work by Gary Raney and his colleagues has further developed this idea (Raney, Therriault, & Minkoff, 2000; Raney, 1998). Raney is interested in how abstract and episodic representations can be combined into a single model of text processing. His *integrated model of text representation* extends the model proposed by van Dijk and Kintsch (1983). They proposed three levels of text representation: a surface form, a propositional text base, and a situation model. The surface-level representations result from the lexical and syntactic analyses of the passage. The propositional text-based representations result from the meaning analysis of the text statements. This propositional representation includes all meaning equivalences or paraphrases of the text, without regard to lexical identity. The situation model combines the text-based information with prior knowledge. It represents the events and actions (episodes) described by the text but goes beyond the contents of the text itself and includes general knowledge, inferences, and the output of processes used to comprehend the text (Raney et al., 2000, p. 64).

Raney (1998) extended this van Dijk and Kintsch (1983) model by proposing that the surface and propositional representations are abstract in form, but the situation model is episodic in form. He basically defined *abstract* as context-independent representation, and *episodic* as context-dependent representation. With these assumptions, he then suggested that Levy's episodic transfer effects resulted from the formation of a situation model because of the "read for meaning" instructions that she used. It is the formation of the situation model that then binds the lower level propositional and surface representations to the episodic text structure. In this case, it is necessary to retrieve the situation model first in order to observe effects of repetitions through the lower levels. If a good situation model is not formed (as for poor readers, difficult text, or instructions for word-by-word reading), then transfer will reflect lower level propositional and surface representations. According to the Raney model, these should be context-free, but this assumption has been hotly debated in the word recognition literature (e.g., Jacoby, 1983; Masson, 1986; Roediger & Blaxton, 1987). This transfer will then cross linguistic contexts, as in Carr et al. (1989) and Faulkner and Levy (1994). I have described here the extreme states, but Raney (1998) suggests that the formation of a situation model is not all or none, but graded in how binding it is in terms of the boundaries it sets on transfer. One could see this as degrees of text organization. A strong situation model leads to more context-dependent transfer than a weak situation model. With a weak situation model, the context-independent surface and propositional levels will carry most of the transfer. Thus it is possible for episodic and abstract transfer to coexist according to Raney. He also argued that maximal transfer will be observed when all three levels of representation are repeated. The magnitude of transfer is determined by the extent of overlap at all three domains across the repetitions. These are clearly a complex set of assumptions, but ones that warrant some testing.

Raney et al. (2000) attempted to show the joint effects of the situation model and the lower level representations by asking undergraduates to read and then reread identical or paraphrased versions of short passages. Here the situation model was always the same, but the lower levels were varied across repetitions. They measured reading time and global fixation times during reading. They reported that both identical repetitions and repetitions involving paraphrased, versions led to repetition effects, but these effects were larger for the identical repetitions. Raney et al. argued that since both versions maintained the same situation model, the difference between paraphrase and identical conditions resulted from the advantage for surface and propositional representations in the identical, compared with the paraphrased versions. They also measured first fixation duration, gaze duration, and total time looking at specific target words during the second reading. These target words were either identical to those read in the first version or they were synonyms of words in the first version. Target words that were identical repetitions yielded repetition benefits irrespective of measure. However, synonyms showed repetition benefits only when multiple fixations occurred. Raney et al. argued that synonyms cannot show facilitation at the lexical level, so the benefit for multiple fixations must be from semantic integration with compatible memory representations. They suggested that these eye movement findings indicate that overall reading time stems from several sources of representation, lexical and conceptual, where the former is abstract and the latter is episodic in form. They argued that these findings are consistent with the integrated text representation model.

The Raney model provides an interesting attempt to integrate text processing with text repetition effects and to specify the memorial representations that influence later reading. Our earlier attempts to describe holistic representations were poorly specified. Raney's notion that a situation model might provide the binding mechanism that sets boundaries on the repetition influences of surface and propositional levels seems worthy of pursuit. To this end, in some recent studies in my laboratory conducted by Shawn Vasdev, we examined the influence of the presence or absence of a good situation model during reading and rereading. Whereas Raney et al. (2000) held the situation model constant and changed the lower levels across repetitions, we examined rereading time benefits when the surface and propositional information was constant. However, we varied whether the situation model was or was not easily instantiated during original reading, and then was or was not cued again during rereading. According to the Raney (1998) model, the amount of transfer should vary with the instantiation and retrieval of the situation model, even though the same propositions and words are read on the two occasions.

☐ Experimental Evidence: Situation Models Influence Repetition Benefits

Because adult readers almost automatically read for meaning and try to interpret the message underlying what they read, we required a manipulation that would make message interpretation easy or difficult while still using coherent statements. The manipulation we chose was one reported by Bransford (1979). Bransford was interested in how the use of *schema* would improve comprehension and memory for passages. He wrote very short passages that described everyday events (e.g., washing clothes), where the individual sentences were coherent but the referent event was ambiguous. Participants then read the passage with or without a title that defined the referent event. Bransford found improvements in reading fluency and comprehension when the title defining the event was given prior to reading the passage. He argued that the presence of a schema organized processing of the passage, and this in turn led to an organized memorial representation that improved later retrieval of that message. Bransford's manipulation defines a situation model, as used in the Raney model. It provides the prior knowledge that is integrated with the stated propositions and surface forms to set up the complete text representation. According to Raney, instantiation of the situation model determines the boundaries on transfer of information across reading encounters. Note that the text representation may include what has been called schema knowledge, but it also includes specific knowledge from an individual's prior history. This prior history sets up the knowledge boundaries for the specific text representation, where prior knowledge is combined with specific text propositions and surface information.

Using Bransford-type passages, Vasdev and I examined the influence on rereading time that resulted from a memorial representation set up during the first reading of that passage. Undergraduate volunteers read texts presented on a computer screen. Each text was 400 words long and was typed, left and right justified, on 34 lines. The texts were then presented line by line on a computer scope. The first key press by the reader revealed the first line of the passage; the second key press presented the next line directly under the first (which stayed on the screen), and so on until the scope's page was filled (after line 24). With the next key press the screen went blank momentarily and then the next line appeared at the top of the screen and the line by line presentation continued down page 2. This simulates turning the page in a book. This presentation method allows naturalistic reading with regressive eye movements. The advantage of the scope presentation is that it allowed us to measure reading time throughout the text, on a line by line basis. The time of each key press was automatically recorded, so that line by line reading times could be measured. This provides some on-line sensitivity during processing compared with the total reading time for the whole passage.

Undergraduate volunteers read and then immediately reread eight different texts. Each text was modeled after Bransford's "washing clothes" passage, in that it described an everyday event, with coherent sentences. However, the sentences were difficult to relate to a referent event unless the title was provided prior to reading (see Appendix A for an example). The main manipulation was the presence or absence of the title on the first reading and then again on the second reading. The orthogonal combination of presence/absence on each occasion yielded four main conditions. We refer to the first condition as title/title, where the title was presented on the screen prior to the first line of text on both reading occasions. In this case the representation formed on the first reading should reflect the appropriate situational model, integrated with the text propositions and surface information to form a text-specific episodic representation. The title given at rereading should cue the same situation model and therefore recruit the text representation formed during the first reading. According to the Raney model, these are the ideal conditions for episodic transfer, and readers should show the maximal rereading benefit. In the second condition, no-title/no-title, for both the initial reading and then for the rereading, no title was given to aid in setting up an appropriate situation model. On both reading occasions, the reader was left to form his or her own best interpretation of the referent situation (with our longer passages, the referent event was sufficiently ambiguous that few subjects would "guess" the "correct" interpretation). This condition is probably most equivalent to Raney's case of little situational constraint, so there should be minimal episodic encoding and therefore little text-level constraint on transfer. The rereading advantage should be mediated largely at the surface and propositional levels, and such transfer should be weaker than in the title/title condition. The contrast in the magnitude of the rereading advantage between the title/title and the no-title/no-title conditions tests the advantage, if any, of reading and rereading with an intact situation model, because the texts read in the two conditions were otherwise identical. Consequently, differences in original reading time and differences in the magnitude of transfer must be credited to the presence of a situational model during reading and rereading.

The final two conditions represent mismatch cases, where the situation model evoked during initial reading was not reinstantiated during rereading. In condition 3, no-title/title, the first reading provides no clue regarding the appropriate situation model, but the second reading cues the appropriate situation model. Thus there will be a mismatch between the situation model used in forming the memorial representation and the situation model evoked at rereading. However, the surface and propositional levels are identical on the two readings. According to Raney's model, episodic transfer should not occur here because the situation models should mismatch and therefore the episodic representation will not be recruited. The second reading should be more fluent than the first because of the availability of the situation model provided prior to the second reading. However, any reprocessing benefits should result entirely from overlap of the lower levels of representation. This transfer should be less than when the memory representation is completely consistent with the current processing event, as in a contrast with the title/title condition. The prediction, then, would be that the no-title/title condition would show less transfer than the title/title condition and should resemble the first reading of a titled passage.

Finally, in condition 4, title/no-title, the reprocessing condition is without a title, but the memory representation was formed with a title and therefore an appropriate situation model. The strong prediction here is that because there will be no overlap at the upper level of representation, all transfer should be mediated by lower level representations, according to Raney's model. However, another reasonable possibility is that as the reader processes the early propositions during the second reading, memory for the "old" interpretation will be recruited; after that point episodic transfer benefits from the first reading will be observed. The line-by-line paradigm used here will allow us to examine this shift in processing as the reader progresses through the second reading. Overall, then, the contrasts tested in this study offer some insight into the interaction of the memorial representation and rereading, so that the influence of memory on current processing is elucidated.

Undergraduate volunteers participated in a session lasting approximately 1.5 hours. After practice in reading using the line-by-line format, each participant silently read and immediately reread eight different passages, two per experimental condition. After the second reading of each passage, ten comprehension questions that tested stated propositions from the text were asked and answered orally. Answers were recorded but no data were analyzed; the questions were used to ensure that participants read for meaning. Participants were aware that their reading time was being recorded with each key press. Instructions indicated that reading should be fluent but for meaning.

The reading times per line were first collapsed into 5-line blocks to yield mean reading time for each of seven blocks (the last block had only four lines). This collapsing was done to "smooth out" differences due to line variations that consisted of different syntactic and semantic segments (e.g., a line might end in the middle or the end of a sentence or an idea unit). Collapsed across 5 lines, reading time influences on a line-by-line basis due to such lower level linguistic and propositional variations were reduced. The graphs presented below will therefore show mean reading time as a function of line block (seven in total), instead of 34 lines.

The first important finding was that on the first reading, collapsed across all conditions, texts with titles were read faster than texts without titles (see Figure 6.1). This finding

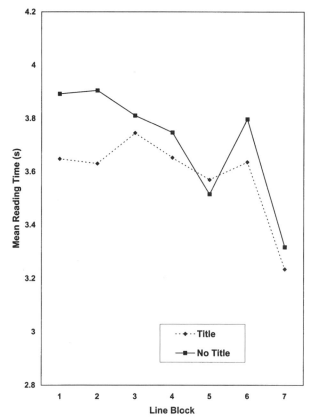

FIGURE 6.1. Mean reading times (in seconds) on the first reading as a function of line-blocks, for the Title and No-Title conditions.

replicated Bransford's (1979) effect of schema, indicating that providing a *situation model* improves reading fluency. Note also that reading times in both conditions declined reliably over the seven line blocks, suggesting that later lines are processed more fluently once a text representation has been set up, allowing later propositions to be more easily integrated into an existing interpretative organization. Finally, the benefit for the title over the no-title condition occurs only in the first few line blocks, when the reader is instantiating this interpretative organization. These findings support the assumption that original processing, and therefore the memorial representation set up during reading, was influenced by the presence or absence of a title.

However, for purposes of exploring the Raney model, the critical comparisons come from the second reading or rereading data. Overall, rereading times were faster than the original reading times for texts of that form. That is, all second reading times in no-title conditions were faster than the first reading times for a no-title passage. Similarly, the rereading times for title passages were faster than the original times for title passages. These findings indicate that irrespective of overlap of the situation model, reliable transfer occurred. Our focus here, however, is on the difference in the magnitude of the transfer benefit that resulted from the prior history or memory representation. To address this matter we will present three individual contrasts, the first comparing cases where the processing conditions were the same on both readings, and the last two, where there was a mismatch of conditions during original reading and rereading.

Title/Title Versus No-Title/No-Title

This contrast asks whether there is a benefit during rereading that stems from having a consistent and easily instantiated situation model provided during both readings, compared with the situation where the reader must form his or her interpretation on each reading. Raney's model would predict an advantage in rereading for the title/title over the no-title/no-title condition. Figure 6.2 shows the first reading times for the title/title and the no-title/no-title conditions. Here there was an advantage over the early line blocks for the Title condition, consistent with Bransford's findings. Importantly, this difference was amplified during rereading (or 2nd reading times). There was reliable transfer in both cases, but the transfer was greater when the memory representation and the rereading cues both provided the appropriate situation model, compared with when the reader had to struggle to form an interpretation of the text on both readings. Again, the greatest advantages are in the early part of the text when an interpretative organization must be

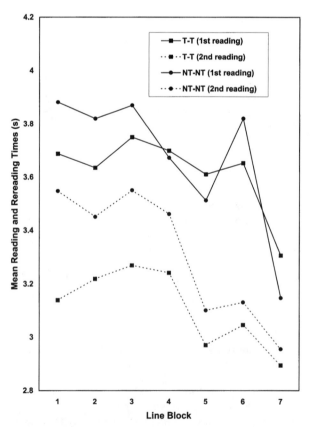

FIGURE 6.2. Mean reading times (in seconds) for the first and second readings as a function of line-blocks, for the Title/Title and the No-Title/No-Title conditions.

set up. The important point, then, is that the memory representation led to the Bransford effect being amplified during reprocessing, compared with original processing. That is, the memory representation affected reading skill in a manner consistent with the Raney model. The presence of a higher level episodic or situational model maximized transfer of skill across experiences.

For the next two contrasts, the *reprocessing* context was held constant, so that the contrast examines the influence of different memorial representations on this reprocessing. The first contrast looks at the memorial influence when the reprocessing context is with a title (provides the situation model), while the second contrast examines the influence of memory when the reprocessing context is without a title (provides little or no situational constraint).

Title/Title Versus No-Title/Title

This contrast addresses the influence of the memorial representation when the rereading passage always cued the appropriate situation model. Figure 6.3 shows a consistent re-reading advantage, over all line blocks (interaction, $p = .09$), when the memory representation was organized around the same situation model (title/title) compared to when the memory representation was formed using the reader's own interpretation (no-title/title).

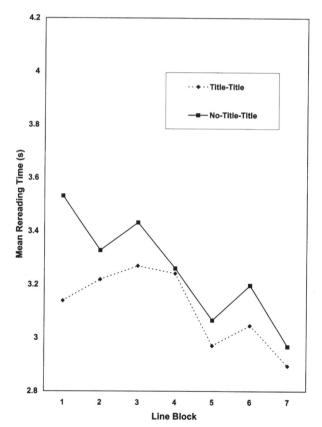

FIGURE 6.3. Mean reading times (in seconds) for the second reading as a function of line-blocks, for the Title/Title and the No-Title/Title conditions.

Even though the rereading conditions here were identical, the different memorial representations influenced the speed of reading the second time. These data are clearly consistent with Raney's model, indicating better transfer when all three levels of representation were repeated, and comprehension and retrieval were guided by a consistent situation model.

No-Title/No-Title Versus Title/No-Title

This contrast addresses the influence of the memory representation on reprocessing a passage when no clue is provided at reprocessing regarding the appropriate situation model. Will the memory from the episodic encoding in the title/no-title case be recruited at some time during rereading to aid in reprocessing the untitled passage? One possibility is that because there is no overlap at the level of the situation model, all transfer will be mediated by the lower level representations, which are the same in these conditions. The conditions would then show the same level of transfer. However, the line-by-line presentation allows us to see on-line changes as the reader progresses through the passage. Figure 6.4 shows an interesting influence of memory. In both of these conditions, the declining slopes of

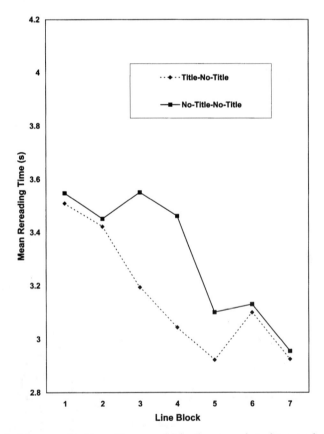

FIGURE 6.4. Mean reading times (in seconds) for the second reading as a function of line-blocks, for the No-Title/No-Title and the Title/No-Title conditions.

the function suggest that a text representation is being formed. Later line blocks are read faster than earlier ones, suggesting that they are being interpreted into a representation, and this becomes easier as the representation develops across lines. Interestingly, while the two conditions have similar reading times for the first two line blocks (or 10 lines), as the Raney model would predict if there is no overlap in situational models, the title/no-title condition then becomes considerably faster than the no-title/no-title condition. This benefit persists over the next few line blocks. These data suggest that initially the original representation was not recruited. However, when the propositional overlap became large enough (about 10 lines here) so that the reader consciously or unconsciously recognized the similarity between passages, then the memory representation was recruited, leading to an advantage for the title over the no-title memorial representation in later line blocks. In fact, after the first two blocks, rereading times for the title/no-title condition were more similar to those for the title/title condition than for the no-title/no-title condition. This changing influence of the memory representation, as the reprocessing proceeded through line blocks, suggests that recruitment of episodic or situation model representations is not "all or none." If sufficient overlap of surface and propositional levels occurs, this may be enough to recruit higher order representational levels as well.

There is considerable support from these data for the use of the van Dijk and Kintsch (1983) text processing model in understanding text repetition effects, as suggested by Raney (1998). However, the main point I want to make here is that in all cases, reading skill development across exposures, as measured by reading time benefits across rereading repetitions, can be viewed as memory representations influencing subsequent processing. Memory acts as a knowledge base to enable more skilled processing of similar events. Thus there is an interplay of processing and memory throughout the development of skilled cognitive performance.

In the experiment just described, the two readings of a passage occurred in immediate succession. This might have led subjects to always recruit the memory representation to aid in reprocessing. Such an intentional strategy would explain the sudden recruitment of the episodic level in the final contrast made above. Perhaps if readers were unable to predict when a repetition would occur, the memorial benefits described above would not be seen. That is, perhaps the memory effects described above were due to use of a strategic reading approach to the second reading. To address this matter, Vasdev and I repeated the experiment above, except that a lag was introduced between original and rereading of a passage. The first readings of the eight texts were distributed across the testing session, with the rereadings interspersed at a lag of 2 or 3 passages. That is, after a passage was read, two or three other passages were read before the repetition or rereading occurred. Thus, there was no predictability as to whether the current passage was a first or a repeated reading. Using a retrieval strategy for second readings was now difficult or impossible. The pattern of results in this lag experiment was almost identical to the one reported above. In most cases the memory influence was larger than in the first study. Thus the reprocessing benefits from different memorial representations do not appear to be strategic in nature. The processing system appears to automatically recruit similar knowledge structures to make current processing more skilled or more fluent.

☐ Conclusions

The experiments described here show the value in using a text processing model to guide the study of text repetition effects, as suggested by Raney (1998). The studies show a clear influence of *episodic interpretation* during original processing. Whether the representation formed from this processing will be fully recruited during reprocessing depends on the amount of overlap between the memory representation and the new text. Transfer is not all or none. It is maximal when the interpretations given on both occasions are concordant. Although the work described here does not settle disputes regarding the abstract versus episodic nature of text reprocessing effects, it reinforces Raney's arguments that questions may be better posed in terms of how different levels of text processing are organized and recruited for later use. Using the paradigm described here, we can explore the contextual dependency of representations at different levels, thus testing further the assumptions made in the Raney (1998) model. There is considerable evidence in the word recognition literature that lower level representations are not abstract, as Raney's model postulates. These questions cry out for further investigation. The evidence we reported here shows the value of using text processing models in understanding repetition effects in reading. It also shows the strong effects of memorial representation on the fluency of later reading, even when there is no instruction to use the prior experience. That is, these are unintentional or implicit memorial influences that may well provide the basis for skill development. In a very real sense, we have just "flipped the relationship" between processing and memory that Craik and Lockhart brought so powerfully to our attention in 1972, with their emphasis on understanding how processing influences memory. Their emphasis was on how memories were formed; ours is on how these memories can be recruited in the service of more skilled processing. While processing established initial representations during learning, these representations are recruited and updated in the constant interplay of memory and processing, as skill develops across experiences. A complete understanding of fluent reading needs to address mechanisms that promote development or growth in skill. Specific memory representations are candidate mechanisms.

☐ References

Bourassa, D. C., Levy, B. A, Dowin, S., & Casey, A. (1998). Transfer effects across contextual and linguistic boundaries: Evidence from poor readers. *Journal of Experimental Child Psychology, 71,* 45–61.

Bransford, J. D. (1979). The role of prior knowledge. In J. D.Bransford (Ed.), *Human cognition: Learning, understanding and remembering* (pp. 129–165). Belmont,CA: Wadsworth.

Carlson, L., Alejano, A., & Carr, T. H. (1991). The level of focal attention hypothesis in oral reading: Influences of strategies on the context specificity of lexical repetition effects. *Journal of Experimental Psychology: Learning, Memory, and Cognition, 17,* 924–931.

Carr, T. H., Brown, J. S., & Charalambous, A. (1989). Repetition and reading: Perceptual encoding mechanisms are very abstract but not very interactive. *Journal of Experimental Psychology: Learning, Memory, & Cognition, 15 ,* 763–778.

Craik, F. I. M., & Lockhart, R. S. (1972). Levels of processing: A framework for memory research. *Journal of Verbal Learning and Verbal Behavior, 11,* 671–684.

Faulkner, H. J., & Levy, B. A. (1994). How text difficulty and reader skill interact to produce differential reliance on word and content overlap in reading transfer. *Journal of Experimental Child Psychology, 58,* 1–24.

Faulkner, H. J., & Levy, B. A. (1999). Fluent and nonfluent forms of transfer in reading: Words and their message. *Psychonomic Bulletin & Review, 6,* 111–116.

Jacoby, L. L. (1983). Remembering the data: Analyzing interactive processing in reading. *Journal of Verbal Learning and Verbal Behaviour, 22,* 485–508.

Kintsch, W. (1991). The role of knowledge in discourse comprehension: A construction-integration model. In G. Denhiere & J. P. Rossi (Eds.), *Text and text processing.* (pp. 107–153). New York: Elsevier Science.

Levy, B. A. (1993). Fluent rereading: An indirect indicator of reading skill development. In P. Graf &

M. E. J. Masson (Eds.), *Indirect memory: New directions in cognition, development, and neuropsychology* (pp. 49–73). Hillsdale, NJ: Erlbaum.

Levy, B. A., Abello, B., & Lysynchuk, L. (1997). Transfer from word training to reading in context: Gains in reading fluency and comprehension. *Learning Disabilities Quarterly, 20,* 173–188.

Levy, B. A., Barnes, L., & Martin, L. (1993). Transfer of fluency across repetitions and across texts. *Canadian Journal of Experimental Psychology, 47,* 401–427.

Levy, B. A., & Burns, K. I. (1990). Reprocessing texts: Contributions from conceptually driven processes. *Canadian Journal of Psychology, 44,* 465–482.

Levy, B. A., Campsall, J., Browne, J., Cooper, D., Waterhouse, C., & Wilson, C. (1995). Reading fluency: Episodic integration across texts. *Journal of Experimental Psychology: Learning, Memory, & Cognition, 21,* 1169–1185.

Levy, B. A., & Kirsner, K. (1989). Reprocessing text: Indirect measures of word and message level processes. *Journal of Experimental Psychology: Learning, Memory, & Cognition, 15,* 407–417.

Levy, B. A., Nicholls, A., & Kohen, D. (1993). Repeated readings: Process benefits for good and poor readers. *Journal of Experimental Child Psychology, 56,* 303–327.

MacLeod, C. M. (1989). Word context during initial exposure influences degree of priming in word fragment completion. *Journal of Experimental Psychology: Learning, Memory, & Cognition, 15,* 398–406.

Masson, M. E. J. (1986). Identification of typographically transformed words: Instance-based skill acquisition. *Journal of Experimental Psychology: Leaning, Memory, and Cognition, 12,* 479–488.

Oliphant, G. W. (1983). Repetition and recency effects in word recognition. *Australian Journal of Psychology, 35,* 393–403.

Rashotte, C. A., & Torgeson, J. K. (1985). Repeated readings and reading fluency in learning disabled children. *Reading Research Quarterly, 20,* 180–202.

Raney, G. E. (1998). An integrated model of memory for text. Paper presented at the Winter Conference on Disourse, Texts, and Cognition, Jackson Hole, WY.

Raney, G. E., & Rayner, K. (1995). Word frequency effects and eye movements during two readings of a text. *Canadian Journal of Psychology, 49,* 151–172.

Raney, G. E., Therriault, D., & Minkoff, S. (2000). Repetition effects for paraphrased text: Evidence for an integrated representation model of text representation. *Discourse Processes, 29,* 61–81.

Roediger, H. L. & Blaxton, T. A. (1987). Effects of varying modality, surface features, and retention interval on priming word fragment completion. *Memory and Cognition, 15,* 379 – 388.

Samuels, S. J. (1979). The method of repeated readings. *The Reading Teacher, 32,* 403–408.

Tenpenny, P. L. (1995). Abstractionist versus episodic theories of repetition priming and word identification. *Psychonomic Bulletin & Review, 2,* 339–363.

van Dijk, T. A., & Kintsch, W. (1983). *Strategies of discourse comprehension.* New York: Academic Press.

☐ Appendix A: Sample Text Used to Measure Repetition Benefits

Beginning in childhood individuals are specifically trained in this age-old tradition. It is important to begin the practice when you are young, as its benefits are not only immediate but long term. Indeed, the pay-off will likely continue long into old-age, and is thought by most people to be very high. For example, consistent practice in the long run may save you significant amounts of money, not to mention undue physical trauma. Gaining full profit from the process, however, is entirely dependent on one's style when completing the job. Proper form is demonstrated by the experts, although we do not always adhere to such strict instruction. As with most tasks in life, it is also important to be thorough. You must take your time since it is crucial to focus on each item *individually* before moving on to the next. While the instructions for execution can be quite stringent, the tools involved are often very simple. Two main items are essential, and they must be used simultaneously for optimum results. Recently, a wide variety of electrically powered devices have been designed to allow the user even greater success. While these items do not necessarily reduce the time needed to complete the job thoroughly, they do significantly increase the power, and thus the effectiveness of the tools involved. Despite the existence of these power tools, most people prefer to stick to the old fashioned method which simply involves a little elbow grease. Further, electrically powered devices are quite expensive. In contrast, more traditional tools are cheap, although they do require frequent replacement. As with most tasks in life, reaping maximal benefit from the execution of *this* task is directly proportional to its *frequency* of execution. It is important, however, not to engage too much or too little in this task. While paying infrequent attention to the activity can have a disastrous effect on your social interaction, executing the task too frequently can damage those items which you are seeking to protect. It is preferable, then, that you adhere to the experts' recommended daily rate. Those closest to you will probably thank you profusely for being so conscientious. Ironically, this practice is not restricted to humans. In fact, it is recommended for some nonhuman mammals as well. As such, some animals *do* engage in this activity, although they are hard-pressed to complete it independently. When assistance is provided, however, everyone involved benefits.

A. Brushing Your Teeth

Robert S. Lockhart

Commentary: Levels of Processing and Memory Theory

It seemed unlikely in 1972 that discussions of levels of processing would extend into the next millenium, much less be the theme of a session graced with eminent speakers from four different countries. In his editorial letter of acceptance of the manuscript for Craik and Lockhart (1972), Tulving wrote, "I predict a bright future for these ideas, at least some of them." The predicted brightness of that future may be a matter for dispute, but its longevity is not.

Something that is often lost in the mists of the distant past is the historical context within which the 1972 levels-of-processing paper was written. Our motivation was very much a negative reaction to the dominance in contemporary thinking of the box-and-arrow style of theorizing, according to which memory was determined by such cognitively impoverished concepts as length of time in a rehearsal buffer, or number of rehearsals. The point of our opposition to such theorizing is captured in an obscure quote from William James which, had we been familiar with it at the time, might have appeared as a battle cry at the beginning of the 1972 paper. "The art of remembering is the art of thinking. . . . Our conscious effort should not be so much to *impress* and *retain* as to *connect* it with something else already there" (James, 1899/1992, p. 793).

A common criticism has been that the concept of "levels" was too vague. One early critic even went to the length of pulling out heavy artillery in the form of a quote from Wittgenstein's *Tractatus* to the effect that we should have been clear about what we meant by levels, or have remained silent. But this sort of attack is a serious misunderstanding of the way science often progresses. Many key scientific ideas begin as vague concepts, and their clarification is the *goal* of research, not its starting point. Concepts such as gravity in physics or the gene in biology come to mind. These are scarcely minor ideas, and science would have been ill served if scientists had heeded the dictum to be clear or silent.

I think, in fact, that in talking about levels, we were not vague enough. Attempts to undermine the central thrust of Craik and Lockhart (1972) with claims that "depth" should be replaced by "breadth" or "elaboration" reveal a failure to grasp the significance of the word "framework" in the paper's title. Note first that the concept of elaboration has been part of the "levels" vocabulary from the outset. More important, terms such as "depth" or "breadth" are best thought of as crude spatial metaphors, serving as promissory notes or place holders awaiting a more detailed theory—a theory about the way qualitatively different forms of processing interact with retrieval conditions to determine memory performance. Velichkovsky's contribution to this volume provides a good example of this kind of endeavor. For this reason, I have no argument with those who think breadth, or some other spatial metaphor, is a preferable label for the place marker. Unfortunately, people became fixated on the idea that "levels of processing" was a theory to be tested in the hypothetico-deductive tradition, rather than a framework within which to develop a theory.

One consequence of this fixation has been the misguided claim that the concept of levels is circular and that before worthwhile research can proceed, "levels" must be given an independent definition. The accusation of circularity and the associated demand for an independent definition of depth of processing has been rather like a mosquito: insubstantial, annoying, but persistent. It is a much-favored criticism among textbook writers. Velichkovsky's chapter 4 has made a valuable contribution to clarifying this matter. I will add just two points.

First, the accusation of circularity has little justification in fact. In every study that I am familiar with in which levels of processing have been manipulated, the conditions that constitute levels have been defined operationally in the form of various orienting tasks and quite independently of any outcome.

Second, while it is true that some people, suffering a writer's block as they faced their discussion section, resorted to levels of processing as a post hoc explanation for some outcome, their strategy is not totally without merit. It exemplifies a line of scientific progress that is both common and legitimate, if rather plodding. With respect to levels of processing, this type of theory development takes the following form: The fact that orienting task A (a synonym judgment, say) leads to better remembering than does orienting task B (say, judging rhyme), tells us something about what is meant by the place marker "depth."

There *is* an element of circularity in such a post hoc analysis, but this sort of circularity is in good company. Natural selection, the single most revolutionary idea that has ever existed, has precisely this property. Appealing to levels of processing to explain memory performance is much the same as appealing to natural selection to explain the extinction of the dodo. Both in their own way can be vacuous post hoc explanations, but they represent the correct designation or demarcation of what needs to be explained. The concept or theoretical framework designates what phenomena are important, and in turn, the details of these phenomena serve to clarify the idea.

The claim that the memory trace was the byproduct of perceptual-cognitive processing is one of the few ideas in Craik and Lockhart (1972) about which I have never had serious doubts. Tulving's analysis in chapter 2 has not changed that conviction, despite the fact that I agree with most of what he said, and that the following comments are shamelessly dependent on his general concept of ecphory as well as Roediger's development of the concept of transfer-appropriate processing (see, e.g., Roediger, 1990).

I should stress, however, that as our ideas have developed over the years, there has been increased emphasis on the claim that the memory trace is a byproduct of *general cognition*, rather than just of perception in the narrow sense (Craik & Lockhart, 1986; Lockhart & Craik, 1978; Lockhart & Craik, 1990). Our everyday cognitive operations involve not only seeing, hearing, etc., but also processes such as comparing, discriminating, noting similarities, inferring, remembering, and detecting novelty. All these processes can occur at degrees of abstraction that would take them well beyond what is normally considered perception.

The inclusion of remembering among this list of cognitive operations warrants a special comment in relation to Levy's contribution in chapter 6. Her analysis of fluent reading is a particularly compelling example of how comprehension and remembering are themselves influenced by memory processes. Not only does the form of processing influence memory (the basic claim of levels of processing) but, equally, the skill of remembering plays a crucial role in determining the processes underlying reading.

The idea that the memory trace is an incidental byproduct amounts to the claim that there is not a process of "committing to memory" in the sense of a distinct memory-encoding operation that can occupy a place in this list of cognitive processes; laying down a memory trace is not one among many distinguishable cognitive processes. A memory trace *is* established, but not by some specialized processing strategy called memory encoding. What we might call a memory trace follows in the continuous wake of the ongoing ship of cognitive activity; it is not the ship itself, of course, but a trail of the cognitive consequences of that activity.

Updated knowledge and changed implicit behavioral propensities are examples of features of this wake. Such features can be said to constitute a pattern of ecphoric affordances. The ecphoric potential to support later episodic remembering is another affordance of the memory trace, at least for noninfant humans with intact brains. In this species-specific and developmental matter, the evidence strongly favors Tulving's claim that episodic memory is a peculiarly human capacity. Moreover, there are undoubtedly some forms of processing that lead to greater episodic ecphoric potential than do others, and novelty detection may well be among them.

Notice the use of the term *episodic remembering* rather than *episodic memory*. There is no difficulty in accepting the idea of an episodic memory system, provided that, as a system, episodic memory refers to the entire interactive relationship between episodic remembering and relevant affordances of the memory trace. The strongest evidence for there being such a distinct system is, in fact, the species-specific nature of episodic remembering. Given this specificity, it is reasonable to expect further support from the study of brain activity.

A strong implication of this byproduct view of the memory trace is that the only distinct "memory process" is retrieval. Thus the most authentic memory researchers are those such as John Gardiner (see chapter 5 of this volume, coauthored with Richardson-Klavehn, Ramponi, & Brooks), who take as their focal point—their point of reference—retrieval processes. Consider an analogy with problem solving. In order to study problem solving you must also study the knowledge base and the existing skills of the problem solver. But the focus of your explanatory efforts is the process of problem solving itself. Analogously, the goal of the memory researcher is to explain retrieval, and although understanding how the cognitive processes lay down a memory trace will play an essential role in that explanation, these processes do not constitute the phenomenon to be explained. Roediger (2000) offered a detailed and convincing argument for this general point of view.

These are not new ideas, especially to Tulving and Craik. But perhaps they provide us with an answer to Roediger and Gallo's metaquestion (see chapter 3 of this volume). He asks why, after 30 years of research, we do not know why or how we get the typical levels-of-processing effect. The reason, I suggest, is that we do not know enough about how retrieval works. Until we know more, debating the relative merits of describing traces as richer, deeper, wider, broader, more elaborated, or whatever, will not get us much further ahead.

If retrieval processing is the focus of memory research, and if we grant the validity of the common general principle underlying both encoding specificity and transfer-appropriate processing, then the problem of trying to predict memory performance on the basis of encoding operations is well known. As Tulving and Roediger among others, have pointed out repeatedly, the conditions of retrieval are unspecified. To continue my problem-solving metaphor, it is rather like trying to predict problem-solving success without specifying the nature of the problem to be solved.

What we do know is that in the world of everyday remembering, the cueing potency of these retrieval conditions—the retrieval context—will be variable across occasions. So one possible starting point for an answer to Roediger and Gallo's question is to take retrieval processing as our point of reference and exploit his own ideas of transfer-appropriate processing. Perhaps, as Schacter (1996, p.63) suggested, a major reason why a semantic orienting task typically works better than a nonsemantic one is because the semantic processing yields a trace that is accessible to a broader range of retrieval cues. Such a trace is more likely to survive variations in the subsequent retrieval context. Rather than a deeper encoding, we might refer to it as a more *robust* encoding, a trace whose ecphoric affordance is less vulnerable to variations in the retrieval environment.

What does the future hold for levels of processing? I do not think "levels" will retire with F. I. M. Craik. I can do no better than to quote a famous psychologist who once wrote, "I predict a bright future for these ideas, at least some of them."

☐ References

Craik, F. I. M., & Lockhart, R. S. (1972). Levels of processing: A framework for memory research. *Journal of Verbal Learning and Verbal Behavior, 11,* 671–684.

Craik, F. I. M., & Lockhart, R. S. (1986). CHARM is not enough. *Psychological Review, 93,* 360–364.

James, W. (1992). Talks to teachers on psychology and to students on some of life's ideals. In *William James: Writings 1878–1899* (pp. 705–887). New York: The Library of America. (Original work published 1898)

Lockhart, R. S., & Craik, F.I.M. (1978). Levels of processing: A reply to Eysenck. *British Journal of Psychology, 69,* 171–175.

Lockhart, R. S., & Craik, F.I.M. (1990). Levels of processing: A retrospective analysis of a framework for memory research. *Canadian Journal of Psychology, 44,* 87–112.

Roediger, H. L. III (1990). Implicit memory: Retention without remembering. *American Psychologist, 45,* 1043–1056

Roediger, H. L. III (2000). Why retrieval is the key process in understanding human memory. In E. Tulving (Ed.), *Memory, consciousness, and the brain: The Tallinn Conference* (pp. 52–75). Philadelphia: Psychology Press.

Schacter, D. L. (1996). *Searching for memory.* New York: Basic Books.

WORKING MEMORY
AND ATTENTION

CHAPTER

Michael T. Turvey

Part II Introduction:
Encoding, Retrieving, and Aging

Understanding how memories are established and subsequently applied constitutes a major challenge confronting a general theory of cognition. Understanding how the two processes alter over the life-span is a major challenge facing a general theory of aging. The chapters in this part indicate the ways in which contemporary research is attempting to meet these challenges. This part is divided into two sections: one on working memory and comprising chapters 9–12, the other on attention at encoding and at retrieval and comprising chapters 14–16.

The key concepts of encoding and retrieval are at an early stage of development. An important influence on present intuitions about encoding is Craik and Lockhart's (1972) levels-of-processing hypothesis. This versatile and enduring hypothesis about memory's nature was inspired, in significant degree, by efforts in the 1960s and early 1970s to comprehend how memory works in the short term. The message of the hypothesis was, roughly, that a person's strategy on encountering new material determined the quality and durability of the established memory. A strategy-oriented approach to encoding implicates options in respect to (a) the type of processing strategy and (b) the type and degree of resource needed to implement the strategy. Experimental questions follow naturally, therefore, for students of memory and cognitive aging. For example, they can ask whether concurrent mental activity impairs encoding (and vice versa) and whether age differences in memory reflect differences in encoding strategy and/or access to resources.

Levels of processing was primarily a hypothesis about encoding's contribution to memory. It had little to say about the retrieval process or about retrieval's relation to encoding. Two other hypotheses of the 1970s, transfer-appropriate processing (Morris, Bransford, & Franks, 1977) and encoding specificity (Tulving, 1972), have grounded modern intuitions about the retrieval process. For both, success of a given type of encoding was not absolute but relative to the circumstances of retrieval. From these hypotheses, it was a small step to the intuition that, at retrieval, memories are not fetched (as a clerk might fetch files from a filing cabinet) but evolved. They evolve (or emerge) from the symbiosis of the circumstances of retrieval and the products of encoding.

Apparently, the complexities at retrieval are not the same kind as the complexities at encoding. To the extent that retrieval is self-organizing and encoding is not, retrieval may impose a smaller demand on cognitive resources than encoding and may undergo different changes with aging than encoding. To the extent that retrieval and encoding are qualitatively distinct, they may not be supported by the same neural mechanisms. For the experimentalist, the charge is clear: examine the mechanisms of encoding and retrieval and determine in what ways they are alike and in what ways they are different.

Of special relevance to these issues of encoding, retrieving, and aging is yet a further hypothesis advanced in the 1970s, the hypothesis of working memory (Baddeley & Hitch, 1974). By this hypothesis, cognitive tasks require the interaction of current and remembered experiences within a system capable of manipulating and holding information in temporary, task-specific forms. In chapter 9 by Baddeley, an episodic buffer is added to the classical formulation of the working memory system. This buffer stores novel combinations of activated long-term memory representations as they arise in the realization of a cognitive task. Working memory thereby makes available temporary arrangements of knowledge for use by conscious strategic processes. It should be evident from reading Baddeley's chapter that encoding and retrieving can assume various forms within working memory dependent upon the precise nature of the working memory function in which they are embedded.

The chapters by Anderson (chapter 16), Moscovitch, Fernandes, and Troyer (chapter 14) and Naveh-Benjamin (chapter 15) are in general agreement that encoding differs from retrieval in its greater susceptibility to secondary tasks in dual-task performance. At first blush, this consensus might suggest that retrieval is more automatic, in the sense of more resource independent, than encoding. But the evidence from retrieval's effect on the secondary task suggests otherwise. Anderson observes that retrieval is equal to encoding in its effects on the secondary task. Anderson's qualification that retrieval is obligatory (it operates indifferently to concurrent cognitive activity) but not automatic (it consumes resources) may itself require qualification. Moscovitch, Fernandes, and Troyer corroborate the observation of Baddeley, Lewis, Eldridge, and Thompson (1984, Experiment 9) that when retrieving necessitates setting up and implementing strategies, it is prone, like encoding, to concurrent cognitive activity.

There are indications, according to Moscovitch, Fernandes, and Troyer that responsibility for distinct forms of retrieval, strategic and nonstrategic, may devolve on different neural subsystems. A modular subsystem composed of the hippocampus and related structures in the medial temporal lobe (MTL) supports the associative retrieval that occurs when an internal or external state automatically elicits an act of remembering. A central executive subsystem anchored in the frontal lobes is responsible for effortful or strategic retrieval; it is often called upon to supply the states that activate the modular MTL subsystem. According to this component-process account, retrieving will suffer from divided attention if it involves the frontal subsystem. For Shallice (chapter 10), this resource-dependent retrieval can be usefully partitioned into component phases and related to subdivisions of the prefrontal cortex. For a given task of retrieving episodic memories, the hypothesized phases are: (a) framing a description of what kind of episodic memory, if it existed, would fit the task, (b) matching the description with episodic memories, and (c) verifying an achieved match. It is conjectured that the ventrolateral and dorsolateral regions of the right prefrontal cortex might accommodate (a) and (c), respectively.

Not surprisingly, the frontal lobe is implicated in encoding. It is of some theoretical significance to cognitive neuroscience, therefore, that the susceptibility of encoding to secondary task performance resists ready interpretation. Naveh-Benjamin (chapter 15) asks whether the susceptibility reflects a restriction on strategic elaboration. Although he found that encoding with elaboration (intentional learning) was superior to encoding without elaboration (incidental learning), the magnitude of the difference was not affected by the availability of attention. Related questions of whether the susceptibility reflected reduced consolidation or a deficit in forming associations were also answered in the negative. The main effects of attention at encoding (full or divided) and delay of recall (short or long) were additive rather than interactive, as were the main effects of attention at encoding and the to-be-remembered information (components or their associations). Apparently, relative to full attention, divided attention simply depresses the effect of a given encoding by a certain amount, whatever that effect might be. The implication is that, with respect to encoding, available attention acts as a scalar.

The aspect of encoding explored by McDowd (chapter 11) is not its resource-dependency but its selectivity. Responding to the lack of support for the idea that the facility to inhibit declines with aging, McDowd pursues the hypothesis that older people encode along different dimensions (or inhibit different dimensions at encoding) than younger people. Age-related differences in encoding selectivity can be found, but it is evident that generalizations are restricted by the task-dependency of such differences. Park and Hedden (chapter 12) are more sanguine about the status of a broad inhibitory deficit but nonetheless highlight the lack of compelling support.

Patently, the potential richness of processes comprising encoding and retrieving gives room for wide speculation about the memory mechanisms and related capacities that might undergo age-related changes. Park and Hedden (chapter 12) focus on the coordinate hypotheses of age-related declines in resources and the efficacy of working memory. Their data are most supportive, however, of a simpler and more unifying hypothesis: Biological processes slow with age. They combined structural modeling with a life-span approach (301 participants from 20 to 90 years of age). Age-related differences in a battery of cognitive tasks involving hypothesized working, and long-term memory functions were explained by speed. No fundamental differences in the organization of memory structures were observed across the life-span. From the perspective of dynamical systems, mean cognitive speed might be viewed as a control parameter that affects the stability and adaptability of self-assembled cognitive states (e.g., Kelso, 1995; Thelen & Smith, 1994; Turvey, 1990).

In overview, the chapters in this part of the book give the reader admiration for the experimental psychology of the 1970s, respect for the concepts of encoding, retrieval, and attention, belief in the possibility of general principles of cognitive aging, and a deep appreciation of Gus Craik's contribution to the science of cognition. The late Jack Turvey would be very proud of his old Edinburgh mate.

References

Baddeley, A. D., & Hitch, G. (1974). Working memory. In G. A. Bower (Ed.), *Recent advances in learning and motivation, Vol. 8*. New York: Academic Press.

Baddeley, A. D., Lewis, V., Eldridge, M., & Thompson, N. (1984). Attention and retrieval from long-term memory. *Journal of Experimental Psychology: General, 113*, 518–540.

Craik, F. I. M., & Lockhart, R. S. (1972). Levels of processing: A framework for memory research. *Journal of Verbal Learning and Verbal Behavior, 11*, 671–684.

Kelso, J. A. S. (1995). *Dynamic patterns*. Cambridge, MA: MIT Press.

Morris, C. D., Bransford, J. D., & Franks, J. J. (1977). Levels of processing versus transfer appropriate processing. *Journal of Verbal Learning and Verbal Behavior, 16*, 519–533.

Thelen, E., & Smith, L. B. (1994). *A dynamic systems approach to the development of cognition and action*. Cambridge, MA: MIT Press.

Tulving, E. (1972). Episodic and semantic memory. In E. Tulving & W. Donaldson (Eds.), *Organization of memory*. New York: Academic Press.

Turvey, M. T. (1990). Coordination. *American Psychologist, 45*, 938–953.

WORKING MEMORY

9

CHAPTER

Alan D. Baddeley

Levels of Working Memory

Gus Craik and I have been friends for many years and have followed very similar career paths. We both completed our Ph.D.s under the aegis of the British Medical Research Council, cut our theoretical teeth on the question of whether there is more than one kind of memory, and went on to do the piece of work for which we are probably best known in the early 1970s. We are both experimentalists at heart, basing our theoretical developments firmly on empirical evidence, and using experimental methods to investigate issues of practical significance, aging in Gus's case and neuropsychology in mine.

However, despite our original interests, there is no doubt that I am currently better known for my research on working memory (WM), and Gus for his contribution to our understanding of long-term memory (LTM), where the concept of levels of processing has had an enormous impact over the last 25 years. Although I have criticized the concept, I continue to find it extremely useful. I occasionally have the job of trying to tell a hall full of 2,000 high school students all about memory in the space of half an hour. I always use the concept of levels of processing, since it captures a huge range of empirical data and summarizes it in a very simple and elegant way, leading to straightforward advice on such practical problems as how one should review for exams. Having done that, I then bore them with the mysteries of WM.

Granted that levels of processing is a major theoretical contribution, I still believe it has limitations. It captures the importance of the nature of coding for the durability of memory very successfully. However, its implication of a succession of coding stages, each deeper than the last, remains problematic, based as it was on the assumption of serial stages of information processing. Although the serial stages approach was influential, I would argue for a much more parallel interpretation of perception and cognition. The paper by Craik and Tulving (1975) confronted this problem squarely, accepting the problems, and proposing instead of a sequential set of processes, an interpretation in terms of richness and elaboration of encoding that is entirely plausible if not novel (James, 1890).

Gus has of course continued to be interested in the processes underlying both learning and retrieval, for example, using the imposition of a secondary load to simulate the effects of aging (Craik & Kester, 1999) and to contrast the attentional demands of learning and retrieval (Craik, Govoni, Naveh-Benjamin, & Anderson, 1996).

Despite my early interest in LTM, and the obvious importance of WM in the process of LTM, I have, until recently, largely neglected the question of the precise interface between WM and LTM. At my own Festschrift last year, Gus chose to present a levels-of-processing account of WM. I would like to return the compliment by addressing the question of how WM and LTM interact. I shall discuss three separate mechanisms that might plausibly be regarded as representing separate levels of WM. In each case the proposed mechanism turns out to be linked with processes that interested me during my pre-WM phase, making it perhaps appropriate to start with a little ancient history.

☐ Some History: Ancient and Modern

I suspect that our theoretical frameworks are perceived as being more different than they are, since Gus has worked principally on LTM while I have concentrated on WM; indeed, others have on occasion interpreted Gus's concept of levels of processing as making the assumption of short-term memory (STM) or WM unnecessary (Postman, 1975), although Gus himself, of course, continued to use the concept of primary memory (Craik & Lockhart, 1972). In fact, we began our careers on the opposite side of the LTM–STM divide, with Gus doing influential work on recency and the concept of primary memory (Craik, 1964), while being one of the first people to study digit recall across contrasting languages (Heron & Craik, 1964). I, on the other hand, earned my Ph.D. working for the British Post Office on factors that might increase the long-term memorability of postal codes; I had the dubious distinction of being the first person to work on the long-term learning of nonsense syllables in Bartlett's old unit.

My Ph.D. research on postal codes was strongly influenced by the concept of information theory (Shannon & Weaver, 1949) and attempted to account for differences in the memorability of nonsense syllables in terms of their approximation to the structure of English, finding that the predictability of a syllable, as measured by its resemblance to the sequential letter structure of English, was a better predictor of subsequent learning than was the apparently dominant predictive measure, association value, which reflected the number of words that were suggested by that syllable to a panel of subjects. On the basis of my findings, I generated predictable and hence comparatively memorable postcodes for every town in Britain. I sent this list to the post office, who completely ignored it, having already made up their minds. They could have made a worse decision, however, as demonstrated by the Canadian Post Office, whose decision to alternate digits and letters was found by my mentor Conrad to be significantly worse than any other digit-letter combination (Baddeley et al., 1962).

During this period, Conrad worked on STM and I worked on LTM. My first immediate memory experiment resulted from dissatisfaction with a paper by Miller, Bruner, and Postman (1954), who tachistoscopically presented their subjects with letter strings of various approximations to English. They observed that the higher the approximation, the better the performance, and given the brevity of presentation, concluded that they had demonstrated the influence of redundancy on perception. The temptation to criticize three such august figures was too much, both for myself and for an up-and-coming young Canadian psychologist called Endel Tulving, who pointed out that Miller et al. had made a mistake in their calculation of redundancy (Tulving, 1963, although for a correction of Endel's correction, see Baddeley, 1964b). In addition, however, I suggested that the redundancy effect they had obtained might well be a memory phenomenon rather than reflecting a perceptual limitation. I presented the material at a speed that was sufficiently slow for the subject to read out the items aloud, hence demonstrating that he had accurately perceived the sequence. I found exactly similar results, hence suggesting a memory rather than a perceptual effect. We went on to extend these results, demonstrating the importance of language-based redundancy using new material (Baddeley, Conrad, & Hull, 1965) and linking it to analogous findings in which approximations to English prose were used (Miller & Selfridge, 1950; Tulving & Patkau, 1962). My early work, therefore, was concerned with the effects of language habits on immediate and long-term memory.

My interests then shifted to contrasting the role of acoustic and semantic coding in LTM and STM. My supervisor, Conrad, had made the important discovery that immediate memory for consonant sequences relied principally on acoustic or phonological coding. I became intrigued by the robust effect of acoustic similarity and decided to contrast it with semantic similarity, largely because both types could readily be manipulated using word sequences. I found that similarity of meaning had little effect in immediate serial recall, but a substantial effect on LTM (Baddeley, 1966a, 1966b). The pre-levels way of interpreting this result was to suggest that there were two separable systems, STM using an acoustic and LTM a semantic code. This clearly could not be the whole story, however; otherwise how could people ever learn new phonological forms, as is needed in acquiring novel vocabulary? I therefore began to manipulate the ease of semantic coding within standard LTM and STM paradigms.

One series of experiments was carried out with Betty Ann Levy, a postdoctoral fellow who came over from Toronto, where she had been warned by Ben Murdock of the barbarous group testing methods used by the Brits, whereby the luckless experimenter was required to hold up cards before a room full of subjects in time to a metronome. Despite (or because of) this primitive practice, we obtained some clear results (see Figure 9.1) indicating that when words fitted together in a readily meaningful way, then semantic coding occurred under standard STM paradigms such as immediate serial recall (Baddeley & Levy, 1971). Thus, serial recall of a sequence such as priest–moral–minister–religious–vicar–pious, etc. was poorer than recall of palace–magnificent–apple–delicious–rattlesnake–deadly, etc., whereas no semantic similarity effect occurred when the nouns and adjectives were not semantically compatible, as in the case of apricot–stubborn etc.

In a subsequent experiment (Baddeley, 1970), it proved possible to demonstrate simultaneous evidence of acoustic and semantic coding, with acoustically similar but meaningful phrases such as "I might fly" and "dry my eye" showing poorer immediate recall than dissimilar meaningful phrases, with an *improvement* in recall over a delay, presumably reflecting a switch from reliance on phonological to a parallel semantic code. At this point, then, it was clear that there was no simple link between paradigm and code, although by assuming separate and additive contributions from STM and LTM, it was possible to give an account of most of the available data (Baddeley, 1972). And then levels of processing burst on the scene!

Meanwhile, Graham Hitch and I had begun the work that led to our concept of WM (Baddeley & Hitch, 1974). We suggested replacing the earlier concept of a unitary short-term or primary memory with a tripartite model in which an attentional control system, the central executive, utilized two subsidiary systems, the phonological loop and the visuospatial sketchpad. The observation by Shallice and Warrington (1970) of grossly impaired STM coupled with apparently preserved LTM seemed to argue for separate WM and LTM systems. However, subsequent study of a patient with a very pure phonological STM deficit showed that LTM was not intact, as she showed a grossly impaired capacity for new phonological learning (Baddeley, Papagno, & Vallar, 1988).

This line of research on the role of WM in long-term phonological learning led in turn to a series of collaborative studies with Susan Gathercole in which we found a close association between impaired capacity of children to perform a task involving the immediate recall of unfamiliar pseudowords and their level of vocabulary development (Gathercole & Baddeley, 1989; 1990). The association held both for children with specific language impairment and for young normal children, encouraging us to propose that the phonological

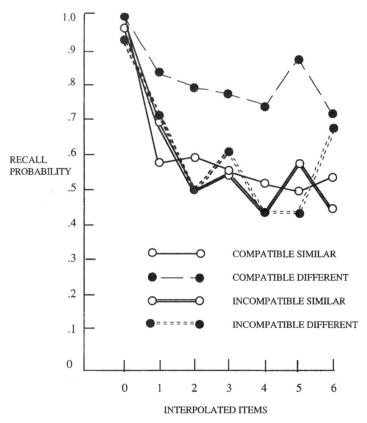

FIGURE 9.1.   Semantic coding in immediate serial recall: When noun–adjective pairs are semantically compatible, recall is enhanced, except when they are also semantically similar. Data from Baddeley and Levy (1971).

loop had evolved as a system for the acquisition of language (Baddeley, Gathercole, & Papagno, 1998).

Our claim did not go unchallenged. Snowling, Chiat, and Hulme, (1991) suggested that a third factor, delayed phonological development, was directly responsible for both poor nonword repetition and delayed vocabulary acquisition. While this is certainly a possibility in the case of the developmental data, this account does not provide an explanation for the impaired vocabulary acquisition in patients whose STM impairment was acquired in adulthood. Such patients can be assumed to have had normal premorbid phonology and may continue to show excellent preservation of phonological perception and language production (Baddeley, Vallar, & Wilson, 1987; Vallar & Shallice, 1990). It is also difficult to see how the phonological deficit hypothesis could account for the observation that variables that influence the phonological loop, namely articulatory suppression, phonological similarity, and word length, all impair the capacity for nonword learning in normal adults, while having no effect on the semantically based acquisition of word pairs (Papagno, Valentine, & Baddeley, 1991; Papagno & Vallar, 1992).

However, although a broad range of evidence appeared to support the hypothesis of a role for the phonological loop in long-term phonological learning (Baddeley et al., 1998), the underlying mechanism remained unclear, principally because the model was silent on the question of how WM and LTM interact. It is this important issue that Susan Gathercole has been addressing in recent years and that bears on the first "level" of interaction between WM and LTM, namely the impact on WM of language habits.

☐ Level I: Language Habits, WM, and the Acquisition of Vocabulary

An important paper by Gathercole (1995) made two very significant observations. First, she noted that the probability that a child would repeat a nonword correctly depended on how wordlike the letter sequence was. Initially, her measure of wordlikeness was based on independent ratings, but it has subsequently been validated using a measure based on the phonological structure of English (Gathercole, Frankish, Pickering, & Peaker, 1999). In some ways, the enhanced memory for wordlike sequences is unsurprising, given the previously described evidence on STM for English letter sequences. However, the result bears on two important theoretical questions. It demonstrates the importance of long-term learning in nonword repetition, and as such might suggest that nonword repetition is itself principally a *result* of prior phonological LTM, rather than a causal predictor of learning as Baddeley et al. (1998) claimed. A second issue concerns the question of how such an impact of long-term language habits on WM can be handled by the existing model.

In the same study, however, a second effect threw further light on the interaction between the phonological STM and the acquisition of vocabulary (Gathercole, 1995). Although there was a general tendency for sequences resembling the structure of English to be easier to recall, the capacity to predict vocabulary acquisition stemmed almost entirely from the less wordlike sequences. Wordlike sequences showed little correlation with vocabulary level. This is consistent with the following interpretation. Nonword repetition depends on at least two forms of storage, one based on prior long-term learning of language structure, and the other based on a separate short-term phonological store. The latter is assumed to reflect the capacity of the system to register and temporarily store novel phonological sequences and then to use this temporary storage to build up new long-term word forms.

If we consider the process of recalling and repeating back an unfamiliar pseudoword, then success will depend on both the support from prior learning, which given their common language background is likely to be broadly equivalent for all subjects, together with the capacity to retain new sounds, and to maintain them long enough to have a potential long-term influence. The contribution from prior learning is likely to be substantial for wordlike sequences, leading to their enhanced retention by all subjects, while the contribution of prior knowledge will be much less for the nonwordlike items. These items will be much more dependent on short-term phonological storage capacity, and hence it is these less wordlike items that will predict new long-term phonological learning.

This was the position when Baddeley et al. (1998) presented their argument for a crucial role for the phonological loop in language acquisition. Since that time, however, Gathercole and her colleagues have made a potentially important new set of observations. Their work stemmed from a concern to measure phonological storage independent of the capacity to articulate the relevant sequence, something that is important if one wishes to separate storage from production limitations, which in turn is necessary if one wishes to identify the nature of certain developmental language disorders. Separation of storage and production was achieved by using a recognition procedure in which a sequence of items was presented, and then repeated, either identically or with two adjacent items switched. The subject's task was to decide whether the sequence was the same or different. Both words and nonwords were tested, hence a word sequence involving change might be dog, hen, hat, pot–dog, hen, pot, hat. Nonwords comprised consonant-vowel-consonant (CVC) letter sequences, e.g., kov, dag, lef, zid–kov, dag, zid, lef. Gathercole et al. first showed that when tested by recall, there was a substantial difference in memory span for word and nonword sequences. However, when tested by recognition, little or no effect of lexicality was detected, a result that has now been replicated several times (Gathercole, Pickering, Hall, & Peaker, 2001).

This result suggests a potential separation of two underlying components, namely a phonological store that is capable of holding information in a sequential form sufficiently well to allow up to five or six nonwords to be stored, together with a second component that is involved in response production. A possible representation of such a model is shown in Figure 9.2. Recognition performance was subsequently proved to correlate with both recall and vocabulary development (S. Gathercole, personal communication, 2001), suggesting that the lexically independent storage component might underpin the acquisition of new words, in contrast to the output process, which depends crucially on existing knowledge of a lexical and sublexical type.

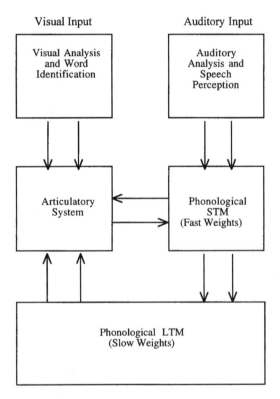

FIGURE 9.2. A suggested model linking the phonological loop with long-term phonological memory. The short-term phonological store holds incoming information, feeding some of it through to long-term phonological memory, which in turn influences performance through the later output stage of the phonological loop.

A case can be made for the desirability of such a separation on the following terms: If we assume that the mechanism has evolved to acquire new phonological representations, then it would be counterproductive to have a store that is dominated by prior habits. Such a store would be inclined to distort incoming representations in the direction of existing knowledge. It would therefore be excessively conservative. On the other hand, it is clearly useful to take advantage of existing knowledge. Having an output and rehearsal process that does so could be said to represent a suitable compromise. Verbal output and, presumably, rehearsal require a relatively complete specification and potentially provide a feedback that allows the rehearser to detect whether the sequence rehearsed is identical or not to the original stimulus. Meanwhile, information from the phonological store is assumed to impinge on long-term representations so as to allow new forms to be created.

It seems likely that such new learning will occur at a series of levels, from setting up representations of novel sounds, through phonological digram and trigram sequences, up to complete new forms, such as occurs with the acquisition of a novel word. This aspect of working memory is assumed to be "low level" in that it principally depends on implicit learning and retrieval processes that do not place heavy additional demands on executive control for either encoding or retrieval.

To what extent does this process equate to the concept of redintegration that has recently come to play an increasingly important role in theorizing about STM (Brown & Hulme, 1995; Schweikert, 1993)? The term is used to refer to the impact on STM of long-term, typically lexical, knowledge. It implies one or both of two mechanisms. The first is an automatic process such as the one just described, whereby existing knowledge shapes and constrains newly presented material. This process, together with the additional assumption that the mechanism is principally one of output rather than storage, reflects my own current view. The second type of redintegrative process involves a more explicit strategy that uses LTM consciously to interpret a noisy or incomplete memory trace. Hence a subject who remembers the sound "ive" in a digit recall experiment will know that since all the items are digits, it must be "five" and not "hive" or "thrive." I would certainly accept that such processes occur but would attribute their operation to the central executive and to the associated storage system termed the episodic buffer, which will be described later.

☐ Level II: Priming and Recency

We have so far proposed one level at which WM and LTM interact through a process of relatively gradual and cumulative implicit learning. The model also, however, includes another level of implicit learning, namely the priming of long-term representations that underlies the recency effect (Baddeley & Hitch, 1977, 1993). This is assumed to operate at the level of existing representations such as words, more complex structures such as proverbs, or indeed high-level concepts such as favorite film stars (Glanzer, 1974; Watkins & Peynircioglu, 1983). The recency effect is defined as the enhanced tendency of the most recently experienced items to be subsequently recalled. It extends from the immediate free recall of lists of unrelated items, through recall over slightly longer periods, when the normal phonological memory processes are disrupted by interpolated verbal activity (Bjork & Whitten, 1974; Glanzer, 1974) to delays operating over days or weeks, as in the study of memory for location of car parking (Pinto & Baddeley, 1991) or remembering rugby game opponents (Baddeley & Hitch, 1977). As Baddeley and Hitch showed, the recency effect is powerful even with incidental learning and is unimpaired by a demanding concurrent digit span task, suggesting that the storage mechanism may be implicit in nature (Baddeley & Hitch, 1993). The process of recall, however, is assumed to be strategy-based and hence presumably explicit, although the strategy is a very simple and robust one, present in patients suffering from moderate Alzheimer's disease (e.g., Spinnler, Della Sala, Bandera, & Baddeley, 1988). There is growing support for the view that the recency retrieval process is limited by the capacity to discriminate between competing memory traces, a process that in turn reflects the constant ratio rule, whereby retrieval depends on the ratio of the delay separating the target item from recall, relative to the delays associated with competing traces (Baddeley, 1976; Baddeley & Hitch, 1993; Crowder, 1976; Glenberg et al., 1980).

I would therefore regard the recency effect as reflecting another level of WM, one that combines an implicit priming process with a very basic and robust, but nevertheless explicit retrieval strategy.

☐ Level III: The Episodic Buffer

The third level of WM I would like to propose is much more obviously explicit in its link to LTM. It involves a newly proposed component of the WM model termed the *episodic buffer* (Baddeley, 2000). The buffer was proposed in order to account for a range of memory phenomena that appear to involve interaction between the slave systems and LTM. In the original version of the WM model, the central executive was assumed to have both control and storage capacities. The storage assumption was subsequently abandoned on the grounds of parsimony and testability; the initial executive seemed to be simply too powerful to be readily investigated (Baddeley & Logie, 1999). While separation of the attentional component was helpful in attempting to fractionate the executive (Baddeley, 1996), it has become increasingly clear that some form of storage mechanism is required to account for the growing evidence for an interaction between the various systems and subsystems.

For example, although memory span for visually presented consonants is principally phonologically based, visual similarity effects can be demonstrated (Logie, Della Sala, Wynn, & Baddeley, 2000). Furthermore, when the phonological loop is disrupted by articulatory suppression, memory span is severely reduced but by no means abolished (Baddeley, Lewis, & Vallar, 1984). Finally, neuropsychological evidence indicates that patients with grossly defective phonological STM nevertheless can remember four or five digits when they are presented visually (Shallice & Warrington, 1970). Since the visuospatial sketchpad does not seem to be effective at storing sequences of items, these results raise the question as to exactly how the relevant information is stored.

A similar problem is caused by the immediate recall of sentences, where a span of 5 or 6 unrelated words increases to 16 or more. My earlier assumption of separate broadly additive contributions from a phonological loop would thus suggest an LTM component of about 10 words. Given a patient with a substantial but pure deficit in phonological STM, one would predict that moving from unrelated words to sentences should increase span from 1 to 11. In fact, the sentence span for such a patient, PV, is five words (Baddeley et al., 1987). This implies some form of interaction between the two stores, rather than additivity, with the capacity of a basic phonological system being symbiotically increased through the utilization of lexical, syntactic, and/or semantic knowledge.

Further problems for a simple additive view of the relationship between working memory and LTM comes from the case of KJ, a patient with a very dense pure amnesic syndrome (Wilson & Baddeley, 1988). Despite his amnesia, KJ performed normally on the immediate recall of a prose paragraph from the Wechsler memory scale, for which he recalled some 12 idea units, an above average performance for his age. On the delayed component of the test, however, he was unable to remember anything, raising the question of how he had performed so well on the initial test. Twelve idea units extending over many more than 15 words is clearly beyond the capacity of the phonological loop, which in any case is assumed to be nonsemantic in nature.

A more extensive investigation of immediate and delayed prose recall in brain injured patients shows that although KJ's performance is unusually high, other broadly similar examples of good immediate and disastrous delayed prose recall occur in other amnesic patients, although it is much more common to find lower levels of initial recall. Analysis of the characteristics of the various patients suggests that good initial prose recall depends on well-preserved intelligence and/or good executive processes (Baddeley & Wilson, in press).

Other examples of surprisingly good immediate recall in densely amnesic patients are also found. Clive Waring, a very talented musician who suffered a devastatingly dense amnesia following encephalitis, nevertheless has extremely well-preserved musical skills. These include the capacity to sight-read a passage on the harpsichord, appropriately repeating a passage when this is signed in the score, and then directly remembering to ignore the repeat on the next occasion (Wilson, Baddeley, & Kapur, 1995). Endel Tulving (personal communication, 2000) reports a striking example of preserved mnemonic skill in a densely amnesic bridge player. When asked to participate in a game with his visitors, he demonstrated that he could not only remember the bid and the trump suit, but also keep track of which cards had been played sufficiently well to win the rubber.

I suggest that each of these examples involves the utilization of LTM to maintain a working record that is sufficiently well maintained as to allow the complex problem in hand to be tackled successfully. The assumption that WM may utilize activated representations within LTM occurs also in the concept of *long-term working memory*, proposed by Ericsson and Kintsch (1995). Indeed, the priming of LTM is assumed by Cowan (1999) to underlie the whole of WM. My own view, I believe, differs from these models, however, in proposing that the sources of information in LTM are actively combined, and that this combination itself requires temporary storage. The storage in question is assumed to depend upon a new component of WM, the episodic buffer, as shown in Figure 9.3.

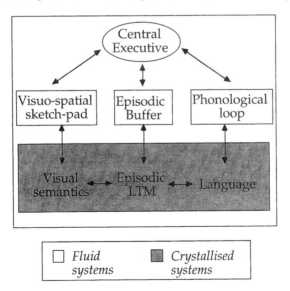

FIGURE 9.3. Suggested architecture for WM (Baddeley, 2000). The episodic buffer is a newly proposed subsystem that provides temporary storage as part of the process of integrating information from the slave systems with that from LTM.

The buffer is assumed to be limited in capacity, although the capacity limit is one based on number of integrated chunks rather than number of items or amount of information. Hence, its functional capacity can be increased by chunking strategies, a view very similar to that proposed by Cowan (in press) and, of course, by Miller (1956). My view also resembles that of Cowan (1999) and of Baars (1988) in suggesting that the system in question may be accessed via conscious awareness, a mechanism that allows a range of options to be entertained simultaneously, and to be used via a process of conscious reflection as a basis for future action.

I differ from Cowan, however, in proposing that it is necessary to do more than simply activate representations in LTM in order to achieve the capacity to reflect on the past and plan the future. It is, for example, possible to combine representations in LTM to create novel items or structures. Imagine, for instance, an elephant who plays ice hockey. Given such a player, we can ask how he holds the stick and what his best playing position might be. He could clearly do a formidable body check, but might be even better as a goal keeper. The essence of this component of WM therefore, is that it allows one to go beyond what already exists in LTM, to combine it in different ways, and to use it to set up novel scenarios on which future action can be based. Unlike Cowan's system which he suggests depends principally on the parietal lobes (Cowan, in press), I would anticipate much more of a dependence on frontal lobe function (Baddeley, 2000). It is important to note, however, that I am not proposing that the buffer reflects a single anatomical location, but rather that it represents a system for combining information from a range of other systems which neuroradiological and lesion evidence suggests are not themselves unitary in their localization (Smith & Jonides, 1996).

If I am not proposing a single location for the episodic buffer, then how is my view different from that proposed by Cowan? In proposing and labelling the episodic buffer, I intend to focus on the need to accept that some form of *temporary storage* is required by the integrative process proposed. Simply saying that it depends upon activation within other memory systems finesses the question of how such information is brought together and integrated. It is this process of active integration and manipulation that continues to represent the core of our WM concept, and while this does not logically need separate WM components, I would suggest that the neuropsychological and neuroradiological evidence suggest that such separable components are in fact involved (Smith & Jonides, 1996). Hence the episodic buffer does not replace our current concept of the central executive, which is still viewed as an attentional control system analogous to the limited-capacity attentional process proposed by Cowan. I propose that in addition, however, there is the need to postulate a separate mechanism for the integration and manipulation of information in WM, and that this additional component depends crucially on short-term storage.

In conclusion, Gus and I continue to share an interest in LTM, STM, and how they are linked. Having avoided this latter question for many years, I am being forced by the evidence to confront it, and like Gus I am proposing a number of levels. Whether our levels coincide will, I suspect, take several mutual pints of beer to decide.

☐ Acknowledgment

The support of MRC grant G9423916 is acknowledged with thanks.

☐ References

Baars, B. J. (1988). *A cognitive theory of consciousness*. New York: Cambridge University Press.

Baddeley, A. D. (1964a). Immediate memory and the "perception" of letter sequences. *The Quarterley Journal of Experimental Psychology, 16*, 4, 364–367.

Baddeley, A. D. (1964b). The redundancy of letter-sequences and space-information. *American Journal of Psychology, 77*, 322.

Baddeley, A. D. (1966a). The influence of acoustic and semantic similarity on long-term memory for word sequences. *Quarterly Journal of Experimental Psychology, 18*, 302–309.

Baddeley, A. D. (1966b). Short-term memory for word sequences as a function of acoustic, semantic, and formal similarity. *Quarterly Journal of Experimental Psychology, 18*, 362–365.

Baddeley, A. D. (1970). Simultaneous acoustic and semantic coding in short-term memory. *Nature, 227*, 288–289.

Baddeley, A. D. (1972). Retrieval rules and semantic coding in short-term memory. *Psychological Bulletin, 78*, 379–385.

Baddeley, A. D. (1976). *The psychology of memory*. New York: Basic Books.

Baddeley, A. D. (1996). Exploring the central executive. *Quarterly Journal of Experimental Psychology, 49A*(1), 5–28.

Baddeley, A. D. (2000). The episodic buffer: A new component for working memory? *Trends in Cognitive Sciences. 4*(11), 417–423.

Baddeley, A. D., Conrad, R., & Hull, A. (1965). Predictability and immediate memory for consonant sequences. *Quarterly Journal of Experimental Psychology, 17*, 175–177.

Baddeley, A. D., Conrad, R., Hull, A. G., Longman, D. J. A., Rabbitt, P. M., Skoulding, B. A., & Stuart, G. A. (1962). *Code design and the design of keyboards*. Report presented to the British Post Office, Medical Research Council Applied Psychology Research Unit, Cambridge, England.

Baddeley, A. D., Gathercole, S. E., & Papagno, C., (1998). The phonological loop as a language learning device, *Psychological Review, 105*(1), 158–173.

Baddeley, A. D., & Hitch, G. J. (1974). Working memory. In G. H. Bower (Ed.), *The psychology of learning and motivation, 8* (pp. 47–90). New York: Academic Press.

Baddeley, A. D., & Hitch, G. J. (1977). Recency re-examined. In S. Dornic (Ed.), *Attention and performance, VI* (pp. 647–667). Hillsdale, NJ: Erlbaum.

Baddeley, A. D., & Hitch, G. J. (1993). The recency effect: Implicit learning with explicit retrieval? *Memory & Cognition, 21*, 146–155.

Baddeley, A. D., & Levy, B. A. (1971). Semantic coding and short-term memory. *Journal of Experimental Psychology, 89*, 132–136.

Baddeley, A. D., Lewis, V. J., & Vallar, G. (1984). Exploring the articulatory loop. *Quarterly Journal of Experimental Psychology, 36*, 233–252.

Baddeley, A. D., & Logie, R. H. (1999). Working memory: The multiple-component model. In A. Miyake & P. Shah (Eds.), *Models of working memory* (pp. 28–61). Cambridge, England: Cambridge University Press.

Baddeley, A. D., Papagno, C., & Vallar, G. (1988). When long term learning depends on short-term storage. *Journal of Memory and Language, 27*, 586–595.

Baddeley, A. D., Vallar, G., & Wilson, B. A. (1987). Sentence comprehension and phonological memory: Some neuropsychological evidence. In M. Coltheart (Ed.), *Attention and performance XII: The psychology of reading* (pp. 509–529). London: Erlbaum.

Baddeley, A. D., & Wilson, B. A. (in press). Prose recall and amnesia: Implications for the structure of working memory. *Neuropsychologia*.

Bjork, R. A., & Whitten, W. B. (1974). Recency-sensitive retrieval processes. *Cognitive Psychology, 6*, 173–189.

Brown, G. D. A., & Hulme, C. (1995). Modelling item length effects in memory span: No rehearsal needed? *Journal of Memory and Language, 34*, 594–621.

Cowan, N. (1999). An embedded-processes model of working memory. In A. Miyake & P. Shah (Eds.), *Models of working memory* (pp. 62–101). Cambridge, England: Cambridge University Press.

Cowan, N. (in press). The magical number 4 in short-term memory: A reconsideration of mental storage capacity. *Behavioral and Brain Sciences*.

Craik, F. I. M. (1964). The fate of primary memory items in free recall. *Journal of Verbal Learning and Verbal Behavior, 5*, 209–217.

Craik, F. I. M., Govoni, R., Naveh-Benjamin, M., & Anderson, N. D. (1996). The effects of divided attention on encoding and retrieval processes in human memory. *Journal of Experimental Psychology: General, 125*, 159–180.

Craik, F. I. M., & Kester, J. D. (1999). Divided attention and memory: Impairment of processing or consolidation? In E. Tulving (Ed.), *Memory, consciousness and the brain* (pp. 38–51). Philadelphia, PA: Psychology Press.

Craik, F. I. M., & Lockhart, R. S. (1972). Levels of processing: A framework for memory research. *Journal of Verbal Learning and Verbal Behavior, 11*, 671–684.

Craik, F. I. M., & Tulving, E. (1975). Depth of processing and the retention of words in episodic memory. *Journal of Experimental Psychology: General, 104*, 3, 268–294.

Crowder, R. G. (1976). *Principles of learning and memory*. Hillsdale, NJ: Erlbaum.

Ericsson, K. A., & Kintsch, W. (1995). Long-term working memory. *Psychological Review, 102*(2), 211–245.

Gathercole, S. E. (1995). Is nonword repetition a test of phonological memory or long-term knowledge? It all depends on the nonwords. *Memory & Cognition, 23*, 83–94.

Gathercole, S. E., & Baddeley, A. D. (1989). Evaluation of the role of phonological STM in the development of vocabulary in children: A longitudinal study. *Journal of Memory and Language, 28*, 200–213.

Gathercole, S. E., & Baddeley, A. D. (1990). Phonological memory deficits in language-disordered children: Is there a causal connection? *Journal of Memory and Language, 29*, 336–360,

Gathercole, S. E., Frankish, C. R., Pickering, S. J., & Peaker, S. M. (1999). Phonotactic influences on short-term memory. *Journal of Experimental Psychology: Learning, Memory & Cognition, 25*, 84–95.

Gathercole, S. E., Pickering, S. J., Hall, J., & Peaker, S. M. (2001). Dissociable lexical and phonological influences on serial recognition and serial recall. *Quarterly Journal of Experimental Psychology, 54A*, 1–30.

Glanzer, M. (1974). Storage mechanisms in recall. In G. H. Bower (Ed.), *The psychology of learning and motivation: Advances in research and theory. 5*. New York: Academic Press.

Glenberg, A. M., Bradley, M. M., Stevenson, J. A., Kraus, T. A., Tkachuk, M. J., Gretz, A. L., Fish, J. H., & Turpin, V. M. (1980). A two-process account of long-term serial position effects. *Journal of Experimental Psychology: Human Learning and Memory, 6*, 355–369.

Heron, A., & Craik, F. I. M. (1964). Age differences in cumulative learning of meaningful and meaningless material. *Scandinavian Journal of Psychology, 5*, 209–216.

James, W. (1890). *The principles of psychology*. New York: Holt, Rinehard & Winston.

Logie, R. H., Della Sala, S. Wynn, V., & Baddeley, A. D. (2000). Visual similarity effects in immediate serial recall. *Quarterly Journal of Experimental Psychology, 53A*(3), 626–646.

Miller, G. A. (1956). The magical number seven, plus or minus two: Some limits on our capacity for processing information. *Psychological Review, 63*, 81–97.

Miller, G. A., Bruner, J. S., & Postman, L. (1954). Familiarity of letter sequences and tachistoscopic identification. *Journal of General Psychology, 50*, 129–139.

Miller, G. A., & Selfridge, J. A. (1950). Verbal context and the recall of meaningful material. *American Journal of Psychology, 63*, 176–185.

Papagno, C., Valentine, T., & Baddeley, A. D. (1991). Phonological short-term memory and foreign language vocabulary learning. *Journal of Memory and Language, 30*, 331–347.

Papagno, C., & Vallar, G. (1992). Phonological short-term memory and the learning of novel words: The effect of phonological similarity and item length. *Quarterly Journal of Experimental Psychology, 44A*, 47–67.

Pinto, A. da C. & Baddeley, A. D.(1991). Where did you park your car? Analysis of a naturalistic long-term recency effect. *European Journal of Cognitive Psychology, 3*, 297–313.

Postman, L. (1975). Verbal learning and memory. *Annual Review of Psychology, 26*, 291–335.

Schweikert, R. (1993). A multinomial processing tree model for degradation and redintegration in immediate recall. *Memory & Cognition, 21*, 168–175.

Shallice, T., & Warrington, E. K. (1970). Independent functioning of verbal memory stores: A neuropsychological study. *Quarterly Journal of Experimental Psychology, 22*, 261–273.

Shannon, C. E., & Weaver, W. (1949). *A mathematical theory of communication.* Urbana: University of Illinois Press.

Smith, E. E., & Jonides, J. (1996). Working memory in humans: Neuropsychological evidence. In M. Gazzaniga (Ed.), *The cognitive neurosciences* (pp. 1009–1020). Cambridge, MA: MIT Press.

Snowling, M., Chiat, S., & Hulme, C. (1991). Words, nonwords, and phonological processes: Some comments on Gathercole, Willis, Emslie and Baddeley. *Applied Psycholinguistics, 12*, 3, 369–373.

Spinnler, H., Della Sala, S., Bandera, R., & Baddeley, A. D. (1988). Dementia, aging and the structure of human memory. *Cognitive Neuropsychology, 5*, 193–211.

Tulving, E. (1963). Familiarity of letter-sequences and tachistoscopic identification. *American Journal of Psychology, 76*, 143–146.

Tulving, E., & Patkau, J. E. (1962). Concurrent effects of contextual constraint and word frequency on immediate recall and learning of verbal material. *Canadian Journal of Psychology, 16*, 2, 83–95.

Vallar, G., & Shallice, T. (1990). *Neuropsychological impairments of short-term memory.* Cambridge, England: Cambridge University Press.

Watkins, M. J., & Peynircioglu, Z. F. (1983). Three recency effects at the same time. *Journal of Verbal Learning and Verbal Behavior, 22*, 375–384.

Wilson, B. A., Baddeley, A. D., & Kapur, N. (1995). Dense amnesia in a professional musician following Herpes Simplex Virus Encephalitis. *Journal of Clinical and Experimental Neuropsychology, 17*, 668–681.

Wilson, B., & Baddeley, A. D. (1998). Semantic, episodic and autobiographical memory in a post-meningitic amnesic patient. *Brain and Cognition, 8*, 31–46.

Tim Shallice

Deconstructing Retrieval Mode

Prior to 1994 there had been little work on the functional imaging of episodic memory. The most important early paper, a position emission-tomography (PET) study by Grasby et al. (1993), had shown a surprising involvement of the frontal lobes in secondary (long-term) verbal memory by comparison with primary (short-term) verbal memory; in this paper the contrast had been made using free recall of different-length lists. However, the procedure involved having encoding and retrieval in the same scan. Interest in the area was really sparked by the demonstration in 1994 of the contrasting involvement of the left and right prefrontal cortices in encoding and retrieval. Three of the four papers on the topic that year including the one on the crucial hemisphere encoding and retrieval assymetry (HERA) generalization, involved Gus Craik (Kapur et al., 1994; Tulving, Kapur, Moscovitch, & Houle, 1994; Tulving, Kapur, Markowitsch et al., 1994). Moreover, the key paper showing left frontal involvement in the encoding process used levels of processing as its manipulation (Kapur et al., 1994). Thus Gus Craik played a major role in the initial establishment of the functional imaging of episodic memory as a scientific field.

The work published in 1994 triggered an explosion of interest in the field. The initial HERA generalization has largely been supported (Cabeza & Nyberg, 2000), but with two provisos. One relates to how far encoding for nonverbal as well as verbal material activates the left rather than right prefrontal cortex (Haxby et al., 1996; Wagner et al., 1998). The second relates to retrieval, the topic of this paper. The involvement of the right rather than left prefrontal cortex has been much less ubiquitously obtained by comparison with the left frontal link to encoding from verbal material. This is particularly so in more complex tasks (Nolde, Johnson, & Raye, 1998). However Lepage, Ghaffar, Nyberg, and Tulving (2000), in a recent meta-analysis, show the right prefrontal dominance still to be present. They define what they consider to be retrieval mode (REMO; Tulving, 1983) regions as those where a particular conjunction of effects holds, namely where an episodic retrieval task with a very high rate of old items and one with a very low rate of old items are both more active than a control task with similar input and output characteristics but no episodic memory requirements. The logic is that it is the attempt to retrieve that is critical for REMO rather than retrieval success.

Lepage et al. (2000) carried out two meta-analyses. One was of four PET recognition memory experiments all containing these three conditions they held to be critical. They found that six regions showed a significant conjunction of effects after allowing for multiple comparisons. Four were in the right frontal lobe and two, which were much smaller in terms of the number of pixels involved, were in the left. Their second analysis used a less constraining comparison; they analyzed PET and functional magnetic resonance imaging (fMRI) studies in the literature in which activation in an episodic retrieval condition had been compared with a control condition. They found 40 such studies and examined the locus of the activation maxima for retrieval minus control comparisons and whether they were within 1.6 cm of the so-called REMO sites, the six maxima obtained in the previous meta-analysis. They then examined the number of studies showing matches. For both areas of frontal cortex where the authors had reported left frontal as well as right frontal activation in their first meta-analysis, they found a fairly large number of studies with bilateral activations but significantly more right-only studies than left-only ones. Thus the HERA generalization was supported as far as retrieval was concerned.

The Lepage et al. (2000) analysis is empirically very interesting. It can be criticized because the basic initial REMO analysis just used recognition tasks. However, as we will see later, the use of recall would not lead to other regions being involved. There are, however, problems with the concept of REMO. It was defined by Lepage et al. as:

> a neurocognitive set, or state, in which one mentally holds in the background of focal attention a segment of one's past, treats incoming and online information as retrieval "cues" for particular events in the past, refrains from task irrelevant processing and becomes consciously aware of the production of successful ecphory.

From this characterization it is not very clear what subprocesses are involved, and even where they are relatively clearly specified, it tends to be in phenomenological terms. To use them as effective theoretical constructs to relate to brain processes, one must first solve the body–mind problem!

A second difficulty with this conceptualization of REMO concerns what it leaves out. Take the process of being given a word as a retrieval cue after being presented with some lists of words. Assume further that the word was in the list just presented. What should the subject do? This would depend critically on the task instructions. If it was a standard recognition experiment, then he or she should say "Yes"; if in a list specification experiment, then respond "last"; if in a Slamecka (1968) type of experiment, where one is examining the effects of being provided with some list words on retrieval of the rest, then give any other words in the last list, if in a serial recall experiment, produce the next word in the last list, and so on. In other words, as Raajimakers and Shiffrin (1981) pointed out, the component processes involved at retrieval need to incorporate the specific retrieval task.

For an initial analysis of the possible subprocesses involved at retrieval, I will therefore use the older formulation of Norman and Bobrow (1979), which has been applied to remembering in children by Barreau and Morton (1999) and to the analysis of confabulations occurring following neurological disease by Burgess and Shallice (1996) (but see Schnider & Ptak, 1999, for a novel alternative view). Norman and Bobrow argued that the subject must set up a characterization of what, if it were to exist in episodic memory, would satisfy the subject's explicit or implicit memory task. This they call the formulation of the "descriptions" of any potentially relevant memory records.

In Burgess and Shallice (1996), this process was considered analogous in the domain of episodic memory to setting up *determining tendencies* in Ach's (1905) theory of thinking (see Humphrey, 1951, for an extensive account in English). This process is then followed by a matching process in which records in the episodic memory store are matched with the descriptions. In a second version of the theory, that of Morton, Hammersley, and Bekerian (1985), it is the "headings" of memory records that are searched to see if they match the retrieval descriptions, and this would accord well with theories of the hippocampus in which it has an indexing function (e.g., Murre, 1996; Taylor & Di Scenna, 1986), especially if one views the hippocampus as the critical storage system required in retrieval in episodic traces and not merely as an intermediate-memory type of store (see for relevant evidence Nadel & Moscovitch, 1997; Cipolotti et al., 2001).

Successfully achieving a match is not, however, the final stage of the process. The typical occurrence of directed episodic memory retrieval in everyday life is not to determine in which list a word was presented. Assume that it is to assist in solving real-life informal problems by providing concrete cases to use in the reasoning process required to produce a strategy (case-based reasoning) (see Schank, 1982; Shallice, 1988). For instance, if asked how a friend you recently saw is doing, then many things in the half-hour you spent with him yesterday may be relevant in answering the question. There is no simple algorithm for specifying exactly what. Thus, articulating specific descriptions is likely to lead to many false positives. For example, if the description system were to request instances of high affect in the half-hour you spent with him, then your friend's tearing his jacket could come to mind. However, it should be rejected as being too temporally specific in its implications to be relevant to the question.

More concretely, in an extended protocol study of remembering specific types of episodes in everyday life, Burgess and I (Burgess & Shallice, 1996) found very high rates of memory errors, typically corrected shortly after they occurred. Norman and Bobrow (1979), in their speculations, expected retrieval from episodic memory to lead to many false positives, and so added a third stage, *memory verification*. Indeed, the related concept of memory monitoring occurs in other analyses of retrieval processes (e.g., Koriat & Goldsmith, 1996). Norman and Bobrow's theory can therefore be seen as a plausible first step in articulating the subprocesses involved in retrieval from episodic memory. Moreover, certain of the syndrome patterns found in the memory disorders of neurological patients can be explained in terms of the theory (see Burgess & Shallice, 1996; Dab, Claes, Morais, & Shallice, 1999, and also Schacter, Norman, & Koutstaal, 1998, for a related framework).

In the work of our London group on the functional imaging of retrieval we have tended to interpret the results in terms of this theory. This was initially for a neuropsychological reason. Our initial work contrasting encoding and retrieval was carried out in parallel to that of the Toronto group. It, however, used the same task at encoding and retrieval—verbal paired associates—and so a more direct comparison could be made. It also showed a left frontal–right frontal contrast between encoding and retrieval in the regions activated. Our interpretation of the right frontal effect at retrieval was influenced by two other pieces of work. One was a meta-analysis by Burgess (1992), which indicated that confabulatory disorders were more common following right frontal than left frontal lesions. The second was our knowledge of the work of Stuss et al. (1994) showing that right frontal patients were particularly likely to repeat previously recalled items in free recall protocols. Together these observations fitted well with an account of the key retrieval processes in the right prefrontal cortex involving checking or verification. As this was the only memory-related process that in 1994 we could plausibly localize in the right prefrontal cortex, at least for verbal material, we speculated that this was the origin of the right prefrontal activation found in our study where we contrasted retrieval of category-cued paired associates with the otherwise equivalent semantic control task of generating any item from an equivalent type of category.

This was merely a speculative interpretation of the results of our first study, but no more so than the REMO speculations of the Toronto group! Moreover, the region activated more in the episodic memory retrieval condition by comparison with a semantic memory control included part of the dorsolateral region, parts of the ventrolateral and anterior cingulate, and three of the four right anterior regions involved in the Lepage et al. (2000) meta-analysis.

A somewhat later study of our group (Fletcher, Shallice, Frith, Frackowiak, & Dolan, 1998a) indicated that these regions are not equipotential. This study and its complement for encoding (Fletcher, Shallice, & Dolan, 1998) were designed to examine the processes involved in making subjective organization so effective in improving episodic memory (Mandler, 1979). One study (Fletcher, Shallice, & Dolan, 1998b) examined the role at encoding; the other (Fletcher, Shallice, Frith, et al., 1998) how retrieval of an organized list occurs. The studies were also motivated by two neuropsychological studies which had indicated that frontal lobe lesions reduce the efficacy with which subjects can use organization in episodic memory (Incisa della Rocchetta & Milner, 1993; Gershberg & Shimamura, 1995). However, in the case of Incisa della Rocchetta and Milner's study, there were suggestions that both the encoding processes involved in the use of organization and how the organization was used at retrieval involved left prefrontal processes.

This view of left lateralization of encoding was compatible with our imaging studies of encoding (Fletcher, Shallice, & Dolan, 1998). However, in Fletcher, Shallice, & Firth, et al. (1998) we contrasted retrieval from an organized list that had been previously presented with retrieval of equivalent items learned as paired associates. The organized list consisted of a set of four items from each of four related categories, such as four types of bread (pitta, ciabatta, wholemeal, nan), four types of fish, four types of fruit, and four types of meat. The list had been presented once, 5 minutes before scanning. During the PET scan, the subject heard "next" every 4 s and had to then give another word from the list. The control condition involved 16 different categories in each list corresponding to more specific categories, e.g., Indian bread, than those used in the experimental internally generated retrieval condition. A single presentation trial had also been given in this condition, and recall was cued by individual category labels presented at the same rate. Two word repetition tasks were used as controls, one for each of the two retrieval conditions.

By comparison with their respective repetition control conditions, both retrieval tasks produced significantly greater activation through a wide swathe of the right prefrontal region. There were no effects in the left prefrontal cortex. However, within the right prefrontal cortex, there was also a surprising double dissociation. Retrieval of the organized list produced significantly greater activation than for the control paired associates in the right dorsolateral prefrontal cortex (see Figure 10.1A). However the effect was significantly reversed in the posterior ventral prefrontal cortex (see Figure 10.1B).

Why might this effect occur? Retrieval from 16 items organized in a 4 × 4 hierarchy led to increased repeats in the output following right frontal lesions. It requires continuous checking of where in the structure one is and which items one has generated from the appropriate four items of the relevant category. By contrast, paired-associate recall, where each item is specified by a different highly restricted category cue, is a situation where monitoring and verification are less critical. A putative response can hardly have been linked to a prior stimulus. "Tennyson" is a plausible response to the category cue "poet" but not to the cue "wine." There is therefore no need to check its relation to items already retrieved. Thus there is a plausible hypothesis for the greater right dorsolateral activation with the internally generated retrieval, namely, that that condition stresses verification processes more.

Free recall from a 16-item list is exactly the situation where Stuss et al. (1994) found that right prefrontal errors produced more repeats in the retrieval process, just what one might expect with impaired verification processes. Why, though, should the posterior ventral right prefrontal region be more activated in the paired associate condition? If subjects are

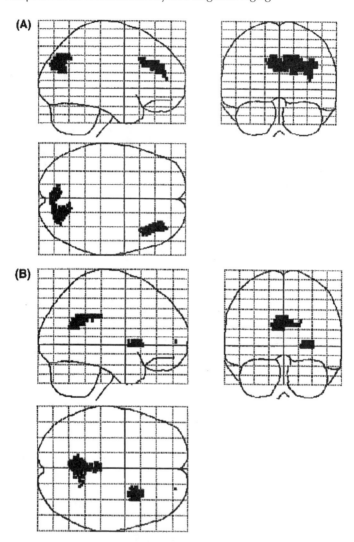

FIGURE 10.1. The regions that were significantly more activated in (A) the organized list retrieval condition by contrast with the paired-associate retrieval condition and (B) the reverse comparison in the Fletcher, Shallice, Frith et al. (1998) study. The diagrams show the regions which were significantly the more activated, projected onto three planes through a "glass brain."

retrieving the items in successive categories, then in the organized list retrieval condition, the recall specification conditions change only four times during retrieval, namely, at the times the subject moves to the following category; when retrieval is of same-category items, then the same recall specification condition will operate, and this can occur for a maximum of 4 items. In the paired-associate condition, however, the recall specification must change with each new category cue and so there will be 16 different specifications. Thus one speculative possibility is that the paired-associate condition stresses the description/

recall specification process more, and that this process is localized in the right ventrolateral regions.

Further studies of our group have shown a differential degree of activation of the right dorsolateral region when two different episodic memory retrieval conditions were contrasted. The first was also a PET study, but this time using a Jacoby (1996) process dissociation framework. "Exclusion" conditions were contrasted with "inclusion" conditions. The exclusion conditions required subjects to respond "Yes" only when the presented word was in the same spatial position (exclusion condition 1) or the same temporal position (List 1 or List 2, exclusion condition 2) as when it was originally presented. These two exclusion conditions did not differ in their activation patterns. They showed strong activation of the dorsolateral prefrontal cortex. Following the initial recognition that a word was presented, this exclusion condition clearly requires an additional checking stage not present in the inclusion one. Thus the finding fits the hypothesis developed earlier.

One way the result differs from the previous one is that the dorsolateral activation was bilateral for the exclusion/inclusion contrast. However even here there was a lateralization effect. In the left hemisphere, activation produced by the exclusion condition was significantly weaker than that in the encoding condition. In the right hemisphere it was far stronger (see Figure 10.2). Thus there was a right hemisphere bias for the exclusion condition by comparison with encoding.

Another study, in this case an event-related fMRI one, gave further and in this case unanticipated, support. In this study (Henson, Rugg, Shallice, Josephs, & Dolan, 1999),

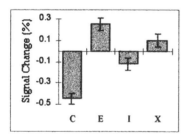
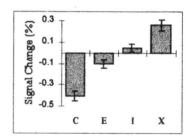
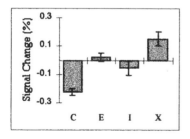
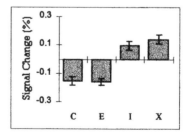

FIGURE 10.2. The contrasting activation patterns at activation maxima in the four regions in Henson, Shallice, and Dolan (1999) memory process dissociation study. C, E, I, X stand for control, encoding, inclusion recall, and exclusion recall. Of particular interest are (i) the contrasts between the two regions on top and (ii) the pattern in the bottom right-hand region. The top left region shows a pixel in the left dorsolateral prefrontal cortex, the bottom left is one in the left posterior parietal cortex, the top right is one in the right dorsolateral prefrontal cortex, and the bottom right is one in right ventral prefrontal cortex.

the paradigm used was a remember–know one modelled on the work of Tulving (1985) and Gardiner (1988). Surprisingly, as far as the frontal cortices are concerned, the remember–know contrast produced only an anterior (area 8) left hemisphere activation and no right frontal activation. This is clearly at odds with any idea that the right frontal effect in the HERA model directly reflects the ecphoric process per se, since the remember judgment but not the know one is held to be based on ecphory. However, more critically, the know–remember contrast activated the same region of the right dorsolateral prefrontal cortex as the exclusion/inclusion contrast of the previous study. We assume, using a Mandler (1987) type of approach to recognition, that when the target word is presented, after an initially positive familiarity impression for a yes response, the subject attempts to make an explicit check of the episodic record if such has not already occurred. For know responses this stage would be longest because it fails, and it is this stage that gives the right dorsolateral prefrontal activation. In broad agreement with this, Allan and Rugg (1997), using electrophysiological techniques, found that both recognition judgments and cued recall ones produced a stronger right than left frontal potential, but only more than 1200 ms after stimulus presentation (see Allan, Wilding, & Rugg, 1998). This led them to suggest also that the source of this right prefrontal potential was involved in postretrieval operations, of which checking is one. The checking hypothesis also fits the electrophysiological findings of Uhl, Podrecka, and Deeke (1994) that the right prefrontal DC shift is greater in conditions with a high degree of proactive interference.

If checking processes are taking place in the right prefrontal cortex, then they should be more likely to occur in situations when the subject has low confidence. In a final fMRI study (Henson, Rugg, Shallice, & Dolan, 2000), subjects had to give a factorially specified response by pressing one of four keys indicating both whether or not they recognized the stimulus and whether they had high or low confidence. As predicted, the right dorsolateral prefrontal region was more activated by low confidence than high confidence responses, and this was independent of whether the subject was recognizing correctly that the stimulus had occurred or recognizing correctly that it had not. Hits and correct rejections, however, differed in the degree to which they activated a more anterior right prefrontal region in area 10, another of the Lepage et al. (2000) REMO regions.

Would these results not be compatible with the activation of right prefrontal cortex being associated with greater retrieval effort (Schacter et al., 1996)? In fact, retrieval effort has been used to explain the left frontal lateralization of retrieval of more shallowly studied words (Schacter et al., 1996; Buckner, Koutsaal, Schacter, Wagner, & Rosen, 1998). Moreover, these hypotheses are not as dissimilar as they might seem. Thus Burgess and Shallice (1996) showed that a variety of different procedures were used to check the veridicality of retrieval attempts. An important one is to search for further related memories to see whether they form a coherent whole with the ones already obtained. Thus a checking procedure could lead to an effortful retrieval process. However, treating the hypotheses as different, if consideration is restricted to memory experiments alone, it is difficult to differentiate them. Take, for example, the confidence study of Henson et al. (2000) just discussed. One could argue that the less confident responses are those where more retrieval effort is made.

One can, however, consider studies other than those on episodic memory. The right dorsolateral region is also involved in other types of experimental studies. Take vigilance operations, as discussed by Posner and Petersen (1990). Lesions in the right frontal cortex affect the subject's ability to carry out monotonous tasks (e.g., Wilkins, Shallice, & McCarthy, 1987). Moreover Pardo, Fox, and Raichle (1991) showed that requiring subjects to be vigilant over the one minute of a PET scan, in order to count the (small) number of faint touches that occurred, led to increased activation in the very same right dorsolateral region. In another domain, when subjects view an anomalous percept unexpectedly, there is strong activation in this region (Fink et al., 1999). This fits a checking hypotheses better than a hypothesis specific to episodic memory retrieval.

What might the checking or verification process consist of? Take the process of checking that an item in a free recall has not previously been recalled earlier in the sequence of responses the process that is impaired in the right frontal patients of Stuss et al. (1994). One possible scenario is that when the repeated response comes to mind, an increased familiarity response occurs. This is detected by some system as being greater than a previously specified threshold, an interrupt occurs, and the subject then explicitly attempts to retrieve items already recalled in the output, detects the match between the implicit response and the previously retrieved item, and so aborts the response. On the assumption that the right dorsolateral region is also involved in checking processes other than those concerned with episodic memory, then there would seem to be three possible stages that may be responsible for the increased activation: the specification of the matching criteria, the matching of the implicit response or external stimulus with the prespecified criteria, or the interrupt process. Which are more plausible must depend on further study.

Returning to the retrieval experiments, Why did activation occur in the right posterior ventral prefrontal cortex? In the exclusion and inclusion conditions of the Jacoby-type experiment, the region was significantly more activated in both conditions by comparison with a memory encoding and a nonmemory control condition. Similarly, it was more active in the know condition than in the no condition of the remember–know experiment. Both effects were bilateral. Both results also fit with the idea that the right posterior ventrolateral cortex is involved in retrieval specification, but they hardly provide strong support.

One subsidiary result of the Henson, Shallice, and Dolan (1999) exclusion/inclusion study is relevant. An analysis was carried out to investigate across conditions whether the regression line relating activation in the right dorsolateral region to activation in any other regions was greater in the exclusion than the inclusion condition. This was found to be the case for the right posterior ventrolateral region. Interestingly, the effect was not found when the analysis was carried out in the reverse direction. This suggests that the right dorsolateral region exerted a unidirectional influence on the right ventrolateral region. This is what one would expect if further examination of episodic memory in the exclusion condition is dependent upon initially deciding to check.

A second phenomenon that fits with the hypothesis is from a functional imaging study our group carried out in a patient with an isolated retrograde amnesia, covering a period of nearly 20 years. Although his memory problem was triggered by a stroke, for a variety of reasons we attributed it to primarily functional causes (Costello, Fletcher, Dolan, Frith, & Shallice, 1998). A key reason was that many very disturbing events occurred in this part of his life. The period affected was the 20-year period preceding the stroke; both his early life and the period since the stroke were unaffected and he was able to remember them in detail. The patient was presented with pictures obtained from his relatives in which he was not personally shown. Some were of events at which he was present, half of these being from the retrograde amnesia period and the other half before or after. A third set of pictures were of family events at which he was not present. He was scanned while being asked whether he recalled the event. When the scans were examined, the condition involving the events where he was present but did not recall the event, as they were in the retrograde amnesic period, differed significantly from both the other two conditions in three respects. One region was more activated for events in the amnesic period. This was the precuneus, a region frequently activated in memory recall (e.g., Shallice et al., 1994; Fletcher, Shallice, Frith, Frackowiak, & Dolan, 1996). The other two were significantly less strongly activated for the events in the critical period at which he was present but of which he had no conscious memory. One was adjacent to his lesion in medial area 8/9 of the left prefrontal cortex and may reflect an artefact of the statistical parametric mapping procedure due to effects of the lesion boundary. The other, however, was the region that has just been discussed, the right posterior ventrolateral prefrontal cortex. In Talairach and Tournoux (1988) coordinates, the activation maximum (26, 26, –4) is little more than 1 cm from the right ventrolateral peaks in the Fletcher, Shallice, Frith, et al. (1998) experiment (36, 18, 0) and in the Henson, Shallice, and Dolan (1999) exclusion/inclusion experiment (36, 24, –9). It was argued that the initial representation of negatively charged events in the critical period led in the patient to suppress the recursive cycle of retrieval specification and memory retrieval that typifies everyday-life episodic recall (Burgess & Shallice, 1996). This meant that fewer retrieval specification processes would occur for the forgotten events from the critical period of his life. This in turn would correspond to reduced activation of the right posterior ventrolateral prefrontal cortex.

Interestingly, activation close to this region is also affected by manipulations in the recent study of Gus Craik and his group (Anderson et al., 2000), which also uses paired-associate recall, as in Fletcher, Shallice, Frith et al. (1998). A bilateral ventrolateral and orbital region is more activated in retrieval than encoding and also shows some effect of a distraction task on retrieval. However, in accordance with earlier findings of Baddeley, Lewis, Eldridge, and Thomson (1984) and Craik, Govoni, Naveh-Benjamin, and Anderson (1996) there was relatively little effect of the distractor on the amount recalled. It is critical for the current theory to examine whether activation in the region was greater than for a control nonmemory task in the distraction condition.

Overall, these studies do not unconditionally support the replacement of the concept of REMO by concepts derived from the Norman–Bobrow theory of retrieval specification and verification. However, given the theoretical insufficiency of the REMO concept, the studies provide a plausible initial replacement for it with a tentative assignment of two regions of right prefrontal cortex, ventrolateral and dorsolateral, respectively, as being where the two control processes of description specification and memory verification are primarily localized.

☐ References

Ach, N. (1905). *Uber die Willenstatigheit und das Denken.* Gottingen, Germany: Vardenhoeck.

Allan, K., & Rugg, M. D. (1997). An event-related potential study of explicit memory on tests of cued recall and recognition. *Neuropsychologia, 35,* 387–397.

Allan, K., Wilding, E. L., & Rugg, M. D. (1998). Electrophysiological evidence for dissociable processes contributing to recollection. *Acta Psychologia, 98,* 231–252.

Anderson, N. D., Iidaka, T., McIntosh, A. R., Kapur, S., Cabeza, R., & Craik, F. I. M. (2000). The effects of divided attention on encoding and retrieval-related brain activity: A PET study of younger and older adults. *Journal of Cognitive Neuroscience, 12,* 775–792.

Barreau, S., & Morton, J. (1999). Pulling Smarties out of a bag. A Headed Records analysis of children's recall of their own past beliefs. *Cognition, 73,* 65–87.

Buckner, R. L., Koutstaal, W., Schacter, D. L., Dale, A. M., Rotte, M., & Rosen, B. R. (1998). Functional-anatomic study of episodic retrieval. II. Selective averaging of event-related fMRI trials to test the retrieval success hypothesis. *NeuroImage, 7,* 163–175.

Buckner, R. L., Koutstaal, W., Schacter, D. L., Wagner, A. D., & Rosen, B. R. (1998). Functional-anatomic study of episodic retrieval using fMRI: I. Retrieval effort versus retrieval success. *NeuroImage, 7,* 151–162.

Burgess, P., & Shallice, T. (1996). Confabulation and the control of recollection. *Memory, 4,* 359–412.

Cabeza, R., & Nyberg, L. (2000). Imaging cognition II: An empirical review of 275 PET and fMRI studies. *Journal of Cognitive Neuroscience, 12,* 1–47.

Cipolotti, L., Shallice, T., Chan, D., Fox, N., Scahill, R., Harrison, G., Stevens, J., & Rudge, P. (2001) Long-term retrograde amnesia: The crucial role of the hippocampus. *Neuropsychologia, 39*, 151–172.

Craik, F. I. M., Gavoni, R., Naveh-Benjamin, M., & Anderson, N. D. (1996). The effects of divided attention on encoding and retrieval processes in human memory. *Journal of Experimental Psychology: General, 125*, 159–180.

Dab, S., Claes, T., Morais, J., & Shallice, T. (1999). Confabulation with a selective descriptor process impairment. *Cognitive Neuropsychology, 16*, 215–242.

Fink, G. R., Marshall, J. C., Halligan, P. W., Frith, C. D., Driver, J., Frackowiak, R. S. J., & Dolan, R. J. (1999). The neural consequences of conflict between intention and the senses. *Brain, 122*, 497–512.

Fletcher, P. C., Shallice, T., & Dolan, R. J. (1998). The functional roles of prefrontal cortex in episodic memory. I. Encoding. *Brain, 121*, 1239–1248.

Fletcher, P. C., Shallice, T., Frith, C. D., Frackowiak, R. S. J., & Dolan, R. J. (1996). Brain activity during memory retrieval: The influence of imagery and semantic cueing. *Brain, 119*, 1587–1596.

Fletcher, P. C., Shallice, T., Frith, C. D., Frackowiak, R. S. J., & Dolan, R. J. (1998). The functional roles of prefrontal cortex in episodic memory. II. Retrieval. *Brain, 121*, 1249–1256.

Gardiner, J.M. (1988). Functional aspects of recollective experience. *Memory and Cognition, 16*, 309–313.

Gershberg, F. B., & Shimamura, A. P. (1995). Impaired use of organizational strategies in free recall following frontal lobe damage. *Neuropsychologia, 33*, 1305–1333.

Grasby, P. M., Frith, C. D., Friston, K. J., Bench, C., Frackowiak, R. S. J., & Dolan, R. J. (1993). Functional mapping of brain areas implicated in auditory-verbal memory function. *Brain, 116*, 1–20.

Haxby, J. V., Ungerleider, L. G., Horwitz, B., Maisog, J. M., Rapoport, S. I., & Grady, C. L. (1996). Face encoding and recognition in the human brain. *Proceedings of the National Academy of Sciences, USA, 93*, 922–927.

Henson, R. N. A., Rugg, M. D., Shallice, T., & Dolan, R. J. (2001). Confidence in word recognition: Dissociating right prefrontal roles in episodic retrieval. *Journal of Cognitive Neuroscience, 12*, 913–923.

Henson, R. N. A., Shallice, T., & Dolan, R. J. (1999). Right prefrontal cortex and episodic memory retrieval: A functional MRI test of the monitoring hypothesis. *Brain, 122*, 1367–1381.

Henson, R. N. A., Ruggs, M. D., Shallice, T. Josephs, O., & Dolan, R. J. (1999). Recollection and familiarity in recognition memory: An event-related functional magnetic resonance imaging study. *Journal of Neuroscience, 19*, 3962–3972.

Humphrey, G. (1951). *Thinking: An introduction to its experimental psychology.* London: Methuen.

Incisa della Rocchetta, A., & Milner, B. (1993). Strategic search and retrieval inhibition: The role of the frontal lobes. *Neuropsychologia, 31*, 503–524.

Jacoby, L. L. (1996). Dissociating automatic and consciously controlled effects of study/test compatibility. *Journal of Memory and Language, 35*, 32–52.

Kapur, S., Craik, F. I., Tulving, E., Wilson, A. A., Houle, S., & Brown, G. M. (1994). Neuroanatomical correlates of encoding in episodic memory: Levels of processing effect. *Proceedings of the National Academy of Sciences, USA, 91*, 2008–2011.

Koriat, A., & Goldsmith, M. (1996). Monitoring and control processes in the strategic regulation of memory accuracy. *Psychological Review, 103*, 490–517.

Lepage, M., Ghaffar, O., Nyberg, E., & Tulving, E. (2000). Prefrontal cortex and episodic memory retrieval mode. *Proceedings of the National Academy of Sciences, USA, 97*, 506–511.

Mandler, G. (1979). Organization and repetition: Organisational principles with special reference to rote learning. In L.-G. Nilsson (Ed.), *Perspectives on memory research.* Hillsdale, NJ: Erlbaum.

Mandler, G. (1987). Determinants of recognition. In E. Van der Meer & J. Hoffman (Eds.), *Knowledge aided information processing* (pp. 3–12). Amsterdam: North Holland.

Morton, J., Hammersley, R. H., & Bekerian, D. A. (1985). Headed records: A model for memory and its failure. *Cognition, 20*, 1–23.

Moscovitch, M., & Melo, B. (1997). Strategic retrieval and the frontal lobes: Evidence from confabulation and amnesia. *Neuropsychologia, 35*, 1017–1034.

Murre, J. M. J. (1996). Trace link: A model of amnesia and consolidation of memory. *Hippocampus, 6,* 675–684.

Nadel, L., & Moscovitch, M. (1997). Memory consolidation, retrograde amnesia and the hippocampal complex. *Current Opinion in Neurobiology, 1,* 217–227.

Nolde, S. F., Johnson, M. K., & Raye, C. L. (1998). The role of prefrontal cortex during tests of episodic memory. *Trends in Cognitive Science, 2,* 399–406.

Norman, D. A., & Bobrow, D. G. (1979). Descriptions: An intermediate stage in memory retrieval. *Cognitive Psychology, 11,* 107–123.

Pardo, L. V., Fox, P. T., & Raichle, M. E. (1991). Localisation of a human system for sustained attention by positron emission tomography. *Nature, 349,* 61–64.

Posner, M. I., & Petersen, S. E. (1990). The attention system of the human brain. *Annual Review of Neurosciences, 13,* 25–42.

Raajimakers, J. G., & Shiffrin, R. M. (1981). Search of associative memory. *Psychological Review, 88,* 93–134.

Schacter, D. L., Norman, K. A., & Koutstaal, W. (1998). The cognitive neuroscience of constructive memory. *Annual Review of Psychology, 49,* 289–318.

Schacter, D. L., Reiman, E., Curran, T., Yun, L. S., Bandy, D., & McDermott, K. B. (1996). Neuroanatomical correlates of veridical and illusory recognition memory: Evidence from positron emission tomography. *Neuron, 17,* 267–274.

Schank, R. C. (1982). *Dynamic memory.* Cambridge, England: Cambridge University Press.

Schnider, A., & Ptak, R. (1999). Spontaneous confabulators fail to suppress currently irrelevant memory traces. *Nature Neuroscience, 2,* 677–681.

Shallice, T. (1988). *From neuropsychology to mental structure.* Cambridge, England: Cambridge University Press.

Shallice, T., Fletcher, P. C., Frith, C. D., Grasby, P., Frackowiak, R. S. J., & Dolan, R. J. (1994). Brain regions associated with the acquisition and retrieval of verbal episodic memory. *Nature, 386,* 633–635.

Slamecka, N. J. (1968). An examinatin of trace storage in free recall. *Journal of Experimental Psychology, 76,* 504–513.

Stuss, D. T., Alexander, M. P., Palumbo, C. L., Buckle, L., Sayer, L., & Pogue, J. (1994). Organizational strategies of patients with unilateral or bilateral frontal lobe injury in word list learning tasks. *Neuropsychology, 8,* 355–373.

Talairach, J., & Tournoux, P. (1988). *Co-planar stereotaxic atlas of the human brain.* Stuttgart, Germany: George Thieme Verlag.

Taylor, T. J., & Di Scenna, P. (1986). The hippocampal memory indexing theory. *Behavioural Neuroscience, 100,* 147–154.

Tulving, E. (1983). *Elements of episodic memory.* New York: Oxford University Press.

Tulving, E. (1985). Memory and consciousness. *Canadian Journal of Psychology, 26,* 1–12.

Tulving, E., Kapur, S., Craik, F. I. M., Moscovitch, M., & Houle, S. (1994). Hemispheric encoding/ retrieval asymmetry in episodic memory: Positron emission tomography findings. *Proceedings of the National Academy of Sciences, USA, 91,* 2016–2020.

Tulving, E., Kapur, S., Markowitsch, J. J., Craik, F. I. M., Habib, R., & Houle, S. (1994). Neuroanatomical correlates of retrieval in episodic memory: Auditory sentence recognition. *Proceedings of the National Academy of Sciences, USA, 91,* 2012–2015.

Wagner, A. D., Poldrack, R. A., Eldridge, I. I., Desmond, J. E., Glover, G. H., & Gabrieli, J. D. E. (1998). Material-specific lateralization of prefrontal activation during episodic encoding and retrieval. *NeuroReport, 9,* 3711–3717.

Wilkins, A., Shallice, T., & McCarthy, R. (1987). Frontal lesions and sustained attention. *Neuropsychologia, 25,* 359–365.

CHAPTER

Joan M. McDowd

Levels of Processing in Selective Attention and Inhibition: Age Differences and Similarities

Many contemporary theories of cognitive aging include notions of qualitative differences in cognitive processing between age groups and/or age-related reductions in information processing resources. The inclusion of these concepts reflects the influence that Gus Craik's work in levels of processing (Craik & Lockhart, 1972; Craik & Simon, 1980; Craik & Tulving, 1975) and cognitive resources (e.g., Craik & Byrd, 1982; Craik, Govoni, Naveh-Benjamin, & Anderson, 1996) has had and continues to have in the development of cognitive aging theories (for reviews, see Craik & Anderson, 1999; Zacks, Hasher, & Li, 2000; McDowd & Shaw, 2000). As will become clear in the present chapter, each of these ideas has also had an influence on my thinking about aging, selective attention, and inhibitory function.

☐ Inhibitory Function in Aging: Negative Priming

The notion that inhibitory function might be an important explanatory concept for understanding cognitive aging was put forth by Hasher and Zacks in 1988. They suggested that age-related declines in inhibitory function account for many age-related cognitive deficits. This framework spawned a variety of studies designed to measure inhibitory processes in old and young adults, and much of this work has been carried out in the context of the negative priming paradigm. In a typical negative priming task, a series of displays are presented in which the participant is required to select and respond to a target stimulus and ignore any distracting stimuli. Negative priming results when the distractor in one display (typically called the "prime" display) is re-presented as a target in the very next display (typically called the "probe" display), producing response slowing. The theoretical interpretation of this lengthening of response times in negative priming is as an indication that inhibitory processes acted to exclude distractors from further processing. This inhibition then delays access to a stimulus when it is re-presented as a target on the next trial. The magnitude of slowing is taken as an index of the strength or efficiency of inhibitory function.

Initial findings with negative priming tasks (Hasher, Stoltzfus, Zacks, & Rypma, 1991;

McDowd & Oseas-Kreger, 1991; Tipper, 1991) supported the hypothesis that older adults were characterized by a decline in inhibitory prowess. However, other findings following this initial set of confirmatory studies indicated that the hypothesis of a general, age-related decline in inhibitory function had to be modified in light of data indicating multiple types of inhibition, as revealed by different types of negative priming tasks. Connelly and Hasher (1993) devised a set of manipulations to illustrate two classes of negative priming tasks: those involving identity suppression and those involving location suppression. Identity negative priming is indexed by slowing relative to control conditions (Figure 11.1a) on trials when the to-be-named target has the same identity as the to-be-suppressed distractor on the just-previous trial (Figure 11.1b). Location negative priming is indexed by a slowing of reaction times on trials in which a target stimulus appears in the same location as the to-be-suppressed distractor has appeared on the just-previous trial (Figure 11.1c). Connelly and Hasher's findings indicated a dissociation in inhibitory function among older adults: Age-related inhibitory deficits were observed in conditions requiring identity suppression, but age equivalence was observed in location suppression conditions. A number of other studies replicated this pattern of results (Kane, Hasher, Stoltzfus, Zacks, & Connelly, 1994; McDowd & Filion, 1995; Stoltzfus, Hasher, Zacks, Ulivi, & Goldstein, 1993).

Although this differentiation of types of inhibition provided a useful framework for describing age differences and similarities, its utility did not last long. Several other studies that did not fit the pattern appeared in the literature. Work by Sullivan and Faust (1993), Schooler, Neumann, Caplin, and Roberts (1997), and Kramer, Humphries, Larish,

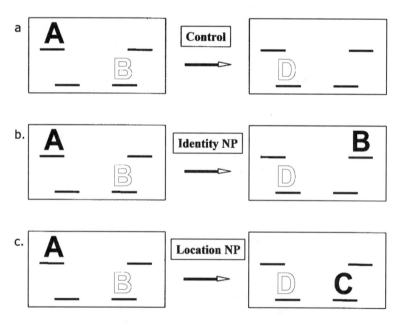

FIGURE 11.1. Stimulus displays from Connelly and Hasher (1993). Target letters to be named are shown in black; distractor letters are shown in outline. The control condition is shown in (a), identity negative priming condition in (b), and location negative priming condition in (c).

and Logan (1994) demonstrated equivalent identity negative priming in young and old adults. These findings appear to put us back to square one in terms of understanding aging and inhibitory function, and the difficulty of integrating these findings into a coherent framework has led to much frustration in the field and a virtual abandonment of the negative priming task in cognitive aging. While recognizing that there are a variety of complexities associated with interpreting data from negative priming tasks (May, Kane, & Hasher, 1995; Neill, Valdes, Terry, & Gorfein, 1992; Park & Kanwisher, 1994), there still may be some things to be learned from already existing literature that would advance the field (cf. McDowd, 1997). The goal of the present analysis is to examine task parameters that may shed some light on the seemingly inconsistent pattern of findings. The remainder of this chapter will describe this task analysis and some emerging theoretical ideas for organizing patterns of data.

☐ Levels of Processing in Selective Attention

To preview, the framework proposed here is based on the idea that whenever possible, older adults adopt an early selection processing mode based on perceptual, or surface, features, whereas young adults adopt a late selection processing mode, based on meaning or stimulus identity. Here the influence of the original levels-of-processing framework is obvious; drawing on a substantial body of work on aging and memory indicates that older adults are more likely to engage in processing of perceptual features of to-be-remembered information, whereas young adults process semantic features of information (e.g., Craik, 1977; Craik & Byrd, 1982; Rabinowitz, Craik, & Ackerman, 1982). In addition, some types of perceptual processing may be more demanding for old than young adults (cf. Maylor & Lavie, 1998; Plude & Doussard-Roosevelt, 1989), reducing resources available for extended semantic analyses (the issue of perceptual load is raised again later in this chapter).

In the context of selective attention, the levels-of-processing framework predicts that the extent of processing differs between old and young adults, with different implications for inhibitory function. When applied to a negative priming task such as that reported by Connelly and Hasher (1993, Experiment 3, described above), this framework provides the following analysis: In very general terms, when faced with the task of naming a red letter and ignoring a green one, the information processing sequence for older adults' early selection requires inhibition on the basis of some physical characteristic such as color, so that nontarget information does not reach identification stages. The late selection version of this process adopted by younger adults has all stimuli reaching identification stages and requires inhibition of a stimulus representation that includes both location and identity information. Hence, both identity- and location-based negative priming are observed among young adults, whereas older adults produce only location-based negative priming.

Logically, then, given this framework, it makes perfect sense that older adults do not show evidence of suppressing the *identity* of the distractor in the Connelly and Hasher (1993) task. The task asks only, "What is the red letter?" Selection of the target for naming requires only an analysis of surface features: the color of the two display objects. Surface-level analysis is sufficient to select target information and to suppress nontarget information. The framework proposed here argues that older adults do not process the nontarget display objects any more deeply than that, and the Connelly and Hasher data showing only location-based suppression among older adults are consistent with that argument.

☐ Age Differences in Features Guiding Selection: Preliminary Findings

One conclusion from this line of reasoning is that older adults do not have an inhibitory deficit; rather, they inhibit different features of the display than young adults do. Given this possibility, it may be that other studies reporting an age deficit in identity suppression may not have considered the possibility of maintained location-based suppression. It may be that the type of inhibition you observe depends on the type of inhibition you look for, and not all studies have examined both identity and location suppression, as Connelly and Hasher (1993) did. For example, Kane, Hasher, Stoltzfus, Zachs, and Connelly (1994) designed a negative priming task using a vertical array of two words. The task was to name the red or green word and ignore the other one. Kane et al. (1994) analyzed naming time data for identity suppression and found none among older adults, concluding that aging is associated with a decline in inhibitory function.

However, in the Kane et al. (1994) task, identity suppression is confounded with location suppression. Because there are only two locations in which words might appear, probe targets appear in either the same location as the prime target (which likely involves location facilitation) or the same location as the prime distractor (which has been shown to produce location suppression). Thus location effects may be producing either speeding or slowing, depending on condition, and these effects may be masked by collapsing across these "location" conditions in the analysis of identity-based effects.

To test the idea that location-based inhibitory function would be observed among older adults, a replication of the Kane et al. (1994) study was designed, with the addition of conditions that would disentangle location-based and identity-based suppression. The stimulus display was modeled after the design of the Connelly and Hasher (1993) task, including four possible locations (Figure 11.2). The word identity task of Kane et al. was

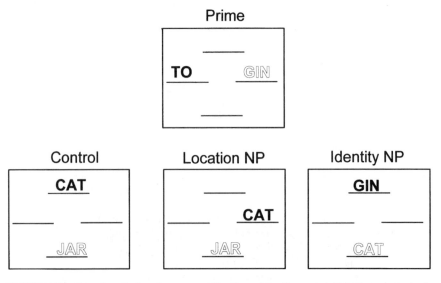

FIGURE 11.2. Stimulus displays from a modification of the Kane et al. (1994) study, including control, location negative priming, and identity negative priming conditions. To-be-named target words are shown in black; distractors are shown in outline.

maintained, requiring participants to name the word in the target color. If older adults use location suppression in support of an early-selection processing mode, then their intact location-based inhibitory function should be observed when given the opportunity to do so, as in the present task.

Preliminary findings based on 22 young adults and 20 older adults are shown in Figure 11.3. Young but not old adults show slowing in the identity suppression condition; although the effect is small (7 ms), it is approximately the same size as reported by Connelly and Hasher (1993), who used a similar display (8 ms). However, old adults do show significant location-based inhibition (34 ms slowing), as do young adults (20 ms slowing). Thus, in the Kane et al. (1994) study, older adults may have had intact (location-based) inhibitory function, but the relevant conditions were not compared in their analysis.

From the point of view of the early/late selection framework presented here, these preliminary results show that when available, older adults will use surface features in an early-selection processing mode that produces location-based negative priming. One alternative to this interpretation is that older adults do process the identity of the distractors, but they do not suppress that information. However, if this were the case, then speeded probe target naming would be expected in the negative priming condition because it becomes, functionally, a repetition priming condition. However, no such speeding is observed in the present data. Thus, this pattern of results indicates that older adults use location suppression to accomplish selective information processing.

Given this interpretation in terms of location suppression, one interesting question might be whether older adults can be forced to process both target and distractor to the level of identity as young adults do, and if so, would the pattern of suppression and negative priming be the same for both age groups? This question was examined (McDowd & Filion, 1995) in a task that required processing of both target and distractor to the level of identity in order to make a correct response. Although a typical identity negative priming task involves displays containing a "target" to be identified and a "distractor" to be ignored, the empirical finding of identity negative priming assumes that *both* target and distractor are identified before the distractor is suppressed. Thus the present task required that both target and distractor be identified in order to simulate the level of processing assumed to underlie identity negative priming. Of interest was the stimulus characteristic (identity and/or location) that would be suppressed by young and old adults.

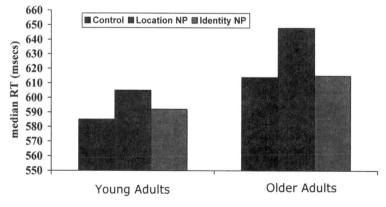

FIGURE 11.3. Data from the four-location word-naming negative priming task, from young and old adults in control, location negative priming, and identity negative priming conditions.

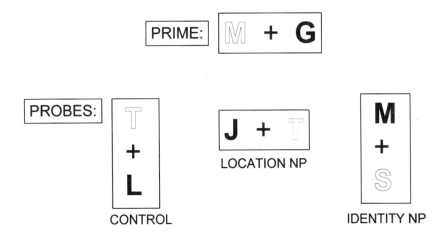

FIGURE 11.4. Stimulus displays for three probe conditions from the alphabet and color tasks. Target letters to be named are shown in black, distractors are shown in outline.

The experimental task, referred to as the alphabet task, required participants to decide which of two letters appears earlier in the alphabet, and to name that letter. Each display contained two letters separated in space, one red and one green (see Figure 11.4). Color and location were irrelevant to the task; both "target" and "distractor" had to be processed to the level of identity in order to perform the task. Trials were set up to assess both identity suppression and location suppression. Of interest is the fate of the distractor: Would it be subject to suppression based on location or identity? Would the pattern of suppression be the same for young and old adults?

A control task was also included, referred to as the color task, which required participants to simply name the letter in the target (red or green) color, so that selection and inhibition could be carried out on color (as in the Connelly & Hasher, 1993, study). Stimulus displays were identical to those used in the alphabet task, and trials were set up as prime-probe pairs designed to assess both location-based and identity-based suppression. In this case it was expected that location suppression would be observed in both young and old adults; in addition, young adults but not older adults would produce identity suppression as they had in Connelly and Hasher (1993).

Data from the color task are presented in Figure 11.5a. These data indicate that when selection can be carried out using a perceptual feature of the display (color), both young and older adults show evidence of location-based distractor suppression. Neither age group shows significant identity-based suppression, a finding that doesn't replicate Connelly and Hasher (1993). However, the present data are consistent with other work outside of the negative priming paradigm showing that distractor location is subject to inhibition in selective attention tasks (e.g., Cave & Pashler, 1995; Cepeda, Cave, Bichot, & Kim, 1998).

Data from the alphabet task are shown in Figure 11.5b. These data suggest that when both stimuli in a display have to be processed in order to perform the task, young and old use different suppression mechanisms to prevent the nontarget from interfering with response processes. Young adults show evidence of suppressing the identity of the nontarget, whereas older adults show evidence of suppression of nontarget location. Thus, when target and distractor occupy separate locations, even though target and distractor identity must be processed for the task, location appears to be the primary stimulus parameter that is subject to inhibition among older adults.

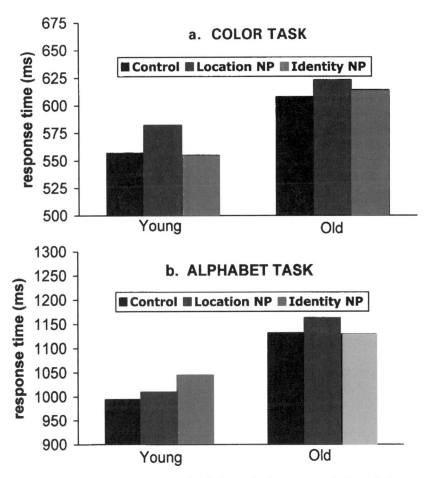

FIGURE 11.5. Data from the color and alphabet tasks for young and old adults in control, location negative priming, and identity negative priming conditions.

The data from young adults in the color and alphabet tasks are very similar to that reported by Cave and Pashler (1995), who reported data from a set of tasks designed to evaluate the role of location in a selective attention task. The first task required subjects to view a series of colored digits, presented in pairs. One digit in each pair was presented in green, the target color, and the other was red, the distractor. At the end of the series, the task was to report the target digit with the largest value, ignoring all distractors. The task was performed under two conditions: (1) all target digits appeared in the same location relative to distractors, intended to maximize performance if selective attention is location-based; and (2) target digits appeared in alternating locations relative to distractors, intended to be more difficult with a location-based attention mechanism. The results (testing only young adults) indicate that performance in the same location condition was better than the alternating location condition, even when location was irrelevant to the task. They conclude from this finding that visual selection is based on location, at least for tasks such as this one.

Cave and Pashler (1995) further tested the role of location in selective attention with a second type of task, similar in structure to the one just described, but involving mixed pairs of digits and letters instead of only digits. Again the task was to focus on the digits, ignoring the letters, and report the digit with the largest value. Across a set of experiments, target and distractor characters in a pair were both black, both red or green but free to vary pair to pair, or one red and one green in each pair. In any case, color did not predict target/distractor category, and both stimuli had to be processed in order to identify the digit and perform the task. In each of these experiments, same versus different target location did not affect task performance (again, only young adults were tested). Cave and Pashler suggested that "by the time a character has been sufficiently processed to determine its category, there may be nothing to gain by subjecting it to location-based facilitation or inhibition" (pp. 427–428). Although their task did not permit assessment of identity-based inhibition, their analysis of location-based inhibition fits the data from the young adults on the present alphabet task.

The older adults, however, do not show the same pattern. That is, even though targets and distractors are both processed to the level of identity in the alphabet task, older adults continue to show evidence of suppression based on stimulus location. Thus for them, even after processing stimuli sufficiently to determine identity, there is apparently something to gain by subjecting the nontarget information to location-based inhibition. In other words, even after deeper processing of display items, inhibition is directed at shallow, perceptual features of the stimuli.

☐ Mechanisms of Levels of Processing in Attention

These general notions about levels of processing, early versus late selection, and identity versus location suppression could be made even more powerful if combined with a specific mechanism that might produce the pattern of results predicted by the framework. There are at least two candidate models already in the literature that might be used to account for the pattern of results described here: LaBerge and Brown's (1989) model of attention in shape identification and Cave's (1999) FeatureGate model. Following is a brief sketch of how the LaBerge and Brown model might account for the pattern of age differences and similarities observed in negative priming.

LaBerge and Brown (1989) proposed a model with four basic components: (1) a feature register, which records features such as lines, colors, contours, and motion, as well as the location of those features; (2) an attentional filter, which facilitates and inhibits the transmission of information at certain locations; (3) a shape identifier to answer "What is it?" questions, and (4) a position analyzer to answer "Where is it?" questions. Higher order processes direct the operation of these components for any given task. To understand how this model works to produce negative priming, consider the Connelly and Hasher (1993) location suppression task (See Figure 11.1c). The task is to name the red letter and ignore the green letter. Higher order processes instruct the feature register to increase the flow of information from the red object to the filter. The filter operates as a spatial map, registering the *location* of the objects detected by the feature register. When the flow of information to the location of the red object represented in the filter map begins to increase, information at the other location begins to be suppressed. This amplification/suppression process produced by the lateral inhibitory network of the filter mechanism eventually produces a sufficient flow of information at the target location to open an attentional channel between the feature register and the shape identifier. Information is passed on to the shape identifier via this channel, the red letter is identified, and an identity response is made.

The suppression of a location at the level of the filter mechanism could produce the phenomenon of negative priming if on the next trial, the target is presented to that suppressed location. That is, the opening of an attentional channel would be delayed while the previous suppression is overcome. Thus the processing of location does not need to be an explicit aspect of the task; location suppression is produced by the characteristics of the filter.

Although this model can produce location negative priming, given the model's function as described above, identity suppression would never be produced when target and distractor differ on some perceptual feature. Thus older adults' data can be accommodated, but some modification of the model is required to explain the empirical finding of identity suppression among young adults. One possible modification would be to postulate an inhibitory function for the shape identifier. If the system uses the shape identifier to consider each object in the array instead of relying solely on color to produce differential activation at the filter mechanism, identity negative priming could be produced. Higher order processes inform the shape identifier that the to-be-named object must be red. If the first item or items to be identified are not red, the shape identifier could exert some inhibitory process against them that is then communicated to the filter, where location suppression is also directed at the rejected item. This process is repeated until a red match is found. Although this inhibitory function in the shape identifier is not part of LaBerge and Brown's (1989) original model, the iterative search process is part of the model that explains performance when target location is uncertain. Inhibition in the shape identifier may be necessary to expand the applicability of the model—with this addition, the model could produce both identity and location negative priming in a manner consistent with the young adults' data of Connelly and Hasher (1993).

A related issue is whether the model can explain the pattern of findings from studies showing comparable identity negative priming in young and old adults. Kramer et al. (1994) used a four-letter stimulus array, with the letters arranged like the four points on a compass. Each display contained one unique target (indicated by an underline) and three identical distractors. According to the LaBerge and Brown (1989) model, at the level of the feature register, there is lateral inhibition of similar features. Because the distractors all have the same identity in this task, their features might be inhibited very early on in the stream of information processing. Identity negative priming could have resulted from an inhibition of perceptual features rather than identity per se, without any "late" inhibition from the shape identifier. This view makes the straightforward prediction that if lateral inhibition was masquerading as identity suppression, presenting different distractors should eliminate the identity-based effects.

A different tack is required to account for the data of Sullivan and Faust (1993) and Schooler et al. (1997). Both of these tasks used displays involving superimposed stimuli; Sullivan and Faust used overlapping pictures, and Schooler et al. used overlapping pictures and overlapping words. In both studies, participants were required to name the picture or word presented in the target color and ignore the other picture or word. In terms of the LaBerge and Brown model, higher order processes may attempt to instruct the feature register to increase transmission of information about the target object. However, because the filter mechanism registers only location information, and because target and nontarget occupy nearly the same location in space, information about both objects may be sent to the shape identifier. There, features will have to be parsed into objects, and both objects may be identified. If both are identified, the identity of the nontarget object must then be inhibited to assure an accurate identity response. In this situation older adults may be forced to use this late selection processing mode because display features are inadequate to depend on the spatial filter. The framework suggested here makes the straightforward prediction that if the two objects are separated in space, older adults would again use the spatial filter and show evidence of location-based suppression of nontarget information.

☐ Resource Accounts of Age Differences in Selective Attention: Perceptual Load

An important question for the framework proposed here is, of course, *why* older adults might prefer an early selection mode, whereas young adults use a late selection mode. Recent ideas about perceptual load may be useful in this regard (e.g., Lavie, 1995). That is, perceptual processing of almost any display may be functionally more demanding for old than young adults, leaving older adults less capacity for processing nontarget information and hence obviating any necessity to suppress meaning-based information. Only when the task requires it will older adults process nontarget information to a level deeper than a perceptual analysis, and only when they have no alternative (i.e., location cues are not present) will they suppress meaning-based information. Young adults, having more spare capacity, may process all display information to the deeper level of meaning, and typically suppress meaning-based nontarget information. Maylor and Lavie (1998) have recently provided one demonstration in which increasing perceptual load affected old adults before young adults. Although more work needs to be done on the parameters of perceptual load that are particularly difficult for older adults, Maylor and Lavie's findings do suggest that this notion may be useful in explaining age differences in selective attention.

☐ Summary

In summary then, the data reviewed here indicate that older adults do not have an inhibitory deficit per se. The pattern of results across studies does suggest that older adults typically use different features for selection and suppression than do young adults, and the presence or absence of age differences appears to depend on the perceptual affordances of the visual display and the processing requirements of the task. It appears that when the task permits, older adults select target information based on perceptual features (such as color), using an early selection processing mode (e.g., Connelly & Hasher, 1993, Experiment 3; Kane et al., 1994). However, regardless of whether the task allows early selection (based on surface features) or requires late selection (based on identity), if target and distractor are spatially separated, older adults suppress information from the location of nontarget information (e.g., the alphabet task described above). Negative priming data from young adults, on the other hand, indicate that they process and suppress both location and meaning-based information regardless of display characteristics or task requirements (Connelly & Hasher, 1993; Kane et al., 1994). And finally, if stimulus displays do not include spatial separation of target and distractor (to support early selection and/or location-based suppression), older adults are able to suppress meaning-based information (Schooler et al., 1997; Sullivan & Faust, 1993). This latter finding is reminiscent of other levels-of-processing studies of age differences in memory, in which older adults are observed not to process information deeply when left to their own devices; but the studies demonstrate that they can process information deeply when required to or encouraged to by an orienting task (e.g., Smith, 1977).

The findings reviewed here demonstrate that different tasks and different task demands can produce different patterns of inhibitory activity. These task demands, along with chronological age, appear to have a role in determining the processing components at which inhibition is directed. The present analysis in terms of shallow and deep processing (corresponding to early and late selection, respectively) suggests that inhibition may exert its influence at various stages in an information processing sequence. Hasher and colleagues (Hasher, Zacks, & May, 1999) have captured some of this variability with their taxonomy of three functions of inhibition: access, deletion, and restraint. The access function prevents irrelevant information from entering working memory; this function may be operating in tasks such as the color task and the modified Kane task described above. The deletion function acts to eliminate once-relevant information from working memory so that it does not interfere with ongoing processing; this function may be operating in tasks such as the alphabet task described here (see also MacDonald, Joordens, & Seergobin, 1999). And finally, the restraint function operates on response processes to prevent dominant response tendencies from always controlling behavior, as when habits must be suppressed to accomplish alternate actions. This taxonomy suggests that a fairly sophisticated analysis of stimulus characteristics and processing demands will be required for a complete understanding of inhibitory function in aging.

The framework presented here provides a basis for integrating the seemingly disparate findings with regard to aging and negative priming in terms of early selection and location-based suppression. The LaBerge and Brown (1989) model provides a mechanism to explain *how* the observed pattern of results might be produced. The more difficult *why* question was broached with the concept of perceptual load, a characteristic of the visual display that could lead to an early selection mode. Together, these ideas provide a direction for research that will lead to a better understanding of age differences in selective attention and inhibitory function.

☐ Acknowledgments

Preparation of this chapter was supported in part by the National Institute on Aging (AG07991).

☐ References

Cave, K. R. (1999). The FeatureGate model of visual selection. *Psychological Research, 62,* 182–194.

Cave, K. R., & Pashler, H. (1995). Visual selection mediated by location: Selecting successive visual objects. *Perception and Psychophysics, 57,* 421–432.

Cepeda, N. J., Cave, K. R., Bichot, N. P., & Kim, M. (1998). Spatial selection via feature-driven inhibition of distractor locations. *Perception & Psychophysics, 60,* 727–746.

Connelly, S. L., & Hasher, L. (1993). Aging and the inhibition of spatial location. *Journal of Experimental Psychology: Human Perception and Performance, 19,* 1238–1250.

Craik, F. I. M. (1977). Age differences in human memory. In J.E. Birren & K.W. Schaie (Eds), *Handbook of the psychology of aging* (pp. 384–420). New York: Van Nostrand Reinhold.

Craik, F. I. M., & Anderson, N. D. (1999). Applying cognitive research to problems of aging. In D. Gopher & A. Koriat (Eds.), *Attention and performance XVII* (pp. 583–615). Cambridge, MA: MIT Press.

Craik, F. I. M., & Byrd, M. (1982). Aging and cognitive deficits: The role of attentional resources. In F. I. M. Craik & S. Trehub (Eds.), *Aging and cognitive processes* (pp. 191–211). New York: Plenum Press.

Craik, F. I. M., Govoni, R., Naveh-Benjamin, M., & Anderson, N. D. (1996). The effects of divided attention on encoding and retrieval processes in human memory. *Journal of Experimenal Psychology: General, 125,* 159–180.

Craik, F. I. M., & Lockhart, R. S. (1972). Levels of processing: a framework for memory research. *Journal of Verbal Learning and Verbal Behavior, 11,* 671–684.

Craik, F. I. M., & Simon, E. (1980). Age differences in memory: The roles of attention and depth of processing. In L. W. Poon, J. L. Fozard, L. S. Cermak, D. Arenberg, & L. W. Thompson (Eds.), *New directions in memory and aging: Proceedings of the George Talland Memorial Conference* (pp. 95–112). Hillsdale, NJ: Erlbaum.

Craik, F. I. M., & Tulving, E. (1975). Depth of processing and the retention of words in episodic memory. *Journal of Experimental Psychology: General, 104,* 268–294.

Hasher, L., Stoltzfus, E. R., Zacks, R. T., & Rypma, B. (1991). Aging and inhibition. *Journal of Experimental Psychology: Learning, Memory, and Cognition, 17,* 163–169.

Hasher, L., & Zacks, R. T. (1988). Working memory, comprehension, and aging: A review and a new view. In G. H. Bower (Ed.), *The psychology of learning and motivation* (Vol. 22, pp. 193–225). Orlando, FL: Academic Press.

Hasher, L., Zacks, R. T., & May, C. P. (1999). Inhibitory control, circadian arousal, and age. In D. Gopher & A. Koriat (Eds.), *Attention and performance XVII* (pp. 653–675). Cambridge, MA: MIT Press.

Kane, M. J., Hasher, L., Stoltzfus, E. R., Zacks, R. T., & Connelly, S. L. (1994). Inhibitory attentional mechanisms and aging. *Psychology and Aging, 9,* 103–112.

Kramer, A. F., Humphrey, D. G., Larish, J. F., & Logan, G. D. (1994). Aging and inhibition: Beyond a unitary view of inhibitory processing in attention. *Psychology & Aging, 9,* 491–512.

LaBerge, D., & Brown, V. (1989). Theory of attentional operations in shape identification. *Psychological Review, 96,* 101–124.

Lavie, N. (1995). Perceptual load as a necessary condition for selective attention. *Journal of Experimental Psychology: Human Perception and Performance, 21,* 451–468.

MacDonald, P.A., Joordens, S., & Seergobin, K.N. (1999). Negative priming effects that are bigger than a breadbox: attention to distractors does not eliminate negative priming, it enhances it. *Memory & Cognition, 27,* 197–207.

May, C. P., Kane, M. J., & Hasher, L. (1995). Determinants of negative priming. *Psychological Bulletin, 118,* 35–54.

Maylor, E. A., & Lavie, N. (1998). The influence of perceptual load on age differences in selective attention. *Psychology and Aging, 13,* 563–573.

McDowd, J. M. (1997). Inhibition in attention and aging. *Journal of Gerontology: Psychological Sciences, 52B,* 265–273.

McDowd, J. M., & Filion, D. L. (1995). Aging and negative priming in a location suppression task: The long and the short of it. *Psychology and Aging, 10,* 34–47.

McDowd, J. M., & Oseas-Kreger, D. M. (1991). Aging, inhibitory processes, and negative priming. *Journal of Gerontology: Psychological Sciences, 46,* 340–345.

McDowd, J. M., & Shaw, R. J. (2000). Attention and aging: a functional perspective. In F. I. M. Craik & T. A. Salthouse (Eds.), *Handbook of aging and cognition* (2nd ed., pp. 221–292). Mahwah, NJ: Erlbaum.

Neill, W. T., Valdes, L. A., Terry, K. M., & Gorfein, D. S. (1992). The persistence of negative priming: II. Evidence for episodic trace retrieval. *Journal of Experimental Psychology: Learning, Memory, and Cognition, 18,* 993–1000.

Park, J., & Kanwisher, N. (1994). Negative priming for spatial location: Identity mismatching, not distractor inhibition. *Journal of Experimental Psychology: Human Perception and Performance, 20,* 613–623.

Plude, D. J., & Doussard-Roosevelt, J. A. (1989). Aging, selective attention, and feature integration. *Psychology and Aging, 4,* 98–105.

Rabinowitz, J. C., Craik, F. I. M., & Ackerman, B. P. (1982). A processing resource account of age differences in recall. *Canadian Journal of Psychology, 36,* 325–344.

Schooler, C., Neumann, E., Caplin, L. J., & Roberts, B. R. (1997). Continued inhibitory capacity throughout adulthood: Conceptual negative priming in younger and older adults. *Psychology and Aging, 12,* 667–674.

Smith, A. D. (1977). Adult age differences in cued recall. *Developmental Psychology, 13,* 326–331.

Stoltzfus, E. R., Hasher, L., Zacks, R. T., Ulivi, M. S., & Goldstein, D. (1993). Investigations of inhibition and interference in younger and older adults. *Journal of Gerontology: Psychological Sciences, 48,* P179–P188.

Sullivan, M. P., & Faust, M. E. (1993). Evidence for identity inhibition during selective attention in old adults. *Psychology and Aging, 8,* 589–598.

Tipper, S. P. (1991). Less attentional selectivity as a result of declining inhibition in older adults. *Bulletin of the Psychonomic Society, 29,* 45–47.

Zacks, R. T., Hasher, L., & Li, K. Z. H. (2000). Human memory. In F. I. M. Craik & T. A. Salthouse (Eds.), *Handbook of aging and cognition* (2nd ed., pp. 293–357). Mahwah, NJ: Erlbaum.

Denise C. Park
Trey Hedden

Working Memory and Aging

There is a large body of scientific evidence, as well as a great deal of anecdotal, self-report data, suggesting that as people age, they are not as mentally "sharp" as they used to be. In a seminal paper on the topic of aging and memory, Craik and Byrd (1982) suggested that with increasing age, the amount of mental energy or cognitive reserves available to perform mental operations declines. According to Craik and Byrd, this reduction in attentional resources (also termed processing resources) accounts for many of the age-related declines observed on a broad range of memory tasks, particularly those tasks that require a great deal of mental effort or "self-initiated processing" (p. 203). Craik and Byrd suggested that there are conditions under which memory tasks can be highly supported (e.g., recognition), and that under these conditions, age differences in memory are smaller. Various types of environmental support can repair some of the memory declines resulting from diminished processing resources that occur with age. Implicit in this view of decreased mental energy with age is the assumption that individuals may vary in the amount of energy or processing resources that they have and that, presumably, individuals with more resources will perform better on memory tasks. Craik, Byrd, and Swanson (1987), in an early study, investigated this individual differences approach to processing resources. They compared the memories of three groups of elderly people who presumably varied in processing resources to those of young adults. They reported that healthy, engaged, high-income adults had performance most similar to young adults, that low income but engaged older adults were intermediate in their cognitive performance, and that older individuals who were both low in income and activities performed most poorly. There was also evidence that memory function was modulated by type of task and the amount of environmental support that it offered. They argued that these findings supported the notion of modulation of aging effects by environmental support and the quantity of processing resources an individual possessed.

At about the same time that the processing resources/environmental support hypothesis of cognitive aging was advanced, Baddeley advanced his conception of working memory. Working memory, according to Baddeley (1986) and Baddeley and Hitch (1974), can be viewed as the amount of cognitive storage and processing capacity that an individual brings to bear in any given situation. It is the amount of information that an individual can simultaneously store, retrieve, and manipulate on his or her mental desktop and is strictly limited in capacity. Moreover, working memory consists of an active central executive processing system with two passive storage or slave components—one visuospatial and one verbal—that feed into the central executive. Many measures of working memory capacity have been developed that include both storage and processing components. Two well known such tasks are reading span (Daneman & Carpenter, 1980) and computation span (Salthouse & Babcock, 1991). Both of these tasks involve the storage of information while simultaneously performing mental operations on other information. In the reading span task, participants must answer questions about sentences while remembering the final word in each sentence. In the computation span task, participants must solve mathematical equations while remembering the second digit in each equation. Span is measured as the number of words or digits that a participant can recall while correctly answering the questions or solving the equations.

These two conceptions—first, that age-related decline in long-term memory and performance on many cognitive tasks is due to decreased mental energy, and second, that this mental energy can be measured or operationalized as working memory—have been the focus of a decade-long research program in our lab. In this chapter, we examine first the role of working memory in understanding age-related declines on a range of cognitive tasks, including picture memory, spatial memory, verbal long-term memory, object assembly, and prospective memory. As our work in this area progressed, we began to develop sophisticated structural equation models to understand the interrelationships among different conceptions of processing resource (e.g., speed of processing compared to working memory) and the relationships of these resource measures to long-term memory. Models of aging, working memory, and long-term memory are the second major focus of this chapter. In the third section, we consider the contributions of inhibitory mechanisms to the function of working memory with age. In the final section, we describe research that addresses the role that changes in working memory function with age have for practical everyday behaviors—making medical judgments and decisions, remembering news information presented in television, radio, and newsprint formats, and taking medications correctly.

☐ Working Memory as an Individual Differences Variable

The interest in working memory as an individual differences variable mediating age-related decrements in performance on a range of cognitive tasks has a long history. First, it is important to note that working memory does decline with age when measures of reading span and computation span (described earlier) are used (Park et al., 1996; Salthouse & Babcock, 1991). In an early study, Stine and Wingfield (1987) reported that working memory mediated age-related variance on a speech recall task. Salthouse and colleagues also demonstrated that working memory mediated age-related differences on laboratory and reasoning tasks (Salthouse 1991, 1992, 1993a; Verhaeghen & Salthouse, 1997). In our own laboratory, we have conducted a number of studies investigating the relationship of working memory function to performance on visuospatial as well as verbal tasks. What is particularly unique to our work is that we have examined sufficient experimental conditions and numbers of subjects to compare the amount of age-related variance explained by working memory across experimental conditions, so that we can determine under what circumstances working memory is more important or less important in explaining age differences. Besides allowing us to determine specific conditions where working memory is important for understanding cognitive aging, these studies generally indicate that working memory explains a great deal of age-related variance on a range of complex tasks, supporting both the fundamental role of working memory in cognition hypothesized by

Baddeley (1986), and Craik and Byrd's (1982) hypothesis that declining "mental energy" (operationalized as working memory) explains age differences on a range of cognitive tasks.

Cherry and Park (1993) studied the contribution of working memory to understanding spatial long-term memory in older adults of two ability levels as well as young adults in a manner analogous to that of Craik et al. (1987). Subjects studied the location of everyday items in a spatial array under impoverished conditions (placed on a map with black and white landmarks) compared to the same items placed in an array with three-dimensional colored blocks hypothesized to provide additional environmental support for remembering the location of the items. Unlike Craik et al. (1987), Cherry and Park found little evidence that the less advantaged elderly were disproportionately influenced by environmental support. They did find, however, that much of the age-related variance on the spatial memory task was mediated by individual differences in working memory (as measured by a composite working memory measure comprised of listening span, size judgment span, and backward digit span). They also reported that working memory attenuated more age-related variance in the contextually rich, environmentally supported colored-block condition (78.9%) compared to the impoverished map condition where working memory explained only 42.7% of the age-related variance. It is as if those with greater working memory capacities were better able to utilize contextual support in this relatively difficult spatial reconstruction task.

In a related study, Frieske and Park (1993) examined the role of working memory in young and older adults' recognition of scenes. Participants studied complex scenes that were organized or unorganized and then made recognition judgments. In this study, unlike Cherry and Park (1993), subjects merely had to recognize information rather than actively recall the location of items in response to cues. Recognition performance was lower for disorganized scenes, in older adults compared to organized scenes and working memory (as measured by computation span) mediated more age-related variance for disorganized scenes (71.8%) compared to organized scenes (17.3%). In this case, it appears that working memory was more important in explaining age differences on the demanding task that was not supported by prior schematic knowledge. Finally, Morrell and Park (1993) examined the ability of young and old subjects to build complex three-dimensional figures from Lego blocks. Subjects received instructions that were entirely text-based, entirely illustrative, or that contained both text and illustrations. In all three conditions, working memory explained at least half of the age-related variance in the ability to correctly build the figures. However, more age-related variance was explained by verbal and spatial measures of working memory in the text only and text plus illustrations condition. In the illustration condition, spatial, but not verbal, working memory explained significant amounts of variance in the errors subjects made in putting together the blocks. Moreover, nearly half of the age-related variance remained unexplained in the illustration condition.

The findings from these studies suggest clearly that working memory is important in explaining age-related variance on a broad range of demanding cognitive tasks. The importance of working memory, however, varies greatly with the task demands, and as Craik and Jennings (1992) have noted, the relationships are not simply explained by the presence or absence of environmental support. To understand conditions under which working memory becomes particularly important for elderly subjects, one must consider the working memory operations required to use the environmental support. For instance, in Cherry and Park (1993), a study that required active recall, working memory was more important in the supported condition where subjects were provided with richer environmental cues. That is, the colored blocks were not related in any conceptual way to the items' spatial locations and therefore required active integration or mediation between the block and the item located near it for successful use of the cue. Thus, performing well on this "supported" task required considerable demands on working memory. Consistent with this explanation, Park, Smith, Morrell, Puglisi, and Dudley (1990) have demonstrated that older adults appear to be deficient in integration operations for unrelated targets and cues, a finding reinforced by A. D. Smith, Park, Earles, Shaw, & Whiting (1998). Working memory may have been less important in the unsupported condition because the task was so difficult that the subjects relied more on passive recognition and feelings of knowing rather than using active rehearsal strategies.

In Frieske and Park (1993), working memory was most important in the more demanding condition. In Frieske and Park (1993), however, participants performed a relatively passive recognition task when presented with a picture they had studied earlier, and they were required to determine if an item on this picture had been relocated. This is in contrast to the active recall task required in Cherry and Park (1993). In the case of an organized picture, participants may have relied on a feeling of familiarity and so working memory played a small role, whereas explicit retrieval processes were required for disorganized pictures. Jacoby (1999) and Jennings and Jacoby (1993) have clearly demonstrated that older adults have intact familiarity judgments and that familiarity processes are automatic, but that effortful processes for explicit retrieval are greatly impaired with age. Thus, working memory was highly related to the age differences in the disorganized but not organized scenes. The limited role of working memory in explaining age-related variance in the Morrell and Park (1993) study for a procedural assembly task when subjects were given only illustrations is also likely due to subjects' reliance on automatic, procedural processes. Working memory was more important in the text-based conditions because it relied on explicit, resource-intensive processes to link textual instructions to a procedural task.

Finally, in two studies on prospective memory, where subjects had to remember to press a key when a particular background pattern appeared while they were performing a working memory task, working memory performance had no relationship to prospective memory performance (Park, Hertzog, Kidder, Morrell, & Mayhorn, 1997; Kidder, Park, Hertzog, & Morrell, 1997). This again is likely due to the strong familiarity-based component of the prospective task in these studies and supports the notion advanced by Craik (1986) that prospective memory, when supported by external cues, does not require the deployment of large amounts of processing resources.

☐ Models of Memory: The Relationship of Aging, Speed of Processing, and Working Memory to Long-Term Memory

One major competing hypothesis to the view that declines in processing resource/working memory account for age-related declines in memory is the speed-of-processing view of cognitive aging (for extensive reviews, see Salthouse, 1993b, 1996). According to this view, it is a decrease in the rate at which mental operations are performed that accounts for age-related cognitive decline. Speed decreases account for cognitive declines on all other cognitive tasks because early mental operations associated with task performance are so slowed that later operations are never performed (limited time mechanism) and because the products of early operations are lost before later operations are completed (simultaneity mechanism). It is plausible that both working memory and speed of processing are different types of cognitive resources that make independent contributions to performance on long-term memory tasks and other higher order cognitive tasks. Surprisingly, there is little work that attempts to determine how these mechanisms operate together to explain age differences in cognitive function. Structural equation modeling (Joreskog, 1993) allows researchers to examine interrelationships among constructs and to determine their relative contributions to an outcome behavior. Park et al. (1996) utilized structural equation modeling to evaluate simultaneously the relative contributions of speed of processing and working memory function to three measures of long-term memory hypothesized to vary in their processing requirements: spatial memory, cued recall, and free recall. Spatial memory is hypothesized to be automatic and to have relatively low resource requirements (Hasher & Zacks, 1979); cued recall requires more cognitive resource than spatial memory, as it relies on explicit traces, but has more environmental support and less processing demand than free recall (Craik, 1986; Craik & Jennings, 1992). We hypothesized that these memory measures represent a continuum of resource requirements and that working memory would increasingly be implicated in explaining age-related variance on these tasks.

In Park et al. (1996), we adopted a life-span approach and tested 301 older adults, aged 20–90. Each subject received a 7-hour cognitive battery across 3 days. We included multiple measures of both perceptual speed and working memory. The working memory measures used had strong central executive demands (reading span, computation span, and backward digit), as they all required active manipulation of information as well as storage. The perceptual speed measures were digit–symbol, letter comparison, and pattern comparison. We thus examined the relationship of the latent constructs of working memory and speed to three types of long-term memory hypothesized to vary in effort and degree of contextual support. The structural model, which had excellent fit ($X^2(46)$ = 74.11, CFI = .99), indicated that all age-related variance operated through speed, in agreement with Salthouse (1996). However, both speed and working memory were important contributors to the three types of long-term memory. Both speed and working memory explained variance in the two more effortful tasks of free and cued recall, but only speed mediated variance in spatial recall. Thus, just as a processing resource view would predict, as memory became more effortful in the cued and free recall conditions, the contribution of working memory increased. By showing such direct connections using an individual differences approach, these findings addressed the complaint that depleted processing resources as a cause of aging is a circular argument (Light, 1991). That is, studies have invoked post hoc explanations such that tasks on which older adults perform more poorly (e.g., free recall) obviously take more processing resources because performance is so poor. We were able to demonstrate independent and joint contributions of two important mechanisms—speed of processing and working memory—to long-term memory, but explained age-related differences in performance on these tasks with the single mechanism of speed.

The use of structural equation modeling techniques to understand the relationship of working memory to long-term memory is an exciting and powerful approach. Park et al. (in press) used this approach to address the possibility that cognitive resources, although highly differentiated in young adults, may dedifferentiate with age. By dedifferentiation, we mean that distinct (e.g., visuospatial vs. verbal) pools of cognitive resource that characterize young adulthood develop into a single, more general resource with age. Behavioral data had provided some evidence for independent domain specificity of working memory function in young adults (Shah & Miyake, 1996). Neuroimaging data, however, supported the organization of working memory primarily in terms of a central executive, as described by Baddeley's (1986) model of working memory. In other words, studies have reported evidence for a strong domain-general central executive (D'Esposito et al., 1995; D'Esposito et al., 1998), with limited organization by content in domain-specific storage/rehearsal buffers that perform only limited functions, as described by D'Esposito et al. (1998) and E. E. Smith and Jonides (1999).

The concept of cognitive resource in aging has generally been one of a single, undifferentiated resource pool. There are two important lines of research that suggest cognitive resource is undifferentiated with age. First, Baltes and Lindenberger (1997) have advanced the common cause hypothesis of aging, suggesting that performance on a broad array of cognitive tasks is mediated by simple measures of visual and auditory acuity. They argue that these simple measures of sensory function reflect the underlying neural integrity of the individual and broadly predict performance on many cognitive tasks. Baltes and Lindenberger (1997) do not directly address the issue of domain specificity of resource, but their hypothesis would certainly argue for dedifferentiation of resources across the life-span. Second, the neuroimaging work on aging also suggests greater neural distribution of processes employed in domain-specific tasks (Madden et al., 1999; Reuter-Lorenz et al., 2000). The imaging literature suggested that one might expect to see well-differentiated behavioral functions for young and older adults for visuospatial and verbal performance on working memory and long-term memory tasks, but that with age, performance would dedifferentiate across content. That is, differentiation between verbal and visuospatial processes would become less pronounced across the adult life-span.

Based on this thinking, Park et al. (in press) conducted an ambitious behavioral study to understand domain specificity of visuospatial and verbal memory across the life-span, at the level of both working memory and long-term memory. They collected multiple measures of visuospatial and verbal working memory, short-term memory, and long-term memory from 345 adults, aged 20–92 over 3 sessions totaling 7 hours, and used structural equation modeling techniques to contrast two different models of domain-specific organization. The latent variable measurement models suggested that all three constructs, working memory, short-term memory, and long-term memory, were distinct with respect to modality (visuospatial or verbal) and should be treated separately in structural models. Structural modeling indicated that visuospatial and verbal working memory were differentiated but highly interrelated. Visuospatial and verbal working memory each had an associated short-term store, with each working memory directly mediating variance in long-term visuospatial or verbal recall. Perhaps the most important finding was that the same structural model fit the data for old and young adult samples separately just as well as it did for the entire sample. This suggested that there were no fundamental organizational differences across the life-span in memory structures. Moreover, the findings indicated that limited differentiation of resource (visuospatial and verbal) exists in young adults and is maintained across the life-span. Although the authors did not find evidence for dedifferentiation or cognitive resource into a single general working memory construct, they nevertheless found that a single mechanism, speed of processing, was the most fundamental in mediating age-related variance in the models. Furthermore, it is entirely possible that dedifferentiation of resource is occurring at the neurobiological level. That is, although behaviorally, visuospatial and verbal differentiation is maintained across the life-span, older adults may be recruiting from diverse, bilateral brain sites to perform tasks of both modalities, whereas young adults maintain neural specificity in their processing (see Park, Polk, Mikels, Taylor, & Marshuetz, in press, for a detailed discussion of this issue). Further neuroimaging studies will permit a better understanding of the relationship between behavioral data and neurobiological function. In summary, these data provide strong evidence for age-related variance medicated by speed, but with differentiation of resource maintained across the life-span into visuospatial and verbal stores.

The other important finding from this study is relatively straightforward and is shown in Figure 12.1. Basically, all measures of processing efficiency (four measures of working

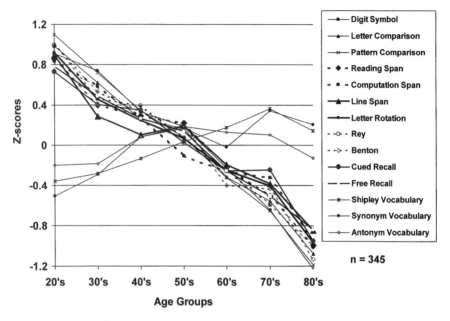

FIGURE 12.1. Performance on measures of speed of processing, working memory, long-term memory, and world knowledge across the life-span.

memory, four measures of long-term memory, and three measures of speed of processing) decline at an equivalent rate and do not have slopes that differ from one another. Declines that occur across all of the processing measures are equivalent across the life-span and occur similarly for working memory and long-term memory in both the visuospatial and verbal modalities. The loss of processing function that occurs from ages 20–29 is approximately the same as the loss that occurs from 60–69. The only difference is that the proportionate loss for the 69 year old is greater than for the 29 year old, given that a 20 year old has more processing resource than a 60 year old. As an analogy, if you start a bank account with a thousand dollars that doesn't accrue interest and withdraw $100 each decade beginning at age 20, you would decrease your financial resources by 10% on your 20th birthday and have $900 remaining. On your 70th birthday, you would have $500 left and your $100 withdrawal would at that point represent a 20% loss of your now meager financial resources, leaving you with only $400. As this analogy illustrates, the absolute decline in working memory function may be equivalent across decades, but the proportion of processing resources lost is greater as one gets older. There is also likely a critical point where the absolute level of processing resource available begins to result in noticeable changes in cognitive function (Park, 1996). This disproportionate loss of resource by decade combined with the notion that there is a threshold beyond which cognitive changes have an obvious impact on cognitive function likely explains why declines in cognitive function are a primary complaint of older but not younger adults, even though rate of decline is continuous across the life-span. Young adults apparently have sufficient cognitive reserves that losses do not result in noticeable deficits in their self-reports of cognitive behavior, but sensitive laboratory tests, such as those depicted in Figure 1, reveal that decline occurs.

Despite the concerns about resource decline so aptly depicted in Figure 12.1, it also portrays the good news of cognitive aging. Measures of world knowledge (vocabulary) show age invariance if not gains across the life-span. Thus, although older adults may have more limited working memory capacity and recall information from long-term memory less efficiently, they have a rich base of information and a wealth of experience that may provide a buffer against the effects of processing declines. This will be particularly true for everyday life, where behaviors are highly supported by the environment and often do not require intensive working memory or long-term memory function, a point further elaborated later in this chapter.

☐ Aging and Inhibitory Function in Working Memory

Hasher and Zacks (1988) have proposed that explaining age-related declines in cognitive function solely in terms of decline of storage and processing capacity in working memory is inaccurate. They argue that older adults show apparent decline in processing and storage capacity of working memory due to inefficient inhibition processes. That is, older adults have more difficulty accessing relevant information in working memory and deleting irrelevant information from working memory (Zacks & Hasher, 1998). Thus what appears to be a storage/capacity limitation in older adults is actually an inability to effectively maintain and process task-relevant information in working memory. There is some support for the Hasher and Zacks (1988) hypothesis. For example, May, Hasher, and Kane (1999) found that working memory span decrements were due to greater susceptibility to proactive interference effects for older adults.

Hedden and Park (in press) studied the role of retroactive interference in the working memory of old and young adults using a variation of the A-B, C-D paradigm (see Kintsch, 1970, and Kausler, 1991 for a discussion of the paradigm). Young and old adults were presented with a study list (the A-B list) of three paired associates. Immediately following the study list, participants were required to read aloud three additional pairs that were either unrelated to the targets (C-D items) or had the same cue (A-C items). This interfering read condition was compared to a rest condition. Following the read or rest condition, participants were tested for recognition of the studied pairs. At recognition, the studied pairs were interspersed with a variety of lure pairs, including the interfering pairs that had just been read. Hedden and Park (in press) found clear evidence for disproportionate interference in the working memories of old adults compared to young adults. Whenever a pair had served as a read item, older adults showed higher false alarms for the pair and were disproportionately slow to correctly reject these pairs relative to young adults. Of particular interest was the finding that A-C pairs in the read condition did not interfere more than did C-D pairs in the read condition for either age group, despite the relationship of A-C pairs to the studied pairs. Finally, Hedden and Park observed equal correct recognition of target pairs in old and young. They concluded that activation processes were intact in older adults in working memory, given the equivalent responding to target pairs, a finding also reported by Zacks, Radvansky, and Hasher (1996) and by Jonides et al. (2000). However, older adults clearly had much more difficulty than young adults deleting the irrelevant read pairs from working memory, and it made little difference whether the interfering pairs were related or unrelated to the target pairs. This suggests that the interference was nonsemantic in nature and likely based on sustained activation of the interfering pairs in working memory due to inefficient deletion operations on the part of older adults.

The effects observed by Hedden and Park (in press) were of sufficient magnitude that this measure of interference might be used effectively as an individual difference variable.

One problem with inhibition paradigms is that although inhibition operations have been demonstrated to be less effective in older compared to younger adults, there is little data relating ineffective inhibition operations to subsequent memory (Park, 2000). Indeed, Salthouse and Meinz (1995) found that inhibition as measured by variants of the Stroop interference task did not uniquely account for age-related variance in working memory. In another study, the majority of age-related variance in working memory performance could not be accounted for by measures of inhibition, interference, or distraction (Earles et al., 1997). Thus, some of the problems that plagued the processing resource argument early on are problematic for inhibition theory at this time. Engle and colleagues have argued that inhibitory deficits are due to reduced attentional capacity rather than vice versa (Conway & Engle, 1994; Engle, Conway, Tuholski, & Shisler, 1995). It is of critical importance to develop models of memory and aging that simultaneously incorporate measures of mechanisms hypothesized to be important in understanding age-related decline in cognitive function (speed of processing, working memory, and inhibitory function). Such an approach would permit an evaluation of the relative importance of speed, working memory storage and processing, and inhibitory function in contributing to the deficits observed in measures of long-term memory and reasoning typical of older adults.

☐ Working Memory and Function in Everyday Life

It seems that one goal of cognitive aging research and theorizing should be to determine the implications of age-related declines in working memory for everyday life. We have done research on the importance of working memory for making medical decisions (Zwahr, Park, & Shifren, 1999) and processing news information on radio, television, and in newsprint (Frieske & Park, 1999), and we have studied the role of working memory in remembering to take medications accurately (Park, Morrell, Frieske, & Kincaid, 1992; Park et al., 1999). The picture is not a simple one. It is the case that working memory plays an important role in some everyday tasks but not others. We argue that many cognitive tasks have a strong familiarity component and are largely driven by automatic processes (Park, 1999; Park & Hall-Gutchess, 2000). Such tasks do not show any relationship between working memory function and task performance, whereas everyday tasks that have substantial processing and storage requirements do show a relationship to working memory.

Zwahr et al. (1999) studied the types of decisions young and older women made about whether or not to take estrogen replacement therapy for menopause after reading detailed information about the pros and cons of the therapy in a carefully designed medical pamphlet. They reported that age had no effect on the decision (to take or not take the therapy), but that older women sought out less information, made fewer comparative judgments, and considered fewer alternatives in making their decisions. In a path analysis, they found that working memory predicted the quality of the decisions made and the number of choices considered. Frieske and Park (1999) looked at the role of sensory function and speed of processing in predicting how much information young and old adults retained from a news story that was presented in newspaper, radio, or television format. They reported that sensory function and speed of processing explained over 85% of the age-related variance in memory for the news information. Moreover, memory for the news information was equivalent in the print, audio, and television conditions, with young adults remembering more than older adults. Source memory (who said what) was better for both young and old adults in the television condition, suggesting that the video/audio format together served as a type of environmental support, but the two age groups profited equally from it. Frieske and Park (1999) did not include working memory as a predictor, but given the close relationship between working memory and speed, it is reasonable to expect that speed and sensory function were good estimates of processing resource. Although the domains of these two studies are quite different (medical information versus news information), both studies have in common that the participants were required to assimilate a great deal of knowledge and then use that knowledge in some fashion (to make a decision in Zwahr et al., 1999, and to perform on a memory test in Frieske & Park, 1999). Under these conditions, one would expect speed and working memory performance to be an important predictor in performance, because the storage and manipulation of novel information were required.

In contrast, let us examine the everyday behavior of remembering to take medications. This is an example of a primarily prospective memory task with many everyday cues to guide the behavior (e.g., taking medications always at the time one brushes one's teeth in the morning and evening). Medication-taking behavior is an example of a real-world behavior that Craik and Jennings (1992) would argue is highly supported. In three studies, Park et al. (1992), Morrell, Park, Kidder, and Martin (1997), and Park et al. (1999) observed a very high level of adherence to complex medication regimens in older adults, using microelectronic monitors. Older adults aged 60–75 made almost no errors. In fact, Morrell et al. (1997) and Park et al. (1999) included middle-aged adults in their studies and found them to be significantly less adherent than their older counterparts, despite evidence of better working memory function. Park et al. (1999) found that the best predictor of nonadherence was self-report of a busy, unpredictable lifestyle. Thus, individuals that do not have stable environmental contexts (e.g., meals at different times, travel, a great deal of multitasking) are much more at risk of not remembering to take medications than older individuals with diminished working memory function. Park (1999) and Park and Hall-Gutchess (2000) argued that reliable environmental cues for a routinely performed behavior result in little cognitive resources being required for the task due to the strong automatic/familiarity component, which is not age sensitive (see chapter 19 of this volume by Jacoby, Marsh, & Dolan).

☐ Conclusion

In the present chapter, we have presented a broad overview of the importance for the working memory construct in understanding aging and cognitive function, both at the basic level as well as in our everyday environments. The Craik and Byrd (1982) conception that aging can be characterized by declining "mental energy" and that this decline has broad implications for many domains of cognitive function has proven itself to be one of the richest and most fruitful avenues of inquiry in understanding cognitive aging, particularly when paired with the construct of environmental support. Future challenges already being addressed by some of the authors in this volume (e.g., Stuss and Binns, chapter 28, Anderson, chapter 16, and Shallice, chapter 10) involve integrating basic behavioral research on working memory with brain imaging. Of particular importance is understanding the role of individual differences in brain activation patterns and how different patterns of activation (e.g., bilateral recruitment for a task where young adults show hemispheric specialization or diffuse neural activation with high signal for a task where young adults are focused and low signal) characterize healthy or less healthy cognitive aging. The future of cognitive aging research seems to lie in integrating the rich conceptual frameworks that exist with new and evolving paradigms that extend the research on one hand to the level of brain and genome, but on the other hand, to complex environmental and social interactions.

☐ Acknowledgments

This research was supported by the National Institute on Aging through grant R01 AG06265 and through grant P50 AG11715 for one of the Edward R. Roybal Centers for Research on Applied Gerontology.

☐ References

Baddeley, A. D. (1986). *Working memory.* Oxford, England: Clarendon Press.

Baddeley, A. D., & Hitch, G. J. (1974). Working memory. In G. Bower (Ed.), *Recent advances in learning and motivation* (Vol. 8, pp. 47–90). New York: Academic Press.

Baltes, P. B., & Lindenberger, U. (1997). Emergence of a powerful connection between sensory and cognitive functions across the adult life span: A new window to the study of cognitive aging? *Psychology & Aging, 12,* 12–21.

Cherry, K. E., & Park, D. C. (1993). Individual difference and contextual variables influence spatial memory in younger and older adults. *Psychology & Aging, 8,* 517–526.

Conway, A. R. A., & Engle, R. W. (1994). Working memory and retrieval: A resource-dependent inhibition model. *Journal of Experimental Psychology: General, 123,* 354– 373.

Craik, F. I. M. (1986). A functional account of age differences in memory. In F. Klix & H. Hagendorf (Eds.), *Human memory and cognitive capabilities, mechanisms, and performances* (pp. 409–422). North Holland: Elsevier.

Craik, F. I. M., & Byrd, M. (1982). Aging and cognitive deficits: The role of attentional resources. In F.I.M. Craik & S. Trehub (Eds.), *Aging and cognitive processes* (pp. 191–211). New York: Plenum.

Craik, F. I. M., Byrd, M., & Swanson, J. M. (1987). Patterns of memory loss in three elderly samples. *Psychology & Aging, 2,* 79–86.

Craik, F. I. M., & Jennings, J. M. (1992). Human memory. In F. I. M. Craik. (Ed.), *The handbook of aging and cognition* (pp. 51–110). Hillsdale, NJ: Erlbaum.

Daneman, M., & Carpenter, P. A. (1980). Individual differences in working memory and reading. *Journal of Verbal Learning and Verbal Behavior, 19,* 450–466.

D'Esposito, M., Aguirre, G. K., Zarahn, E., Ballard, D., Shin, R. K., & Lease, J. (1998). Functional MRI studies of spatial and nonspatial working memory. *Cognitive Brain Research, 7,* 1–13.

D'Esposito, M., Detre, J. A., Alsop, D. C., Shin, R. K., Atlas, S., & Grossman, M. (1995). The neural basis of the central executive system of working memory. *Nature, 378,* 279–281.

Earles, J. L., Connor, L. T., Frieske, D., Park, D. C., Smith, A. D., & Zwahr, M. (1997). Age differences in inhibition: Possible causes and consequences. *Aging, Neuropsychology, and Cognition, 4,* 45–57.

Engle, R. W., Conway, A. R. A., Tuholski, S. W., & Shisler, R. J. (1995). A resource account of inhibition. *Psychological Science, 6,* 122–125.

Frieske, D. A., & Park, D. C. (1993). Effects of organization and working memory on age differences in memory for scene information. *Experimental Aging Research, 19,* 321–332.

Frieske, D. A., & Park, D. C. (1999). Memory for news in young and old adults. *Psychology & Aging, 14,* 90–98.

Hasher, L., & Zacks, R. T. (1979). Automatic and effortful processes in memory. *Journal of Experimental Psychology: General, 108,* 356–388.

Hasher, L., & Zacks, R. T. (1988). Working memory, comprehension, and aging: A review and a new view. In G. H. Bower (Ed.), *The psychology of learning and motivation* (Vol. 22, pp. 193–225). San Diego, CA: Academic Press.

Hedden, T., & Park, D. C. (in press). Aging and interference in verbal working memory. *Psychology & Aging.*

Jacoby, L. L. (1999). Ironic effects of repetition: Measuring age-related differences in memory. *Journal of Experimental Psychology: Learning, Memory, and Cognition, 25,* 3–22.

Jennings, J. M., & Jacoby, L. L. (1993). Automatic versus intentional uses of memory: Aging, attention, and control. *Psychology & Aging, 8,* 283–293.

Jonides, J., Marshuetz, C., Smith, E. E., Reuter-Lorenz, P. A., Koeppe, R. A., & Hartley, A. (2000).

Age differences in behavior and PET activation reveal differences in interference resolution in verbal working memory. *Journal of Cognitive Neuroscience, 12,* 188–196.

Joreskog, K. G. (1993). *Testing structural equation models.* Newbury Park, CA: Sage.

Kausler, D. H. (1991). *Experimental psychology, cognition, and human aging* (2nd ed.). New York: Springer-Verlag.

Kidder, D. P., Park, D. C., Hertzog, C., & Morrell, R. W. (1997). Prospective memory and aging: The effects of working memory and prospective memory task load. *Aging, Neuropsychology, & Cognition, 4,* 93–112.

Kintsch, W. (1970). *Learning, memory, and conceptual processes.* New York: Wiley.

Light, L. L. (1991). Memory and aging: Four hypotheses in search of data. *Annual Review of Psychology, 42,* 333–376.

Madden, D. J., Turkington, T. G., Provenzale, J. M., Denny, L. L., Hawk, T. C., Gottlob, L. R., & Coleman, R. E. (1999). Adult age differences in the functional neuroanatomy of verbal recognition memory. *Human Brain Mapping, 7,* 115–135.

May, C. P., Hasher, L., & Kane, M. J. (1999). The role of interference in memory span. *Memory & Cognition, 27,* 759–767.

Morrell, R.W., & Park, D. C. (1993). The effects of age, illustrations, and task variables on the performance of procedural assembly tasks. *Psychology & Aging, 8,* 389–399.

Morrell, R. W., Park, D. C., Kidder, D. P., & Martin, M. (1997). Adherence to antihypertensive medications across the life span. *Gerontologist, 37,* 609–619.

Park, D. C. (1996). Aging, health, and behavior: The interplay between basic and applied science. In R. J. Resnick & R. H. Rozensky (Eds.), *Health psychology through the life span: Practice and research opportunities* (pp. 59–75). New York: Springer-Verlag.

Park, D. C. (1999). Aging and the controlled and automatic processing of medical information and medical intentions. In D. C. Park (Ed.), *Processing of medical information in aging patients: Cognitive and human factors perspectives* (pp. 3–22). Mahwah, NJ: Erlbaum.

Park, D. C. (2000). The basic mechanisms accounting for age-related decline in cognitive function. In D. C. Park & N. Schwarz (Eds.), *Cognitive aging: A primer* (pp. 3–21). Philadelphia: Psychology Press.

Park, D. C., Lautenschlager, G., Hedden, T., Davidson, N. S., Smith, A. D., & Smith, P. K. (2001). *Models of visuospatial and verbal memory across the adult life span.* Submitted for publication.

Park, D. C., & Hall-Gutchess, A. (2000). Cognitive aging and everyday life. In D. C. Park & N. Schwarz (Eds.), *Cognitive aging: A primer* (pp. 217–232). Philadelphia: Psychology Press.

Park, D. C., Hertzog, C., Kidder, D. P., Morrell, R. W., & Mayhorn, C. (1997). Effect of age on event-based and time-based prospective memory. *Psychology & Aging, 12,* 314-327.

Park, D.C., Hertzog, C., Leventhal, H., Morrell, R.W., Leventhal, E., Birchmore, D., Martin, M., & Bennett, J. (1999). Medication adherence in rheumatoid arthritis patients: Older is wiser. *Journal of American Geriatrics Society, 47,* 172–183.

Park, D. C., Morrell, R. W., Frieske, D. A., & Kincaid, D. (1992). Medication adherence behaviors in older adults: Effects of external cognitive supports. *Psychology & Aging, 7,* 252–256.

Park, D. C., Polk, T. A., Mikels, J. A., Taylor, S. F., & Marshuetz, C. (in press). Cerebral aging: Integration of brain and behavioral models of cognitive functions. *Dialogues in Clinical Neuroscience: Cerebral Aging.*

Park, D. C., Smith, A. D., Lautenschlager, G., Earles, J. L., Frieske, D., Zwahr, M., & Gaines, C. L. (1996). Mediators of long-term memory performance across the life span. *Psychology & Aging, 11,* 621–637.

Park, D. C., Smith, A. D., Morrell, R. W., Puglisi, J. T., & Dudley, W. N. (1990). Effects of contextual integration on recall of pictures by older adults. *Journal of Gerontology: Psychological Sciences, 45,* P52–P57.

Reuter-Lorenz, P. A., Jonides, J., Smith, E. E., Hartley, A., Miller, A., Marshuetz, C., & Koeppe, R. A. (2000). Age differences in the frontal lateralization of verbal and spatial working memory revealed by PET. *Journal of Cognitive Neuroscience, 12,* 174–187.

Salthouse, T. A. (1991). Mediation of adult age differences in cognition by reductions in working memory and speed of processing. *Psychological Science, 2,* 179–183.

Salthouse, T. A. (1992). Working memory mediation of adult age differences in integrative reasoning. *Memory & Cognition, 20,* 413–423.

Salthouse, T. A. (1993a). Influence of working memory on adult age differences in matrix reasoning. *British Journal of Psychology, 84,* 171–199.

Salthouse, T. A. (1993b). Speed mediation of adult age differences in cognition. *Developmental Psychology, 29,* 722–738.

Salthouse, T. A. (1996). The processing-speed theory of adult age differences in cognition. *Psychological Review, 103,* 403–428.

Salthouse, T. A., & Babcock, R. L. (1991). Decomposing adult age differences in working memory. *Developmental Psychology, 27,* 763–776.

Salthouse, T. A., & Meinz, E. J. (1995). Aging, inhibition, working memory, and speed. *Journal of Gerontology: Psychological Sciences, 50B,* P297–P306.

Shah, P., & Miyake, A. (1996). The separability of working memory resources for spatial thinking and language processing: An individual differences approach. *Journal of Experimental Psychology: General, 125,* 4–27.

Smith, A. D., Park, D. C., Earles, J. L. K., Shaw, R. J., & Whiting, W. L. (1998). Age differences in context integration in memory. *Psychology & Aging, 13,* 21–28.

Smith, E. E., & Jonides, J. (1999). Storage and executive processes in the frontal lobes. *Science, 283,* 1657–1661.

Stine, E. L., & Wingfield, A. (1987). Process and strategy in memory for speech among younger and older adults. *Psychology & Aging, 2,* 272–279.

Verhaeghen, P., & Salthouse, T. A. (1997). Meta-analyses of age-cognition relations in adulthood: Estimates of linear and nonlinear age effects and structural models. *Psychological Bulletin, 122,* 231–249.

Zacks, R. T., & Hasher, L. (1998). Cognitive gerontology and attentional inhibition: A reply to Burke and McDowd. *Journal of Gerontology, 52B,* P274–P283.

Zacks, R. T., Radvansky, G., & Hasher, L. (1996). Studies of directed forgetting in older adults. *Journal of Experimental Psychology: Learning, Memory, and Cognition, 22,* 143–156.

Zwahr, M. D., Park, D. C., & Shifren, K. (1999). Judgments about estrogen replacement therapy: The role of age, cognitive abilities, and beliefs. *Psychology & Aging, 14,* 179–191.

CHAPTER

13

Meredyth Daneman

Commentary: Working Memory, Long-Term Memory, and the Effects of Aging

When I was first asked to act as discussant of the four preceding chapters that comprise this section of Part II, I tried to find a common theme or themes, a set of defining features that characterize all four contributions. And I couldn't do it. I felt like Wittgenstein (1953), who tried to come up with a fixed set of features that cover all the things we would consider a *game*, such as basketball, tennis, chess, scrabble, poker, solitaire, and couldn't do it. But as Wittgenstein pointed out, even if there is no fixed set of features that is common to all games, what organizes the separate instances into the game category is a set of *family resemblances* among the members. Just as Johnny might resemble his mother, and his mother might resemble her brother but in different ways so that Johnny and his uncle bear little resemblance to each other, so basketball shares something in common with tennis, tennis with chess, chess with scrabble, scrabble with poker, and poker with solitaire, and yet basketball and solitaire seem very different things (see also, Anderson, 1980; Rosch & Mervis, 1975). Using this logic, I decided that what holds these four contributions together is a set of family resemblances: Shallice's contribution is related to Baddeley's through their mutual interest in long-term memory, Baddeley's contribution is related to Park and Hedden's through their mutual interest in working memory; and Park and Hedden's contribution is related to McDowd's through their mutual interest in aging. But then suddenly it dawned on me. Of course, there *is* a defining feature that characterizes these four contributions. The defining feature is Fergus Craik. All four chapters deal with work that is related in one way or another to the work of Fergus Craik, whom we are honoring in this volume. And I think this is testimony to the impressive breadth of Gus's work and the impressive influence his work has had on the field.

Of the four contributors to this section of the volume, Alan Baddeley shares the longest and possibly the most complex professional relationship with Gus Craik. Baddeley and Craik are often viewed as theoretical adversaries; remember Craik's highly influential levels-of-processing papers (e.g., Craik & Lockhart, 1972; Craik & Tulving, 1975) and Baddeley's high-profile rebuttal (Baddeley, 1978). However, Baddeley provides an entertaining and informative summary of their joint histories in his chapter, and we see that their career paths have some rather interesting convergences as well as divergences. Both completed their doctoral studies in Britain, both "cut their theoretical teeth" on the question of whether there is one kind of memory or two, and both produced the pieces of work for which they are probably best known in the early 1970s. Craik is, of course, best known for his contribution to our understanding of long-term memory processes, with his concept of levels-of-processing having had an enormous impact dating back to the publication of the seminal Craik and Lockhart (1972) paper. And Baddeley is, of course, best known for his contribution to our understanding of short-term memory processes, with his model of working memory having had an enormous impact dating back to the publication of the seminal Baddeley and Hitch (1974) paper. However, a perhaps less well known fact is that both Craik and Baddeley began their careers on opposite sides of the "long-term memory–short-term memory divide." As Baddeley reminds us, Craik did some early important work on short-term memory phenomena, such as recency and digit recall across different languages, whereas Baddeley's doctoral research involved investigating the long-term memorability of different types of postal codes for the British Post Office. Given that they have found themselves on opposite sides of the long-term memory–short-term memory divide at all points in their careers, I think it is entirely fitting that Baddeley uses his chapter to reach across the divide by addressing the question of how working memory and long-term memory interact.

Borrowing the Craik metaphor of "levels," Baddeley frames his discussion of the interaction between working memory and long-term memory in terms of three levels of interaction that vary in the extent to which they implicate the central executive at encoding or retrieval. Level I deals with the interaction of phonological working memory and long-term memory language habits in the acquisition of new vocabulary. This level is assumed to be "low-level" because working memory and long-term memory interact through "a process of relatively gradual and cumulative implicit learning" that places little if any demands on the central executive for either encoding or retrieval. Level II deals with the interaction of working memory and long-term memory in producing what is commonly referred to in the memory literature as *the recency effect*, that is, the enhanced probability of recalling recently experienced information. Baddeley classifies this as an intermediate level of interaction because it combines an implicit priming of long-term memory representations with a basic but nevertheless explicit retrieval strategy. Level III deals with a much more explicit interaction between working memory and long-term memory via a newly proposed component called the *episodic buffer*. It is this level that I will comment on here.

The original Baddeley and Hitch (1974) model had three components: the central executive and its two subsidiary systems, the phonological loop and the visuospatial sketchpad. Now Baddeley proposes a purportedly new component, the episodic buffer (see also Baddeley, 2000), which he defines as "a limited capacity system that provides temporary storage of information held in a multimodal code, which is capable of binding information from the subsidiary systems, and from long-term memory, into a unitary episodic buffer" (Baddeley, 2000, p. 417). So, according to Baddeley, the new buffer addresses the problem of how information from long-term memory and from the various subsystems of working memory gets integrated. It is a temporary storage system that is linked to long-term memory but not dependent on it, so densely amnesic patients with grossly impaired episodic long-term memory may have an unimpaired episodic buffer.

I like the fact that Baddeley is trying to specify the relation between working memory and long-term memory. If working memory is to fulfill its promise of being an ecologically valid construct (see Baddeley & Hitch, 1974), if it is to play a role in meaningful and complex everyday cognitive tasks, and not just in how we temporarily store and rehearse telephone numbers, the system needs to interact with long-term memory, and so I welcome the new attention Baddeley is giving to this question. However, I do have some questions about the episodic buffer and whether in fact Baddeley is introducing a new component or simply reverting to an earlier version of the model. In earlier versions (e.g., Baddeley, 1986; Baddeley & Hitch, 1974), the central executive had temporary storage capabilities and a whole host of processing capabilities beyond the mere attentional executive capabilities it has in more recent versions (e.g., Baddeley, 1993; Baddeley & Logie, 1999). I never quite understood why Baddeley abandoned the view of a central executive that has temporary storage capacity.[1] The whole idea of the tradeoff between processing and storage functions in the Baddeley and Hitch (1974) model is what got me "hitched" onto the concept of working memory in the first place and got me to develop measures that assess the processing–storage tradeoff in working memory during the performance of tasks such as reading comprehension, mathematical computations, and so on (e.g., Daneman & Carpenter, 1980; Daneman & Tardif, 1987). And I never quite understood why Baddeley started taking all the work out of the working memory concept either. In other words, I never quite understood why he converted a process-rich central executive that could perform all sorts of task-specific manipulations and computations in addition to the more general attention and coordination functions into a process-poor central executive that has only attentional executive capabilities. If the central executive has only attentional executive capabilities, and the slave systems have only rehearsal and maintenance capabilities, where in working memory is the rest of the work performed? So I see the concept of an episodic buffer as a positive reversion to an earlier model, because Baddeley is putting more temporary memory back into the system, and some more work too (these so-called integration or binding processes). Whether one wants this episodic buffer to be its own system, or part of the central executive, still remains to be seen.

Tim Shallice's chapter deals with functional neuroimaging studies of long-term memory retrieval processes. Although we don't tend to think of Gus Craik as a cognitive *neuroscientist*, Shallice reminds us that Craik has played a prominent role in establishing the functional imaging of long-term memory as a scientific field. Indeed, the recent flurry of interest in the functional imaging of episodic memory was precipitated by the finding that the left prefrontal cortex appears to be involved in encoding processes, whereas the right prefrontal cortex appears to be involved in retrieval processes, and Craik was involved in three of the four initial studies published on this topic. Shallice takes the right prefrontal cortex–retrieval process association as his starting point and then proceeds to make the argument that the ventrolateral region of the right prefrontal cortex may be involved in retrieval specification processes, whereas the dorsolateral region of the right prefrontal cortex may be involved in retrieval verification.

Work showing right prefrontal dominance during retrieval has depended on contrasting tasks in which the subject is or is not "in retrieval mode" (Tulving, 1983). Shallice challenges the basic assumption that retrieval mode is some monolithic, task-independent state. Borrowing from Norman and Bobrow (1979), Shallice suggests that retrieval from episodic memory can be decomposed into three stages or subprocesses. During the first stage, the individual formulates a retrieval "description," that is, a specification of the criteria that would constitute a memory. This process is followed by a matching process in which records in episodic memory are matched with the retrieval descriptions. However, retrieval does not end with a successful match. Given that retrieval from episodic memory is likely to lead to many false positives, Norman and Bobrow included a memory checking or verification stage. Shallice uses some interesting findings from his research group's

---

[1] In this chapter, Baddeley's only rationale is that "the storage assumption was abandoned on the grounds of parsimony and testability."

functional imaging studies to support Norman and Bobrow's distinction between retrieval specification and retrieval verification. Although Shallice's studies have shown the typical right prefrontal activation during retrieval, some of the studies have also shown an interesting double dissociation, namely, that certain retrieval tasks (e.g., paired associate recall) produce greater activation in the right ventrolateral prefrontal cortex, whereas other retrieval tasks (e.g., organized list recall) produce greater activation in the right dorsolateral prefrontal cortex. According to Shallice, greater activation in the ventrolateral region of the right prefrontal cortex occurs when the task stresses retrieval specification more than verification, whereas greater activation in the dorsolateral region of the right prefrontal cortex occurs when the task stresses retrieval verification more than specification. Shallice's argument is more convincing with respect to the dorsolateral–verification link. Nevertheless, his argument is provocative, and the message against assuming a single or simple retrieval mode remains an important one.

Whereas we may not immediately associate Gus Craik with cognitive neuroscience, we most certainly do associate him with cognitive aging, the topic of Denise Park and Trey Hedden's chapter. Craik has made a substantial contribution to the field of cognitive aging, and Park and Hedden use two early and influential papers by Craik (Craik & Byrd, 1982; Craik, Byrd, & Swanson, 1987) as a springboard to their arguments. In these early papers, Craik argued that the amount of "mental energy" or "attentional resources" available to perform mental operations declines with age, and it is this decline in attentional resources that is responsible for age-related declines on a wide range of memory tasks. However, Craik also recognized that tasks might differ in the degree to which they make demands on attentional resources, and individuals might differ in the amount of resources they possess, so that aging effects can be attenuated for memory tasks that offer sufficient environmental support and for individuals who possess larger amounts of attentional resources. Substitute Craik's construct of mental energy or attentional resources with Baddeley's (1986) construct of working memory capacity, and you have much of the argument being proposed by Park and Hedden here.

Park and Hedden use the results of a series of studies conducted in their laboratory to argue for the importance of the working memory construct in understanding aging and cognitive function. I think they make a convincing case for the involvement of working memory in accounting for individual differences in performance on a wide range of effortful verbal and spatial long-term memory tasks. However, I think they make a less convincing case for the involvement of working memory in accounting for age-related declines in cognitive function. It's not that working memory capacity did not account for a substantial proportion of age-related variance in a range of complex cognitive tasks. It did in all the studies Park and Hedden report here. However, in one of their most ambitious studies of 301 adults ranging in age from 20–90 years (see Park et al., 1996), they pitted working memory capacity against speed of processing and showed that speed of processing explained all the *age-related* variance in performance on the complex verbal and spatial memory tasks (see also Salthouse, 1996). Park and Hedden present this finding at the midpoint of their chapter, and then they appear to ignore it for the remainder of the chapter because they resume the argument that working memory is important in understanding age-related declines in effortful cognitive tasks. So I remain confused as to whether they are positing one mechanism for age-related declines in cognitive function or two. This said, I really like the life-span, multimeasure approach to studying cognitive aging that Park and colleagues have adopted in several of their studies. And I think they have convincing evidence that working memory, long-term memory, and speed of processing decline at a constant and equivalent rate across the adult lifespan (20–92 years).

Of the four contributors to this section of the volume, Joan McDowd is the only person to have directly collaborated with Gus Craik and to have coauthored scientific papers with him.[2] Craik was McDowd's Ph.D. supervisor, and his persisting influence on her work is readily apparent in her chapter on selective attention, inhibition, and aging. McDowd draws on Craik's levels-of-processing framework in an attempt to understand the seemingly contradictory findings in the literature with respect to aging and negative priming. Some studies have shown that old adults do not show the typical negative priming effect that young adults do, a finding that has been taken to support Hasher and Zack's (1988) claim that age-related declines in inhibitory function account for many age-related cognitive deficits. However, other studies have shown that old and young adults show equivalent negative priming effects, a finding that is inconsistent with the inhibitory-decline hypothesis of cognitive aging. Through an interesting analysis of the literature and a clever series of experiments of her own, McDowd makes the case that older adults might not have an inhibitory deficit per se. She argues that older adults typically use different features for selection and suppression than do young adults, and the presence or absence of age differences in negative priming tasks appears to depend on the processing requirements of the task. McDowd argues that whenever the task permits, older adults adopt an early selection processing mode, selecting target information based on surface or perceptual features, whereas younger adults adopt a late selection processing mode, selecting target information based on meaning or stimulus identity. Thus, older adults will tend to show evidence of suppression based on stimulus location but not stimulus identity, whereas younger adults will tend to show evidence of suppression based on stimulus location and stimulus identity. McDowd doesn't have any direct evidence for why older adults might prefer an early selection mode, but she speculates that it may have to do with the fact that "perceptual processing may be more demanding" for the older adults. If perceptual processing were very demanding for older adults, this would leave the older adults with less capacity for processing nontarget information, and so there would be no need for them to suppress meaning-based information. In contrast, if perceptual processing were not as demanding for younger adults, then they would not find perceptual processing as demanding as do older adults; consequently, young adults would have more residual capacity for processing target and nontarget information to a deeper level of meaning and would typically suppress meaning-based nontarget information in negative priming tasks.

This notion of a greater perceptual load for older adults fits nicely with some of my own recent work done in collaboration with Bruce Schneider and others (Pichora-Fuller, Schneider, & Daneman, 1995; Schneider, Daneman, Murphy, & Kwong-See, 2000; Speranza, Daneman, & Schneider, 2000; see also Schneider, chapter 24 of this volume). Our research confirms McDowd's speculation that older adults may find perceptual tasks more demanding than younger adults do. Indeed, not only have we shown that older adults are at a disadvantage when it comes to auditory and visual processing, but we have also shown that age-related declines in perceptual processes may be responsible, in large part, for the frequently observed age-related declines in cognitive and linguistic processing. In Schneider et al. (2000), we had younger and older adults listen to discourse in quiet or against a background of conversational noise (12-people babble), and then we assessed their comprehension and memory of the discourse afterwards. When younger and older adults were tested under identical physical conditions (the passages were presented at the same sound pressure level to all participants, and the noise, when present, was the same for all participants), older participants answered fewer questions correctly, a finding which could be interpreted to mean that there are age-related declines in comprehending and/or

---

[2]Alan Baddeley and Gus Craik did coauthor an obituary notice for Donald Broadbent, which was published in *American Psychologist* in 1995.

remembering spoken discourse. However, when we equated young and old for perceptual stress by adjusting the listening situation to take into account each individual's hearing status, the age-related comprehension differences were largely eliminated (see also Schneider, chapter 24 of this volume). These findings suggest that the speech understanding difficulties of the elderly may be attributed to perceptual deficits rather than cognitive-linguistic deficits. They are consistent with McDowd's view that older adults tend to focus more on perceptual features of the negative priming task at the expense of meaning-based features because they find the perceptual processes so demanding.

The influence of Gus Craik's work is readily apparent in the chapters by Baddeley, Shallice, Park and Hedden, and McDowd. That these four chapters span such a wide range of topics and constructs attests to the enormous influence Gus has had and continues to have on the development of theories about cognition, memory, and cognitive aging.

☐ References

Anderson, J. R. (1980). *Cognitive psychology and its implications.* San Francisco: Freeman.

Baddeley, A. D. (1978). The trouble with "levels": A re-examination of Craik and Lockhart's framework for memory research. *Psychological Review, 85,* 139–152.

Baddeley, A. D. (1986). *Working memory.* Oxford, England: Clarendon Press.

Baddeley, A. D. (1993). Working memory or working attention? In A. Baddeley & L. Weiskrantz (Eds.), *Attention: Selection, awareness, and control. A tribute to Donald Broadbent* (pp. 152–170). Oxford, England: Oxford University Press.

Baddeley, A. D. (2000). The episodic buffer: A new component of working memory? *Trends in Cognitive Sciences, 4,* 417–423.

Baddeley, A. D., & Hitch, G. (1974). Working memory. In G. H. Bower (Ed.), *The psychology of learning and motivation: Advances in research and theory* (Vol. 8, pp. 47–89). New York: Academic Press.

Baddeley, A. D., & Logie, R. H. (1999). Working memory: The multi-component model. In A. Miyake & P. Shah (Eds.) *Models of working memory: Mechanisms of active maintenance and executive control,* pp. 28–61. Cambridge, England: Cambridge University Press.

Craik, F. I. M., & Byrd, M. (1982). Aging and cognitive deficits: The role of attentional resources. In F. I. M. Craik & S. Trehub (Eds.), *Aging and cognitive processes* (pp. 191–211). New York: Plenum.

Craik, F. I. M., Byrd, M., & Swanson, J. M. (1987). Patterns of memory loss in three elderly samples. *Psychology & Aging, 2,* 79–86.

Craik, F. I. M., & Lockhart, R. S. (1972). Levels-of-processing: A framework for memory research. *Journal of Verbal Learning and Verbal Behavior, 11,* 671–684.

Craik, F. I. M., & Tulving, E. (1975). Depth of processing and the retention of words in episodic memory. *Journal of Experimental Psychology: General, 104,* 268–294.

Daneman, M., & Carpenter, P. (1980). Individual differences in working memory and reading. *Journal of Verbal Learning and Verbal Behavior, 19,* 450–466.

Daneman, M., & Tardif, T. (1987). Working memory and reading skill re-examined. In M. Coltheart (Ed.), *Attention and performance XII: The psychology of reading* (pp. 491–508). Hove, England: Erlbaum.

Hasher, L., & Zacks, R. T. (1988). Working memory, comprehension , and aging: A review and a new view. In G. H. Bower (Ed.), *The psychology of learning and motivation* (Vol. 22, pp. 193–225). Orlando, FL: Academic Press.

Norman, D. A., & Bobrow, D. B. (1979). Descriptions: An intermediate stage in memory retrieval. *Cognitive Psychology, 11,* 107–123.

Park, D. C., Smith, A. D., Lautenschlager, G., Earles, J. L., Frieske, D., Zwahr, M., & Gaines, C. L. (1996). Mediators of long-term performance across the life span. *Psychology & Aging, 11,* 621–637.

Pichora-Fuller, M. K., Schneider, B. A., & Daneman, M. (1995). How young and old adults listen to and remember speech in noise. *Journal of the Acoustical Society of America, 97,* 593–608.

Rosch, E., & Mervis, C. B. (1975). Family resemblances: Studies in the internal structure of categories. *Cognitive Psychology, 7,* 573–605.

Salthouse, T. A. (1996). The processing-speed theory of adult age differences in cognition. *Psychological Review, 103,* 403–428.

Schneider, B. A., Daneman, M., Murphy, D. R., & Kwong-See, S. (2000). Listening to discourse in distracting settings: The effects of aging. *Psychology and Aging, 15,* 110–125.

Speranza, F., Daneman, M., & Schneider, B. A. (2000). How aging affects the reading of words in noisy backgrounds. *Psychology and Aging, 15,* 253–258.

Tulving, E. (1983). *Elements of episodic memory.* Oxford, England: Oxford University Press.

Wittgenstein, L. (1953). *Philosophical investigations.* New York: Macmillan

ATTENTION AT ENCODING
AND RETRIEVAL

Morris Moscovitch
Myra Fernandes
Angela Troyer

CHAPTER

Working-With-Memory and Cognitive Resources: A Component-Process Account of Divided Attention and Memory

This chapter is divided into two parts. Part 1 recounts some of the early history that Morris Moscovitch and Gus Craik shared at Erindale, the influence that Gus had on Morris, and Morris's development of the component process model, which provides a neuropsychological account of memory and aging that is compatible with many aspects of Craik's cognitive theories on aging. Part 2 is concerned with more recent empirical and theoretical developments on divided attention, memory, and aging that had their origin in those theories and model. Part 1 is told from Morris's perspective in the first person, whereas Part 2 is related by all of us.

☐ Part 1: Reminiscence and Models

Gus and I joined the faculty at Erindale College in the fall of 1971 along with two other colleagues, which gives you some idea of how expansive and optimistic governments and universities were in those days. Whereas the rest of us were rookies out of graduate school, Gus was already a seasoned veteran. I was familiar with some of his research, particularly a review paper on primary memory that appeared in the *British Medical Bulletin* (Craik, 1971). He had not yet published his landmark paper with Lockhart on levels of processing (Craik & Lockhart, 1972), though he was working on it during that academic year and presented it publicly for the first time at the Annual Erindale Symposium on Communication and Affect (Craik, 1973). I must confess I do not remember Gus's paper at the conference, probably because I was too preoccupied with my own presentation on laterality (hemispheric specialization), which was the first one I had ever given to a large audience (Moscovitch, 1973). However, another presentation that Gus gave that year that did stick in my mind. It is one he gave just to the dozen or so Erindale psychologists in a small room on the third floor during a seminar whose purpose was to acquaint ourselves with each others' work. Drawing on research he completed in London with Birtwistle and Gardiner,

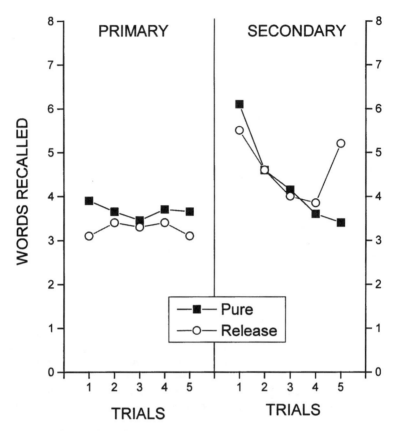

FIGURE 14.1. The number of words recalled from primary (PM) and secondary memory (SM) as a function of trials and material. Trials 1–4 were from the same list and Trial 5 was from either the same (pure) or a different (release) list (from Craik & Birtwistle, 1970).

Gus demonstrated that build-up and release of proactive inhibition (PI) in recall of a list of words affected only the primacy and middle portions of the serial position curve. He concluded that the build-up and release of PI affects only secondary memory, not a single, undifferentiated memory, as others had speculated (Melton, 1963, 1970) and provided evidence against a one-process, or single-storage, model of memory (see Figure 14.1). A subsequent study suggested that release from PI was determined by retrieval processes (Gardiner, Craik & Birtwistle, 1972). The experiments were elegant and the effects were large, which, in part, may explain the great impression they made on me, since at that time I was struggling to obtain laterality effects of about 10–30 ms between visual fields.

I mention these old studies and controversies only partly for their nostalgic value, but mainly because they had a direct impact on the first studies I conducted on memory. The influence of those studies are also evident in the more recent work on neuropsychological aspects of divided attention and memory, which we report in this chapter. The latter studies, in turn, are related closely to some of Gus's own current work on divided attention and on the role of the frontal lobes in retrieval. In short, what I have to say about the past has a direct bearing on the present.

PI, Retrieval, and the Frontal Lobes

After two years at Erindale, I took a leave of absence to work with Brenda Milner at the Montreal Neurological Institute. By then, Craik and Lockhart's (1972) paper on levels of processing had appeared and its impact was felt immediately. Its relevance to studies of memory disorder, however, seemed limited to me because most amnesics and people with unilateral temporal lobectomy could process information as deeply as normal people, yet still had a profound memory disorder. Whatever benefit depth of processing conferred on memory, it could not do so without the medial temporal lobes.

On the other hand, Gus's studies on PI had a direct application to testing neuropsychological theories of amnesia which were current at the time. In a paper presented at the Annual Meeting of the American Psychological Association in Montreal in 1973, Cermak and his colleagues showed that Korsakoff amnesic patients do not have a normal release from PI unless the stimulus categories were widely divergent from one another. On this basis they argued that amnesia resulted from an encoding deficit rather than a deficit in retrieval or consolidation (Cermak, Butters, & Moreines, 1974). Gardiner et al.'s (1972) demonstration that release from PI occurred at retrieval suggested an alternative interpretation to that offered by Cermak et al. (1974). Korsakoff's syndrome is associated not only with amnesia but also with impaired frontal functions that is likely to lead to heightened interference in memory (Lhermitte & Signoret, 1972; Luria, 1971), which, in turn, may account for their failure to release from PI. If this interpretation was correct, then patients with frontal lobe damage who are not amnesic should also fail to release from PI. On the other hand, patients with damage restricted to the medial temporal lobe, who suffer memory loss, should show impaired overall performance but normal release.

Using a modified version of Craik and Birtwistle's (1971) procedure, Milner and I presented four lists of 12 items each from a single category followed by a fifth list from a different category. The results in controls replicated Craik and Birtwistle's findings. We used Tulving and Colotla's (1970) method of distinguishing between items recalled from primary and secondary memory and found that build-up and release from PI occurred in secondary memory (see Figure 14.2). Contrary to predictions based on Cermak et al. (1974),

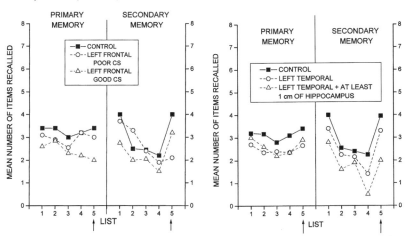

FIGURE 14.2. Number of words recalled from primary and secondary memory for each list by normal controls and by patients with different lesions. PI was built during Lists 1–4, which contained words from the same lexical category and released during List 5, which contained words from a different category (from Moscovitch, 1982a).

patients with verbal memory loss following left medial temporal lobe lesions performed similarly to controls except that their memory was worse overall, the extent of loss being related to the size of the hippocampal lesion. On the other hand, patients with left frontal damage who were poor at card-sorting were the only ones who did not show a normal release-from-PI. We concluded that the release-from-PI test could not be used to make inferences about the nature of amnesia but could tell us something about the contribution of the frontal lobes to memory. Drawing on Craik et al.'s findings, our results suggested that the frontal lobes play a crucial role in memory retrieval, whereas the medial temporal lobes are needed for memory retention (Moscovitch, 1982a).

The idea that the frontal and medial temporal lobes have complementary functions in memory was relatively new in 1973, so that even in its crude and simple formulation it was a useful guide for research and an impetus to theory development. For example, Winocur and I (Moscovitch, 1982b; Winocur, 1982) recognized that memory deficits associated with aging are likely the result of the deterioration of frontal and medial temporal lobes that occurs in old age (see also Naveh-Benjamin, chapter 15 of this volume). Consequently, older adults should be impaired on tests sensitive to frontal and medial temporal lobe damage. Thus, on tests of release from PI, older adults who live in institutions show both an overall reduction in the amount of material that is recalled and a failure to release (Moscovitch & Winocur, 1983; see also Figure 14.3).

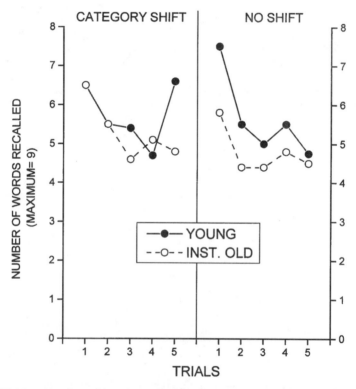

FIGURE 14.3. Number of words recalled by young and institutionalized old people on each trial in the category shift and no shift conditions. PI is built up on Trials 1–4 and released on Trial 5 in the shift condition (from Moscovitch & Winocur, 1983).

This theme was also picked up by Craik and his colleagues, who showed that source memory, which was selectively impaired in people with frontal lobe damage (Schacter, Harbluck, & McLachlan, 1984), was also decreased in older adults (McIntyre & Craik, 1987). The extent of decline was correlated with their performance on tests sensitive to frontal function such as verbal fluency and some measures from the Wisconsin Card Sorting Test (WCST; Craik, Morris, Morris, & Loewen, 1990).

On the other hand, performance on perceptual implicit tests of memory, which are presumed to be mediated primarily by perceptual modules or representation systems in the posterior neocortex, should be relatively well-preserved in old age, as Winocur and I were the first to show (Moscovitch, 1982b; Moscovitch, Winocur, & McLachlan, 1986; see also Figure 14.4). If, however, implicit tests of memory also have a retrieval component that requires generating, searching, or selecting among response alternatives, then they are likely to implicate the prefrontal cortex and be impaired with aging. Borrowing another idea from Craik et al. (1990) as well as from Davis et al. (1990), Winocur, Moscovitch, and Stuss (1996) correlated performance on tests of stem-completion which had many possible solutions with performance on verbal fluency and the WCST in older adults. As predicted, the worse their performance on these frontal-sensitive tests, the worse they did on stem completion. Performance on fragment completion which was more perceptually driven and had only one solution, was not influenced by the functional integrity of the frontal lobes (see also Nyberg, Moscovitch, & Winocur, 1997). In subsequent studies, we found similar results in young people with traumatic brain injury and frontal lobe dysfunction (Winocur, Stuss, & Moscovitch, unpublished observations).

The most striking evidence of the effects of frontal lesions on memory comes from

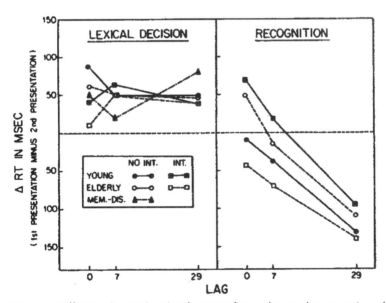

FIGURE 14.4. Difference in reaction time between first and second presentation of a word in lexical decision (repetition priming) and recognition tasks. The second word was presented at lags of 0, 7, and 29 items. INT refers to interference produced by an interpolated math task between each trial. The difference between young and elderly was evident only on the explicit recognition task. Memory-disordered patients could not perform the recognition task reliably at a level above chance, so their data are not shown (from Moscovitch, 1982b).

studies of patients who confabulate. Although a variety of disorders can lead to confabulation, including Korsakoff's amnesia, the most common is aneurysm of the anterior communicating artery, which spares the medial temporal lobes but injures the basal forebrain and ventromedial aspects of the frontal lobes. Confabulation is a form of gross, and often bizarre, memory distortion that is produced without the intention to deceive, a kind of "honest lying" that especially affects episodic memory but can also affect semantic memory. Because these patients confabulate about remote events that they experienced long before the lesion occurred as much as about recent events, and because their memory improved greatly with cueing, confabulation was considered to result from deficits in retrieval processes involving search, monitoring, and verification (Moscovitch, 1989, 1995; Moscovitch & Melo, 1997).

Memory and Working-With-Memory: A Component Process Model

In reviewing the literature on the effects of frontal and medial-temporal lesions on memory, Moscovitch and Winocur (Moscovitch, 1989, 1992, 1994; Moscovitch & Winocur, 1992) placed the studies on memory in the context of a more general framework of modules and central systems that Moscovitch and Umiltà (1990, 1991) developed based on the work of Fodor (1983, 1985). Moscovitch and Winocur proposed a *component process model* in which the medial temporal lobes are considered to be modules that obligatorily encode information that is consciously apprehended and retrieve it with relatively little effort in response to a cue that clearly specifies the target. It is an *associative-cue-dependent* memory system whose domain is explicit, episodic memory. It lacks organization except that of simple and immediate contiguity between items (see Figure 14.5). By contrast, the frontal lobes are "intelligent," central system structures that *"work-with-memory"* delivered to the medial temporal lobes or recovered from it, performing much the same functions in the episodic memory domain as they do in other domains. The frontal lobes are needed for strategic aspects of encoding and retrieval which include orienting attention and organizing information at encoding; initiating and guiding search at retrieval, monitoring, endorsing, and verifying the output from the medial temporal lobes to determine if it meets the goals (description) of the memory task; and placing recovered memories in their proper temporal and spatial context. Unlike modules, central system structures, such as the frontal lobes, are defined by their function, not by the type of information they represent. Because frontal processes are strategic and reflective, rather than "reflexive," they are more effortful, requiring greater resources than medial temporal lobe modules to complete their operation (see Figure 14.5).

Perceptual modules or representation systems in the posterior neocortex are also domain-specific structures, but each is concerned with representing either faces, words, objects, places, or some other material. Processing material in one domain modifies the corresponding structures so that the same material is processed more efficiently and accurately when it is encountered subsequently, even if the individual is not aware of having encountered it before. In this way, perceptual modules mediate performance on domain-specific, perceptual implicit tests of memory.

According to the model, performance on any given task is determined by the component processes that are recruited, which in turn depends on the stimulus material, the demands of the task, and the integrity and activation of the structures that mediate the component processes. Having been based on evidence from the neuropsychological literature, the component process model clearly was able to account for the pattern of deficits and spared abilities in people with memory loss caused by medial temporal, frontal or

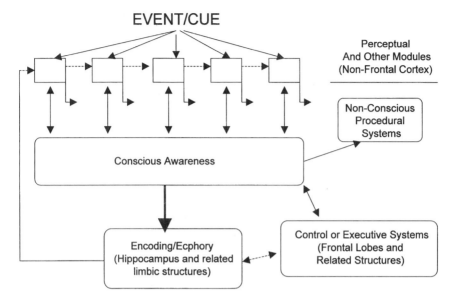

FIGURE 14.5. A schematic model of memory (from Moscovitch, 1989). See text for details.

posterior neocortical lesions (for review, see Moscovitch, 1994; Moscovitch, Gosher-Gottstein, & Vriezen, 1993; Moscovitch, Vriezen, & Gosher-Gottstein, 1994). With respect to aging, the model predicted accurately that deficits would be evident on explicit tests of memory that are mediated by the medial temporal lobes, such as free recall and recognition of randomly related words, and especially so if tests also required strategic, effortful processing by the frontal lobes as in retrieving categorized lists (see Moscovitch, 1982a; Moscovitch & Winocur, 1992, 1995; West, 1996). Performance on perceptual implicit tests of memory that did not have a strategic component, such as perceptual identification or fragment completion, would be relatively spared. The model was also applied successfully to animal models of memory (Moscovitch & Winocur, in press).

Cognitive Resources and Environmental Support

Many readers will see a resemblance between the component process model as applied to aging and Craik's theory of cognitive resources and environmental support (Craik & Jennings, 1992). According to that theory, aging is accompanied by a reduction of cognitive resources needed to initiate and implement encoding and retrieval strategies. As a result, memory in older adults is most impaired on tests of memory that make the greatest demand on those resources, namely, those that depend on self-initiated processing strategies and internally generated cues. Environmental support, in the form of external cues, structured context, and clearly defined processing strategies, can help ameliorate, and sometimes eliminate, age-related memory impairment. If one associates depletion of cognitive resources with deterioration of frontal function in old age, then the component-process model provides a neuropsychological account of the central principles of Craik's theory. Whatever the source of depletion of cognitive resources, its effect, according to the component-process model, will be greatest on central system structures such as the frontal lobes, which mediate the very processes assumed to be most affected by aging in Craik's theory. Although no deliberate attempt was made to have the component process model correspond to Craik's theory (as I recall, despite our close association, the two were developed independently of one another), it is fitting that they do so given the influence Craik's ideas and paradigms had on my first experiments on the neuropsychology of memory. Despite the obvious resemblance, it was not until we both, again independently, embarked on a series of experiments on the effects of divided attention on memory, that we turned to each other's ideas and data to help test and modify our theories and account for our findings.

☐ Part 2: Recent Empirical Studies and Theory Development

The Effects of Divided Attention on Encoding and Retrieval: Component Processes and Competition for Cognitive Resources

It has long been known that diverting attention from to-be-remembered items at encoding to some secondary task severely impairs memory for those items. What is surprising, and less well known, is that in many but not all instances, dividing attention at retrieval has little or no effect on memory performance, even though retrieval is often experienced as effortful. As we shall see, the exceptions to this rule are illuminating.

According to the component process model, only information that is consciously apprehended can be encoded by the hippocampus and related structures in the medial temporal lobes and diencephalon (Moscovitch, 1992, 1995). The frontal lobes are a crucial component in the voluntary control of attention which influences what information is attended, as well as the extent to which it is apprehended consciously and how it is organized. In so doing, the frontal lobes determine, either directly or indirectly, the type of information that is made available to the medial temporal lobe system. Diverting attention to a secondary task reduces conscious awareness of to-be-remembered items and limits access to the medial temporal lobe system. In addition, the type of information that penetrates the system when attention is divided may not be especially conducive to later memory. Thus, the information may be processed at a shallower level, or not be well organized, or be less distinctive (see Craik & Kester, 1999; Naveh-Benjamin, chapter 15 of this volume). Indeed, Craik's theory of cognitive resources predicts that dividing attention would most affect those processes that make the greatest demands on cognitive resources. It is these very processes, such as those needed to organize the material, to derive its meaning, and elaborate upon it, that promote good memory, though these alone may not be sufficient. As Craik and Kester noted in their own studies and in their review of the literature, the extent of memory loss under conditions of divided attention exceeds that accounted for by diminished depth of processing or organization. Some added factor, perhaps conscious awareness of the material itself, may be needed to activate the hippocampal system and allow it to bind the neural elements that mediate that conscious experience into a coherent memory trace, and then consolidate it (see Naveh-Benjamin, chapter 15 of this volume and Figure 14.6).

Thus, the effects of divided attention on encoding, though not fully understood, are broadly consistent with the component process model and the cognitive resource theory. The situation at retrieval is more complicated and will be the focus of the remainder of the paper.

The component process model predicts that the effects of dividing attention at retrieval will vary depending on the extent to which the frontal or medial temporal lobes are implicated. Being modular, the medial temporal lobes process information obligatorily and with relatively little effort in response to an external or internal cue. Thus, for memory tasks

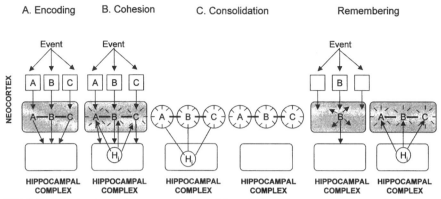

FIGURE 14.6. A schematic representation of the relation of memory and consciousness as it occurs during registration (encoding), cohesion, consolidation, and remembering. The illustration highlights the roles of the hippocampal complex and neocortex during these processes. The speckled area and sparkles represent consciousness. Hi is the hippocampal complex index for the bound engram or memory trace (A-B-C). The closed circles represent the consolidated memory trace which contains elements or features of the event with consciousness bound to it. See text, p. 183 (from Moscovitch, 1995, 1999).

that are associative-cue dependent (i.e., cue-driven either by externally or internally generated cues) and mediated primarily by the medial temporal lobe, dividing attention at retrieval should have little effect on memory performance. If, however, retrieval requires strategic processing mediated by the frontal lobes, then performance will suffer under conditions of divided attention at retrieval.

The evidence from the literature is generally consistent with these predictions. On memory tests that had little organization or strategic component, such as free recall or recognition of randomly selected words (e.g., Baddeley, Lewis, Eldridge, & Thomson, 1984), performance was not altered much by dividing attention at retrieval. If the test involved retrieval of categorized lists (Park, Smith, Dudley, & LaFronca, 1989) or list discrimination, which requires source assignment or temporal classification (Dywan & Jacoby, 1990), then performance suffered when attention was divided. (For additional references see Moscovitch, 1994, and Fernandes & Moscovitch, 2000.)

To test the component process model directly, Craik and Birtwistle's (1971) version of the release-from-PI test was enlisted again (Moscovitch, 1994). If release from PI occurs at retrieval and is dependent on the frontal lobes, then according to the component process model, dividing attention at retrieval should hamper release from PI in normal people. Overall memory performance, however, should be relatively preserved since it does not rely exclusively on the frontal lobes but is also hippocampally dependent. Using sequential finger tapping as the concurrent task, Moscovitch (1994) showed that release from PI, but not overall memory, was impaired only if tapping occurred during both retrieval and encoding (see Figure 14.7), but not during either alone. Because dividing attention at retrieval was effective only if attention was also divided at encoding, the results suggest that although release from PI may occur at retrieval, it is also dependent, in part, on how information was encoded. In retrospect, these results vindicate Cermak et al. (1974): They were partially correct in attributing the failure to release from PI in Korsakoff's amnesia to a deficit in encoding.

Similar results were obtained in a number of other dual-task memory experiments in which either sequential finger-tapping or tapping to randomly occurring visual signals (continuous visual reaction time [VRT] task) served as the interfering concurrent task.

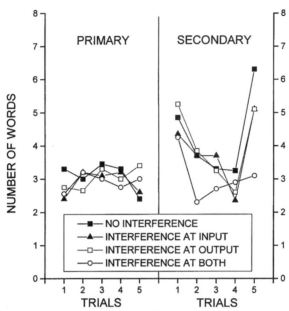

FIGURE 14.7. Mean number of words recalled from primary and secondary memory in each trial in a release-from-PI test under different interference conditions. Words were recalled from the same category on Trials 1–4 (build-up if PI) and from a different category on Trial 5 (release from PI).

Free recall of a categorized list of words from the California Verbal Learning Test was reduced equally at each of five learning trials due in part to deficient clustering, a frontally mediated organizational process (Moscovitch, 1994; Stuss et al., 1994). Rate of learning, which may be more hippocampally dependent, was intact. Likewise, Troyer, Moscovitch, Winocur, Alexander, and Stuss (1998) found that source memory, which is frontally mediated, was more impaired by divided attention than item recognition, which is more dependent on the medial temporal lobes. The effect was especially pronounced when source was assessed by the word's spatial location (left or right, see Figure 14.8), though it was also noticeable for voicing (male or female) and color. Similarly, Downey-Lamb & Woodruff-Pak (1999) showed that sequential finger-tapping led to a reduction in stem-completion, as predicted by Winocur et al.'s (1996) finding that stem completion has a frontal component. Even on tests of semantic memory, concurrent, sequential finger tapping led to a reduction in phonemic fluency, a frontally-mediated task, but not on semantic fluency which has a strong temporal lobe component (Moscovitch, 1994; Martin, Wiggs, Lalonde, & Mack, 1994). In later studies, Troyer, Moscovitch, and their colleagues showed that this difference arises because switching from one subcategory to another, a resource-demanding, frontally-mediated operation, is implicated more in tests of phonemic, than of semantic, fluency (Troyer, Moscovitch, & Winocur, 1997; Troyer et al., 1998). Interestingly, aging is also associated with decrements in switching (Troyer et al., 1998) but only on semantic fluency tasks and in source memory (Spencer & Raz, 1995), supporting the idea that aging is associated with a reduction in cognitive resources that affect frontal lobe functions.

As a note of caution, not all age-related reductions in memory can be attributed to loss of cognitive resources at retrieval or to deterioration of frontal functions. As we noted, cognitive aging is associated with reduced medial temporal, as well as frontal, function,

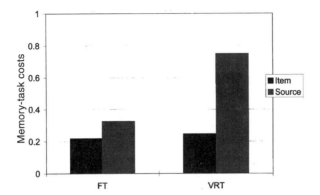

FIGURE 14.8. Memory task costs expressed in proportion decline from the undivided attention condition for item and source (location) information under two conditions of divided attention: sequential finger tapping (FT) and visual reaction time (VRT). Costs are calculated by subtracting accuracy under divided attention from full attention.

and it is expected that some age-related changes in memory may be related to medial temporal function (Craik & Kester, 1999; Moscovitch, 1982a; Moscovitch & Wincour, 1992; Naveh-Benjamin, chapter 15 of this volume). For example, free and cued recall are strongly affected by age, but very little by frontal lobe damage and by diverted attention at retrieval except under certain conditions (see below).

The effects of divided attention on recognition memory are more complicated. Recognition has both a recollective and a familiarity component (Mandler, 1980; Tulving, 1985) which can be distinguished from one another by having participants respond either "remember" (R) or "know" (K) to items that they recognize. R responses indicate that the person can recover contextual details of the event leading to a sense of reexperiencing it, whereas K responses indicate only that the person was aware that the event had occurred but no more than that. Taken at face value, the prediction, borne out by a number of studies, is that frontal lesions (Levine et al., 1998), aging (Parkin & Walter, 1992; Perfect, William, & Anderson-Brown, 1995), and divided attention at encoding (Gardiner & Parkin, 1990) would all affect R responses more than K. Indeed, Moroz and Moscovitch (Moroz, 1999) found that if the to-be-remembered material is self-referential, consisting of adjectives that may describe a person, dividing attention only at retrieval is sufficient to lead to a reduction in R, but not K, responses.[1]

---

[1]What makes the situation more complicated, however, is that both R and K responses are not pure reflections of frontal and medial temporal involvement, respectively. R responses are rapid and confident, suggesting that they may reflect recovery of a detailed memory trace via the medial temporal lobes in addition to the derived source information which is dependent on the frontal cortex. K responses, on the other hand, are slower, suggesting that once the memory on which they are based has been recovered via the medial temporal lobes, they are subject to monitoring and verification, both of which are frontally mediated. To underscore the fact that both R and K responses are hippocampally mediated, Knowlton and Squire (1996; Knowlton, 1998) showed that both are impaired in amnesia.

In addition, Henson, Rugg, Shallice, Josephs, and Dolan (1999) and Moroz, Moscovitch, Kohler, Craik, and McIntosh (in Moroz, 1999) showed that the dorsolateral frontal cortex is activated more during K than R responses. Aging and divided attention at retrieval, therefore, can have variable effects on R and K responses depending on the extent to which each is mediated by the frontal lobes and medial temporal lobes. Thus, Moroz and Moscovitch (Moroz, 1999) found that the results of the

Craik and his colleagues were also exploring the effects of divided attention at encoding and retrieval but, understandably, from a more cognitive perspective (see chapters 16 by Anderson and chapter 15 by Naveh-Benjamin in this volume). Craik, Govini, Naveh-Benjamin, and Anderson (1996) reasoned that if retrieval recapitulates processes that occurred at encoding, as many theories assert, then dividing attention at retrieval should have the same effect as it does at encoding. There already was some evidence to indicate that dividing attention at retrieval was much less debilitating than dividing attention at encoding as far as memory was concerned (Baddeley et al., 1984). Other investigators, however, noted that retrieving memories led to a substantial decrement in performance on a secondary, concurrent task. In an elegant series of experiments, Craik et al. (1996) had participants conduct two tasks simultaneously, the target memory task and a concurrent, visual, four-choice continuous reaction time (VRT) task. The memory tasks varied from free recall, to cued recall of paired associates, to recognition. Craik et al. (1996) also had participants vary the amount of attention they allocated to each task. They could divide attention evenly between the tasks or allocate it primarily to one or the other, and do so at both encoding and retrieval. By noting the effects of divided attention on the memory and distracting task, Craik et al. (1996) could determine how resource-demanding each was and derive a more accurate measure of retrieval demands than any one had yet obtained by examining each effect separately.

The results, which were replicated in subsequent studies (e.g., Naveh-Benjamin, Craik, Perretta, & Tonev, 2000) using different paradigms, were counterintuitive yet illuminating. Dividing attention at encoding had the expected, debilitating effect on memory whether tested by free recall, cued recall, or recognition: The more attention was allocated to the digit-monitoring task, the worse memory became. The opposite pattern, however, was observed at retrieval: Memory remained relatively stable across changes in attention, dropping only by a small but significant amount, although performance on the distracting task varied according to how much attention was paid to it.

Craik and his colleagues drew a number of different conclusions from these studies, but I will focus on only two of them. Because divided attention had different effects on encoding and retrieval, retrieval cannot simply be a reinstatement of the processes that occurred at encoding. More importantly, whereas encoding is both voluntary and resource demanding, retrieval, though resource demanding, seems to be obligatory. That is, once initiated, retrieval processes run to completion without being impeded by dividing attention, though the retrieval process itself requires cognitive resources as indicated by its effect on the concurrent VRT task.

That retrieval is obligatory on associative-cue-dependent tests, such as cued and free recall and recognition of random items, is consistent with the component process model; but that retrieval is also resource-demanding would, at first glance, seem to contradict it. On reflection, however, there are alternative and equally plausible interpretations that are consistent with the model. Retrieval itself consists of a number of component processes that include establishment and maintenance of a retrieval mode (see Moscovitch & Winocur, in press; Shallice, chapter 10 of this volume), recovery of a memory trace that results from

---

divided attention experiments supported the component process model by showing that divided attention at retrieval has different effects depending on the components that are involved. Divided attention leads to reduced memory performance on tests that have a strategic component, typically R responses, that are sensitive to frontal lobe damage, and that demand considerable cognitive resources for their operation. Divided attention has little effect on tests that are associative-cue dependent, typically K responses, and mediated by the medial temporal lobes and posterior neocortex since their operation makes little demand on cognitive resources.

the interaction of the cue with the engram, a process termed "ecphory," and postecphoric processes, such as monitoring, verification, and response selection. Only ecphory is associated with the medial temporal lobes by the model and is posited to require minimal resources for their operation. Initiation and maintenance of a retrieval model, as well as monitoring and response selection, are dependent on the frontal lobes and thus are in need of cognitive resources. Indeed, Craik et al. (1996) favor the interpretation that recovery of the memory trace or ecphory is obligatory and demands few resources, as the component process model asserts, but that maintenance of the retrieval mode (Craik et al., 1996) or postecphoric response selection (Anderson, chapter 10 of this volume) requires the allocation of cognitive resources. To explain why divided attention at retrieval does not lead to performance deficits on the memory task, one also needs to assume that resources are allocated preferentially to (or automatically usurped by) the memory task over the concurrent, distracting task.

Component Processes and Competition for Representations or Structures

This hypothesis led us to consider whether there are conditions under which divided attention can interfere with recovering of memory traces (ecphory) mediated by the medial temporal lobes, particularly the hippocampal complex. Almost all the studies that we reviewed had the underlying assumption that competition for limited but general resources is at the root of the divided attention effect on memory. Competition, however, can also exist at a structural level: Two tasks which vie for access to a common structure will interfere with one another even if the structures that the processes support do not demand many cognitive resources for their operation (Moscovitch, 1979). The component process model suggests two possibilities, neither of which appeals to competition for cognitive resources, but rather to competition for the structures needed to recover the memory trace. According to the model, the memory trace consists of a bound, coherent ensemble of medial temporal lobes and neocortical (and other) neurons that represent the conscious experience of a past event. Medial temporal lobe neurons act as an index (Hi) or pointer to the neocortical neurons that represent the content of the event and the conscious experience that accompanied it (Moscovitch, 1995, 1999; and Figures 14.5 and 14.6). An internal or external cue activates the medial temporal lobes index or pointer via which the memory trace is recovered. A concurrent task may interfere with retrieval by competing for one or both of the structures whose neurons comprise the memory trace: the medial temporal lobes or the neocortex. At a functional level, the first possibility is that memory will be impaired only by a concurrent memory task that competes with the primary task for the medial temporal lobes. The second possibility is that memory will be impaired by attending to any stimulus at retrieval that shares an underlying representation with the items being retrieved from memory. That is, at retrieval, it is competition for memory or representational systems, rather than for cognitive resources, that leads to memory decrement.

Fernandes and Moscovitch (Fernandes & Moscovitch, 2000; Fernandes & Moscovitch, submitted) tested these hypotheses in a series of experiments that borrowed some of the procedures from Craik et al. (1996) and to which he provided advice and support. In the first of the experiments, participants studied a set of 16 auditorily presented words under full attention which they had to recall freely aloud after a 55 s, filled delay (15 s of arithmetic and 40 s of the distracting task). In the divided attention condition, recall began after 15 seconds of the arithmetic task and participants were given 40 seconds to recall the words. During recall, participants also had to monitor simultaneously a list of visually-presented words in a running recognition test. In one divided attention condition, some words were repeated after at a lag of 3 or less, and in the other, at a lag of 7 or more, making it a test of short-term or long-term memory, respectively (see Tulving & Colotla, 1970). Both divided attention conditions were successful in producing a substantial decrement in recall of about 30% in comparison to the full attention condition. That there was no difference between the short and long lag conditions suggested that medial temporal lobes, which are involved in long-term but not short-term memory, was not the locus of the competition effect between the target and interfering memory tasks. Instead, the results suggested that the locus of the effect was at the level of neocortical representational systems involved in word perception and production.

This conclusion was confirmed in subsequent studies. Instead of using running recognition as the interference task, we used word monitoring. In the animacy monitoring task, participants monitored a list of visually presented words and indicated whenever words denoting living things occurred three times in succession. The effects of this interfering task, at encoding and retrieval, were compared with those of a similar odd-digit-monitoring task used by Craik et al. (1996), which was equally demanding (for details, see Fernandes & Moscovitch, 2000). The results in the digit-monitoring condition replicated those of Craik et al. (1996). Recall dropped by about 50% when digit monitoring occurred at encoding but only by about 10% when it occurred at retrieval. By contrast, the animacy monitoring task, which had similar effects to digit monitoring at encoding, led to a substantial 30% drop in recall at retrieval. Thus, the results showed that interference effects of divided attention at retrieval were material specific, but the effects at encoding were general. That interference at retrieval was material specific confirmed that it is competition for representational structures, presumably in the neocortex, that accounts for effects of divided attention at retrieval in associative-cue-dependent tests of memory. In contrast, at encoding, it is competition for general cognitive resources that largely determines the effects of divided attention on subsequent recall (see Figure 14.9).[2]

These results can be accommodated easily by the component process model. According

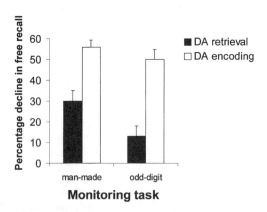

FIGURE 14.9. (a) Percentage decline in accuracy of free recall of words when attention is divided (as compared to undivided) at encoding or retrieval by concurrent monitoring tasks: man-made and odd-digit decisions.

---

[2] The effect of the target memory task on the interfering tasks was complementary, Performance on both interfering tasks dropped little at encoding but substantially at retrieval, replicating Craik et al. ((1996); see also Figure 14.9b).

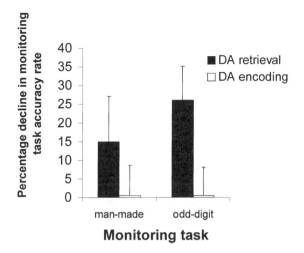

FIGURE 14.9. (b) Percentage decline in monitoring task performance at encoding and retrieval when attention is divided between the monitoring and target memory task as compared to when attention is devoted fully to the monitoring task.

to the component process model, conscious awareness of the target event is a pre-requisite for activation of the medial temporal lobes (Moscovitch 1994, 1995). Reduction of conscious awareness by any means leads to reduced formation of long-lasting memory traces or engrams, thereby explaining the general effects of divided attention at encoding. At retrieval, recovery of memory traces via the medial temporal lobes is obligatory and automatic unless a concurrently attended stimulus competes with neocortical representations that either form part of the recovered memory trace or are needed to gain access to it. This would explain the material-specific effects at retrieval (see Figures 14.9, 14.10).

In more recent experiments, Fernandes and Moscovitch (submitted) have attempted to

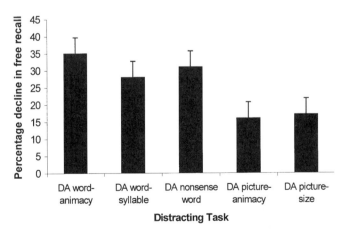

FIGURE 14.10. Percentage decline in accuracy of free recall when attention was divided at retrieval by different interfering tasks, as compared to when attention was focused only on the target memory task.

determine more precisely the nature of the representations for which the divided attention and free recall tasks compete at retrieval. Consistent with our working hypothesis, we showed that divided attention effects on memory, comparable to those obtained with the animacy monitoring tasks, can also be had on concurrent word-decision tasks made item by item that have no memory component. While recalling a list of words, participants had to indicate as each word appeared on the computer monitor whether it was living or had three or more syllables. We found that the reduction in free recall was as large on the phonological, syllable decision task as on the more semantic, animacy decision task, even if the syllable decisions involved nonsense words. The results suggested strongly that the primary locus of the interference effect is at the level of phonological representations, with semantic representations being implicated to a lesser extent. This conclusion was confirmed in a recently completed set of studies using line drawings from Snodgrass and Vanderwort (1980) as the stimuli in the interfering task. Participants made either semantic decisions about the drawings, about animacy, or about the real-world size of the depicted objects, or syllable decisions about the name of the depicted object. Recall was reduced somewhat for animacy and size decisions, but most for phonological decisions (Figure 14.10).

That the locus of the primary interfering effects of divided attention on free recall (and possibly recognition, Fernandes and Moscovitch, unpublished observation, May 1998) was phonological suggests that the effect occurred at output, after the memory trace was recovered but before it could be specified phonologically. This explanation is consistent with Pashler's (1998) model of response selection and output interference in divided attention, and with Anderson's (chapter 16 of this volume) application of it to account for some of her and Craik's findings. Alternatively, the competition may involve the phonological loop of working memory (Baddeley, 1986), which may also implicate regions of the inferior left frontal cortex needed for cue specification (Fletcher & Henson, 2001; Shallice, chapter 10 of this volume; Wagner, 1999). We plan to test these hypotheses more directly in subsequent studies.

There remains one puzzling recurring finding in Fernandes and Moscovitch's (2000, submitted) studies that was not mentioned until now and that needs to be explained. If material-specific interference effects simply blocked retrieval, memory should be restored to the level it attained under full attention once the interfering task is completed, and the interference was removed. Although participants were given the opportunity to recall more items after the concurrent task ended, they rarely recalled even a single additional word. The effects of divided attention at retrieval seemed permanent. Performance improved if recognition was tested, as was expected, but even then it did not attain the level of recognition under full attention.

One possibility is that decay may account for the effect. We do not believe this is the case because the same amount of time elapsed between presentation and final recall under full and divided attention conditions. The only difference between the two conditions was that in the full attention condition, participants performed the interfering and recall tasks successively, whereas in the divided attention condition, they performed the tasks concurrently.

Another possible explanation is that participants have difficulty discriminating between the items in the concurrent task and those in memory. Although this explanation may be applicable when words are used in both the interfering and memory tasks, it does not completely account for the equally large interference effects on memory when the items in the interfering task are nonsense words or pictures. Also, the discrimination hypothesis would predict greater effects of the target task on the interfering tasks when the two are similar as compared to different, but this, too, was not the case.

A highly speculative, but intriguing explanation is that recently learned material is in a vulnerable state, capable of disruption by procedures or stimuli that interact with the memory trace. Studies on consolidation in rodents have shown that when previously acquired, well-consolidated memories are retrieved, they are momentarily in a vulnerable state. Administration at this time of amnesic agents such as electroconvulsive shock (Lewis, Misanin, & Miller, 1968; Miller & Springer, 1973), protein inhibitors (Nader, Schafe, & LeDoux, 2000, Sara, 2000), or hippocampal lesions (Land, Bunsey, & Riccio, 2001) will either make these memories inaccessible or possibly eliminate them entirely (see discussion by Nadel and Land [and others] in 2000). Although material-specific interference does not have such a profound effect, it may operate on similar principles. The concurrent interfering material may alter the trace sufficiently to make it inaccessible on free recall, and possibly on recognition. Such an interpretation predicts that the effects will be observed only if they occur concurrently with memory retrieval, even if the memories were acquired long ago.

Evidence Concerning the Neurological Basis of Divided Attention

The component process model provides a neuropsychological account of the effects of divided attention at encoding and retrieval that is also compatible with Craik's cognitive resources theory. Although the predictions that followed from the model were generally confirmed by the studies we reviewed, almost all of the studies tested the model at a behavioral or functional level in normal people, rather than more directly at a level that takes neuroanatomy into account. For example, we do not know what the effects of frontal or medial temporal lobes lesions are on memory under conditions of divided attention, though some clear predictions follow from the model.

For lack of patients, some investigators, ourselves included, have turned to older adults to test their neuropsychologically based theories, because aging leads to deterioration of the frontal lobes and medial temporal lobes. Glisky, Polster, & Routhieaux (1995) adopted the sensible approach of screening older adults on tests sensitive to frontal and medial temporal lobe damage and divided them into groups according to their performance, the assumption being that test performance will reflect the integrity of the mediating structures. Although this approach has been used successfully in other contexts (McDaniel, Glisky, Rubin, Guynn, & Routhieaux, 1999), as far as we know it has not been applied to memory under conditions of divided attention. Preliminary results from our own study in collaboration with Glisky and Davidson suggest that frontal dysfunction in older adults has little effect on memory when attention is divided at retrieval, as the component process model predicts.

Functional neuroimaging provides another technique for testing some of the neuroanatomical predictions of the model. Yet here, too, there is less than a handful of studies on divided attention. Nonetheless, the results of even these few studies are dramatic and consistent with the model.

In a position emission tomography (PET) study, Shallice et al. (1994) found greater activation in the dorsolateral prefrontal cortex (DLPFC) during encoding of a categorized list of words. Activation in this region was unaffected by an easy distracting task but significantly reduced by a difficult distracting task, which also led to a decrement in memory performance. Shallice et al. concluded that the DLPFC is implicated in organizational processes at encoding which are disrupted by a difficult concurrent task.

In a subsequent PET study, Fletcher, Shallice, and Dolan (1998) used two different word lists: one that the participant had to organize at encoding, and the other that already was organized into its separate categories. As predicted, the list that required the implementation of an organizational strategy activated the left DLPFC as well as the ventrolateral PFC (VLPFC), whereas the already organized list only activated the VLPFC. A concurrent finger-tapping task reduced DLPFC activity only during encoding of the list that emphasized organizational processing, whereas it reduced VLPFC equally for both tasks. Similar reductions in activity of the left VLPFC were noted in PET studies by Craik and Anderson and their collaborations (see Anderson, chapter 16 of this volume) both during a concurrent task and in aging (see also Shallice, chapter 10 of this volume).

The latter finding is interesting in light of the observation that activity in VLPFC at encoding is correlated with subsequent memory even for single words (Wagner et al., 1998) or complex pictures (Brewer, Zhao, Desmond, Glover, & Gabrieli, 1998). Whereas the presumed function of DLPFC is to manipulate information held in working memory and thus help implement encoding strategies, the function of VLPFC is cue specification or description. If this hypothesis is correct, decreased activation in VLPFC by a concurrent task, or by aging, leads to poor memory because the distinctive aspects of the item are poorly specified at encoding, making it difficult to retrieve it (Moscovitch & Craik, 1976; Moscovitch & Winocur, in press).

To our knowledge, there is only one published study on the effects of divided attention on memory at retrieval. Anderson, Craik, Idaka, and their colleagues (Anderson, chapter 16 of this volume) examined both young and older adults. They found that memory performance in young adults was associated with activity in the right fronto-polar cortex (BA 10), whereas in older adults it was associated with additional activity in the left mid-DLPFC (BA 46) and the VLPFC (BA 45/47). What is interesting is that in contrast to encoding, a concurrent task at retrieval did not alter activity in these regions (see Anderson, chapter 16).

The results from these studies, sparse as they are, are consistent with predictions of the component process model. Dividing attention by imposing a concurrent task affects frontal processes needed for encoding on any type of memory task, though the affected regions may depend on the extent of strategic processing that the task demands. At retrieval, however, dividing attention by a nonspecific concurrent task has little effect on frontal function unless strategic retrieval processes are involved. It remains to be determined whether non-specific concurrent tasks will alter the level of DLPFC at retrieval, as they did at encoding, if strategic processes are invoked. Material-specific concurrent tasks, however, should lead to changes in cerebral activation in the posterior neocortex, and possibly VLPFC, even on tests of memory that are associative-cue dependent.

☐ Conclusion

In writing this chapter, we could not help but be struck by how much some of the empirical and theoretical work emanating from Craik's and Moscovitch's labs were interweaved with one another. Ideas and themes, even material and procedures, developed by one are picked and reworked by the other. Sometimes this is done deliberately, and we have tried to note as best we could those instances in which we felt Gus's influence directly. Sometimes the labs joined forces on collaborative ventures leading to joint publications. More often, however, the influences were more subtle and pervasive. This chapter is a testimony to the open and free exchange of ideas that existed between us—and the advantages of having Gus as a colleague and friend. Happily, this relationship shows no sign of diminishing. If anything, Gus's increased interest in cognitive neuroscience indicates that there will be even more to share in the future.

☐ Acknowledgment

Preparation of this paper and the research reported in it was supported by an NSERC of Canada grant to MM, an MRC and CIHR of Canada grant to MM and Gordon Winocur, an NSERC of Canada fellowship to MF, and a Rothman postdoctoral fellowship to AT. We thank Marilyne Ziegler and Heidi Roesler for help in collecting and analyzing the data and making the figures.

☐ References

Anderson, N. D., Craik, F. I. M., & Naveh-Benjamin, M. (1998). The attentional demands of encoding and retrieval in younger and older adults: I. Evidence from divided attention costs. *Psychology and Aging, 13*, 405–423.

Balleley, A. D. (1986). *Working memory.* Oxford: Oxford University Press.

Baddeley, A. D., Lewis, V., Eldridge, M., & Thomson, N. (1984). Attention and retrieval from long-term memory. *Journal of Experimental Psychology: General, 113*(4), 518–540.

Brewer, J. B., Zhao, Z., Desmond, J. E., Glover, G. H., & Gabrieli, J. D. E. (1998). Making memories: Brain activity that predicts how well visual experience will be remembered. *Science, 281*, 1185–1187.

Cermak, L. S., Butters, N., & Moreines, J. (1974). Some analyses of the verbal encoding deficit of alcoholic Korsakoff patients. *Brain and Language, 1*, 141–150.

Craik, F. I. M. (1970). Primary memory. *British Medical Bulletin, 27*, 232–236.

Craik. F. I. M. (1973). A "levels of analysis" view of memory. In P. Pliner, L. Kramer, & T. Alloway (Eds.), *Communication and affect: Language and thought* (pp. 45–65). New York: Academy Press.

Craik, F. I. M., & Birtwistle, J. (1971). Proactive inhibition in free recall. *Journal of Experimental Psychology, 91*, 120–123.

Craik, F. I. M., Govoni, R., Naveh-Benjamin, M., & Anderson, N. D. (1996). The effects of divided attention on encoding and retrieval processes in human memory. *Journal of Experimental Psychology: General, 125*(2), 159–180.

Craik, F. I. M., & Kester, J. D. (1999). Divided attention and memory:Impairment of processing or consolidation? In E. Tulving (Ed.), *Memory, consciousness, and the brain: The Tallinn conference.* (pp. 38–51). Philadelphia: Psychology Press.

Craik, F. I. M., & Lockhart, R. S. (1972). Levels of processing: A framework for memory research. *Journal of Verbal Learning and Verbal Behavior, 11*, 671–684.

Craik, F. I. M., Morris, L. W., Morris, R. G., & Loewen, E. R. (1990). Relations between source amnesia and frontal lobe functioning in older adults. *Psychology and Aging, 5*, 148–151.

Craik. F. I. M., & Jenning, J. M. (1992). Human memory. In F. I. M. Craik & T. A. Salthouse (Eds.), *The handbook of aging and cognition* (pp. 51–110). Hillsdale, NJ: Erlbaum.

Davis, H. P., Cohen, A., Gundy, M., Colombo, P., Van Dusseldorp, G., Simolke, N., & Romanao, J. (1990). Lexical priming deficits as a result of age. *Behavioral Neuroscience, 104*, 299–297.

Downey-Lamb & Woodruf-Pak, D. S. (1999). Dual-task performance of nondeclarative tasks in young and older adults. *Society for Neuroscience Abstracts, 25*, 1896.

Dywan, J., & Jacoby, L. L. (1990). Effects of aging on source monitoring: Differences in susceptibility to false fame. *Psychology and Aging, 5*, 379–387.

Fernandes, M. A., & Moscovitch, M. (2000). Divided attention and memory: Evidence of substantial interference effects at retrieval and encoding. *Journal of Experimental Psychology: General, 129*(2), 155–176.

Fernandes, M. A., & Moscovitch, M. (submitted). Factors modulating the effect of divided attention at retrieval: mnemonics, semantics, phonemics or word-forms?

Fletcher, P. C., Shallice, T., & Dolan, R. J. (1998). The functional roles of prefrontal cortex in episodic memory I. Encoding. *Brain, 121*, 1239–1248.

Fodor, J. (1983) *The modularity of mind.* Cambridge, MA: MIT Press.

Fodor, J. (1985). Precis of "The modularity of mind." *Behavioral and Brain Sciences, 8,* 1–42.

Gardiner, J. M., Craik, F. I. M., & Birtwistle, J. (1972). Retrieval cues and release from proactive inhibition. *Journal of Verbal Learning and Verbal Behavior, 11,* 778–783.

Gardiner, J. M., & Parkin, A. (1990). Attention and recollective experience in recognition memory. *Memory and Cognition, 18,* 579–583.

Glisky, E. L., Polster, M. R., & Routhieaux, B. C. (1995). Double dissociation between item and source memory. *Neuropsychologia, 9,* 229–235.

Henson, R. N. A., Rugg, M. D., Shallice, T., Josephs, O., & Dolan, R. A. (1999). Recollection and familiarity in recognition memory: An event-related functional magnetic resonance imaging study. *The Journal of Neuroscience, 19,* 3962–3972.

Knowlton, B. J. (1998). The relationship between remembering and knowing: A cognitive neuroscience perspective. *Acta Psychologica, 98,* 253–266.

Knowlton, B. J., & Squire L. R. (1995). Remembering and knowing: Two different expressions of declarative memory. *Journal of Experimental Psychology: Learning, Memory, and Cognition, 21,* 699–710.

Land, C., Bunsey, M., & Riccio, D. C. (2001) Anomalous properties of hippocampal lesion-induced retrograde amnesia. *Psychobiology, 28,* 476–485.

Lhermitte, F., & Signoret, J. L. (1972) Analyse neuropsychologique et doffereciation des syndromes amnestiques. *Revue Neurologique, 126,* 161–178.

Levine, B., Black, S. E., Cabeza, R., Sinden, M., McIntosh, A. R., Toth, J. P., Tulving, E., & Stuss, D. T. (1998). Episodic memory and the self in a case of isolated retrograde amnesia. *Brain, 121,* 1951–1973.

Lewis, D. J., Misanin, J. R., & Miller, R. R. (1968). The recovery of memory following amnestic treatment. *Nature, 220,* 704–705.

Luria A. R. (1971). Memory disturbances in local brain lesions. *Neuropsychologia, 9,* 367–376.

Mandler, G. (1980). Recognizing: The judgement of previuos occurrence. *Psychological Review, 87,* 252–271.

Martin, A., Wiggs, O. I., Lalonde, F., & Mack, C. (1994). Word retrieval to letter and semantic uses: A double dissociation in normal subjects using interference tasks. *Neuropsychologica, 32,* 1487–1494.

McDaniel, M. A., Glisky, E. L., Rubin, S. R., Guynn, M. J., & Routhieaux, B. C. (1999). Prospective memory: A neuropsychological study. *Neuropsychology, 13,* 103–110.

McIntyre, J. S., & Craik, F. I. M. (1987). Age differences in memory for item and source information. *Canadian Journal of Psychology, 41,* 175–192.

Melton, A. W. (1963). Implications of short-term memory for a general theory of memory. *Journal of Verbal Learning and Verbal Behavior, 2,* 1–21.

Melton, A. W. (1970). Short- and long-term post-perceptual memory: Dichotomy or continuum? In K. H. Pribram & D. E. Broadbent (Eds.), *Biology of memory.* New York: Academic Press.

Miller, R. R., & Springer, A. D. (1973). Amnesia, consolidation and retrieval. *Psychological Review, 80,* 69–79.

Moroz, T. M. (1998). *Episodic memory fort persoannly relevant information: Evidence from aging, divided attention at retrieval, and position emission tomography.* Unpublished doctoral dissertation, University of Toronto.

Moscovitch, M. (1973). Language and the cerebral hemisphere: Reaction-time studies and their implications for models of cerebral dominance. In P. Pliner, L. Rames, and T. Alloway (Eds.), *Communication and affect: Language and thought* (pp. 89–126). New York: Academic Press.

Moscovitch, M. (1979). Information processing in the cerebral hemispheres. In M. S. Gazzaniga (Ed.), *Hanbook of Behavioral Neurobiology, Volume 2: Neuropsychology* (pp. 379–446). New York: Plenum Press.

Moscovitch, M. (1982a). Multiple dissociation of function in the amnesic syndrome. In L. S. Cermak (Ed.), *Human memory and amnesia* (pp. 337–370). Hillsdale, NJ: Erlbaum.

Moscovitch, M. (1982b). Neuropsychological approaches to perception and memory in normal and pathological aging. In F. I. M. Craik & S. Trehub (Eds.), *Aging and cognitive processes* (pp. 55–78). Plenum Press.

Moscovitch, M. (1989). Confabulation and the frontal system: Strategic vs, associative retrieval in neuropsychological theories of memory. In H. L Roediger III & F. I. M. Craik (Eds.), *Varieties of memory and consciousness: Essays in honour of Endel Tulving* (pp. 133–160). Hillsdale, NJ: Erlbaum.

Moscovitch, M. (1999). Theories of memory and consciousness. In E. Tulving & F. I. M. Craik (Eds.), *The Oxford handbook of memory.* Oxford: Oxford University Press.

Moscovitch, M. (1992). Memory and working-with-memory: A component process model based on modules and central systems. *Journal of Cognitive Neuroscience, 4,* 257–267.

Moscovitch, M. (1994). Cognitive resources and dual-task interference effects at retrieval in normal people: The role of the frontal lobes and medial temporal cortex. *Neuropsychology, 8,* 524-534.

Moscovitch, M. (1995). Recovered consciousness: A hypothesis concerning modularity and episodic memory. *Journal of Clinical and Experimental Neuropsychology, 17*(2), 276–290.

Moscovitch, M., & Craik, F. I. M. (1976). Depth of processing, retrieval cues and uniqueness of encoding as factors in recall. *Journal of Verbal Learning and Verbal Behavior, 15,* 447–458.

Moscovitch, M., Goshen-Gottstein, Y., & Vriezen, E. (1994). Memory without conscious recollection: A tutorial review from a neuropsychological perspective. In C. Umilta & M. Moscovitch (Eds.), *Attention & performance XV: Conscious and nonconscious processes in cognition* (pp. 619–660). Cambridge, MA: MIT/Bradford Press.

Moscovitch, M., & Melo, B. (1997). Strategic retrieval and the frontal lobes: Evidence from confabulation and amnesia. *Neuropsychologia, 35,* 1017–1034.

Moscovitch, M., & Umiltà, C. (1990). Modularity and neuropsychology: Implications for the organization of attention and memory in normal and brain-damaged people. In M. F. Schwartz (Ed.), *Modular processes in dementia* (pp. 1–59). Cambridge, MA: MIT/Bradford.

Moscovitch, M., & Umiltà, C. (1991). Conscious and nonconscious aspects of memory: A neuropsychological framework of modules and central systems. In R. Lister & H. Weingartner. (Eds.), *Perspectives in cognitive neuroscience* (pp. 229–266). London: Oxford University Press.

Moscovitch, M., Vriezen, E., & Goshen-Gottstein, Y. (1993). Implicit tests of memory in patients with focal lesions or degenerative brain disorders. In F. Boller & H. Spinnler (Eds.), *The handbook of neuropsychology, Vol. 8* (pp. 133–173). Amsterdam: Elsevier Press.

Moscovitch, M., & Winocur, G. (1983). Contextural cues and release from proactive inhibition in young and old people. *Canadian Journal of Psychology, 37,* 338–344.

Moscovitch, M., & Winocur, G. (1992). The Neuropsychology of memory and aging. In F. I. M. Craik & T. A. Salthouse (Eds.), *The handbook of aging and cognition* (pp. 315–372). Hillsdale, NJ: Erlbaum.

Moscovitch, M., & Winocur, G. (1995). Frontal lobes, memory, and aging. In J. Grafman, K.J. Holyoak, & F. Boller (Eds.), *Structure and function of the human prefrontal cortex. Annals of the New York Academy of Sciences, 769* (pp. 119–150). New York: New York Academy of Sciences.

Moscovitch, M., & Winocur, G. (in press). Working-with-memory and the frontal lobes. In D. T Stuss & R. Knight (Eds.), *The frontal lobes: Proceedings of the Rotman conference.*

Moscovitch, M., Winocur, G., & McLachlan, D. (1986). Memory as assessed by recognition and by reading time of normal and transformed script: Evidence from normal young and old people, and patients with severe memory impairment due to Alzheimer's Disease and other neurological disorders. *Journal of Experimental Psychology: General, 115,* 331–347.

Nadel, L., & Land, C. (2000). Memory traces revisited. *Nature Reviews: Neuroscience, 1,* 209–212.

Nader, K., Schafe, G. E., & LeDoux, J. E. (2000). Fear memories require protein synthesis in the amygdala for reconsolidation after retrieval. *Nature, 406,* 722–726.

Naveh-Benjamin, M., Craik, F. I. M., Perretta, J. G., & Tonev, S. (2000). The effects of divided attention on encoding and retrieval processes: The resiliency of retrieval processes. *Quarterly Journal of Experimental Psychology, 53A,* 609–635.

Nyberg, L., Moscovitch, M., & Winocur, G. (1997). When do the frontal lobes contribute to priming? *Neuropsychology, 11,* 70–76.

Park, D. C., Smith, A. D., Dudley, W. N., & Lafronza, V. N. (1989). Effects of age and a divided attention task presented during encoding and retrieval on memory. *Journal of Experimental Psychology: Learning, Memory, and Cognition, 15,* 1185-1191.

Parkin, A., & Walter, B. M. (1992). Recollective experience, normal aging, and frontal function. *Psychology and Aging, 17,* 290–298.

Pashler, H. E. (1998). *The psychology of attention.* Cambridge, MA: MIT Press.

Perfect, T. J., Williams, R. B., & Andeerson-Brown, C. (1995). Age differences in recollective experience are due to encoding effects, not response bias. *Memory, 3,* 169–186.

Sara, S. J. (2000). Retrieval and reconsolidation: Toward a neurobiology of remembering. *Learning and Memory, 7,* 73–84.

Schacter, D. L., Harbluck, J. L., & McLachlan, D. R. (1984). Retrieval without recollection: An experimental analysis of source amnesia. *Journal of Verbal Learning and Verbal Behavior, 23,* 593–611.

Shallice, T., Fletcher, P., Frith, C. D., Grasby, P., Frackowiak, R. S. J., & Dolan, R. J. (1994). Brain regions associated with acquisition and retrieval of verbal episodic memory. *Nature, 368,* 633–635.

Snodgrass, J. G., & Vanderwart, M. (1980). A standardized set of 260 pictures: Norms for name agreement, image agreement, familiarity, and visual complexity. *Journal of Experimental Psychology: Human Learning and Memory, 6(2),* 174–215.

Spencer, W. D., & Raz, N (1995). Differential effects of age on memory for content and context: A meta-analysis. *Psychology and Aging, 10,* 527–539.

Stuss, D. T., Alexander, M. P., Palumbo, C. L., Buckle, L. Sayer, L., & Pogue, J. (1994). Organizational strategies of patients with unilateral or bilateral frontal lobe injury in word list learning tasks. *Neuropsychology, 8,* 355–373.

Troyer, A. K., Moscovitch, M., & Winocur, G. (1997). Clustering and switching as two components of verbal fluency: Evidence from younger and older healthy adults. *Neuropsychology, 11,* 138–146.

Troyer, A. K., Moscovitch, M., Winocur, G., Alexander, M. P., & Stuss, D. (1998). Clustering and switching on verbal fluency: The effects of focal frontal- and temporal-lobe lesions. *Neuropsychologia, 36,* 449–504.

Troyer, A. K., Winocur, G., Craik, F. I. M., & Moscovitch, M. (1999). Source memory and divided attention: Reciprocal costs to primary and secondary tasks. *Neuropsychology, 13,* 467–474.

Tulving, E. (1985). Memory and consciousness. *Canadian Psychology, 26,* 1–12.

Tulving, E., & Colotla, V. (1970). Free recall of trilingual lists. *Cognitive Psychology, 1,* 86–98.

Wagner, A. D. (1999). Working memory contributions to human learning and remembering. *Neuron, 22,* 19–22.

West, R. L. (1996). An application of prefrontal cortex function theory to cognitive aging. *Psychological Bulletin, 120,* 272–292.

Wagner, A. D., Schacter, D. L., Rotte, M., Koutstaal, W., Maril, A., Dale, A. D., Rosen, B. R., & Buckner, R. L. (1998). Building memories: Remembering and forgetting of verbal experiences as predicted by brain activity. *Science, 281,* 1188–1191.

Winocur, G. (1982). Learning and memory deficits in institutionalized old people: An analysis of interference effects. In F. I. M. Craik & S. Trehub (Eds.), *Aging and Cognitive Processes* (pp. 155–182). New York: Plenum Press.

Winocur, G., Moscovitch, M., & Stuss, D. T. (1996). A neuropsychological investigation of explicit and implicit memory in institutionalized and community-dwelling old people. *Neuropsychology, 10,* 57–65.

CHAPTER

Moshe Naveh-Benjamin

The Effects of Divided Attention on Encoding Processes: Underlying Mechanisms

This chapter examines some issues related to the effects of divided attention on memory, including some recent work that I have conducted on memory encoding and retrieval. Although I have been interested in the question of the relationships between attention and encoding and retrieval processes in human memory for many years, the current research stems from issues that Gus Craik and I have investigated in recent years, starting in 1992, when I spent two years at the University of Toronto. This collaboration and interaction with Gus inspired further research of my own, and I am indebted to Gus for his counsel and support.

The work reported in this article relates mostly to the effects of divided attention (DA) on encoding processes, although occasionally the effects of DA on retrieval processes are mentioned as well. After describing some empirical results concerning the effects of DA on encoding and retrieval, I would like to evaluate several hypotheses concerning the underlying mechanisms mediating the effects of DA at encoding on memory performance. Although the detrimental effects of DA are well documented (see below, and also Anderson, chapter 16 of this volume), I will contend that the status of the hypotheses explaining these effects is not entirely clear. In particular, I will evaluate the validity of two well-established dichotomies in memory research in explaining results concerning the effects of DA at encoding on memory performance. One dichotomy is related to the distinction between strategic-effortful and nonstrategic-automatic encoding behavior, and the other is related to the distinction between processing of item and associative information.

☐ Memory and DA

Studies using the DA paradigm have shown marked differences between encoding and retrieval processes. Dividing participants' attention between the encoding of the information presented and performing a secondary task has been shown to have a clear detrimental effect on free recall, cued recall, and recognition memory performance compared to conditions where full attention is paid to encoding the items (e.g., Baddeley, Lewis, Eldridge, & Thomson, 1984; Craik, Govoni, Naveh-Benjamin, & Anderson, 1996; Murdock, 1965; Naveh-Benjamin, Craik, Guez, & Dori, 1998; Naveh-Benjamin, Craik, Gavrilescu, & Anderson, 2000; see also Anderson, chapter 16 of this volume). DA at encoding has a similar effect on a variety of memory features, including memory for frequency of occurrence (Naveh-Benjamin & Jonides, 1986), memory for spatial location (Naveh-Benjamin, 1987, 1988), and memory for temporal order information (Naveh-Benjamin, 1990).

For example, Murdock (1965) had participants sort cards into one, two, or four piles during presentation of a list of words, and showed that free recall performance declined under DA conditions as compared to a case in which a full attention condition was used. In addition, free recall performance declined as secondary-task card sorting was emphasized. Likewise, Craik et al. (1996) showed that encoding single words and word pairs results in a reliable decrease in secondary task performance. Furthermore, manipulating emphasis by instructing participants to emphasize either the memory task, the secondary task, or both tasks equally has complementary effects on the two tasks: As attention is switched to the secondary task and away from the memory task, memory performance declines and secondary task performance improves. These results indicate that encoding processes require attention and that the allocation of attention to encoding processes is under the participant's conscious control.

The effects of DA on retrieval processes are quite different. When attention was divided at retrieval, participants in Baddeley et al. (1984), Craik et al. (1996), Naveh-Benjamin et al. (1998), Naveh-Benjamin, Craik, Perretta, and Tonev (2000), and Naveh-Benjamin, Craik, Gavrilescu, and Anderson (2000) showed only small reductions in free recall, cued recall, and recognition performance (but see results reported by Fernandes & Moscovitch, 2000). This relative immunity of memory to DA at retrieval was shown by Craik et al. (1996) and Naveh-Benjamin, Craik, Perretta, and Tonev (2000) to be accompanied by substantial secondary-task reaction time (RT) costs, which decreased from free recall to cued recall to recognition (see also Anderson, chapter 16 of this volume; Griffith, 1976; Johnston, Greenberg, Fisher, & Martin, 1970; Johnston, Griffith, & Wagstaff, 1972).

☐ The Effects of DA on Encoding: Underlying Mechanisms

One suggested mediating factor for the effects of DA at encoding on later memory performance is reduced processing time. According to this suggestion, the decrease in memory performance under DA at encoding is due to the subjects spending some of their time performing the secondary task, leaving less time available for processing the relevant information. However, using a shared-time model analysis, Craik et al. (1996) showed that the decrease in processing time could explain only part of the deficit (in contrast to the effects of DA at retrieval, see Anderson, chapter 16 of this volume). Likewise, Naveh-Benjamin, Craik, Gavrilescu, and Anderson (2000), using a similar approach, showed that the reduced memory performance as a result of DA at encoding was only partially related to the reduced functional time available for encoding (for details, see Anderson, this volume). In order to shed some light on possible mechanisms underlying these DA effects, in the following sections I will discuss three possible mediating mechanisms for the effects of DA at encoding: impaired strategic-effortful processing, impaired automatic-nonstrategic processing, and impaired associative processing.

Impaired Strategic-Effortful Encoding

One possibility is that the decrease in memory performance when attention is divided at encoding is related to a decrease in strategic-effortful processing (Hasher & Zacks, 1979). In other words, as subjects are trying to perform the secondary task, they do not have enough resources left to allow them to use strategic-effortful processes. According to this view, those aspects of encoding that do not require strategic-effortful processes will be much less affected by the division of attention.

This idea is intuitively appealing as it relates directly to the notion of limited attentional resources; the fewer the resources available for encoding, the less participants can engage in strategic-effortful encoding processing, resulting in poorer memory performance. This idea has received support from several studies that manipulated the difficulty of the secondary task at encoding. For example, Craik was one of the first researchers (C. M. B. Anderson & Craik, 1974) to show that the difficulty of a secondary RT task (and thus the amount of processing capacity required to carry it out) is inversely related to later memory performance. Similarly, more recently, we have shown (Naveh-Benjamin, Craik, Gavrilescu, and Anderson, 2000) that the difficulty of the secondary task at encoding (but not at retrieval) affects memory performance. Participants listened to lists of 12 word pairs each, to be learned under conditions of either full attention or DA. In the DA conditions, participants performed a continuous-choice RT task that involved a visual display on a computer screen and a manual response on a computer keyboard. The display consisted of either 3 or 6 boxes arranged horizontally. An asterisk appeared at random in one of the boxes and the participants' task was to press the corresponding key on the keyboard. A correct response caused the asterisk to move immediately to one of the other boxes at random. The results, which appear in Figure 15.1, indicate that cued recall memory performance was worse in the condition where 6 boxes were used rather than 3 (interestingly, no such effect was obtained when attention was divided at retrieval). The most straightforward interpretation of these results is that the 6-box condition requires more attentional resources, leaving fewer resources available for strategic-effortful processing of the encoded words.

Note, however, that this interpretation of the results assumes that the fewer attentional resources are left for encoding, the lower the probability that strategic encoding processes will be used for the words. Therefore, the above results provide only indirect evidence, as they do not reflect the direct measurement or manipulation of underlying strategic-effortful processes. Do we have any direct evidence that strategic-effortful processes are the ones affected by DA at encoding? In a series of elegant studies during the 1980s, Craik provided such evidence, showing that under DA at encoding, participants use shallower and less semantic processes to encode the information.

In a typical study, Craik (1982) used the orienting task procedure, where for each item presented, participants were asked a question relating to either the graphemic, phonemic, or semantic aspects of a word, with half of the words yielding a positive answer and the other half a negative answer. Participants performed the task either paying full attention to the words or attending also to an auditory secondary task at the same time. Recall performance demonstrated that the DA participants showed the greatest memory deficit under deeper levels of processing; this indicated that strategic-effortful semantic processes are the ones most affected under DA. Similar results, indicating a shallower level of processing under DA at encoding conditions, were reported by Craik and Byrd (1982) and Rabinowitz, Craik, and Ackerman (1982). In addition, a recent study conducted by us (Naveh-Benjamin, Craik, Gavrilescu, & Anderson, 2000; described in Anderson, chapter

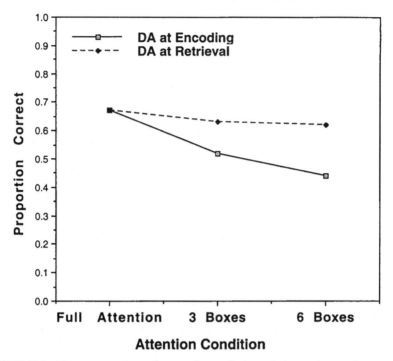

FIGURE 15.1. Mean proportions of correctly recalled words for each attention condition as a function of number of boxes in the display.

16 of this volume) supported the notion that DA at encoding changes the qualitative nature of encoding such that it becomes less semantic in nature. Finally, recent studies using neuroimaging techniques (e.g., Fletcher et al., 1995; N. D. Anderson et al., 2000) have shown that DA at encoding reduces encoding-related brain activity in the left inferior prefrontal cortex, an area shown in other studies to be associated with deep strategic semantic processing (e.g., Kapur et al., 1994).

All of this provides converging evidence, coinciding with our intuitions, that DA at encoding interrupts the deep-level strategic-effortful processes necessary for an adequate encoding of incoming information. However, the results of several recent studies complicate this picture.

For example, a recent series of studies carried out by Craik and Kester (2000) provide some counter-results. In a typical study in this series, participants were presented with word pairs and asked to rate the elaborateness of the connection they could create for each word pair. This was done under either full attention or DA, where participants simultaneously performed an auditory digit-monitoring task. Results indicated that later unexpected cued recall performance improved as the rated degree of elaboration increased, and that this happened for both full attention and DA conditions. However, in contrast to what is expected by the strategic-effortful hypothesis, memory performance for the DA condition was substantially lower than under the full attention condition at every level of elaboration. In other words, for the same degree of strategic semantic elaboration, fewer words were recalled after being encoded under DA conditions; this implies that there is a different mechanism, other than the amount of strategic elaboration, underlying the effects of DA at encoding on later memory performance.

Similarly, several studies carried out recently in my laboratory do not support the hypothesis that the effects of DA at encoding on memory performance are mediated by reduced strategic-effortful processing. In all of these studies, we employed a dual-task paradigm with the following features: We used well-understood memory paradigms in which encoding and retrieval phases could be clearly separated. To avoid modality-specific interference, we presented the memory lists auditorily and asked for spoken recall, while the concurrent task employed visual stimuli and manual responses. The concurrent task was a continuous choice reaction time (CRT) task reported in previous studies (Craik et al., 1996; Naveh-Benjamin et al., 1998; Naveh-Benjamin, Craik, Gavrilescu, & Anderson, 2000; Naveh-Benjamin, Craik, Perretta, & Anderson, 2000; Naveh-Benjamin & Guez, 2000), in which the participant's response immediately caused the next stimulus to appear. As performance did not reach ceiling on either task performed singly, we argue that each task required full attention. When performed together, the tasks allowed for assessment of performance throughout the dual-task interval.

The idea behind the first two experiments was to evaluate the degree to which the type of instructions given to the participants modulates the effects of DA at encoding on memory performance. Specifically, we tested the hypothesis that if strategic-effortful processes are the ones mediating these DA effects, then one way of reducing the effect would be to provide instructions (conditions) under which participants would not use strategic-effortful processes. In this case, we would expect DA to have either a reduced effect or no effect at all, as there is no apparent reason for participants to employ strategic-effortful processes under either full or DA conditions.

In one such experiment carried out by Iris Lowenschuss, half of the participants listened to a list of words under intentional learning instructions, where they were told to try to learn the words for an upcoming memory test. The other half listened to the words under pure incidental learning instructions, where they were told that the experimenter was interested in their physiological response to the words (they were hooked up, as was the "intentional" group, to electrodes). Half of the subjects in each learning group were presented with the words under full attention and the other half performed a concurrent secondary visual four-choice reaction-time task, as described above. All subjects received an item recognition test at the end.

The results of this experiment (Figure 15.2), show the expected large effects of both DA and intention to learn. Interestingly, there is no sign of an interaction between the two factors. In particular, the effect of DA on memory performance was as large in the incidental as in the intentional learning condition, despite the fact that in the former condition no strategic-effortful processing was used, as participants did not expect to be tested later. In the postexperiment debriefing, participants confirmed that under incidental learning instructions they did not in any way try to learn the information. In contrast, most of the subjects under intentional learning instructions reported using different elaborative strategies. Such a result suggests that DA at encoding affects other types of processing than those associated with effortful strategic ones.

A second experiment carried out by Ido Ziv, Ariel Hartman, and Jonathan Guez used a more complicated design with six combinations of encoding instructions (incidental or intentional) and encoding strategy (no strategy, rehearsal, and sentence generation). Subjects studied lists of word pairs under either full attention or DA at encoding and then received an item recognition test. The results of this study were similar to the previously discussed experiment in that intention to learn did not interact with the DA effects. In particular, this pattern was seen in the two conditions where no study strategy was used (pure incidental and pure intentional conditions), despite the strong effects of both intention and DA.

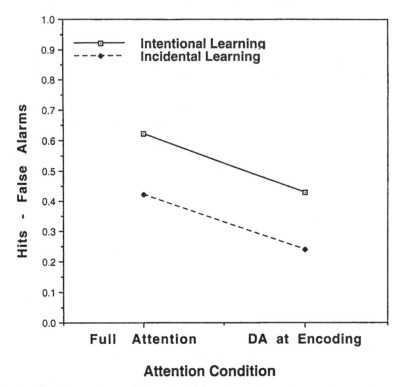

FIGURE 15.2. Proportions of hits minus false alarms for each attention condition, as a function of the type of learning at encoding (pure incidental vs. intentional).

The above results are not in line with the hypothesis that DA at encoding has its greatest effect on strategic-effortful processing. DA appears to have considerable effect on memory even when participants are not expecting a memory test and show no indication that they are using any strategy-related processing at encoding. At a minimum, these results do not support across-the-board adverse effects of DA at encoding on strategic-effortful processing; instead, it seems that DA may affect types of processing other than strategic-effortful ones.

Impaired Automatic-Nonstrategic Processing

The above-mentioned studies raise the possibility that the effects of DA at encoding on later memory performance might be mediated by automatic-nonstrategic processes. One possibility is that the effects of DA are downstream in the continuum of processing, after strategic processing and other types of processing are completed. Specifically, one possibility is that the operations interrupted during DA at encoding are consolidation processes that bind aspects of the coherent memory trace. Although consolidation has been accepted and usefully used in physiologically oriented studies of memory (e.g., McGaugh, 1966; Alvarez & Squire, 1994; Weingartner & Parker, 1984), it has not been used much until very recently in cognitive studies (see Kroll, Knight, Metcalfe, Wolf, & Tulving, 1996). According to the consolidation hypothesis, when information that is encoded under DA conditions does not support a strong memory record, this record is susceptible to interruption—for example, by other memory traces—and hence will show more forgetting over time relative to information encoded under full attention.

What evidence is there for this hypothesis? Rosi Itzhaki in my laboratory looked at this issue. Itzhaki had participants listen to a list of word pairs under either full attention or DA at encoding conditions. In the DA condition, the 4-CRT task described above was used. After the encoding phase and a further 30 seconds of interpolated activity to abolish recency, participants performed an item recognition test using half of the words studied and a similar number of distractors. After this test, a 30-minute activity period was employed in which participants performed different visual tasks. Then a second recognition memory test was given with the other half of the words from the study phase intermixed with new distractor items. This resulted in large effects of both DA and retention interval. Interestingly, there was no indication of an interaction between the two variables; in particular, forgetting rates were not faster for the DA condition, as might be expected from the consolidation hypothesis. Recent results obtained by Craik and Naveh-Benjamin, indicate that the lack of interaction of DA at encoding and forgetting rates happen even when the initial retention interval is as short as 4 seconds. Note, however, that we don't have an indication of whether performance in the two attention conditions was equated at the very start of the retention interval.

Despite the fact that these results do not support the claim that the effect of DA at encoding is mediated by an automatic consolidation hypothesis, another possibility is that DA has its effect on another nonstrategic encoding component, more upstream in the continuum of processing. In particular, it may be the case that DA interrupts the initial registration of the information; that is, it is possible that DA conditions impede the full registration of the presented event when participants' attention is focused on the secondary task.

Pnina Grinzeig in my laboratory tested this possibility by presenting participants with lists of words, each of which was presented in one of two computer fonts. Participants encoded the information under conditions of either full attention or DA. In the latter condition, an auditory version of the 4-CRT task with four tones was used simultaneously with encoding. After an interpolated activity, participants were shown the words intermixed with new distractor words in one of two fonts, where each word was presented either in the original font used at encoding or in the other font. Distractors were presented randomly in one of the fonts, and participants were instructed to recognize the originally presented words. Nothing was said about the different fonts used and participants later indicated that they had not paid attention to them. The results of the recognition test (seen in Figure 15.3), showed clear effects of DA and of similarity of font: Words presented at test in the same font as at encoding were remembered better than those words presented in a different font from the one used at encoding. There was, however, no interaction of the two variables, implying that DA at encoding does not disrupt the initial processing of perceptual aspects, in this case font information. Such an interaction, showing a smaller advantage of same over different font recognition in the DA condition than in the full attention condition, would be expected if DA interrupts the initial perceptual registration of the information. Using perceptual priming procedures, Mulligan (1998) reached similar conclusions about the lack of DA effects on perceptual analysis.

To summarize, it seems that the results described here do not provide support for the claim that the effects of DA at encoding on memory performance are mediated by the interruption of automatic-nonstrategic processes. Instead, they suggest that neither the initial perceptual registration of the information nor later consolidation processes are differentially affected by DA at encoding, at least within the context of the manipulations employed.

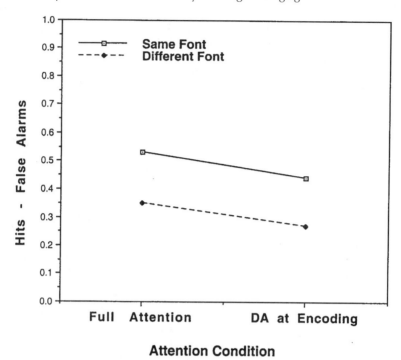

FIGURE 15.3. Proportions of hits minus false alarms for each attention condition as a function of the voice at test (same vs. different than at study).

As the above studies indicate, it seems that we are still in need of an adequate explanation of the underlying mechanisms that mediate the effects of DA at encoding on memory performance. In the next section, I will address the question of whether these effects might be mediated by the disruption of associative processing. In particular, I seek to determine whether DA at encoding has a greater effect on the processes required to relate together different components of the episode, than on processes required to encode each of the components separately.

Impaired Associative Processing

This associative deficit hypothesis (ADH; see Naveh-Benjamin, 2000) is based on the notion that complex events consist of many kinds of information that are bound together. A dominant view in cognitive psychology (e.g., Underwood, 1969) is that an episode consists of several attributes (e.g., semantic, acoustic, contextual) that are connected to create a coherent, distinctive unit. An event can include the semantic content, information about the time of the event, the place in which it occurred, the acting agents, their characteristics, etc. All these aspects, together with the internal cognitive state of the person, are encoded as an episode. Remembering such an episode requires that at least some of the components be retained, as well as their relationships to each other (see Moscovitch, 1995).

Several suggestions in the literature are in line with a within-memory separation of information about single units from information about associative relationships among these units (e.g., J. R. Anderson & Bower, 1973; Chalfonte & Johnson, 1996; Gillund &

Shiffrin; 1984; Humphreys, 1976; Johnson, 1992; Johnson & Chalfonte, 1994; Murdock, 1974, 1982; 1993; Naveh-Benjamin, 2000). This distinction between item and associative information has been supported by several experiments that yielded different patterns of results for the two types of information (e.g., Dosher, 1988; Gronlund & Ratcliff, 1989; Hockley, 1991, 1992, 1994; Hockley & Cristi, 1996; Naveh-Benjamin, 2000).

One plausible possibility is that an associative deficit is a mediating factor in the effects of DA at encoding on memory. Using task analysis, it seems reasonable that what is disrupted during DA at encoding is the cohesiveness of the episode created; that is, since participants have to alternate between processing the primary encoding task and the secondary task, they are not capable of uninterrupted encoding and binding together of the different components of the episode. This results in the creation of a fragmented encoding unit. According to this hypothesis, DA at encoding will be more disruptive to the activity of the associative mechanism, which binds together the components of the episode, than to that of the mechanism which encodes each component separately. Such an ADH has recently been offered to explain older adults' degraded episodic memory performance (Naveh-Benjamin, 2000).

In order to directly compare memory for item and for associative information we have used item and associative recognition tests, with the former requiring the encoding and retrieval of component information and the latter requiring the encoding and retrieval of associative information (see Naveh-Benjamin, 2000).

Two experiments were conducted in my laboratory to explore this issue, with two different types of episodic relationships being created and tested. In one experiment, participants under either full attention or DA at encoding conditions studied lists of unrelated word pairs. Participants were told to study the pairs in preparation for the upcoming word and associative recognition tests, the nature of which was explained. The test phase included tasks that require either memory for the components of each pair (item recognition test) or memory for the associations between the components in each pair (associative recognition test). Item memory was tested by a recognition test in which half of the words were studied (targets) and half were not (distractors). Associative memory was tested by presenting participants with target items only, either as intact pairs (two words presented together at study) or as recombined pairs (two words presented in different pairs at study) and asking them to recognize the intact pairs. The order of the two tests was counterbalanced. As described earlier, the ADH predicts an interaction between DA and type of test. Specifically, the resulting memory differences between full attention and DA at encoding conditions are expected to be larger in the word–word association test, than in the word recognition one. Note that different words were used in the item and associative recognition tests.

Figure 15.4 shows recognition memory performance in each DA condition for each test. The results show that the effect of attention was significant but that the interaction of attention and test was not. As can be seen in Figure 15.4, this absence of interaction reflects a similar pattern of reduced memory performance in the two memory tests under DA conditions.

This pattern of results, especially the absence of a significant interaction of attention condition and test, indicates that participants under DA at encoding do not show a differentially poorer performance in recognition of associative than of item information compared to their performance under full attention. Apparently, DA at encoding affects component processing (word) to the same degree as it affects the processing of associations among the components. These results do not, therefore, support the associative deficit as the locus of the effects of DA at encoding on memory performance.

In the second experiment, we extended these results to other types of associations; the

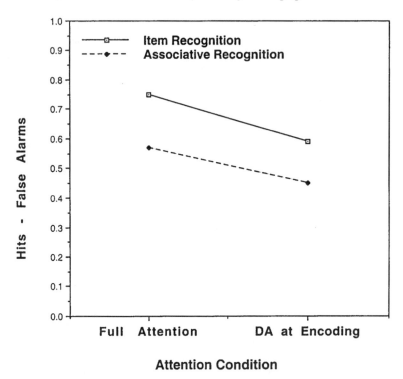

Figure 15.4. Proportions of hits minus false alarms for each attention condition in the item and the associative recognition tests.

associations used were between a focal attribute (word) and a perceptual-contextual attribute (font). In this experiment participants studied lists of word–font pairs and were then tested on either their memory for the components (word or font recognition tests) or the relationships among them (word–font pair recognition test). Words were presented for study in one of several fonts under either full attention or DA conditions, followed by three memory tests. One test was a recognition test on the words. In this test some of the original words (targets) appeared with new words (distractors). All the words at test appeared in a neutral font (one which had not been presented at study). The second test was a recognition test on the fonts. In this test the original fonts (targets) were mixed with other new fonts (distractors) and were presented without the words (using XXXX) for a recognition test. The third test was a recognition test on the associations of words and fonts. In this test only original (target) words and fonts were presented. In half of the cases, the word was presented in the original font (intact events), and in the other half of the cases the word was presented in a different font from the one in which it had appeared at the study phase; in this case, a font that appeared with another word at study was used (recombined events). Such a test requires that participants have information about the relationships between the words and the fonts, and it is similar in nature to the recognition test for inter-item associations employed in the previously described experiment. The order of the tests was counterbalanced and each word or font appeared in only one of the tests.

As in the first experiment, the ADH predicts an interaction of attention condition and test, in the sense that the detrimental effects of attention are expected to be greatest in the word–font association test. Results of recognition memory performance indicated an effect of DA. The type of test was also significant, with performance on the word test being better than performance on both the font test and the word–font combination test. Performance on the latter two tests did not differ. Finally, the interaction of attention and test was not significant, indicating that DA had the same effect on the associative test (word–font combinations) as on the item tests (separate word and font tests).

Overall, these results indicate that when information is encoded under DA conditions, a similar deficit emerges in a task requiring the merging of contextual elements as in tasks requiring memory for each of the contextual elements separately. Such results are not consistent with the notion that an associative deficit is the locus of the DA effects.

The results of the last two experiments are not consistent with the ADH; participants who encode the information under DA conditions do not show a disproportionally larger deficit in memory for associations among components compared to participants who encoded the information under full attention. These results demonstrate that a deficit in the processing of relationships or associations between single units (the components of an episode) probably does not play an important role in explaining the poor memory performance of participants who encoded the information under DA conditions. The components can be either two separate units (e.g., words) or more integrated ones (a word and its context).

The results of the last two experiments are consistent with evidence and models emerging from the literature on neuropsychology and neuroscience. For example, one noteworthy model is the one suggested by Moscovitch (1992, 1995), which proposes that episodic memory performance is mediated by two principal components: a modular medial temporal/hippocampal component whose operations are essentially automatic, and a frontal lobe component whose operations are strategic, organizational, and accessible to consciousness and voluntary control. As mentioned earlier, recent neuroimaging studies indicate that the DA effects at encoding result mostly in decreased brain activation in the left prefrontal region but not in the medial temporal/hippocampal regions (N. D. Anderson et al., 2000; Fletcher et al., 1995). Such studies are in line with the results reported in this section, showing no differential effects of DA on associative information; they are also consistent with the notion that the medial temporal/hippocampal region, which was thought to mediate the merging of different components of an episode into a cohesive unit (Cohen & Eichenbaum, 1993), is not differentially affected by DA at encoding. Interestingly, neuroimaging studies do indicate effects of age on the temporal/hippocampal region activity, in line with the results reported (Naveh-Benjamin, 2000), showing a disproportionally larger age-related deficit in memory for associative than for item information (Naveh-Benjamin, 2000).

These results from neuroimaging studies, combined with the ones described in this chapter (see also Moscovitch, Fernandes, & Troyer, chapter 14 of this volume, and Anderson, chapter 16), point to a strategic type of encoding process as a possible locus for the effects of DA at encoding on memory performance. However, as shown in the previous sections, we still need an exact characterization of these processes in order to allow predictions of the conditions in which the withdrawal of attention during encoding has a detrimental effect on memory.

It should be noted that there is a least one study that shows a somewhat different pattern from the one reported here on the effect of DA at encoding on item and associative information. Reinitz, Morrissey, and Demb (1994) reported that when participants are presented with faces under conditions of full attention or DA, performance on a memory test that required information about conjunctions of facial features was affected by DA to a greater degree than a memory test that required information about specific features. However, this study differs from the ones discussed here in several respects. First, faces are integral-holistic stimuli which may be processed differently from stimuli composed of separate components (see Tanaka & Sengco, 1997). Second, in their experiment, the new distractor faces contained several new features that made the feature (item) recognition test easier than the associative test. Nevertheless, these results indicate that further studies employing different types of stimuli, both feature-like and holistic, should be conducted in order to investigate the effects of DA on encoding processes.

☐ Summary

Encoding processes were shown in previous research (Craik et al., 1996; Naveh-Benjamin et al., 1998; Naveh-Benjamin, Craik, Gavrilescu, & Anderson, 2000; Naveh-Benjamin, Craik, Perratta, & Tonev, 2000) to be consciously controlled and attention demanding. This was reflected in the findings that division of attention is associated with a reduction in memory performance and also with a slowing of the concurrent RT task. Moreover, changes in emphasis result in systematic and complementary changes in both tasks. In this article I have tried to elucidate the possible mechanisms underlying these detrimental effects of DA at encoding, using two sets of processing classifications: One involves the distinction between strategic-effortful and automatic-nonstrategic processes, and the other involves the distinction between item and associative information. In particular, I attempted to determine whether impaired strategic-effortful processing and impaired associative processing could be the mediating mechanisms for the effects of DA at encoding.

In general, the results convey a complex picture with no one specific mechanism implicated as the sole mediator of these DA effects. Although previous results indicate that strategic-effortful processes are those most affected by DA, the studies described in this chapter show that this is not always the case. In particular, the large effects of DA at encoding on memory performance when a pure incidental learning paradigm is employed, and when strategic elaboration activity is equated in the full attention and DA groups, indicate that effortful strategic processes are not the only ones affected by DA. Likewise, it seems that the encoding of associative information is not particularly vulnerable to the effects of DA as it was disrupted by DA to the same degree as component information. It seems that despite the robust and replicable empirical results regarding the detrimental effects of DA at encoding on memory performance, to which Gus Craik has contributed significantly, we still need studies that further explore the different cognitive mechanisms mediating these effects.

☐ Acknowledgments

This research was supported in part by a grant from the Ben-Gurion University Faculty of Humanities and Social Sciences as well as a grant from the Zlotowski Center for the Neurosciences. I am grateful to members of the memory research group at Ben-Gurion University of the Negev for their help in conducting the research and to Morris Moscovitch for his helpful comments on an earlier version of this chapter. This chapter was written while I was a visiting scientist at the Rotman Research Institute, Baycrest Centre for Geriatric Care, Toronto, Canada.

☐ References

Alvarez, P., & Squire, L. R. (1994). Memory consolidation and the medial temporal lobe: A simple network model. *Proceedings of the National Academy of Sciences of the United States of America, 91,* 7041–7045.

Anderson, C. M. B., & Craik, F. I. M. (1974). The effect of a concurrent task on recall from primary memory. *Journal of Verbal Learning and Verbal Behavior, 13,* 107–113.

Anderson, J. R., & Bower, G. H. (1973). *Human associative memory.* Washington, DC: Winston.

Anderson, N. D., Iidaka, T., Cabeza, R., Kapur, S., McIntosh, A. R., & Craik, F. I. M. (2000). The effects of divided attention on encoding–and retrieval-related brain activity: A PET study of younger and older adults. *Journal of Cognitive Neuroscience, 12,* 775–792.

Baddeley, A. D., Lewis, V., Eldridge, M., & Thomson, N. (1984). Attention and retrieval from long-term memory. *Journal of Experimental Psychology: General, 13,* 518–540.

Chalfonte, B. L., & Johnson, M. K. (1996). Feature memory and binding in young and older adults. *Memory and Cognition, 24,* 403–416.

Cohen, N. J., & Eichenbaum, H. (1993). *Memory, amnesia, and the hippocampal system.* Cambridge, MA: MIT Press.

Craik, F. I. M. (1982). Selective changes in encoding as a function of reduced processing capacity. In F. Klix, J. Hoffman, & E. Van der Meer (Eds.), *Cognitive research in psychology* (pp.152–161). Berlin: DVW.

Craik, F. I. M., & Byrd, M. (1982). Aging and cognitive deficits: The role of attentional resources. In F. I. M. Craik & S. E. Trehub (Eds.), *Aging and cognitive processes* (pp. 191–211). New York: Plenum Press.

Craik, F. I. M., Govoni, R., Naveh-Benjamin, M., & Anderson, N. D. (1996). The effects of divided attention on encoding and retrieval processes in human memory. *Journal of Experimental Psychology: General, 125,* 159–180.

Craik F. I. M., & Kester, J. D. (2000). Divided attention and memory: Impairment of processing or consolidation? In E. Tulving (Ed.), *Memory, consciousness, and brain: The Tallinn conference.* Philadelphia, PA: Psychology Press.

Dosher, B. A. (1988). *Retrieval dynamics of item and associative information.* Unpublished manuscript.

Fernandes, M. A., & Moscovitch, M. (2000). Divided attention and memory: Evidence of substantial interference effects at retrieval and encoding. *Journal of Experimental Psychology: General, 129,* 155–176.

Fletcher, P. C., Frith, C. D., Grasby, P. M., Shallice, T., Frackowiak, R. S., & Dulan, R. J. (1995). Brain systems for encoding and retrieval of auditory-verbal memory: An in vivo study in humans. *Brain, 118,* 401–416.

Gillund, G., & Shiffrin, R. M. (1984). A retrieval model for both recognition and recall. *Psychological Review, 91,* 1–67.

Griffith, D. (1976). The attentional demands of mnemonic control processes. *Memory and Cognition, 4,* 103–108.

Gronlund, S. D., & Ratcliff, R. (1989). Time course of item and associative information: Implications for global memory models. *Journal of Experimental Psychology: Learning, Memory, and Cognition, 15,* 846–858.

Hasher, L., & Zacks, R. T. (1979). Automatic and effortful processes in human memory. *Journal of Experimental Psychology: General, 108,* 356–388.

Hockley, W. E. (1991). Recognition memory for item and associative information: A comparison of forgetting rates. In W. E. Hockley & S. Lewandowsky (Eds.), *Relating theory and data: Essays on human memory in honor of Bennet B. Murdock* (pp. 227–248). Hillsdale, NJ: Erlbaum.

Hockley, W. E. (1992). Item versus associative information: Further comparisons of forgetting rates. *Journal of Experimental Psychology: Learning, Memory, & Cognition, 18,* 1321–1330.

Hockley, W. E. (1994). Reflections of the mirror effect for item and associative recognition. *Memory and Cognition, 22,* 713–722.

Hockley, W. E., & Cristi, C. (1996). Tests of encoding tradeoffs between item and associative information. *Memory and Cognition, 24,* 202–216.

Humphreys, M. S. (1976). Relational information and the context effect in recognition memory. *Memory and Cognition, 4,* 221–232.

Johnson, M. K. (1992). MEM: Mechanisms of recollection. *Journal of Cognitive Neuroscience, 4,* 268–280.

Johnson, M. K., & Chalfonte, B. L. (1994). Binding complex memories: The role of reactivation and the hippocampus. In D. L. Schacter & E. Tulving (Eds.), *Memory systems 1994* (pp. 311–350). Cambridge, MA: MIT Press.

Johnston, W. A., Greenberg, S. N., Fisher, R. P., & Martin, D. W. (1970). Divided attention: A vehicle for monitoring memory processes. *Journal of Experimental Psychology, 83,* 164–171.

Johnston, W. A., Griffith, D., & Wagstaff, R. R. (1972). Speed, accuracy, and ease of recall. *Journal of Verbal Learning and Verbal Behavior, 11,* 512–520.

Kapur, S., Craik, F. I. M., Tulving, E., Wilson, A. A., Houle, S., & Brown, G. M. (1994). Neuroanatomical correlates of encoding in episodic memory: Levels of processing effect. *Proceedings of the National Academy of Sciences, USA, 91,* 2008–2011.

Kroll, E. A., Knight, R. T., Metcalfe, J., Wolf, E. S., & Tulving, E. (1996). Cohesion failure as a source of memory illusions. *Journal of Memory and Language, 35,* 176–196.

McGaugh, J. L. (1966). Time-dependent processes in memory storage. *Science, 153,* 1351–1358.

Moscovitch, M. (1992). Memory and working-with-memory: A component process model based on modules and central systems. *Journal of Cognitive Neuroscience, 4,* 257–267.

Moscovitch, M. (1995). Recovered consciousness—a hypothesis concerning modularity and episodic memory. *Journal of Clinical Experimental Neuropsychology, 17,* 276–290.

Mulligan, N. W. (1998). The role of attention during encoding in implicit and explicit memory. *Journal of Experimental Psychology: Learning, Memory, & Cognition, 24,* 27–47.

Murdock, B. B., Jr. (1965). Effects of a subsidiary task on short-term memory. *British Journal of Psychology, 56,* 413–419.

Murdock, B. B., Jr. (1974). *Human memory: Theory and data.* Potomac, MD: Erlbaum.

Murdock, B. B., Jr. (1982). A theory of storage and retrieval of item and associative information. *Psychological Review, 89,* 609–626.

Murdock, B. B., Jr. (1993). TODAM2: A model for the storage and retrieval of item, associative, and serial-order information. *Psychological Review, 100,* 183–203.

Naveh-Benjamin, M. (1987). Coding of spatial location information: An automatic process? *Journal of Experimental Psychology: Learning, Memory and Cognition, 13,* 595–605.

Naveh-Benjamin, M. (1988). Recognition of spatial location information: Another failure to support automaticity. *Memory and Cognition, 16,* 437–445.

Naveh-Benjamin, M. (1990). Coding of temporal order information: An automatic process? *Journal of Experimental Psychology: Learning, Memory and Cognition, 16,* 117–126.

Naveh-Benjamin, M. (2000). Adult-age differences in memory performance: Tests of an associative deficit hypothesis. *Journal of Experimental Psychology: Learning, Memory and Cognition, 26,* 1170–1187.

Naveh-Benjamin, M., Craik, F. I. M., Gavrilescu, D., & Anderson, N. D. (2000a). Asymmetry between encoding and retrieval processes: Evidence from a divided attention paradigm and a calibration analysis. *Memory and Cognition, 28,* 965–976.

Naveh-Benjamin, M., Craik, F. I. M., Guez, J., & Dori, H. (1998). Effects of divided attention on encoding and retrieval processes in human memory: Further support for an asymmetry. *Journal of Experimental Psychology: Learning, Memory and Cognition, 24,* 1091–1104.

Naveh-Benjamin, M., Craik, F. I. M., Perretta, J., & Tonev, S. (2000). The effects of divided attention on encoding and retrieval processes: The resiliency of retrieval processes. *Quarterly Journal of Experimental Psychology, 53,* 609–626.

Naveh-Benjamin, M., & Guez, J. (2000). The effects of divided attention on encoding and retrieval processes: Assessment of attentional costs and a componential analysis. *Journal of Experimental Psychology: Learning, Memory and Cognition, 26,* 1461–1482.

Naveh-Benjamin, M., & Jonides, J. (1986). On the automaticity of frequency coding: Effects of competing task load, encoding strategy, and intention. *Journal of Experimental Psychology: Learning, Memory and Cognition, 12,* 378–386.

Rabinowitz, J. C., Craik, F. I. M., & Ackerman, B. P. (1982). A processing resource account of age differences in recall. *Canadian Journal of Psychology, 36,* 325–344.

Reinitz, M. T., Morrissey, J., & Demb, J. (1994). Role of attention in face encoding. *Journal of Experimental Psychology: Learning, Memory and Cognition, 20,* 161–168.

Tanaka, J. W., & Sengco, J. A. (1997). Features and their configuration in face recognition. *Memory and Cognition, 25,* 583–592.

Underwood, B. J. (1969). Attributes of memory. *Psychological Review, 76,* 559–573.

Weingartner, H. S., & Parker, E. S. (1984). *Memory consolidation.* Hillsdale, NJ: Erlbaum.

Nicole D. Anderson

The Attentional Demands and Attentional Control of Encoding and Retrieval

A basic question about the nature of memory encoding and retrieval concerns whether they are similar operations. Many cognitive theories champion the view that encoding and retrieval are comparable processes, such that retrieval is successful to the extent that encoding processes are reinstated (Bransford, Franks, Morris, & Stein, 1979; Craik, 1983; Kolers, 1973; Roediger, Weldon, & Challis, 1989; Tulving & Thomson, 1973). There is growing evidence, however, that these mnemonic operations differ in important ways. The divided attention paradigm has three primary advantages that make it ideally suited to address the similarity of encoding and retrieval. First, one can compare the vulnerability of encoding and retrieval to disruption by having subjects perform a secondary task only during encoding or only during retrieval. Second, one can examine the attentional control of encoding and retrieval by asking participants to vary their emphasis between the memory task and the secondary task across trials. If encoding and retrieval are under voluntary control, then as they are given more emphasis, memory performance should increase and secondary task performance should decrease. Third, one can examine the resource demands of encoding and retrieval, if secondary task costs are taken as an index of their resource demands (Kahneman, 1973; Kerr, 1973). The more central resources encoding or retrieval demand, the more they should disrupt performance on a secondary task.

The similarity and differences between encoding and retrieval in terms of their vulnerability to disruption, their attentional control, and their attentional demands will be discussed in the first three sections and summarized in the fourth section of the current chapter. These discussions will reveal that episodic encoding and retrieval are *not* similar in these regards. Episodic retrieval, in particular, is obligatory in the sense that it is relatively immune to disruption, does not operate under attentional control, but has significant attentional demands. A shared-time model of memory and current processing (Craik, Govoni, Naveh-Benjamin, & Anderson, 1996) is described in the fourth section of this chapter, and it is shown that memory performance under conditions of divided attention at retrieval can be predicted from the amount of time theoretically available for retrieval. Finally, in the fifth section of this chapter, a new theoretical explanation of these somewhat surprising features of episodic retrieval is proposed.

☐ The Vulnerability of Encoding and Retrieval to Disruption by a Secondary Task

Divided attention during episodic encoding results in significant reductions in later memory performance (e.g., N. D. Anderson, Craik, & Naveh-Benjamin, 1998; C. M. B. Anderson & Craik, 1974; Baddeley, Lewis, Eldridge, & Thomson, 1984; Craik et al., 1996; Murdock, 1965). By contrast, episodic retrieval is often remarkably immune to the effects of divided attention (e.g., N. D. Anderson et al., 1998; Baddeley et al., 1984; Craik et al., 1996; Kellogg, Cocklin, & Bourne, 1982; Naveh-Benjamin, Craik, Guez, & Dori, 1998; Naveh-Benjamin, Craik, Perretta, & Tonev, 2000). Table 16.1 shows the results from studies that compared the effects of divided attention at encoding and retrieval. The data are presented as the percentage decline in memory performance due to divided attention during encoding or retrieval, relative to memory performance under full attention conditions. As seen in the table, divided attention at encoding leads to significant declines in memory performance regardless of the type of memory task (i.e., free recall, cued recall, or recognition), the list type (unrelated words or related words), or the age of the subjects. By contrast, divided attention at retrieval usually results in much smaller and sometimes nonsignificant decrements in memory performance, again regardless of the type of memory task, list type, or subject population. There are cases in which significant memory decrements are found due to divided attention at retrieval (Fernandes & Moscovitch, 2000; Park, Smith, Dudley, & Lafronza, 1989); these exceptions will be discussed later in this chapter.

Recent advances in neuroimaging techniques allow one to examine brain activity associated with encoding and retrieval and to investigate the effects of divided attention on encoding-related and retrieval-related brain activity. Shallice, Fletcher, and their colleagues used positron emission tomography (PET) to study the effects of divided attention during encoding (Fletcher et al., 1995; Shallice et al., 1994). Subjects learned a list of paired associates while performing either an easy or a difficult secondary task. Encoding during the easy secondary task was associated with activity in the left inferior prefrontal cortex, a finding that is consistent with much previous work showing activation of this region during episodic encoding, particularly during deep, semantic learning (e.g., Kapur et al., 1994). Moreover, and of particular importance, the difficult secondary task all but obliterated activation of this region in the left prefrontal cortex. These results suggest that memory performance is diminished by a difficult secondary task because it interferes with brain activity mediating semantic encoding processes.

We found these results intriguing and wondered what effect divided attention during retrieval would have on retrieval-related brain activity. Given that memory performance is relatively immune to disruption, we hypothesized that retrieval-related brain activity would also withstand disruption. Our PET studies (N. D. Anderson et al., 2000; Iidaka, Anderson, Kapur, Cabeza, & Craik, 2000) included healthy younger (21–31 years old) and older (63–76 years old) adults who were scanned during encoding or retrieval. We used a cued recall task, in which subjects learned lists of moderately related word pairs (e.g., dentist–glove) and then were given the first word of each pair as a cue to recall the second word. The secondary task was an auditory tone discrimination task. In an "easy" condition, a low tone was presented every 2 seconds and subjects repeatedly pressed a button in response to each tone. In a "difficult" condition, a low and a high tone were presented randomly every 2 seconds and subjects pressed the corresponding button in response to each tone. The auditory-motor demands of these 2 conditions were thus equated, but given the relative automaticity of the easy version of the task, we regarded it as the full attention condition, and given the relative complexity of the difficult version of the task,

TABLE 16.1. Memory costs due to divided attention at encoding or retrieval, expressed as the percentage decline in memory performance from full attention conditions.

Study	#	Memory task	Secondary task	Age	DA at encoding	DA at retrieval
Baddeley 1984	1	FR - UR	Card sorting	Y	35	8
	2	FR - UR	Card sorting	Y	24	14
	2	FR - Rel	Card sorting	Y	22	9
	3	FR - UR	Digit WM	Y	18	7
	4	CR - Rel	Digit WM	Y	24	13
	5	FR - UR	Card sorting	Y	13	3
Park 1989	1	FR - Rel	Odd/Even	Y	38	30
				O	55	15
	2	CR - Rel	Odd/Even	Y	34	19
				O	55	21
Craik 1996	1	FR - UR	Visual RT	Y	43	13
	2	FR - UR	Visual RT	Y	35	11
	3	CR – UR	Visual RT	Y	33	9
	4	Rn – UR	Visual RT	Y	22	1
Anderson 1998	1	FR - UR	Visual RT	Y	28	9
				O	38	10
	2	CR - UR	Visual RT	Y	26	2
				O	49	8
	4	Rn - UR	Visual RT	Y	22	1
				O	18	−1
Naveh-Benjamin 1998	1	CR - UR	Visual RT	Y	35	2
		CR - UR	Visual RT	Y	40	9
		CR - UR	Visual RT	Y	35	2
		CR - UR	Visual RT	Y	43	2
Fernandes 2000	2-3	FR - UR	Word WM	Y	53	37
			Word WM	Y	52	33
	4-5	Rn - UR	Word WM	Y	56	30
			Digit WM	Y	50	13
Naveh-Benjamin 2000[a]	1	CR - UR	Visual Tracking	Y	19	4
	2	CR - UR	Visual Tracking	Y	10	1
	2	CR - UR	Visual Tracking	Y	11	−2
Naveh-Benjamin 2000[b]	1	CR - UR	Visual RT*	Y	23	5
		CR - UR	Visual RT*	Y	31	6
Naveh-Benjamin 2000[c]	1	CR-UR	Digit WM[‡]	Y	60	15
Naveh-Benjamin 2000[c]	1	CR-UR	Digit WM[‡]	Y	31	4
	2	CR-Med-Intra	Visual RT	Y	16	0
	2	CR-Med-Extra	Visual RT	Y	19	6
	2	CR-Low-Intra	Visual RT	Y	23	2
	2	CR-Low-Extra	Visual RT	Y	19	9

Note. Studies are identified by the first author, year of publication, and experiment number within publication (Naveh-Benjamin 2000[a] = Naveh-Benjamin & Guez, 2000; Naveh-Benjamin 2000[b] = Naveh-Benjamin, Craik, Gavrilescu, & Anderson, 2000a; Naveh-Benjamin 2000[c] = Naveh-Benjamin, Craik, Perretta, & Tonev, 2000). DA = divided attention, FR = free recall, CR = cued recall, Rn = recognition, UR = unrelated word lists, Rel = related word lists, Intra = Intralist word cues, Extra = Extralist word cues, WM = working memory, RT = reaction time, Y = young, O = old. *Results from the 1-press conditions of Naveh-Benjamin, Craik, Gavrilescu, & Anderson (2000) are shown. [‡]Results from the second trial of Naveh-Benjamin, Craik, Perretta, & Tonev (2000, Exp. 1) are shown.

we regarded it as the divided attention condition (cf. Fletcher et al., 1995; Shallice et al., 1994). Subjects learned and recalled two lists of word pairs under each of four conditions: *full encoding*, full retrieval; *divided encoding*, full retrieval; full encoding, *full retrieval*; full encoding, *divided retrieval* (the italics denotes the memory phase during which scanning took place).

The behavioral data replicated those in Table 16.1. Specifically, relative to full attention conditions (0.79 words for the younger adults, 0.60 for the older adults), divided attention during encoding led to significant reductions in memory performance (0.58 words for the younger adults, 0.36 for the older adults). By contrast, divided attention during retrieval had much smaller and unreliable effects on memory performance for both age groups (0.75 words for the younger adults, 0.51 for the older adults).

Figure 16.1 (see color plate I) shows the imaging data. We first identified brain regions in which activity was associated with full attention encoding and retrieval in younger and older adults, using an Age × Full Attention Encoding/Full Attention Retrieval design. Panels A and B in Figure 16.1 show regions that were more activated by encoding than retrieval (yellow), and areas that were more activated by retrieval than encoding (blue). For the younger adults (panel A), prefrontal activity during encoding was lateralized to the left hemisphere (the inferior frontal gyrus in particular), whereas prefrontal activity during retrieval was lateralized to the right hemisphere (middle frontal gyrus), consistent with previous findings (Tulving, Kapur, Craik, Moscovitch, & Houle, 1994), although retrieval did include some areas of left prefrontal activity. The older adults revealed a very different pattern (panel B); relative to their younger counterparts (panel A), the older adults had less encoding-related brain activity in the left prefrontal cortex, less retrieval-related brain activity in the right prefrontal cortex, but *more* retrieval-related brain activity in the left prefrontal cortex. This combination of age-related *reductions* in encoding-related and retrieval-related brain activity and age-related *increases* of brain activity in regions not activated by the young is consistent with other reports of dedifferentiation of neurocognitive functioning in older adults (Bäckman et al., 1997; Cabeza et al., 1997; Madden et al., 1999).

Our next analysis identified the effect of divided attention during encoding on brain activity in younger and older adults. The yellow in panels C and D in Figure 16.1, for younger and older adults, respectively, identifies regions that were more active during full than divided attention conditions at encoding, and blue identifies regions that were more active during divided than full attention conditions at encoding. Here we see results that replicate those of Shallice et al. (1994; Fletcher et al., 1995). Specifically, divided attention at encoding reduced encoding-related brain activity in the left prefrontal cortex. The data from the older adults are especially intriguing, because although their left inferior prefrontal cortex was not activated more during encoding than retrieval (panel B), divided attention during encoding nevertheless disrupted activity in this region (panel D). These results indicate that although there are definite age-related differences in encoding-related (and retrieval-related) brain activity, divided attention during encoding affects brain activity similarly in both age groups.

Finally, what about the effects of divided attention on retrieval-related brain activity? Divided attention at retrieval had comparable effects on brain activity in younger and older adults; that is, the interaction of age group and full/divided attention during retrieval on brain activity was not significant. Thus, panel E in Figure 16.1 shows regions that were more activated by full attention retrieval than divided attention retrieval (yellow) and vice versa (blue) for the two age groups combined. This analysis showed that divided attention at retrieval had essentially no effect on retrieval-related brain activity in the prefrontal cortex. Specifically, of the seven prefrontal regions in which activity was reduced by divided attention during retrieval, only one of these, in the left orbital frontal gyrus, was preferentially active during retrieval relative to encoding. These results demonstrate that retrieval-related prefrontal brain activity is relatively immune to disruption by divided attention in both age groups.

In summary, divided attention during encoding reduces memory performance and reduces encoding-related brain activity in the left inferior prefrontal cortex. These results, combined with other research showing that divided attention during encoding reduces levels-of-processing effects (Craik, 1982), increases false alarm rates to semantically related lures (Mandler & Worden, 1973), reduces conscious recollection but not familiarity (e.g., Jacoby, 1991; Jacoby, Woloshyn, & Kelley, 1989), and disrupts conceptual but (usually) not perceptual priming (e.g., Mulligan, 1998), all suggest that divided attention during encoding interferes with deep, semantic processing. By contrast, divided attention at retrieval has small or unreliable effects on memory performance and has essentially no effect on retrieval-related processes mediated by the right prefrontal cortex.

☐ The Attentional Control of Encoding and Retrieval

If encoding and retrieval operate under attentional control, then one should be able to control how much emphasis these processes receive, and memory performance should be affected accordingly. Specifically, in a dual task situation, as one gives more emphasis to encoding or retrieval, memory performance should increase, but secondary task performance should decrease. The results of studies that have compared the attentional control of encoding and retrieval are presented in Table 16.2. These studies have found that memory performance is quite sensitive to modulations in task emphasis when attention is divided during encoding (see also Murdock, 1965) but is less sensitive to modulations in task emphasis when attention is divided during retrieval (N. D. Anderson et al., 1998; Craik et al., 1996). Note that it is not the case that subjects "protect" retrieval, thereby making it insensitive to task emphasis effects, because secondary task performance is affected by task emphasis as much during retrieval as it is during encoding. That is, subjects are com-

TABLE 16.2. Task emphasis effects at encoding or retrieval, expressed as the percentage change between conditions in which the memory task was emphasized and conditions in which the secondary task was emphasized.

Study	#	Memory task	Secondary task	Age	Memory		RT	
					Enc	Ret	Enc	Ret
Craik 1996	2	FR - UR	Visual RT	Y	26	1	14	15
	3	CR - UR	Visual RT	Y	31	3	16	13
	4	Rn - UR	Visual RT	Y	17	3	9	6
Anderson 1998	1	FR - UR	Visual RT	Y	26	14	16	15
				O	29	0	17	8
	2	CR - UR	Visual RT	Y	24	0	18	15
				O	11	0	21	15
	4	Rn - UR	Visual RT	Y	36	3	9	7
				O	12	-2	11	9

Note. Studies are identified by the first author, year of publication, and experiment number within publication. FR = free recall, CR = cued recall, Rn = recognition, UR = unrelated word lists, RT = reaction time, Y = young, O = old.

plying with the instructions to vary their emphasis between the two tasks, but in the case of divided attention at retrieval, only secondary task performance, and not memory performance is affected. These results indicate that although encoding operates under attentional control, retrieval does not.

☐ The Attentional Demands of Encoding and Retrieval

In a divided attention paradigm, disruptions to secondary task performance are taken as an index of the central attentional demands of the memory task (Kahneman, 1973; Kerr, 1973). Table 16.3 shows the results from a number of studies that compared secondary task costs during encoding and retrieval. Both encoding (see also C. M. B. Anderson & Craik, 1974; Griffith, 1976; Johnston, Greenberg, Fisher, & Martin, 1970; Johnston, Griffith, & Wagstaff, 1972; Johnston, Wagstaff, & Griffith, 1972; Martin, 1970; Trumbo & Milone, 1971) and retrieval (see also Griffith, 1976; Johnston et al., 1970; Martin, 1970; Trumbo & Milone, 1971) cause significant disruptions in secondary task performance. These results indicate that both memory processes are quite demanding of attention. However, most studies have found that secondary task costs are greater during retrieval than during encoding, and particular variables such as aging and the type of memory task have different effects on secondary task costs during encoding and retrieval. These results suggest that encoding and retrieval may place different demands on central resources. In particular, as Table 16.3 shows, secondary task costs are larger for older than younger adults, especially during retrieval (N. D. Anderson et al., 1998), and secondary task costs during retrieval are inversely related to the quality of the retrieval cue. Large costs are found during free recall tasks, smaller costs are found during cued recall tasks, and even smaller costs are found during recognition tasks (N. D. Anderson et al., 1998; Craik et al., 1996), and this is particularly true for older adults (N. D. Anderson et al., 1998; Craik & McDowd, 1987).

Two major conclusions can be drawn from these results. First, although retrieval is typically undisrupted by another task and does not operate under attentional control, it is not "automatic" as Baddeley et al. (1984) suggested, because the large secondary task costs indicate that retrieval can be very demanding of attention. Second, the attentional demands of encoding and especially retrieval are greater for older than younger adults, but age-related increases in the attentional demands of retrieval are attenuated by cues that guide retrieval.

☐ The Nature of Episodic Encoding and Retrieval: An Interim Summary

Thus far, the evidence presented indicates that encoding and retrieval differ in terms of their susceptibility to disruption, their attentional control, and their attentional demands. Encoding is prone to disruption by other ongoing tasks and causes significant disruption to a secondary task, both of which suggest that encoding and the secondary task compete for central resources. Encoding is also sensitive to task emphasis instructions, such that subjects remember more when they emphasize learning and remember less when they emphasize the secondary task, indicating that encoding operates under attentional control. By contrast, retrieval is surprisingly immune to disruption by another ongoing task and operates outside of attentional control, although it nevertheless requires central resources. Craik et al. (1996) described retrieval as "obligatory" in the sense that it seems to

TABLE 16.3. Secondary task costs due to divided attention at encoding or retrieval, expressed as the percentage increase relative to full attention conditions.

Study	#	Memory task	Secondary task	Age	DA at encoding	DA at retrieval
Craik 1996	1	FR - UR	Visual RT	Y	10	35
	2	FR - UR	Visual RT	Y	14	29
	3	CR - UR	Visual RT	Y	18	15
	4	Rn - UR	Visual RT	Y	6	8
Anderson 1998	1	FR - UR	Visual RT	Y	19	35
				O	32	101
	2	CR - UR	Visual RT	Y	13	10
				O	31	50
	4	Rn - UR	Visual RT	Y	7	6
				O	15	15
Naveh-	1	CR - UR	Visual Tracking	Y	10	18
Benjamin 2000[a]	2	CR - UR	Visual Tracking	Y	7	9
	2	CR - UR	Visual Tracking	Y	14	19
Naveh-	1	CR - UR	Visual RT*	Y	4	8
Benjamin 2000[b]	1	CR - UR	Visual RT*	Y	3	10
Naveh-	2	CR-Med-Intra	Visual RT	Y	1	5
Benjamin 2000[c]	2	CR-Med-Extra	Visual RT	Y	3	8
	2	CR-Low-Intra	Visual RT	Y	3	1
	2	CR-Low-Extra	Visual RT	Y	2	11

Note. Studies are identified by the first author, year of publication, and experiment number within publication (Naveh-Benjamin 2000[a] = Naveh-Benjamin & Guez, 2000; Naveh-Benjamin 2000[b] = Naveh-Benjamin, Craik, Gavrilescu, & Anderson, 2000; Naveh-Benjamin 2000[c] = Naveh-Benjamin, Craik, Perretta, & Tonev, 2000). DA = divided attention, FR = free recall, CR = cued recall, Rn = recognition, UR = unrelated word lists, Intra = Intralist word cues, Extra = Extralist word cues, RT = reaction time, Y = young, O = old. * Results from the 1-press condition in Naveh-Benjamin, Craik, Gavrilescu, & Anderson (2000) are shown.

occur regardless of other ongoing activity and task emphasis, while nevertheless consuming attentional resources.

One could argue that if retrieval is obligatory, it should be relatively immune to disruption in all situations. However, some investigators have found rather large decrements in memory performance due to divided attention at retrieval (see Table 16.1). Fernandes and Moscovitch (2000) reported substantial decrements in memory performance due to divided attention at retrieval (up to 37%), and found that the magnitude of these retrieval costs differed across secondary tasks (see also chapter 14 of this volume by Moscovitch, Fernandes, & Troyer). Specifically, word-based secondary tasks such as word recognition and word monitoring resulted in very large decrements to memory performance, while a digit-based monitoring task led to smaller but reliable memory decrements. Park et al. (1989) found that an odd/even digit classification task significantly disrupted free recall and cued recall for both younger and older adults. Both Fernandes and Moscovitch and Park et al. found that divided attention disrupted encoding more than retrieval, but the point here is that the decrements during retrieval were much larger than have been found by N. D. Anderson et al. (1998), Baddeley et al. (1984), Craik et al. (1996). Thus, the question is, Why is retrieval immune to disruption in some experimental paradigms but not others? What sort of theoretical framework can account for these seemingly disparate findings?

☐ A Shared-Time Model of Memory and Concurrent Processing

My thinking about retrieval has been influenced both by the results presented above and by one more result that was first reported by Craik et al. (1996) and was later replicated in my doctoral studies (Anderson, 1998). Craik et al. (1996) presented a "shared-time" model of memory and secondary task reaction time, developed by Richard Govoni. In the model, it was assumed that time is a resource that is shared between the memory task and the secondary task in divided attention conditions. We first derived time-accuracy functions relating encoding or retrieval time to memory performance under full attention conditions. For encoding, and for retrieval in cued recall and recognition, we varied the presentation rate and examined memory performance as a function of the amount of time provided to encode or retrieve. For retrieval in free recall, we plotted cumulative memory performance over a 30-second free recall period. We then investigated the extent to which memory performance under divided attention conditions could be predicted from the combination of the amount of time by which reaction time on the secondary task slowed from single-task to dual-task conditions and the time devoted to the motor demands of the secondary task. This investigation was based on the assumption that secondary task slowing from single- to dual-task conditions reflects the amount of time devoted to the memory task and that subjects can also use the mechanical motor time for memory encoding or retrieval. For example, if a subject's mean reaction time on the secondary task under full attention conditions (i.e., the secondary task performed alone) was 400 ms and under divided attention at retrieval conditions was 600 ms, then we assumed that 200 ms per secondary task response was available for retrieval. If the subject's motor speed (assessed by having subjects repeatedly press a button in response to a predictable pattern of stimuli) was 100 ms per response, then we assumed that this time was also available for retrieval. If the subject made 70 responses to the secondary task during retrieval, then we assumed that she had 21 seconds in total for retrieval (70 responses × (200 ms + 100 ms)). The validity of the shared-time model was then assessed by comparing the recall level under this divided attention condition to the recall level predicted by the time-accuracy functions (e.g., the free recall level corresponding to 21 seconds).

Craik et al. (1996) reported that the shared-time model consistently *overpredicted* memory performance in conditions of divided attention during encoding. That is, subjects recalled fewer words in divided attention at encoding conditions than would be expected, given the amount of time the model predicted they had for encoding. Furthermore, memory performance under conditions of divided attention at encoding fell progressively further from the predicted levels as subjects were instructed to switch their task emphasis from memory encoding to the secondary task. These results showed that divided attention during encoding does more than simply reduce the amount of time available for learning. We suggested that divided attention during encoding may cause subjects to learn words in a less deep or semantic manner, especially when their emphasis is on the secondary task, and we later found tentative support for this hypothesis (Naveh-Benjamin, Craik, Gavrilescu, & Anderson, 2000). Craik et al. (1996) found a very different pattern of results for conditions of divided attention at retrieval. In this case, memory performance was essentially exactly what would be expected on the basis of the shared-time model, and this was true for divided attention during retrieval in free recall, cued recall, and recognition.

These results were replicated as part of my doctoral studies (N. D. Anderson, 1998), in which attention was divided at encoding or retrieval under each of three task emphasis conditions (emphasize the memory task, emphasize the secondary reaction time task, or emphasize the two tasks equally). I also found that the shared-time model overestimated memory performance in divided attention at encoding conditions but almost perfectly estimated memory performance in divided attention at retrieval conditions. Furthermore, this pattern held for both younger and older adults.

The results from the retrieval conditions in free recall and cued recall are shown in Figure 16.2. The solid curves depict cumulative recall functions for free recall (top panel) and time-accuracy functions for cued recall (bottom panel) for younger and older adults. Although the figure shows the average functions for each age group, it is important to note that the functions were derived for each individual subject. The points on the curves show memory performance in conditions of divided attention at retrieval plotted as a

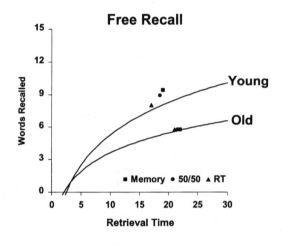

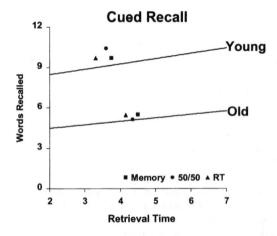

FIGURE 16.2. Solid lines show time-accuracy functions derived from full attention conditions. The data points show memory performance under conditions of divided attention at retrieval in three task emphasis conditions (Mem = memory; RT = reaction time), plotted as a function of the amount of time available for retrieval (see text). From N. D. Anderson (1998).

function of the amount of time available for retrieval, as described above. The important finding, shown in Figure 16.2, is that subjects recalled exactly as much as predicted given the amount of time they had to retrieve. In no case did observed memory performance and predicted memory performance differ reliably. Furthermore, the correlations between predicted and observed memory performance ranged from .31 to .72 and were significant in 11 of the 12 conditions (created by the combination of free recall/cued recall × young/ old × the three task emphasis conditions).

Craik et al. (1996) concluded from their results that memory retrieval and secondary task performance can operate somewhat in parallel and that the large secondary task costs associated with retrieval reflect the maintenance of retrieval mode (Tulving, 1983) and other strategic retrieval operations perhaps mediated by the frontal lobes. However, a significant problem with the conclusion that retrieval operates in parallel with other on-going tasks is that it does not account for the fact that retrieval is drastically compromised by divided attention in some situations but not others. What is needed is a theoretical account of retrieval that can explain why it is immune to disruption in many but not all situations, why it operates outside attentional control, why it is highly demanding of attention, and why the shared-time model predicts memory performance under conditions of divided attention at retrieval.

☐ A Bottleneck Model of Retrieval and Concurrent Processing

It is proposed that these disparate findings can be accounted for by applying Pashler's (1994) extension of the psychological refractory period to memory retrieval. Specifically, Carrier and Pashler (1995) found that memory retrieval and response selection on a secondary task could not occur in parallel. The current model proposes that there is a bottleneck encompassing memory retrieval and "central processes" required for response selection on the secondary task. These central processes may include evaluating the significance of the secondary task stimulus (e.g., its position in a four-box array), decision-making processes required for determining a response, and response planning, initiation, and monitoring. For simplicity's sake, I will refer to these operations collectively as response selection, as Pashler (e.g., 1994) does, but the reader should bear in mind that this term encompasses all processes between perception and response production. Neither retrieval nor secondary response selection takes automatic priority over the other, but whichever commences first wins temporary priority, and until it is completed or terminated, the other operation must be suspended. Moreover, although retrieval and secondary task response selection cannot coincide, the relationship between retrieval costs and secondary task costs is not straightforward but is mediated through the participant's retrieval-time-accuracy functions (as shown by Craik et al., 1996). That is, one must know both the amount of time that was available for retrieval and the level of memory performance corresponding to that amount of time. The first component is estimated from the sum of secondary task retrieval costs and motor times, and the second component is estimated from time-accuracy functions.

The model makes a number of predictions, some of which can be assessed vis-à-vis existing data and some of which await future testing. Figure 16.3 diagrams theoretical component operations involved in secondary task performance and memory retrieval and their proposed time-sharing in dual-task conditions. It is assumed that the component operations involved in a secondary task are stimulus identification (denoted as "S" in the figure), "response selection" as described above, and response execution (denoted as "R"

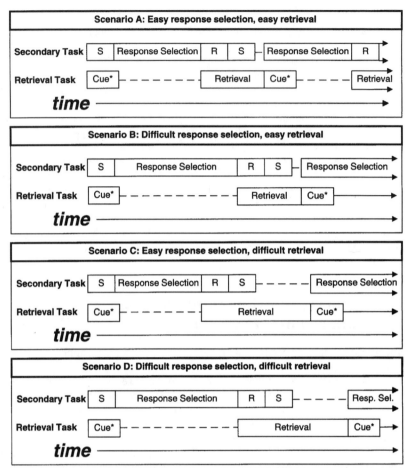

Note: The retrieval cue can be either experimenter provided, as is the case in cued recall and recognition tasks, or subject-generated, as is the case in free recall tasks.

FIGURE 16.3. Theoretical component operations involved in secondary task performance and memory retrieval, and their proposed temporal relationship according to the bottleneck model of memory retrieval and concurrent processing.

in the figure). The component operations involved in memory retrieval are assumed to be cue identification or generation (depending on whether the cue is experimenter provided or subject generated), and retrieval, which in turn is assumed to include ecphory, monitoring, and response output. In the figure, a dashed horizontal line indicates the suspension of operations when a bottleneck between secondary task response selection and memory retrieval occurs.

The primary predictions made by the bottleneck model are as follows:

1. Memory performance in divided attention at retrieval conditions can be predicted from the amount of time remaining after response selection on the secondary task. This is the broadest prediction made by the model, and as described in the preceding section

of this chapter, this prediction was upheld by the success of the shared-time model in Craik et al. (1996) and N. D. Anderson (1998).

2. A secondary task involving response selection will slow retrieval relative to full attention retrieval conditions. This prediction can be seen diagrammatically in any of the scenarios shown in Figure 16.3. Indeed, Baddeley et al. (1984) reported that divided attention slowed retrieval, and Carrier and Pashler (1995) and Naveh-Benjamin and Guez (2000) replicated these results. Furthermore, Baddeley et al. (1984) found that retrieval latency increased with increasing secondary task demands, a prediction that would also fall out of the current model.

3. Secondary task costs will increase as retrieval becomes more difficult and more time consuming (see scenarios A and C in Figure 16.3). Specifically, the model predicts that secondary task response selection will be suspended during memory retrieval, and thus more difficult, slower retrieval will result in slower secondary task response times. This prediction has been confirmed by findings of greater secondary task costs during recall than recognition (N. D. Anderson et al., 1998; Craik et al., 1996; Craik & McDowd, 1987), greater secondary task costs during the cued recall of low-frequency than high-frequency words (Naveh-Benjamin et al., 1998; Naveh-Benjamin & Guez, 2000), and greater secondary task costs during recall cued by extralist cues than recall cued by intralist cues (Naveh-Benjamin, Craik, Perretta, & Tonev, 2000b).

4. Memory retrieval costs will increase as secondary task response selection demands increase (see scenarios A and B in Figure 16.3). The model predicts that retrieval will be suspended during secondary task response selection, and thus more time-consuming secondary tasks will lead to greater memory costs. This prediction has not been properly tested. Naveh-Benjamin, Craik, Gavrilesau, and Anderson (2000) compared the effects of a three-choice and a six-choice visual reaction time task on encoding and retrieval in a cued recall task of unrelated word pairs. Relative to the three-choice task, the six-choice task led to longer single-task and dual-task reaction times and caused greater disruptions to memory performance when combined with encoding, but not when combined with retrieval. At first blush, these results are inconsistent with the proposed bottleneck model. However, it must be pointed out that the difference in secondary task costs during retrieval between the two tasks was only 16 milliseconds. Given an estimated average of 12.20 secondary task responses per word retrieved (6,000 ms cue presentation rate divided by the mean reaction time of 492 ms), the amount of time available for retrieval of each word in these two conditions differed by only 195 ms (16 ms × 12.20 responses). Naveh-Benjamin, Craik, Gavrilesau, and Anderson did not collect the data necessary to derive time-accuracy functions, but the functions should be similar to those for retrieval of unrelated word pairs in Figure 16.2 (bottom panel). Inspection of those functions makes it clear that a 195 ms difference between the three- and six-choice task in the time available for retrieval would have little effect on the number of words recalled. According to the model, a more powerful manipulation of secondary task difficulty would be needed to produce differences in retrieval costs.

Fernandes and Moscovitch (2000) proposed a component-process model, which essentially states that verbal secondary tasks activate the same neocortical brain regions as verbal memory traces activated by retrieval, thus producing interference. According to their model, word-based secondary tasks cause particularly substantial interference because of the greater overlap between brain regions activated by the memory task and the secondary task. Their secondary tasks involved monitoring a string for (a) three consecutive odd two-digit numbers, (b) three consecutive two-syllable words, and (c) three consecutive man-made objects. Each of these tasks interfered substantially with retrieval, but the effects were greatest when the secondary task involved words.

Their model is appealing, and it may indeed turn out that memory retrieval costs depend on the overlap among primary and secondary task representations. However, I suggest that the current model offers a more parsimonious explanation, in that the nature of the secondary task is unimportant—what matters is how long the secondary task operations take. Fernandes and Moscovitch did not obtain time-accuracy functions for memory retrieval or measure secondary task latencies. The current model predicts that response selection (i.e., all of the central processes involved in making decisions on the secondary task) on their word-based secondary tasks takes longer than it does on their digit-based secondary tasks (see also Park et al., 1989, who used an odd-even decision secondary task), which in turn takes longer than on visual reaction time tasks. Moreover, the current model predicts that if one used a relatively simple and hence quick word-based secondary task (e.g., press a button if the word "monkey" is presented among a string of words), one would find little cost to memory retrieval.

5. Regardless of a secondary task's response selection demands, memory costs should be larger for free recall than for cued recall or recognition. This prediction has been upheld by N. D. Anderson et al. (1998) and by Craik et al. (1996) and is based on the fact that the slope of time-accuracy functions is generally much greater for free recall than for cued recall or recognition (see Figure 16.2, and Craik et al., 1996). In standard cued recall and recognition paradigms, retrieval runs off quickly, and the provision of additional retrieval time affords little benefit to memory performance. Thus, a reduction in the amount of time available for retrieval due to a secondary task will have little impact on memory performance. Indeed, the results of the shared time model are not shown for the recognition experiment included in N. D. Anderson (1998) because they were flat and near ceiling (~92% hit minus false alarm rate) even at presentation rates of 2 s per item. Of course, at extreme time deadlines (e.g., around 1 s or less), memory performance will be degraded merely because a certain amount of time is needed for cue identification/generation and response output.

   Modified cued recall or recognition procedures (e.g., extralist cuing in which the cue words were not shown during the encoding phase, or same-different recognition discriminations for intact or recombined word pairs) which involve greater generation or monitoring demands should be more susceptible to divided attention at retrieval than their standard counterparts if they lead to steeper time-accuracy functions. This hypothesis has not been properly tested, and at this point, only speculative connections between existing work and the hypothesis can be made. Naveh-Benjamin, Craik, Perretta, and Tonev (2000) found that a visual reaction time task disrupted recall by 0.1 words when cued with intralist cues, and by 0.5 words when cued by extralist cues, a difference that was not significant. Had they analyzed relative costs (1% and 7%, respectively), this difference may have been reliable, but more important to the present point is the fact that time-accuracy functions might be able to shed some light on the reason for the small difference in retrieval costs between these two conditions. For example, it might be that the difference in the amount of time estimated for retrieval in these two conditions (estimated to be only 349 ms: 11.62 responses per word × 30 ms difference in secondary task cost) is not enough if the slopes of the time-accuracy functions are too similar. In a different study, Jacoby (1991) found that divided attention at retrieval impaired recognition of words that had been solved as anagrams but not words that had been read during the learning phase. He furthermore showed that divided attention exerted its effect on recognition judgments based on recollection but not familiarity. According to the current model, these results would be predicted if the slope of the recognition time-accuracy function is much steeper for words originally solved as anagrams than read. If that is the case, then the reduction in the amount of retrieval time due to the secondary task would have much greater consequences for words originally solved as anagrams than read.

6. If memory retrieval and secondary task response selection cannot occur in parallel, performance on a secondary task that allows continuous response measurement should show sharp disruptions during memory retrieval. In the studies conducted by Craik et al. (1996) and N. D. Anderson et al. (1998), the timing of the visual reaction time secondary task relative to the retrieval task operations was not under experimental control. Hence, it was not feasible to measure reaction time as a function of coincident memory operation (e.g., cue identification or generation vs. memory retrieval). In a cued recall paradigm, Naveh-Benjamin & Guez (2000) used a visual-motor tracking task as their secondary task and recorded performance (defined as the distance between the subject-controlled cursor and the target) every 20 ms. They found that secondary task deviations rose sharply during the cue-elaboration/retrieval phase between the presentation of a retrieval cue and the subjects' spoken recall. Carrier and Pashler (1995) used a psychological refractory period design, in which memorized word pairs were tested individually with cued recall or recognition. Memory "strength" was varied by presenting the stimuli for learning once or twice for cued recall, or once or five times for recognition. During the retrieval phase, at experimenter-controlled times prior to the presentation of the retrieval cue (50, 250, or 1250 ms), a high or low tone was played for a two-choice auditory reaction time response. Memory retrieval was slowed when the stimulus-onset-asynchrony (SOA) between the tone and the cue word was shorter, and parallel retrieval latency × SOA functions were obtained for "weak" and "strong" items. That is, retrieval of both strong and weak items was slowed when it was coincident with auditory tone response selection at the shorter SOAs, a finding that provides strong support for a bottleneck between response selection and memory retrieval. Although in this paradigm memory retrieval was the "secondary" task on which processing was slowed by a preceding primary reaction time task, the opposite results should hold if the order of the tasks was reversed. Namely, reaction times to an auditory or visual discrimination task should be slowed until memory retrieval is completed if memory retrieval is initiated first, as shown in Figure 16.3. Both of these methods, a continuous secondary task and an experimenter-choreographed secondary task, allow for more direct observation of the response selection/retrieval bottleneck.

In summary, a bottleneck model, derived from that of Pashler (1994), is proposed in which memory retrieval and secondary task response selection cannot occur in parallel. The strengths of the current model are that it can explain why retrieval is typically (N. D. Anderson et al., 1989; Baddeley et al., 1984; Craik et al., 1996) but not always (Fernandes & Moscovitch, 2000; Jacoby, 1991; Park et al., 1989) immune to disruption by other ongoing tasks, why retrieval causes disruption to secondary task performance, and why retrieval operates outside attentional control. Divided attention sometimes does and sometimes does not lead to significant reductions in memory performance relative to full attention conditions depending on the difficulty of secondary task response selection (e.g., evaluation of the stimulus, decision making, initiation, monitoring, etc.) and on the time-accuracy functions of the memory task. Simply put, more difficult secondary tasks "steal" more time away from memory retrieval, and if the memory task is one in which retrieval is strongly time dependent, large memory costs will be incurred. Retrieval disrupts secondary task performance because it temporarily suspends secondary task response selection. It operates outside attentional control because the bottleneck is not under attentional control. And finally, under conditions of divided attention at retrieval, memory performance is exactly what one would predict given the amount of time remaining for retrieval, because retrieval and secondary task response selection share retrieval time. Time is of greater or lesser importance depending on the nature of the memory task and the individual. It is therefore critical that the relationship between memory retrieval and secondary task performance be interpreted in the context of subject- and task-specific relationships between time and memory performance.

Although bottleneck models of cognitive processing traditionally have been proposed as alternatives to resource models, the fundamental mechanism underlying the current model—time—is a resource that is shared between memory retrieval and response selection on a concurrent task. Retrieval requires time, particularly in more impoverished retrieval environments, and during its operation it forces the suspension of ongoing subsidiary response selection. In a sense, retrieval captures attention, and thus phrases such as "attention demanding" are appropriate descriptions of memory retrieval.

The primary strengths of the proposed model of memory retrieval and concurrent processing are that it accounts for a wide array of seemingly incongruent results and that it generates a number of specific, testable predictions, as outlined above. Nevertheless, what has been described in the current chapter is but an introduction, and thus many important issues have not been addressed. Chief among them is an explanation of why encoding and retrieval differ so drastically in the nature of their vulnerability to disruption, attentional demands, and attentional control. The existing data suggest that encoding is mediated by resources other than or additional to time, but the current model does not specify what those resources may be. The current model, particularly the application of time-accuracy functions as proposed, is also limited because it describes the overall competition between memory retrieval and secondary task response selection for a person and task. It does not take into account the obvious fact that a given person, within a given task, recalls some memoranda quickly and others slowly and may not recall some information at all no matter how much time is provided. Naveh-Benjamin and Guez (2000) found that secondary task tracking costs differed between slow and fast retrievals and between successful and unsuccessful retrievals, with greater and longer sustained costs for slow and unsuccessful retrievals. It is now well established that two processes (recollection and familiarity, or conscious and unconscious, or effortful and automatic) mediate memory retrieval (Atkinson & Juola, 1974; Hasher & Zacks, 1979; Jacoby & Dallas, 1981; Mandler, 1980). Although the current model does not specify how a secondary task differentially affects these processes, it has already been established that a secondary task affects recollection but not familiarity (Jacoby, 1991; Jacoby et al., 1989) and affects explicit and conceptual-implicit but not perceptual-implicit memory (e.g., Mulligan, 1998). Yonelinas and Jacoby (1994) furthermore showed that familiarity is a faster mediator of retrieval than is recollection. The fact that it is recollection and not familiarity that takes time and that is disrupted by divided attention suggests that only the former process shares time as a resource with a secondary task. This suggests that the bottleneck may encompass only recollection and not familiarity, such that familiarity-based retrieval processes (including perceptual-implicit) can operate in parallel with secondary task response selection. That is, the greater, sustained costs associated with slow and unsuccessful retrieval (Naveh-Benjamin & Guez, 2000) may arise when familiarity fails, and recollection plods along in its slow and error-prone way. Finally, what has been described is a cognitive model, not a functional neuroanatomical model. Future research will determine whether retrieval-related activity in the right prefrontal cortex is undisrupted by divided attention because that region mediates both retrieval and response selection, or because it mediates a higher order function such as multitasking, working memory, and monitoring necessary for a wide array of complex cognitive functions (see chapter 10, by Shallice).

☐ Acknowledgment

I am grateful to Fergus Craik, by whom I had the extremely good fortune to be supervised during my doctoral studies, for his support and encouragement, and to Drs. Craik and Moshe Naveh-Benjamin for their helpful comments on an earlier version of this chapter.

☐ References

Anderson, C. M. B., & Craik, F. I. M. (1974). The effect of a concurrent task on recall from primary memory. *Journal of Verbal Learning and Verbal Behavior, 13*, 107–113.

Anderson, N. D. (1998). The attentional demands of encoding and retrieval in younger and older adults (Doctoral dissertation, University of Toronto, 1997). *Dissertation Abstracts International, 59*, 3080.

Anderson, N. D., Craik, F. I. M., & Naveh-Benjamin, M. (1998). The attentional demands of encoding and retrieval: 1. Evidence from divided attention costs. *Psychology and Aging, 13*, 405–423.

Anderson, N. D., Iidaka, T., Cabeza, R., Kapur, S., McIntosh, A. R., & Craik, F. I. M. (2000). The effects of divided attention on encoding- and retrieval-related brain activity: A PET study of younger and older adults. *Journal of Cognitive Neuroscience, 12*, 775–792.

Atkinson, R. C., & Juola, A. F. (1974). Search and decision processes in recognition memory. In D. H. Krantz, R. C. Atkinson, R. D. Luce, & P. Suppes (Eds.), *Contemporary developments in mathematical psychology: Vol. 1. Learning, memory, & thinking* (pp. 242–293). San Francisco: Freeman.

Baddeley, A. D., Lewis, V., Eldridge, M., & Thomson, N. (1984). Attention and retrieval from long-term memory. *Journal of Experimental Psychology: General, 113*, 518–540.

Bäckman, L., Almkvist, O., Andersson, J., Nordberg, A., Windblad, B., Reinick, R., & Långström, B. (1997). Brain activation in young and older adults during implicit and explicit retrieval. *Journal of Cognitive Neuroscience, 9*, 378–391.

Bransford, J. D., Franks, J. J., Morris, C. D., & Stein, B. S. (1979). Some general constraints on learning and memory research. In L. S. Cermak & F. I. M. Craik (Eds.), *Levels of processing in human memory* (pp. 331–354). Hillsdale, NJ: Erlbaum.

Cabeza, R., Grady, C. L., Nyberg, L., McIntosh, A. R., Tulving, E., Kapur, S., Jennings, J. M., Houle, S., & Craik, F. I. M. (1997). Age-related differences in neural activity during memory encoding and retrieval: A positron emission tomography study. *Journal of Neuroscience, 17*, 391–400.

Carrier, L. M., & Pashler, H. (1995). Attentional limits in memory retrieval. *Journal of Experimental Psychology: Learning, Memory, and Cognition, 21*, 1339–1348.

Craik, F. I. M. (1982). Selective changes in encoding as a function of reduced processing capacity. In F. Klix, J. Hoffman, & E. van der Meer (Eds.), *Cognitive research in psychology* (pp. 152–161). New York: Elsevier North-Holland.

Craik, F. I. M. (1983). On the transfer of information from temporary to permanent memory. *Philosophical Transactions of the Royal Society of London, B 302*, 341–359.

Craik, F. I. M., Govoni, R., Naveh-Benjamin, M., & Anderson, N. D. (1996). The effects of divided attention on encoding and retrieval processes in human memory. *Journal of Experimental Psychology: General, 125*, 159–180.

Craik, F. I. M., & McDowd, J. M. (1987). Age differences in recall and recognition. *Journal of Experimental Psychology: Learning, Memory, and Cognition, 13*, 474–479.

Fernandes, M. A., & Moscovitch, M. (2000). Divided attention and memory: Evidence of substantial interference effects at retrieval and encoding. *Journal of Experimental Psychology: General, 129*, 155–176.

Fletcher, P. C., Frith, C. D., Grasby, P. M., Shallice, T., Frackowiak, R. S. J., & Dolan, R. J. (1995). Brain systems for encoding and retrieval of auditory-verbal memory: An *in vivo* study in humans. *Brain, 118*, 401–416.

Griffith, D. (1976). The attentional demands of mnemonic control processes. *Memory & Cognition, 4*, 103–108.

Hasher, L., & Zacks, R. T. (1979). Automatic and effortful processes in memory. *Journal of Experimental Psychology: General, 108,* 356–388.

Iidaka, T., Anderson, N. D., Kapur, S., Cabeza, R., & Craik, F. I. M. (2000). The effect of divided attention on encoding and retrieval in episodic memory revealed by positron emission tomography. *Journal of Cognitive Neuroscience, 12,* 267–280.

Jacoby, L. L. (1991). A process dissociation framework: Separating automatic from intentional uses of memory. *Journal of Memory and Language, 30,* 513–541.

Jacoby, L. L., & Dallas, M. (1981). On the relationship between autobiographical memory and perceptual learning. *Journal of Experimental Psychology: General, 110,* 306–340.

Jacoby, L. L., Woloshyn, V., & Kelley, C. (1989). Becoming famous without being recognized: Unconscious influences of memory produced by divided attention. *Journal of Experimental Psychology: General, 118,* 115–125.

Johnston, W. A., Greenberg, S. N., Fisher, R. P., & Martin, D. W. (1970). Divided attention: A vehicle for monitoring memory processes. *Journal of Experimental Psychology, 83,* 164–171.

Johnston, W. A., Griffith, D., & Wagstaff, R. R. (1972). Speed, accuracy, and ease of recall. *Journal of Verbal Learning and Verbal Behavior, 11,* 512–520.

Johnston, W. A., Wagstaff, R. R., & Griffith, D. (1972). Information-processing analysis of verbal learning. *Journal of Experimental Psychology, 96,* 307–314.

Kahneman, D. (1973). *Attention and effort.* Englewood Cliffs, NJ: Prentice-Hall.

Kapur, S., Craik, F. I. M., Tulving, E., Wilson, A. A., Houle, S., & Brown, G. M. (1994). Neuroanatomical correlates of encoding in episodic memory: Levels of processing effect. *Proceedings of the National Academy of Sciences, 91,* 2008–2011.

Kellogg, R. T., Cocklin, T., & Bourne, L. E. Jr. (1982). Conscious attentional demands of encoding and retrieval from long-term memory. *American Journal of Psychology, 95,* 183–198.

Kerr, B. (1973). Processing demands during mental operation. *Memory & Cognition, 1,* 401–412.

Kolers, P. A. (1973). Remembering operations. *Memory & Cognition, 1,* 347–355.

Madden, D. J., Turkington, T. G., Provenzale, J. M., Denny, L. L., Hawk, T. C., Gottlob, L. R., & Coleman, R. E. (1999). Adult age differences in the functional neuroanatomy of verbal recognition memory. *Human Brain Mapping, 7,* 115–135.

Mandler, G. (1980). Recognizing: The judgment of previous occurence. *Psychological Review, 87,* 252–271.

Mandler, G., & Worden, P. E. (1973). Semantic processing without permanent storage. *Journal of Experimental Psychology, 100,* 277–283.

Martin, D. W. (1970). Residual processing capacity during verbal organization in memory. *Journal of Verbal Learning and Verbal Behavior, 9,* 391–397.

Mulligan, N. W. (1998). The role of attention during encoding in implicit and explicit memory. *Journal of Experimental Psychology: Learning, Memory, and Cognition, 24,* 27–47.

Murdock, B. B. (1965). Effects of a subsidiary task on short-term memory. *British Journal of Psychology, 56,* 413–419.

Naveh-Benjamin, M., Craik, F. I. M., Gavrilescu, D., & Anderson, N. D. (2000). Asymmetry between encoding and retrieval processes: Evidence from divided attention and a calibration analysis. *Memory & Cognition, 28,* 965–976.

Naveh-Benjamin, M., Craik, F. I. M., Guez, J., & Dori, H. (1998). Effects of divided attention on encoding and retrieval processes in human memory: Further support for an asymmetry. *Journal of Experimental Psychology: Learning, Memory, and Cognition, 24,* 1091–1104.

Naveh-Benjamin, M., Craik, F. I. M., Perretta, J. G., & Tonev, S. T. (2000). The effects of divided attention on encoding and retrieval processes: The resiliency of retrieval processes. *The Quarterly Journal of Experimental Psychology, 53A,* 609–625.

Naveh-Benjamin, M., & Guez, J. (2000). The effects of divided attention on encoding and retrieval processes: Assessment of attentional costs and a componential analysis. *Journal of Experimental Psychology: Learning, Memory, and Cognition, 26,* 1461–1482.

Pashler, H. (1994). Graded capacity-sharing in dual-task interference? *Journal of Experimental Psychology: Human Perception and Performance, 20,* 330–342.

Park, D. C., Smith, A. D., Dudley, W. N., & Lafronza, V. N. (1989). Effects of age and a divided attention task presented during encoding and retrieval on memory. *Journal of Experimental Psychology: Learning, Memory, and Cognition, 15,* 1185–1191.

Roediger III, H. L., Weldon, M. S., & Challis, B. H. (1989). Explaining dissociations between implicit and explicit measures of retention: A processing account. In H. L. Roediger & F. I. M. Craik (Eds.), *Varieties of memory and consciousness: Essays in honor of Endel Tulving* (pp. 3–42). Hillsdale, NJ: Erlbaum.

Shallice, T., Fletcher, P., Frith, C. D., Grasby, P., Frackowiak, R. S. J., & Dolan, R. J. (1994). Brain regions associated with acquisition and retrieval of verbal episodic memory. *Nature, 368,* 633–635.

Trumbo, D., & Milone, F. (1971). Primary task performance as a function of encoding, retention, and recall in a secondary task. *Journal of Experimental Psychology, 91,* 273–279.

Tulving, E. (1983). *Elements of episodic memory.* New York: Oxford University Press.

Tulving, E., Kapur, S., Craik, F. I. M., Moscovitch, M., & Houle, S. (1994). Hemispheric encoding/retrieval asymmetry in episodic memory: Positron emission tomography findings. *Proceedings of the National Academy of Sciences, USA, 91,* 2016–2020.

Tulving, E., & Thomson, D. M. (1973). Encoding specificity and retrieval processes in episodic memory. *Psychological Review, 80,* 352–373.

Yonelinas, A. P., & Jacoby, L. L. (1994). Dissociations of processes in recognition memory: Effects of interference and response speed. *Canadian Journal of Experimental Psychology, 8,* 516–534.

A. Young: FA-Enc vs FA-Ret.

B. Old: FA-Enc. vs. FA-Ret.

C. Young: FA-Enc vs DA-Enc.

D. Old: FA-Enc. vs. DA-Enc.

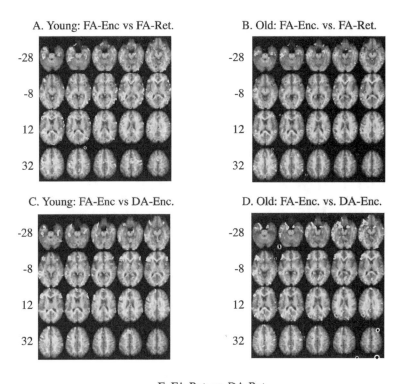

E. FA-Ret. vs. DA-Ret.

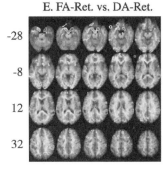

FIGURE 16.1 (See Color Plate I). Panels A and B show images from full attention conditions for younger and older adults, respectively. Regions that were more active during encoding than retrieval are shown in yellow, and regions that were more active during retrieval than encoding are shown in blue. Panels C and D show images from the encoding conditions, for younger and older adults, respectively. Regions that were more active during full than divided attention encoding are shown in yellow, and regions that were more active in divided than full attention encoding are shown in blue. Panel E shows images from the retrieval conditions for both age groups combined (see text). Regions that were more active during full than divided attention retrieval are shown in yellow, and regions that were more active in divided than full attention are shown in blue. The PET data are superimposed on standard MR images, plotted from z = −28 to z = +48 mm relative to the AC-PC line, in 4 mm increments. Numbers to the left of each row are the z value of the leftmost image in each row. The left side of each image represents the left side of the brain. From N. D. Anderson et al. (2000).

Colin M. MacLeod

Commentary: Dividing Attention to Study the Resource Demands of Memory Processes

How can we determine the processing demands of different component processes involved in remembering? This is a huge question, but certainly one that is critical to address in developing a full understanding of memory. It has long been one of the central questions motivating the research of Fergus Craik, so it is fitting that the three preceding chapters by his frequent collaborators take on one central aspect of this question: How do resource demands, in the form of attentional requirements, influence encoding versus retrieval? The answer offered in all three chapters is that resource demands ordinarily are considerably greater at encoding than at retrieval, but that the picture is not simple and that the exceptions are particularly informative.

The conclusion that retrieval is less resource demanding than encoding derives largely from research contrasting full attention, where there is no secondary task to distract from the primary memory task, to divided attention, where a secondary task must be performed in conjunction with the primary memory task. Thus, the resource in question seems closely related to attention. The research technique is referred to as the divided attention paradigm, an instance of a broader category of situations—dual task or secondary task methodologies (see Pashler, 1994a, 1994b)—where participants must cope with two tasks. Because these procedures require the coordination of two tasks, this research is necessarily quite complex, as indeed is the underlying concept of resources. With this complexity, however, comes a richness that has the potential to provide us with insight into the demands made by different memory tasks in a way that other standard cognitive procedures cannot readily do.

In this brief commentary, I will consider what has been learned from divided attention studies of memory, a domain of research in which Fergus Craik and his collaborators continue to be leaders. The domain has a long association with the University of Toronto, both through Craik himself (Anderson & Craik, 1974) and through his colleagues (e.g., Murdock, 1965). For much of the recent past, Craik and his colleagues have used the divided attention procedure to explore the encoding–retrieval contrast as part of Craik's ongoing program of memory research, which emphasizes encoding–retrieval interactions. Craik has long been interested in encoding processes (Craik & Lockhart, 1972) and in retrieval processes (see Gardiner, Craik, & Birtwistle, 1972) from the standpoint of basic processes. And uniquely, because of his "parallel career" as a leader in the study of cognitive aging, Craik has used the aging work to inform his basic work and vice versa. Thus, his notion of environmental support in the cognitive aging literature (Craik, 1986) also highlights encoding–retrieval interactions, emphasizing the degree to which different remembering situations provide different types of cues to assist in remembering.

In these three chapters, emphasis shifts from encoding (Naveh-Benjamin, chapter 15), to the relation between encoding and retrieval (Anderson, chapter 16), to retrieval (Moscovitch, Fernandes, & Troyer, chapter 14), providing nice coverage of the whole sequence involved in remembering. Emphasis also shifts from behavioral data (Naveh-Benjamin), to models and brain imaging (Anderson), to neuropsychological evidence and theory (Moscovitch, Fernandes, & Troyer), providing a broad perspective on the domains in which these ideas have been considered. There is a wealth of information here, and I certainly cannot do it justice in these comments. But let us consider some of what is known and some of what needs to be addressed, working our way from encoding to retrieval.

☐ Divided Attention at Encoding

In centering his attention on encoding, Naveh-Benjamin carefully evaluates a number of possible bases for the cost to encoding of a secondary task, from the methodological to the theoretical. An intuitively appealing basis is that dividing attention at encoding reduces the time available for encoding, but he argues that this can account for only part of the cost of dividing attention, based on his collaborative work with Craik (Craik, Govoni, Naveh-Benjamin, & Anderson, 1996; Naveh-Benjamin, Craik, Gavrilescu, & Anderson, 2000; Naveh-Benjamin, Craik, Perretta, & Tonev, 2000).

Accepting that the problem at encoding is not solely insufficient time, Naveh-Benjamin considers other more qualitative reasons, working through the most likely suspects. Intriguingly, he is forced by the existing data to discard all of them. He initially considers that divided attention may reduce effortful, strategic processing that results in well-elaborated encoding—an instance of which would be reflected in the work of another of Craik's longstanding University of Toronto colleagues, Norman Slamecka, on the "generation effect" (Slamecka & Graf, 1978). But Naveh-Benjamin concludes after an extended examination of the literature that divided attention "may affect types of processing other than strategic-effortful ones," basing this on careful attempts to equate strategy under full and divided attention and also to minimize strategy via incidental learning.

If the problem is not with strategic processing, then it makes sense to turn to automatic processing, which Naveh-Benjamin does next. Once again, however, he rejects this as the answer: "The results described here do not provide support for the claim that the effects of DA [divided attention] at encoding on memory performance are mediated by the interruption of automatic nonstrategic processes." He bases this on attempts to examine both initial perceptual registration of information and its consolidation, neither of which appears differentially influenced by the division of attention. This results in something of a conundrum, given that his analysis would appear to eliminate the entire continuum from strategic through automatic as underlying the divided attention cost in encoding.

Naveh-Benjamin considers, however, that the automatic–strategic distinction may not be valuable in this context and turns instead to a distinction that relies more on the nature of the material to be remembered. Could it be that dividing attention impairs associative encoding as opposed to item encoding? This distinction, long a central emphasis in the theorizing of Craik's colleague at the University of Toronto, Bennet Murdock (1982), also provides a plausible way to explain why the disruption of encoding leads to poorer retention. The idea is that associative encoding leads to better memory than item encoding, so being forced to rely more on item encoding due to divided attention would reduce memory. But Naveh-Benjamin eventually rejects this possibility as well: "Such results are not consistent with the notion that an associative deficit is the locus of the DA effects [on memory performance at encoding]." In so doing, he emphasizes association within items (e.g., between two words of a pair); I wondered whether deficits in associations across all of the items thoughout the entire encoding experience would be a good place to look for costs due to divided attention.

In discarding all of these possible accounts, Naveh-Benjamin reaches the conclusion that "the results convey a complex picture with no one specific mechanism implicated as the sole mediator of these DA effects." He is, nevertheless, optimistic that we can still discover the causes(s) of the harm done to encoding by dividing attention. One factor that I would point to is rehearsal or elaboration. Once an item is encoded, given that a memory test is usually expected, subjects are likely to rehearse or in some way further elaborate the encoded item. The presence of the secondary task, and the requirement to respond to it even *subsequent* to encoding, may also disrupt later memory. Indeed, Posner and Boies (1971) demonstrated this 30 years ago using a secondary probe task to estimate demands of various processing components. They concluded that rehearsal and response production or decision were most taxing. Thus, it may be postencoding processes like rehearsal that are most attention demanding. Interestingly, this would parallel the conclusion that Moscovitch, Fernandes, and Troyer offer with regard to retrieval—that it is not the retrieval itself but the postretrieval processes that are most vulnerable to disruption by dividing attention. I will return to this important point.

☐ Divided Attention at Retrieval

Anderson does a very good job of defining the terms and the fundamental issues in the domain of divided attention and memory, considering task effects, material effects, and even subject effects (aging differences). Indeed, one virtue of her chapter is the bringing together of pointers to so many of the relevant issues, particularly notable in the three tables that roughly correspond to the beginnings of a meta-analysis, an endeavour well worth pursuing. She also adds discussion of new work on brain imaging to the standard behavioral data on the effects of divided attention on memory (Iidaka, Anderson, Kapur, Cabeza, & Craik, 2000; Tulving, Kapur, Craik, Moscovitch, & Houle, 1994). In the context of Tulving's HERA model in which the left prefrontal cortex is associated more with encoding and the right prefrontal cortex more with retrieval, she describes the complex pattern of brain activity as a function of aging.

Picking up the encoding thread from Naveh-Benjamin, Anderson argues that "divided attention during encoding interferes with deep, semantic processing," an argument also put forth by Moscovitch, Fernandes, and Troyer. For me, there is a paradox in this conclusion, resting on the episodic-semantic distinction (Tulving, 1972). It would seem that deep semantic encoding would necessitate the retrieval of related information from semantic memory, otherwise it is hard to see how elaboration of the input could occur. Does this not suggest that retrieval from *semantic* memory is therefore affected by divided attention? Or is it the postretrieval *use* of this retrieved information that is disrupted? This distinction between, on the one hand, encoding or retrieval itself, and on the other hand, the processes surrounding (particularly following) encoding and retrieval is one that is certainly recognized in all three chapters. Indeed, Craik et al. (1996) raised this issue and suggested that retrieval itself—what Tulving (1991) called *ecphory*—does not demand attention, but that maintenance of retrieval mode and other retrieval-related activities does require attention. Breaking down encoding and retrieval into their component parts is without question an important direction for this research to pursue, as all of these chapters readily acknowledge.

Anderson proposes a model along the lines of a Pashler (1994a, 1994b) bottleneck model in which retrieval and the response to the secondary task cannot occur in parallel. By "retrieval" here, she means something more akin to ecphory—just the accessing of memory, not the use of what is recovered from memory. It will be important in future to discriminate between these two uses of "retrieval." She makes the reasonable prediction that if ecphory and secondary task response cannot co-occur, then a continuous secondary task might reveal this, whereas a discrete-response secondary task might not. This is an interesting observation in that secondary tasks always require responses and so does memory retrieval in a test phase, but encoding in a study phase does not. Could it be that retrieval is more able to accommodate an interruption than is encoding because of this difference in response conflict? (Indeed, it might even be the case that retrieval would occasionally *benefit* from interruption, if this causes the subject to shift from an unsuccessful to a more successful retrieval path.) On accuracy measures at the time of test, this may mean that memory will suffer more when encoding as opposed to retrieval has been disrupted. Classical memory research tends not to rely on retrieval latency as a dependent measure, but it is possible that latency would be useful in addressing this concern, as might the techniques of cognitive neuroscience, such as evoked response potentials (ERPs) or the like.

In keeping with Roediger's (2000) argument that retrieval is the "critical mystery" of memory, Moscovitch, Fernandes, and Troyer emphasize retrieval and the relevant neuropsychological evidence in the context of Moscovitch's component process model (see, e.g., Moscovitch, 1994; Moscovitch & Winocur, 1992). The essence of the model is that the medial temporal lobes are a kind of modular slave system that necessarily encodes inputs and then retrieves these encoded representations in a rather ballistic manner. In contrast, the frontal lobes are "intelligent" and nonmodular, having as one responsibility the task of working on the products of the medial temporal lobes in strategic ways: directing attention, organizing, searching, monitoring, and verifying. Under this view, the medial temporal lobes require little attention, whereas the frontal lobes make extensive demands on attention. Moscovitch, Fernandes, and Troyer point out the possibility of mapping this account onto Craik's environmental support account of aging, with resource depletion corresponding to the deterioration of frontal lobe function with age.

In their chapter, Moscovitch, Fernandes, and Troyer raise the interesting puzzle that we experience retrieval as difficult despite the evidence presented in all three chapters that retrieval requires little in the way of attentional resources. Once again, I see the distinction between "pure" retrieval and the other processes also occurring at the time of test as critical here. A great deal goes on at the time of test other than retrieval, and the effort we experience in retrieval may actually derive from these other processes. Moscovitch, Fernandes, and Troyer recognize this by saying that "retrieval itself consists of a number of component processes," but I would suggest that, despite their admirably pointing out the problem, it is still conceptually ambiguous. We must either reserve "retrieval" for the pure act of recovery from memory and then refer to the collection of processes surrounding this pure retrieval as "test-related processes" (or the like) or we must adopt a new term for the pure act of retrieval (as Tulving suggests with ecphory) and preserve the more common usage of "retrieval" as coincident with test-related processes. My vote is for the second option because it highlights the component processes.

There are two further ideas in the Moscovitch, Fernandes, and Troyer chapter that particularly caught my interest, one in a positive way and one in a negative way. On the positive side, they say that "At retrieval, it is competition for memory or representational systems, rather than for cognitive resources, that leads to memory decrement." I very much prefer this perspective. My sense is that the concept of resources is overly flexible, a problem discussed by Kahneman (1973) in his excellent and still very relevant treatment of the issues. He described how task demands potentially influence allocation of resources to a task. Once resources are seen as expandable in a given setting, measuring or manipulating them becomes much more complicated. How are we to differentiate when further resources *cannot* be allocated from when further resources simply *are not* allocated? But competition for memories or for memory systems, as an explanatory idea, holds the potential for keeping the explanation based firmly in the domain of memory.

The idea with which I disagree is their statement that "Because divided attention had different effects on encoding and retrieval, retrieval cannot simply be a reinstatement of the processes that occurred at encoding." This directly challenges the view of memory championed by another of Craik's long-time University of Toronto colleagues, Paul Kolers (Kolers, 1976; Kolers & Roediger, 1984), a view that has clearly influenced Craik's own thinking (e.g., Tardif & Craik, 1989). For Kolers, all events that constitute memory are processing or reprocessing events. Thus, to encode is to engage a set of processes, the actions of which are then themselves retained in memory. To retrieve is again to engage a set of processes, the actions of which may lead to "remembering." To the degree that the encoding-retrieval match is a good one, remembering will be good as well. This view remains very influential today in the transfer-appropriate processing framework (e.g., Roediger, Weldon, & Challis, 1989). Moscovitch, Fernandes, and Troyer contest this view. As they argue themselves, however, both encoding and retrieval consist of multiple processes. Moreover, we do not yet know which processes are affected and which are not affected by dividing attention. Different constellations of processes will always be invoked at study and test, such that the encoding–retrieval match will never be perfect. Therefore, that divided attention apparently influences encoding differently from retrieval cannot be diagnostic concerning whether retrieval consists of the *attempted* reinstatement of processes engaged during encoding.

The most intriguing idea put forth by Moscovitch, Fernandes, and Troyer is that there may be two quite different kinds of retrieval, retrieval that is strategic and heavily involves the frontal lobes, and retrieval that is quite ballistic and relies on the medial temporal lobes. This leads to the nice prediction that the former kind of retrieval should indeed require resources and hence be affected by divided attention, whereas the latter should not. They also present some evidence that is consistent with this view. This is clearly a direction that should be pursued, given its potential for drawing together the cognitive, cognitive neuropsychology, and cognitive neuroscience empirical and theoretical work.

☐ Memory Processes and Divided Attention

As Craik and all of the authors of these chapters have increasingly emphasized, encoding and retrieval are not themselves processes but rather collections of processes assembled for a particular memory-related task. It is for this reason that I find the Kolers perspective a particularly compelling one: Memory is not trying to match encoding and retrieval, but rather it is trying to deploy suitable processes to perform the task at hand (be it encoding or retrieval). To the extent that similar constellations of processes are deployed at encoding and retrieval, remembering will be more successful. Retrieval is not a weaker reinstatement of encoding; rather, retrieval is a new situation that can put into play some of the same processes as encoding, but the degree of overlap is subject to a great many influences.

Under such a view, how do we deal with the results of divided attention manipulations at encoding versus retrieval? It may be that the pure act of retrieval does not require attention, or even that the pure acts of both encoding and retrieval do not require attention, though the literature on indirect, implicit tests of memory indicates that this is not a straightforward issue and that subtle changes in attention can have dramatic effects on memory (see, e.g., MacDonald & MacLeod, 1998; Szymanski & MacLeod, 1996). In contrast, it may be that the "supporting players" that surround encoding at the time of study and retrieval at the time of test do require much more in the way of attention. Rehearsing an already encoded item would appear to be very attention demanding, as would making a decision or producing a response (see Posner & Boies, 1971). For this reason, it is crucial to break down the activities at the time of study and at the time of test into their component processes and not to equate encoding with study and retrieval with test. This is where the research must go and, to their credit, like Craik himself, this is very evidently where the authors of these three chapters are taking their research.

Research must also put the divided attention technique itself under scrutiny, as the authors of these chapters are well aware. As always, we must be critical not just of our theories but also of the methods that we use to evaluate those theories. Very recent work indicates that dual task situations are remarkably complex. Thus, Rah, Reber, and Hsiao (2000) suggest that secondary tasks do not stay independent from primary tasks but rather that the two tasks become intertwined with each other, complicating analysis. In addition, Hegarty, Shah, and Miyake (2000) sound a cautionary note. They observed the counterintuitive result that secondary tasks considered on the basis of psychometric work to make the greatest resource demands (i.e., to most heavily tax the central executive) exerted less effect on primary tasks than did secondary tasks associated with lower resource demands. On this basis, they argued that there is a considerable problem of tradeoff between the two tasks. We must thoroughly understand the procedure if we are to be able to unambiguously interpret results derived from it.

☐ Concluding Comments

In her chapter, Anderson cites a recent article by Naveh-Benjamin and Guez (2000) wherein the secondary task indicated increased attentional demands during the period between the presentation of a retrieval cue and recall. She rightly notes how increasingly complex the patterns are becoming as researchers delve deeper into the attentional requirements of encoding and retrieval with both standard chronometric approaches and the new imaging approaches of cognitive neuroscience. Naveh-Benjamin raises the problems of binding and of intra-item association as important, correctly recognizing that we must go beneath the global domains of encoding and retrieval to unpack the processes that compose them. Moscovitch, Fernandes, and Troyer (see Fernandes & Moscovitch, 2000) point to the exceptions where retrieval clearly does make resource demands as being particularly informative and consistent with neuropsychological findings about the roles of various brain areas in encoding versus retrieval.

All three of these chapters are state-of-the-art statements of where we have come from and where we are now in terms of understanding the complex nature of attentional demands in remembering. Most importantly, all three chapters point to the path we must take to understand the resource demands of memory processes, a topic to which Fergus Craik has devoted so much of his incisive research throughout his career. As such, these chapters are a fitting tribute to one of the most influential of memory researchers, and to the profound impact that he and his University of Toronto colleagues have had in moving encoding–retrieval interactions to center stage in the study of human memory.

☐ References

Anderson, C. M., & Craik, F. I. M. (1974). The effect of a concurrent task on recall from primary memory. *Journal of Verbal Learning & Verbal Behavior, 13,* 107–113.

Craik, F. I. M. (1986). A functional account of age differences in memory. In F. Klix & H. Hagendorf (Eds.), *Human memory and cognitive capabilities, mechanisms, and performances* (pp. 409–422). North Holland: Elsevier.

Craik, F. I. M., Govoni, R., Naveh-Benjamin, M., & Anderson, N. D. (1996). The effects of divided attention on encoding and retrieval processes in human memory. *Journal of Experimental Psychology: General, 125,* 159–180.

Craik, F. I. M., & Lockhart, R. S. (1972). Levels of processing: A framework for memory research. *Journal of Verbal Learning & Verbal Behavior, 11,* 671–684.

Fernandes, M. A., & Moscovitch, M. (2000). Divided attention and memory: Evidence of substantial interference effects at retrieval and encoding. *Journal of Experimental Psychology: General, 129,* 155–176.

Gardiner, J. M., Craik, F. I. M., & Birtwistle, J. (1972). Retrieval cues and release from proactive inhibition. *Journal of Verbal Learning & Verbal Behavior, 11,* 778–783.

Hegarty, M., Shah, P., & Miyake, A. (2000). Constraints on using the dual-task methodology to specify the degree of central executive involvement in cognitive tasks. *Memory & Cognition, 28,* 376–385.

Iidaka, T., Anderson, N. D., Kapur, S., Cabeza, R., & Craik, F. I. M. (2000). The Effect of divided attention on encoding and retrieval in episodic memory revealed by positron emission tomography. *Journal of Cognitive Neuroscience, 12,* 267–280.

Kahneman, D. (1973). *Attention and effort.* Englewood Cliffs, NJ: Prentice-Hall.

Kolers, P. A. (1976). Reading a year later. *Journal of Experimental Psychology: Human Learning & Memory, 2,* 554–565.

Kolers, P. A., & Roediger, H. L., III (1984). Procedures of mind. *Journal of Verbal Learning & Verbal Behavior, 23,* 425–449.

MacDonald, P. A., & MacLeod, C. M. (1998). The influence of attention at encoding on direct and indirect remembering. *Acta Psychologica, 98,* 291–310.

Moscovitch, M. (1994). Cognitive resources and dual-task interference effects at retrieval in normal people: The role of the frontal lobes and medial temporal cortex. *Neuropsychology, 8,* 524–534.

Moscovitch, M., & Winocur, G. (1992). The neuropsychology of memory and aging. In F. I. M. Craik and T. A. Salthouse (Eds.), *The handbook of aging and cognition* (pp. 315–372). Hillsdale, NJ: Erlbaum.

Murdock, B. B., Jr. (1965). Effects of a subsidiary task on short-term memory. *British Journal of Psychology, 56,* 413–419.

Murdock, B. B. (1982). A theory for the storage and retrieval of item and associative information. *Psychological Review, 89,* 609–626.

Naveh-Benjamin, M., & Guez, J. (2000). Effects of divided attention on encoding and retrieval processes: Assessment of attentional costs and a componential analysis. *Journal of Experimental Psychology: Learning, Memory, & Cognition, 26,* 1461–1482.

Naveh-Benjamin, M., Craik, F. I. M., Gavrilescu, D., & Anderson, N. D. (2000). Asymmetry between encoding and retrieval processes: Evidence from divided attention and a calibration analysis. *Memory & Cognition, 28,* 965–976.

Naveh-Benjamin, M., Craik, F. I. M., Perretta, J. G., & Tonev, S. T. (2000). The effects of divided attention on encoding and retrieval processes: The resiliency of retrieval processes. *Quarterly Journal of Experimental Psychology: Human Experimental Psychology, 53A,* 609–625.

Pashler, H. (1994a). Dual-task interference in simple tasks: Data and theory. *Psychological Bulletin, 116,* 220–244.

Pashler, H. (1994b). Graded capacity-sharing in dual-task interference? *Journal of Experimental Psychology: Human Perception & Performance, 20,* 330–342.

Posner, M. I., & Boies, S. J. (1971). Components of attention. *Psychological Review, 78,* 391–408.

Rah, S. K.-Y., Reber, A. S., & Hsiao, A. T. (2000). Another wrinkle on the dual-task SRT experiment: It's probably not dual-task. *Psychonomic Bulletin & Review, 7,* 309–313.

Roediger, H. L., III (2000). Why retrieval is the key process in understanding human memory. In E. Tulving (Ed.), *Memory, consciousness, and the brain: The Tallinn conference* (pp. 52–75). Philadelphia: Psychology Press.

Roediger, H. L., III, Weldon, M. S., & Challis, B. H. (1989). Explaining dissociations between implicit and explicit measures of retention: A processing account. In H. L. Roediger, III & F. I. M. Craik (Eds.), *Varieties of memory and consciousness: Essays in honour of Endel Tulving* (pp. 3–41). Hillsdale, NJ: Erlbaum.

Slamecka, N. J., & Graf, P. (1978). The generation effect: Delineation of a phenomenon. *Journal of Experimental Psychology: Human Learning and Memory, 4,* 592–604.

Szymanski, K. F., & MacLeod, C. M. (1996). Manipulation of attention at study affects an explicit but not an implicit test of memory. *Consciousness & Cognition, 5,* 165–175.

Tardif, T., & Craik, F. I. M. (1989). Reading a week later: Perceptual and conceptual factors. *Journal of Memory & Language, 28,* 107–125.

Tulving, E. (1972). Episodic and semantic memory. In E. Tulving & W. Donaldson (Eds.), *Organization of memory.* New York: Academic Press.

Tulving, E. (1991). Concepts of human memory. In L. R. Squire, N. M. Weinberger et al. (Eds.), *Memory: Organization and locus of change* (pp. 3–32). New York: Oxford University Press.

Tulving, E., Kapur, S., Craik, F. I. M., Moscovitch, M., & Houle, S. (1994). Hemispheric encoding/retrieval asymmetry in episodic memory: Positron emission tomography findings. *Proceedings of the National Academy of Sciences (USA), 91,* 2016–2020.

AGE-RELATED CHANGES IN MEMORY AND COGNITION

CHAPTER **18**   Aaron S. Benjamin

Part III Introduction: Toward a Taxonomy of Research on Memory and Aging

Even before the effects of nonpathological aging became a *cause célèbre* for granting agencies, there were a few lonely (and unfunded) souls who pioneered the use of empirical approaches to understanding the effects of aging on cognition in general and on memory in particular. Very early work by our fêted honoree included analyses of word retrieval and aging (Craik & Masani, 1969), language and aging (Craik & Masani, 1967), dichotic listening and aging (Craik, 1965), recall of Finnish digits and aging, and even personality and aging (Craik, 1964). So, lest the uninformed reader suggest that the many references to and citations of Craik in the chapters that follow be nothing more than an overt attempt to curry his favor on the occasion of his Festschrift, I submit to you that this is nothing more than a half-truth.

Although Fergus Craik has never been one to hector his colleagues into his point of view, modern research on cognition and aging has nonetheless come to follow in the footsteps of his early work. The six excellent contributions to this section on aging represent some of the best that the field has to offer, and each of the authors acknowledges a substantial debt to Professor Craik, as either a mentor, a colleague, or simply a good friend. These chapters divide themselves into one of two approaches to the study of memory and aging, each of which I will briefly introduce.

☐ Global Changes Underlying Memory Deficits

One approach to understanding and characterizing age-related deficits in memory is to look for common elements that underlie seemingly disparate deficits. A particularly appealing aspect of this approach is its parsimony: Rather than construe the myriad of apparent age-related changes in memory in a piecemeal manner, these explanations specify global factors, the effects of which cascade through the cognitive system and give rise to superficially very different effects on memory.

Cognitive Changes

This strategy is exemplified by the work described in chapter 22 by Salthouse, in which he reviews evidence that a wide variety of tasks—some of which have a mnemonic component and some of which do not—share a substantial portion of the total age-related variance in performance. The relative lack of age-related variance unique to any particular task, and to memory tasks in general, suggests that the existence of a global variable that mediates effects of aging on cognition and memory. He suggests this mystery variable might be something akin to the notion of "self-initiated processing" suggested by Craik (e.g., 1986).

Another suggestion is provided in chapter 24 by Schneider; namely, that perceptual deficits underlie memory deficits. His proposal is that, even when the perceptual demands in a memory experiment appear minimal and no age-related perceptual effects are apparent, there may be different ways in which the young and the old arrive at a coherent perception. If the elderly supplement their declining perceptual faculties in a top-down manner with input from semantic systems, then they may be compromising those very resources that are used to effect good memory. He reviews evidence that, when perceptual demands on the subjects are meaningfully equated across the old and the young, some of the apparent age-related differences in memory no longer obtain.

Hasher, Tonev, Lustig, and Zacks offer in chapter 23 a view of cognitive aging that stresses the loss of inhibitory control. Because older adults have less control over what they attend to and thereby what information enters memory, they suffer from an overload of information, some of which may be irrelevant. Furthermore, they are less able to volitionally "forget" information that is no longer current or relevant, and thus suffer from additional mental clutter. Haster et al. review evidence that stimulus displays that minimize distracting and irrelevant information attenuate age differences in cognitive performance and that lessening the effects of proactive interference in working memory tasks actually eliminates age differences in working memory span estimates.

Noncognitive Changes

The chapter by Nilsson and Söderlund reviews evidence that certain indices of health, including hypertension, diabetes, vitamin deficiencies, and physical activity, among others, correlate with performance on cognitive tasks, including tests of memory. Given that many of these impairments and risk factors are more likely in the elderly, they suggest that some of the cognitive changes associated with aging reflect more general health and lifestyle changes. It is worth noting, however, that they conclude health status to be an important but not primary determinant of age-related memory problems.

☐ Specificity of Memory Deficits

The second strategy used in understanding aging and memory is to tease out ways in which memory is selectively impaired in the elderly. Many gross physical and cognitive functions decline with age to some degree; thus, the focus of this approach is on the elicitation of *dissociations*. Such dissociations are thought to reveal cognitively and perhaps neuroanatomically separable functions of memory, some of which degrade in the course of normal aging and some of which do not.

Chapter 19, by Jacoby, Marsh, and Dolan, illustrates this approach. Jacoby et al. discuss interesting differences in aware and unaware forms of bias on recognition in young subjects, as well as deficits in the elderly with the *controlled* use of memory, such as in recollection. They conclude that it is this failure—and not a lack of inhibition, as suggested by Hasher et al.—that underlies the greater susceptibility of the elderly to the effects of proactive interference. One particularly interesting aspect of this chapter is the discussion of rehabilitation of memory deficits in the elderly. Jacoby et al. suggest that the route to effective rehabilitation may not lie in improving inhibitory capacity, but rather in training older adults to adopt cognitive goals that compete with those in which habit-driven action slips are likely to occur, thereby constraining what thoughts come to mind.

A similar argument is advanced by Glisky, who reviews in chapter 21 a research program addressing whether older adults have a particular difficulty with remembering the source of acquired information, and whether such a decline is mediated by individual differences in degradations of prefrontal cortex. She shows that such individual differences do not correlate with performance on tests of *item* memory—that is, memory for information that was focally under study—but do with tests of *source* memory, or the ability to remember peripheral details about the study materials. One major advancement in this work over previous demonstrations of age-related dissociations of source memory is the use of atypical—and theoretically interchangable—dimensions of "source" and "item" information.

These chapters provide a "slice of life" view of current research on aging and memory. Although sharp differences between some of the views espoused here are apparent, the ultimate arbiter—a reliable, replicable body of data—is still being assembled.

☐ References

Craik, F. I. M. (1964). An observed age difference in responses to a personality inventory. *British Journal of Psychology, 55,* 453–462.

Craik, F. I. M. (1965). The nature of the age decrement in performance on dichotic listening tasks. *Quarterly Journal of Experimental Psychology, 17,* 227–240.

Craik, F. I. M. (1986). A functional account of age differences in memory. In F. Klix & H. Hagendorf (Eds.), *Human memory and cognitive capabilities, mechanisms, and performances* (pp. 409–422). Amsterdam: Elsevier.

Craik, F. I. M., & Masani, P. A. (1967). Age differences in the temporal integration of language. *British Journal of Psychology, 58,* 291–299.

Craik, F. I. M., & Masani, P. A. (1969). Age and intelligience differences in coding and retrieval of word lists. *British Journal of Psychology, 60,* 315–319.

19

Larry L. Jacoby
Elizabeth J. Marsh
Patrick O. Dolan

Forms of Bias: Age-Related Changes in Memory and Cognition

During the academic year of 1973–1974, I (Jacoby) worked with Gus Craik as a Research Associate at Erindale College, University of Toronto. That opportunity arose from a conversation that Gus and I had at a meeting of the Psychonomics Society. I was on the faculty at Iowa State University and had done experiments to show that, contrary to the dual-store models that were popular at the time, repeatedly saying a word is not an optimal means of transferring information to long-term memory (Jacoby & Bartz, 1972). Rather, we found that processing of meaning is important (Jacoby & Goolkassian, 1973). We were very excited by these findings—I believed they would place me on the road to fame or, at least, tenure. During my conversation with Gus, it became clear that I had been "scooped." His "levels" paper with Bob Lockhart (Craik & Lockhart, 1972), which was soon to be published, described results that were similar to ours. Fortunately, I decided it was unlikely that their paper would be ignored, and that, regardless, it would be fun to work with Gus. I gained a close friend and a valued collaborator. The conversations we had about research during that year at Erindale continue to heavily influence my thinking.

The research described here could be cast as a follow-up to research that Gus did for his thesis. His thesis research used signal-detection theory to investigate the possibility that poorer memory performance of older adults results from their using a higher criterion for responding, being less willing to guess. Age-related differences in criterion are not consistently found (e.g., Le Breck & Baron, 1987). However, the focus on criterion differences is important in ways that have not been generally appreciated.

To illustrate this, suppose you were preparing a colloquium and considering two alternative topics. One possibility would be to talk about false memory along with its relationship to implicit memory. Further, you would talk about how older adults are more susceptible to false memories and how this makes them more vulnerable to scams and to action slips. A second possibility would be to talk about means of correcting memory performance for guessing. For that talk, you would talk about models for separating effects of discriminability and bias. You would start by describing the two-high-threshold theory that underlies the common practice of subtracting false alarms from hits to measure memory accuracy, corrected for guessing.

The first talk would likely draw a much larger audience than would the second. However, we will argue that the two talks should be one and the same, in that our guesses are often influenced by our prior experiences. In some situations, such biasing effects are best characterized as automatic, unconscious influences of memory, similar to those measured by indirect or implicit tests of memory.

Unfortunately, biases have traditionally been treated as uninteresting nuisances that need to be controlled for or eliminated. The interest in measuring "true memory" has left bias effects maligned and ignored. However, it has been noted that the relative neglect of bias effects has left them poorly understood (e.g., Hirshman, 1995). By highlighting the similarity between biases and implicit memory, we demonstrate the importance of studying bias effects and the utility of procedures that separate the influence of biases from other, intentional uses of memory. We begin by showing that implicit learning can serve as a source of bias effects. Rather than using signal-detection theory to measure bias, as Craik did, we used a two-high-threshold model. Later, we describe advantages of the two-high-threshold model, and relate that model to the process-dissociation procedure (Jacoby, 1991).

☐ Acquisition of Bias: Is Bias "Automatic"?

To some, it might seem unwarranted to refer to a bias effect as an unconscious influence of memory. The objection is that we are aware of our biases, and effects of biases are intentional rather than automatic. However, consider the following example involving students' responding on a multiple-choice test. One of us read someplace that given four alternatives, the probability of alternative "c" being correct is far above one quarter. Supposedly, it is common for test-makers to easily generate two plausible, incorrect alternatives but to have difficulty thinking of a third incorrect alternative. They write down the first two incorrect alternatives and the correct alternative, making "c" correct, and then return to the task of generating another, plausible, incorrect alternative. Do students know that alternative "c" is correct more than 25% of the time? Even if they do guess "c" above chance, they are not necessarily aware of doing so. Rather, their preference could reflect a form of implicit learning.

Implicit learning refers to the phenomenon of learning new information independent of awareness and has been demonstrated in a variety of tasks and situations (see Stadler & Frensch, 1998, for a review). These tasks typically provide extensive practice with material containing probabilistic information that, over time, comes to guide (bias) performance on the task, just as students may come to be biased to choose "c" on a multiple-choice exam. Amnesics provide some of the most compelling evidence that this type of learning can occur without awareness, as they demonstrate learning in the absence of any explicit knowledge of prior experience with the material (Knowlton, Mangels, & Squire, 1996; Knowlton, Ramus, & Squire, 1992; Knowlton, Squire, & Gluck, 1994; Nissen & Bullemer, 1987).

We (Dolan & Jacoby, 2001) have done experiments to show the importance of distinguishing between aware and unaware biases in a task akin to those used in the implicit learning literature. During the course of one experiment, participants studied multiple lists of words, with each study list being followed by a test of recognition memory. During study, all words were presented in white. Words were tested in green or red, and the color of the test item provided potentially biasing information. The probability of a word being old was greater for words tested in green, P(old/green) = .67, than for words tested in red, P(old/red) = .33. Participants' performance suggested that they had learned this relationship between item color and old/new status (i.e., that 2/3 of green words were studied). They maintained two different and opposite biases in their responding: hits and false alarms were higher for green (mostly old) than for red (mostly new) items. However, extensive postexperiment questioning suggested that participants were unaware that the color of a test item was correlated with whether it was old.

A second experiment was conducted to further characterize participants' awareness by means other than self-report. In that experiment, participants were assigned to one of two conditions, only one of which encouraged awareness of the color relationship. In the standard, "unaware" condition, the recognition memory test allowed participants to ignore the colors of the test items. In contrast, the "aware" condition forced participants to explicitly attend to the test item's color. This was accomplished by requiring participants to use different response keys depending on the color of the test item. Critically, after over 400 trials of training, both groups were given a speeded test that required them to respond much more quickly than did earlier tests. When recognition was speeded, participants who were aware of their biases might adopt a simpler rule of responding based primarily on color. The notion is that awareness of the source of bias allows them to better adapt to a special circumstance. However, participants who were unaware of their biases should not respond differently under speeded conditions. Thus, the prediction was that speeded conditions would result in exaggerated differential bias for red and green test items in the aware, but not the unaware, condition.

Table 19.1 provides the hit rate and false-alarm (FA) rate along with discriminability and bias measures for the two groups, for both the training phase and the speeded transfer phase. The two-high-threshold theory was used to compute measures of discriminability and bias (Snodgrass & Corwin, 1988). Discriminability (Pr) was estimated as Hits – FA. Bias (Br) was estimated as FA/(1- Pr). First, note that the manipulation of neither training color nor awareness significantly influenced discriminability. Discriminability was reduced when participants were required to respond rapidly. Statistically, none of the differences in discriminability between the aware and unaware conditions were significant.

Of greater interest, training influenced bias equally for the aware and unaware condi-

TABLE 19.1. Proportion of "yes" responses for studied (Hits) and nonstudied (FA) words and resulting discrimination (P$_r$) and bias (B$_r$) measures for the different groups and conditions. Data from Dolan and Jacoby (2001, Experiment 2).

Conditions and groups	Hits	FA	Pr.	Br.	Difference in bias
Training phase					
Unaware group					
Green	.80	.29	.51	.57	.12
Red	.71	.24	.47	.45	
Aware group					
Green	.78	.32	.45	.58	.13
Red	.68	.26	.43	.45	
Transfer phase					
Unaware group					
Green	.78	.52	.26	.70	.12
Red	.67	.42	.25	.58	
Aware group					
Green	.78	.57	.21	.72	.33
Red	.53	.29	.23	.39	

tions. Training increased Hits and FAs for the mostly-old, green items, as compared to red items, indicating biases in responding related to the test item's color. Results from the transfer phase supported that one group was aware of their biases whereas the other was not. Under speeded conditions, participants in the unaware condition were more likely to call a test word "old." Critically, however, the increase in bias was identical for red and green test items. Participants in the aware condition showed a strikingly different pattern of results. When fast responding was required, these participants used their explicit knowledge of the color relationship as a basis for responding. This was reflected in an increase in bias for the green words in conjunction with a large decrease in bias for the red words. Under speeded conditions, differential bias was increased almost threefold in the aware condition but remained constant in the unaware condition.

These results demonstrate the importance of distinguishing between aware and unaware forms of bias. Awareness bestows flexibility in the strategic use of biasing information. Faced with a short deadline that compromised the gathering of evidence about the "oldness" of a test item, aware participants relied more heavily on their explicit knowledge of the correlation between color and oldness by being much less willing to respond "old" to red items—items that they knew were infrequently old. In contrast, unaware participants were less flexible. It was as if the biasing influence was "in their fingers"—not under conscious control.

Older adults acquire biases in the same manner as younger adults, although they do so at a slower rate. Using procedures similar to those described here, Dolan (1998) found that older and younger adults were equally biased to respond differently to the two colors of test items after extensive training. However, whereas younger adults showed differences in bias after as few as 100 test items, older adults required close to 300 test items to show differences in bias. Age-related differences in the rate of implicit learning have also been reported by Howard and Howard (1997).

☐ Dissociating Accessibility Bias from Recollection and Perception

The experiments described above show that implicit learning can result in bias effects that are unaccompanied by awareness of their source. The goal of the process-dissociation procedure (Jacoby, 1991) is to separate the contributions of automatic and controlled processes within the confines of a single task. Doing so is akin to separating effects of discriminability and bias. The equations used by the process-dissociation procedure (Jacoby, 1991) to gain estimates of recollection and automatic influences of memory are the same as those used by the two-high-threshold model to separate discriminability and bias effects. However, the process-dissociation approach rests on a two-process model and uses the equations to separate the contributions of automatic and controlled processes (Jacoby, Toth, & Yonelinas, 1993, pp. 150–151).

For us, "guessing" reflects automatic influences of memory and is at least as interesting as are differences in discrimination. Guessing or bias reflects memory, as does discriminability, but the two reflect qualitatively different forms or uses of memory. We refer to "accessibility bias" as a willingness to make a particular response rather than a general willingness to respond. When recollection fails, people produce the response that is most accessible. Next, we illustrate the process-dissociation procedure by examining the possibility that, sometimes, proactive interference is an accessibility bias effect that reflects habit.

Proactive Interference as a Bias Effect

In several talks, I (Jacoby) have introduced experiments of the sort that are described in this section by telling a story about an elderly math professor who was returning to Winnipeg after attending a conference in Chicago. At the end of the conference, he went to the airport only to discover that he could not locate his return air ticket. He bought a new ticket, flew home, and called his wife from the airport. When asked to pick him up at the airport, she replied: "I would, except that you drove our only car to Chicago." Gus Craik heard several of those talks, and so, was well acquainted with my "returning to Winnipeg" story. By his account, knowledge of the story had an interesting influence on his own behavior. Gus was in Scotland and unable to locate his return plane ticket to Toronto. He relates that his response was to say to himself: "Wait, did I drive here?" Not likely, since doing so would require driving across the ocean.

Hay and Jacoby (1999) used the "returning to Winnipeg" story to introduce experiments that examined the effects of aging on action slips. However, the story could also be used as an example of proactive interference. Anderson and Neely (1996) provided an excellent review of results and theorizing about interference effects (see also Crowder, 1976). They illustrated such effects with the example of remembering where one's car was last parked. Due to proactive interference, one might mistakenly return to yesterday's more typical parking spot, rather than to today's spot. Similarly, our math professor's mistake likely resulted from his typically flying, rather than driving, to conferences.

Jacoby, Debner, and Hay (2001) showed that proactive interference is sometimes due to a reliance on habit in the absence of recollection. Studies of proactive interference typically have three phases: participants learn a list of stimulus-response pairs (A-B), then learn a second set of responses to the same stimuli (A-D), and finally are asked to recall the most recent pairs (A-D). Participants in a control condition rest during the first part of the experiment; they learn and are tested only on the second set of pairs (A-D). Proactive interference is measured by comparing memory for A-D in the control and experimental groups. Traditionally, performance in these conditions has rarely been compared to performance in a facilitation condition, in which the first phase of the experiment exposes participants to the to-be-remembered set of responses (A-D) rather than a competing set (A-B). In order to separate recollection and bias, however, all three conditions are required.

Jacoby et al. (2001) included all the necessary conditions required for use of the process-dissociation procedure, and thus for the separation of controlled (recollection) and automatic (bias) processes. Their experiment began with a training phase, in which participants were presented with context cues and fragments (e.g., knee-b_n_). Participants were instructed to guess the completion and received informative feedback. In the 75–25 condition, the typical response (e.g., bend) was presented on 75% of the trials, whereas the atypical response (e.g., bone) was presented on 25% of the trials. In the 50–50 condition, typical and atypical responses were presented equally often. The manipulation of training was meant to create "habits" of different strengths, akin to those that would result from our math professor flying to varying proportions of conferences.

Participants then studied a series of short lists and took a cued recall test following each list. The context word and fragment were presented (e.g., knee-b_n_) and participants were instructed to complete the fragment with the word studied in the immediately preceding list. Participants studied the lists either under full or divided attention. On congruent trials, the to-be-remembered response was the typical response from training. On incongruent trials, the to-be-remembered response was the atypical response from training. On guessing trials, the word pair had not been presented in the immediately preceding list.

For congruent trials, a facilitation condition, participants could give a correct response either by recollecting (R) the prior event or by relying on automatic influences of memory (habit, H) when recollection failed (1-R): P(Hit | facilitation) = R + H(1-R). For incongruent trials, an opposition condition, errors in the form of false alarms (FA) are made when recollection fails and participants rely on automatic influences of memory: P(FA | opposition) = H(1-R). Recollection can be estimated by subtracting the false alarm rate in the opposition condition from the hit rate in the facilitation condition: R = P(Hit | facilitation) – P(FA | opposition). Given the estimate of recollection, an estimate of the automatic influences of memory can be obtained by dividing the false alarm rate in the opposition condition by the estimated probability of a failure of recollection: H = P(FA | opposition)/(1-R). These equations are the same as used by the two-high-threshold model to measure the biasing effects of implicit learning in the experiments described in the preceding section although the letters have been changed to refer to underlying processes.

As shown in Table 19.2, both hits and false alarms were less frequent in the 50–50 condition, and divided attention reduced hits while increasing false alarms. These are the comparisons that would be made using standard procedures for investigating proactive interference. The 50–50 condition serves the same role as does the traditional "rest" control for showing effects of further training of an interfering response (75–25 condition). Results of these traditional comparisons might be described as showing that both proactive interference and divided attention reduced memory by the same means, and as further showing that dividing attention during study increased susceptibility to proactive interference. However, as shown in Table 19.3, application of the process-dissociation equations revealed a very different picture. The estimate of recollection, R, was reduced by divided attention during study but was unaffected by prior training probabilities. The estimates of bias (habit) showed the opposite pattern. Habit was affected by prior training probabilities but unaffected by the manipulation of attention. The process-dissociation approach was supported by the convergence of the habit estimates with training probabilities and the convergence of guessing trials with habit.

Results reported by Hay and Jacoby (1996) suggest that effects of habit reflect an automatic influence of memory. They found that only estimates of recollection, and not habit, are affected by a requirement to respond rapidly. Because fast responding did not affect estimated habit, we believe its effects are automatic.

How did older adults perform on this task? Younger adults studying with divided attention often perform similarly to older adults (Craik & Anderson, 1999); Jacoby et al. (2001) showed that divided attention reduced recollection but left habit unaffected. This led to the prediction that older adults would be more susceptible to proactive interference due to a deficit in recollection.

TABLE 19.2. Proportion of typical responses on congruent trials (Hits) and incongruent trials (FA) for full and divided attention conditions. Data from Jacoby, Debner, and Hay (2001, Experiment 1).

Condition	Full attention		Divided attention	
	Congruent Hits	Incongruent FA	Congruent Hits	Incongruent FA
50–50	.72	.32	.59	.43
75–25	.83	.40	.75	.57

TABLE 19.3. Estimates of recollection (R) and habit (H) and probabilities for responding with the typical response on guessing trials, for full and divided attention conditions. Data from Jacoby, Debner, and Hay (2001, Experiment 1).

Condition	Full attention			Divided attention		
	R	H	Guess	R	H	Guess
50–50	.40	.54	.52	.17	.51	.52
75–25	.43	.69	.74	.18	.70	.70

Jacoby et al. (2001) tested this prediction in an experiment in which older and younger adults saw the typical response 67% of the time during training and then studied a series of short lists followed by cued recall tests. Younger adults showed more hits and fewer false alarms than did older adults. However, this effect was fully driven by a difference in the recollection parameter (.44 vs. .29). Younger (.63) and older adults (.62) did not differ in their estimates of habit.

These results are consistent with general findings that older participants are more susceptible to proactive interference (e.g., Hasher & Zacks, 1988; Winocur, 1982). Older participants were more likely to falsely recall words made typical by prior training. However, our results go beyond those from earlier investigations by showing that this greater susceptibility to interference reflected a deficit in recollection. Both young and older participants were likely to produce a typical response as a guess when recollection failed. The only difference between the two groups is that older participants were less able to recollect.

Recollection Deficit Versus Inhibition Deficit as a Cause of Proactive Interference

Our finding that differences in recollection account for age-related differences in susceptibility to interference conflicts with a currently popular account of interference effects. Hasher and Zacks (1988) have explained age-related increases in susceptibility to interference effects as due to a deficit in inhibitory processes. They suggested that the larger Stroop interference effects shown by older adults provide evidence for a lessened ability to inhibit preponderant responses. However, even if older participants do show larger Stroop interference effects (for a meta-analysis, see Verhaeghen & De Meersman, 1998), Stroop interference does not always have the same cause as does proactive interference.

Jacoby et al. (2001) cast both the recollection/habit and the inhibition-deficit accounts into multinomial models, and compared the fits of the two models. The inhibition-deficit model was the same as the model used by Lindsay and Jacoby (1994) to describe performance in Stroop tasks. The recollection/habit model clearly fit the data from their experiments much better than the inhibition (Stroop) model. Consequently, they concluded that the automaticity of habit, as manipulated in their experiments, is different from word reading in Stroop tasks. That is, they concluded that age-related differences in interference effects were due to a deficit in recollection in combination with accessibility bias, not a deficit in inhibition.

Awareness and Control: Effects of Aging.   In the experiment by Jacoby et al. (2001), older and younger participants indicated when they actually "recalled" their responses.

This estimate of subjective recollection was compared to the estimate of objective recollection. Across both age groups, the correlation was surprisingly high ($r > .7$); we label this as "surprising" because of the recent interest in false memories that seem subjectively real (e.g., Roediger & McDermott, 1995). However, subjective recollection was lower than objective recollection, and this difference was larger for older, as compared to younger, participants.

Knowing when versus when not to respond is important for controlling memory accuracy. It is possible to improve accuracy by simply allowing participants to withhold responses (Koriat & Goldsmith, 1996). Theoretically, this effect can be framed in two different ways. Within an inhibition model, the option to withhold responses would cause participants to more stringently evaluate retrieved memory traces for qualities associated with remembered events (e.g., Johnson, Foley, Suengas, & Raye, 1988; Johnson, Hashtroudi, & Lindsay, 1993). Such an account depends on late-correction strategies. A second possibility is that increases in memory accuracy that result from allowing participants to not respond result from early-selection mechanisms. The option to withhold a response may change the strategies with which a subject approaches the task in ways that further constrain what comes to mind. In a later section, we further contrast these "late correction" and "early selection" models of cognitive control (see also Jacoby, Kelley, & McElree, 1999), and relate deficits in early selection to goal neglect (Duncan, Emslie, Williams, Johnson, & Freer, 1996).

Our lab has contrasted performance under free- versus forced-responding instructions to highlight the importance of cognitive control in laboratory memory tasks (e.g. Jacoby, 1999). One finding is that older adults, as compared to college students, are less able to take advantage of the opportunity to not respond. Their failure to do so makes them more susceptible to scams that rely on the creation of memory illusions.

☐ Bias Effects in Perception

Historically, there has been a parallel between false perception and false memory (see Roediger, 1996). Both what people report perceiving and what they claim to remember is shaped by their prior knowledge, expectations, and attitudes (e.g., Bartlett, 1932). The idea that expectations guide perception is an old one, popularized by the "New Look" movement in perception (e.g., Bruner, 1957). An important question is how to separate actual seeing from effects of expectations that reflect general knowledge. The process-dissociation equations allow for separation of effects on perception (discriminability) and expectations (bias). Jacoby, McElree, and Trainham (1999) discuss the relation between the process-dissociation procedure and other models of bias effects, including Ratcliff and McKoon's (1997) counter model.

Jacoby and Debner (2001) used the process-dissociation procedure to examine the contributions of discriminability and bias in a repetition-priming task. Their experiment nicely parallels the memory experiment of Jacoby et al. (2001) described earlier. As in that experiment, participants in the perception experiment began by learning the typical and atypical fragment completions during the training phase. In the 75–25 condition, participants received typical feedback more often than atypical; typical and atypical feedback occurred equally often in the 50–50 condition. Following training, all participants were instructed that they would again be asked to complete the fragments, but this time with the masked word flashed immediately prior to the presentation of the fragment. Congruent trials were ones in which the flashed word was the typical response, whereas incongruent trials were ones in which the flashed word was the atypical response. Guessing

TABLE 19.4. Proportion of typical responses on congruent trials (Hits) and incongruent trials (FA) across flash durations. Data from Jacoby and Debner (2001, Experiment 1).

| Condition | Flash durations | | | |
| | 28 ms | | 43 ms | |
	Congruent Hits	Incongruent FA	Congruent Hits	Incongruent FA
50–50	.51	.51	.69	.32
75–25	.68	.65	.81	.43

trials were ones in which no word was flashed prior to presentation of the to-be-completed fragment. Trial type was crossed with flash duration; the flash lasted either 28 or 43 ms.

Correct and false perception data are presented in Table 19.4. Both correct and false perception were higher in the 75–25 condition than in the 50–50 condition. Increased flash duration improved perception; there were more hits and fewer false alarms in the 43 ms condition than following 28 ms flashes. The process-dissociation equations were used to describe these results in terms of effects on perception and bias. Simply put, as shown in Table 19.5, flash duration affected estimates of perception (P) but not habit or implicit memory (M), whereas training probabilities affected estimates of implicit memory but not perception. Supporting the process-dissociation approach, guessing trials converged with estimates of M. That is, results for perception parallel those found for memory. Results from follow-up experiments showed that perception was reduced for older adults—words had to be flashed for a longer duration to achieve the same level of perception. Otherwise, the pattern of results was the same as found for young adults.

☐ Conclusions and Future Directions

Our experiments demonstrated how people easily acquire both aware and unaware biases, and how these biases affect performance on a wide range of tasks. Participants implicitly learned the relationship between a test item's color and its old/new status, and this implicit knowledge affected bias but not discriminability. Proactive interference is sometimes "just" a bias effect; reflecting a reliance on habit following the failure of recollection. Results for perception paralleled those from memory: Increasing flash duration

TABLE 19.5. Estimates of perception (P) and implicit memory (M) derived from the process-dissociation procedure across flash durations. Data from Jacoby and Debner (2001, Experiment 1).

| Condition | Flash Durations | | | | |
| | 28 ms | | 43 ms | | |
	P	M	P	M	Guess
50–50	−.01	.51	.37	.50	.51
75–25	.03	.67	.37	.69	.67

affected discriminability but not bias, whereas manipulating training probabilities only influenced bias.

The process-dissociation equations for separating the contributions of automatic and controlled processes are the same as those used by a two-high-threshold model for separating effects on discriminability and bias. Snodgrass and Corwin (1988) chose the two-high-threshold model over alternative models because of its ability to show effects on discriminability with estimated bias being unchanged and vice versa. Such selective effects are the same as showing dissociations. Identifying discriminability and bias with controlled and automatic forms or uses of memory gives reasons to predict when selectivity of effects (dissociations) will be found.

"Bias" has generally been defined in formal models as unitary, without acknowledging the possibility that there are multiple forms of bias. In the next section, we distinguish between forms of bias by considering the difference between accessibility bias and "Stroop" bias. In a final section, we discuss the importance of bias effects for understanding and rehabilitating age-related differences in memory.

Accesibility Bias Versus "Stroop" Bias

Although we have labeled accessibility bias as a relatively automatic basis for responding, we believe the automaticity of accessibility bias differs from the automaticity revealed by Stroop interference (Jacoby et. al., 2001). As hypothesized in Stroop tasks, the inhibition model (e.g., Hasher & Zacks, 1988) suggests that a particular response or action is activated automatically, and then controlled cognitive processes are required to suppress it. This inhibition model may provide a good framework for thinking about instances of "behavior capture," in which a particular action is strongly elicited, almost coerced, by the environment or other cues. As an example, confronted by knitting needles that she should ignore, the frontal patient is compelled to start knitting and is unable to suppress this action (Lhermitte, 1986). Just as in the Stroop model, habitual motor programs prevail when controlled processes fail to suppress them. For the Stroop task and for behavior capture, action seems to have become functionally autonomous.

When do actions become functionally autonomous and require inhibition? Many cases are ambiguous as to whether they involve inhibition. Gollwitzer (1999) gave the example of a person who always discusses work at parties. As framed within the inhibition model, this workaholic needs to actively suppress thoughts of work, which automatically come to mind during parties. However, the workaholic can also avoid this bad habit by setting a competing goal prior to entering the social situation: She can decide to focus her cognitive processes on the goal of socializing and thus constrain up-front what thoughts will come to mind. In this framework, inhibition is not required—the inappropriate work thoughts never come to mind. Thus, there are two reasons why the workaholic may slip and begin to discuss work at the party: such action slips may be due to a failure to inhibit work-related thoughts, or due to a failure of controlled cognitive processes to keep the socializing goal active.

We believe the example of the workaholic may be a case of "goal neglect," in that the workaholic loses track of the socializing goal rather than fails to inhibit inappropriate comments. In these types of scenarios, we believe the recollection/habit model likely fits. Consistent with this, manipulations that reduce one's ability to form and maintain intentions result in goal neglect. For example, people with divided attention are less able to switch tasks at a target cue (Duncan et. al., 1996). Similarly, older adults are less able to task-switch. Just like in the habit-recollection model, habitual motor programs prevail when controlled processes are overloaded.

In the experiments by Jacoby et al. (2001), habit served as a form of bias that was important only when recollection failed, rather than as a source of preponderant responses that had to be inhibited or suppressed. This has implications for the steps taken to rehabilitate the memory performance of older adults. A deficit in inhibitory processes would suggest a need to improve editing processes and to teach older adults to "correct" the responses that automatically come to mind. Application of the recollection/habit model, in contrast, would involve the front-end use of consciously controlled processes to constrain what comes to mind. This suggests that the appropriate rehabilitative strategies are those that boost recollection and therefore increase the likelihood that target items come to mind. For example, Hay and Jacoby (1999) showed that older adults failed to elaborate on the semantic relations of stimulus–response pairs and thus showed lower estimates of recollection, unless given additional study time and explicitly informed about the semantic relations of the to-be-remembered material (see also Law, Hawkins, & Craik, 1999).

Biases and Aging

We believe that Craik's thesis research relied on an overly restricted notion of bias. The signal-detection theory that guided Gus's research is a single-process model that portrays bias effects as only reflecting a quantitative difference in willingness to respond, without acknowledging qualitative differences among bases for responding. In contrast, our approach treats recollection and bias as relying on qualitatively different bases for responding and further distinguishes between automatic and strategic bias effects.

Contrary to Craik's thesis, older adults are not always more conservative. Automatic bias effects are generally the same for young and older adults. However, older adults are less strategic (Jacoby, 1999). It seems likely that strategic bias relies on consciously controlled processing just as does recollection. Thus, the current research converges upon the conclusion that older adults are impaired in controlled cognitive processes.

Having arrived at the above conclusions, I (Jacoby) momentarily felt that I now had ammunition to avenge my earlier being "scooped" by Gus, described at the start of this chapter: Gus's thesis research was flawed! Perhaps he should not have been granted a Ph.D.! Our work shows that Gus was and is wrong in his view of age differences in memory! However, our notion of a deficit in controlled cognitive processes is similar to Craik's claim that older adults have reduced cognitive resources (e.g., Craik & Byrd, 1982). The major change is that rather than appealing to a difference in resources, we seek to better specify age-related differences in processing. As was true many years ago, the similarities between my views and Gus's views are striking. Fortunately, being honored by a volume such as the present one does not mean that Gus is forced to truly retire, and so continued collaboration with him is still possible.

☐ Acknowledgments

The writing of this chapter was supported by a grant to Larry L. Jacoby from the National Institute on Aging (NIA) (#AG13845). Elizabeth J. Marsh is supported by a NRSA postdoctoral fellowship from the National Institute of Mental Health (NIMH) (#1F32MH12567-01). Patrick O. Dolan is supported by an NIA training grant (#55690).

☐ References

Anderson, M. C., & Neely, J. H. (1996). Interference and inhibition in memory retrieval. In E. L. Bjork & R. A. Bjork (Eds.), *Handbook of perception and cognition* (pp. 237–313). San Diego, CA: Academic Press.

Bartlett, F. C. (1932). *Remembering: A study in experimental and social psychology*. New York: Cambridge University Press.

Bruner, J. S. (1957). On perceptual readiness. *Psychological Review, 64*, 123–152.

Craik, F. I. M., & Anderson, N. D. (1999). Applying cognitive research to problems of aging. In A. Koriat & D. Gopher (Eds.), *Attention and performance XVII* (pp. 583–615). Cambridge, MA: MIT Press.

Craik, F. I. M., & Bryd, M. (1982). Aging and cognitive deficits: The role of attentional resources. In F. I. M. Craik & S. Trehub (Eds.), *Aging and cognitive processes* (pp. 191–211). New York: Plenum.

Craik, F. I. M., & Lockhart, R. S. (1972). Levels of processing: A framework for memory research. *Journal of Verbal Learning and Verbal Behavior, 11*, 671–684.

Crowder, R. G. (1976). *Principles of learning and memory*. Hillsdale, NJ: Erlbaum.

Dolan, P. O. (1998). *Response biases, implicit learning, and the effects of age*. Unpublished Ph.D. thesis, New York University.

Dolan, P. O., & Jacoby. L. L. (2001). *Aware and unaware biases in recognition memory*. Manuscript in preparation.

Duncan, J., Emslie, H., Williams, P., Johnson, R., & Freer, C. (1996). Intelligence and the frontal lobe: The organization of goal-directed behavior. *Cognitive Psychology, 30*, 257–303.

Gollwitzer, P. M. (1999). Implementation intentions: Strong effects of simple plans. *American Psychologist, 54*, 493–503.

Hasher, L., & Zacks, R. T. (1988). Working memory, comprehension, and aging: A review of a new view. In G. H. Bower (Ed.), *The psychology of learning and motivation* (Vol. 22, pp. 193–225). New York: Academic Press.

Hay, J. F., & Jacoby, L. L. (1996). Separating habit and recollection: Memory slips, process dissociations and probability matching. *Journal of Experimental Psychology: Learning, Memory, and Cognition, 22*, 1323–1335.

Hay, J. F., & Jacoby, L. L. (1999). Separating habit and recollection in young and elderly adults: Effects of elaborative processing and distinctiveness. *Psychology and Aging, 14*, 122–134.

Hirshman, E. (1995). Decision processes in recognition memory: Criterion shifts and the List-Strength paradigm. *Journal of Experimental Psychology: Learning, Memory, and Cognition, 21*, 302–313.

Howard, J. H., & Howard, D. V. (1997). Age differences in implicit learning of higher order dependencies in serial patterns. *Psychology and Aging, 12*, 634–656.

Jacoby, L. L. (1991). A process dissociation framework: Separating automatic from intentional uses of memory. *Journal of Memory & Language, 30*, 513–541.

Jacoby, L. L. (1999). Deceiving the elderly: Effects of accessibility bias in cued-recall performance. *Cognitive Neuropsychology, 16*, 417–435.

Jacoby, L. L., & Bartz, W. H. (1972). Rehearsal and transfer to LTM. *Journal of Verbal Learning and Verbal Behavior, 11*, 561–565.

Jacoby, L., & Debner, J.A. (2001). *Discussing perception and memory: The importance of subjective experience*. Manuscript in preparation.

Jacoby, L. L., Debner, J. A., & Hay, J. F. (2001). Proactive interference, accessibility bias, and process dissociations: Valid subjective reports of memory. *Journal of Experimental Psychology: Learning, Memory, and Cognition, 27*, 686–700.

Jacoby, L. L., & Goolkassian, P. (1973). Semantic vs. acoustic coding: Retention and conditions of organization. *Journal of Verbal Learning and Verbal Behavior, 12*, 324–333.

Jacoby, L. L., McElree, B., & Trainham, T. N. (1999). Automatic influences as accessibility bias in memory and Stroop-like tasks: Toward a formal model. In A. Koriat & D. Gopher (Eds.), *Attention and performance XVII* (pp. 461–486). Cambridge, MA: MIT Press.

Jacoby, L. L., Toth, J. P., & Yonelinas, A. P. (1993). Separating conscious and unconscious influences of memory: Measuring recollection. *Journal of Experimental Psychology: General, 122*, 139–154.

Jacoby, L. L., Kelley, C. M., & McElree, B. D. (1999). The role of cognitive control: Early selection vs late correction. In S. Chaiken & Y. Trope (Eds.), *Dual-process theories in social psychology* (pp. 383–400). New York: Guilford

Johnson, M. K., Foley, M. A., Suengas, A. G., & Raye, C. L. (1988). Phenomenal characteristics of memories for perceived and imagined autobiographical events. *Journal of Experimental Psychology: General, 117*, 371–376.

Johnson, M. K., & Hashtroudi, S., & Lindsay, D. S. (1993). Source monitoring. *Psychological Bulletin, 114*, 3–28.

Knowlton, B. J., Mangels, J. A., & Squire, L. R. (1996). A neostriatal habit learning system in humans. *Science, 273*, 1399–1402.

Knowlton, B. J., Ramus, S. J., & Squire, L. R. (1992). Intact artificial grammar learning in amnesia: Dissociation of classification learning and explicit memory for specific instances. *Psychological Science, 3*, 172–179.

Knowlton, B. J., Squire, L. R., & Gluck, M. A. (1994). Probabilistic classification learning in amnesia. *Learning & Memory, 1*, 106–120.

Koriat, A., & Goldsmith, M. (1996). Monitoring and control processes in the strategic regulation of memory accuracy. *Psychological Review, 103*, 490–517.

Law, S., Hawkins, S. A., & Craik, F. I. M. (1999). Repetition-induced belief in the elderly: Rehabilitating age-related memory deficits. *Journal of Consumer Research, 25*, 91–107.

Le Breck, D. B., & Baron, A. (1987). Age and practice effects in continuous recognition memory. *Journal of Gerontology, 42*, 89–91.

Lhermitte, F. (1986). Human autonomy and the frontal lobes: Part II. Patient behavior in complex and social situations: The "Environmental Dependency Syndrome." *Annals of Neurology, 19*(4), 335–343.

Lindsay, S. D., & Jacoby, L. L. (1994). Stroop process dissociations: The relationship between facilitation and interference. *Journal of Experimental Psychology: Human Perception & Performance, 20*, 219–234.

Nissen, M. J., & Bullemer, P. (1987). Attentional requirements of learning: Evidence from performance measures. *Cognitive Psychology, 19*, 1–32.

Ratcliff, R., & McKoon, G. (1997). A counter model for implicit priming in perceptual word identification. *Psychological Review, 104*, 319–343.

Roediger, H. L., III (1996). Memory illusions. *Journal of Memory and Language, 35*, 76–100.

Roediger, H. L., III, & McDermott, K. B. (1995). Creating false memories: Remembering words not presented in lists. *Journal of Memory and Cognition, 21*, 803–814.

Snodgrass, J. G., & Corwin, J. (1988). Pragmatics of measuring recognition memory: Applications to dementia and amnesia. *Journal of Experimental Psychology: General, 117*, 34–50.

Stadler, M. A., & Frensch, P. A. (Eds.). (1998). *Handbook of implicit learning*. Thousand Oaks, CA: Sage.

Verhaeghen, P., & De Meersman, L. (1998). Aging and the Stroop effect: A meta-analysis. *Psychology & Aging, 13*, 120–126.

Winocur, G. (1982). Learning and memory deficits in institutionalized and noninstitutionalized old people: An analysis of interference effects. In F. I. M. Craik & S. Trehub (Eds.), *Aging & cognitive processes* (pp. 155–181). New York: Plenum.

CHAPTER

20

Lars-Göran Nilsson
Hedvig Söderlund

Aging, Cognition, and Health

Many epidemiological studies have demonstrated that somatic morbidity and functional incapacity are more frequent in old than in young age (e.g., Bell, Rose, & Damon, 1972; Branch, Katz, Kniepeman, & Papsidero, 1984; Palmore, 1986; Steinhagen-Thiessen & Borchelt, 1993). It has been shown that more than 80% of those who are 65 years of age and older, on the average, have a chronic disease, and many of these have multiple diseases (Fozard, Metter, & Brant, 1990). It has also been well known for a long time that increasing age is associated with an increasing prevalence of diseases that affect cognitive functions (e.g., Brody & Schneider, 1986; Fries & Crapo, 1981; Nolan & Blass, 1992). The increasing health problems in old age most likely contribute to the well-known increase in variability in cognitive performance in old age (Bäckman, Small, Wahlin, & Larsson, 1999). It goes without saying, however, that the interrelations between aging, health, and cognitive functions are complex. Only the first steps have been taken to understand the mechanisms behind these interrelations.

Given the fact that extensive health examinations are infrequent in individual studies of cognitive aging, it might be the case that at least some portion of the well-documented deficits in cognitive performance are due to physiological pathology rather than to normal aging (e.g., Abrahams, 1976). In some studies it has been argued that normal health variation in a population may account for a considerable portion of both age-related variation (e.g., Lindenberger & Baltes, 1994) and other variation in cognitive performance (Wahlin, Robins-Wahlin, Small, & Bäckman, 1998).

In order to examine the role of health in cognitive function, health should ideally be defined and assessed on the basis of some general consensus. Unfortunately, there is no real agreement as how to define and assess health. On the basis of a general medical model, the most common definition is that of absence of disease.

This medical definition is still dominating, although a more multidimensional conceptualization of health has been suggested in more recent years. The dimensions commonly included involve biology, psychology, and sociology. Whereas the biological dimension stresses physiological adaptation in relation to environmental demands, the psychological dimension incorporates behavioral aspects in general and lifestyle behaviors in particular. The sociological dimension relates to performance of individuals with respect to various roles in the society, for example, as consumers of health care.

Assessment of health to date has primarily been pragmatical in the sense that it is based on the particular setting in which the study is conducted, i.e., medical, psychological, or sociological. In this chapter, examples from all these orientations will be discussed. The first section includes data based on reports of various diseases, followed by a section on biochemical analyses for estimating various deficiencies leading to poor health. In the third section, different aspects of lifestyle are discussed in relation to health and cognition. The final part of the chapter contains a description of an ongoing prospective cohort study (Nilsson et al., 1997), in which attempts have been made to integrate and compare subjective and objective indices of health and their respective contribution to the understanding of the relationship between health and cognitive functioning.

☐ Reports About Diseases

Several health-related factors have been demonstrated to be associated with cognitive dysfunction. In many studies it has been shown that chronic diseases of various sorts lead to low cognitive performance. Vascular diseases (e.g., hypertension, diabetes, heart disease) are thoroughly studied in this context, and it has been shown that hypertension (cf. Starr & Whalley, 1992; Waldstein, 1995) decreases cognitive performance. Hypertension is the most important risk factor for brain hemorrhage, infarction (Gorelick, 1995), and vascular dementia (Skoog, 1994). Case-control studies (cf., Waldstein, 1995) have demonstrated that hypertension is associated with low scores primarily on tasks assessing attention, learning, and memory, whereas performance on other cognitive tests is less affected. Elias, Robbins, Schultz, and Pierce (1990) found that diastolic blood pressure even in the normal to borderline range was negatively associated with some cognitive functions, and particularly so in younger subjects. Swan, Carmelli, and Larue (1998) demonstrated that subjects who have remained at a high level of systolic blood pressure (140 mm Hg or more) over a period of 30 years performed less well on composite memory measures than those who have remained stable at a lower level of systolic blood pressure during the same period of time. However, the relationship between blood pressure and cognition may not be linear, since participants with a decrease in systolic blood pressure over time performed worse in psychomotor speed tasks than those with no decrease (Swan et al., 1998).

Such cases of high blood pressure over a long period in midlife have been demonstrated to lead to cerebral white matter lesions in old age, which in turn may affect cognitive function (Swan et al., 1998). It was concluded from this study that long-term impact of elevated systolic blood pressure on late-life cognitive performance is likely to be mediated through its chronic, negative effect on structural characteristics of the brain. In a study carried out in our own lab, a similar result was obtained (Söderlund, Nyberg, Adolfsson, Nilsson, & Launer, 2001). Subcortical and periventricular lesions were detected in 90% and 69%, respectively, of 139 subjects, aged 64–74 years. For both locations, brain damage could be related to past elevated blood pressure. The subcortical lesions were associated with impaired cognitive speed whereas the periventricular lesions were negatively related to episodic memory. When adjusting for blood pressure, there was no longer a significant association between cerebral damage and cognitive performance. Thus, it was concluded that white matter lesions may, at least in part, mediate the negative relationship between hypertension and cognitive performance.

It is worth noticing that that the two studies cited (Söderlund et al., 2001; Swan et al., 1998) are based on longitudinal data. In a cross-sectional study, van Boxtel (1997) found no significant relationship between current blood pressure and cognitive function and concluded that prospective studies are needed to examine this relationship.

The fact that blood pressure can interact with other factors in the internal and external environment indicates a very complex picture with respect to underlying mechanisms.

One study by Pierce and Elias (1993), in particular, has illustrated this complexity. Persons with a history of parental hypertension, but no actual hypertension of their own, performed at a lower level in tasks on memory search than control subjects without such a parental history.

With respect to diabetes, several studies have shown a decrease in cognitive performance (e.g., U'ren, Riddle, Lezak, & Bennington-Davis, 1990; Widom & Simonson, 1990). Biessels, Kapelle, Bravenboer, Erkelens, and Gispen (1994) found disorders associated with diabetes at neurochemical, electrophysiological, and cognitive levels. Although both the nature and the extent of the cognitive deficits, as a function of diabetes, vary across studies, the general pattern of data seems to be that performance is impaired on tasks assessing memory, psychomotor speed, and problem solving (cf. van Boxtel, 1997). However, cognitive performance in these studies has been assessed with relatively crude measures. For example, Kalmijn, Feskens, Launer, Stijnen, and Kromhout (1995) showed in a study involving 462 men aged 69–89 years of age that scores on the Mini-Mental State Examination (MMSE; Folstein, Folstein, & McHugh, 1975) were significantly lower in diabetic subjects than in age-matched controls. Furthermore, the pathophysiological mechanism of diabetes seems to be rather complex and, as of yet, largely unclear. As summarized by McCall (1992), acute effects of diabetes on the central nervous system, due to extreme levels of glucose, include seizures, impaired consciousness, or coma. Diabetes also increases the risk of stroke and brain damage. In addition, the medication given to diabetic patients, insulin and oral hypoglycemic agents, may, if overdosed, cause permanent brain damage due to hypoglycemia. Taken together, the relatively crude measures of cognitive function and the complex pathophysiological pattern of diabetes complicate the interpretation of the effect of diabetes on cognitive performance. More research is certainly needed on this topic.

Other chronic diseases are also known to impair cognitive performance. Both hypo and hyper forms of thyroid function are known to decrease performance in cognitive tests (e.g., Beckwith & Tucker, 1988). In some single studies, diseases like cancer (Berg, 1988), liver failure (Tarter, Edwards, & Van Thiel, 1988), renal failure (Moe & Sprague, 1994), and obstructive pulmonary disease (Incalzi et al., 1993; Stuss, Peterkir, Guzman, Guzman, & Troyer, 1997) have also been demonstrated to produce lower cognitive performances when compared to age-matched controls without these diseases.

☐ Laboratory Indices of Health

Deficiencies of various kinds should also be mentioned as important causes to impairment in cognitive performance. Vitamin deficiencies (primarily vitamins B and E) are known to reveal a negative effect on cognition (Carney, 1990). Vitamin B_{12} and folic acid are particularly interesting in this context. Vitamin B_{12} is found in food of animal origin, and folic acid is rich in milk, fresh leafy vegetables, fruits, yeast, and liver. Both vitamins are important to nerve and brain function and are required as coenzymes related to the synthesis of serotonin and chatecolamine neurotransmitters (Levitt & Joffe, 1989; Shane & Stokstad, 1985). Deficiencies in vitamin B_{12} and folic acid are associated with memory disorders (Goodwin, Goodwin, & Garry, 1983; Hassing, Wahlin, Winblad, & Bäckman, 1999; Wahlin, Hill, Winblad, & Bäckman, 1996). Other deficiencies have also been reported as having negative effects on cognitive function. Persons who are short on micronutrients like zinc and cobalt have been reported to show cognitive impairment (Sandstead, 1986).

Blood cholesterol is a major constituent of cell membranes, some hormones, bile salts, and vitamins; it is largely of endogenous origin but can be modified on the basis of food intake. Low-density lipoprotein (LDL) carries most of the cholesterol in the blood. It is the "bad" form of cholesterol since high levels lead to cholesterol build-up and an increased risk of myocardial infarction. High-density lipoprotein (HDL) is the benign form of cholesterol since its return to the liver prevents cholesterol build-up in arteries. Low levels of HDL cholesterol is a known risk factor for cardiovascular disease (van Boxtel, 1997). The relation between blood lipids and cognitive function has been explored in several studies. The overall picture is, however, quite mixed. For example, when controlling for various demographic factors, Desmond, Tatemichi, Paik, and Stern (1993) showed that high levels of cholesterol in a group of 249 stroke-free community volunteers (age = 70.8 +/– 6.7 years) was associated with poor memory performance but unaffected performance levels in tasks assessing verbal functions, visuospatial abilities, and attention. Snowdon, Belcher, Tully, and Greiner (1996) showed in a study of 89 nuns, 77–99 years of age, that low levels of total cholesterol were associated with substantial decline in cognitive performance. The mixed results obtained on the role of cholesterol in cognitive function may depend on a complex underlying mechanism involving genetic factors related to ApolipoproteinE. It has been shown that ApoE2 lowers the total cholesterol level, whereas ApoE4 increases it (Walden & Hegele, 1994).

Intoxication of various sorts might also be mentioned in this health context as causing cognitive impairment (Hartman, 1988). Alcohol is perhaps the most common cause of intoxication known to decrease cognitive performance (cf. Molina et al., 1994). Excessive alcohol consumption exerts a direct toxic effect on the brain with irreversible tissue damage and with a possible negative effect on cerebral blood flow (Rogers, Meyer, & Shaw, 1985). A lower intake of important nutrients such as vitamin B is typically associated with alcoholism, with specific cognitive disorders such as dementia and Wernicke-Korsakow encephalopathy characterized by severe memory dysfunction (Butterworth, 1995). According to Molina et al., 1994) clinical studies reveal that 50% to 70% of chronic alcohol users show mild to moderate cognitive impairment. In contrast, in studies of normal aging, controlling for stroke, dementia, and encephalophathy, the general pattern seems to be a lack of association between mild to heavy alcohol intake and cognitive decline (e.g., Desmond et al., 1993; Herbert et al., 1993). In one study by Elias, Wolf, D'Agostino, Cobb, and White (1993), moderate alcohol intake was even weakly associated with better overall cognitive performance.

Other substances known to lower cognitive performance in cases of intoxication have also been reported. For example, Lewis, Worobey, Ramsay, and McCormack (1992) found that metals like lead, manganese, and aluminum lead to a decreased performance in various cognitive tasks. Ganzevles and Geus (1991) demonstrated that high doses of organic solvents lead to a lower cognitive performance. Individuals with high doses of pesticides also show inferior cognitive performance than age-matched controls without such intoxication (Mearns, Dunn, & Lees Haley, 1994).

☐ Lifestyle Variables

Lifestyle variables are potentially important factors for understanding the relationship between health and cognitive function. Overweight, physical inactivity, and smoking are generally indicators of an unhealthy life style and a poor vascular risk profile. The overall picture is relatively complex because of confounding factors in some cases and no such confounding factors in other cases. For example, obese individuals are often less physically active, have high total cholesterol levels in general, and are more often afflicted by diabetes and hypertension (van Boxtel, 1997). The effect of overweight, as assessed by body mass index or waist-to-hip ratio, on cognitive function is still unclear, because studies are scarce and the general cause-effect picture is too complex. In a recent study, however, involving more than 2,000 hypertensive subjects, aged 65–74 years, Prince, Lewis, Bird, Blizard, and Mann (1996) failed to find any association between body mass index and cognitive performance. It should be noted, though, that this result could be due to the selective group of hypertensive persons, who, according to the earlier-mentioned reviews (Starr & Whalley, 1992; Waldstein, 1995), do not perform as well in cognitive tasks.

With respect to physical activity, Rogers, Meyer, and Mortel (1990) have demonstrated that inactive retired individuals, aged 62–70 years, showed a gradual decline in regional cerebral blood flow and cognitive performance. Those individuals who were engaged in sport activities maintained both cerebral perfusion and cognitive function over a 4-year period. Two hypotheses have been proposed to account for the beneficial effects of physical activity (see Chodzko-Zajko & More, 1994). One hypothesis, usually referred to as the oxygen hypothesis, states that neuromuscular activity may alter cerebral circulation. The other hypothesis, called the neurotropic stimulation hypothesis, states that physical activity directly enhances the efficiency of higher brain centers. The literature on the role of physical activity is steadily increasing, but as of yet, many studies have been criticized for failure to account for differences in background variables (e.g., health habits, psychological variables like anxiety and depression) between active and inactive persons. Keeping these potential confounding factors in mind, it might be concluded that physical activity does have a small positive effect on cognitive performance in complex, attention-demanding tasks, given that the exercise is extensive and that it is being carried out over a long period of time.

Smoking is generally regarded as an important lifestyle factor with high risk of hypertension, stroke (e.g., Gorelick, 1995), and vascular dementia (Skoog, 1994). Studies of the effect of smoking on cognitive function in normal aging have not yet revealed a consistent picture. For example, Hill (1989) demonstrated that old smokers performed less well than old nonsmokers on speeded performance tasks. On a wide variety of other cognitive tasks, there were no differences between the two groups. Herbert et al. (1993) failed to demonstrate a significant relationship between smoking and cognitive performance in a large-scale study involving more than 1,000 subjects 65 years of age and older. In a recent study in our own lab, smokers and nonsmokers were compared with respect to performance on episodic memory tasks and semantic memory tasks, after having controlled for demographics, indices of health, mental status, and lifestyle behavior (Hill, Nilsson, Nyberg, & Bäckman, 2000). The data from this study revealed that nonsmokers outperformed smokers on episodic memory tasks. For semantic memory tasks, there was no difference between smokers and nonsmokers.

The data for this study by Hill et al. (2000) emanate from an ongoing longitudinal study on memory, health, and aging called the Betula study (Nilsson et al., 1997). In this study the relationship between memory, health, and aging has been explored in a way that is somewhat different from the studies reported to this point. A core feature of the studies reported is that they are based primarily on reports about diseases, consumption of alcohol and cigarettes, exposure to organic solvents, etc. Such data are also included in the Betula study, but in addition to this, assessment of health is also to a large extent based on objective indices of health from a biochemical lab. A crucial feature of the Betula study is also that an extensive battery of cognitive tests is included to investigate various components of memory and cognition more thoroughly.

☐ The Betula Study

The Betula project is a prospective cohort study examining the development of memory and health in adulthood and old age with participants being 35, 40, 45, . . . , 80 years of age when first tested. The project started in 1988 and is currently planned to continue until 2003. The chief objectives of the study are to (a) examine the development of health and memory in adulthood and old age, (b) determine early preclinical signs of dementia, (c) determine risk factors for dementia, and (d) assess premorbid memory function in subjects who are in accidents or acquire diseases during the course of the study.

To accomplish these goals, the Betula study was designed on the basis of the assumption of continuous interactions between the individual and the environment in which the individual lives. The individual factors include medical, physiological, and psychological parameters, age, gender, and genetic markers. The environmental factors include a chain of events that the individual is exposed to and the experiences that the individual accumulates from these exposures throughout life. These environmental factors are manifested in family history, education, occupation, residential area, previous morbidity, risk factors, socioeconomical status, social networks, lifestyle and habits, and use and availability of social and medical facilities.

The design of the study includes three waves of data collection. The first of these waves was conducted in 1988–1990, the second in 1993–1095, and the third in 1998–2000. One sample of 1,000 subjects in 10 age cohorts (35, 40, 45, . . . , 80 years of age) underwent testing in 1988–1990 (100 subjects per cohort). This sample and two additional samples were tested in 1993–1995 and in 1998–2000. A fourth sample was tested for the first time in 1998–2000.

This design presents clear advantages when compared to traditional cross-sectional or purely longitudinal designs. With this design it is possible to make cross-sectional, cross-sequential, cohort-sequential, time-sequential, and longitudinal analyses with proper control for practice effects. These analyses can be made after the third wave of data collection has been completed in 1998–2000.

In addition to an extensive examination of cognitive functions in general and memory functions in particular, the participants in the Betula study were given a health examination, including blood sample testing, an interview about health status and activities of daily living, and questionnaires about social and economic issues and about critical life events.

Health examination by a nurse took 1.5 to 2 hours for each participant. Blood samples were taken for blood chemistry and were deep-frozen for future use. The health examination was extensive so as to provide a good picture of the health of each subject. Selection of lab tests was aimed at disclosing unknown somatic disorders, which might be associated with cognitive impairment, and screening for abnormal laboratory values known to be associated with cognitive impairment (e.g., vitamin B12, blood folate, T4/TSH, blood glucose, serum calcium levels). The evaluation of health was also done by means of subjective rating scales and self-report about various symptoms of a somatic and psychic nature.

Assessment of memory function was based on a large-scale test battery. This battery was composed in such a way that tests were theoretically motivated and that a wide variety of processes and hypothetical memory systems could be explored analytically. The memory tests selected and a few traditional psychometric tests were thoroughly described in Nilsson et al. (1997).

In brief, the test battery includes a large number of episodic memory tasks involving prospective memory, face recognition, name recognition, action memory, sentence memory, word recall with or without a distractor task, source recall, and memory for activities.

Short-term memory is assessed by means of the Tulving and Colotla (1970) method on tasks involving free recall of 12- and 16-item lists. General knowledge questions, a vocabulary test, and four-word fluency tests are used for assessing semantic memory. One word-stem completion task and one word-fragment completion task are used for assessing unconscious forms of memory.

The basis for subjective ratings of health are first discussed, followed by the results obtained in the Betula study and in other studies. The objective health indicators as predictors of cognitive performance are then examined and discussed.

☐ Subjective Ratings of Health

Large-scale evaluations of physical health are rarely done because of the costs and the time needed to carry out these examinations. Subjective ratings of health have therefore often been used as an alternative to objective measures, with the rationale that such ratings are highly related to the health ratings done by physicians (LaRue, Bank, Jarvik, & Hetland, 1979). Another reason for using subjective ratings of health is that such ratings are reasonably good predictors of longevity or death (Ljungquist, Berg, & Steen, 1995).

Perlmutter and Nyquist (1990) have reported that self-rated health status declines as a function of age. Significant relations between subjective ratings of health and cognitive performance in samples of healthy old adults have been demonstrated (e.g., Field, Schaie, & Leino, 1988; Hultsch, Hammer, & Small, 1993; Perlmutter & Nyquist, 1990). Other studies have failed to find such relations (e.g., Salthouse, Kausler, & Saults, 1990). Earles and Salthouse (1995) have recently demonstrated that self-rated health is only partially related to cognitive performance, and then only to performance in speeded cognitive tasks.

In the Betula study subjective health was assessed in three different ways. First, subjects were asked whether they currently felt healthy or not. Then they were asked whether they had experienced symptoms of a somatic nature (e.g., heart pain, back pain, stomach pain) and whether they had experienced symptoms categorized as being of a psychiatric nature (e.g., difficulties in sleeping, feelings of loneliness, anxiety).

The results showed that the proportion of subjects feeling healthy was relatively stable across age cohorts, with the exception that 55-year-old subjects reported a lower level of feeling healthy. The correlation between subjective health and age was nonsignificant ($r = -.06$). At a follow-up data collection 5 years after the first wave of data collection, there was again a lower proportion of 55-year-old subjects feeling healthy, and again, there was no significant correlation between subjective health and age. In addition, the same data pattern was found in another two independent Betula samples tested for the first time at the second wave of data collection (Molander et al., 2000). As of yet, there is no obvious explanation available for this lower level of subjective feeling of health for middle-aged 55-year-old subjects. It should be noted, though, that self-reports on pain (primarily pain in neck, shoulder, and back) are more frequent among middle-aged subjects than in any of the young and old age cohorts (Söderfjell et al., 2000). Controlling for education level, the correlations between subjective health and three different composite memory scores for episodic memory, semantic memory, and priming were all nonsignificant ($r_s = .05-.09$).

☐ Objective Health Measures

Subjective rating scales of health have been questioned as biased when used as measures of general health over a wide age range. For example, Hooker and Siegler (1992) pointed out that young and old persons may rate their own health from quite different perspectives. Given such problems with subjective rating scales, the use of more objective measures might be a more adequate way to quantify the health variable in order to assess its effects on cognitive function. However, one basic problem with all such objective measures in this context is which indicators to use. There is no consensus concerning which are the most adequate indicators of health status. The concept of health is indeed difficult to define in terms of objective indicators.

In Nilsson et al. (1997), a total of 42 blood parameters, five urine parameters, systolic blood pressure, diastolic blood pressure, pulse rate, health care consumption, use of prescribed medication, and measures of sensory function were used. The blood parameters included six different measures of red cells, six different measures of white cells, four measures of hormones, two measures of vitamins, two blood fat measures, one measure of blood sugar, six measures of the immune system, seven measures of liver function, and eight measures of electrolytes and minerals. The five urine measures included leukocytes, glucose, protein, electrolytes, and hemoglobin.

Only four of these objective indicators of health correlated significantly (using Bonferroni correction) with subjective ratings of health. These were erythrocyte sedimentation rate (a red blood cell measure) and haptoglobin (an immune system measure), health care consumption, and medication. These two blood measures are both acute response reactants to infection or inflammation.

Twelve of the objective measures of health showed significant simple correlations with performance in episodic memory tests. These were sedimentation rate ($r = -.18$), glycolized hemoglobin ($r = -.21$), cholesterol ($r = -.20$), triglycerides($r = -.14$), glucose($r = -.20$), alpha-1-antitrypsin ($r = -.19$), alanine-amino-transferase (ALAT) ($r = -.23$), alkaline phosphatase (ALP) ($r = -.19$), systolic ($r = -.34$) and diastolic blood pressure ($r = -.15$), medication ($r = -.27$), and sensory function ($r = -.27$). After controlling for age by means of partial correlations, none of these correlations reached significance ($r_s = -.07 - .01$). None of the correlations between objective health measures and semantic memory performance or priming reached significance.

Hierarchical regression analyses, with significantly associated objective health indicators entered before age, indicated that these variables reduced the age-related variance in memory, although age still made a significant contribution to the variance. The age-related variance associated with episodic memory was 34% when age was entered first in the simple analysis and 35% when entered after four blocks of health-related factors in the hierarchical analysis. These health factors (sensory function, blood pressure, medication, and blood parameters) accounted for 22% in this second analysis. This means that 62% (.216/.350) of the age-related variance was accounted for by the health indicators. It should be noted, however, in this context, that none of the health indicators was independent of age, and none of the β weights for the health indicators reached significance when age was entered into the final equation. Moreover, the change in R^2 for age between the simple and the hierarchical analyses was nonsignificant, $p > .25$, whereas the change R^2 between the fourth block (health, blood parameters) and the fifth block (age) was significant, $p < .001$. In all, the Nilsson et al. (1997) study revealed that the health–memory relationship is completely mediated by age and that the age–memory relationship is partially mediated by health (cf. Earles & Salthouse, 1995). Jelicic, Jonker, and Deeg (1999) recently confirmed this overall conclusion, that health factors have only a weak relationship with memory performance in older adults.

☐ Conclusion

The overall picture of the literature on the effects of health variables on cognitive function is somewhat mixed. When the definition of health is formulated in medical terms as absence of disease, there is certainly a considerable effect to take into account. This is seen most obviously in the effect of vascular factors like hypertension. There are reliable data showing that high blood pressure in midlife will have negative effect on some cognitive functions in late life. It should be noted, though, that this effect might be mediated via white matter lesions. The mechanisms underlying the relationship between vascular factors and cognitive function are complex and need further exploration. Poor health as defined by deficiencies in vitamin B_{12} and folic acid also leads to a lower cognitive performance in comparison to cases with no such deficiencies. It can also be concluded that subjective ratings of health show weak relationships to cognitive functions like memory. Various blood substances as indices of variation in health also show weak associations to cognitive function, at least in a relatively healthy population and after having controlled for the age variable.

Fergus I. M. Craik was quite right in stating that "for normal aging, health status may be a contributing factor but is not the prime determinant of age-related memory loss" (Craik, Anderson, Kerr, & Li, 1995, p. 235).

☐ References

Abrahams, J. P. (1976). Health status in aging research. *Experimental Aging Research, 2,* 63–71.

Bäckman, L., Small, B., Wahlin, Å., & Larsson, M. (1999). Cognitive functioning in very old age. In F. I. M. Craik & T. A. Salthouse (Eds.), *Handbook of cognitive aging* (Vol. 2, pp. 499–558). Hillsdale, NJ: Erlbaum.

Beckwith, B. E., & Tucker, D. M. (1988). Thyroid disorders. In R. E. Tarter, D. H. van Thiel, & K. L. Edwards (Eds.), *Medical neuropsychology: The impact of disease on behavior* (pp. 197–218). New York: Plenum Press.

Bell, B., Rose, C. L., & Damon, A. (1972). The normative aging study: An interdisciplinary and longitudinal study of health and aging. *Aging and Human Development, 3,* 5–17.

Berg, R. A. (1988). Cancer. In R. E. Tarter, D. H. van Thiel, & K. L. Edwards (Eds.), *Medical neuropsychology: The impact of disease on behavior* (pp. 265–290). New York: Plenum Press.

Biessels, G. J., Kapelle, A. C., Bravenboer, B., Erkelens, D. W., & Gispen, W. H. (1994). Cerebral function in diabetes mellitus. *Diabetologia, 37,* 643–650.

Branch, L. G., Katz, S., Kniepeman, K., & Papsidero, J. A. (1984). A prospective study of functional status among community elders. *American Journal of Public Health, 74,* 266–268.

Brody, J. A., & Schneider, E. L. (1986). Disease and disorders of aging: A hypothesis. *Journal of Chronic Diseases, 39,* 871–876.

Butterworth, R. F. (1995). Pathophysiology of alcholic brain damage: Synergistic effects of ethanol, thiamine deficiency and alcoholic liver disease. *Metabolic Brain Diseases, 10,* 1–8.

Carney, M. W. (1990). Vitamin deficiency and mental symptoms. *British Journal of Psychiatry, 156,* 878–882.

Chodzko-Zajko, W. J., & More, K. A. (1994). Physical fitness and cognitive functioning in aging. In J. O. Holloszy (Ed.), *Exercise and sport science reviews* (Vol. 2, pp. 195–220). Baltimore: Williams & Wilkins.

Craik, F. I. M., Anderson, N. D., Kerr, S. A., & Li, K. Z. H. (1995). Memory changes in normal aging. In A. D. Baddeley, B. A. Wilson & F. N. Watts (Eds.), *Handbook of memory disorders* (pp. 211–241). Chichester, England: Wiley.

Desmond, D. W., Tatemichi, T. K., Paik, M., & Stern, Y. (1993). Risk factors for cerebrovascular disease as correlates of cognitive function in a stroke-free cohort. *Archives of Neurology, 50,* 162–166.

Earles, J. L., & Salthouse, T. A. (1995). Interrelations of age, health, and speed. *Journal of Gerontology: Psychological Sciences, 50B,* P33–P41.

Elias, M. F., Robbins, M. A., Schultz, J. N. R., & Pierce, T. W. (1990). Is blood pressure an important variable in research on aging and neuropsychological test performance? *Journal of Gerontology, 45,* P128–P135.

Elias, M. F., Wolf, P. A., D'Agostino, R. B., Cobb, J., & White, L. R. (1993). Untreated blood pressure level is inversely related to cognitive functioning: The Framingham Study. *American Journal of Epidemiology, 138,* 353–364.

Field, D., Schaie, K. W., & Leino, E. V. (1988). Continuity in intellectual functioning: The role of self-reported health. *Psychology and Aging, 4,* 385–392.

Folstein, M. G., Folstein, S. E., & McHugh, P. R. (1975). "Mini-mental state": A practical method for grading the cognitive state of patients for the clinician. *Journal of Psychiatric Research, 12,* 189–198.

Fozard, J. L., Metter, E. J., & Brant, L. J. (1990). Next steps describing aging and disease in longitudinal studies. *Journal of Gerontology, 45,* P116–P127.

Fries, J. F., & Crapo, L. M. (1981). *Vitality and aging.* New York: Freeman.

Ganzevles, P. G., & Geus, B. W. J. (1991). Clinical neuropsychological assessment of patients chronically exposed to organic solvents. *Archives of Toxicology Suppl., 15,* 54–57.

Goodwin, J. S., Goodwin, J. M., & Garry, P. J. (1983). Association between nutritional status and cognitive functioning in a healthy elderly population. *Journal of the American Medical Association, 249,* 2917–2921.

Gorelick, P. B. (1995). Stroke prevention. *Archives of Neurology, 52,* 347–355.

Hartman, D. E. (1988). *Neuropsychological toxicology: Identification and assessment of human neurotoxic syndromes.* New York: Pergamon Press.

Hassing, L., Wahlin, Å., Winblad, B., & Bäckman, L. (1999). Further evidence for the effects of vitamin B$_{12}$ and folate status on episodic memory functioning: A population based study of very old adults. *Biological Psychiatry, 45,* 1472–1480.

Herbert, L. E., Scherr, P. A., Beckett, L. A., Albert, M. S., Rosner, B., Taylor, J. O., & Evans, D. A. (1993). Relation of smoking and low-to-moderate alcohol consumption to change in cognitive function: A longitudinal study in a defined community of older persons. *American Journal of Epidemiology, 137,* 881–891.

Hill, R. D. (1989). Residual effects of cigarette smoking on cognitive performance in normal aging. *Psychology and Aging, 4,* 251–254.

Hill, R. D., Nilsson, L.-G., Nyberg, L., & Bäckman, L. (2000). *Cigarette smoking as a predictor of cognitive performance across age cohorts in a cross-sectional sample of Swedish adults.* Manuscript submitted for publication.

Hooker, K., & Siegler, I. C. (1992). Separating apples from oranges in health ratings: Perceived health includes psychological well-being. *Behavior, Health and Aging, 2,* 81–92.

Hultsch, D. F., Hammer, M., & Small, B. J. (1993). Age differences in cognitive performance in later life: Relationships to self-reported health and activity life style. *Journal of Gerontology: Psychological Sciences, 48,* P1–P11.

Incalzi, R. A., Gemma, A., Marra, C., Muzzolon, R., Capparella, O., & Carbonin, P. (1993). Chronic obstructive pulmonary disease: An original model of cognitive decline. *American Review of Respiratory Disease, 148,* 418–424.

Jelicic, M., Jonker, C., & Deeg, D. J. H. (1999). Do health factors affect memory performance in old age. *International Journal of Geriatric Psychiatry, 14,* 572–576.

Kalmijin, S., Feskens, E. J. M., Launer, L. J., Stijnen, T., & Kromhout, D. (1995). Glucose intolerance, hyperinsulinaemia and cognitive function in a general population of elderly men. *Diabetologia, 38,* 1096–1102.

LaRue, A., Bank, L., Jarvik, L., & Hetland, M. (1979). Health in old age: How do physicians' ratings and self-ratings compare? *Journal of Gerontology, 34,* 687–691.

Levitt, A. J., & Joffe, R. T. (1989). Folate, vitamin B-12, and life course of depressive illness. *Biological Psychiatry, 25,* 867–872.

Lewis, M., Worobey, J., Ramsay, D. S., & McCormack, M. K. (1992). Prenatal exposure to heavy metals: Effect on childhood cognitive skills and health status. *Pediatrics, 89,* 1010–1015.

Lindenberger, U., & Baltes, P. B. (1994). Sensory functioning and intelligence in old age: A strong connection. *Psychology and Aging, 9*, 339–355.

Ljungquist, B., Berg, S., & Steen, B. (1995). Prediction of survival in 70-year olds. *Archives of Gerontology and Geriatrics, 20*, 295–307.

McCall, A. L. (1992). The impact of diabetes on the CNS. *Diabetes, 41*, 557–570.

Mearns, J., Dunn, J., & Lees Haley, P.R. (1994). Psychological effects of organophosphate pesticides: A review and call for research by psychologists. *Journal of Clinical Psychology, 50*, 286-294.

Moe, S. M., & Sprague, S. M. (1994). Uremic encephalopathy. *Clinical Nephrology, 42*, 251–256.

Molander, B., Andersson, R., Forsgren, L., Holmgren, S., Marklund, P., & Nilsson, L.-G. (2000). Subjective health as a function of age and time of measurement. *International Journal of Psychology, 35*, 367.

Molina, J. A., Bermejo, F., del Ser, T., Jimenez, F. J., Herranz, A., Fernández Calle, P., Ortuno, B., Villanueva, C., & Sainz, M. J. (1994). Alcoholic cognitive deterioration and nutritional deficiencies. *Acta Neurologica Scandinavica, 89*, 384–390.

Nilsson, L.-G., Bäckman, L., Erngrund, K., Nyberg, L., Adolfsson, R., Bucht, G., Karlsson, S., Widing, M., & Winblad, B. (1997). The Betula prospective cohort study: Memory, health and aging. *Aging, Neuropsychology, and Cognition, 4*, 1–32.

Nolan, K. A., & Blass, J. P. (1992). Preventing cognitive decline. *Clinics in Geriatric Medicine, 8*, 19–34.

Palmore, E. B. (1986). Trends in the health of the aged. *Gerontologist, 26*, 289–302.

Perlmutter, M., & Nyquist, L. (1990). Relationships between self-reported physical and mental health and intelligence performance across adulthood. *Journal of Gerontology: Psychological Sciences, 45*, P145–P155.

Pierce, T. W., & Elias, M. F. (1993). Cognitive function and cardiovascular responsivity in subjects with a parental history of hypertension. *Journal of Behavioral Medicine, 16*, 277–294.

Prince, M., Lewis, G., Bird, A., Blizard, R., & Mann, A. (1996). A longitudinal study of factors predicting change in cognitive test scores over time, in an older hypertensive population. *Psychological Medicine, 26*, 555–568.

Rogers, R. L., Meyer, J. S., & Mortel, K. F. (1990). After reaching retirement age physical activity sustains cerebral perfusion and cognition. *Journal of the American Geriatrics Society, 38*, 123–128.

Rogers, R. L., Meyer, J. S., & Shaw, T.G. (1985). Reductions in cerebral blood flow associated with chronic alchohol consumption. *Journal of the American Geriatrics Society, 31*, 540–543.

Salthouse, T. A., Kausler, D. H., & Saults, J. S. (1990). Age, self-assessed health status, and cognition. *Journal of Gerontology: Psychological Sciences, 45*, P156–P160.

Sandstead, H. H. (1986). A brief history of the influence of trace elements on brain function. *American Journal of Clinical Nutrition, 43*, 293–298.

Shane, B., & Stokstad, E. L. R. (1985). Vitamin B-12-folate interrelationships. *Annual Review of Nutrition, 5*, 115–141.

Skoog, I. (1994). Risk factors for vascular dementia: A review. *Dementia, 5*, 137-144.

Snowdon, D. A., Belcher, J. D., Tully, C. L., & Greiner, L. H. (1996, April). *Plasma cholesterol and cognitive function in the elderly: Findings from the nun study.* Paper presented at the Cognitive Aging Conference, Atlanta, GA.

Söderfjell, S., Molander, B., Barnekow-Bergkvist, M., Lyskov, E., Johansson, H., & Nilsson, L.-G. (2000). Aging, stress, and musculoskeletal problems. *International Journal of Psychology, 35*, 368.

Söderlund, H., Nyberg, L., Adolfsson, R., Nilsson, L.-G., & Launer, L. (2001). *White matter hyperintesities, blood pressure, and cognition.* Manuscript submitted for publication.

Starr, J. M., & Whalley, L. J. (1992). Senile hypertension and cognitive impairment: An overview. *Journal of Hypertension (Suppl.), 10*, S31–S42.

Steinhagen-Thiessen, E., & Borchelt, M. (1993). Health differences in advanced old age. *Aging and Society, 13*, 619–655.

Stuss, D.T ., Peterkin, I., Guzman, D. A., Guzman, C., & Troyer, A. K. (1997). Chronic obstructive pulmonary disease: Effects of hypoxia on neurological and neuropsychological measures. *Journal of Clinical Experimental Neuropsychology, 19*, 515–524.

Swan, G. E., Carmelli, D., & LaRue, A. (1998). Systolic blood pressure tracking over 25 to 30 years and cognitive performance in older adults. *Stroke, 29*, 2334–2340.

Tarter, R. E., Edwards, K. L., & Van Thiel, D. H. (1988). Perspective and rationale for neuropsychological assessment of medical disease. In R. E. Tarter, D. H. van Thiel, & K. L. Edwards (Eds.), *Medical neuropsychology: The impact of disease on behavior* (pp. 1–10). New York: Plenum Press.

Tulving, E., & Colotla, V. A. (1970). Free recall of trilingual lists. *Cognitive Psychology, 1,* 86–98.

U'ren, R. C., Riddle, M. C., Lezak, M. D., & Bennington-Davis, M. (1990). The mental efficiency of the elderly person with Type II diabetes mellitus. Journal of the *American Geriatrics Society, 38,* 505–510.

van Boxtel, M. P. J. (1997). *Physical health, vascular risk factors, and age-related cognitive decline.* Unpublished doctoral dissertation, University of Maastricht, the Netherlands.

Wahlin, Å. Hill, R., Winblad, B., & Bäckman, L. (1996). Effects of serum vitamin B_{12} and folate status on episodic memory performance in very old age: A population based study. *Psychology and Aging, 11,* 487–496.

Wahlin, Å., Robins-Wahlin, T.-B., Small, B., & Bäckman, L. (1998). Influences of Thyroid Stimulating Hormone on cognitive functioning in very old age. *Journal of Gerontology: Psychological Sciences, 53B,* 234–239.

Walden, C. C., & Hegele, R. A. (1994). Apolipoprotein E in hyperlipidemia. *Annals of Internal Medicine, 120,* 1026–1036.

Waldstein, S. R. (1995). Hypertension and neuropsychological function: A lifetime perspective. *Experimental Aging Research, 21,* 321–352.

Widom, B., & Simonson, D. C. (1990) Glycemic control and neuropsychologic function during hypoglycemia in patients with insulin-dependent diabetes mellitus. *Annals of Internal Medicine, 112,* 904–912.

CHAPTER 21

Elizabeth L. Glisky

Source Memory, Aging, and the Frontal Lobes

In 1978–1979, when I was a first-year graduate student at the University of Toronto, Gus Craik commented on a paper I wrote that, "Questions have to do with what aspects of the situation, the event, and the context require effort to integrate." At the time, he was interested in the qualitative "aspects" of a memory, in particular, its semantic properties; I was struggling to understand the construct of "effort." Neither of us, I believe, knew or had thought a whole lot about how various aspects of an experience might be "integrated." Ten years later, however, at a conference celebrating Endel Tulving's 60th birthday, Craik (1989) stated that "the integration of event and context is . . . of crucial importance in the understanding of memory processes" (p. 43). In the present paper, I am concerned with how various aspects of an experience are integrated and what cognitive and neural processes contribute to and ensure that integration. In particular, I argue that the processes necessary to integrate content and context decline with age as a result of reduced frontal lobe function, at least in a subset of older adults. Consequently, performance on memory tasks that are dependent on that integration—source memory, for example—shows corresponding declines.

☐ What is Source Memory?

Although source memory has sometimes been defined as "a special case of contextual memory" involving specification of the "circumstances under which information was acquired" (Spencer & Raz, 1994, p. 149), it has also been more broadly characterized as any aspect of the context of an event as opposed to its content (Johnson, Hashtroudi, & Lindsay, 1993). Distinguishing between content and context, however, is not always straightforward and may be dependent on the particular situation and the goals of the perceiver. In most source memory experiments, the content–context relation is determined by the many-to-few mapping between items and sources. So, for example, people may hear many words in one of two voices, in which case words are perceived as content and voices represent source or context. Focal content may also be defined through instructions. If people are asked to perform an orienting task with respect to some aspect of a stimulus, its meaning, for example, that aspect of the stimulus may be perceived as focal whereas other aspects, such as the voice, may be considered peripheral. Conversely, if people are oriented to features of the voice, the voice may be viewed as focal and the meaning of the stimulus as peripheral. Remembering the source or context of a memory is virtually always more difficult than remembering its content, because it requires the retrieval of additional detail. The content of a memory may be recollected without its context, but memory for context requires retrieval of both content and context and of the spatiotemporal link between the two. In the typical many words–two voices source memory experiment, the source task is not to recall whether a particular voice occurred in the experiment, but to identify which voice was associated with which item. Source memory may therefore require integrative processes at encoding and retrieval that may not be necessary for item memory.

☐ Source Memory and Aging

In 1987, McIntyre and Craik reported that older adults, although as able as young adults, under some conditions, to remember recently presented facts about the world, were nevertheless impaired in their ability to attribute their knowledge of these facts to the correct source. McIntyre and Craik speculated that this source amnesia may have been caused by ineffective integration of focal and contextual information, which occurred as a result of declining attentional resources associated with the aging process. Since that time, a number of other studies have confirmed that source memory is more affected by aging than item or fact memory (Brown, Jones, & Davis, 1995; Ferguson, Hashtroudi, & Johnson, 1992; Henkel, Johnson, & DeLeonardis, 1998; Naveh-Benjamin, 2000; Schacter, Kaszniak, Kihlstrom, & Valdiserri, 1991; Spencer & Raz, 1995; Trott, Friedman, Ritter, & Fabiani, 1997; Trott, Friedman, Ritter, Fabiani, & Snodgrass, 1999), but the reasons for the differential effects are uncertain. One possibility is that source memory relies to a greater extent on the frontal lobes than does item memory and the frontal lobes are particularly susceptible to the deleterious effects of aging (e.g., Raz, 2000).

☐ Source Memory and the Frontal Lobes

Studies of source memory in patients with frontal lobe lesions (Janowsky, Shimamura, & Squire, 1989; Johnson, O'Connor, & Cantor, 1997) have found that, despite equivalent memory for new factual information, frontal patients show a disproportionate number of source memory errors. In a related vein, source memory deficits have been observed in amnesic patients only if, in addition to their basic memory deficits, they exhibit impaired performance on tasks thought to rely on the frontal lobes (Schacter, Harbluk, & McLachlan, 1984; Shimamura & Squire, 1987). Further support for a relation between source memory and the frontal lobes comes from recent studies of event-related potentials (ERPs) and functional magnetic resonance imaging (fMRI) in normal young individuals (Johnson, Kounios, & Nolde, 1996; Nolde, Johnson, & D'Esposito, 1998; Senkfor & Van Petten, 1998; Trott et al., 1997; Trott et al., 1999; Van Petten, Senkfor, & Newberg, 2000), which have noted responses in prefrontal brain sites during source memory tasks that are absent in item memory tasks.

In an attempt to establish a connection between source memory deficits and reduced frontal function in older adults, Craik, Morris, Morris, and Loewen (1990) noted a correlation between source memory performance and performance on tests of frontal lobe function in a group of individuals over the age of 60. They also reported a lack of any correlation between source memory and fact memory, a finding suggesting that source memory and item memory may rely on different cognitive and neural processes. Similarly, we (Glisky, Polster, & Routhieaux, 1995) found item and source memory to be uncorrelated in older adults and dependent on different underlying processes. Whereas item memory in older adults was related to performance on classical tests of memory typically associated with medial temporal brain regions, source memory was related to performance on tests of executive function that are normally associated with the frontal lobes. Other investigators, however, have failed to find such an association between source memory and frontal function but instead have found source memory to be related to fact recall (e.g., Degl'Innocenti & Bäckman, 1996; Johnson, DeLeonardis, Hashtroudi, & Ferguson, 1995) and correlated with performance on tasks thought to be dependent on medial temporal lobe function—standard tests of memory (Henkel et al., 1998). Reasons for the variable findings may relate to task, material or individual differences, and/or may be a function of the extent to which item and source memory tasks require similar or different processes in particular situations. The experiments reported in this paper consider the nature of the processes required for source memory and how these may be similar to or different from those required for item memory.

☐ Aging and the Frontal Lobes

If source memory is dependent at least partly on the frontal lobes, then the decline in source memory among older adults may reflect the declining frontal function that appears to occur as a consequence of normal aging. Evidence with respect to the integrity of different brain regions in older adults provides some support for the view that the frontal lobes may be preferentially affected by aging (for review, see Raz, 2000). Structural neuroimaging studies have generally reported greater volumetric reductions with age in prefrontal cortex than in other cortical regions (Coffey et al., 1992; Raz et al., 1997), although temporal and parietal association cortices are also affected. There is also some evidence from positron emission tomography (PET) and single photon emission computerized tomography (SPECT) studies that reduced regional cerebral blood flow (rCBF) associated with aging is greater in prefrontal regions (Madden & Hoffman, 1997; Waldemar, 1995). In addition, both PET and MRI studies of memory in older adults, have consistently demonstrated reduced activation in prefrontal cortex in older as compared to younger adults particularly during memory encoding, although medial temporal regions also show reductions (for overviews, see Anderson & Craik, 2000; Raz, 2000). In an ERP study of memory for temporal source, Trott et al. (1997) reported that older adults failed to show the late onset frontal effect associated with memory for temporal source in young adults, yet showed an equivalent item memory effect at posterior scalp sites. Taken together, these in vivo studies of the aging brain, although still few in number, suggest that prefrontal cortex may be more affected by aging than other brain regions. Nevertheless, it is important to note that not all older adults show these declines in brain structure or function, and there may be considerable variability in patterns of age-related change across individuals. These individual differences in brain aging may be partly responsible for some of the conflicting findings concerning the effects of aging on source memory.

☐ Individual Differences Among Older Adults

In studies in my laboratory, we have tried to take advantage of this variability among older adults to explore the relation between frontal lobe function and source memory and to delineate more precisely what aspects of memory processing may be particularly dependent on the frontal lobes. In the studies that I am reporting in this chapter, all of the older adults have been characterized as high or low in frontal functioning on the basis of their performance on neuropsychological tests. Although performance on these tests almost certainly relies on multiple processes and brain regions, their loading together in a factor analysis indicates that they share a common variance. We have hypothesized that this common variance reflects processes dependent on the frontal lobes. Nevertheless, the composite measure that we have derived is only an indirect indicator of the integrity of the frontal lobes. We are currently gathering neuroanatomical evidence to provide further support for this relation.

The five neuropsychological tests comprising the frontal factor are number of categories achieved on the modified Wisconsin Card Sorting Test (Hart, Kwentus, Wade, & Taylor, 1988), number of words produced on a test of verbal fluency (commonly referred to as the FAS test; Spreen & Benton, 1977), Mental Arithmetic from the Wechsler Adult Intelligence Scale—Revised (Wechsler, 1981), and Mental Control and Backward Digit Span from the Wechsler Memory Scale—Revised (Wechsler, 1987). The composite score assigned to each of our older adults represents an average z-score for the five tests relative to a 100-member normative group of adults over the age of 65. Scores above the mean (i.e., positive z-scores) are referred to as representing high frontal function, and scores below the mean (i.e., negative z-scores) as representing low frontal function. Individuals with scores very close to the mean (i.e., between –.08 and +.08) are not included. By comparing the performance of these subsets of older adults on memory tasks, we may be able to obtain additional evidence of the involvement of the frontal lobes in source memory and to identify more precisely the particular role that the frontal lobes play. An initial study (Glisky et al., 1995) demonstrated the potential usefulness of this methodology. After hearing several sentences spoken in one of two voices, older adults with low frontal function were impaired relative to those with high frontal function in memory for the voice but not in memory for the sentence. In that study, older adults were also divided on the basis of their medial temporal lobe function, and results indicated that medial temporal function predicted item memory but not source memory. Thus, it appeared that item memory and source memory were dependent on different underlying processes, with source memory requiring processes represented by our composite frontal scores.

☐ What Role Do the Frontal Lobes Play in Source Memory?

Given the mounting evidence implicating the frontal lobes in source memory, the interesting questions now concern the specific role(s) that this brain region plays. In particular, we are interested in whether the frontal lobes are involved at encoding, retrieval, or both and what the nature of their role might be. Four experiments addressing these questions are outlined below (Glisky, Rubin, & Davidson, 2001).

Difficult or Nonroutine Encoding Operations

We first considered that the frontal lobes may be involved when encoding operations are difficult or nonroutine (Shallice, 1982), as may be the case with novel voices. If this were so, then the difficult task of encoding novel voices should involve the frontal lobes, whether the task is one of source memory or item memory. To test this hypothesis, we reversed the usual mapping of sentences and voices by presenting multiple voices speaking one of two sentences. Participants in the experiment were also given an orienting task that required a judgment about the voice rather than the sentence, further defining voice as content and sentence as context. If the encoding of novel voices requires frontal input, then we would expect that our low frontal performers would be impaired on the difficult item (i.e., voice) memory task. On the other hand, if there is something special about source memory that involves the frontal lobes, then the effect of reduced frontal functioning should again be evident only on the source memory task, which in this case required memory for the sentence that each voice spoke.

Thirty-two older adults (mean age = 72), half with frontal composite scores above the mean (the HiF group) and half with frontal scores below the mean (the LoF group), participated in this experiment. A young college-student control group was also included. Because of the difficulty of the task, list length was relatively short—12 voices, half male and half female, each speaking one of two sentences—and each list was presented three times. Two study-test sessions were conducted, each with a different 12-voice list. In both study sessions, people were asked to judge the likelihood that each voice would be heard on the radio. The memory tests were two-alternative forced-choice (2AFC) recognition tests. For the item test, each target voice was paired with a novel voice. The target voice spoke either the same sentence as at study or the other sentence. People were asked to identify the voice that they had heard earlier. On the 2AFC source/context test, each voice was re-presented at test speaking each of the two sentences that occurred during study. People were asked to identify which sentence the voice had spoken in the study phase.

As shown in Table 21.1, on the item memory task (i.e., the voice task), older adults were impaired relative to young, but equally so in the HiF and LoF group. Thus, goodness of frontal function appeared not to be implicated in performance on the difficult item memory task. On the source memory task (i.e., memory for the sentence), however, the LoF group was significantly impaired relative to the HiF group, and did not perform significantly above chance. The HiF group on the other hand, did not differ significantly from the young controls. Thus it appears that the frontal function tapped by our frontal composite score is not required for all difficult memory tasks but instead has a particular role to play in source memory. Results of the same/different manipulation provide a clue as to what that role might be. Both HiF and LoF groups showed an equivalent benefit in memory for the voice when it spoke the same sentence at study and test. This finding suggests that information about the voice and the sentence was encoded and integrated by both groups and was subsequently available to facilitate item memory performance. Only the HiF group, however, was able to make use of that information to support source memory performance. These results suggest that the problem experienced by the LoF group may be at

TABLE 21.1. Proportion of items correctly identified (SD) in item and source memory tasks in the multiple voices/two sentences experiment.

	Young	HiF	LoF
Voice	.83 (.17)	.71 (.16)	.69 (.15)
Same	.93 (.14)	.75 (.23)	.75 (.20)
Different	.73 (.23)	.68 (.17)	.64 (.20)
Sentence	.74 (.15)	.66 (.10)	.54 (.12)

Note. HiF = Older adults with above average frontal function; LoF = Older adults with below average frontal function.

retrieval. The two sentences in the 2AFC test had been presented many times during study and were equally familiar. Thus a recognition decision could not be made on the basis of the familiarity of the sentence, but instead would require a search process to retrieve information about the particular voice–sentence pairing. People with low frontal function may fail to initiate the search process and simply resort to guessing—thus the chance performance. Alternatively, the problem may be at the level of decision processes. Frontal control processes may be necessary to evaluate retrieved information, particularly when such information is weak or impoverished, as may be the case when encodings have been difficult or novel. Frontal lobes may also be needed to reduce interference from highly confusable alternatives (cf. Shimamura, 1994).

Difficult Retrieval Processes

The previous experiment suggested that, in source memory tasks, the frontal lobes might have a particular role to play at retrieval. In general, contextual information will be encoded less well than focal content, and so its retrieval will be more difficult. Additionally, in 2AFC recognition tests, the task can be made particularly challenging when the alternatives are highly confusable. In the previous experiment, although there was some evidence that both groups of older adults had encoded some aspects of the context, as evidenced by the equivalent same/different effect, it may be that the encoded contextual information, although sufficient to improve item memory when it was re-presented at test (a kind of implicit memory effect) was not sufficient to support explicit retrieval of the context. Under these conditions, retrieval and decision processes may be increasingly demanding and may benefit from frontal control.

To test the generality of the findings from the previous experiment and ensure that they were not specific to the verbal-linguistic domain, we conducted another study using visuospatial materials. In this experiment, photographs of chairs located in one of two readily discriminable rooms served as stimuli. The item memory task was a 2AFC recognition test of the chairs and the source memory task was a 2AFC test of the locations of those chairs. The procedure was identical to the previous experiment, except for list length and number of presentations: 16 stimuli for the item memory test and 12 for the source test, presented only once during study. People were asked an item-orienting question in both cases, namely, "How comfortable is this chair likely to be?"

The results, illustrated in the left part of Table 21.2, replicated the findings of the previous experiment in important respects. There was no difference between the HiF and LoF groups in item memory, but in source memory, the LoF group performed at chance, whereas the HiF older adults were not significantly different from young controls. Once again in this paradigm, therefore, frontal function was important for source memory but not item memory. This time, however, there was no hint of a same/different effect. Memory was equally good whether chairs were re-presented in the same room or in a different room at test. Thus, the retrieval explanation that seemed the most likely interpretation of the findings in the previous voice/sentence experiment could not be supported. We thought that perhaps spatial context was indeed different from verbal-linguistic context in that space may be separable from the visual objects that occupy it, whereas a voice may be integrally linked with what it is saying. Thus, in the present experiment, the spatial context may have been only superficially encoded if at all and may not have been well linked with the target object, particularly in the LoF group.

The findings of this experiment thus raise the possibility that the poor source memory performance of the LoF group may be partly attributable to an encoding deficit. Individuals with reduced frontal function may be more likely to ignore spatial context at study and

TABLE 21.2. Proportion of items correctly identified (SD) in item and source memory tasks in the multiple chairs/two rooms experiments.

	Item orienting question			Integrative orienting question		
	Young	HiF	LoF	Young	HiF	LoF
Chair	.77 (.11)	.66 (.14)	.67 (.15)	.83 (.11)	.72 (.14)	.64 (.16)
Same	.78 (.16)	.65 (.24)	.68 (.20)	.84 (.16)	.75 (.16)	.69 (.19)
Different	.76 (.15)	.67 (.13)	.67 (.19)	.82 (.14)	.69 (.19)	.59 (.20)
Room	.64 (.16)	.58 (.13)	.51 (.16)	.65 (.18)	.58 (.08)	.69 (.14)

Note. HiF = Older adults with above average frontal function; LoF = Older adults with below average frontal function.

therefore be unable to recognize it at test. Accordingly, we decided to repeat the experiment, altering the orienting task at encoding to ensure that people noticed and encoded the spatial environment in which the chairs were located.

Integrating Content and Context at Encoding

Naveh-Benjamin and Craik (1996) suggested that older adults may have problems dividing attention between two components of the stimulus environment and may therefore process one at the expense of the other. In most source memory experiments, attention is focused on the primary content information. Source or context information may therefore be unattended and only superficially encoded. Failure to take account of contextual information may be particularly likely in older adults with reduced frontal function.

In the next experiment, we tried to circumvent the divided attention problem by focusing participants on the information that was relevant to the ensuing memory task. The experiment was identical to the previous one except for the orienting tasks presented to participants. Thus, when the test was an item memory test, the orienting question focused attention on the item (viz., "How comfortable is this chair likely to be?"). Alternatively, when the test was to be a test of source, people were oriented to the relation between item and source (viz., "How well does the chair fit in the room?"). Note that this latter question requires people to encode the relation between item and source, the precise information required by the source task.

The results of this experiment are shown on the right side of Table 21.2. The critical finding to note here is that the context memory deficit that was found in the LoF group in both previous experiments is completely absent. Further, orienting people to the information relevant to the source memory task, namely, the item–source conjunction, benefited the LoF group selectively. Neither the HiF nor the young group was affected. This finding suggests that, in the previous experiment, those individuals with intact frontal function spontaneously encoded the relation between the object and its spatial context, whereas those with compromised frontal function did not. Nevertheless, those in the LoF group were able to encode item and source interactively when given the appropriate orienting task, and their source memory benefited accordingly. These results appear to place the locus of the source memory deficit at encoding rather than at retrieval. Further, it does not seem to be the case that older adults in the LoF group are unable to encode more than one aspect of a stimulus at a time, but rather that they do not do so in the absence of specific instruction. Specifically, they appear not to initiate the appropriate processes necessary to integrate the focal object with its spatial context. When encoding processes are directed by an appropriate orienting question, however, the LoF group appears able to achieve a well-integrated encoding that can support unimpaired memory for source in a later recognition test.

To provide converging evidence of an encoding problem in the LoF group, we repeated the multiple voices–two sentence experiment that we had conducted earlier, changing the orienting question for the source task so that it required integration of the voice and sentence. For the item memory test, people were asked to judge the likelihood that each voice would be heard on the radio, as in Experiment 1. For the source test, however, they were asked to judge the likelihood that each voice would have spoken that particular sentence. The results, shown in Table 21.3, were virtually identical to those obtained with spatial context. The provision of the task-relevant orienting task benefited only the LoF group, completely eliminating the source memory deficit. Once again, these findings suggest that older adults with reduced frontal function do not spontaneously initiate the processes necessary to achieve a well-integrated encoding of item and source, although they do so when given an appropriate orienting task. In the case of auditory or verbal materials, some information about the voice–sentence conjunction appears to be weakly encoded—enough to enhance item memory when context is repeated but not enough to support the explicit retrieval of source. Spatial context, however, may be largely ignored. In either case, provision of the integrative orienting question is completely sufficient to enable normal source memory performance in the impaired group of older adults.

Why do some older adults fail to encode the content–context relation? Craik (1986) has argued that one of the consequences of aging is declining attentional resources that limit the processing that older adults engage in spontaneously. In source memory tasks, they may focus on core content information to the exclusion of peripheral background information in order to optimize their performance on what they perceive to be the primary task (i.e., the item memory task). This strategy may enable unimpaired item recognition, but if all resources are allocated to the encoding of focal information, encoding of peripheral information will be limited or absent. Alternatively, they may process both focal and peripheral information but fail to integrate them (cf. Naveh-Benjamin, 2000). In either case, the integrative orienting question may provide a more efficient strategy for the allocation of resources and enable the encoding of the critical item–source conjunction. Note

TABLE 21.3. Proportion of items correctly identified (SD) in item and source memory tasks in the multiple voices/two sentences experiment with an integrative orienting question.

	Young	HiF	LoF
Voice	.73 (.17)	.71 (.16)	.70 (.18)
Same	.83 (.21)	.84 (.11)	.74 (.19)
Different	.63 (.20)	.58 (.24)	.66 (.11)
Sentence	.68 (.15)	.65 (.12)	.64 (.15)

Note. HiF = Older adults with above average frontal function; LoF = Older adults with below average frontal function.

that we did not ask specifically for item information following the source-relevant orienting task. If this task does in fact create a strong link between content and context, we would expect to observe a strong same/different effect in item memory. If item and context are encoded as a tightly bound unit, the item will likely be well recognized when re-presented with its context but poorly recognized when out of context (cf. Tulving & Thomson, 1973).

In our experiments, the failure to integrate context with content seems not to be an inevitable consequence of aging, however, but rather a particular problem of older adults with reduced frontal lobe function. Frontal control processes such as the construction and initiation of encoding strategies may be particularly demanding of attentional resources. The decline in frontal lobe function in a subset of older adults may represent a reduction in resources that may not occur, or may occur to a much lesser extent in other older adults.

Search and Decision Processes at Retrieval?

Is it possible that the source memory deficit observed in older adults with reduced frontal function is entirely attributable to an encoding problem, namely the failure to initiate the encoding operations necessary to integrate item and source? At least at one level, this would seem to be the case. When encoding is appropriately supported, the LoF group performs normally. Yet, at the same time, there is evidence suggesting that the frontal lobes are involved in retrieval as well. In our own studies, in the absence of a relevant orienting task, the LoF performers were impaired relative to the HiF despite what appeared to be equivalent encoding as evidenced by the same/different effect. This finding suggests a role for the frontal lobes at retrieval (see also Dodson, Holland, and Shimamura, 1998; Dodson & Shimamura, 2000). Evidence from ERP and fMRI studies also implicates the frontal lobes in the retrieval of source (Johnson et al., 1996; Nolde et al., 1998; Senkfor & Van Petten, 1998; Trott et al., 1997; Van Petten et al., 2000). We speculate that the frontal lobes may come into play at test when the retrieval task is particularly challenging. In general, 2AFC is a relatively easy test of recognition memory, but it can be particularly difficult under two conditions: (a) when the distractors are very similar to the target, and (b) when the discriminating information has not been well encoded. The item memory task that we have used is thus relatively easy. The distractors at test are new and the item-orienting task has ensured a reasonably elaborate encoding. The source memory task is more difficult, however, particularly following an item-orienting question. Source information in this condition may be poorly encoded, not well linked with item information, and thereby unable to support an easy discrimination between equally familiar alternatives at retrieval. Under these conditions, frontal control processes may be used at retrieval to initiate either a search for relevant contextual information or a strategy to guide decision processes and reduce interference from similar alternatives. If, on the other hand, the orienting task facilitates the binding of an item to its source, then the recognition decision may be much simpler and require much less frontal control.

☐ Concluding Comments

Source memory deficits are not an inevitable consequence of aging, but instead appear to represent a specific problem associated with reduced frontal function in a subset of older adults. For these individuals, encoding of the integrative relation between an item and its context seems not to occur spontaneously, and so they do not have access to the information necessary to make an accurate identification of source. When they are given an orienting task that requires them to encode that relation, however, their source memory performance improves to normal levels. These findings suggest that at least some memory deficits may be alleviated by careful attention at encoding, not only to the central or core aspects of experience, but to the contextual aspects of an event as well. The problem for older adults with declining frontal lobe function may lie in a narrowing of attentional focus to the center of experience, perhaps to optimize performance on what is perceived to be most important and to conserve resources. If these older adults are trained to broaden their attention and to process item and context in an integrative fashion, such processing may become increasingly less resource demanding, and source memory deficits may ultimately be reduced or eliminated.

☐ Acknowledgments

I am grateful to Sue Rubin and Patrick Davidson, who collaborated on the research reported in this chapter. Preparation of the chapter and the research reported herein was supported by grant AG14792 from the National Institute on Aging.

☐ References

Anderson, N. D., & Craik, F. I. M. (2000). Memory in the aging brain. In E. Tulving & F. I. M. Craik (Eds.), *The Oxford handbook of memory* (pp. 411–425). Oxford, England: Oxford University Press.

Brown, A. S., Jones, E. M., & Davis, T. L. (1995). Age differences in conversational source monitoring. *Psychology and Aging, 10,* 111–122.

Coffey, C. E., Wilkinson, W. E., Parashos, I. A., Soady, S. A. R., Sullivan, R. J., Patterson, L. J., Figiel, G. S., Webb, M. C., Spritzer, C. E., & Djang, W. T. (1992). Quantitative cerebral anatomy of the aging human brain: A cross-sectional study using magnetic resonance imaging. *Neuropsychology, 42,* 527–536.

Craik, F. I. M. (1986). A functional account of age differences in memory. In F. Klix & H. Hagendorf (Eds.), *Human memory and cognitive capabilities, mechanisms and performances* (pp. 409–422). Amsterdam: Elsevier.

Craik, F. I. M. (1989). On the making of episodes. In I. H. L. Roediger & F. I. M. Craik (Eds.), *Varieties of memory and consciousness* (pp. 43–57). Hillsdale, NJ: Erlbaum.

Craik, F. I. M., Morris, L. W., Morris, R. G., & Loewen, E. R. (1990). Relations between source amnesia and frontal lobe functioning in older adults. *Psychology and Aging, 5,* 148-151.

Degl'Innocenti, A., & Bäckman, L. (1996). Aging and source memory: Influences of intention to remember and associations with frontal lobe tests. *Aging, Neuropsychology, and Cognition, 3,* 307–319.

Dodson, C. S., Holland, P. W., & Shimamura, A. P. (1998). On the recollection of specific- and partial-source information. *Journal of Experimental Psychology: Learning, Memory, and Cognition, 24,* 1121–1136.

Dodson, C. S., & Shimamura, A. P. (2000). Differential effects of cue dependency on item and source memory. *Journal of Experimental Psychology: Learning, Memory, and Cognition, 26,* 1023–1044.

Ferguson, S., Hashtroudi, S., & Johnson, M. K. (1992). Age differences in using source-relevant cues. *Psychology and Aging, 7,* 443–452.

Glisky, E. L., Polster, M. R., & Routhieaux, B. C. (1995). Double dissociation between item and source memory. *Neuropsychology, 9,* 229–235.

Glisky, E. L., Rubin, S. R., & Davidson, P. S. R. (2001). Source memory in older adults: An encoding or retrieval problem? *Journal of Experimental Psychology: Learning, Memory, and Cognition, 27,* 1131–1146.

Hart, R. P., Kwentus, J. A., Wade, J. B., & Taylor, J. R. (1988). Modified Wisconsin Card Sorting Test in elderly normal, depressed and demented patients. *Clinical Neuropsychologist, 2,* 49–56.

Henkel, L. A., Johnson, M. K., & DeLeonardis, D. M. (1998). Aging and source monitoring: Cognitive processes and neuropsychological correlates. *Journal of Experimental Psychology: General, 127,* 251–268.

Janowsky, J. S., Shimamura, A. P., & Squire, L. R. (1989). Source memory impairment in patients with frontal lobe lesions. *Neuropsychologia, 27,* 1043–1056.

Johnson, M. K., DeLeonardis, D. M., Hashtroudi, S., & Ferguson, S. A. (1995). Aging and single versus multiple cues in source monitoring. *Psychology and Aging, 10,* 507–517.

Johnson, M. K., Hashtroudi, S., & Lindsay, D. S. (1993). Source monitoring. *Psychological Bulletin, 114,* 3–28.

Johnson, M. K., Kounios, J., & Nolde, S. F. (1996). Electrophysiological brain activity and memory source monitoring. *NeuroReport, 7,* 2929–2932.

Johnson, M. K., O'Connor, M., & Cantor, J. (1997). Confabulation, memory deficits, and frontal dysfunction. *Brain and Cognition, 34,* 189–206.

Madden, D. J., & Hoffman, J. M. (1997). Application of positron emission tomography to age-related cognitive changes. In K. R. R. Krishnan & P. M. Doraiswamy (Eds.), *Brain imaging in clinical psychiatry* (pp. 575–613). New York: Marcel Dekker.

McIntyre, J. S., & Craik, F. I. M. (1987). Age differences in memory for item and source information. *Canadian Journal of Psychology, 41,* 175–192.

Naveh-Benjamin, M. (2000). Adult age differences in memory performance: Tests of an associative deficit hypothesis. *Journal of Experimental Psychology: Learning, Memory, and Cognition, 26,* 1170–1187.

Naveh-Benjamin, M., & Craik, F. I. M. (1996). Effects of perceptual and conceptual processing on memory for words and voice: Different patterns for young and old. *The Quarterly Journal of Experimental Psychology, 49A,* 780–796.

Nolde, S. F., Johnson, M. K., & D'Esposito, M. (1998). Left prefrontal activation during episodic remembering: An event-related fMRI study. *NeuroReport, 9,* 3509–3514.

Raz, N. (2000). Aging of the brain and its impact on cognitive performance: Integration of structural and functional findings. In F. I. M. Craik & T. A. Salthouse (Eds.), *The handbook of aging and cognition* (2nd ed., pp. 1–90). Mahwah, NJ: Erlbaum.

Raz, N., Gunning, F. M., Head, D., Dupuis, J. H., McQuain, J., Briggs, S. D., Loken, W. J., Thornton, A. E., & Acker, J. D. (1997). Selective aging of the human cerebral cortex observed in vivo: Differential vulnerability of the prefrontal gray matter. *Cerebral Cortex, 7,* 268–282.

Schacter, D. L., Harbluk, J. L., & McLachlan, D. R. (1984). Retrieval without recollection: An experimental analysis of source amnesia. *Journal of Verbal Learning and Verbal Behavior, 23,* 593–611.

Schacter, D. L., Kaszniak, A. W., Kihlstrom, J. F., & Valdiserri, M. (1991). The relation between source memory and aging. *Psychology and Aging, 6,* 559–568.

Senkfor, A. J., & Van Petten, C. (1998). Who said what? An event-related potential investigation of source and item memory. *Journal of Experimental Psychology: Learning, Memory, and Cognition, 24,* 1005–1025.

Shallice, T. (1982). Specific impairments of planning. *Philosophical Transactions of the Royal Society of London, B, 298,* 199–209.

Shimamura, A. P. (1994). Memory and frontal lobe function. In M. S. Gazzaniga (Ed.), *The cognitive neurosciences* (pp. 803–813). Cambridge, MA: MIT Press.

Shimamura, A. P., & Squire, L. R. (1987). A neuropsychological study of fact memory and source amnesia. *Journal of Experimental Psychology: Learning, Memory, and Cognition, 13,* 464–473.

Spencer, W. D., & Raz, N. (1994). Memory for facts, source and context: Can frontal lobe dysfunction explain age-related differences? *Psychology and Aging, 9,* 149–159.

Spencer, W. D., & Raz, N. (1995). Differential effects of aging on memory for content and context: A meta-analysis. *Psychology and Aging, 10,* 527–539.

Spreen, O., & Benton, A. L. (1977). *Neurosensory Center Comprehensive Examination for Aphasia.* (revised ed.). Victoria, BC, Canada: University of Victoria Neuropsychology Laboratory.

Trott, C. T., Friedman, D., Ritter, W., & Fabiani, M. (1997). Item and source memory: Differential age effects revealed by event-related potentials. *NeuroReport, 8,* 3373–3378.

Trott, C. T., Friedman, D., Ritter, W., Fabiani, M., & Snodgrass, J. G. (1999). Episodic priming and memory for temporal source: Event-related potentials reveal age-related differences in prefrontal functioning. *Psychology and Aging, 14,* 390–413.

Tulving, E., & Thomson, D. M. (1973). Encoding specificity and retrieval processes in episodic memory. *Psychological Review, 80,* 352–373.

Van Petten, C., Senkfor, A. J., & Newberg, W. M. (2000). Memory for drawings in locations: Spatial source memory and event-related potentials. *Psychophysiology, 37,* 551–564.

Waldemar, G. (1995). Functional brain imaging with SPECT in normal aging and dementia: Methodological, pathophysiological and diagnostic aspect. *Cerebrovascular and Brain Metabolism Reviews, 7,* 89–130.

Wechsler, D. (1981). *Wechsler Adult Intelligence Scale–Revised.* New York: Psychological Corporation.

Wechsler, D. (1987). *Wechsler Memory Scale–Revised.* New York: Psychological Corporation.

CHAPTER

Timothy A. Salthouse

The Broader Context of Craik's Self-Initiated Processing Hypothesis

I am delighted to participate in the conference and contribute to the resulting volume honoring Gus Craik, who is widely recognized as a leading experimental psychologist investigating both basic processes in memory and the effects of increased age on memory. I have long been an admirer of Craik's creative experiments and intuitively appealing theoretical interpretations, and like many others I have enjoyed and benefited from collaborations with him, in my case as a coeditor of the first and second editions of the *Handbook of Aging and Cognition* (Craik & Salthouse, 1992, 2000). Because he is as nice interpersonally as he is esteemed scientifically, I can think of no person more deserving of this type of recognition.

This event is intended to commemorate Gus's retirement from the University of Toronto, and it is often appropriate when such a distinguished individual completes an important phase of his career to attempt to classify and evaluate his contributions. I will leave it to others to evaluate his contributions, and instead I will attempt a preliminary classification of where he stands with respect to major schools or systems within psychology. Although Craik is indeed an outstanding experimental psychologist, I suggest that he may have at least as much in common with Charles Spearman, one of the pioneers of psychometric or individual difference psychology, as with Wilhelm Wundt, who is often considered the founding father of experimental psychology.

I will explain this perhaps surprising claim by first describing two broad approaches that have been used to investigate and explain adult age differences in memory and other aspects of cognitive functioning. One approach can be characterized as largely analytical and specific, in that it is designed to seek interpretations based on processes hypothesized to be involved in the task under investigation. The second approach is more general, in that it tends to emphasize influences that have an impact at a level broader than that of individual variables.

Most research concerned with adult age differences in memory has focused on variants of the specific approach because the goal has been to decompose or fractionate the task to identify constituent processes, and then determine the magnitude of the age-related effects on each process. This *micro* approach has frequently been successful in identifying processes with differential sensitivity to advancing age. For example, age-related effects are typically greater on controlled processes than on automatic processes, and on processes associated with explicit memory than on processes associated with implicit memory. The micro perspective is represented in this volume by the contributions of Jacoby, Marsh, and Dolan (chapter 19); McDowd (chapter 11); Naveh-Benjamin (chapter 15); and Koustaal and Schacter (chapter 30).

The alternative *macro* approach tends to emphasize age-related effects that operate on several different types of variables. These broader influences may be related to effects on a critical process or theoretical construct, such as encoding or goal maintenance, or they may be linked to an attribute such as working memory capacity, effectiveness of deploying or inhibiting attention, or speed of processing. The common feature of these more general perspectives is that they postulate that at least some of the age-related effects on a given variable are not specific to that variable, but instead are shared with several different kinds of variables.

Figure 22.1 contains a schematic illustration of the micro and macro perspectives in cognitive aging. The top panel portrays the decomposition of a variable into a number (in this case, three) of hypothesized processes or components, and the bottom panel represents age-related effects operating on several different types of cognitive variables.

Although much of Craik's research has attempted to fractionate memory tasks to isolate the age-related effects to specific processes, he has also been sympathetic to, and sometimes even an ardent advocate of, the macro or general perspective because he has hy-

Micro

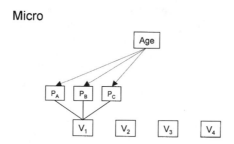

Decompose the task into constituent processes, and examine the age sensitivity of each component

Macro

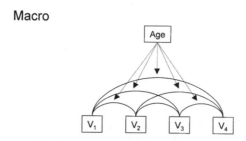

Examine age-related influences that simultaneously operate on several different variables

FIGURE 22.1. Schematic illustration of micro (decompositional) and macro (integrative) approaches to investigating adult age differences in cognition.

pothesized that in addition to task-specific processes, there are also age-related influences on some form of processing resource that is needed for the effective performance of many different types of memory tasks. Craik can therefore be considered similar to Spearman (e.g., 1927) because both he and Spearman have argued that individual differences in variables representing different cognitive tasks or abilities are attributable to a combination of general and specific influences. Spearman and Craik are also similar in that both have used the term *mental energy* to refer to the basis of individual differences in the general influences. However, they differ in their proposals about what it is that varies across people and across variables.

As most psychologists know, Spearman proposed the concept of g, which refers to the general factor manifested in different degrees across most variables and which is presumably related to the amount of mental energy available to an individual. Craik's equivalent of g is self-initiated processing (sometimes referred to as SIP), which he hypothesized is required in different amounts across different types of memory tasks, and which is also presumably related to the amount of mental energy an individual possesses. Craik (e.g., 1986) portrayed his self-initiated processing hypothesis in the form of a table in which the rows represented different memory tasks and the columns indicated that as the amount of self-initiated processing increased, so did the expected magnitude of the age-related differences. A major goal of the hypothesis was to account for an ordering of the magnitude of age differences in memory variables, ranging from priming with the smallest differences, with progressively larger differences for relearning, recognition, and cued recall, and finally the largest age differences for free recall. Another aspect of Craik's self-initiated processing hypothesis is the notion of environmental support because successive positions along the self-initiated processing dimension were postulated to be associated with varying amounts of environmental support. This support existed in the form of cues, context, etc., that serve to reduce the amount of self-initiated processing required to perform the task, and hence also to decrease the magnitude of the resulting age-related differences.

Craik's self-initiated processing hypothesis is intriguing because it implies that memory aging phenomena might be explained once the nature of self-initiated processing was understood. The concept of self-initiated processing shares some similarities with a number of other proposals such as controlled processing, effortful processing, deliberate processing, and reflective processing. In every case, memory or other cognitive tasks are hypothesized to differ in the amount of this processing needed for successful performance, and on average, the effectiveness of carrying out this type of processing is postulated to decrease with increasing age. Each of these proposals has plausibility, but they all face the difficulties of how to operationalize the relevant construct and how to obtain independent measures of the construct to avoid problems of circularity in which the existence of the construct is inferred from the same pattern of results that it is supposed to explain.

Craik and his colleagues have recognized these issues and have attempted to deal with them in a number of ingenious experiments. For example, Craik and McDowd (1987) found that when research participants were asked to perform a reaction time task during a memory task not only were older adults slowed more than young adults by the requirement to perform the two tasks simultaneously, but the reaction times in both groups were larger for a free recall memory task than for a recognition memory task. These results were replicated and extended in a series of experiments by Anderson, Craik, and Naveh-Benjamin (1998), in which the secondary reaction time costs decreased from free recall to cued recall to recognition. The discovery that the magnitude of age differences on a series of memory tasks can be predicted from a variable (i.e., secondary task reaction time) presumed to reflect self-initiated processing demands provides impressive support for Craik's self-initiated processing hypothesis.

In the remainder of this article I will describe a different approach to the study of adult age differences in memory and other cognitive variables. I will start with a quite different question and will rely on a different methodological approach, but I will end up with an empirical function similar to that implied by Craik's self-initiated processing hypothesis. In order to highlight the correspondence between my approach and the Craikian self-initiated processing hypothesis, I will first transform Craik's hypothesis into the graph portrayed in Figure 22.2 in which self-initiated processing and age are positively related to one another, and different memory variables are located at different positions along the function. Note that this representation embodies the key principle of Craik's hypothesis, namely, that there is a systematic relationship between the amount of self-initiated processing required and the magnitude of the age differences on the variable, but it is easier to illustrate the similarity to my approach with this form of representation.

A fundamental assumption of my perspective is that all variables have at least two types of age-related influences: unique influences that are specific to a particular variable and shared influences that are common to many different types of cognitive variables. I also assume that not only do variables differ in the total magnitude of their relation with age but also in the relative contributions of the two types of influences, such that some variables primarily have unique age-related influences, whereas other variables have largely shared influences.

Several analytical methods can be used to estimate the relative contributions of the two

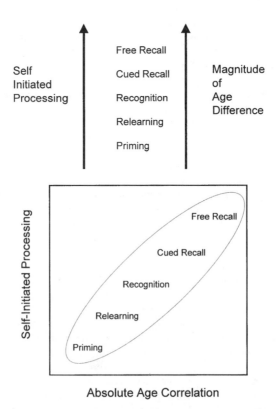

FIGURE 22.2. Alternative representation of Craik's self-initiated processing hypothesis.

types of influences, but it is simplest to illustrate how the estimates can be derived with what can be termed the shared influences method (see Salthouse, 1998; Salthouse, Hambrik, & McGuthry, 1998). The first step in this procedure is to obtain an estimate of the variance that all variables have in common. This can be achieved with a variety of statistical procedures such as principal components analysis, factor analysis, or structural equation modeling. The next step in the procedure is to control an estimate of this common variance before examining age-related effects on individual variables. Effects of age on individual variables in this type of analysis that are evident after controlling what the variables have in common correspond to direct or unique age-related effects, whereas effects that are mediated through the common factor represent shared effects. This analytical method is not necessarily informative about the nature of what is shared among different cognitive variables, but it does provide a means of allowing age-related influences to be partitioned into unique (direct) and shared (indirect) aspects.

Application of the method can be illustrated with data from a study by Salthouse, Fristoe, and Rhee (1996), which involved 259 adults between 19 and 94 years of age. A total of 14 variables were examined in this study, including three measures of episodic memory from

TABLE 22.1. Proportions of total, shared, and unique age-related variance from study by Salthouse, Fristoe, and Rhee (1996).

Variable	Age-related variance (r^2)		
	Total	Shared	Unique
RVLT2	.220	.217	.003
RVLT6	.199	.196	.003
Recog	.108	.096	.012
PA1	.261	.257	.004
PA2	.123	.114	.009
WCST	.167	.166	.001
TrailsA	.256	.256	.000
TrailsB	.348	.344	.004
Shipley	.199	.184	.015
BlkDes	.219	.216	.003
ObjAssm	.170	.167	.003
DigSym	.429	.418	.011
LetCom	.243	.241	.002
PatCom	.436	.395	.041
Median	.220	.220	.004

Note: RVLT2 refers to the number of words recalled in the second trial of the Rey Verbal Learning Test; RVLT6 to the number of words recalled in the sixth (postinterference) trial of the Rey Verbal Learning Test; Recog to the score in the recognition test of the Rey Verbal Learning Test; PA1 and PA2 to the number of response terms correctly recalled in two lists of paired associates; WCST to the number of categories completed in the Wisconsin Card Sorting Test, TrailsA and TrailsB to the time needed to complete versions A and B, respectively, of the Trail Making Test; Shipley to the abstraction (series completion) score from the Shipley Institute of Living Scale; BlkDes to the block design score from the WAIS-R; ObjAssm to the object assembly score from the WAIS-R; DigSym to the digit symbol substitution score from the WAIS-R; LetCom to the number of items completed in the letter comparison test; and PatCom to the number of items completed in the pattern comparison test. See original article for details on these tests.

the Rey Auditory Verbal Learning Test: free recall on the second trial, free recall after an interference list, and recognition. The estimate of the common variance in the shared influence analysis was based on the (unrotated) first principal component obtained from a principal components analysis on the 14 variables. Table 22.1 contains the total age-related variance and the estimates of shared and unique age-related variance for each variable. Notice that the median proportion of age-related variance across the 14 variables was .220, which corresponds to an age correlation of -.47. However, the median proportion of unique age-related variance was only .004, which is less than 2% of the total age-related variance and corresponds to an (absolute) age correlation of .06. The results summarized in Table 22.1 are typical of many analyses of this type because it has frequently been found that only a small proportion of the total age-related effects on a given variable are unique to that variable and independent of the age-related effects on other variables (e.g., Salthouse, 1998, 2001; Salthouse, et al., 1998).

An interesting implication of the finding that a large proportion of the age-related effects on one variable is shared with the age-related effects on other variables is that there should be a positive relation between the magnitude of the age relation on a variable and the degree to which that variable is related to other variables. That is, if large proportions of the age-related effects on different cognitive variables are shared, then the magnitude of the age relation on a variable should closely correspond to the degree to which that variable is related to, or has aspects in common with, other variables. Stated somewhat differently, if a substantial amount of the age-related effects on a particular variable is mediated through a factor representing what is common to all variables, then the size of the age relation for that variable should be proportional to the strength of the relation between the target variable and the common factor. This reasoning leads to the prediction that there should be a strong positive relation between the absolute magnitude of the age relation on the variable and the degree to which that variable is related to other variables. I refer to these predicted functions as AR functions because the axes represent relations of the variable to age (A) and to relatedness (R).

The prediction of positive AR functions across different combinations of cognitive variables has recently received a considerable amount of empirical support. For example, Figure 22.3 illustrates the AR function with data from 14 variables in the Salthouse et al.

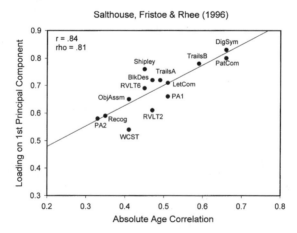

FIGURE 22.3. Variables plotted in terms of their absolute correlation with age (horizontal axis) and their degree of relatedness to other variables (vertical axis). Data from Salthouse, Fristoe, and Rhee (1996).

(1996) study (see Table 22.1 for a description of the variables). Each point in this figure corresponds to a single variable, with its absolute correlation with age along the abscissa and its loading on the first principal component, representing what is statistically common to all variables, along the ordinate. Note that there is a clear positive relation between the two sets of values, as the Pearson *r* was .84 and Spearman's rank-order *rho* correlation was .81.

A similar pattern was evident in a later study by Salthouse, Toth, Hancock, & Woodard (1997), involving an independent sample of participants and a different combination of variables. The data from this study are illustrated in Figure 22.4, where it can be seen that the Pearson *r* was .83 and Spearman's rank-order *rho* correlation was .93. An interesting aspect of this latter study was that it included measures of automatic and controlled processing in a stem completion memory task derived from Jacoby's (1991) process-dissociation procedure. Although the measure of controlled processing (i.e., Stem-Cont) was located close to the center of the AR function and thus can be considered similar to other variables, the measure of automatic processing (i.e., Stem-Auto) was a clear outlier from the function, indicating that the variable had little or no relation to other variables. This finding is therefore consistent with the assumption that automatic processing represents a qualitatively different type of processing than that involved in many variables, and that age-related effects are minimal to nonexistent in the effectiveness of automatic processing. It is important to note that the automatic processing variable in this study had a respectable level of reliability (i.e., .82), and thus its lack of relation to age and to other variables cannot be attributed to a low level of systematic variance (i.e., reliability) available to be shared with other variables.

Similar patterns of positive AR functions are evident in other studies from my laboratory, as the median rank-order correlation across 30 different data sets was .80, and the phenomenon is not an artifact of differential reliability of the variables because the correlations were nearly the same magnitude after partialling estimates of reliability (see Salthouse, 2001). Moreover, the phenomenon is not restricted to data from my laboratory because it is evident in analyses of data from other investigators. Data from two recent large-scale studies by Park and her collaborators can be used to illustrate this point. A

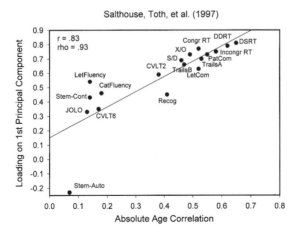

FIGURE 22.4. Variables plotted in terms of their absolute correlation with age (horizontal axis) and their degree of relatedness to other variables (vertical axis). Data from Salthouse, Toth, Hancock, and Woodard (1997).

study published in 1996 (Park et al., 1996) contained data on 11 variables from 301 adults and yielded a Pearson *r* of .54 and a Spearman rank-order *rho* correlation of .52. A study reported in 1998 (Park, Davidson, Lantenschlager, Smith, & Smith, 1998) contained data on 13 variables from 345 adults, and yielded a Pearson *r* of .88, and a Spearman *rho* of .91.

It should be apparent that these empirical AR functions closely resemble the relations predicted by Craik's self-initiated processing hypothesis, as portrayed in Figure 22.2. In both cases the horizontal axis represents the absolute magnitude of the relation of the variable to age. The vertical axes in the two types of functions differ, because with the hypothetical self-initiated processing functions, the axis corresponds to the amount of self-initiated processing, and with the empirical AR functions the axis corresponds to how closely related the variable is to other variables. However, the two situations may be similar in that in each case the vertical dimension can be interpreted as representing the degree of reliance on aspects of processing common to many different types of cognitive variables. That is, the vertical axis in both functions may reflect the need to develop and execute a sequence of processing operations that require the control or allocation of attention. The hypothetical construct of self-initiated processing represents this capability directly, whereas the empirically determined relatedness index may represent it indirectly if it is assumed that variables are related to one another to the extent that they rely on controlled or deliberate processing.

The discovery of positive AR functions can therefore be interpreted as empirical evidence consistent with Craik's self-initiated processing hypothesis. As Craik has predicted, the age differences are larger when there is greater reliance on something necessary for effective performance on different memory tasks. However, it should also be noted that the results I have described suggest that Craik's self-initiated processing hypothesis represents only a limited portion of a broader phenomenon. That is, positive AR relations are not restricted to memory variables, and in fact, memory variables tend to be located toward the lower left region of AR functions. Across a number of analyses of this type, involving a mixture of different kinds of cognitive variables, the upper right region of the function is usually occupied by variables derived from reasoning tasks and perceptual speed tasks (see Salthouse, 2001). This finding also seems consistent with the controlled processing interpretation of AR functions because reasoning tasks can be assumed to require controlled processing to assemble a novel sequence of processes to solve a problem, and perceptual speed tasks require controlled or effortful processing to ensure efficient execution of a simple sequence of processing operations.

In conclusion, despite the dominance of the micro or task-oriented perspective in contemporary cognitive aging research, there is considerable evidence that at least some age-related effects on memory and other cognitive variables are shared and are not completely specific to a particular task. Explanations are therefore needed to account for both shared (or general) and unique (or specific) age-related effects in cognitive aging. The discovery of strong positive relations between the magnitude of the age relation on a variable and the degree to which the variable shares variance with other variables (i.e., AR functions) may provide a valuable window into understanding the basis for shared age-related influences. Furthermore, one promising candidate that might account for these general effects is Craik's notion of self-initiated processing because the dimension underlying the AR functions may correspond to the amount of controlled or self-initiated processing required by a task.

☐ References

Anderson, N. D., Craik, F. I. M., & Naveh-Benjamin, M. (1998). The attentional demands of encoding and retrieval in younger and older adults: 1. Evidence from divided attention costs. *Psychology and Aging, 13*, 405–423.

Craik, F. I. M. (1986). A functional account of age differences in memory. In F. Klix & H. Hagendorf (Eds.), *Human memory and cognitive capabilities* (pp. 409–422). Amsterdam: Elsevier.

Craik, F. I. M., & McDowd, J. M. (1987). Age differences in recall and recognition. *Journal of Experimental Psychology: Learning, Memory and Cognition, 13*, 474–479.

Craik, F. I. M., & Salthouse, T. A. (Eds.). (1992). *Handbook of aging and cognition.* Hillsdale, NJ: Erlbaum.

Craik, F. I. M., & Salthouse, T. A. (2000). *Handbook of aging and cognition* (2nd ed.). Hillsdale, NJ: Erlbaum.

Jacoby, L. L. (1991). A process dissociation framework: Separating automatic from intentional uses of memory. *Journal of Memory and Language, 30*, 513–541.

Park, D. C., Davidson, N., Lautenschlager, G., Smith, A. D., & Smith, P. (1998, April) *Differentation of visuo-spatial and verbal working memory and long-term memory across the life span.* Paper presented at the 1998 Cognitive Aging Conference, Atlanta, Georgia.

Park, D. C., Smith, A. D., Lautenschlager, G., Earles, J. L., Frieske, D., Zwahr, M., & Gaines, C. L. (1996). Mediators of long-term memory performance across the life span. *Psychology and Aging, 11*, 621–637.

Salthouse, T. A. (1998). Independence of age-related influences on cognitive abilities across the life span. *Developmental Psychology, 34*, 851–864.

Salthouse, T. A. (2001). Structural models of the relations between age and measures of cognitive functioning. *Intelligence, 29*, 93–115.

Salthouse, T. A., Fristoe, N., & Rhee, S. H. (1996). How localized are age-related effects on neuropsychological measures? *Neuropsychology, 10*, 272–285.

Salthouse, T. A., Hambrick, D. Z., & McGuthry, K. E. (1998). Shared age-related influences on cognitive and noncognitive variables. *Psychology and Aging, 13*, 486–500.

Salthouse, T. A., Toth, J. P., Hancock, H. E., & Woodard, J. L. (1997). Controlled and automatic forms of memory and attention: Process purity and the uniqueness of age-related influences. *Journal of Gerontology: Psychological Sciences, 52B*, P216–P228.

Spearman, C. (1927). *The nature of "intelligence" and the principles of cognition.* London: MacMillan.

23
CHAPTER

Lynn Hasher
Simon T. Tonev
Cindy Lustig
Rose T. Zacks

Inhibitory Control, Environmental Support, and Self-Initiated Processing in Aging

The phrase "senior moment" is increasingly common in everyday conversations among people of a certain age. Most such "moments" center on the kinds of errors that adults of all ages make, such as forgetting where you left your keys or parked your car, or the name of a person you've just been introduced to. Nonetheless, older adults believe that such moments are increasingly common (Hertzog, Lineweaver, & McGuire, 1999), and much of the cognitive gerontology literature would agree with this observation (see Balota, Dolan, & Duchek, 2000; Craik & Jennings, 1992; Kausler, 1994; Zacks, Hasher, & Li, 2000). There are, indeed, many circumstances under which the memory performance of older adults is poorer than that of younger adults.

In addition to these senior "memory moments," older adults also are more likely than young adults to complain about what might be called "attention moments," or difficulties in concentrating on intended events. Noise in theaters, restaurants, and at cocktail parties is reportedly more bothersome to older adults than to younger adults. This phenomenon has also been well documented in the laboratory for both visual and auditory distraction (e.g., Connelly, Hasher, & Zacks, 1991; Rabbit, 1965; Tun, O'Kane, & Wingfield, 2001; Tun & Wingfield, 1999; Zacks & Hasher, 1994; see Hartley, 1992, for a review). Indeed, a central focus of theorizing in the cognitive gerontology literature has been to explain the empirical findings that are consistent with these sorts of self-reports.

Recently, three major perspectives have attempted to integrate a broad range of findings of age differences in the cognitive gerontology literature, including both memory and attention moments. Proponents of theories that focus on processing speed deficits (e.g., Cerella, 1985; Myerson, Hale, Wagstaff, Poon, & Smith, 1990; Salthouse, 1991, 1996) argue that slowing of basic-level cognitive processes negatively impacts more complex functions, such as handling distraction, with the result of slowed and inaccurate retrieval. Another class of theories (e.g., N. D. Anderson & Craik, 2000; Craik, 1986; Craik & Byrd, 1982) suggests that older adults' deficits are due to age-related declines in the functional capacity of processing resources, such as working memory. Finally, our own view, stressing inhibitory control, also uses working memory as a central explanatory construct (e.g.,

Hasher & Zacks, 1988; Hasher, Zacks, & May, 1999). However, rather than focusing on the *capacity* of working memory (or reductions therein), the inhibitory view concentrates on the *contents* of working memory with a particular focus on the relevance of those contents for current goals. Specifically, this view argues that (a) older adults have particular difficulty in controlling what information enters and leaves working memory and (b) inhibitory processes are fundamental in determining both "memory" and "attention" moments, as well as apparent differences in mental capacity and, to some degree at least, in speed as well.

Here we focus on the relationship between the inhibitory viewpoint and ideas central to Craik's viewpoint: self-initiated processing and environmental support. Our conclusion from this evaluation is that there is rather more similarity between these views than a surface consideration might suggest.

☐ The Limited Resource View

The limited resource model of aging posits that older adults are deficient with respect to the amount of mental workspace or energy they have available to perform cognitive tasks. Specifically, Craik and colleagues (e.g., Craik, 1986; Craik, Anderson, Kerr, & Li, 1995; Craik & Byrd, 1982) have suggested that as a result of age-related reductions in this workspace, older adults are less able to engage in the kinds of self-initiated processes that are important for remembering and, as a result, their memory performance is greatly influenced by the amount of support available from the physical environment. In particular, the more support the environment offers, the less the deficit in capacity matters since the environmental cues can drive memory performance.

In this framework, self-initiated processes include retrieval searches and reconstructive activities that individuals execute in the service of a task such as remembering. They may also include processes engaged at encoding, such as the formation of novel connections between and among stimuli, such that several retrieval pathways are created for a particular item. To the degree that these processes are effortful, they require the use of cognitive resources (Craik, 1986; Hasher & Zacks, 1979). Because older adults generally have fewer cognitive resources available to them than do younger adults, older adults have greater difficulty initiating such effortful processes.

However, when environmental support is available for memory, older adults (and others with reduced capacity) can do very well. Some common laboratory tasks, such as cued recall, recognition, and most implicit tasks, provide a great deal of environmental support in the form of cues and context, whereas others, such as free recall and most prospective memory tasks, provide very little. Craik suggested that as environmental support decreases, individuals must increasingly rely on self-initiated processes instead. Not surprisingly, reliable age differences are much more common on tasks in which environmental support is low (and hence the demand for self-initiated processing is high) than on tasks in which environmental support is high (e.g., Craik, 1986; Humphrey & Kramer, 1999; Morrow, Leirer, Andrassy, Hier, & Menard, 1998; Sharps & Antonelli, 1996; Stine-Morrow, Miller, & Nevin, 1999).

☐ The Inhibitory Deficit View

The inhibitory deficit view (Hasher & Zacks, 1988) suggests that a major cause of the cognitive declines associated with aging, including those in memory and comprehension, is inhibitory in nature. Specifically, Hasher and Zacks (1988) argued that compared to younger adults, older adults have spared excitatory attentional mechanisms but less efficient inhibitory mechanisms.

At the core of this view is the argument that attention requires inhibitory constraints over automatically engaged, broad-spread, preattentive activation in order for working memory to function optimally (Cowan, 1995). Efficient inhibition constrains the contents of working memory to information relevant to the immediate goals and demands of a task. In a recent update of the theory, Hasher, Zacks, and May (1999) described three general inhibitory functions that operate at different times in the flow of an information processing sequence, allowing individuals to achieve control over working memory's contents. One function of inhibition operates when information is first presented (or when ideas are activated), preventing the initial access of irrelevant and marginally relevant information into working memory. Evidence suggests that older adults are indeed deficient with respect to this *access function*; this evidence includes a substantial literature on selective attention (see Hartley, 1992, and McDowd & Shaw, 2000, for a review of aging and selective attention; see also Carlson, Hasher, Connelly, & Zacks, 1995; May, 1999).

A second function of inhibition, the *deletion function*, operates when information active in working memory is either irrelevant or only marginally relevant or when information in working memory becomes irrelevant, as occurs when the task or topic changes or when the person's goals change. Bjork (1989) has argued that the ability to discard old information is a crucial step in the process of updating memory representations; by ridding ourselves of nonrelevant information from the current focus in working memory, we make room for more relevant information to enter. A number of studies, including those employing working memory span measures (e.g., Lustig, Hasher, & May, 2001; May, Hasher, & Kane, 1999), garden path sentence and prose materials (Hamm & Hasher, 1992; Hartman & Hasher, 1991; May & Hasher, 1998; Zacks, Hasher, Doren, Hamm, & Attig, 1987), and the directed forgetting paradigm (Beerten, Van Der Linden, & Lagae, 1995; Zacks, Radvansky, & Hasher, 1996; Zacks & Hasher, 1994), have demonstrated age-related deficits in the ability to discard no-longer-relevant information from working memory.

The access and deletion functions of inhibition are relevant to the classic memory finding that the more facts or items attached to a single cue, the slower and more inaccurate retrieval will be (J. R. Anderson, 1974; Watkins & Watkins, 1975). More specifically, a person with inefficient access and deletion functions is likely to have a substantially larger number of facts hooked to each cue compared to a person with efficient access and deletion functions, at least in part because working memory was far more likely to contain information that was nonrelevant along with information that was relevant to the task or goal. As these arguments suggest, the inhibitory framework is able to account for the substantial memory deficits that older adults often demonstrate in laboratory tasks, particularly when environmental support is limited.

The final function of inhibition, the *restraint function*, operates when strong responses are triggered by a familiar cue (e.g., Butler, Zacks, & Henderson, 1999; May & Hasher, 1998). The ability to restrain such responses is especially important whenever the most potent response is not the most appropriate and when alternative responses need to be considered. However, because it is not entirely germane to the current focus, the restraint function is not discussed further.

☐ Deficient Access Control: An Example of Environmental Nonsupport

The access function of inhibition has important implications not only for online performance but also for retrieval. When efficient, the access function permits only task-relevant information (whether that information originates in the environment or in thought) to enter into the focus of attention or working memory. If the access function is not efficient, as is the case for older adults, then irrelevant information enters working memory and, for example, can slow the processing of relevant information. As a result, irrelevant information in working memory will be bound to or associated with relevant information in working memory. When a retrieval cue is presented sometime later, the irrelevant information competes with the task-relevant information, impeding its retrieval.

On this view, then, older adults can be thought of as functioning under more or less continuous divided attention circumstances. Indeed, dividing young adults' attention at encoding—in essence, disrupting their ability to control access to working memory by forcing them to attend to irrelevant information—disrupts their later retrieval of the relevant information, simulating the performance of older adults under normal encoding circumstances (e.g., N. D. Anderson, Craik, & Naveh-Benjamin, 1998; Naveh-Benjamin, chapter 15 of this volume).

Can environmental support help reduce these inhibitory-based age differences in distraction? Recent work by Rahhal, Hasher, and Colcombe (in press) suggests that a small change in instructions given to older adults might be helpful in at least some memory situations. Older adults are typically quite concerned about their memory performance, and thus under the standard ("memory"-intensive) instructions used in laboratory studies, intrusive thoughts and worries are quite likely to serve as highly salient but irrelevant information that distracts them from the memory task. Thus, when older adults are told that they will be required to remember something, their attention may well be divided between the memory task and their concerns about performing well. Rahhal et al. found that reducing the usual emphasis on words related to memory in the instructions (e.g., "remember," "retrieve," etc.) boosted the memory performance of older adults substantially, with little impact on the performance of younger adults. It is possible that reducing the emphasis on memory in the instructions reduced the degree to which older adults were distracted by these irrelevant thoughts during encoding and retrieval, resulting in higher levels of recall than when more standard instructions are used. Thus, task instructions can vary in their degree of environmental support. Indeed, it may not just be task instructions that influence this type of environmental support, it can be the name on the door of a laboratory in which people are tested or the wording of informed consent forms or of telephone calls and letters used to recruit and schedule older adults.

We turn now to another consequence of deficient inhibitory control over access: slowing. One potential inhibitory-based source of the slowing typically shown by older adults is tied to the availability of too much information in the environment. An example of the disruptive effect of too much information is seen in a reading-with-distraction task (Connelly et al., 1991; see also Carlson, Hasher, Zacks, & Connelly, 1995; Li, Hasher, Jonas, Rahhal, & May, 1998) in which younger and older adults read passages embedded with one of four types of visual distraction: blank spaces, strings of Xs, words unrelated to the theme of the passage, and words related to the passage. Older adults are more bothered by distraction (as indicated by slower reading times) than are younger adults, although this is especially true to the extent that the distractors match the target material on a dimension (here, meaning) relevant for the goals of the task.

Other contexts in which distraction may differentially affect apparent processing include measures of cognitive speed that are widely used in the group and individual differences literatures. In most such tasks, many highly similar stimuli are presented at once on a single sheet of paper or in a single computer display, with participants instructed to solve as many problems as possible in a limited amount of time (see e.g., Salthouse, 1996). Thus, the standard speed tasks implicitly require participants to ignore many other currently irrelevant items while solving the single item that is currently relevant. If older adults are less able than young adults to ignore distracting information on a page in order to focus only on the current stimulus (and the selective attention literature would suggest this is so), this will interfere with their ability to complete each item on the test, and this interference may well be seen as a slowdown in responding. The multistimulus displays of standard speed tasks (and "busy" displays in many laboratory or real-life situations) may then constitute a form of environmental "nonsupport."

To test this possibility, we varied the distraction present in the displays of a variety of traditional speed tasks (Lustig, Tonev, & Hasher, 2000; Tonev, Lustig, & Hasher, 2000). Such tasks typically require participants to make simple, rapid decisions about a series of stimuli. For example, in the Letter Comparison Test (see Salthouse, 1993), individuals are instructed to decide whether two strings of letters are identical. On the standard version of the test, many pairs of letter strings are presented in columns on the page; participants work their way down the columns deciding whether the two members of each pair are the same or different.

We compared the performance of younger and older adults across two different versions of the Letter Comparison task. The first, "high-distraction" version simulated the standard, paper-and-pencil test: Pairs of letter strings of varying lengths were presented in columns on the screen. In the second, "low-distraction" version, each pair was presented individually. The logic was simple: If age differences on tests of "cognitive speed" are influenced by age differences in inhibitory control over access to working memory, then age differences in performance should be reduced in the low-distraction version relative to the high-distraction version. This was indeed the case (see Figure 23.1). The presence versus absence of distraction had little or no effect on the performance of younger adults. By contrast, older adults were reliably slower on the standard, high-distraction version than on the low-distraction version. These findings suggest that age-related reductions in the efficiency of the access function of inhibition may contribute to age-related slowing on many tests designed to measure cognitive speed.

In the above examples, extraneous, distracting information from the environment impaired the performance of older adults. It is worth noting, however, that distracting information can either *help or hurt* the performance of older adults, depending on the nature of the distraction in conjunction with the nature of the test task. When environmental information is congruent with the requirements of the task, older adults' greater tendency to take in additional information (due to poor inhibitory control over access) may improve rather than harm their performance. For instance, May (1999) found that if nominally irrelevant, to-be-ignored words were presented on the same computer screen with word problems, the success of older adults on the task depended on the relationship between the distraction and the solution to the problem. When the distracting information led towards solutions (to word problems presented on the Remote Associates Test; Mednick, 1962), older adults benefited to a greater degree than did younger adults. Conversely, older adults were more negatively affected than younger adults when the distracting information led away from solutions.

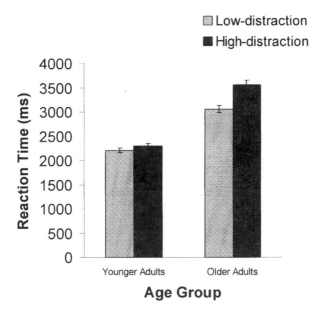

FIGURE 23.1. Younger and older adults' mean correct reaction time on a letter comparison task as a function of distraction.

The access function of inhibitory control constrains how much nonrelevant information enters working memory. The nonrelevant information can actually occur in the external environment or can be triggered by objects and events in the external environment and can even be irrelevant thoughts in response to relevant information. In any event, task-irrelevant information can disrupt performance in a variety of ways. It can reduce subsequent recall by permitting thoughts about performance levels to enter working memory (Rahhal et al., 2000) or by permitting off-track thoughts in response to target information.[1] It can slow performance on a variety of speed tasks whether they are unfamiliar (as in the Letter Comparison task) or quite familiar (as in reading with distraction; e.g., Connelly et al., 1991). It can also alter verbal problem-solving success (as in May, 1999). Thus the external environment can be helpful for performance, as Craik and his collaborators have often shown, but if the information in the environment is irrelevant or only marginally relevant to the current task and goals, it can also disrupt performance. This is particularly so for older adults who are less efficient than younger adults at preventing extraneous contextual information from entering into the focus of attention or working memory (e.g., Hasher et al., 1999; May, 1999).

---

[1]Because of the connection being made here with Craik's notion of environmental support, we have emphasized the importance of the access function in controlling activation of extraneous events in the environment. It is possible that both the environmental support/interference ideas and the inhibitory ideas can explain these effects equally well. In addition, however, the access function also controls irrelevant thoughts in response to ongoing relevant processing. Thus, an experimental sentence about a doctor who slices an apple pie into six pieces is more likely to trigger irrelevant thoughts (when's my doctor's appointment? My doctor's too thin; she can't possibly eat pie) in older than in younger adults. It is not clear that the environmental support notion handles such phenomena with as much ease as does the inhibitory control notion.

☐ Deficient Deletion: An Example of Poor Self-Initiated Processing

The *deletion function* of inhibition serves to remove marginally relevant, irrelevant, and no longer relevant information from working memory. No longer relevant information is suppressed whenever there is a switch in tasks, topics, or goals. A number of findings indicate that older adults are impaired at this function relative to younger adults.

For instance, using garden path sentences, Hartman and Hasher (1991; see also May, Zacks, Hasher, & Multhaup, 1999) found that older adults were less able than younger adults to forget the recent past when explicitly instructed to do so. As the name suggests, experiments involving "garden path" materials involve misleading individuals to entertain a conceptual representation that is then subsequently disconfirmed. The disconfirmation requires adopting a different conceptual representation. Hartman and Hasher (1991) presented participants with sentence frames such as, "Before you go to bed, be sure to turn off the _____," and instructed them to generate the missing final word. As anticipated on the basis of norms, most participants predicted the likely ending, "lights." Participants were asked to remember the completion word that was then actually provided by the experimenter. For critical sentences, the ending was always a plausible, but less probable ending (e.g., "stove") than the one most participants generated.

Retention of the critical, final words (both the ones that were generated and the ones that were provided by the experimenters) was determined by an implicit memory task. In this task, participants were given medium cloze sentence frames and were asked to complete the missing, final word for purposes connected to what they thought was an entirely different study. The particular sentence frames were normed to have baseline completion rates with the critical words of approximately 50% among naive control subjects. There was a long series of such sentences, and participants were asked to provide a final word, using in each instance the first word that came to mind. Embedded among sentences, with no connection to items in the first part of the experiment were experimental sentences that were used to test for access to the subject-generated ("lights") or experimenter-provided ("stove") critical items from the first part of the study. Using data from participants who showed no awareness of any connection between the two critical parts of the study, Hartman and Hasher (1991) found that younger adults showed greater priming for target endings than for disconfirmed endings, indicating that they were successfully able to discard their original representation. In contrast, older adults showed equal priming for both target and disconfirmed endings (see also May & Hasher, 1998; May, Zacks, et al., 1999).

Thus, older adults carry along the recent past with them, as indicated by greater priming for no-longer-relevant information relative to younger adults, who may show little or no priming for such information. Within the context of the present discussion, such failures can arise as a result of poor self-initiated processing of the sort that would ordinarily serve to delete no-longer-relevant information from working memory. The failure to successfully delete such information has a number of consequences. Perhaps the most profound among these is the heightened interference at retrieval from still partially active, but not currently relevant, information which became part of the memory representation that now includes both relevant, and no-longer-relevant information. This pattern—an increase in the number of elements in a single memory bundle—is sometimes called a "fan," and fan size is known to be inversely related to recall speed and success (J. R. Anderson, 1974). In accordance with the inhibitory deficit perspective, a number of studies have indicated that older adults are more vulnerable to fan effects than are younger adults (Gerard, Zacks, Hasher, & Radvansky, 1991). In addition, these fan effects are widely seen as the basis for proactive interference, a major source of retrieval failures (Zechmeister & Nyberg, 1982). It is not surprising, then, that older adults are more vulnerable to proactive interference effects than younger adults (for reviews, see Kane & Hasher, 1995; Lustig & Hasher, 2001).

Older adults' vulnerability to proactive interference can have a wide range of consequences, including difficulties on tasks traditionally used to assess working memory capacity, namely, working memory span. On a typical working memory span task (e.g., Daneman & Carpenter, 1980), participants are exposed to multiple trials in which they are required to both process (e.g., comprehend a series of sentences) and store information (e.g., the last word of each sentence) for a recall test that follows each of a series of sentences. This multiple trial methodology carries with it the possibility that information from earlier trials may proactively interfere with recall of information from later trials (May, Hasher, & Kane, 1999a). Specifically, May, Hasher, and Kane suggested that while individuals are attempting to complete later trials, information from earlier trials might still be active, disrupting retrieval of the current trial's information. It follows that individuals will perform efficiently on this task to the extent that they can delete prior trials from working memory.

To test their claim, May, Hasher, and Kane (1999) attempted to reduce the effect of proactive interference on memory span via an alteration in the way in which lists were presented: Span tests typically begin with the participant having to remember few items, with the memory load (or list length) gradually increasing as test trials proceed. This creates the potential for items from the briefer, earlier trials to proactively interfere with those on the longer, later trials that are critical for getting a high span score. Thus, May, Hasher, and Kane simply reversed the presentation such that testing began with longer list-length trials and then gradually proceeded to briefer trials. In this way, longer trials were administered before proactive interference was built up, and the shorter list-length trials (e.g., those with two items) were simple enough that they were not adversely affected by proactive interference.

For participants tested using the standard administration (long trials last), the standard age differences were obtained: Older adults had reliably smaller working memory span scores than did young adults (see, e.g., Gick, Craik, & Morris, 1988; Salthouse & Babcock, 1991). However, older adults' performance was much improved when the span task was administered using the alternative, interference-reducing method (see Figure 23.2). Indeed, the performance of older adults tested in the interference-reducing method was not statistically different from that of young adults (see also Lustig et al., 2001).

These results clearly show that the age deficits in working memory span often obtained in the commonly used reading span task (see, e.g., Daneman & Merikle, 1996) are at least partially the result of older adults' reduced ability to delete now-irrelevant information from previous trials from working memory. This poses a particular problem for capacity-based explanations of age declines in cognitive performance, at least to the extent that these explanations rely on working memory span as an estimate of capacity: When the inhibitory (deletion) demands of the span task were reduced, older adults showed equivalent capacities (span scores) as young adults. Together with other findings of older adults' reduced deletion efficiency (e.g., Hartman & Hasher, 1991; May, Zacks, et al., 1999, these results strongly suggest that age differences in many tasks, including working memory span, are not due to reduced capacity but are instead the result of age differences in initiating the deletion process that removes irrelevant information from working memory.

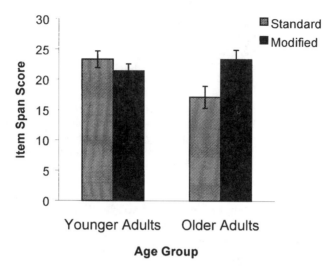

FIGURE 23.2. Younger and older adults' mean item span score on reading span task as a function of format: Standard (ascending) versus Modified (descending). (Adapted from May, Hasher, & Kane, 1999.)

☐ Conclusions

From a theoretical standpoint, the findings presented here are consistent with the idea that inhibitory control over attention is an important cognitive function that probably differs among individuals but that certainly differs with age, manifesting itself as slowing in some instances and as reduced working memory span in others.

We note especially that in some ways, these ideas map rather nicely onto Craik's views (e.g., Craik, 1986; Craik et al., 1995) of aging and of age differences in cognition. Older adults may be slower on most speed tasks because the environment not only doesn't support the particular task, but in fact actively disrupts performance even more for older adults than for younger adults (Carlson et al., 1995; Connelly et al., 1991; Lustig et al., 2000; Tonev et al., 2000). Such findings are quite in agreement with the age-related increase in sensitivity to environmental cues that Craik has noted (e.g., Craik, 1986). We would attribute these age differences to declines in inhibitory control over access to focal attention or working memory, declines that result in the physical and mental environments (e.g., Rahhal et al., in press) playing bigger roles in the performance of older than of younger adults.

In addition, when tasks shift their focus, for example from list 1 to 2, or passages shift their topics, older adults are much less able to stop the processing of the earlier task than are younger adults. This reduced ability (as the inhibitory framework would suggest) to suppress the no-longer-relevant past may be an instance of older adults' reduced ability to engage in self-initiated processing.[2] In the present instance, a major consequence is a

---

[2]We note this parallel with some reservation because the Craik notion of self-initiated processing may in general have a rather more deliberate, effortful, strategic quality to it than does the Hasher et al. notion of inhibition.

decrease in the ability to recall in a wide range of tasks, including even working memory span tasks (e.g., Lustig et al., 2001; May, Hasher, & Kane, 1999a).

Thus, as we see it, Craik's ideas and the inhibitory framework of Hasher and Zacks have some key ideas in common. The views differ in their ultimate explanation (or possibly in their level of explanation), of course, with Craik and his collaborators relying on the notion of capacity and reductions in capacity that presumed to be associated with aging, and with the inhibitory framework relying on what we take to be the underlying determinant of the apparent age-related (or even individual) capacity differences, inhibitory-based attentional processes.

☐ Acknowledgments

The research reported here was largely supported by grants from the National Institute on Aging (R37 AG 2753 to LH and RTZ and RO1 2753 to LH and Cindi May) and by a graduate fellowship (to CL) from the National Science Foundation.

☐ References

Anderson, J. R. (1974). Retrieval of propositional information from long-term memory. *Cognitive Psychology, 6*, 451–474.

Anderson, N. D., & Craik, F. I. M. (2000). Memory in the aging brain. In E. Tulving & F. I. M. Craik (Eds.), *The Oxford handbook of memory* (pp. 411–422). New York: Oxford University Press.

Anderson, N. D., Craik, F. I. M., & Naveh-Benjamin, M. (1998). The attentional demands of encoding and retrieval in younger and older adults: 1. Evidence from divided attention costs. *Psychology and Aging, 13*, 405–423.

Balota, D. A., Dolan, P. O., & Duchek, J. M. (2000). Memory changes in healthy older adults. In E. Tulving & F. I. M. Craik (Eds.), *The Oxford handbook of memory* (pp. 395–409). New York: Oxford University Press.

Beerten, A., Van Der Linden, M., & Lagae, C. (1995). Vieillissement et oubli dirigé. *Bulletin de Psychologie, 48*, 496–497.

Bjork, R. A. (1989). Retrieval inhibition as an adaptive mechanism in human memory. In H. L. Roediger, III & F. I. M. Craik (Eds.), *Varieties of memory and consciousness: Essays in honour of Endel Tulving* (pp. 309–330). Hillsdale, NJ: Erlbaum.

Butler, K. M., Zacks, R. T., & Henderson, J. M. (1999). Suppression of reflexive saccades in younger and older adults: Age comparisons in an antisaccade task. *Memory & Cognition, 27*, 584–591.

Carlson, M., Hasher, L., Zacks, R. T., & Connelly, S. L. (1995). Aging, distraction, and the benefits of predictable location. *Psychology and Aging, 10*, 427–436.

Cerella, J. (1985). Information processing rates in the elderly. *Psychological Bulletin, 98*, 67–83.

Connelly, S. L., Hasher, L., & Zacks, R. T. (1991). Age and reading: The impact of distraction. *Psychology & Aging, 6*, 533–541.

Cowan, N. (1995). *Attention and memory: An integrated framework.* New York: Oxford University Press.

Craik, F. I. M. (1986). A functional account of age differences in memory. In F. Klix & H. Hagendorf (Eds.), *Human memory and cognitive capabilities* (pp. 409-422). Amsterdam: Elsevier.

Craik, F. I. M., Anderson, N. D., Kerr, S. A., & Li, K. Z. H. (1995). Memory changes in normal ageing. In A. D. Baddeley, B. A. Wilson, & F. N. Watts (Eds.), *Handbook of memory disorders* (pp. 211–241). New York: Wiley.

Craik, F. I. M., & Byrd, M. (1982). Aging and cognitive deficits: The role of attentional resources. In F. I. M. Craik & S. Trehub (Eds.), *Aging and cognitive processes* (pp. 191–211). New York: Plenum.

Craik, F. I. M., & Jennings, J. M. (1992). Human memory. In F. I. M. Craik & T. A. Salthouse (Eds.), *The handbook of aging and cognition* (pp. 51–110). Hillsdale, NJ: Erlbaum.

Daneman, M., & Carpenter, P. A. (1980). Individual differences in working memory and reading. *Journal of Verbal Learning and Verbal Behavior, 19*, 450–466.

Daneman, M., & Merikle, P. (1996). Working memory and language comprehension: A meta-analysis. *Psychonomic Bulletin and Review, 3*, 422–433.

Gerard, L., Zacks, R. T., Hasher, L., & Radvansky, G. A. (1991). Age deficits in retrieval: The fan effect. *Journal of Gerontology: Psychological Sciences, 46*, P131–P136.

Gick, M. L., Craik, F. I. M., & Morris, R. G. (1988). Task complexity and age differences in working memory. *Memory & Cognition, 16*, 353–361.

Hamm, V. P., & Hasher, L. (1992). Age and the availability of inferences. *Psychology & Aging, 7*, 56–64.

Hartley, A. A. (1992). Attention. In F. I. M. Craik & T. A. Salthouse (Eds.), *The handbook of aging and cognition* (pp. 3–49). Hillsdale, NJ: Erlbaum.

Hartman, M., & Hasher, L. (1991). Aging and suppression: Memory for previously relevant information. *Psychology & Aging, 6*, 587-594.

Hasher, L., & Zacks, R. T. (1979). Automatic and effortful processes in memory. *Journal of Experimental Psychology: General, 108*, 356–388.

Hasher, L., & Zacks, R. T. (1988). Working memory, comprehension, and aging: A review and a new view. In G. H. Bower (Ed.), *The psychology of learning and motivation* (Vol. 22, pp. 193–225). New York: Academic Press.

Hasher, L., Zacks, R. T., & May, C. P. (1999). Inhibitory control, circadian arousal, and age. In D. Gopher & A. Koriat (Eds.), *Attention and performance XVII: Cognitive regulation of performance: Interaction of theory and application* (pp. 653–675). Cambridge, MA: MIT Press.

Hertzog, C., Lineweaver, T. T., & McGuire, C. L. (1999). Beliefs about memory and aging. In T. M. Hess & F. Blandard-Fields, (Eds.), *Social cognition and aging* (pp. 43–68). San Diego, CA: Academic Press.

Humphrey, D. G., & Kramer, A. (1999). Age-related differences in perceptual organization and selective attention: Implications for display segmentation and recall performance. *Experimental Aging Research, 25*, 1–26.

Kane, M. J., & Hasher, L. (1995). Interference. In G.L. Maddox (Ed.), *Encyclopedia of aging* (2nd ed., pp. 514–516). New York: Springer-Verlag.

Kausler, D. H. (1994). *Learning and memory in normal aging*. San Diego: Academic Press.

Li, K. Z. H., Hasher, L., Jonas, D., Rahhal, T. A., & May, C. P. (1998). Distractibility, circadian arousal, and aging: A boundary condition? *Psychology and Aging,13*, 574–583.

Lustig, C., & Hasher, L. (2001). Interference. In G. Maddox (Ed.), *Encyclopedia of Aging* (3rd ed.). New York: Springer-Verlag.

Lustig, C., Hasher, L., & May, C. P. (2001). Working memory span and the role of proactive interference. *Journal of Experimental Psychology: General, 130*, 149–207.

Lustig, C., Tonev, S. T., & Hasher, L. (2000, April). *Visual dDistraction and processing speed I.* Poster presented at the Cognitive Aging Conference, Atlanta.

May, C. P. (1999). Synchrony effects in cognition: The costs and a benefit. *Psychonomic Bulletin & Review, 6*, 142–147.

May, C. P., & Hasher, L. (1998). Synchrony effects in inhibitory control over thought and action. *Journal of Experimental Psychology: Human Perception & Performance, 24*, 363–379.

May, C. P., Hasher, L., & Kane, M. J. (1999). The role of interference in memory span. *Memory & Cognition, 27*, 759–767.

May, C. P., Zacks, R. T., Hasher, L., & Multhaup, K. S. (1999). Inhibition in the processing of garden-path sentences. *Psychology and Aging, 14*, 304–313.

McDowd, J. M., & Shaw, R. J. (2000). Attention and aging: A functional perspective. In F. I. M. Craik & T. A. Salthouse (Eds.), *The handbook of aging and cognition* (2nd ed., pp. 221–292). Hillsdale, NJ: Erlbaum.

Mednick, S. A. (1962). The associative basis of the creative process. *Psychological Review, 69*, 220–232.

Morrow, D. G., Leirer, V. O., Andrassy, J. M., Hier, C. M., & Menard, W. E. (1998). The influence of list format and category headers on age differences in understanding medication instructions. *Experimental Aging Research, 24*, 231–256.

Myerson, J., Hale, S., Wagstaff, D., & Poon, L. W., & Smith, G. A. (1990). The information-loss model: A mathematical theory of age-related cognitive slowing. *Psychological Review, 97*, 475–487.

Rabbit, P. M. (1965). An age-related decrement in the ability to ignore irrelevant information. *Journal of Gerontology, 20*, 233–238.

Rahhal, T. A., Hasher, L., & Colcombe, S. (in press). Age differences in memory: Now you see them, now you don't. *Psychology and Aging.*

Salthouse, T. A. (1991). *Theoretical perspectives on cognitive aging.* Hillsdale, NJ: Erlbaum.

Salthouse, T. A. (1993). Speed mediation of adult age differences in cognition. *Developmental Psychology, 29*, 722–738.

Salthouse, T. A. (1996). The processing-speed theory of adult age differences in cognition. *Psychological Review, 103*, 403–428.

Salthouse, T. A., & Babcock, R. L., (1991). Decomposing adult age differences in working memory. *Developmental Psychology, 27*, 763–776.

Sharps, M. J., & Antonelli, J. R. S. (1996). Visual and semantic support for paired-associates recall in young and older adults. *Journal of Genetic Psychology, 58*, 347–355.

Stine-Morrow, E. A. L., Miller, L. M. S., & Nevin, J. A. (1999) The effects of context and feedback on age differences in spoken word recognition. *Journal of Gerontology: Psychological Sciences, 54*, 125–134

Tonev, S. T., Lustig, C., & Hasher, L. (2000, April). *Visual distraction and processing speed II.* Poster presented at the Cognitive Aging Conference, Atlanta, GA.

Tun, P. A., O'Kane, G., & Wingfield, A. (2001). Distraction by competing speech in younger and older listeners. Manuscript submitted for publication.

Tun, P. A., & Wingfield, A. (1999). One voice too many: Adult age differences in language processing with different types of distracting sounds. *Journals of Gerontology, Series B: Psychological Sciences and Social Sciences, 54B*, P317–P327.

Watkins, O. C., & Watkins, M. J. (1975). Buildup of proactive inhibition as a cue-overload effect. *Journal of Experimental Psychology: Human Learning & Memory, 1*, 442–452.

Zacks, R. T., & Hasher, L. (1994). Directed ignoring: Inhibitory regulation of working memory. In D. Dagenbach & T. H. Carr (eds.), *Inhibitory mechanisms in attention, memory, and language* (pp. 241–264). New York: Academic Press.

Zacks, R. T., Hasher, L., Doren, B., Hamm, V., & Attig, M. S. (1987). Encoding and memory of explicit and implicit information. *Journal of Gerontology, 42*, 418–422.

Zacks, R. T., Hasher, L., & Li, K. Z. H. (2000). Aging and memory. In T. A. Salthouse & F. I. M. Craik (Eds.), *Handbook of Aging and Cognition* (pp. 293-357). Hillsdale, NJ: Erlbaum.

Zacks, R. T., Radvansky, G., & Hasher, L. (1996). Studies of directed forgetting in older adults. *Journal of Experimental Psychology: Learning, Memory and Cognition, 22*, 143–156.

Zacks, R. T., Hasher, L., Doren, B., Hamm, V., & Attig, M. S. (1987). Encoding and memory of explicit and implicit information. *Journal of Gerontology, 42*, 418–422.

Zacks, R. T., Radvansky, G., & Hasher, L. (1996). Studies of directed forgetting in older adults. *Journal of Experimental Psychology: Learning, Memory, and Cognition, 22*, 143–156.

Zechmeister, E. B., & Nyberg, S. E. (1982). *Human memory: An introduction to research and theory.* Monterey, CA: Brooks/Cole.

CHAPTER

Bruce A. Schneider

Sensation, Cognition, and Levels of Processing in Aging

Both sensory psychologists and cognitive psychologists study how intact organisms detect, encode, process, store, and recall information. Yet, in spite of this common interest, there has been, until recently, relatively little interaction between the two groups. For well over a century, sensory psychologists have concentrated their efforts on understanding how patterns of energy initiate sensory activity and how the information available in the discharge patterns of the sensory receptors is used to build up a representation of the external world. To the sensory psychologist, the end product is this representation: the figures we detect, locate, identify, and separate from the background; the voices we hear, the words we recognize; and the objects we touch, smell, and taste. Cognitive psychologists, on the other hand, typically begin to study how information is processed *after* a perceptual representation has been achieved. To the cognitive psychologist, the stimuli *are* the seen objects or the heard words. Their interests lie in how, for example, the heard word is stored in memory to be later recalled, and how sequences of words are integrated to extract meaning from a conversation. Thus, cognitive psychologists concentrate on how information is processed *after* the perceptual representation has been achieved, whereas sensory psychologists concentrate on how the sensory and perceptual systems arrive at that representation.

If perceptual processing merely set the stage for cognitive processing by developing a perceptual representation, there would be little need for cognitive psychologists to consider the intricacies of perceptual processing. Conversely, if the perceptual representation is achieved in a more or less automatic fashion (bottom-up processing), with little interference or control exerted by more central processes (top-down control), there would be little need for the sensory psychologist to be concerned with the complexities of top-down influences. While both groups know that this division of the information processing stream into two stages (perceptual and cognitive) grossly oversimplifies the complexity of the system, both consider the division to be convenient and have developed procedures and techniques to minimize the effects of one domain on the other. Perception researchers do this by simplifying the nature of the stimuli used in their experiments (e.g., using pure tones and noises so that semantic systems are not activated) and by developing techniques, such as signal detection, to separate sensory acuity from response biases. Cognitive researchers minimize the contribution of sensory factors in most of their experiments by using stimuli that are easily perceived (words printed in black on high-contrast paper, or clearly enunciated in a quiet background), and by testing only homogenous groups of participants (young, healthy, university students), thereby minimizing variations in perceptual representations across participants.

Recently, however, researchers have begun to investigate how aging affects perceptual and cognitive processing, calling into question assumptions concerning the separability of the two domains (see Schneider & Pichora-Fuller, 2000, for a recent review). Perception researchers now have to consider how age differences in cognitive processes contribute to age-related declines in perception, especially in more complex visual or auditory environments. Cognitive researchers, when comparing performance across age groups, cannot easily assume that the perceptual representation of the world remains invariant with age. Age-related changes in sensory systems could very well lead to inadequate or error-prone representations of external events. These inadequacies and errors at the perceptual level may cascade upwards and lead to declines in cognitive performance because the information available to the cognitive system is degraded or distorted. Hence researchers interested in perceptual and cognitive aging are going to be compelled to examine more closely the relationship between perception and cognition.

☐ A Levels-of-Processing Approach to Cognitive Aging

The Craik and Lockhart (1972) paper on levels of processing provides a good theoretical formulation for considering how interactions between the perceptual and cognitive domains might affect cognitive aging. Craik and Lockhart argued that "the memory trace can be understood as a by-product of perceptual analysis and that trace persistence is a positive function of the depth to which the stimulus has been analyzed" (p. 671). This approach, which emphasizes that cognitive processing flows from a perceptual analysis of the stimulus, is very amenable to sensory and perceptual psychologists who often consider cognition to be a relatively recent (in evolutionary terms) elaboration of the perceptual systems, so that an intimate relationship between the two is to be expected. Thus, rather than viewing perception and cognition as separate modules (or boxes in a flow chart), it makes more sense to consider them as a unitary information-processing system in which those processes we call sensory or perceptual occur relatively early in the processing sequence, whereas those that are labelled cognitive could be considered as elaborations of these early processes (see Figure 24.1).

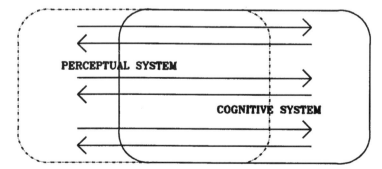

FIGURE 24.1. An integrated model of perception and cognition in which both the perception and cognition components are highly interconnected and may even share some overlapping resources. From Schneider and Pichora-Fuller (2000).

With respect to questions of aging, there are at least three major implications of this kind of approach. First, if memory is a byproduct of perceptual processing, it follows that any factor that might alter the nature of perceptual processing can, and most likely will, affect memory and other cognitive functions. Thus, age-related changes in sensory function could result in age-related declines in cognitive performance. Second, Craik and Lockhart (1972) assume that there are limitations on processing efficiency and/or on the availability of processing resources. Consequently, age-related reductions in processing at any level could lead to age-related declines in perceptual and/or cognitive performance. Third, the specific processes that are engaged are assumed to depend on the processing demands imposed by the testing situation. Hence, an age-related loss of sensory function could lead to changes in the *effective* processing demands imposed by a particular task. For example, consider a task where the participant is asked to decide whether a heard sentence is true or false. If an older adult mishears some of the words because of a hearing problem, he or she can often recover the misheard words from the context of the sentence. This would mean that the older adult would have to engage semantic and syntactic processes to a greater degree than a younger adult in order to simply resolve these perceptual ambiguities or errors. This may deplete the processing resources available to perform other aspects of the task and/or delay the application of these processing resources to other aspects of the task. Thus, older adults could be slower in making true/false decisions simply because their sensory systems are in decline.

These three implications of a levels-of-processing approach suggest that it may be inappropriate to attribute age-related changes in higher level cognitive tasks to changes in cognitive function if age-related changes in the early stages of sensory or perceptual processing (i.e., before perceptual representations of the objects have been achieved) have not been taken into account. Of course, if sensory aging and cognitive aging were shown to be independent of one another, we would not have to worry that one was causally related to the other. However, a number of recent correlational studies, have established a strong linkage between sensory and cognitive aging. Indeed, the relationship is so strong that in many studies auditory and visual acuity can account for almost all of the age-related variance in cognitive functioning (Baltes & Lindenberger, 1997; Lindenberger & Baltes, 1994; Salthouse, Hancock, Meinz, & Hambrick, 1996). For example, in the 1994 Berlin Aging study (Lindenberger & Baltes, 1994), the hierarchical model that provided the best account of age-related declines in cognitive function was one in which age effects on cognitive tasks were completely mediated by age-related changes in auditory-visual function.

Of course, the covariance of perceptual and cognitive declines does not necessarily indicate that sensory processing difficulties are the cause of declines in cognitive performance. There are at least four possible explanations for the correlation. The first possibility is that long-term perceptual declines cause the cognitive systems to decline (the sensory deprivation hypothesis; Lindenberger & Baltes, 1994; Sekuler & Blake, 1987). The second possibility is that both perceptual and cognitive declines reflect either widespread degeneration in the central nervous system or changes in specific functions or circuitry that have system-wide consequences (the common-cause hypothesis; Baltes & Lindenberger, 1997; Lindenberger & Baltes, 1994; Salthouse et al., 1996). Third, cognitive declines could contribute to age-related differences in sensory measures (the cognitive load on perception hypothesis; Lindenberger & Baltes, 1994; Salthouse et al., 1996). The fourth possibility, and the one that is most consistent with a levels-of-processing approach, is that there is a decline in cognitive performance because unclear and distorted perceptual information is delivered to the cognitive systems, thereby compromising cognitive performance (the information-degradation hypothesis; Pichora-Fuller, Schneider, & Daneman, 1995;

Salthouse et al., 1996; Schneider, Daneman, Murphy, & Kwong-See, 2000; Schneider & Pichora-Fuller, 2000).

☐ Information Degradation and Cognitive Performance

Because of the strong correlation between sensory and cognitive aging, we need to consider the information-degradation hypothesis more closely. Before we can attribute age-related differences in cognitive performance to age-related differences in cognitive processing, we must show experimentally that age-related changes in sensory function have a negligible effect on cognitive performance. One way to do this would be to find a group of older adults with intact sensory systems. If these older adults showed the same age-related differences in performance on cognitive tasks as found in other studies, then it would be appropriate to conclude that sensory declines are not responsible for cognitive declines. Unfortunately, age-related changes in sensory function are so pervasive that it would be extremely difficult to find older adults with sensory systems anywhere near equivalent to those of younger adults (Schneider, 1997; Schneider & Pichora-Fuller, 2000). For example, in our laboratories, where we attempt to select older adults with good hearing, only about one third of the older adults who report that they have no hearing difficulties are able to meet our criterion of good hearing (audiometric thresholds < 30 dB for frequencies less than or equal to 3 kHz). Even the select group who pass the screening criteria have thresholds that are at least 10 dB higher than those of younger adults for frequencies < 3 kHz, and more than 30 dB higher for frequencies over 6 kHz. Finally, even this select group of older adults have problems with respect to temporal aspects of hearing (e.g., Gehr & Sommers, 1999; Schneider & Hamstra, 1999; Schneider, Pichora-Fuller, Kowalchuk, & Lamb, 1994). Thus, it will certainly be extremely difficult, if not virtually impossible, to find a group of older adults with sensory systems as good as those of younger adults.

A second way of investigating the information-degradation hypothesis would be to simulate the sensory deficits of older adults in younger adults. This approach also has its difficulties. In order to be effective, all of the sensory declines found in older adults would have to be simulated, as well as the distribution of these declines in the population. Although we are beginning to explore this approach, we have opted for a third approach, namely, to test older and younger adults under equivalent levels of perceptual stress.

Consider, for the moment, an older person whose auditory system is in decline. Because of these declines, that person may not be able to hear and correctly identify some of the words presented aurally during testing. As a result, this individual will have to engage other resources (i.e., semantic and linguistic processes) in order to recover these lost words, placing her or him at a disadvantage relative to a younger adult who experiences no difficulty in hearing the individual words. Rather than concerning ourselves with the reasons for this hearing disadvantage, we have chosen to make it equally difficult for the younger adult to hear these individual words by changing the listening situation. If this manipulation is successful, we can then test younger and older adults under conditions of *equivalent perceptual stress*. If under such conditions older adults continue to perform less well than younger adults, we can infer that this age difference is not due to the inability of older adults to hear the individual words. Rather, we can attribute it to age-related changes in cognitive functioning. If, on the other hand, age-related differences disappear under this kind of manipulation, it then becomes reasonable to attribute age-related difference in cognitive performance to the higher degree of perceptual stress usually experienced by older adults.

We have also attempted, whenever possible, to use tasks that represent a closer approximation to tasks and functions that older adults need to carry out in everyday life. Thus, we have concentrated on recognition of and memory for words presented in sentences and on comprehension and memory of connected discourse. In order to test younger and older adults under equal levels of perceptual stress, we have individually adjusted listening conditions so that it is equally difficult (or easy) for each person (young or old) to identify individual words when these words are presented in the absence of supportive context.

☐ Perceptual Stress and the Use of Context

One of the reasons why older adults may appear to depend more on context than younger adults could be that they may have to use it more often in order to perform the task. Consider, for instance, a task in which younger and older adults are asked to repeat the last word of a sentence heard in a background of 12 people talking at once (a 12-talker babble). In this Speech Perception in Noise (SPIN) test (Bilger, Nuetzel, Rabinowitz, & Rzeczkowski, 1984), participants are presented with sentences and asked to repeat the last word of the sentence immediately after hearing it. In some of the sentences, the last word is predictable from the context ("Stir your coffee with a spoon"), in others it is not ("Jane was thinking about the spoon"). The ratio of the signal to the noise (SNR) is varied, and a psychometric function is constructed relating percentage of correct identification to SNR in decibels (dB). As expected, percentage correct identification increases with increasing SNR for the younger adult, the older good-hearing adult, and the presbycusic adult (see Figure 24.2). (Presbycusis refers to a variety of hearing disorders, including hearing loss, that affect the elderly; Willott, 1991, p. 2). Moreover, the function for low-context sentences is displaced to the right relative to that for high-context sentences; i.e., listeners need a higher SNR to hear a word with a given degree of accuracy when it is not supported by context than when it is supported by context. Finally, younger adults need less of a SNR to maintain a good level of performance than do older adults and presbycusics individuals.

The degree of contextual benefit experienced by a person can be estimated by computing the extent of the difference between the high- and low-context psychometric functions. For all three listeners shown in Figure 24.2, the degree of contextual benefit first increases and then decreases as SNR increases. Note, however, that the low-context psychometric function of the presbycusic individual asymptotes at about 65%. This means that this individual will miss approximately 35% of the low-context sentence-final words even when these sentences are presented in quiet. Moreover, the perceptual problem experienced by this individual would not be evident in situations where there is low noise and good contextual support, because he or she can identify 100% of the words so long as the SNR is greater than +10 dB. By way of contrast, the younger adult can identify 100% of the low-context words when the SNR is greater than 10 dB. Thus, at high SNRs, younger adults are not perceptually stressed when listening to sentences, whereas the presbycusic individuals are operating under considerable perceptual stress and *must* depend on context to identify the individual words. Older, good-hearing adults will fall between these two extremes in terms of perceptual stress.

Figure 24.2 shows that older adults, even when they are able to identify 100% of the words that they are hearing, may be under some degree of perceptual stress and can only maintain such high degrees of accuracy by using context to disambiguate incorrectly heard words. Given that high SNRs are rare in the modern world, older listeners are more often

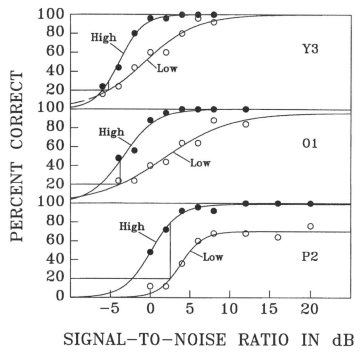

FIGURE 24.2. The percentage of high-context and low-context words correctly identified as a function of SNR for three participants. The top panel shows the performance of a young adult with good hearing; the middle panel shows the performance of an older adult whose hearing is in the normal range; the bottom panel shows the performance of an older, presbycusic adult. The horizontal lines intersect the low-context psychometric functions at the SNRs that result in 20% correct identification for each participant The vertical lines connecting the low- and high-context functions indicate the increments in identification accuracy that result when context is introduced at the SNRs that produce 20% identification accuracy in the low-context situation for each of the three participants. Adapted from Pichora-Fuller, Schneider, and Daneman (1995).

likely to find themselves in environments that are perceptually stressful to them but not to their younger counterparts. Moreover, because they must use contextual cues more often than younger adults, it is possible that they become more skilled in the use of context. One way to evaluate this hypothesis is to find the SNR for each individual that results in the same identification accuracy for low-context sentence-final words, so that each individual can be evaluated under equivalent levels of perceptual stress. The horizontal lines intersecting the low-context psychometric functions identify the SNR for that individual that results in an identification accuracy of 20%. The length of the vertical line between the low- and high-context conditions at this SNR specifies the beneficial aspect of context for this level of perceptual stress. In Figure 24.2, it is clear that for this level of stress, the presbycusic and the older normal hearing participants are much more adept at using context than the younger individual.

If we use the accuracy with which participants identify low-context sentence-final words as a measure of the degree of perceptual stress (low accuracy implies high perceptual stress), we can plot the degree to which individuals can use context to disambiguate words for different levels of perceptual stress. To do this, we take a particular level of perceptual stress, say the SNR that results in 30% correct detection of low-context words. The difference between the percentage of high- versus low-context words correctly identified at that SNR represents the degree of contextual advantage enjoyed at that level of perceptual stress. Figure 24.3 (top) plots the advantage afforded by context (percentage correct for high-context sentences minus percentage correct for low-context sentences) for younger and older listeners as a function of the percentage of words correctly identified in the low-context situation. Note that even when the percentage of low-context words correctly identified is very low (high degree of perceptual stress), older adults appear to be better able to use context to disambiguate words. As the percentage of low-context words correctly identified increases, so does the degree of contextual benefit until a maximum is reached at around 20% to 40% and then decreases thereafter. Note that over most of the range, older adults show a higher contextual advantage than younger adults, a result also reported by Sommers and Danielson (1999). The extent of this age difference in the ability to use context is shown in Figure 24.4.

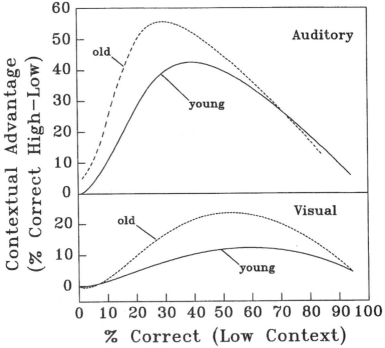

FIGURE 24.3. Contextual advantage as a function of the number of low-context words correctly identified. Contextual advantage at a particular level of low-context identification accuracy is obtained by first determining the SNR that results in a particular level of accuracy in the low-context condition, and then subtracting this level of accuracy from the level of accuracy found at the same SNR for high-context words. Top. Contextual advantage for younger and older adults in the Pichora-Fuller et al. (1995) SPIN study. (The results for older, normal hearing and presbycusic individuals were averaged together because of a lack of a statistically significant difference between these two groups). Bottom. Contextual advantage for older and younger adults when the same SPIN sentences were presented in visual noise (Speranza et al., 2000).

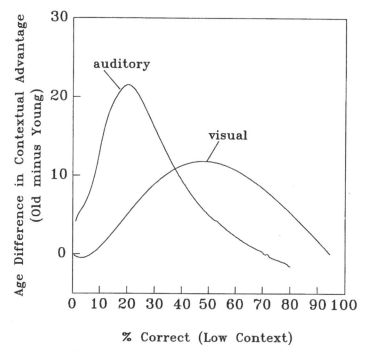

FIGURE 24.4. Age difference in contextual advantage as a function of the percent correct identification of low-context words. The age difference is defined as the contextual advantage shown by older adults minus the contextual advantage shown by younger adults. Data from Pichora-Fuller et al. (1995) and Speranza et al. (2000).

We have also looked for age differences in the ability to use the context provided by sentences when the sentences are presented visually rather than aurally (Speranza, Daneman, & Schneider, 2000). In this study the same sentences, masked by Gaussian noise, were presented on a monitor. Again, psychometric functions were constructed for low- and high-context sentences and these functions were used to determine how contextual advantage varied with the percentage of correctly identified low-context sentence-final words (Figure 24.3, bottom) and the extent of the age difference in the visual modality (Figure 24.4). Figure 24.3 shows less of a contextual advantage for visually presented words. Older adults outperformed younger adults but not to the same degree as for auditory presentation (Figure 24.4). The greater effects in the auditory modality might be due to the greater frequency with which individuals encounter difficult listening situations as compared to difficult reading situations.

To investigate how perceptual stress might affect working memory span (Daneman & Carpenter, 1980), in a separate experiment we also asked participants to recall the last n sentence-final words they had heard in the SPIN test for $n = 2, 4, 6,$ and 8. For example, participants were told that after having heard four sentences ($n = 4$) in a row, they would be asked to repeat the last word of each of these four sentences. The number of sentences so recalled can be considered as a measure of working memory span. Correct answers were those in which the participant repeated the word they had heard and reported following each sentence presentation, independent of whether or not they had correctly heard the word. An interesting feature of the data was that memory load (the number of words to be recalled) had no effect on word identification. That is, word identification immediately following sentence presentation was not affected by the number of sentence-final words they were supposed to be memorizing for later recall. However, working memory span (the number of sentence-final words recalled) was reduced by equal amounts in younger and older adults when noise level was increased. Thus, the level of perceptual stress affected working memory, but the working memory task demands had no effect on the level of word recognition.

A reduction in working memory span with increasing levels of perceptual stress suggests that perceptual difficulties do indeed cascade upward and adversely affect cognitive functions such as working memory. In addition, the results depicted in Figures 24.3 and 24.4 suggest that older adults are better than younger adults at using contextual information to support word recognition.

☐ Listening to Discourse When Perceptual Stress Is Equalized

The previous studies show that older adults can outperform younger adults with respect to the use of context when all individuals are equated for level of perceptual stress. To investigate whether equating younger and older adults for perceptual stress might reduce or eliminate negative age differences (poorer performance by older adults) in other cognitively demanding situations, we (Schneider et al., 2000) tested the abilities of younger and older adults to comprehend and remember connected discourse.

Younger and older adults (> 65 years of age) with good hearing (audiometric thresholds < 30 dB for frequencies less than or equal to 3 kHz) listened to passages read by a professional actor either in quiet or in noise. The passages were excerpts from previously published works and were from 1,050 to 1,866 words in length. After listening to a passage, participants were asked to answer a set of questions based on information presented in the passage. There were two types of questions: detail and integrative. Detail questions asked for a specific detail presented only once during the story or lecture. Integrative questions, however, were of the sort that required information to be integrated over the entire passage. Previous research (Daneman & Newson, 1992) had found that integrative (gist) questions are more difficult than detail questions. However, because older adults were shown to be more proficient than younger adults at making use of redundancies when comprehending sentences, we thought that we might find smaller age differences on the integrative questions.

In a control experiment we presented these passages in quiet and in noise. In both instances, the passages were presented at the same sound pressure level to all participants, and the noise, when present, was the same for all participants. Figure 24.5 plots the average number of correct answers (out of a total of 10) for younger and older listeners and for detail and integrative questions. The number of both kinds of questions answered correctly decreased in the presence of noise for both age groups, and the integrative questions proved to be more difficult for both younger and older participants. There was also a strong age effect: Older listeners answered fewer questions correctly than younger listeners, with the extent of this difference being larger for detail than for integrative questions. However, the extent of any age difference in noise for "gist" questions may have been limited by a floor effect (chance responding in these experiments was 2.5 questions correct).

The results of the control experiment indicate that independent of whether the passages are presented at high level in quiet or are embedded in a background of babble, older adults are unable to recall as much detail as younger adults and may not be able to

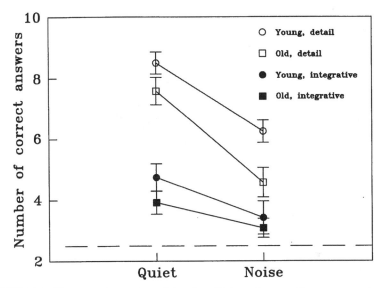

FIGURE 24.5. The average number of detail and integrative questions answered correctly by younger and older participants with good hearing in quiet and in noise. The signal level and the level of background babble were identical for all participants. Standard error bars are also shown. The dotted line indicates chance performance. From Schneider et al. (2000).

answer as many integrative questions as younger adults. This finding would not be surprising to those interested in cognitive aging where it is thought that factors such as generalized slowing and/or failure of inhibition should adversely affect the comprehension and recall of material (Cohen, 1987; Hasher & Zacks, 1988, Kwong See & Ryan, 1996; Wingfield, 1996). In other words, the negative age effect could easily be attributed to cognitive aging.

However, this negative aging effect, according to the arguments presented above, could be due to subclinical changes in hearing in older adults. If, for example, they were missing 10% of the words because of auditory problems, they might have to reallocate resources to the recovery of those words from context, leaving fewer resources for integrating words and phrases into sentences and for extracting and storing information from the passage for later recall. To investigate this possibility, in a second experiment we presented the passages after adjusting the listening situation to make it equally difficult for both young and old adults to identify individual words when these words were unsupported by context.

When sounds are presented at a fixed level to individuals with varying degrees of sensitivity, the sounds may be well above threshold for some, but near threshold for others. Because performance on an auditory test is often influenced by proximity of the stimulus to the listener's threshold, it is a common practice to present stimuli in auditory experiments at a fixed number of dB above threshold (at a fixed sensation level, SL) to make it equally audible to all participants. Hence, in the following experiment the passages were presented at 50 dB SL to all listeners.

When sounds are presented in a background noise, their audibility, as we have seen above, depends on the SNR. Our intent, when words were presented in a background babble, was to adjust the SNR so that the words were equally intelligible to all participants regardless of their hearing status or their age. We accomplished this in the following way.

Consider, first, a listener such as Y3 in Figure 24.2, listening to low-context SPIN sentences. Define the threshold for identifying low-context sentence final words as the SNR corresponding to 50% correct identification. For Y3, the threshold for identifying individual words unsupported by context occurs at SNR = 0 dB. Now consider listener P2, whose low-context threshold occurs at a SNR of approximately 5 dB. If we wanted both of these listeners to be able to hear and identify the same number of words in a passage when these words were unsupported by context, we would have to present the passage to observer P3 at an SNR that was 5 dB greater than the SNR used for observer Y3. Under these circumstances, both observers should find it equally difficult to identify and process individual words. In other words, they would be listening to the passages under conditions of equivalent perceptual stress. In this experiment, the passages were always presented at a SL of 50 dB, and when noise was presented, the level of the babble was individually adjusted to take into account individual differences in low-context SPIN thresholds so that each listener was operating under equivalent levels of perceptual stress (see Schneider et al., 2000, for details).

Figure 24.6 plots the number of correct answers for both detail and integrative questions for younger and older adults listening to passages in quiet and in two levels of a background babble. A comparison of Figures 24.5 and 24.6 shows that when listeners are tested at equivalent levels of perceptual stress (Figure 24.6), age differences in performance, for the most part, disappear. Performance still decreases with noise and integrative questions are more difficult to answer than detail questions. However, with the possible exception of detail questions at the highest noise level, there are no age differences in performance. Hence, when tested under equivalent levels of perceptual stress, older adults are able to answer as many questions as their younger counterparts.

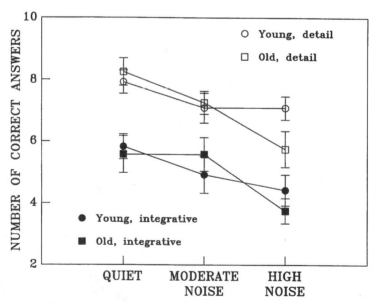

FIGURE 24.6. The average number of detail and integrative questions answered correctly by younger and older adults with good hearing in quiet and in two levels of noise. Both the signal level and the level of the background babble (when present) were adjusted for individual differences in hearing (see text). Standard error bars are also shown. Chance performance was 2.5 items correct. Adapted from Schneider et al. (2000).

We have seen that when younger and older adults are tested under physically equivalent listening conditions, younger adults perform better than older adults. However, when the listening conditions are adjusted to take into account individual differences in the ability to identify words in noise, the negative age differences on this cognitive task disappear. Hence, the poorer memory for connected discourse shown by older adults in Figure 24.5 can be attributed to subclinical hearing problems in this population.

These results emphasize the importance of considering both perceptual and cognitive processing as part of an integrated information processing system when examining cognitive aging. If sensory and perceptual factors are neglected, one is likely to attribute negative age differences on a cognitive task to an age-related cognitive decline. Such an attribution, however, assumes that the contribution of any sensory and perceptual declines to cognitive performance is negligible. No doubt, in some instances, this is likely to be true. However, in those cases that involve a great deal of "on-line" sensory processing (such as listening to or reading passages), it is quite likely that some, if not all, of the negative age difference in cognitive performance might be due to sensory problems.

☐ Memory Versus Comprehension

In the previous study, the number of detail and integrative questions answered correctly declined with increases in noise level. However, because the questions were asked subsequent to the presentation of the passage, we do not know whether increases in noise level (increases in perceptual stress) interfered with comprehension or with recall of the material. Higher noise level may have disrupted on-line comprehension, so that the information was never acquired or erroneous information was acquired, memorized, and later recalled. On the other hand, higher noise levels may have exerted their effect by disrupting the encoding of correctly apprehended information into long-term memory. More than likely, both processes were operating. While our preference is to study situations that more closely represent events in everyday life, it is sometimes necessary to use a simpler paradigm so that, for example, the memory component can be separated from the comprehension component. For these reasons we have also looked at memory for heard words in a paired-associates paradigm.

Murphy, Craik, Li, and Schneider (2000) tested younger and older adults in a paired-associates memory task modelled on Madigan and McCabe's (1971) study of serial position effects. In this task, listeners heard sets of five paired associates. After each set, the first member of one of the paired-associates was presented to the listener, who was asked to supply the other word in the pair. When the paired-associate tested was the last from the set of five, performance was very good. However, when paired associates from earlier in the set were presented, listeners often failed to recall the second member of the pair, giving rise to a serial position effect. Figure 24.7 (left panel) plots the percentage of items correctly recalled as a function of their serial position in the set for younger and older adults tested in quiet. Note that the performance of younger and older adults in quiet is equivalent for serial positions 4 and 5. However, at the earlier serial positions, older adults perform more poorly than younger adults, giving rise to an age–serial position interaction.

According to the information-degradation hypothesis, the perceptual representations of these paired associates may be degraded in older adults but not in younger adults. Therefore, it is theoretically possible that poorer perceptual representation of these words in older adults is preventing the words from being efficiently encoded into long-term storage. If so, then degrading the perceptual representation in younger adults should have an

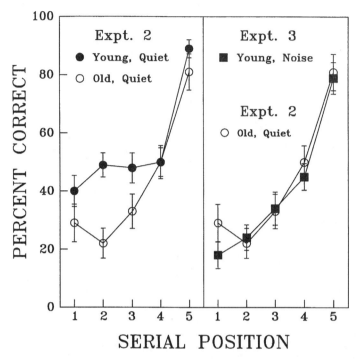

FIGURE 24.7. Percentage correct in a paired-associates learning task as a function of serial position for older and younger adults. Left panel. The paired associates were presented in a quiet background to both younger and older adults. From Experiment 2 of Murphy et al. (2000). Right panel: Percentage correct as a function of serial position for paired associates presented in quiet to older adults and in a background babble to younger adults. From Experiments 2 and 3 of Murphy et al. (2000).

equivalent effect on their performance. To test this, we added a background babble (the babble from the SPIN test) and replicated this experiment with another group of younger subjects. Figure 24.7 (right panel) plots the data from the young adults tested in noise along with the data of the older adults tested in quiet. Clearly, the performance of younger adults in noise is equivalent to that of older adults in quiet.

The data presented in Figure 24.7 are consistent with the notion that a degraded perceptual representation impedes the encoding of remote items into long-term storage. When we obtained these results, we did not know whether the degree of degradation that occurs in the perceptual representation when the young adults hear the words in noise is equivalent to that experienced by older adults in quiet. To resolve this question, it was necessary to test both younger and older adults under equal degrees of perceptual stress. Therefore, we determined a noise level for older adults that resulted in the same percentage of misheard words (9%) as that found for younger adults when these words were presented singly in a background babble. As in the previous experiment, older adults required a higher SNR than younger adults to obtain the same percentage of correct identifications (91%). Figure 24.8 shows the results when younger and older adults were tested at SNRs producing equivalent levels of identification. Younger adults performed better than older adults at all serial positions. Thus, equating both younger and older adults in terms of

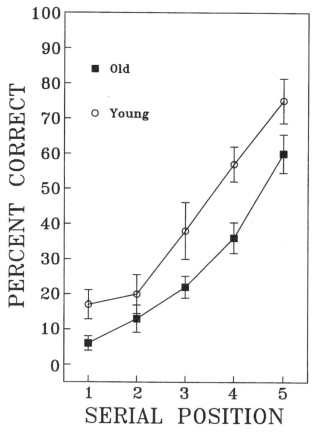

FIGURE 24.8. Percentage correct as a function of serial position for younger and older adults listening to paired associates in a background babble. The level of the babble was adjusted so that both the younger and older adults were, on average, able to correctly identify the same percentage of words when these words were presented individually. From Murphy et al. (2000).

perceptual stress did not eliminate the negative age difference. However, it did eliminate the age–serial position interaction. Apparently, degrading the stimulus representation (masking the words by babble noise) removed the relative advantage enjoyed by younger adults at the temporally remote serial positions.

The results of the serial position experiment suggest that perceptual noise can interfere with memory and that the degree of interference depends on the serial position of the word to be recalled. It is not too difficult to imagine that, in older adults, accumulated errors in sensory processing increase internal noise. If so, adding external noise when presenting the words to young adults might simulate, at least to a first approximation, the effects of increased internal noise in older adults. Why the effect of either external or internal noise is stronger for words presented in the earlier serial positions remains to be determined and is now being investigated.

☐ Implications of an Integrated Sensory and Cognitive System

In a levels-of-processing approach, there are no clear lines of demarcation between sensation, perception, and cognition. Cognitive processing is seen as a continuation and elaboration of perceptual processing. The Craik and Lockhart (1972) formulation also emphasizes that the extent and/or level of processing should be sensitive to task demands, and there is no reason to suspect that this susceptibility to task demands is limited to higher order cognitive processes. Of course, the more peripheral the process, the more automatic and obligatory it is likely to be. For example, independent of whether the task involves letter recognition (does the letter "a" appear or not?) or lexical decision, it is likely that certain stimulus features have to be processed in both cases in order to identify the letter "a" in the first task, or to make a lexical decision about a word in the second task. However, because the first task does not require semantic processing of the letter sequences, whereas the second most likely does, we would expect the degree of semantic processing to be greater in the second task than in the first.

That some processes may be more automatic than others does not mean that they cannot be affected by task demands, expectations, or context. For example, whether or not a person will hear a low-intensity tone whose frequency is 950 Hz will depend on whether he or she expects the tone to be at this frequency or to be at 1 kHz (Dai, Scharf, & Buus, 1991; Hafter & Schlauch, 1991). This suggests that the participant can "tune" her or his hearing to a particular frequency. In more general terms, sensory systems should not be considered as passive bottom-up processors of information, but rather as "information seekers" under central control, capable of searching for a required piece of information in a complex world. Indeed, in the auditory realm this central control over information seeking extends all the way down to the level of the basilar membrane.

Because of the pervasiveness of top-down control in the sensory and perceptual systems, it is also possible that age-related differences in performance on sensory tasks may be a consequence of age-related deterioration in top-down control. However, if age-related differences in top-down processes, such as the ability to maintain attentional focus, were responsible for negative-age effects on sensory tasks, then age-related differences should be observed for all sensory abilities so long as task demands are held constant. The available evidence suggests that this is not the case in many circumstances. For example, Pichora-Fuller and Schneider (1991) determined monaural thresholds for pure tones in quiet and for the same tones in a noise background for younger and older adults using the same two-alternative, forced-choice procedure. If anything, the cognitive demands placed on the subjects should have been higher for the detection of tones in noise than for the detection of tones in quiet. Yet, no age differences were found for the detection of pure tones in noise, whereas there was a substantial negative age effect for the detection of the same pure tones in quiet. However, results such as these do not eliminate the possibility that some of the age-related declines found in peripheral sensory processes reflect age-related declines in top-down control over these processes. Indeed, further work is needed to determine the extent of age-related changes in the top-down control of sensory function.

If we conceive of the sensory-cognitive system as under top-down control so that both the flow of processing and the emphasis given to certain kinds of processing may change according to context and task demands, we would expect the ways in which stimuli are processed to be influenced by the level of either external or internal noise. For example, in the absence of noise, there would be little need to tune the auditory system to select the frequency regions that are required to identify the stimuli in the stimulus set. However, as the situation becomes noisier, tuning will be required. Now, if the extent of executive control is limited, the tuning requirement may reduce the capacity of the system to exercise control elsewhere. In such a model, a sufficient increase in the amount of noise should produce performance decrements in higher order tasks because more processing resources are required for controlling and improving lower level functions. Thus, we would expect performance decrements in working memory span (Pichora-Fuller et al., 1995, Speranza et al., 2000), memory for connected discourse (Schneider et al., 2000), and paired-associate memory (Murphy et al., 2000) as the noise level increases.

With aging, we have seen that there are declines in sensory and perceptual processing. Within an integrated model such declines could result in a greater degree of top-down control over early stages of sensory and perceptual processing. For example, if the peripheral nervous system becomes noisy, it may be necessary to invoke "tuning" nearly all of the time. Other changes or "redirection" of processing may also be required because of deterioration in other systems. One consequence of such deterioration is that the particular processes by which older adults accomplish a task may be quite different from those used by younger adults even when both groups are performing equivalently. Indeed, McIntosh et al. (1999) have shown that the pattern of interconnectedness among brain structures involved in performing a visual task differed substantially between younger and older adults even when they were performing the task at the same level of accuracy. The use of different pathways or strategies by older adults may be a consequence of deterioration in the pathways normally used by younger adults to solve such tasks.

Thus, within an integrated model of sensory and cognitive processing, changes in sensory and perceptual processing could have far-reaching consequences for cognitive performance. In particular some portion of the declines seen in cognitive functions could be a direct consequence of sensory deterioration. Moreover, age-related changes in top-down control could exacerbate these effects. The results from the studies reviewed here are clearly consistent with this viewpoint and researchers interested in either perceptual or cognitive aging need to take into account the interconnectedness between these two levels of processing.

☐ Acknowledgments

The preparation of this chapter was supported by grants from the Natural Sciences and Engineering Research Council and the Canadian Institutes of Health Research.

☐ References

Baltes, P. B., & Lindenberger, U. (1997). Emergence of a powerful connection between sensory and cognitive functions across the adult life span: A new window to the study of cognitive aging? *Psychology and Aging, 12,* 12–21.

Bilger, R. C., Nuetzel, M. J., Rabinowitz, W. M., & Rzeczkowski, C. (1984). Standardization of a test of speech perception in noise. *Journal of Speech and Hearing Research, 27,* 32–48.

Cohen, G. (1987). Speech comprehension in the elderly: The effects of cognitive changes. *British Journal of Audiology, 21,* 221–226.

Craik, F. I. M., & Lockhart, R. S. (1972). Levels of processing: A framework for memory research. *Journal of Verbal Learning and Verbal Behavior, 11,* 671–684.

Dai, H., Scharf, B., & Buus, S. (1991). Effective attenuation of signals in noise under focused attention. *Journal of the Acoustical Society of America, 89,* 2837–2842.

Daneman, M., & Carpenter, P. A. (1980). Individual differences in working memory and reading. *Journal of Verbal Learning and Verbal Behavior, 19,* 450–466.

Daneman, M., & Newson, M. (1992). Assessing the importance of subvocalization during normal silent reading. *Reading and Writing: An Interdisciplinary Journal, 4,* 55–77.

Gehr, S. E., & Sommers, M. S. (1999). Age differences in backward masking. *Journal of the Acoustical Society of America, 106,* 2793–2799.

Hafter, E.R., & Schlauch, R. S. (1991). Cognitive factors and selection of auditory listening bands. In A. L. Dancer, D. Henderson, R. J. Salvi, & R. P. Hammernik (Eds.), *Noise- induced hearing loss* (pp. 303–310). Philadelphia: B. C. Decker.

Hasher, L., & Zacks, R. T. (1988). Working memory, comprehension, and aging: A review and a new view. In G. H. Bower (Ed.), *The psychology of learning and motivation* (Vol. 22, pp. 193–225). New York: Academic Press.

Kwong See, S., & Ryan, E. B. (1996). Cognitive mediation of discourse processing in later life. *Journal of Speech-Language Pathology and Audiology, 20,* 109–117.

Lindenberger, U., & Baltes, P.B. (1994). Sensory functioning and intelligence in old age: A strong connection. *Psychology and Aging, 9,* 339–355.

Madigan, S. A., & McCabe, L. (1971). Perfect recall and total forgetting: A problem for models of short-term memory. *Journal of Verbal Learning and Verbal Behavior, 10,* 101–106.

McIntosh, A. R., Sekuler, A. B., Penpeci, C., Rajah, M. N., Grady, C. L., Sekuler, R., & Bennett, P. J. (1999). Recruitment of unique neural systems to support visual memory in normal aging. *Current Biology, 9,* 1275–1278.

Murphy, D. R., Craik, F. I. M., Li, K. Z. H., & Schneider, B. A. (2000). Comparing the effects of aging and background noise on short-term memory performance. *Psychology and Aging, 15,* 323–334.

Pichora-Fuller, M. K., & Schneider, B. A. (1991). Masking-level differences in the elderly: A comparison of antiphasic and time-delay methods with burst and with continuous masking noise. *Journal of Speech and Hearing Research, 34,* 1410–1422.

Pichora-Fuller, M. K., Schneider, B. A., & Daneman, M. (1995). How young and old adults listen to and remember speech in noise. *Journal of the Acoustical Society of America, 97,* 593–608.

Salthouse, T. A., Hancock, H. E., Meinz, E. J., & Hambrick, D. Z. (1996). Interrelations of age, visual acuity, and cognitive functioning. *Journal of Gerontology: Psychological Sciences, 51B,* P317–P330.

Schneider, B. A. (1997). Psychoacoustics and aging: Implications for everyday listening. *Journal of Speech-Language Pathology and Audiology, 21,* 111–124.

Schneider, B. A., Daneman, M., Murphy, D. R., & Kwong-See, S. (2000). Listening to discourse in distracting settings: The effects of aging. *Psychology and Aging, 15,* 110–125.

Schneider, B. A., & Hamstra, S. (1999). Gap detection thresholds as a function of tonal duration for young and old. listeners. *Journal of the Acoustical Society of America, 106,* 371–380.

Schneider, B. A., & Pichora-Fuller, M. K. (2000). Implications of perceptual deterioration for cognitive aging research. In F. I. M. Craik & T. A. Salthouse (Eds.), *The handbook of aging and cognition* (2nd ed., pp. 155–219). Mahway, NJ: Erlbaum.

Schneider, B. A., Pichora-Fuller, M. K., Kowalchuk, D., & Lamb, M. (1994). Gap detection and the precedence effect in young and old adults. *Journal of the Acoustical Society of America, 95,* 980–991.

Sekuler, R., & Blake, R. (1987). Sensory underload. *Psychology Today, 21,* 48–51.

Sommers, M. S., & Danielson, S. M. (1999). Inhibitory processes and spoken word recognition in young and older adults: The interaction of lexical competition and semantic context. *Psychology and Aging, 14,* 458–472.

Speranza, F., Daneman, M., & Schneider, B. A. (2000). How aging affects the reading of words in noisy backgrounds, *Psychology and Aging, 15,* 253–258.

Willott, J. F. (1991). *Aging and auditory system: Anatomy, physiology, and psychophysics.* San Diego, CA: Singular.

Wingfield, A. (1996). Cognitive factors in auditory performance: Context, speed of processing, and constraints of memory. *Journal of the American Academy of Audiology, 7,* 175–182.

CHAPTER

25

Leah L. Light

Commentary: Some Observations on the Self-Initiated Processing Hypothesis

In an important paper, Craik (1986) argued that, due to limitations in processing resources, self-initiated processing at both encoding and retrieval is especially problematic for older adults. Six classes of memory tests were ordered as affording decreasing amounts of environmental support, correspondingly increasing needs for self-initiated activity, and increasing age-related deficits: procedural memory (priming tasks), relearning, recognition, cued recall, free recall, and remembering to remember. The six chapters in this section can be seen as exegeses of the self-initiated processing deficit hypothesis. They constitute unpackings, extensions, and amplifications of this hypothesis. In this commentary, I will begin by summarizing ways, both explicit and implicit, in which chapters in this section elaborate the self-initiated processing hypothesis and will then ruminate on the contribution and current status of this hypothesis.

One indicator of the profound influence of the self-initiated processing hypothesis is that longitudinal studies of memory typically include a variety of measures, running the full gamut from tasks that are thought to involve a heavy dose of self-initiated processing to those thought to be less dependent on such processing. For instance, an incomplete list of memory measures used in the Betula study discussed by Nilsson and Söderlund (Nilsson et al., 1997) includes cued recall, free recall, recognition for enacted and nonenacted sentences, source memory for whether each sentence was enacted or not, recognition memory for names and faces, priming in word-stem completion, and prospective memory. Estimated omega-squares for some of the measures are presented. Consistent with what one would expect based on the self-initiated processing deficit hypothesis, age effects were ordered from (greatest to least) free recall of elements of enacted sentences (omega-squares of .35 and .39 for verbs and nouns), free recall of nonenacted sentences (omega-squares of .18 and .20), recognition memory of first and last names (omega-squares of .12 and .14), to word-stem completion (.02).

The use of multiple tasks within a study gives rise to the question of how tasks may be ordered on self-initiated processing, an issue to which we now turn briefly and to which we will return later. Salthouse has analyzed a large number of measures derived from memory tasks, as well as from tasks in other domains tapping reasoning and perceptual speed, to determine the extent to which these share age-related variability. Interestingly, he reports that there is a positive relation between the extent of age-related deficit on a variable and the extent to which that variable shares variability with other measures. That is, there is a positive relation between the magnitude of the effect of aging exhibited by a variable and the strength of the relation between that variable and the common factor. In interpreting this empirical finding, Salthouse suggests that loadings on the common factor may reflect "the need to develop and execute a sequence of processing operations that require the control or allocation of attention" or, in other words, self-initiated processing. One important finding is that reasoning and perceptual speed tasks have higher loadings on the common factor and show larger age effects than the memory tasks studied. This serves as a reminder that memory is only one of several domains of cognitive function in which self-initiated processing may play a role, and it suggests that extensions of the self-initiated processing hypothesis to other domains may yield important insights.

Although Craik has focused on positive environmental support, Hasher points out that the environment can also have negative effects on memory. Inhibition deficit theory postulates that aging is accompanied by a specific deficit in inhibitory control, making it more difficult for older adults to prevent competing thoughts or information from environmental events (as in divided attention tasks) from entering working memory, to delete or suppress no-longer-relevant ideas or to keep strong responses from being triggered by familiar cues. Inhibitory control is one aspect of self-initiated processing, so the connection with Craik's work is clear and the extension of self-initiated processing constructs to harmful aspects of the environment enlarges the explanatory potential of this approach. Irrelevant information in the environment is distracting in that goal-relevant information cannot be as easily isolated and acted upon. In a real tour de force, Hasher, Tonev, Lustig, and Zacks demonstrate that inhibition deficits can contribute both to age-related declines in working memory and to age-related slowing in tasks used as measures of perceptual slowing.

In the chapter by Jacoby, Marsh, and Dolan, the construct of self-initiated processing is unpacked further by describing mechanisms underlying performance on memory, attention, and perceptual identification tasks. Jacoby and his colleagues (e.g., Jacoby & Hollingshead, 1990) have argued convincingly that memory tasks are not process pure and that both strategic and automatic processes contribute to performance in a variety of memory tasks. This implies that processes, rather than tasks per se, should be the focus of cognitive aging theory and research. Jacoby's approach is exemplified in the use of process dissociation procedures to obtain estimates of habit and recollection in many experimental procedures in studies comparing young and older adults. Such studies generally support the view that recollection, a strategic and self-initiated set of mechanisms, but not habit, is reduced in old age.

Failures in self-initiated processing can occur on either the encoding side or the retrieval side. Glisky's chapter examines the possibility that older adults' difficulties with source memory are associated with deficits in self-initiated processes attendant on impaired frontal lobe function, whereas problems with item memory are not. Glisky concludes that older adults who score lower on a battery of neuropsychological tests thought to tap frontal lobe functions have reduced attentional resources, leading to less spontaneous integration of content and context, a problem that can be remediated by structuring encoding tasks appropriately. The presence of a same/different effect for item memory in some experiments, which was age invariant, also suggests that source information may be encoded, so it is possible that the frontal lobes may be important in retrieval as well as encoding when the test task is sufficiently difficult. In sum, Glisky's findings fit nicely into the self-initiated processing framework.

Schneider's chapter deals with the interface between sensory and cognitive systems. Schneider argues that subclinical hearing losses in older adults can account for all or part of their apparent deficits in cognition. For instance, when young and older adults are tested at equal levels of perceptual (auditory) stress, age differences on fact and inference questions that are manifest when both age groups are tested in silence pretty much disappear. At first blush, these results might not seem relevant to the self-initiated processing hypothesis. However, Schneider makes a strong case for a scenario in which sensory impairments necessitate the diversion of processing resources to compensatory top-down processes to improve lower level function. When this occurs, strategic self-initiated processing needed for such activities as working memory, paired-associate learning, prose comprehension, and memory are compromised. Hence, Schneider highlights the importance of considering the entire sensory–cognitive continuum when theorizing about age-related changes in performance.

My own work also bears on the self-initiated processing hypothesis. For the last decade and a half, my research has centered on differentiating aspects of episodic memory that are relatively spared by aging from those that are more age sensitive. In particular, I have been interested in the dissociation between age effects on priming tasks, thought to be low in self-initiated processing demands, and recall and recognition, both of which involve deliberate recollection. Also, in a meta-analysis, La Voie and Light (1994) calculated effect sizes for recall, recognition, and a variety of priming tasks that measure memory indirectly. To explain the fact that effect sizes for recall and recognition were larger than those for priming tasks, we argued that these three classes of memory tasks were differentially subserved by deliberate recollection, with recall having the greatest contribution from recollection, and priming tasks the least. This line of argument bears an obvious family resemblance to the self-initiated processing approach. Recently, in a series of studies on bias effects in word-stem completion, Robert Kennison, Michael Healy, and I have found age differences in benefits of prior experience on the typical production version of the task, but not on a forced-choice word-stem completion task, a result also in keeping with the self-initiated processing deficit hypothesis (Light, Kennison, & Healy, 1998).

One of the byproducts of working on priming tasks has been the realization that the self-initiated processing hypothesis is a very useful tool for organizing and summarizing what we know about age differences in episodic memory, but that when examined up close, it proves to have limitations. A short discussion of some of these is now offered (see also Burke & Light, 1981; Light, 1991; Light, 1996).

First, as I have noted elsewhere, the ideas of environmental support and self-initiated processing can be separated, so they should not be viewed as being linked as tightly as Craik (1986) suggested. In several studies in my own laboratory and elsewhere, environmental support has been held constant across cued recall and indirect measures of memory thought to require different degrees of self-initiated processing. For instance, Light and Albertson (1989) presented young and older adults with words drawn from several taxonomic categories. At test, participants were presented with the names of the categories from which the words had been drawn, as well as some new category names, and were asked to generate category exemplars. Later, they were tested for cued recall with the names of categories serving as cues. What varied between these two tasks was the instructions provided. For exemplar generation, an indirect measure of memory, participants were asked to produce the first category members that came to mind, whereas for cued recall they were asked to produce words they had studied that fit the relevant categories. Older adults recalled reliably fewer words than young adults, but there was no reliable age effect on exemplar generation. A similar pattern has been observed for word-stem completion (Light & Singh,1987). These results, and others now in the literature, argue for the decoupling of self-initiated processing from environmental support as explanatory devices. When environmental support is held constant, self-initiated processing demands can vary across tasks, and the magnitude of age decrements may vary with the latter but not the former. Similarly, when environmental support is varied within a task such as word-stem completion or cued recall, older adults may not benefit more from increased support (Park & Shaw, 1992).

Second, as discussed above, some tasks involve a mixture of processes. So, one can see Jacoby et al.'s process dissociation methodology as a way of experimentally obtaining estimates of processes that involve greater and lesser amounts of self-initiated processes. Rather than comparing performance across tasks to study such processes, Jacoby et al.'s process dissociation procedure affords the advantage of studying processes that require self-initiated recollective processes and more activation-based familiarity processes within a single task. The fact that tasks are not process pure also argues against trying to order tasks rather than processes on the extent of self-initated processes required. This, of course, raises the question of whether we can order processes rather than tasks, using some a priori criterion of degree of self-initiatedness and immediately leads to my next point.

Despite the fact that I have used meta-analysis to do just this, it is no longer obvious to me that there is much utility in trying to order experimental tasks or measures in terms of the extent of their dependence on particular processes. Nelson (1977), in an oft-cited paper on levels of processing, noted the difficulty of deciding a priori the relative positions of different tasks on a "depth" dimension. Absent a yardstick for doing that, he pointed to the interpretive problems faced by the levels hypothesis and the potential for circularity of argument. A similar situation may exist for the hypothesis that age-related deficits covary with the extent of how much recollection or self-initiated processing is required. Within a given experiment or within a single paradigm, it is often relatively easy, at least on an intuitive level, to argue that a given condition involves more or less self-initiated processing. For instance, it seems straightforward to argue that restricting search in a word-stem completion task by providing more letters in the cue constitutes an operationalization of degree of self-initiated processing. It seems less clear, however, how we can order tasks that involve vastly different processes such as prospective memory (remembering to remember), free recall, single-stimulus recognition, three-alternative forced-choice recognition, memory for the room in which a chair was pictured, verifying that a word belongs to a semantic category, and generating members of various categories. Salthouse's use of factor loadings provides an estimate of the amount of variability shared by tasks but does not itself provide an index of any hypothetical processes that might underlie the tasks. Thus, factor loadings do not give us an independent measure of self-initiated processing. The advent of functional neuroimaging of cognitive processes holds out the potential for using activation of the frontal lobes during a task as an index of self-initiated processing, but this seems unlikely to prove useful given the diversity of functions subserved by the frontal lobes (see, e.g., Miyake et al., 2000, for a discussion of the varieties of executive functions).

Third, without an independent measure of how much self-initiated processing is involved, it is not clear what to do when tasks within a class show differences or when tasks show inversions in their hypothesized order of sensitivity to aging. Here are two examples of what I have in mind. In a recent meta-analysis, Light, Prull, La Voie, and Healy (2000) found that some kinds of priming tasks produced larger effect sizes than others. Tasks categorized as involving identification had, on average, smaller d's than those requiring production (see also Fleischman & Gabrieli, 1998). Quite arguably, production tasks (such as category exemplar production) have heavier self-initiated processing demands than do identification tasks (such as category verification; but see Light, Prull, & Kennison, 2000). However, there seems no simple way to decide a priori whether the self-initiated processing demands of exemplar generation are greater than those of word-stem completion or single-item recognition or event-based prospective memory tasks. Cued recall is thought to require less self-initiated processing than free recall. Nonetheless, Naveh-Benjamin (2000) found smaller age differences in free recall than in cued recall for unrelated word pairs.

Fourth, the self-initiated processing deficit hypothesis was formulated at a time when, as a field, we were more convinced that age-related memory problems were all episodic memory problems. Difficulties in retrieving information from semantic memory were not a focus of investigation, and it was widely believed that semantic memory is well preserved in old age (see, e.g., Light, 1992, for a review). It is, but this does not mean that there are not age-related changes within domains that we think of as semantic memory. For instance, older people have more tip-of-the-tongue experiences than young ones (Burke, MacKay, Worthley, & Wade, 1991) and also are more likely to misspell words (MacKay & Abrams, 1998; MacKay, Abrams, & Pedroza, 1999). Interestingly, older adults can detect spelling errors as well as young ones, so that there is an asymmetry between error perception and error production in the orthographic domain. Burke and MacKay and their colleagues postulated specific mechanisms operating within a particular cognitive architecture to explain both tip-of-the-tongue experiences and spelling errors. According to node structure theory, these are the result of deficits in the transmission of activation. Asymmetries between perception and production are the product of transmission failures when there are one-to-many connections rather than many-to-one connections within the network. Error production could be viewed as relying more on self-initiated processing because orthography must be retrieved. However, transmission deficits involve the failure of automatic processes. There are two points that I want to make here. One is that identifying production with self-initiated processing and perception with its lack is just too simplistic. The fact that speech perception, for instance, can involve strategic (or at least top-down) processes has been forcefully brought home by Schneider's chapter. The second is that there is a need for the embedding of the construct of self-initiated processing within a plausible cognitive architecture and the clearer specification of its central ideas of strategic and automatic processing at encoding and retrieval within such an architecture.

So where does this leave us? I've suggested here and elsewhere that the empirical data do not always support the self-initiated processing deficit hypothesis and that some of the research goals suggested by this hypothesis may prove to be unattainable. Despite these somewhat critical remarks, however, the papers in this section of the Festschrift for Gus Craik serve as an index of the durability of the ideas encompassed by the self-initiated processing hypothesis. For several decades, Craik has set an agenda for cognitive aging researchers. His openness to challenge and revision of ideas has encouraged investigations that provide exegeses and elaborations of the constructs he has used to explain stability and change in memory with increasing age. In sum, he has forced researchers in cognitive aging to engage in self-initiated processing and has provided the environmental support needed for this enterprise.

☐ Acknowledgment

Preparation of this chapter was supported by National Institute on Aging Grant RO1 AG02452.

☐ References

Burke, D. M., & Light, L. L. (1981). Memory and aging: The role of retrieval. *Psychological Bulletin, 90,* 513–546.

Burke, D. M., MacKay, D. G., Worthley, J. S., & Wade, E. (1991). On the tip of the tongue: What causes word finding failures in young and older adults? *Journal of Memory and Language, 30,* 542–579.

Craik, F. I. M. (1986). A functional account of age differences in memory. In F. Klix & H. Hagendorf (Eds.), *Human memory and cognitive capabilities* (pp. 409–422). Amsterdam: Elsevier.

Fleischman, D. A., & Gabrieli, J. D. E. (1998). Repetition priming in normal aging and Alzheimer's disease: A review of findings and theories. *Psychology and Aging, 13,* 88–119.

Jacoby, L. L., & Hollingshead, A. (1990). Toward a generate/recognize model of performance on direct and indirect tests of memory. *Journal of Memory and Language, 29,* 433–454.

La Voie, D., & Light, L. L. (1994). Adult age differences in repetition priming: A meta-analysis. *Psychology and Aging, 9,* 539–553.

Light, L. L. (1991). Memory and aging: Four hypothesis in search of data. *Annual Review of Psychology, 42,* 333–376.

Light, L. L. (1992). The organization of memory in old age. In F. I. M. Craik & T. Salthouse (Eds.), *Handbook of aging and cognition* (pp. 111–165). Hillsdale, NJ: Erlbaum.

Light, L. L. (1996). Memory and aging. In E. L. Bjork & R. A. Bjork (Eds.), *Handbook of perception and cognition* (2nd ed., Vol. 10: *Memory,* pp. 443–490). San Diego, CA: Academic Press.

Light, L. L., & Albertson, S. A. (1989). Direct and indirect tests of memory for category exemplars in young and older adults. *Psychology and Aging, 4,* 487–492.

Light, L. L., Kennison, R. F., & Healy, M. (1998, April). *Are there age differences in word-fragment completion priming?* Paper presented at the 1998 Cognitive Aging Conference, Atlanta, GA.

Light, L. L., Prull, M. W., & Kennison, R. F. (2000). Divided attention, aging, and priming in exemplar generation and category verification. *Memory & Cognition, 28,* 856–872.

Light, L. L., Prull, M. W., La Voie, D. J., & Healy, M. (2000). Dual process theories of memory in old age. In T. J. Perfect & E. A. Maylor (Eds.), *Models of cognitive aging* (pp. 239–300). Oxford, England: Oxford University Press.

Light, L. L., & Singh, A. (1987). Implicit and explicit memory in young and older adults. *Journal of Experimental Psychology: Learning, Memory, and Cognition, 13,* 531–541.

MacKay, D. G., & Abrams, L. (1998). Linked declines in retrieving orthographic knowledge: Empirical, practical, and theoretical implications. *Psychology and Aging, 13,* 647–662.

MacKay, D. G., Abrams, L., & Pedroza, M. J. (1999). Aging on the input versus output side: Theoretical implications of age-linked asymmetries between detecting versus retrieving orthographic information. *Psychology and Aging, 14,* 3–17.

Miyake, A., Friedman, N. P., Emerson, M. J., Witzki, A. H., Howerter, A., & Wager, T. D. (2000). The unity and diversity of executive functions and their contributions to complex "frontal lobe" tasks: A latent variable analysis. *Cognitive Psychology, 41,* 49–100.

Naveh-Benjamin, M. (2000). Adult age differences in memory performance: Tests of an associative deficit hypothesis. *Journal of Experimental Psychology: Learning, Memory, and Cognition, 26,* 1170–1187.

Nelson, T. O. (1977). Repetition and depth of processing. *Journal of Verbal Learning and Verbal Behavior, 16,* 151–171.

Nilsson, L.-G., Backman, L., Erngrund, K., Nyberg, L., Adolfsson, R., Bucht, G., Karlsson, S., Widing, M., & Winblad, B. (1997). The Betula Prospective Cohort Study: Memory, health, and aging. *Aging, Neuropsychology, and Cognition, 4,* 1–32.

Park, D. C., & Shaw, R. J. (1992). Effect of environmental support on implicit and explicit memory in younger and older adults. *Psychology and Aging, 7,* 632–642.

NEUROSCIENCE PERSPECTIVES ON MEMORY AND AGING

CHAPTER

Anthony Randal McIntosh

Part IV Introduction:
How the Study of Brain Function
Is Influenced by
the Function of Craik's Brain

Cognitive neuroscience represents a concerted effort to merge cognitive theory with different fields of neuroscience. Neuropsychological studies of patient populations, and functional neuroimaging are two of the main methodologies used in this rapidly expanding field. Like any scientific approach, these studies have their greatest immediate impact when integrated with cognitive theory. It is here that the work of Fergus Craik has had significant influence. Cognitive phenomena, such as levels of processing, provide a means to tap into the brain dynamic of human memory in a controlled manner. Moreover, the orientation provides new avenues to investigate the neurobiological changes in aging and in mental disorders that affect cognitive function. The four chapters in this section exemplify how Craik's cognitive theories have served as the foundation for understanding the link between brain and cognition. The chapters also illustrate how different cognitive neuroscience approaches can be used to study memory function and dysfunction in different populations. A common theme running through them is that cognitive theory provides an important framework for the study of brain function.

Chapter 28, by Stuss and Binns, follows from careful observations of neuropsychological studies of frontal lobe damage. Stuss and colleagues observed that deficits from prefrontal damage could be fractionated depending on damage location. Stuss and Binns raise the possibility that the effects of aging on cognition may also be approached from this perspective where multiple changes can occur that reflect the involvement of multiple brain areas.

Chapter 27, by Grady, demonstrates the use of Craik's theoretical foundation in neuroimaging studies of memory and aging. The intriguing observation from Grady's work is the apparent reorganization of memory circuits in the aging brain. Such reorganization is observed even when memory performance is the same as that of young participants. As with the Stuss and Binns work, Grady's neuroimaging results imply that cognitive changes in aging cannot be easily accounted for by a single mechanism.

In chapter 30, Koutstaal and Schacter provide an engaging account of memory distortions that accompany advanced age. These memory distortions include false recognition and misattribution of memories, where the event is recalled but mislabeled in time or in its source. Using a combination of neuropsychological and neuroimaging studies, Koutstaal and Schacter provide strong converging evidence that memory errors encountered in the old adults may be caused by functional changes in the prefrontal cortex. The chapter also discusses the dual-task paradigm that was used by Craik to evaluate which memory processes were most sensitive to reduced attentional resources in aging. A thorough review of these studies presents a picture that is congruent with the conclusions in the Stuss and Binns and Grady chapters, where it appears that memory changes in aging may be a multidimensional effect. Indeed, Koutstaal and Schacter argue that memory errors in old adults may reflect reduced processing efficiency in the hippocampal formation, which occur in conjunction with prefrontal lobe changes. A second important component of the Koutstaal and Schacter chapter is the elegant demonstration of how basic behavioral, neuropsychology, and neuroimaging studies can complement one another to develop and elucidate fundamental cognitive operations.

Chapter 29, by Vidailhet, Christensen, Danion, and Kapur, illustrates how cognitive theory, including Craik's theoretical framework, has been used to examine episodic memory dysfunction in schizophrenia. The authors first review the literature to emphasize that memory dysfunction in schizophrenia is selective and appears to affect explicit memory operations. As with the cognitive changes in aging, it appears that memory difficulties in schizophrenia may represent multiple effects, which range from difficulties in strategic processes at encoding to the inability to spontaneously use an organizational strategy during retrieval. Ongoing neuroimaging studies, where patients and controls are matched for memory performance, suggest that patients show both reduced activation of encoding-related brain areas and unique activations during retrieval that are not found in controls. Among the areas singled out for distinction were prefrontal and parietal cortices, hippocampus, and thalamus. These preliminary results support ideas of a large-scale network dysfunction in schizophrenia. An interesting suggestion from this chapter is that examination targeted at memory function in schizophrenia may be of great clinical value, although it has not traditionally been considered. The authors cite recent clinical work demonstrating that impairment of episodic memory is closely related to measures of functional outcome in schizophrenia.

The findings from these clinical chapters demonstrate the utility of bridging basic cognitive theory, neuroimaging, and clinical studies in the study of patient populations. Collectively, the four chapters in this section provide a salient demonstration for the profound impact Craik's work has had on a broad range of research.

Cheryl L. Grady

Age-Related Changes in the Functional Neuroanatomy of Memory

☐ Introduction

An impressive amount of effort over the years has gone toward the study of age-related changes in memory, especially episodic memory. Episodic memory, or the conscious recollection of events that a person has experienced (Tulving, 1983), is thought to be the result of several stages of processing. The initial stage is encoding, in which the features of the incoming stimulus are analyzed and related to previously encountered information. The final stage is retrieval, in which stored information is searched for and brought to consciousness to be acted upon. Age-related difficulties in episodic memory thus could be related to deficits in encoding the to-be-remembered material (Craik & Byrd, 1982) as well as to reductions in the adequacy of retrieval (Burke & Light, 1981). One proposed reason for encoding failure in older people is that they are less able to initiate adequate encoding strategies or to organize material in their attempt to learn it (Hultsch, 1969; Sanders, Murphy, Schmitt, & Walsh, 1980). Using the well-known levels-of-processing manipulation (Craik & Lockhart, 1972; Craik & Tulving, 1975), or other methods to provide older adults with support for memory at the encoding stage, can result in smaller age-related differences in their performance compared to young adults (Backman, 1986; Craik & Simon, 1980; Park, Smith, Morrell, Puglisi, & Dudley, 1990).

In terms of retrieval, older individuals have consistently been found to have more severe decrements on memory tasks requiring free recall than those tapping recognition (Craik & McDowd, 1987; Rabinowitz, 1984; Schonfield & Robertson, 1966). This difference may be due to the more effortful nature of recall. Several studies using dual task paradigms have shown that performing a recall task is more detrimental to a concurrent reaction time task in older subjects compared to younger subjects (Craik & McDowd, 1987; Macht & Buschke, 1983). This suggests that older people have greater difficulty in managing tasks requiring greater effort, consistent with the idea that they have a reduction in the cognitive resources necessary for task completion (Craik, 1983, 1986).

As this very brief review makes clear, the work of Gus Craik has been foremost in this field. Recently, functional neuroimaging has become an increasingly popular method to examine age-related changes in memory, and many of the results from these experiments can be viewed in light of some of Craik's ideas about aging and memory. The three aspects that I will discuss are: (a) encoding deficits in age-related memory changes; (b) the reduction with age in processing resources available for cognition; and (c) the effect of levels of processing on memory function.

☐ Effects of Age on Encoding

A number of experiments have examined both encoding and retrieval in elderly adults and have found support for Craik's idea that older individuals are particularly disadvantaged during encoding (Craik & Byrd, 1982). In one such experiment (Grady et al., 1995), young and old participants saw a series of unfamiliar faces, presented one at a time, and were instructed to memorize them. During a later scan they were shown these faces, as well as new faces, and they had to identify the previously learned ones. Young adults showed greater increases of blood flow in the right hippocampal gyrus, left inferior prefrontal cortex, and left temporal cortex during encoding, compared to the older group. In fact, the older adults showed no significant activation in any of these regions during encoding. During recognition of the faces, however, both groups showed activation of the right prefrontal cortex, and young subjects showed activation of parietal cortices as well. These results were consistent with the poorer memory performance in the older people and suggested that reduced face recognition was due in large part to a failure to encode the stimuli adequately. On the other hand, activation in the older participants was not entirely normal during recognition, which could have reflected a specific deficit in retrieval or simply that fewer items were successfully recognized. Thus, the results suggested that reduced activation was more extensive in the elderly during encoding, reflecting a greater problem with the initial stage of memory.

In a more recent experiment, young and old adults were scanned during encoding and retrieval of paired associates (Cabeza et al., 1997). Participants were shown a series of word pairs and were instructed to learn these pairs by making some meaningful association between the words in each pair. In a later condition they were shown the first word in the pair and had to recall the second (cued recall task). In contrast to the study of face memory, the old group was as accurate as the young group during retrieval, most likely because the encoding strategy was equally effective for both groups. However, as in the face memory study, the old adults showed less activation during encoding in the areas that were active in young adults, i.e., left prefrontal and temporal regions. During cued recall of the paired associates, both groups had increased activity in the right prefrontal cortex, indicating again the relatively preserved activity in this region during retrieval in the older adults. Thus, for both verbal and nonverbal memory, older adults have reduced levels of activity in those brain areas that presumably mediate encoding, notably in the prefrontal cortex, but can engage prefrontal regions involved in retrieval relatively normally. Interestingly, the behavioral results of these two studies were different: reduced memory for faces in the elderly but preserved memory for paired associates. This finding is discussed below.

☐ Reduced Processing Resources in the Elderly

Another hypothesis proposed by Craik and his colleagues that has been influential in the field of cognitive aging is that older adults have reduced cognitive resources available to them, which could affect a variety of tasks (Craik & Byrd, 1982). Consistent with this idea, neuroimaging experiments have shown that episodic encoding is not the only effortful cognitive process in which older adults appear to have a reduction in available resources, as indexed by brain activity. Other tasks on which older adults have shown reduced activity include visual perceptual (Grady et al., 1994; Ross et al., 1997) and attention tasks (Madden et al., 1997), where older adults have reduced activity in occipital regions. Reduced activity in the parietal and prefrontal cortex during the Wisconsin Card Sort Task (Esposito, Kirkby, Van Horn, Ellmore, & Berman, 1999; Nagahama et al., 1997), and in the left prefrontal cortex during interference tasks requiring inhibition of prepotent responses (Jonides et al., 2000) also has been reported in older adults. In addition, a recent study of working memory found that older adults had reduced activity in the dorsolateral prefrontal cortex compared to young adults, but only during the period of time in each trial when a response to the probe stimulus was required (Rypma & D'Esposito, 2000). A further example of reduced resources in the elderly in the context of divided attention tasks can be found in chapter 16 of this volume by Anderson.

In contrast to these *reductions* in brain activation, which imply a reduction in processing resources, a number of investigators have now reported *increased* utilization of prefrontal regions by older adults, primarily during memory retrieval. The study of paired-associate memory mentioned above (Cabeza et al., 1997) found that both young and old adults had right prefrontal activity during retrieval, but only the old adults also had left prefrontal activity in this condition. A similar experiment was carried out by Madden and colleagues (1999), who examined encoding and recognition of single words. Young adults had right prefrontal activation during word recognition, whereas the old adults had bilateral prefrontal activation. Backman and colleagues (1997) also reported bilateral prefrontal activation in older adults during cued recall of learned words, compared to right hemisphere activation in young adults. Another experiment (Cabeza, Anderson, Houle, Mangels, & Nyberg, 2000) that examined memory for words as well as the context in which the words were presented found increased activity in both young and old adults in the ventral temporal cortex bilaterally during the item memory conditions and in the parietal and left prefrontal cortices during the temporal order conditions. However, during the item memory condition, the old adults also had increased activity in the left prefrontal cortex, whereas the young adults did not. These experiments, together with the ones examining encoding mentioned above, indicate that older adults do not engage the left prefrontal cortex during encoding, but often do so during retrieval and to a greater extent than do young adults. This suggests that the cognitive processes mediated by the left prefrontal cortex are not necessarily unavailable to the elderly, but they are utilized differently.

Differential utilization of the prefrontal cortex also has been found in short-term or working memory experiments. One such experiment involved short-term recognition of unfamiliar faces using a delayed match-to-sample (DMS) paradigm (Grady et al., 1998). When all the delay conditions were averaged and compared to a baseline condition, both young and old adults had activation of occipitotemporal and prefrontal cortices bilaterally. However, young adults had greater activation of the right ventral prefrontal cortex, and old individuals showed greater activation in the left dorsolateral prefrontal cortex. This study is therefore an interesting example of both reduced use of resources (in right frontal) and increased use of resources (left frontal) in the elderly. Reuter-Lorenz and colleagues (2000) examined working memory for verbal and spatial information. They found that young adults had lateralized prefrontal activity during these tasks, in the left hemisphere during the verbal task and in the right hemisphere during the spatial task. Older adults, on the other hand, had bilateral prefrontal activity during both tasks.

The results of these experiments provide rather dramatic evidence to support Craik's idea that older adults have reduced processing resources under some conditions and further suggest that a response to this reduction might be to increase activation elsewhere, in regions not typically used by young adults for the specific task in question. The obvious question raised by these data is how one should interpret this recruitment of brain activity in the elderly. In some cases this additional activity occurs during a task that the older adults are able to perform normally, leading to the suggestion that recruitment of additional areas is compensatory (Cabeza et al., 1997; Grady et al., 1994). That is, older adults might have reduced processing resources in the form of less brain activity in some task-specific regions but be able to recruit some other areas to compensate for these reduced resources. As a consequence of this compensation, task performance would be maintained. On the other hand, the area most often recruited by older adults is the prefrontal cortex, a region that increases its activity when tasks emphasize executive functions (e.g., D'Esposito et al., 1995; D'Esposito, Postle, Ballard, & Lease, 1999) or become more difficult (e.g., Braver et al., 1997; Grady et al., 1996). It is possible, then, that increased prefrontal activity in the elderly reflects greater need or use of executive functions at lower levels of task demand than would be necessary for activation of this area in young adults. This might be the most likely explanation in those situations where older adults have increased prefrontal activation yet show reduced performance levels compared to younger adults (e.g. Madden, Gottlob et al., 1999).

☐ Effect of Levels of Processing on Memory

The third example of how Craik's work has influenced the neuroimaging field can be found in studies that have used the levels-of-processing manipulation (Craik & Lockhart, 1972) to study brain activity during memory tasks (e.g. Buckner, Koutstaal, Schacter, Wagner, & Rosen, 1998; Nyberg et al., 1995; Rugg et al., 1998). A more recent study examined this manipulation in old as well as young adults. This experiment required participants to encode words and pictures of objects using deep and shallow encoding strategies (Grady, McIntosh, Rajah, Beig, & Craik, 1999). The deep encoding task was a living/nonliving decision, and the shallow task was a size judgment for pictures (large/small) and a case judgment for words (upper/lower). In a third encoding condition, participants were instructed to memorize lists of objects and words (intentional learning). Recognition accuracy was better after deep encoding and memorization compared to shallow encoding in both young and old groups (Table 27.1). There was an age-related decrement in recognition of words, but memory for objects was equivalent in the two groups. Brain activity was analyzed with a multivariate method that identifies patterns of activity across the whole brain, which characterize the different task conditions (partial least squares, McIntosh, Bookstein, Haxby, & Grady, 1996). The predominant brain activity patterns for each stimulus type are shown in Figure 27.1 (see color plate II). There are two aspects of these data that are worth noting. First, the different encoding strategies have distinct effects on brain activity, which are specific to each stimulus type. During object encoding the deeper processing conditions were differentiated from the shallow condition, whereas during word encoding, the most prominent strategy-related difference was between deep encoding and intentional learning. The brain areas that were activated also were distinct. Deeper object encoding was accompanied by a large area of activation in the left lateral prefrontal cortex and in the left inferior temporal regions. Deep word encoding, on the other hand, was associated with activity in the left anterior prefrontal cortex and posterior visual regions near the occipital poles. The second notable aspect of these data is that old and young adults have similar patterns of activity across the encoding conditions. However,

TABLE 27.1. Recognition accuracy (hits–false alarms).

Pictures Encoding Task	Young	Old
Shallow	0.49 ± 0.15	0.41 ± 0.19
Learn	0.68 ± 0.17	0.64 ± 0.21
Deep	0.57 ± 0.21	0.55 ± 0.16

Words Encoding Task	Young	Old
Shallow	0.28 ± 0.23	0.09 ± 0.16
Learn	0.58 ± 0.21	0.42 ± 0.23
Deep	0.55 ± 0.16	0.40 ± 0.20

Note: Data are from Grady et al., 1999.

the strength of the expression of these patterns is reduced in older adults during word encoding, consistent with their reduced memory for words. Thus a levels-of-processing approach to encoding affects both behavior and brain activity in young and old adults in a similar manner, although not necessarily to the same degree.

☐ How Do These Findings Relate to Other Theories of Cognitive Aging?

Up to this point, the results of functional neuroimaging studies have been discussed in relation to Craik's notions about cognitive aging. However, these data also can be viewed in light of other theories about how age affects cognitive processing. One of these theories is that the frontal lobes are particularly vulnerable to the effects of aging. This idea has emerged in part from structural imaging studies, mostly magnetic resonance imaging (MRI) experiments, that have shown age-related loss of brain tissue to be more severe in the frontal lobes than elsewhere in the brain (e.g. Coffey et al., 1992; Raz, 2000). In addition, some behavioral experiments examining memory and other cognitive functions in the elderly have found patterns of deficit that suggest a more pronounced reduction on those tests that rely on the integrity of the frontal lobes (for reviews see Moscovitch & Winocur, 1995; West, 1996). Interestingly, the neuroimaging experiments listed above have shown reductions in the frontal lobe activation in older adults compared to young adults, consistent with the idea that the frontal lobes are vulnerable to the effects of age. However, there also are reports of greater activation in frontal cortex in older individuals during more than one type of cognitive activity, often in the context of equivalent performance between young and old adults. It is difficult to reconcile this type of finding with the idea of particular vulnerability of the frontal lobes, at least if vulnerability is defined in its usual sense as having an increased sensitivity to damage reflected in reduced function. The frontal lobe theory also does not take into account that the prefrontal cortex is made up of a number of distinct functional areas that may be differentially affected by age. In addition, some current concepts of cognition emphasize the involvement of networks of brain areas rather than any one region acting independently (Friston, Frith, Liddle, & Frackowiak, 1993; Horwitz, 1994; McIntosh & Gonzalez-Lima, 1994), suggesting that the frontal lobe theory of aging is too narrowly focused. Perhaps a more broadly conceived notion of an age-related increase in the demand on cognitive networks involving the prefrontal cortex is closer to the complexity revealed by imaging experiments.

Another theory of cognitive aging that has relevance to neuroimaging studies is that of age-related slowing of information processing. Several investigators have suggested that a large proportion of the cognitive changes seen with age can be explained on the basis of slowed processing (Cerella, 1985; Salthouse, 1991; Salthouse, Fristoe, & Rhee, 1996). Similar to the frontal lobe theory, the neuroimaging results do not fall easily into this framework. For example, increased activity in the prefrontal cortex has been associated with both increased and decreased response times in both young and old adults. In the study of working memory for faces described above, increased activity in the prefrontal regions was associated with reduced response times in young adults and increased times in older adults (Grady et al., 1998). In contrast, the study reported by Rypma and D'Esposito (2000) found just the opposite, that increases in prefrontal activity were correlated with reduced response times in the elderly and increased times in younger adults. In addition, older adults routinely have longer response times on almost every task yet show a wide range of brain activity differences, from reduced activity to greater activity, depending on the specific task. Thus, it is difficult to explain the imaging results in terms of a single mechanism of cognitive slowing that presumably would affect all processes in the same manner.

A third theory of cognitive aging is that of altered inhibitory processes as suggested by Zacks and Hasher (1988). If older adults have reduced inhibition, then one might expect to see reduced activity in those brain areas that usually inhibit and increased activity in those areas that are normally inhibited. Since the prefrontal cortex has the capacity to inhibit thalamically driven activity in other cortical areas via its connections with the basal ganglia (Feifel, 1999), one might expect that reduced inhibition in the elderly would be accompanied by reduced activity in the frontal cortex. While there is evidence that this may indeed occur under some conditions (Jonides et al., 2000), it is harder to account for increased prefrontal activity in the elderly using this conception of the inhibitory model of aging. On the other hand, one could argue that the reduced activity in the visual cortex seen in older adults during a task involving visual search for a target among distractors (Madden et al., 1997) leads to a reduction in the ability to focus on specific visual stimuli and an increase in the salience of distracting stimuli. In this case, increased activity in the prefrontal cortex of older adults, also found in the Madden et al. (1997) study, could reflect an increase in the inhibitory function of this area to refocus attention appropriately. Thus, neuroimaging results are consistent with the idea of altered inhibition in the elderly, but the mechanism of this effect depends on how one thinks about inhibition. Clearly, our current knowledge of inhibition on both the neural and behavioral levels is insufficient to adequately address this issue as it applies to aging and brain activity.

☐ Conclusions

The neuroimaging experiments discussed here provide ample evidence that older people can be readily distinguished from young people in terms of brain activity during cognitive tasks, even when performing the task at the same level of proficiency. Many of Craik's ideas about aging and memory have been supported by the results of these experiments, but there have also been surprises. Perhaps the most interesting of these surprises is that older adults appear able, under some conditions, to recruit new areas into their cognitive networks, which may indicate that an age-related compensatory mechanism is at work. However, in some cases, older adults show recruitment of different brain areas but nevertheless have reduced performance, indicating that our knowledge of the brain mechanisms underlying age-related changes in cognition is far from complete. Nevertheless, it seems clear that if we continue to explore age-related changes in brain activity in light of Craik's theories of cognitive aging, the future holds still more interesting and useful discoveries.

☐ Acknowledgments

This work was supported in part by the Canadian Institutes for Health Research (MOP14036).

☐ References

Backman, L. (1986). Adult age differences in cross-modal recoding and mental tempo, and older adults' utilization of compensatory task conditions. *Experimental Aging Research, 12*, 135–140.

Backman, L., Almkvist, O., Andersson, J., Nordberg, A., Winblad, B., Reineck, R., & Langstrom, B. (1997). Brain activation in young and older adults during implicit and explicit retrieval. *Journal of Cognitive Neuroscience, 9*, 378–391.

Braver, T. S., Cohen, J. D., Nystrom, L. E., Jonides, J., Smith, E. E., & Noll, D. C. (1997). A parametric study of prefrontal cortex involvement in human working memory. *NeuroImage, 5*, 49–62.

Buckner, R. L., Koutstaal, W., Schacter, D. L., Wagner, A. D., & Rosen, B. R. (1998). Functional-anatomic study of episodic retrieval using fMRI. I. Retrieval effort versus retrieval success. *NeuroImage, 7*, 151–162.

Burke, D. M., & Light, L. L. (1981). Memory and aging: The role of retrieval processes. *Psychological Bulletin, 90*, 513–546.

Cabeza, R., Anderson, N. D., Houle, S., Mangels, J. A., & Nyberg, L. (2000). Age-related differences in neural activity during item and temporal-order memory retrieval: a positron emission tomography study. *Journal of Cognitive Neuroscience, 12*(1), 197–206.

Cabeza, R., Grady, C. L., Nyberg, L., McIntosh, A. R., Tulving, E., Kapur, S., Jennings, J. M., Houle, S., & Craik, F. I. M. (1997). Age-related differences in neural activity during memory encoding and retrieval: A positron emission tomography study. *Journal of Neuroscience, 17*, 391–400.

Cerella, J. (1985). Information processing rates in the elderly. *Psychological Bulletin, 98*, 67–83.

Coffey, C. E., Wilkinson, W. E., Parashos, I. A., Soady, S. A., Sullivan, R. J., Patterson, L. J., Figiel, G. S., Webb, M. C., Spritzer, C. E., & Djang, W. T. (1992). Quantitative cerebral anatomy of the aging human brain: A cross-sectional study using magnetic resonance imaging. *Neurology, 42*, 527–536.

Craik, F. I. M. (1983). On the transfer of information from temporary to permanent memory. *Philosophical Transactions of the Royal Society of London (Series B), 302*, 341–359.

Craik, F. I. M. (1986). A functional account of age differences in memory. In F. Klix & H. Hagendorf (Eds.), *Human memory and cognitive capabilities: Mechanisms and performances* (pp. 403–422). Amsterdam: Elsevier Science.

Craik, F. I. M., & Byrd, M. (1982). Aging and cognitive deficits: The role of attentional resources. In F. I. M. Craik & S. Trehub (Eds.), *Aging and cognitive processes* (pp. 191–211). New York: Plenum Press.

Craik, F. I. M., & Lockhart, R. S. (1972). Levels of processing: A framework for memory research. *Journal of Verbal Learning and Verbal Behavior, 11*, 671–684.

Craik, F. I. M., & McDowd, J. M. (1987). Age differences in recall and recognition. *Journal of Experimental Psychology: Learning, Memory and Cognition, 13*, 474–479.

Craik, F. I. M., & Simon, E. (1980). Age differences in memory: The roles of attention and depth of processing. In L. W. Poon, J. L. Fozard, L. Cermak, D. Arenberg, & L. W. Thompson (Eds.), *New directions in memory and aging: Proceedings of the George Talland memorial conference* (pp. 95–112). Hillsdale, NJ: Erlbaum.

Craik, F. I. M., & Tulving, E. (1975). Depth of processing and the retention of words in episodic memory. *Journal of Experimental Psychology: General, 104*, 268–294.

D'Esposito, M., Detre, J. A., Alsop, D. C., Shin, R. K., Atlas, S., & Grossman, M. (1995). The neural basis of the central executive system of working memory. *Nature, 378,* 279–281.

D'Esposito, M., Postle, B. R., Ballard, D., & Lease, J. (1999). Maintenance versus manipulation of information held in working memory: An event-related fMRI study. *Brain and Cognition, 41,* 66–86.

Esposito, G., Kirkby, B. S., Van Horn, J. D., Ellmore, T. M., & Berman, K. F. (1999). Context-dependent, neural system-specific neurophysiological concomitants of ageing: Mapping PET correlates during cognitive activation. *Brain, 122,* 963–979.

Feifel, D. (1999). Neurotransmitters and neuromodulators in frontal-subcortical circuits. In B. L. Miller & J. L. Cummings (Eds.), *The human frontal lobes* (pp. 174–186). New York: Guilford Press.

Friston, K. J., Frith, C. D., Liddle, P. F., & Frackowiak, R. S. J. (1993). Functional connectivity: the principal-component analysis of large (PET) data sets. *Journal Cerebral Blood Flow and Metabolism, 13,* 5–14.

Grady, C. L., Horwitz, B., Pietrini, P., Mentis, M. J., Ungerleider, L. G., Rapoport, S. I., & Haxby, J. V. (1996). The effect of task difficulty on cerebral blood flow during perceptual matching of faces. *Human Brain Mapping, 4,* 227–239.

Grady, C. L., Maisog, J. M., Horwitz, B., Ungerleider, L. G., Mentis, M. J., Salerno, J. A., Pietrini, P., Wagner, E., & Haxby, J. V. (1994). Age-related changes in cortical blood flow activation during visual processing of faces and location. *Journal of Neuroscience, 14,* 1450–1462.

Grady, C. L., McIntosh, A. R., Bookstein, F., Horwitz, B., Rapoport, S. I., & Haxby, J. V. (1998). Age-related changes in regional cerebral blood flow during working memory for faces. *NeuroImage, 8,* 409–425.

Grady, C. L., McIntosh, A. R., Horwitz, B., Maisog, J. M., Ungerleider, L. G., Mentis, M. J., Pietrini, P., Schapiro, M. B., & Haxby, J. V. (1995). Age-related reductions in human recognition memory due to impaired encoding. *Science, 269,* 218–221.

Grady, C. L., McIntosh, A. R., Rajah, M. N., Beig, S., & Craik, F. I. M. (1999). The effects of age on the neural correlates of episodic encoding. *Cerebral Cortex, 9,* 805–814.

Horwitz, B. (1994). Data analysis paradigms for metabolic-flow data: Combining neural modeling and functional neuroimaging. *Human Brain Mapping, 2,* 112–122.

Hultsch, D. F. (1969). Adult age differences in the organization of free recall. *Developmental Psychology, 1,* 673–678.

Jonides, J., Marshuetz, C., Smith, E. E., Reuter-Lorenz, P. A., Koeppe, R. A., & Hartley, A. (2000). Age differences in behavior and PET activation reveal differences in interference resolution in verbal working memory. *Journal of Cognitive of Neuroscience, 12*(1), 188–196.

Macht, M. L., & Buschke, H. (1983). Age differences in cognitive effort in recall. *Journal of Gerontology, 38,* 695–700.

Madden, D. J., Turkington, T. G., Provenzale, J. M., Denny, L. L., Hawk, T. C., Gottlob, L. R., & Coleman, R. E. (1999). Adult age differences in the functional neuroanatomy of verbal recognition memory. *Human Brain Mapping, 7,* 115–135.

Madden, D. J., Turkington, T. G., Provenzale, J. M., Hawk, T. C., Hoffman, J. M., & Coleman, R. E. (1997). Selective and divided visual attention: Age-related changes in regional cerebral blood flow measured by $H_2^{15}O$ PET. *Human Brain Mapping, 5,* 389–409.

McIntosh, A. R., Bookstein, F. L., Haxby, J. V., & Grady, C. L. (1996). Spatial pattern analysis of functional brain images using Partial Least Squares. *NeuroImage, 3,* 143–157.

McIntosh, A. R., & Gonzalez-Lima, F. (1994). Structural equation modeling and its application to network analysis in functional brain imaging. *Human Brain Mapping, 2,* 2–22.

Moscovitch, M., & Winocur, G. (1995). Frontal lobes, memory, and aging. *Annals of New York Academy of Sciences, 769,* 119–150.

Nagahama, Y., Fukuyama, H., Yamauchi, H., Katsumi, Y., Magata, Y., Shibasaki, H., & Kimura, J. (1997). Age-related changes in cerebral blood flow activation during a card sorting test. *Experimental Brain Research, 114,* 571–577.

Nyberg, L., Tulving, E., Habib, R., Nilsson, L.-G., Kapur, S., Houle, S., Cabeza, R., & McIntosh, A. R. (1995). Functional brain maps of retrieval mode and recovery of episodic information. *NeuroReport, 7,* 249–252.

Park, D. C., Smith, A. D., Morrell, R. W., Puglisi, J. T., & Dudley, W. N. (1990). Effects of contextual integration on recall of pictures by older adults. *Journal of Gerontology, 45,* P52–P57.

Rabinowitz, J. C. (1984). Aging and recognition failure. *Journal of Gerontology, 39,* 65–71.

Raz, N. (2000). Aging of the brain and its impact on cognitive performance: Integration of structural and functional findings. In F. I. M. Craik & T. A. Salthouse (Eds.), *Handbook of Aging and Cognition - II.* Mahwah, NJ: Erlbaum.

Reuter-Lorenz, P. A., Jonides, J., Smith, E. E., Hartley, A., Miller, A., Marshuetz, C., & Koeppe, R. A. (2000). Age differences in the frontal lateralization of verbal and spatial working memory revealed by PET. *Journal of Cognitive Neuroscience, 12*(1), 174–187.

Ross, M. H., Yurgelun-Todd, D. A., Renshaw, P. F., Maas, L. C., Mendelson, J. H., Mello, N. K., Cohen, B. M., & Levin, J. M. (1997). Age-related reduction in functional MRI response to photic stimulation. *Neurology, 48,* 173–176.

Rugg, M. D., Walla, P., Schloerscheidt, A. M., Fletcher, P. C., Frith, C. D., & Dolan, R. J. (1998). Neural correlates of depth of processing effects on recollection: Evidence from brain potentials and positron emission tomography. *Experimental Brain Research, 123,* 18–23.

Rypma, B., & D'Esposito, M. (2000). Isolating the neural mechanisms of age-related changes in human working memory. *Nature Neuroscience, 3*(5), 509–515.

Salthouse, T. A. (1991). *Theoretical perspectives on cognitive aging.* Hillsdale, NJ: Erlbaum.

Salthouse, T. A., Fristoe, N., & Rhee, S. H. (1996). How localized are age-related effects on neuropsychological measures? *Neuropsychology, 10,* 272–285.

Sanders, R. E., Murphy, M. D., Schmitt, F. A., & Walsh, K. K. (1980). Age differences in free recall rehearsal strategies. *Journal of Gerontology, 35,* 550–558.

Schonfield, D., & Robertson, B. A. (1966). Memory storage and aging. *Canadian Journal of Psychology, 20,* 228–236.

Tulving, E. (1983). *Elements of Episodic Memory.* New York: Oxford University Press.

West, R. L. (1996). An application of prefrontal cortex function theory to cognitive aging. *Psychological Bulletin, 120,* 272–292.

Zacks, R. T., & Hasher, L. (1988). Capacity theory and the processing of inferences. In L. L. Light & D. M. Burke (Eds.), *Language, memory and aging* (pp. 154–170). New York: Cambridge University Press.

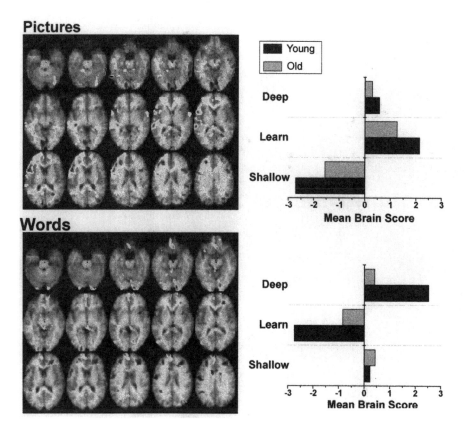

FIGURE 27.1 (See Color Plate II). Areas of differential blood flow during picture and word encoding carried out using three different strategies (Grady et al., 1999). Areas are shown on magnetic resonance imaging (MRI) templates. Levels relative to the intercommissural line are from –28 mm (top left of images) to +40 mm (bottom right of images). Regions shown in yellow/red have increased activity in those conditions where the mean brain scores (shown in graphs on the right of the figure) are positive. Regions shown in blue have increased activity in those conditions where the mean brain scores are negative. Thus, during both deep picture and deep word encoding, activity was increased in the yellow/red areas seen in the images.

28

CHAPTER

Donald T. Stuss
Malcolm A. Binns

Aging: Not an Escarpment, But Many Different Slopes

One of the major gifts Fergus Craik has given to neuropsychologists, and neuropsychological research, is the lesson that processing and processing capacity are important concepts for understanding changes in memory. A second benefit is the application of this approach to the study of aging. In the latter area, Craik (among others) has emphasized the critical role of the frontal lobes in at least some of the cognitive changes that occur with aging (e.g., Craik, Morris, Morris, & Loewen, 1990; McIntyre & Craik, 1987; Moscovitch & Winocur, 1992; Stuss, Craik, Sayer, Franchi, & Alexander, 1996; R. L. West, 1996). We extended this approach by assessing whether recent findings of fractionation of frontal lobe processes could be used to define further the pattern, or patterns, of cognitive changes with aging.

☐ Hypotheses

A Global Hypothesis

A working hypothesis to explain the pattern of cognitive aging is that the profiles of the various changes resemble a slope more closely than an escarpment. That is, there is not some abrupt temporal brim after which processes change; the transition is more gradual. Evidence for such an hypothesis derives from the important research of Salthouse (chapter 22 of this volume), Park and Hedden (chapter 12 of this volume), and others on cognitive changes with aging. For example, full-scale IQ seems to decline gradually over time (Doppelt & Wallace, 1955). This "decline hypothesis" was strongly stated by Wechsler (1958), who suggested that there is a progressive deterioration in most human abilities after approximately age 25. Indeed, age changes in digit symbol do not start at 70, but at 25 (Salthouse, 1992). This linearly increasing effect of aging is evident with neurophysiological measures. In a study using the detection of "oddball" (infrequent target among nontarget) stimuli, Picton, Stuss, Champagne, and Nelson (1984) reported a linear decrease in P300 amplitude and increase in P300 latency starting in young adulthood.

The argument of a gradual decline with aging is buttressed by research on the interaction of aging with neurological disease. This was evidenced in a study of a cognitive change associated with Parkinson's disease called "bradyphrenia," or increased mental slowing (Lafleche, Stuss, Nelson, & Picton, 1990). When patients with Parkinson's disease were studied on the Sternberg memory search task, a general slowing was noted, but there was no significant difference from a control group in the slope of the memory retrieval function related to the number of items in memory storage. That is, there was no "mental" slowing; the results could be explained by motor dysfunction. However, when patients with similar levels of severity of Parkinson's disease were divided according to their chronological age, bradyphrenia was more notable in the older patients. Age appeared to interact with the neurological disease.

The idea of an interaction between age and neurological dysfunction revealing cognitive decline was investigated more directly in a study of the effects of traumatic brain injury. We examined what factors were important in predicting when a patient with traumatic brain injury would be able to recall correctly three words after a 24-hour delay (Stuss, Binns et al., 2000). Patients ranging in age from 16 to 65, with head injuries of varying severity, were examined daily until they had achieved this level of performance. Several factors, including age, were investigated for their value in predicting recovery of continuous memory. We had anticipated, based on previous literature (Katz & Alexander, 1994), that the effect of age would be somewhat dichotomous, with age having an effect on the speed of recovery only after middle age. While the number of subjects in our study was weighted toward the younger group, the definite linear trend illustrated in Figure 28.1 suggests that time to recovery of this seemingly simple ability was directly related to the age of the individual even from young adulthood.

The examples from the neurological literature are drawn from populations with diffuse

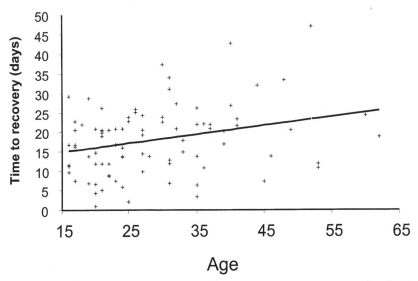

FIGURE 28.1. Changes in time to recovery of continuous memory, measured as the ability to recall three words after a 24-hour delay, was partially attributable to an effect of age in individuals who had suffered various degrees of severity of traumatic brain injury. There was a linear increase in the time to recovery of about two days per decade conditional on injury severity. Age affected recovery of memory even in young adulthood.

brain pathology. Biological evidence suggests that normal aging is associated with diffuse brain dysfunction. For example, there is a linear age-related decline in brain weight and volume, as well as blood flow (see Raz, 2000, for review). Therefore, both biological and psychological evidence support the hypothesis that some cognitive functions decline gradually starting in young adulthood, and that this gradual decline interacts with diffuse neurological damage. This notion of a gradual decline is, however, likely an oversimplification.

A Refinement of the Hypothesis

Several sources of information imply a refinement of the hypothesis of the pattern of cognitive changes with aging, a pattern that is not an escarpment, not even a slope, but possibly many slopes of different trajectories related to different functions. In addition to the gradual progressive decline described above, a "no decline" profile of certain abilities has been reported (Botwinick, 1977). Research using the Primary Abilities test indicated a different profile: no age decline from age 20 to 50 years, with a relatively systematic drop after age 50 (Schaie, 1958). A "terminal drop" has also been described, in which certain abilities such as vocabulary decrease in the period prior to death (White & Cunningham, 1988). Biological studies provide further evidence of different patterns of biological changes: "Against the backdrop of generalized age-related deterioration, numerous differential changes loom, like multiple islands of relative preservation and decline" (Raz, 2000, p. 13).

One possible reason for distinct patterns derives from the different functions measured (Botwinick, 1977). For example, tests that do not change with age typically involve verbal functions, while perceptual-motor and speed tests tend to fall with age. Another possible hypothesis, as Craik and others have argued, is based on the role that the frontal lobes play in cognitive changes with aging. The multiple slopes might relate to the different functions of the frontal lobes. A brief review of more recent findings of frontal lobe anatomy and functions is presented as supporting evidence.

The frontal lobes in general appear to show greater age-related reductions in volume and resting cerebral blood flow than most other cortical regions (Raz et al., 1997; Shaw et al., 1984). The frontal lobes are, however, anatomically heterogeneous, with architectonic specificity (Petrides & Pandya, 1994) as well as distinct connectivity to other brain regions (Pandya & Barnes, 1987), strongly implying functional differences within the frontal lobes. The known specificity of the various dopamine systems and changes with aging also imply a potential regional specificity in function (Arnsten, 1999).

This biological diversity is reflected in functional distinctiveness within the frontal lobes (Shallice & Burgess, 1991; Stuss & Benson, 1986). Functional heterogeneity has been documented in animal research (Goldman-Rakic, 1993; Fuster, 1997; Petrides, 1994), human imaging research (D'Esposito, Postle, & Rypma, 2000; Kapur et al., 1994; Tulving, Kapur, Craik, Moscovitch, & Houle, 1994), and neuropsychological studies of frontal lobe–damaged humans (for reviews, see Alexander & Stuss, 2000; Stuss & Alexander, 1994, 2000b; Stuss, Eskes, & Foster, 1994). The evidence from focal lesion studies provides the most compelling evidence of this functional heterogeneity. Different cognitive processes identified in various neuropsychological tasks are related to distinct frontal lobe regions. For example, in a study of word-list learning, frontal lesions in the left dorsolateral and inferior medial-septal regions resulted in an encoding deficit, while right frontal lesions revealed problems in retrieval consistency and monitoring (Stuss, Alexander, et al., 1994). Problems in shifting concepts were caused not only by lesions in left and right dorsolateral areas, but also by superior medial damage; patients with inferior medial damage had no problems with cognitive shifting, but did have difficulty staying on task (Stuss, Levine, et al., 2000). Damage to the left dorsolateral and superior medial regions affected the ability to generate words in a semantic category or beginning with a specific letter. Right dorsolateral damage, on the other hand, significantly affected only semantic generation (Stuss et al., 1998). In a simple spatial location identity test, three different attentional measures were affected by different frontal brain regions: presence of distracting stimuli—bilateral and right frontal; negative priming—right frontal; inhibition of return—left frontal (Stuss et al., 1999). Humor appreciation and self-awareness have been associated with right frontal lobe functions (Shammi & Stuss, 1999; Stuss & Alexander, 1999, 2000a, 2000b; Wheeler, Stuss, & Tulving, 1997). Strategy application in unstructured tasks appeared most sensitive to inferior medial frontal and right hemisphere lesions (Levine et al., 1998).

There has also been some evidence that frontal or executive functions are among the first, if not the first, to deteriorate with aging (Raz, 2000). Three possibilities of the effect of aging on these functions exist: (a) all frontal functions start to change at approximately the same time and decline at a similar rate, (b) different functions start to decline at various times; (c) independent functions deteriorate at different rates. The early developmental literature strongly suggests that frontal, or executive, functions phase in differentially over time (Smith, Kates, & Vriezen, 1992; Stuss, 1992). One might also hypothesize, then, that distinct frontal lobe abilities (as well as others) phase out differentially with increasing age.

The aim is not to relate cognitive decline in aging to specific frontal regions. At this early stage, the objective is to use the knowledge of frontal lobe functional heterogeneity to assess whether different classes of behavioral profiles of separate frontal functions may help us to understand cognitive aging.

☐ Profile Classification

We propose four basic profiles of change that might occur in cognitive functions during the aging process. These profiles, depicted in Figure 28.2, are not quantitative. They are

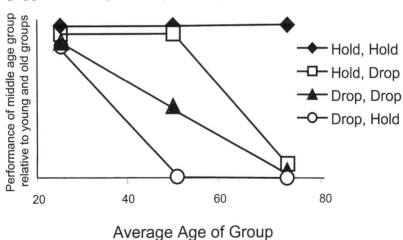

FIGURE 28.2. Four potential profiles of performance are suggested as templates for differential patterns of changes in cognitive processes with aging. The abscissa indicates increasing age from 20 to 80 years. The three points in each profile indicate performance of three age groups, defined globally as young adulthood (average age approximately 22–29), middle age (40–55), and older age (around 60–72). The ordinate is relative and not a quantitative index, with the top indicating performance of the young group on any task. The bottom of the scale indicates significant impairment in the older group. The rest of the scale suggests intermediate levels of change in performance of the middle age group.

hypothesized schematic profiles of functions across three age groups: young adulthood (approximate age range 20–40), middle age (40–60), and older age (60–80). Performance of the younger group was chosen as the benchmark against which the performance of the older group was compared. All profiles, therefore, start with the performance of the young group at the top of the graph. The older group's performance anchors the other end of the profile with performance depicted at the bottom of the graph if it is significantly impaired relative to the young group, and at the top of the graph if it is normal. The vertical location of the middle-aged group is determined by their average performance relative to the average performances of both the younger and older groups. A "hold–hold" profile represents no detectable change in function between the young and older groups. A "hold–drop" profile would represent maintenance of performance through middle age, with a decrease in the older group. A "drop–drop" profile depicts lower performance in the middle age group, with further deterioration in performance in the older group. Profiles clearly could have different slopes depending on the relative change in the middle age group. Finally, a "drop-hold" profile would indicate lower performance in the middle group, with relatively consistent performance from middle to older age.

☐   Evidence for the Profiles

If frontal lobe functions have been demonstrated to be dissociable using a particular task, then an aging study using the same task would seem to be a reasonable way to test our hypothesized profiles. We reviewed our past studies on "frontal lobe" tests on which we had data on the three modal age groups (most studies had 20 subjects per group) to see if there was some supportive evidence for our model.

We first examined set shifting processes. Problems in shifting as one ages have been reported (Haaland, Vranes, Goodwin, & Garry, 1987), but there are different types of shifting (e.g., Dias, Robbins, & Roberts, 1997). We examined how our identified patterns of change might apply to different types of shifts, those that are required by the Wisconsin Card Sorting Test (WCST) and those that are required by the Trail Making Test (TMT) Part B. The WCST is preferentially sensitive to frontal lobe pathology if compared to posterior patients who do not have significant neglect or comprehension deficits (Stuss, Levine et al., 2000). In the WCST, the subject must learn, by trial and error based on feedback from the examiner, to sort a deck of cards by one of three criteria. After 10 consecutive sorts, the examiner alters the sorting criterion simply by indicating that any responses based on the previous criterion are now wrong. The subject must change his or her set and develop new hypotheses to test. The number of sorting categories achieved provides one index of set shifting abilities. Potential reasons for any difficulty, in addition to problems in learning the criterion, are revealed in other measures, such as losing set after a correct shift has been made, or perseverating on the previous sorting criterion.

Different measures in the WCST revealed different profiles of change with aging (Levine, Stuss, & Milberg, 1995; see Figure 28.3, top). The older group achieved significantly fewer categories than the young group. At the same time, older individuals lost set more often (i.e., made errors after they apparently had achieved the correct sorting criterion) and tended to perseverate on the previously correct response category. The old age end of the profile for perseverations is not anchored at normal or impaired since the reported statistical evidence for impairment is inconclusive.

Another task requiring shifting, and sometimes related to the frontal lobes, is the TMT. In Part A, the subject must rapidly draw a line joining, in numerical order, numbered circles (1 to 13) pseudorandomly arranged on a page. In Part B, numbers from 1 to 13 and

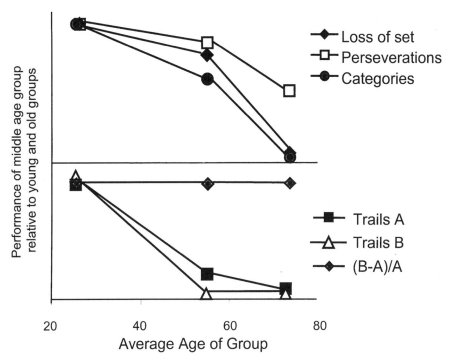

FIGURE 28.3. The three age groups are as defined in Figure 28.2. Top: Measures from the WCST are presented: loss of set—the occurrence of an erroneous response after at least 3 consecutively correct responses, one of which is unambiguous (that is, a single criterion matching); perseverations—an erroneous response based on the previous response criterion; categories—the number of correct sorting changes made, defined as the number of times 10 consecutive correct responses in a row were made. Bottom: A comparison of the three age groups on the time to completion of the TMT is depicted. While both Trails A and B suggest a drop-hold profile, the proportional time score of B relative to A (time to complete Part B minus time for Part A over time for Part A) indicates a hold-hold profile.

letters from A to L are also pseudorandomly arranged on a page, and the subject is required to join numbers and letters in alternating sequential order (1-A-2-B-3 . . .). Several different processes are required for both measures, including rapid visual-motor coordination and visual search (Crowe, 1998). Part B has an added demand of switching between numbers and letters. Total time to complete each task is the common mode of measurement. Both Parts A and B of the TMT followed a drop–hold pattern, suggesting that whatever problems this test elicited were evident by middle age (see Figure 28.3, bottom). However, to isolate the shifting demands of Part B independent of visual search, rapid motor responses, and other processes common to both tasks, the increased time to complete B was taken as a ratio of A (i.e., (B-A)/A). When this was estimated, a hold–hold pattern was revealed (see Figure 28.3, bottom). That is, with increasing age, there was no independent shifting impairment on Part B of the TMT. The age decline elicited by the TMT can be reduced to more basic processes. The WCST and TMT Part B have different set shifting demands, and the shifting requirements of the WCST are more sensitive to aging. Part B of the TMT may be less reactive to aging because it requires shifting between two overlearned response patterns, both of which are continually relevant. The WCST, on the other hand, requires the ability to abstract rules, keep track of past sorts, reject the previous relevant sorting criterion, and select a criterion that had previously been irrelevant (Elliott, McKenna, Robbins, & Sahakian, 1995).

Another example of our approach derives from the theoretical notion that the frontal lobes are necessary when tasks are complex (Shallice, 1988; Stuss & Benson, 1986) and from the findings that this brain region is more sensitive to distracting information (Chao & Knight, 1995). A reaction time (RT) paradigm was devised to explore the effects of distractibility and increasing complexity in feature integration and detection at different ages (Stuss, Stethem, Picton, Leech, & Pelchat, 1989). A simple RT condition, in which one symbolic shape was presented repeatedly, was followed by an easy feature detection task requiring a dominant hand response to one defined target shape (e.g., a cross) and a nondominant hand response to three other shapes. Complexity was then increased by having three features define the target, such as a blue circle with horizontal lines in the shape, all other stimuli having 0, 1, or 2 features in common with the target (complex RT). In a fourth "redundant" condition, three features defined the target shape, but there were no common features in the nontargets. In essence, then, one feature out of the three could be used to identify the target, and the other two bits of information were unnecessary, with the potential to be distracting.

The RT performance profiles on these four conditions for the three age groups are depicted in Figure 28.4. Simple RT performance was not significantly different between the young and old groups. The older group was significantly impaired in both the complex and redundant conditions, and borderline deficient in the easy RT condition. In the complex task, the middle age group showed about 30% of the age-related slowing of the older group. In other words, different task demands revealed different RT profiles: Simple RT was hold–hold; easy RT was hold–drop (borderline); redundant RT was hold–drop; complex RT was drop–drop.

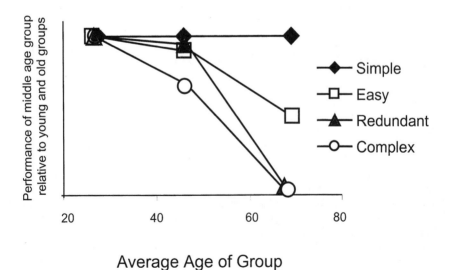

FIGURE 28.4. Four different reaction time conditions are compared across the three age groups (defined as in Figure 28.2). The four conditions are described in the text.

Both medial temporal and frontal lobe functions decline with aging (Moscovitch & Winocur, 1992; Winocur, 1992; Winocur, Moscovitch, & Stuss, 1996). Our approach enables us to address the relative changes of these functions with age. We (Stuss et al., 1996) compared three age groups on the same word-list learning task that had been used previously to assess functional specificity in patients with focal frontal lobe lesions (Stuss, Alexander, et al., 1994). We also assessed other abilities in the same subjects. Figure 28.5, top, illustrates that the NART IQ scores and performance on the Boston Naming Test were not significantly different between young and old groups (hold–hold), demonstrating the high level of functioning in the older group. Two other language tasks revealed different profiles. On phonological fluency (generation of as many words as possible beginning with a defined letter), there was a drop–hold pattern. The older group was significantly different from the young group, and the middle age group was at least as impaired as the older age group. Semantic fluency (generation of animal names) was impaired in the older group, with an impairment about half as large in the middle group (drop–drop). Phonological fluency has been associated with left dorsolateral and superior medial frontal pathology (as well as other areas). Semantic fluency has demonstrated less specificity within the frontal lobes (Stuss et al., 1998).

For the word-list learning test, we compared two measures that were hypothesized to be dependent on different mechanisms and brain regions. Secondary memory (SM), defined as the recall of a word from the list if eight or more words intervened between presenta-

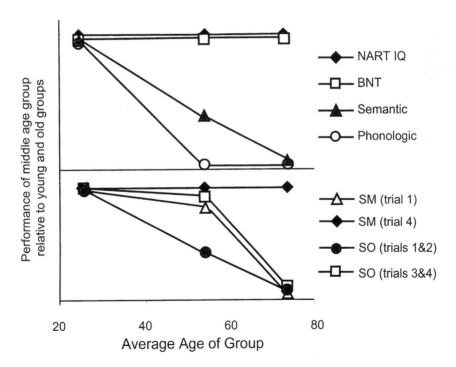

FIGURE 28.5. The three age groups (see Figure 28.2) are compared on different measures of intelligence and language (top), and a word-list memory task with four trials (bottom: SM: secondary memory; SO: subjective organization). The different measures in the same individuals reveal different profiles of performance related to age.

tion and recall, is typically considered a measure of medial temporal lobe memory (Winocur et al., 1996). One additional contributor to the SM deficit in older individuals could be a deficiency in the ability to impose self-initiated strategic retrieval (Craik, 1983), a "working with memory" problem (Moscovitch & Winocur, 1992) that is compatible with frontal lobe dysfunction. Subjective organization (SO), defined as the recall of two words together in one trial that were successfully recalled together in the immediately following trial, has been shown to be related to the frontal lobes (Stuss, Alexander, et al., 1994). This SO measure would reflect self-initiated strategic retrieval. By analyzing SM and SO separately over the learning trials in the different age groups, a potential dissociation of the medial temporal/hippocampal and frontal contributions may be possible.

The same list of words was given for four successive trials, with immediate recall tested after each trial. SM scores were obtained from trials 1 and 4. For SO, the first score relates to the SO between trials 1 and 2, and the second score between trials 3 and 4. Different profiles for the two measures were evident (Figure 28.5, bottom). The middle age group performed more similarly to the young group for both SM measures. For the older group, SM was impaired on the first trial, but by the fourth trial, the SM score of this older group was not significantly different from the young group. For SM, therefore, there is a hold–drop pattern for trial 1 and a hold–hold profile for trial 4. A different pattern was revealed on the SO measure. For the SO measures from the trial 1–2 comparison, there is a drop–drop pattern. That is, the older group was significantly impaired, and the performance of the middle group fell midway between the young and old groups. For the SO comparing trials 3 and 4, the pattern is more hold and drop. There are comparative profile differences for the various measures, although some ceiling effect in the younger group may have minimized the age effect.

☐ Implications

The brain and its functions age globally as well as differentially (Raz, 2000). Emphasis on the commonality of variance in function would likely reflect the more global changes. A focus on the separation of processes has suggested that distinct processes that have been associated with the frontal lobes appear to change at different maturational times. Although there is surely individual variation, there appears to be some group commonality in the profile, analogous to the commonality and differences reported in the childhood maturation of these processes. There are several implications of our approach.

Our motivation to use this approach derived from the evidence of anatomical and functional heterogeneity within the frontal lobes as indicated in focal lesion studies. Is it possible, then, to infer from our findings of the decline of different functions at different times in aging that specific regions within the frontal lobes also deteriorate at different times? Such a claim is not warranted at present. Frontal lobe or executive functions may also be disrupted for reasons other than focal brain damage, for example, by general brain deterioration and by factors such as pain and sleep disturbance (Goldberg & Bilder, 1987; Herscovitch, Stuss, & Broughton, 1980). Nevertheless, both our approach and work with animals relating specific behavioral impairments to distinct anatomical locations in the frontal lobes and different neurotransmitter systems (Arnsten, 1999; Petrides, 1994) support this as a potential research goal. Functional imaging would be the experimental method of choice to test this hypothesis (e.g., McIntosh, Sekuler et al., 1999).

Can some indication be gleaned from our data as to which functions deteriorate and which don't? The hold–hold profile, as noted in many earlier studies, is most common for "crystallized" functions, such as general verbal intellectual functioning, basic semantic knowledge, and simple motor speed measures. The drop–hold, indicating notable difficulties on the task as early as middle age, appears to be more related to tasks requiring speeded sustained response (phonological fluency, TMT Parts A and B). This profile, however, may be confounded by our method of establishing the profiles. In addition to changes in speeded responses, tasks requiring some level of top-down strategic influences, as measured by subjective organization, complex RT, and semantic fluency, also start to reveal deficiencies by middle age, with a drop–drop profile. Further clarification of the relation of specific processes to our hypothesized profiles of change requires a more controlled investigation.

A second implication relates to the use of different measures in memory tests to dissociate further the role of frontal or medial/temporal biological changes and the subsequent behavioral consequences. Such dissociations would have significant application to the rehabilitation of cognitive processes in aging, for *both* the middle and older groups. For example, the comparative profiles of performance for different types of shifting indicate that set shifting is impaired under certain task demands or conditions. Analogous to Craik's emphasis on environmental support to minimize impaired functioning (Craik, 1983, 1986), ability to shift is less affected when the task is constrained by having the subjects alternate between two overlearned tasks.

The SM/SO results in the memory study provide another example. SM is quite vulnerable to aging. However, this measure may reflect the input of two anatomical areas and different processes: medial temporal/hippocampal areas for the "binding" aspect of encoding, as well as self-initiated strategic retrieval associated with the frontal lobes. For the older group in the first trial, SM and SO are impaired. By the fourth trial, SO is impaired but SM is at least relatively intact. This implies some level of intact medial temporal ability in this high-functioning group, despite their deficiency in imposing top-down strategic retrieval. Several hypotheses for this relatively preserved performance in SM for the older group can be proposed: a limited effect of aging on medial temporal lobe regions (Morrison & Hof, 1997; West, 1993); a biological compensatory effort of the hippocampal memory region, perhaps secondary to dendritic sprouting (Coleman & Flood, 1987); or use of different brain regions to achieve the same end (Cabeza et al., 1997; Grady, chapter 27 of this volume). The normal SO performance on the fourth trial for the middle age group might reflect, not biological compensation, but a natural psychological adaptation to the use of strategic processes, e.g., learning what works. The memory complaints in the elderly (at least in a rather intact group like ours) might be primarily complaints of changes in strategic abilities, and this may not accurately reflect their encoding competence associated with medial temporal functions. Would enriched environmental support maximize biological compensation? What if strategic retrieval strategies were taught? Would it be helpful if such teaching began in the middle years while abilities were only mildly affected? The research by Grady (chapter 27 of this volume) suggests the use of functional imaging to assess these possibilities.

☐ Conclusions

Our primary goal has been to present a potential profile classifications of how different processes change with aging. The data are presented as suggestive, since we did not test a priori hypotheses. Moreover, the sample size in each study is relatively small compared to that of other studies investigating cognitive differences in aging; the subjects were not always the same in the different examples, and the data are cross-sectional, not longitudinal. Our profiles may be context related; that is, they may depend on the quality of the group and the difficulty of the task. In any case, the possibility of such dissociations opens future research doors.

There appears to be little doubt that one or two basic factors such as general slowing and diminished working memory can explain a large percentage of the variance in changes in cognitive functioning with age (e.g., Verhaeghen & Salthouse, 1997). Our proposed profile classification theme is based on a different premise and a different focus, derived from the separation of processes and anatomy provided by our neuropsychological research. The model implies an approach to the study of cognitive changes with aging that emphasizes not similarities but differences. It was such a focus on individual differences in performance that led us to define more precise brain-behavior relations (see Alexander & Stuss, 2000, and Stuss & Alexander, 2000b, for the value of this approach in neuropsychological research). This approach calls for an emphasis on different profiles in performance, to be followed by studies using functional imaging, as well as studies of the genetic, environmental, and other changes related to such profiles. In so doing, we might reveal not only the common threads of change with aging, but also the richness of diversity that may lead to new insights into cognition and perhaps also into new methods of treatment and rehabilitation.

☐ Acknowledgments

The various projects summarized in the grant were possible because of the funding of the Canadian Institutes of Health Research and the Ontario Mental Health Foundation. We are grateful to all our coauthors who contributed to the different studies that we have referenced. Fergus Craik and Gordon Winocur reviewed early drafts and provided important editorial suggestions. Agnes Borowiec, Carole Copnick, Natasha Fansabedian, and Susan Gillingham assisted with manuscript preparation.

☐ References

Alexander, M. P., & Stuss, D. T. (2000). Disorders of frontal lobe functioning. *Seminars in Neurology, 20,* 427–437.

Arnsten, A. F. T. (1999). Age-related cognitive deficits and neurotransmitters: The role of catecholamine mechanisms in prefrontal cortical cognitive decline. In A. Peters, & J. Morrison (Eds.), *Cerebral cortex: Vol 14. Neurodegenerative and age-related changes in structure and function of cerebral cortex* (pp. 89–110). New York: Plenum Press.

Botwinick, J. (1977). Intellectual abilities. In J. E. Birren & K. Schaie (Eds.), *Handbook of the psychology of sging* (pp. 580–605). New York: Van Nostrand Reinhold.

Cabeza, R., Grady, C. L., Nyberg, L., McIntosh, A. R., Tulving, E., Kapur, S., Jennings, J. M., Houle, S., & Craik, F. I. M. (1997). Age-related differences in neural activity during memory encoding and retrieval: A positron emission tomography study. *Journal of Neuroscience, 17,* 391–400.

Chao, L. L., & Knight, R. T. (1995). Human prefrontal lesions increase distractibility to irrelevant sensory inputs. *NeuroReport, 6,* 1605–1610.

Coleman, P. D., & Flood, D. G. (1987). Neuron numbers and dendritic extent in normal aging and Alzheimer's disease. *Neurobiology of Aging, 8,* 521–545.

Craik, F. I. M. (1983). On the transfer of information from temporary to permanent memory. *Philosophical Transactions of the Royal Society of London, Series B, 302,* 341–359.

Craik, F. I. M. (1986). A functional account of age differences in memory. In F. Klix, & H. Hagendorf (Eds.), *Human memory and cognitive capabilities: Mechanisms and performances* (pp. 409–422). Amsterdam: Elsevier.

Craik, F. I. M., Morris, L. W., Morris, R. G., & Loewen, E. R. (1990). Relations between source amnesia and frontal lobe functioning in older adults. *Psychology and Aging, 5*, 148–151.

Crowe, S. (1998). The differential contribution of mental tracking, cognitive flexibility, visual search, and motor speed to performance on parts A and B of The Trail Making Test. *Journal of Clinical Psychology, 54*, 585–591.

D'Esposito, M., Postle, B. R., & Rypma B. (2000). Prefrontal cortical contributions to working memory: Evidence from event-related fMRI studies. *Experimental Brain Research, 133*, 3–11.

Dias, R., Robbins, T. W., & Roberts, A. C. (1997). Dissociable forms of inhibitory control within prefrontal cortex with an analog of the Wisconsin Card Sorting Test: Restriction to novel situations and independence from "on-line" processing. *Journal of Neuroscience, 17*, 9285–9287.

Doppelt, J. E., & Wallace, W. L. (1955). Standardization of the Wechsler Adult Intelligence Scale for older persons. *Journal of Abnormal and Social Psychology, 51*, 312–330.

Elliott, R., McKenna. P. J., Robbins, T. W., & Sahakian, B. J. (1995). Neuropsychological evidence for frontostriatal dysfunction in schizophrenia. *Psychological Medicine, 25*, 619–630.

Fuster, J. M. (1997). *The prefrontal cortex: Anatomy, physiology and neuropsychology of the frontal lobe* (3rd ed.). New York: Lippincott-Raven.

Goldberg, E., & Bilder, R. M. Jr. (1987). The frontal lobes and hierarchical organization of cognitive control. In E. Perecman (Ed.), *The frontal lobes revisited* (pp.159–187). New York: IRBN Press.

Goldman-Rakic, P. S. (1993). Specification of higher cortical functions. *Journal of Head Trauma Rehabilitation, 8*, 13–23.

Haaland, K. Y., Vranes, L. F., Goodwin, J. S., & Garry, P. J. (1987). Wisconsin Card Sort Test performance in healthy elderly population. *Journal of Gerontology, 42*, 345–346.

Herscovitch, J., Stuss, D. T., & Broughton, R. (1980). Changes in cognitive processes following short-term cumulative partial sleep deprivation and recovery oversleeping. *Journal of Clinical Neuropsychology, 2*, 301–319.

Kapur, S., Rose, R., Liddle, P. F., Zipursky, R. B., Brown, G. M., Stuss, D. T., Houle, S., & Tulving, E. (1994). The role of the left prefrontal cortex in verbal processing: Semantic processing or willed action. *NeuroReport, 5*, 2193–2196.

Katz, D. I., & Alexander, M. P. (1994). Traumatic brain injury: Predicting course of recovery and outcome for patients admitted to rehabilitation. *Archives of Neurology, 51*, 661–670.

Lafleche, G., Stuss, D. T., Nelson, R. F., & Picton, T. W. (1990). Memory scanning and structured learning in Alzheimer's disease and Parkinson's disease. *Canadian Journal on Aging, 9*, 120–134.

Levine, B., Stuss, D.T., & Milberg, W.P. (1995). Concept generation: Validation of a test of executive functioning in a normal aging population. *Journal of Clinical and Experimental Neuropsychology, 17*, 740–758.

Levine, B., Stuss, D. T., Milberg, W. P., Alexander, M. P., Schwartz, M., & Macdonald, R. (1998). The effects of focal and diffuse brain damage on strategy application: Evidence from focal lesions, traumatic brain injury and normal aging. *Journal of the International Neuropsychological Society, 4*, 247–264.

McIntosh, A.R., Sekuler, A.B., Penpeci, C., Rajah, M.N., Grady, C.L., Sekuler, R., & Bennett, P.J. (1999). Recruitment of unique neural systems to support visual memory in normal aging. *Current Biology, 9*, 1275–1278.

McIntyre, J. S., & Craik, F. I. M. (1987). Age differences in memory for item and source information. *Canadian Journal of Psychology, 41*, 175–192.

Morrison, J. H., & Hof, P. R. (1997). Life and death of neurons in the aging brain. *Science, 278*, 412–419.

Moscovitch, M., & Winocur, G. (1992). The neuropsychology of memory and aging. In F. I. M. Craik & T. A. Salthouse (Eds.), *The handbook of aging and cognition.* (pp. 315–372). Hillsdale, NJ: Erlbaum.

Pandya, D. N., & Barnes, C. L. (1987). Architecture and connections of the frontal lobe. In E. Perecman (Ed.), *The frontal lobes revisited* (pp. 41–72). New York: IRBN Press.

Petrides, M. (1994). Frontal lobes and working memory: Evidence from investigations of the effects of cortical excisions in nonhuman primates. In F. Boller & J. Grafman (Eds.), *Handbook of neuropsychology* (Vol. 9, pp. 59–82). Amsterdam: Elsevier.

Petrides, M., & Pandya, D. N. (1994). Comparative architectonic analysis of the human and macaque frontal cortex. In F. Boller & J. Grafman (Eds.), *Handbook of neuropsychology* (Vol. 9, pp. 17–57). Amsterdam: Elsevier.

Picton, T. W., Stuss, D. T., Champagne, S. C., & Nelson, R. F. (1984). The effects of age on human event-related potentials. *Psychophysiology, 21*, 312–325.

Raz, N. (2000). Aging of the brain and its impact on cognitive performance: Integration of structural and functional findings. In F. I. M. Craik & T. A. Salthouse (Eds.), *The Handbook of aging and cognition* (2nd ed., pp. 1–90). Mahwah, NJ: Erlbaum.

Raz, N., Gunning, F. M., Head, D., Dupuis, J. H., McQuain, J., Briggs, S. D., Loken, W. J., Thornton, A. E., & Acker, J. D. (1997). Selective aging of the human cerebral cortex observed in vivo: Differential vulnerability of the prefrontal gray matter. *Cerebral Cortex, 7*, 268–282.

Salthouse, T. A. (1992). What do adult age differences in the Digit Symbol Substitution Test reflect? *Journal of Gerontology, 47*, 121–128.

Schaie, K. W. (1958). Rigidity – flexibility and intelligence: A cross-sectional study of the adult life-span from 20 to 70. *Psychological Monographs, 72* (9, Whole. No. 462).

Shallice, T. (1988). *From neuropsychology to mental structure*. New York: Cambridge University Press.

Shallice, T., & Burgess, P. W. (1991). Deficits in strategy application following frontal lobe damage in men. *Brain, 114*, 727–741.

Shammi, P., & Stuss, D. T. (1999). Humour appreciation: A role of the right frontal lobe. *Brain, 122*, 657–666.

Shaw, T. G., Mortel, K. F., Meyer, J. S., Rogers, R. L., Hardenberg, J., & Cutaia, M. M. (1984). Cerebral blood flow changes in benign aging and cerebrovascular disease. *Neurology, 34*, 855–862.

Smith, M. L., Kates, J. H., & Vriezen, E. R. (1992). The development of frontal-lobe functions. In F. Boller & J. Grafman (Eds.), *Handbook of neuropsychology* (Vol. 7, pp. 309–330). Amsterdam: Elsevier.

Stuss, D. T. (1992). Biological and psychological development of executive functions. *Brain and Cognition, 20*, 8–23.

Stuss, D. T., & Alexander, M. P. (1994). Functional and anatomical specificity of frontal lobe functions. In L. S. Cermak (Ed.), *Neuropsychological explorations of memory and cognition: Essays in honor of Nelson Butters* (pp. 191–200). New York: Plenum Press.

Stuss, D. T., & Alexander, M. P. (1999). Affectively burnt in: A proposed role of the right frontal lobe. In E. Tulving (Ed.), *Memory, consciousness, and the brain: The Tallinn conference* (pp. 215–227). Philadelphia: The Psychology Press.

Stuss, D. T., & Alexander, M. P. (2000). The anatomical basis of affective behavior, emotion and self-awareness: A specific role of the right frontal lobe. In G. Hatano, N. Okada, & H. Tanabe (Eds.), *Affective minds. The 13th Toyota conference* (pp 13–25). New York: Elsevier.

Stuss, D. T., & Alexander, M. P. (2000b). Executive functions and the frontal lobes: A conceptual view. *Psychological Research, 63*, 289–298.

Stuss, D. T., Alexander, M. P., Palumbo, C. L., Buckle, L., Sayer, L., & Pogue, J. (1994). Organizational strategies of patients with unilateral or bilateral frontal lobe injury in word list learning tasks. *Neuropsychology, 8*, 355–373.

Stuss, D. T., Alexander, M. P., Hamer, L., Palumbo, C., Dempster, R., Binns, M., Levine, B., & Izukawa, D. (1998). The effects of focal anterior and posterior brain lesions on verbal fluency. *Journal of the International Neuropsychological Society, 4*, 265–278.

Stuss, D. T., & Benson, D. F. (1986). *The frontal lobes*. New York: Raven Press.

Stuss, D. T., Binns, M. A., Carruth, F. G., Levine, B., Brandys, C. E., Moulton, R. J., Snow, W. G., & Schwartz, M. L. (2000). Prediction of recovery of continuous memory after traumatic brain injury. *Neurology, 54*, 1337–1344.

Stuss, D. T., Craik, F. I. M., Sayer, L., Franchi, D., & Alexander, M. P. (1996). Comparison of older people and patients with frontal lesions: Evidence from word list learning. *Psychology and Aging, 11*, 387–395.

Stuss, D. T., Eskes, G. A., & Foster, J. K. (1994). Experimental neuropsychological studies of frontal lobe functions. In F. Boller & J. Grafman (Eds.), *Handbook of neuropsychology* (Vol. 9, pp. 149–185). Amsterdam: Elsevier.

Stuss, D. T., Levine, B., Alexander, M. P., Hong, J., Palumbo, C., Hamer, L., Murphy, K. J., & Izukawa, D. (2000). Wisconsin Card Sorting Test performance in patients with focal frontal and posterior brain damage: Effects of lesion location and test structure on separable cognitive processes. *Neuropsychologia, 38,* 388–402.

Stuss, D. T., Stethem, L. L., Picton, T. W., Leech, E. E., & Pelchat, G. (1989). Traumatic brain injury, aging and reaction time. *Canadian Journal of Neurological Sciences, 16,* 161–167.

Stuss, D. T., Toth, J. P., Franchi, D., Alexander, M. P., Tipper, S., & Craik, F. I. M. (1999). Dissociation of attentional processes in patients with focal frontal and posterior lesions. *Neuropsychologia, 37,* 1005–1027.

Tulving, E., Kapur, S., Craik, F. I. M., Moscovitch, M., & Houle, S. (1994). Hemispheric encoding/ retrieval asymmetry in episodic memory: Positron emission tomography findings. *Proceedings of National Academy of Sciences U.S.A., 91,* 2016–2020.

Verhaeghen, P., & Salthouse, T.A. (1997). Meta-analyses of age-cognition relations in adulthood: Estimates of linear and nonlinear age effects and structural models. *Psychological Bulletin, 122,* 231–249.

Wechsler, D. (1958). *The Measurement and Appraisal of Adult Intelligence* (4th ed.). Baltimore: Williams & Wilkins.

West, M. J. (1993). Regionally specific loss of neurons in the aging human hippocampus. *Neurobiology of Aging, 14,* 287–293.

West, R. L. (1996). An application of prefrontal cortex function theory to cognitive aging. *Psychological Bulletin, 120,* 272–292.

Wheeler, M. A., Stuss, D. T., & Tulving, E. (1997). Toward a theory of episodic memory: The frontal lobes and autonoetic consciousness. *Psychological Bulletin, 121,* 331–354.

White, N., & Cunningham, W. R. (1988). Is terminal drop pervasive or specific? *Journal of Gerontology: Psychological Sciences, 43,* 141–144.

Winocur, G. (1992). Conditional learning in aged rats: Evidence of hippocampal and prefrontal impairment. *Neurobiology of Aging, 13,* 131–135.

Winocur, G., Moscovitch, M., & Stuss, D. T. (1996). Explicit and implicit memory in the elderly: Evidence for double dissociation involving medial temporal and frontal lobe lesions. *Neuropsychology, 10,* 57–65.

Pierre Vidailhet
Bruce K. Christensen
Jean-Marie Danion
Shitij Kapur

Episodic Memory Impairment in Schizophrenia: A View from Cognitive Psychopathology

☐ Introduction

Schizophrenia is a chronic and disabling mental disease that typically first manifests during adolescence and young adulthood. It occurs worldwide, in approximately 0.5% to 1% of the general population (American Psychiatric Association, 1994), and affects all social classes. The costs for society are considerable: direct and indirect costs for Canada alone have been estimated at $4.3 billion yearly (Schizophrenia Society of Canada, 2000). The disease is also highly distressing and disabling for individuals and families. Clinically, schizophrenia is characterized by the presence of delusions and hallucinations (positive symptoms), incoherence of thoughts, speech and behavior (disorganization), lack of motivation, poverty of speech, poor self-care, affective flattening, motor retardation, and disinterest in interpersonal interactions (negative symptoms).

The conceptualization of schizophrenia has recently changed. Cognitive deficits, and in particular memory impairment, are now considered to be core symptoms (McKenna et al., 1990) and among the major disabilities of the disease (Green, 1996; McGurk et al., 2000). Despite researchers' more recent emphasis on memory impairment, its existence was recognized by early pioneers. For example, Hull (Hull, 1917) observed, in three hospitalized patients who were diagnosed with "dementia praecox" (the original term for schizophrenia), the existence of difficulties in learning associations between Chinese ideograms and nonsense syllables. However, memory impairment was generally considered as secondary to the lack of motivation or cooperativeness, the distraction, and/or the psychotic symptoms displayed by patients. It was not until the late 1970s that the first comprehensive review of memory in schizophrenia was written (Koh, 1978).

The reemergence of interest in memory and schizophrenia is likely related to several factors. First, severe memory impairment is common among patients with schizophrenia (J. M. Gold, Randolph, Carpenter, Goldberg, & Weinberger, 1992). Second, memory impairment appears to account for much of the functional disability in patients with schizophrenia (Green, 1996). Third, a large part of clinical work (e.g., collecting historical information; conducting psychodynamic, behavioral, or cognitive therapies; ensuring medication compliance) relies on the ability of the patient to learn and remember. Finally, the substantive advances made by memory researchers have radically altered our ability to understand and measure memory functions in diseased populations. In this respect, Fergus Craik is one of the cognitive psychologists whose work has been highly influential. For instance, the level-of-processing framework (Craik & Lockhart, 1972; Lockhart & Craik, 1990) has been fruitfully applied for studying the cognitive deficits associated with various psychiatric diseases (e.g., Koh & Peterson, 1978; Weingartner, Cohen, Murphy, Martello, & Gerdt, 1981) or the administration of psychotropic drugs (e.g., Curran, Barrow, Weingartner, Lader, & Bernik, 1995; Malone, Kershner, & Siegel, 1988) and for exploring the neuroanatomical correlates of these memory deficits (e.g., Heckers et al., 1998).

Memory impairment is not an isolated cognitive deficit in schizophrenia. A recent meta-analysis of 204 studies exploring cognition in schizophrenia revealed significant deficits in memory, executive functions, motor functions, attention, spatial abilities, and language (Heinrichs & Zakzanis, 1998). These data have led some researchers to consider memory impairment as simply one component of this generalized cognitive deficit (e.g., Andreasen, 1999; Blanchard & Neale, 1994; Mohamed, Paulsen, O'Leary, Arndt, & Andreasen, 1999). However, all cognitive abilities are not equally altered, and several studies have shown that memory functions are disproportionately impaired (e.g., Bilder et al., 2000; J. M. Gold et al., 1992; Heinrichs & Zakzanis, 1998; Palmer et al., 1997; Saykin et al., 1991, 1994). For instance, Saykin and colleagues (Saykin et al., 1991) measured the performance of 36 drug-free patients on a large number of neuropsychological tasks. Using standardized residual scores (Chapman & Chapman, 1989) and grouping the different tasks by cognitive functions, the authors showed the existence of a specific memory impairment against the background of generalized cognitive deficit.

In the remaining sections of this chapter, we will first briefly describe a theoretical framework for memory functions. Many cognitive psychologists and cognitive neuropsychologists posit that memory consists of several separate, but cooperative, systems. Within this framework, we will show that not all memory abilities are impaired in patients with schizophrenia, but that these patients demonstrate particular difficulties in explicit memory tasks. We will also demonstrate how a cognitive psychopathological approach, based on the concepts and methods developed by cognitive psychologists and neuropsychologists, helps to elucidate the functional mechanisms underlying this memory deficit. Studies using this approach point to a disruption of autonoetic awareness as a fundamental cognitive deficit in schizophrenia. Finally, we will emphasize the clinical relevance of exploring episodic memory in patients with schizophrenia.

☐ A Theoretical Framework for Exploring Memory

As a result of the work conducted by cognitive psychologists with normal subjects and by neuropsychologists in clinical populations, our knowledge of memory function has dramatically evolved in the past 30 years. Consequently, any research aimed at exploring memory in schizophrenia can now benefit from these modern memory concepts and theories.

Memory is no longer considered a unitary function (but see Foster & Jelicic, 1999, for a debate on unitary vs. multiple memories). Dissociations between different forms of memory have been repeatedly demonstrated in normal subjects (for a review, see Roediger & McDermott, 1993), brain-damaged patients (for a review, see Richardson-Klavehn & Bjork, 1988), persons under the influence of psychotropic drugs (e.g., Vidailhet et al., 1994), and, more recently, in functional brain imaging studies (for a review, see Schacter & Buckner, 1998). These results have led many researchers to consider memory as composed of distinct memory systems that rely on independent neurobiological and neuroana-tomical substrates. For instance, Schacter and Tulving (Schacter & Tulving, 1994) have described five major memory systems; that is, working memory (a system of limited ca-pacity that stores and allows on-line manipulation of information), semantic memory (a system concerned with general and encyclopedic knowledge), episodic memory (a system concerned with personal events and experiences in their temporal and spatial context, and characterized by autonoetic awareness), perceptual representation system (a system subserving perceptual priming; that is, the unconscious facilitation of information pro-cessing as a consequence of previous perceptual experience), and procedural memory (several systems involving diverse forms of skills and habit learning). Tasks that explore these memory systems have been broadly categorized as implicit or explicit as a function of the instructions given to subjects (Schacter, 1987). In explicit memory tasks, subjects have to voluntarily and consciously retrieve previously learned information. In contrast, implicit memory tasks do not explicitly refer to any previous learning experience but sim-ply measure the increase in performance that arises as a consequence of this previous experience. Therefore, classic episodic memory tasks that utilize cued and free recall or recognition are considered explicit tasks, whereas tasks such as word-completion or puzzle solving, which involve priming and procedural memory, respectively, are implicit.

Within the different memory systems, separate temporal stages also exist. In episodic memory, the stages are described as encoding, storage, and retrieval. Performance in re-call or recognition largely depends on the type of strategies that are used at the time of encoding. This was shown by Craik and Lockhart (Craik & Lockhart, 1972) in their now-classic paper on the levels-of-processing framework. As they stated in a later paper (Lockhart & Craik, 1990), "greater enrichment or elaboration of encoding is associated with en-hanced memory performance" and "performance depends on the qualitative type of en-coding achieved, not time or effort as such" (p 97). Retrieval is also a crucial stage in the memory process (Roediger, 1999). Recently, functional brain imaging studies have shown that encoding and retrieval of episodic information are associated with separate neuroana-tomical structures. Encoding is mostly associated with left hemispheric activation, while retrieval is mainly accompanied by right hemispheric activation, particularly in prefrontal regions (Kapur et al., 1994, 1995; Tulving, Kapur, Craik, Moscovitch, & Houle, 1994). Other brain regions also mediate episodic memory processes, forming large-scale neural net-works including prefrontal, limbic, parietal, and cerebellar areas (Desgranges, Baron, & Eustache, 1998; Nyberg et al., 2000).

Episodic memories are not exact transcriptions of past personal experiences, but are transitory and modifiable mental representations (Schacter, Norman, & Koutstaal, 1998). In other words, memory is not a passive encoding and retrieving process, but a dynamic one that depends on past experiences and takes into account the present reality. The effectiveness of episodic retrieval is determined not only by the nominal identity of the target information but also by the links that were established with its episodically and semantically encoded context (e.g., the type of cognitive processing used at the time of encoding, the emotions provoked by the experience, when and where the information was acquired). Retrieval cues also play a central role in the quality of the memories that are produced. For instance, Loftus and colleagues (Loftus, Miller, & Burns, 1978) have shown that questions and information given to the subject at the time of retrieval modify the memory of a past event. Thus, memories can be incomplete, partially false, or even correspond to events that never happened (Conway, 1997).

An individual's experience of retrieving his or her own past manifests itself as two distinct subjective states: conscious recollection (or autonoetic awareness [Tulving, 1985]) and feeling of familiarity (or noetic awareness). According to Wheeler and colleagues

(Wheeler, Stuss, & Tulving, 1997), "autonoetic consciousness affords individuals the possibility to apprehend their subjective experiences throughout time and to perceive the present moment as both a continuation to their past and as a prelude to their future" (p. 335). This unique ability to travel mentally through one's own past and future confers to autonoetic awareness a close relationship both with the sense of time and with the sense of self. Following Tulving's initial proposal (Tulving, 1985), Gardiner and colleagues (Gardiner & Java, 1993; Gardiner, Java, & Richardson-Klavehn, 1996) used the remember/know paradigm to dissociate conscious recollection from feelings of familiarity and to assess experimentally subjective experiences of awareness. In this paradigm, subjects have to specify their state of awareness at the time they recognize previously learned items. If recognition is accompanied by conscious recollection (i.e., the subject recollects an association made with an event or an experience related to the study moment), they indicate that they "remember" the item. Items retrieved in the absence of conscious recollection, but which are familiar in the context of the task, are regarded as "know" responses. Responses that are based simply on guessing are denoted as "guess" responses. The validity of this distinction is attested to by the dissociations of these states in normal subjects (Gardiner & Java, 1993) and neurological populations (Schacter, Verfaellie, & Anes, 1997) and by their distinct neuroanatomical correlates (Duzel, Yonelinas, Mangun, Heinze, & Tulving, 1997; Henson, Rugg, Shallice, Josephs, & Dolan, 1999).

☐ A Characterization of the Episodic Memory Deficit in Schizophrenia

When explored within the framework of modern concepts and theories, the memory impairment associated with schizophrenia reveals interesting features. First, the impairment is selective: Whereas patients with schizophrenia display a marked deficit of performance in explicit memory tasks, their performance in implicit tasks is normal. Second, a few studies, using tasks other than item recall and recognition to explore episodic memory, allow a better understanding of the functional mechanisms underlying memory performance in patients with schizophrenia. These studies point to a disruption of autonoetic awareness in schizophrenia; that is, the state of awareness that characterizes episodic memory. The neuroanatomical abnormalities underlying the impairment of episodic memory are currently being explored using functional brain imaging techniques. Third, general factors such as medications cannot explain the memory deficit associated with schizophrenia. Finally, exploring episodic memory has direct clinical implications in schizophrenia. The remainder of this section will address each of these points in more detail.

The Memory Deficit Associated With Schizophrenia Is Selective

Whether patients with schizophrenia display a deficit of performance depends on the tasks that are used. Several studies have shown that patients display normal performances in implicit memory tasks. This has been demonstrated in tasks exploring perceptual priming (Gras-Vincendon et al., 1994), conceptual priming (Schwartz, Rosse, & Deutsch, 1993), and procedural memory (Michel, Danion, Grange, & Sandner, 1998), as well as in implicit learning tasks (Keri et al., 2000). In accordance with these findings, Kazès and colleagues (Kazès et al., 1999), using the process dissociation procedure (Jacoby, 1991) to obtain uncontaminated estimates of memory processes, found that consciously controlled use of memory, but not automatic influences of memory, was impaired in schizophrenia.

On the other hand, the magnitude of impairment typically seen with explicit memory tasks is severe. This has been consistently demonstrated in free recall (Koh, 1978) and cued recall (Schwartz et al., 1993) tasks. Although early studies reported that patients with schizophrenia had poor recall and normal recognition performances (Koh, 1978), these studies typically lacked adequate diagnostic specificity and did not control for task difficulty. Equating task difficulty is an important issue when attempting to reveal a differential deficit (Chapman & Chapman, 1978, 1989). Calev (1984), using recall and recognition tasks that were matched for their discrimination power, showed that recognition is actually impaired in schizophrenia, albeit to a lesser degree than recall. This was confirmed in a recent meta-analysis carried out in 70 studies exploring memory in schizophrenia (Aleman, Hijman, de Haan, & Kahn, 1999): The effect sizes obtained (i.e., magnitude of the difference between control and patient group) were 1.21 and 0.64 for recall and recognition respectively. Furthermore, memory impairment exists for verbal material, such as nonsense syllables, words, word pairs, sentences (Koh & Peterson, 1978), and stories (Abbruzzese & Scarone, 1993), as well as for visual material such as abstract designs (Saykin et al., 1991) or faces (Addington & Addington, 1998). When verbal and nonverbal tasks are matched for difficulty (Calev, Edelist, Kugelmass, & Lerer, 1991), the deficit does not appear to be disproportionate in one domain, arguing against a hemispheric lateralization of the deficit (Taylor & Abrams, 1984). This deficit of performance has been observed in immediate as well as in delayed recall tasks (Aleman et al., 1999), and remote memories are also affected (Feinstein, Goldberg, Nowlin, & Weinberger, 1998). For example, in the study by Feinstein and colleagues (Feinstein et al., 1998), patients with schizophrenia displayed an inverse U memory curve when compared to healthy individuals: Where the most severe impairment affected early adulthood memories, childhood memories were quasi-normal, and recent past memories were altered to a lesser extent. Finally, it should be noted, that despite their severe episodic memory impairment, patients with schizophrenia remain able to learn (Goldberg, Weinberger, Pliskin, Berman, & Podd, 1989; Hawkins, 1999), although their learning curve is lower than normal (Aleman et al., 1999).

Functional Mechanisms Underlying the Explicit Memory Impairment in Schizophrenia

By far, item recall and recognition performances have been the most common laboratory measures used to assess the status of episodic memory in schizophrenia. However, performance in those tasks depends not only on episodic memory, but also on other kinds of memory, such as semantic memory (Wheeler et al., 1997).

A few studies have assessed memory for contextual information in schizophrenia; that is, the dimensions of the learning episode that are not central to the target information at the time of encoding, such as when, where, and how the information was acquired. These studies have shown that memory for context is impaired in schizophrenia and that this impairment is often disproportionately greater than decrements in item recall and recognition (Rizzo, Danion, Van der Linden, & Grange, 1996; Rizzo, Danion, Van der Linden, Grange, & Rohmer, 1996). As memory for contextual information underlies the ability of the subject to consciously recollect a personally experienced episode, these studies point to a possible impairment in autonoetic awareness (Wheeler et al., 1997).

Huron and colleagues (Huron et al., 1995) used the remember/know procedure to investigate the state of awareness experienced by patients with schizophrenia while they were engaged in a word recognition task. The results demonstrated that the recognition deficit in patients with schizophrenia was associated with a decrease in the number of items consciously recollected (i.e., "remember" responses) but not of items associated with feeling of familiarity (i.e., "know" responses), indicating an impairment of autonoetic awareness but not of noetic awareness. Furthermore, the number and quality of interitem associations were significantly diminished in patients with schizophrenia, indicating impairment in the relational binding of the information to be learned. The inability of patients with schizophrenia to link the separate aspects of an event into a cohesive, distinctive, and autonoetically memorable whole has been recently confirmed (Danion, Rizzo, & Bruant, 1999). In this study, common objects were paired either by the experimenter or by the subjects themselves. In a subsequent memory task, subjects had to indicate their state of awareness while they were recognizing identical and reorganized pairs of objects and the source of their pairing. Patients with schizophrenia displayed a profound deficit in recognizing pairs of objects, particularly when the experimenter previously did the pairing. In contrast, their source memory and single-item recognition performance were less impaired. The coherence of the state of awareness associated with the recognition of pairs of objects on the one hand and with the source of the pairing on the other hand was also diminished in patients with schizophrenia.

Since patients have difficulty spontaneously organizing information to be remembered (Russell, Bannatyne, & Smith, 1975; Russell & Beekhuis, 1976; Traupmann, Berzofsky, & Kesselman, 1976), an impairment of strategic processes (Moscovitch, 1992; Moscovitch & Melo, 1997) has been hypothesized to be a mechanism for the impairment of autonoetic awareness in schizophrenia. This hypothesis is consistent with the decrease of false memories associated with conscious recollection, but not of false memories associated with familiarity, in patients with schizophrenia, since only the former depend on constructive, strategic processes (Huron & Danion, 2001). These strategic processes are involved in various cognitive functions, such as perception, attention, language, executive functions and working memory and are influenced by global factors, such as speed of processing or attentional resources, that are themselves impaired in schizophrenia (e.g., Brebion, Smith, Malaspina, Sharif, & Amador, 2000). The impairment of autonoetic awareness, arising from a variety of cognitive deficits, could therefore represent a fundamental cognitive deficit in schizophrenia (see Danion et al., 2001).

The disturbance of strategic processes might occur at the level of encoding and/or retrieval of information. The fact that recall is more impaired than recognition first led researchers to favor a retrieval deficit hypothesis in schizophrenia (Barker, 1977; Bauman & Murray, 1968). However, the observation that patients display an inability to spontaneously organize the to-be-remembered material (Koh, 1978) suggests an impairment of encoding processes. McClain (1983) conducted a study in which patients with schizophrenia and healthy control subjects had to learn word lists formed by six instances of three semantic categories. Words were presented in two different encoding conditions: at random or blocked by category. Following each encoding condition, subjects had to recall the words either in a cued recall task (with category names given as cues) or in a free recall task. When words were presented at random, recall performance was profoundly impaired in the patient group, and cues given at retrieval did not help patients to improve their performance. However, when words were blocked by category at encoding, patients' performance significantly improved and, when retrieval cues were provided, their recall performance no longer differed from that observed in healthy controls. These results suggest the existence of both encoding and retrieval defects. They also confirm that patients with schizophrenia have a decreased ability to spontaneously adopt efficient organizational mnemonic strategies to encode and/or retrieve information, but they can dramatically improve their memory performance when possibilities to organize material are made sufficiently salient (Koh & Peterson, 1978).

Functional brain imaging techniques, such as Positron Emission Tomography (PET) and functional Magnetic Resonance Imaging (fMRI), allow one to explore the neuroanatomical correlates of encoding and retrieval processes separately. Using these techniques, recent studies have confirmed the existence of brain activation abnormalities during encoding and retrieval of information in schizophrenia. For instance, using PET and a cued-recall task, Heckers and colleagues (1998) showed that patients displayed higher right prefrontal and lower hippocampal recruitment when consciously recollecting words. However, memory performance differed between patients and normal controls in their study, making it difficult to infer whether activation abnormalities were due to low task performance or to an actual functional brain defect associated with schizophrenia. In an ongoing PET study, our group is using the levels-of-processing procedure (Craik & Lockhart, 1972) to explore the neuroanatomical correlates of encoding and recognition in schizophrenia. Eight patients with schizophrenia and 8 healthy control subjects have been scanned while they were encoding and subsequently recognizing word pairs. Neither encoding accuracy, nor recognition performance, significantly differed between the two groups. In both groups, recognition performance was significantly better for deeply than for shallowly encoded word pairs, indicating that patients, as controls, benefited from the levels-of-processing effect (see also Koh & Peterson, 1978). Preliminary analysis of the PET images shows that, in conditions where accuracy did not significantly differ between the two groups, patients with schizophrenia displayed less activation than healthy controls in several brain regions during the encoding of information. These regions include prefrontal, hippocampal, parietal, and thalamic areas, that is, brain regions that have been shown to be neuropathologically and structurally abnormal in schizophrenia (Pearlson, 2000). During recognition, brain activation was also different between the two groups in several regions, even though their memory performance did not differ significantly. These results indicate that schizophrenia is associated with brain activation abnormalities, during both encoding and retrieval of information, even in conditions where patients manage to perform the memory task efficiently. In line with the disconnection hypothesis of schizophrenia (Andreasen, Paradiso, & O'Leary, 1998; Friston, 1996), our study also points to the existence of a large-scale network dysfunction in patients with schizophrenia. Multivariate methods such as partial least squares and structural equation modeling have been recently applied to brain imaging studies (McIntosh, 1999). These methods will be instrumental in understanding the abnormalities of neural connectivity associated with schizophrenia-related memory deficits.

Can the Episodic Memory Deficit Be Explained by Medication Effects?

Noncognitive factors may also play a role in the impairment of memory performance in schizophrenia. The most frequently considered factor is pharmacotherapy, given that the vast majority of patients are chronically treated with neuroleptics and many often receive other psychotropic medications, such as antiparkinsonian agents (Stip, 1996). Several reviews have been published on the topic (e.g., Goldberg & Weinberger, 1996; Spohn & Strauss, 1989) and suggest that, as a whole, neuroleptics have little, if any, deleterious effect on episodic memory. Antiparkinsonian agents do interfere with memory and learning, but their deleterious effect remains weak (Paulsen et al., 1995). Further evidence that medications cannot account for the entire memory deficit associated with schizophrenia stems from the fact that the deficit was observed before the era of psychotropic drugs and that it has been found in studies carried out in drug-free and/or drug-naive patients (Saykin et al., 1994). Furthermore, in the meta-analysis by Aleman and colleagues (1999), medication use did not moderate the magnitude of memory impairment.

The Clinical Relevance of Exploring Episodic Memory in Schizophrenia

Results of the studies exploring the severity of episodic memory deficit in schizophrenia have been somewhat equivocal (e.g., J. M. Gold et al., 1992; Hawkins, 1999; McKenna et al., 1990). Most of the studies showed a large overlap of memory performances between patients and healthy controls (Heinrichs & Zakzanis, 1998). However, the level of impairment borders on severe amnesia in a significant proportion of patients. For instance, J. M. Gold and colleagues (1992) found a discrepancy of 20 or more points between intelligence and memory quotients in 23% of their 45 patients. Furthermore, in monozygotic twins discordant for schizophrenia, Goldberg and colleagues (1990) showed that the memory performance of the ill twin was almost always significantly impaired compared to his or her sibling. Thus, the memory deficit appears to be profound and reliable.

A number of studies have been interested in the relationships between cognitive deficits and other clinical variables in schizophrenia. Concerning episodic memory, the deficit is already present in drug-naive (Mohamed et al., 1999) as well as in clinically stabilized (Bilder et al., 2000) first-episode patients, and does not deteriorate during the first years of illness evolution (S. Gold, Arndt, Nopoulos, O'Leary, & Andreasen, 1999). This indicates that the memory deficit is more consistent with a static encephalopathy of neurodevelopmental origin than with a neurodegenerative process (Rund, 1998). The recent meta-analysis by Aleman and colleagues (1999) revealed that memory impairment was independent of most of the clinical variables that were explored. In particular, age, duration of illness, patient status (in- vs. out-patients), and positive symptoms did not significantly influence the magnitude of memory impairment. Only negative symptoms showed a significant, though weak, relationship with memory performance. However, the influence of these clinical variables, as well as others such as age of onset of the illness, length and frequency of hospitalization, and tardive dyskinesia (Krabbendam, van Harten, Picus, & Jolles, 2000), is still under debate. Also, other clinical symptoms of schizophrenia, such as disorganization of behavior, could be closely associated to the impairment of episodic memory (Danion et al., 2001). The question of whether different subpopulations of patients with schizophrenia can be identified on the basis of their profile of cognitive and memory abilities (Buchanan et al., 1994) is still being explored and appears far from being answered (Zalewski, Johnson-Selfridge, Ohriner, Zarrella, & Seltzer, 1998).

Although the episodic memory deficit in schizophrenia shows weak correlation with positive and negative symptoms, it certainly has clinical consequences. For instance, the impairment of consciously controlled use of memory, in the context of preserved automatic influences of memory, can lead to inappropriate and abnormal behavior (Jacoby, Jennings, & Hay, 1996). As autonoetic awareness is linked to one's ability to travel through one's past and future (Wheeler et al., 1997), its impairment could explain the decreased ability displayed by patients with schizophrenia to define personal future plans and to link them to their own past. The impairment of autonoetic awareness could also account for the abnormal constitution of the self in schizophrenia (Danion et al., 2001). Such clinical consequences have recently been highlighted in studies showing that the impairment of episodic memory is more closely related to various measures of functional outcome than are positive symptoms, such as delusions and hallucinations, or negative symptoms (e.g., Bryson, Bell, Kaplan, & Greig, 1998; Green, 1996; McGurk et al., 2000; Tsuang,

1982, Velligan et al., 1997). Green and Nuechterlein (Green & Nuechterlein, 1999) have suggested that the choice of a particular cognitive deficit as a target for cognitive rehabilitation and/or for pharmacological intervention could be guided by its associations with an outcome area of interest and/or by the knowledge we have of its neural substrates. The understanding of the functional mechanisms underlying the impairment of performance on cognitive tasks is also an important factor to take into account. Thus, episodic memory appears to be a particularly valuable target for cognitive rehabilitation (O'Carroll, Russell, Lawrie, & Johnstone, 1999) and/or future pharmacological treatment design (Friedman, Temporini, & Davis, 1999). It is already an important factor when evaluating the therapeutic effects of medications in schizophrenia (Sharma, 1999).

Finally, it should be noted that there is still little knowledge concerning memory deficits in aged patients, although a substantial proportion of elderly patients with schizophrenia develop profound intellectual impairments that were described in the past as "vesanic dementia" (Harvey et al., 1998). Advances in the understanding of memory and aging (Grady & Craik, 2000) will be instrumental in guiding this area of research (Lindenmayer et al., 1997; Putnam & Harvey, 1999).

☐ Conclusion

Schizophrenia is a chronic psychiatric disease with severe consequences for individuals, families and society. The concepts and methods developed in recent years by cognitive neuroscientists now permit us to explore and understand the cognitive deficits associated with this disease in an original way. This approach not only consists of describing the cognitive deficits, but also seeks to explore their functional mechanisms at a cognitive and a neuroanatomical level. It also aims to link cognitive deficits with clinical symptoms on the one hand and with neurobiological abnormalities on the other hand, thereby promoting integrated models of the disease. In the memory domain, this approach has led to a better characterization of the memory deficit in schizophrenia. All memory abilities are not equally affected in the disease. Patients with schizophrenia perform normally on implicit memory tasks. In contrast, their performance in explicit memory tasks is profoundly impaired. The impairment has been shown in recall and recognition tasks, for verbal and nonverbal material, and for recent and remote memories. Studies that have explored the functional mechanism of this deficit of memory performance point to an impairment of autonoetic awareness, that is, the state of awareness that characterizes episodic memory. The neural correlates of the episodic memory impairment are currently being explored using functional brain imaging techniques. Its clinical consequences have been emphasized recently by studies showing the close relationship memory impairment bears with measures of functional outcome. Therefore, episodic memory deficit appears to be a potential target for cognitive rehabilitation programs and pharmacological treatments in schizophrenia.

☐ References

Abbruzzese, M., & Scarone, S. (1993). Memory and attention dysfunctions in story recall in schizophrenia: Evidence of a possible frontal malfunctioning. *Biological Psychology, 35*, 51–58.

Addington, J., & Addington, D. (1998). Facial affect recognition and information processing in schizophrenia and bipolar disorder. *Schizophrenia Research, 32*, 171–181.

Aleman, A., Hijman, R., de Haan, E. H., & Kahn, R. S. (1999). Memory impairment in schizophrenia: A meta-analysis. *American Journal of Psychiatry, 156*, 1358–1366.

American Psychiatric Association. (1994). *Diagnostic and statistical manual of mental disorders* (4th ed.). Washington, DC: Author.

Andreasen, N. (1999). A unitary model of schizophrenia. *Archives of General Psychiatry, 56,* 781–787.

Andreasen, N. C., Paradiso, S., & O'Leary, D. S. (1998). "Cognitive dysmetria" as an integrative theory of schizophrenia: a dysfunction in cortical-subcortical-cerebellar circuitry? *Schizophrenia Bulletin, 24,* 203–218.

Barker, W. J. (1977). The role of retrieval in schizophrenic memory deficit. *Canadian Journal of Behavioral Sciences, 9,* 176–186.

Bauman, E., & Murray, D. J. (1968). Recognition versus recall in schizophrenia. *Canadian Journal of Psychology, 22,* 18–25.

Bilder, R. M., Goldman, R. S., Robinson, D., Reiter, G., Bell, L., Bates, J. A., Pappadopulos, E., Willson, D. F., Alvir, J. M., Woerner, M. G., Geisler, S., Kane, J. M., & Lieberman, J. A. (2000). Neuropsychology of first-episode schizophrenia: Initial characterization and clinical correlates. *American Journal of Psychiatry, 157,* 549–559.

Blanchard, J. J., & Neale, J. M. (1994). The neuropsychological signature of schizophrenia: generalized or differential deficit? *American Journal of Psychiatry, 151,* 40–48.

Brebion, G., Smith, M. J., J.M., G., Malaspina, D., Sharif, Z., & Amador, X. (2000). Memory and schizophrenia: Differential link of processing speed and selective attention with two levels of encoding. *Journal of Psychiatric Research, 34,* 121–127.

Bryson, G., Bell, M. D., Kaplan, E., & Greig, T. (1998). The functional consequences of memory impairments on initial work performance in people with schizophrenia. *Journal of Nervous and Mental Disease, 186,* 610–615.

Buchanan, R. W., Strauss, M. E., Kirkpatrick, B., Holstein, C., Breier, A., & Carpenter, W. T., Jr. (1994). Neuropsychological impairments in deficit vs nondeficit forms of schizophrenia. *Archives of General Psychiatry, 51,* 804–811.

Calev, A. (1984). Recall and recognition in chronic nondemented schizophrenics: Use of matched tasks. *Journal of Abnormal Psychology, 93,* 172–177.

Calev, A., Edelist, S., Kugelmass, S., & Lerer, B. (1991). Performance of long-stay schizophrenics on matched verbal and visuospatial recall tasks. *Psychological Medicine, 21,* 655–660.

Chapman, L. J., & Chapman, J. P. (1978). The measurement of differential deficit. *Journal of Psychiatric Research, 14,* 303–311.

Chapman, L. J., & Chapman, J. P. (1989). Strategies for resolving the heterogeneity of schizophrenics and their relatives using cognitive measures. *Journal of Abnormal Psychology, 98,* 357–366.

Conway, M. A. (1997). Past and present: recovered memories and false memories. In M. A. Conway (Ed.), *Recovered memories and false memories* (pp. 150–191). New York: Oxford University Press.

Craik, F. I. M., & Lockhart, R. S. (1972). Levels of processing: a framework for memory research. *Journal of Verbal Learning and Verbal Behavior, 11,* 671–684.

Curran, H.V., Barrow, S., Weingartner, H., Lader, M., & Bernik, M. (1995). Encoding, remembering and awareness in lorazepam-induced amnesia. *Psychopharmacology, 122,* 187–193.

Danion, J. M., Huron, C., & Robert, P. (2001). Schizophrenia as a disorder of autonetic awareness. *Schizophrenia Research, 49*(Abstract).

Danion, J. M., Rizzo, L., & Bruant, A. (1999). Functional mechanisms underlying impaired recognition memory and conscious awareness in patients with schizophrenia. *Archives of General Psychiatry, 56,* 639–644.

Desgranges, B., Baron, J. C., & Eustache, F. (1998). The functional neuroanatomy of episodic memory: The role of the frontal lobes, the hippocampal formation, and other areas. *Neuroimage, 8,* 198–213.

Duzel, E., Yonelinas, A. P., Mangun, G. R., Heinze, H. J., & Tulving, E. (1997). Event-related brain potential correlates of two states of conscious awareness in memory. *Proceedings of National Academy of Sciences USA, 94,* 5973–5978.

Feinstein, A., Goldberg, T. E., Nowlin, B., & Weinberger, D. R. (1998). Types and characteristics of remote memory impairment in schizophrenia. *Schizophrenia Research, 30,* 155–163.

Foster, J. K., & Jelicic, M. (Eds.). (1999). *Memory: Structure, function, or process?* Oxford, England: Oxford University Press.

Friedman, J. I., Temporini, H., & Davis, K. L. (1999). Pharmacologic strategies for augmenting cognitive performance in schizophrenia. *Biological Psychiatry, 45*, 1–16.

Friston, K. J. (1996). Theoretical neurobiology and schizophrenia. *British Medical Bulletin, 52*, 644–655.

Gardiner, J. M., & Java, R. I. (1993). Recognition memory and awareness: An experiential approach. *European Journal of Cognitive Psychology, 3*, 337–346.

Gardiner, J. M., Java, R. I., & Richardson-Klavehn, A. (1996). How level of processing really influences awareness in recognition memory. *Canadian Journal of Experimental Psychology, 50*, 114–122.

Gold, J. M., Randolph, C., Carpenter, C. J., Goldberg, T. E., & Weinberger, D. R. (1992). Forms of memory failure in schizophrenia. *Journal of Abnormal Psychology, 101*, 487–494.

Gold, S., Arndt, S., Nopoulos, P., O'Leary, D. S., & Andreasen, N. C. (1999). Longitudinal study of cognitive function in first-episode and recent-onset schizophrenia. *American Journal of Psychiatry, 156*, 1342–1348.

Goldberg, T. E., Ragland, J. D., Torrey, E. F., Gold, J. M., Bigelow, L. B., & Weinberger, D. R. (1990). Neuropsychological assessment of monozygotic twins discordant for schizophrenia. *Archives of General Psychiatry, 47*, 1066–1072.

Goldberg, T. E., & Weinberger, D. R. (1996). Effects of neuroleptic medications on the cognition of patients with schizophrenia: A review of recent studies. *Journal of Clinical Psychiatry, 57*, S62–S65.

Goldberg, T. E., Weinberger, D. R., Pliskin, N. H., Berman, K. F., & Podd, M. H. (1989). Recall memory deficit in schizophrenia. A possible manifestation of prefrontal dysfunction. *Schizophrenia Research, 2*, 251–257.

Grady, C. L., & Craik, F. I. (2000). Changes in memory processing with age. *Current Opinion in Neurobiology, 10*, 224–231.

Gras-Vincendon, A., Danion, J. M., Grange, D., Bilik, M., Willard-Schroeder, D., Sichel, J. P., & Singer, L. (1994). Explicit memory, repetition priming and cognitive skill learning in schizophrenia. *Schizophrenia Research, 13*, 117–126.

Green, M. F. (1996). What are the functional consequences of neurocognitive deficits in schizophrenia? *American Journal of Psychiatry, 153*, 321–330.

Green, M. F., & Nuechterlein, K. H. (1999). Should schizophrenia be treated as a neurocognitive disorder? *Schizophrenia Bulletin, 25*, 309–319.

Harvey, P. D., Howanitz, E., Parrella, M., White, L., Davidson, M., Mohs, R. C., Hoblyn, J., & Davis, K. L. (1998). Symptoms, cognitive functioning, and adaptive skills in geriatric patients with lifelong schizophrenia: a comparison across treatment sites. *American Journal of Psychiatry, 155*, 1080–1086.

Hawkins, K. A. (1999). Memory deficits in patients with schizophrenia: Preliminary data from the Wechsler Memory Scale-Third Edition support earlier findings. *Journal of Psychiatry and Neurosciences, 24*, 341–347.

Heckers, S., Rauch, S. L., Goff, D., Savage, C. R., Schacter, D. L., Fischman, A. J., & Alpert, N. M. (1998). Impaired recruitment of the hippocampus during conscious recollection in schizophrenia. *Nature Neuroscience, 1*, 318-323.

Heinrichs, R. W., & Zakzanis, K. K. (1998). Neurocognitive deficit in schizophrenia: A quantitative review of the evidence. *Neuropsychology, 12*, 426-445.

Henson, R. N., Rugg, M. D., Shallice, T., Josephs, O., & Dolan, R. J. (1999). Recollection and familiarity in recognition memory: An event-related functional magnetic resonance imaging study. *Journal of Neurosciences, 19*, 3962–3972.

Hull, C. L. (1917). The formation and retention of associations among the insane. *American Journal of Psychology, 87*, 419–435.

Huron, C., & Danion, J. M. (2001). *False memories in schizophrenia.* Submitted.

Huron, C., Danion, J. M., Giacomoni, F., Grange, D., Robert, P., & Rizzo, L. (1995). Impairment of recognition memory with, but not without, conscious recollection in schizophrenia. *American Journal of Psychiatry, 152*, 1737–1742.

Jacoby, L. L. (1991). A process dissociation framework: Separating automatic from intentional uses of memory. *Journal of Memory and Language, 30*, 513–541.

Jacoby, L. L., Jennings, J. M., & Hay, J. F. (1996). Dissociating automatic and consciously controlled processes: Implications for diagnosis and rehabilitation of memory deficits. In D. J. Hermann,

C. McEvoy, C. Hertzog, P. Hertel, & M. K. Johnson (Eds.), *Basic and applied memory research theory in context* (Vol.1, pp. 59–69). Mahwah, NJ: Erlbaum.

Kapur, S., Craik, F. I. M., Jones, C., Brown, G. M., Houle, S., & Tulving, E. (1995). Functional role of the prefrontal cortex in retrieval of memories: A PET study. *Neuroreport, 2,* 1880–1884.

Kapur, S., Craik, F. I. M., Tulving, E., Wilson, A. A., Houle, S., & Brown, G. M. (1994). Neuroanatomical correlates of encoding in episodic memory: Levels of processing effect. *Proceedings of National Academy of Sciences USA, 91,* 2008–2011.

Kazes, M., Berthet, L., Danion, J. M., Amado, I., Willard, D., Robert, P., & Poirier, M. F. (1999). Impairment of consciously controlled use of memory in schizophrenia. *Neuropsychology, 13,* 54–61.

Keri, S., Kelemen, O., Szekeres, G., Bagoczky, N., Erdelyi, R., Antal, A., Benedek, G., & Janka, Z. (2000). Schizophrenics know more than they can tell: Probabilistic classification learning in schizophrenia. *Psychological Medicine, 30,* 149–55.

Koh, S. D. (1978). Remembering of verbal materials by schizophrenic young adults. In S. Schwartz (Ed.), *Language and cognition in schizophrenia* (pp. 52–75). Hillsdale, NJ: Erlbaum.

Koh, S. D., & Peterson, R. A. (1978). Encoding orientation and the remembering of schizophrenic young adults. *Journal of Abnormal Psychology, 87,* 303–313.

Krabbendam, L., van Harten, P. N., Picus, I., & Jolles, J. (2000). Tardive dyskinesia is associated with impaired retrieval from long-term memory: The Curacao Extrapyramidal Syndromes Study: IV. *Schizophrenia Research, 42,* 41–46.

Lindenmayer, J. P., Negron, A. E., Shah, S., Lowinger, R., Kennedy, G., Bark, N., & Hyman, R. (1997). Cognitive deficits and psychopathology in elderly schizophrenic patients. *American Journal of Geriatric Psychiatry, 5,* 31–42.

Lockhart, R. S., & Craik, F. I. M. (1990). Levels of processing: A retrospective commentary on a framework for memory research. *Canadian Journal of Psychology, 44,* 87–112.

Loftus, E. F., Miller, D. G., & Burns, H. J. (1978). Semantic integration of verbal information into a visual memory. *Journal of Experimental Psychology: Human Learning, 4,* 19–31.

Malone, M. A., Kershner, J. R., & Siegel, L. (1988). The effects of methylphenidate on levels of processing and laterality in children with attention deficit disorder. *Journal of Abnormal Child Psychology, 16,* 379–395.

McClain, L. (1983). Encoding and retrieval in schizophrenics' free recall. *Journal of Nervous and Mental Disease, 171,* 471–479.

McGurk, S. R., Moriarty, P. J., Harvey, P. D., Parrella, M., White, L., & Davis, K. L. (2000). The longitudinal relationship of clinical symptoms, cognitive functioning, and adaptive life in geriatric schizophrenia. *Schizophrenia Research, 42,* 47–55.

McIntosh, A. R. (1999). Mapping cognition to the brain through neural interactions. *Memory, 7,* 523–548.

McKenna, P. J., Tamlyn, D., Lund, C. E., Mortimer, A. M., Hammond, S., & Baddeley, A. D. (1990). Amnesic syndrome in schizophrenia. *Psychological Medicine, 20,* 967–972.

Michel, L., Danion, J. M., Grange, D., & Sandner, G. (1998). Cognitive skill learning and schizophrenia: implications for cognitive remediation. *Neuropsychology, 12,* 590–599.

Mohamed, S., Paulsen, J. S., O'Leary, D., Arndt, S., & Andreasen, N. (1999). Generalized cognitive deficits in schizophrenia: A study of first-episode patients. *Archives of General Psychiatry, 56,* 749–754.

Moscovitch, M. (1992). Memory and working-with-memory: A component process model based on modules and central systems. *Journal of Cognitive Neuroscience, 4,* 257–267.

Moscovitch, M., & Melo, B. (1997). Strategic retrieval and the frontal lobes: Evidence from confabulation and amnesia. *Neuropsychologia, 35,* 1017–1034.

Nyberg, L., Persson, J., Habib, R., Tulving, E., McIntosh, A. R., Cabeza, R., & Houle, S. (2000). Large scale neurocognitive networks underlying episodic memory. *Journal of Cognitive Neuroscience, 12,* 163–173.

O'Carroll, R. E., Russell, H. H., Lawrie, S. M., & Johnstone, E. C. (1999). Errorless learning and the cognitive rehabilitation of memory-impaired schizophrenic patients. *Psychological Medicine, 29,* 105–112.

Palmer, B. W., Heaton, R. K., Paulsen, J. S., Kuck, J., Braff, D., Harris, M. J., Zisook, S., & Jeste, D. V. (1997). Is it possible to be schizophrenic yet neuropsychologically normal? *Neuropsychology, 11,* 437–446.

Paulsen, J. S., Heaton, R. K., Sadek, J. R., Perry, W., Delis, D. C., Braff, D., Kuck, J., Zisook, S., & Jeste, D. V. (1995). The nature of learning and memory impairments in schizophrenia. *Journal of the International Neuropsychological Society, 1,* 88–99.

Pearlson, G. D. (2000). Neurobiology of schizophrenia. *Annals of Neurology, 49,* 556–566.

Putnam, K. M., & Harvey, P. D. (1999). Memory performance of geriatric and nongeriatric chronic schizophrenic patients: A cross-sectional study. *Journal of the International Neuropsychological Society, 5,* 494–501.

Richardson-Klavehn, A., & Bjork, R. A. (1988). Measures of memory. *Annual Review of Psychology, 39,* 475–543.

Rizzo, L., Danion, J. M., Van Der Linden, M., & Grange, D. (1996). Patients with schizophrenia remember that an event has occurred, but not when. *British Journal of Psychiatry, 168,* 427–431.

Rizzo, L., Danion, J.M., Van Der Linden, M., Grange, D., & Rohmer, J.-G. (1996). Impairment of spatial context in schizophrenia. *Neuropsychology, 10,* 376–384.

Roediger, H.L. (1999). Why retrieval is the key process in understanding human memory. In E. Tulving (Ed.), *Memory, consciousness and the brain: The Tallin conference.* Philadelphia: Psychology Press.

Roediger, H. L., & McDermott, K. B. (1993). Implicit memory in normal human subjects. In H. Spinnler & F. Boller (Eds.), *Handbook of neuropsychology* (Vol. 8). Amsterdam: Elsevier.

Rund, B. R. (1998). A review of longitudinal studies of cognitive functions in schizophrenia patients. *Schizophrenia Bulletin, 24,* 425–435.

Russell, P. N., Bannatyne, P. A., & Smith, J. F. (1975). Associative strength as a mode of organization in recall and recognition: A comparison of schizophrenics and normals. *Journal of Abnormal Psychology, 84,* 122–128.

Russell, P. N., & Beekhuis, M. E. (1976). Organization in memory: A comparison of psychotics and normals. *Journal of Abnormal Psychology, 85,* 527–534.

Saykin, A. J., Gur, R. C., Gur, R. E., Mozley, P. D., Mozley, L. H., Resnick, S. M., Kester, D. B., & Stafiniak, P. (1991). Neuropsychological function in schizophrenia. Selective impairment in memory and learning. *Archives of General Psychiatry, 48,* 618–624.

Saykin, A. J., Shtasel, D. L., Gur, R. E., Kester, D. B., Mozley, L. H., Stafiniak, P., & Gur, R. C. (1994). Neuropsychological deficits in patients with first-episode schizophrenia. *Archives of General Psychiatry, 51,* 124–131.

Schacter, D. L. (1987). Implicit memory: history and current status. *Journal of Experimental Psychology: Learning Memory and Cognition, 11,* 501–518.

Schacter, D. L., & Buckner, R. L. (1998). On the relations among priming, conscious recollection, and intentional retrieval: Evidence from neuroimaging research. *Neurobiology of Learning and Memory, 70,* 284-303.

Schacter, D. L., Norman, K. A., & Koutstaal, W. (1998). The cognitive neuroscience of constructive memory. *Annual Review of Psychology, 49,* 289–318.

Schacter, D. L., & Tulving, E. (1994). What are the memory systems of 1994? In D. L. Schacter & E. Tulving (Eds.), *Memory systems.* Cambridge, MA: MIT Press.

Schacter, D. L., Verfaellie, M., & Anes, M. D. (1997). Illusory memories in amnesic patients: False recall and recognition in amnesic patients. *Journal of Memory and Language, 35,* 319–334.

Schizophrenia Society of Canada. (2000). http://www.schizophrenia.ca

Schwartz, B. L., Rosse, R. B., & Deutsch, S. (1993). Limits of the processing view in accounting for dissociations among memory measures in a clinical population. *Memory and Cognition, 21,* 63–72.

Sharma, T. (1999). Cognitive effects of conventional and atypical antipsychotics in schizophrenia. *British Journal of Psychiatry, 174,* S44–S51.

Spohn, H. E., & Strauss, M. E. (1989). Relation of neuroleptic and anticholinergic medication to cognitive functions in schizophrenia. *Journal of Abnormal Psychology, 98,* 367–380.

Stip, E. (1996). Memory impairment in schizophrenia: Perspectives from psychopathology and pharmacotherapy. *Canadian Journal of Psychiatry, 41,* 27–34.

Taylor, M. A., & Abrams, R. (1984). Cognitive impairment in schizophrenia. *American Journal of Psychiatry, 141,* 196–201.

Traupmann, K. L., Berzofsky, M., & Kesselman, M. (1976). Encoding of taxonomic word categories by schizophrenics. *Journal of Abnormal Psychology, 85,* 350–355.

Tsaung, M. T. (1982). Memory deficit and long-term outcome in schizophrenia: A preliminary study. *Psychiatry Research, 6,* 355–360.

Tulving, E. (1985). Memory and consciousness. *Canadian Psychology, 1,* 1–12.

Tulving, E., Kapur, S., Craik, F. I. M., Moscovitch, M., & Houle, S. (1994). Hemispheric encoding/ retrieval asymmetry in episodic memory: Positron emission tomography findings. *Proceedings of the National Academy of Sciences USA, 91,* 2016–2020.

Velligan, D. I., Mahurin, R. K., Diamond P. L., Hazleton, B. C., Eckert, S. L., & Miller A. L. (1997). The functional significance of symptomatology and cognitive function in schizophrenia. *Schizophrenia Research, 25,* 21–31.

Vidailhet, P., Danion, J. M., Kauffmann-Muller, F., Grange, D., Giersch, A., Van der Linden, M., & Imbs, J. L. (1994). Lorazepam and diazepam effects on memory acquisition in priming tasks. *Psychopharmacology (Berl), 115,* 397–406.

Weingartner, H., Cohen, R. M., Murphy, D. L., Martello, J., & Gerdt, C. (1981). Cognitive processes in depression. *Archives of General Psychiatry, 38,* 42–47.

Wheeler, M. A., Stuss, D. T., & Tulving, E. (1997). Toward a theory of episodic memory: The frontal lobes and autonoetic consciousness. *Psychological Bulletin, 121,* 331–354.

Zalewski, C., Johnson-Selfridge, M. T., Ohriner, S., Zarrella, K., & Seltzer, J. C. (1998). A review of neuropsychological differences between paranoid and nonparanoid schizophrenia patients. *Schizophrenia Bulletin, 24,* 127–145.

30

CHAPTER

Wilma Koutstaal
Daniel L. Schacter

Memory Distortion and Aging

Memory is often, but not invariably, a trustworthy guide to the past. Understanding the basis of memory's errors, involving mistakes of both omission and commission, is an important focus of contemporary research (cf., Johnson, Hashtroudi, & Lindsay, 1993; Koriat & Goldsmith, 1996; Koriat, Goldsmith, & Pansky, 2000; Koutstaal & Schacter, 1997b; Roediger, 1996; Schacter, 1999). Developing a theoretical account of memory errors requires understanding the nature of fundamental processes involved in the initial perception and interpretation of events (memory encoding), and processes involved in recognition or recall when we "re-collect" aspects of earlier experienced events (memory retrieval). Fergus Craik has contributed immensely to our understanding of these fundamental memory processes, and in so doing has also provided important insights into the basis of memory's imperfections.[1]

Craik's contributions to the understanding of imperfections in memory deriving from the loss of information, or errors of omission, are perhaps the most widely known. There are three especially prominent streams of work that we would like to consider briefly here, and then examine further with regard to errors of commission. First, according to the levels-of-processing framework (Craik & Lockhart, 1972; Jacoby & Craik, 1979; Lockhart & Craik, 1990; cf. White, 1983), shallow encoding may often be a substantial contributor to errors of omission. It may also, as we shall show—particularly when combined with a failure to encode "distinctive" features of an event or context—be a substantial contributor to errors of commission.

Second, and equally prominent, is Craik's extensive work examining the effects of nor-

---

[1]Perhaps ironically, although many of us may especially think of Fergus Craik in connection with his contributions to our understanding of "memory encoding," he and his collaborators have strongly emphasized the inseparability of the processes that lead to memory retention from the processes involved in cognition and perception more generally, arguing that there is no separably identifiable cognitive process of memory encoding. Thus: "There are many cognitive operations and functions, but . . . among these various processes there is nothing that corresponds to committing to memory. There is no distinct process of memorizing that can take its place alongside other cognitive operations" (Lockhart & Craik, 1990, p. 89), and "a second implication of the view that the memory trace is the by-product of perceptual/conceptual analysis, rather than the consequence of a special memory-encoding process, is that the only cognitive operation that can legitimately be referred to as 'remembering' is that of retrieval" (Lockhart & Craik, 1990, p. 89).

mal cognitive aging on memory. One influential account of age-related memory impairments, proposed by Craik and others, attributes age-related performance deficits to limited processing resources (Craik & Byrd, 1982; Salthouse, 1982). On this account, successful memory performance requires that an individual, during the initial processing of an item, encode sufficiently "distinctive" contextual information and then draw upon this at the time of retrieval. A concomitant of the reduced processing resources account is that age-related deficits may be manifested to a greater or lesser degree in a given situation depending on the amount of environmental support that is present to encourage adequate encoding and/or retrieval. In accord with this, age-related errors of omission may be less frequent under conditions where there is greater retrieval support, such as recognition, where "copy cues" of the studied items are presented, than in cases where little retrieval support is provided, such as free recall, where little beyond a general spatial-temporal context cue is provided (e.g., Craik, 1977; Craik & McDowd, 1987). As we will show, enhanced environmental support—at either encoding or retrieval—may likewise reduce errors of commission in both older and younger adults.

Third, associated with the notion of reduced processing resources induced by cognitive aging is the extensive work by Craik and his collaborators investigating the effects of *divided attention* or dual-task performance on memory. In agreement with the notion that memory performance may be impaired by a reduction in available processing resources, the pattern of effects found in younger adults working under dual-task conditions often resembles the pattern found in older adults working under full attention conditions (Anderson, Craik, & Naveh-Benjamin, 1998; Craik, 1982; Craik & Byrd, 1982; Whiting & Smith, 1997). Also, errors of omission are significantly more frequent when encoding takes place under dual-task than single-task conditions (e.g., Baddeley, Lewis, Eldridge, & Thomson, 1984; Craik, Govoni, Naveh-Benjamin, & Anderson, 1996; Mulligan, 1998). By contrast, dual-task performance during retrieval often yields no or comparatively smaller decreases in memory (e.g., Baddeley et al., 1984; Craik et al., 1996; Iidaka et al., 1999; Naveh-Benjamin, Craik, Guez, & Dori, 1998; Nyberg, Nilsson, Olofsson, & Backman, 1997; but see also Moscovitch, 1994; Moscovitch, Fernandes, & Troyer, chapter 14 of this volume; Fernandes & Moscovitch, 2000).

The effects of dual-task requirements on memory errors in the form of errors of commission are also complex: in some instances, secondary task performance has led to an increment in errors of commission, but as will be discussed below, this is not invariably observed. Further, under some conditions, although dual-task requirements simulate the effects of cognitive aging with regard to errors of omission in memory, they may simultaneously *fail to mimic* aging with respect to memory distortion (see Naveh-Benjamin, chapter 15 of this volume).

☐ Misattributions, Source Confusions, and False Recognition

Misattribution refers to situations in which some form of memory is present but is misattributed to an incorrect time, place, or person (e.g., Jacoby, Kelley, & Dywan, 1989; Johnson et al., 1993; Roediger, 1996; Schacter, 1999; Schacter, Norman, & Koutstaal, 1998). A common form of memory misattribution involves source confusions, in which an experience is "misaligned" or "misassigned" to an origin, context, or "source" other than that actually associated with the experience, as when we remember a particular statement, but mistakenly believe that it was (say) Penelope who told us this when, in fact, it was Marianne, or when we believe that we read something in a particular book but, in fact, read it elsewhere. Source misattributions appear to "straddle" the categories of errors of omission and errors of commission because they may derive from missing information regarding the context or origins of acquired information, but they also comprise a form of distortion, where information is incorrectly ascribed to an origin or context other than that in which it occurred. In the late 1980s, Craik and colleagues reported that older adults are more likely to forget source information than are younger adults (McIntyre & Craik, 1987). They further reported that age-related increases in source misattributions are correlated with declines on neuropsychological measures that are sensitive to frontal lobe dysfunction (Craik, Morris, Morris, & Loewen, 1990; also see Schacter, Harbluk, & McLachlan, 1984).[2]

During the mid-1990s, research in our lab began to link frontal lobe dysfunction with increased susceptibility to the phenomenon of false recognition: incorrectly claiming that a novel item or event was encountered earlier when it was not (cf., Roediger & McDermott, 1995; Underwood, 1965). First, we described a series of experiments concerning a patient with damage to the right frontal lobe who exhibited extremely high levels of false recognition across a wide range of laboratory tests (Curran, Schacter, Norman, & Galluccio, 1997; Schacter, Curran, Galluccio, Milberg, & Bates, 1996). Second, we carried out neuroimaging studies of false recognition using a procedure initially described by Deese (1959), and later revived and modified by Roediger and McDermott (1995), that produces extremely high levels of false alarms in healthy volunteers. In this procedure, participants first study word lists comprised of semantic associates, such that all of the 15 or so words in a list associatively "converge" on a given nonpresented theme word or critical lure. On a subsequent recognition test, participants frequently claim, with high confidence, that they previously studied the critical lure. Our imaging results generally indicated that the same brain regions are activated during true recognition of words from the study list and false recognition of critical lure words (Schacter, Reiman et al., 1996; Schacter, Buckner, Koutstaal, Dale, & Rosen, 1997). However, under certain testing conditions, false recognition elicited greater right frontal activity than did true recognition.

In light of Craik's earlier observations concerning the possible role of frontal lobe dysfunction in source misattributions by older adults, these neuropsychological and neuroimaging findings suggested to us that older adults might be more susceptible to false recognition than younger adults. Consistent with this, a search of the literature yielded several early reports of increased false alarm rates among older relative to younger adults (Bartlett, Leslie, Tubbs, & Fulton, 1989; G. Cohen & Faulkner, 1989; Rankin & Kausler, 1979; Smith, 1975; for review, see Schacter, Koutstaal, & Norman, 1997). This view was

---

[2]A more recent exploration of misattribution in older adults was reported by Law, Hawkins, and Craik (1998) and involved "repetition-induced belief" (also termed the "truth effect"), a phenomenon in which individuals show greater belief in fictitious statements that have been presented previously than in nonrepeated fictitious statements. In this study, consistent with many other studies, compared with younger adults older adults were found to make more false alarms during recognition testing, were more prone to source-confusion errors (judging where they had seen the claims before: outside the experiment, in the first part of the experiment, or never) and more prone to conditionalized source-confusion errors (judging the origins of a claim *given that* they correctly identified it as previously presented). Older adults also showed a greater effect of repetition (greater "truth-inflation") than did younger adults in part because of their greater likelihood of (incorrectly) attributing statements to extraexperimental sources. (For both younger and older adults, truth ratings tended to be highest for items perceived to have been encountered outside the experiment.) However, use of an imagery-related encoding task yielded equivalent memory performance in older and younger adults (hits, false alarms, and source memory were similar in the two age groups under imagery instructions); the age-related difference in "truth-inflation" was also eliminated in the imagery condition.

also encouraged by further neuroimaging findings indicating that, under conditions of difficult retrieval, older adults exhibit different patterns of right frontal activation than younger adults (Schacter, Savage, Alpert, Rauch, & Albert, 1996). Neuropsychological comparisons of older adults and patients with frontal lesions likewise appeared to implicate frontal system dysfunction in older adults (Stuss, Craik, Sayer, Franchi, & Alexander, 1996; for review, see Moscovitch & Winocur, 1992, 1995, West, 1996). We next discuss, in some detail, recent studies from our laboratory and others that focus on false recognition in older adults in relation to two areas explored by Fergus Craik: the effect of "levels of encoding" (particularly in conjunction with the notion of distinctiveness, as advanced by Jacoby and Craik (1979) in a revision of the 1972 levels-of-processing approach), and the effect of dual-task performance (divided attention) during encoding and/or retrieval.

☐ Levels of Encoding, Distinctiveness, and False Recognition

In a paper titled, "Effects of Elaboration of Processing at Encoding and Retrieval: Trace Distinctiveness and Recovery of Initial Context," Jacoby and Craik (1979) began by outlining several observations—and qualifications—concerning the levels-of-processing framework as it was initially proposed by Craik and Lockhart (1972). Jacoby and Craik noted two early-emerging difficulties: first, problems in specifying exactly what was meant by "deep" processing and, second, problems posed by the presence of *within-level* variability in how well material was remembered. Given that material was meaningfully or semantically processed, why did recall nonetheless sometimes vary with the particular type of encoding task that was performed? These difficulties led to an attempt to incorporate additional mechanisms. These included, first, an acknowledgement of the importance of the *breadth* of elaboration, not only depth (Craik & Tulving, 1975; Lockhart, Craik, & Jacoby, 1976, proposed that whereas the notion of depth might well capture differences in across-domain levels of processing, such as phonemic vs. semantic coding, the notion of breadth might better capture within-domain differences in the extensiveness of processing) and, second, an acknowledgment of the significant role played by the factor of *distinctiveness*, or the extent to which an item is encoded so as to allow its differentiation from other, possibly quite similar, items (cf. Einstein & Hunt, 1980; Nelson, 1979; see also Klein & Saltz, 1976; Moscovitch & Craik, 1976).

In developing this viewpoint further, Jacoby and Craik (1979) underscored a conception of the memory trace as essentially a description, or *set of contrasts*, as in the multicomponent view of memory proposed by Bower (1967) or the attribute approach of Underwood (1969), but with the additional emphasis that such contrasts necessarily must be construed relative to the particular context or task in which they occur:

> A description that is highly distinctive for a particular set of alternatives is not necessarily distinctive for another set. Consequently, the distinctiveness of the description of an event cannot be specified without considering the alternatives from which it has been contrasted. If the set of alternatives is changed drastically, a previously distinctive description may be of very little use. (Jacoby & Craik, 1979, p. 5)

These key points are very similar to those that we recently stressed in relation to the conditions that may lead to high levels of *false recognition* or *false recall*, where we further linked these notions with the need to develop nonoverlapping representations of the study items (McClelland, McNaughton, & O'Reilly, 1995; O'Reilly & McClelland, 1994; Schacter et al., 1998; see also Gluck & Myers, 1996). Several experiments from our lab have examined the effects of encoding manipulations intended to enhance the availability of item-specific or distinctive information for reducing false recognition. One set of experiments used the converging semantic associates paradigm described above, in which participants encounter lists of words, where all of the words in each list are associatively related to a nonpresented theme word, and where individuals typically show high levels of false recognition responding. However, a key manipulation in these experiments (Israel & Schacter, 1997; Schacter, Israel, & Racine, 1999) involved provision of distinctive information, in the form of black-and-white line drawings, that accompanied the words in one of the conditions (pictures + words encoding condition, words presented auditorily, simultaneously with visual presentation of the picture) but not in another condition (words-only encoding condition, words presented auditorily simultaneously with visual presentation of the word). False recognition in the low-distinctive words-only condition was markedly higher than in a condition where the list items were accompanied by distinctive pictorial information. Further, this decrease in false recognition responses for words accompanied by distinctive pictorial information relative to the words-only condition was also strongly shown by older adults.[3]

Perhaps even more convincing as an illustration of the importance of "distinctiveness" in errors of commission, particularly construed as a set of contrasts between a given set of target items and an overall larger set of items (Jacoby & Craik, 1979), are data showing that the converse combination—verbal elaborations of highly detailed pictures—may likewise act to reduce false recognition. All else being equal, pictures are, indeed, highly distinctive. But all else is *not* equal if many pictures are derived from a given object category (for example, 18 different teddy bears, or 18 different teapots, or chairs): Here the "contrasts" that are spontaneously coded in perceiving the objects might be sufficient to allow differentiation of, for example, a teapot from other types of objects, or from quite different objects within the same class, but not necessarily the particular teapots that were encountered versus others that were not shown but are very similar to those that were shown. And, indeed, relatively high levels of false recognition of pictured objects from categories where numerous exemplars of the same sort have been presented have been

---

[3]It would be remiss on our part not to remark upon a certain methodological "regression" in many, although not all, of the recent experiments using the converging semantic associates paradigm, namely, the use of *intentional learning instructions* in the absence of a further orienting task. This was the procedure that we, too, adopted in our neuroimaging studies of false recognition using this paradigm (Schacter, Reiman, et al., 1996; Schacter, Buckner, et al., 1997) and in the experiments exploring the effects of distinctive pictorial information on false recognition (Israel & Schacter, 1997; Schacter et al., 1999). However, for several reasons, this is clearly a less-than-ideal experimental design, given the early—and convincing—arguments of Craik and Lockhart (1972), and reiterated in Lockhart and Craik (1990, p. 89), that intentional instructions represent a loss of experimental control over processing operations, confounding as they do the subject's choice of processing strategy on the one hand, with the differential consequences (for subsequent tests of memory) of that particular form of processing on the other. Orienting task instructions provide better, if not perfect, experimental control over input processing. Such tasks provide an independent variable that can be operationally defined, described in functional processing terms, and, through monitoring subjects' responses during the orienting task, provide some check that the designated processing is being performed. Another virtue of incidental instructions lies in their capacity to model the cognitive operations that occur in everyday cognition. Given these concerns, and the further possibility that older adults may be especially disadvantaged under conditions involving simple intentional learning instructions that provide little environmental support, it is important to note that in the subsequently discussed experiments demonstrating a consistent age-related increase in false recognition using categorized pictures, an orienting task was always used (most often, participants rated how much they liked each picture, comprising a relatively strong "item-specific" encoding task).

observed (Koutstaal & Schacter, 1997a). Both older and younger adults frequently incorrectly endorse as having been "studied" new items from categories where they have studied many similar items, with rates of false recognition to lures from many-exemplar categories averaging 29% (across three experiments) for younger adults (compared to baseline rates of false alarms of about 5% for novel categories) and 64% for older adults (compared to baseline rates of 10% to 22%).

In this situation, verbal information that helps to single out features or aspects of an object that are comparatively rare may help to differentiate the items and later assist in the discrimination of studied items from similar but not studied items of the same sort. Results of an experiment testing this prediction yielded just this result. Participants in the experimental condition first encountered pictured items in the context of distinctive verbal elaborators—instructions calling their attention to two differentiating or individuating features of the object, which they were then asked to notice during the subsequent presentation of the object (e.g., "Notice the compact, pudgy body and round feet of this teddy bear" or "Notice the silvery-white color and attached seat cover of this motorcycle"). Both older and younger adults in this experimental condition showed lower levels of false recognition than in a control condition, where they first performed an unrelated filler task, then read the object name and indicated whether or not they liked the particular item (Koutstaal, Schacter, Galluccio, & Stofer, 1999). Nonetheless, although both age groups benefited from the verbal elaborators, older adults (as found in several previous experiments with these materials and also with semantically related words) continued to show elevated false recognition relative to that shown by the young.

However, there is an important qualification that must be made regarding both of these experiments—a qualification stemming from an apparently minor aspect of the experimental design, but possibly quite important in determining how the task was performed and thus the implications that can be drawn regarding memory. In both of the experiments described thus far, the manipulation of encoding task occurred on a *between-subjects* basis. Under these conditions, it is possible that participants in the more distinctive encoding conditions demonstrated lower levels of false recognition simply as a result of an overall change in their response criteria for designating items as "old." That is, individuals in both the pictures-plus-words condition of the semantic associates paradigm and the verbal elaborators condition of the categorized pictures paradigm may simply have changed their decision criteria regarding how much they needed to "recollect" or the type of information they believed they needed to recollect, before designating an item as "old" relative to that used by participants in the control conditions. Indeed, using the semantic associates paradigm, Schacter et al. (1999) found a reduction in false recognition for items accompanied by pictures only when the encoding task was varied between subjects. When, instead, a given participant was presented some study lists with accompanying pictures and others without such distinctive pictorial information, then neither younger nor older adults showed a reduction in false recognition compared to the word-only encoding condition.

Schacter et al. (1999) hypothesized that the divergent findings from these conditions could be explained if the reduction of false recognition in the between-subjects condition reflected the use of a *distinctiveness heuristic*: a mode of responding in which, because individuals are aware that they can sometimes recollect items with a high degree of specificity (considerable richness or vividness), they come to consistently demand such high-quality recollective material to justify a positive recognition response. The possible role of heuristics, or "rules of thumb," in many areas of cognition is widely acknowledged. Individuals may often "focus on that subset of available information that enables them to use simple inferential rules, schemata, or cognitive heuristics to formulate their judgments and decisions" (Chaiken, Lieberman, & Eagly, 1989, p. 212). The possible role of heuristics has also been emphasized in connection with memory judgments by several research-ers (Johnson et al., 1993; see also Jacoby, Kelley, & Dywan, 1989; Whittlesea & Leboe, 2000). Schacter et al. (1999) proposed that, in the between-subjects condition, where all of the words were accompanied by drawings, participants may have adopted such a heuristic, becoming especially attuned to whether they could recollect distinctive details about an item and using a criteria of the sort, "If I do not remember seeing a picture of an item, it is probably new." A similar account could be proposed for the reduction in false recognition of pictures that we observed for pictures that were accompanied with verbal elaborators rela-tive to those without such elaborators: because participants in this experiment either saw all of the pictures with accompanying distinctive elaborators, or performed the liking rating control task for all of the items, false recognition suppression in these experiments could be attributed to the operation of a distinctiveness heuristic (cf. Schacter et al., 1999, p. 20).

To examine the issue, we conducted another experiment using the categorized pictures and again using the distinctive verbal elaborators, but now adopting a within-subject de-sign. For any given participant, objects from some categories were accompanied with dis-tinctive verbal information, but, for objects from other categories, no distinctive verbal information was provided and participants simply evaluated whether they did or did not like the particular item presented. However, postexperimental questioning during pilot testing with younger adults uncovered a slight complication. If the "liking rating" items were randomly interspersed with the "verbal elaboration" items, then participants began to generate their own verbal elaborations for the liking task items, thereby invalidating our experimental comparison.[4] To circumvent this difficulty, we decided to temporally block the items by encoding task. We first presented all of the items for the liking rating task with no prior mention of the verbal elaborator task, and then, immediately after these items, with only a brief interval required to provide instructions for the verbal elaborator encoding condition, we presented the items for the verbal elaboration task. Note that, even in this temporally blocked paradigm, individuals saw different types of objects interspersed throughout the list; only the encoding task, not the categories, were blocked. Then, following a three-day retention interval, participants were given an old/new recognition test consisting of items from both the liking rating task and the verbal elaboration task, with items from the two encoding tasks randomly intermixed throughout the list.

Critically, under these conditions, an overall shift in criteria will not allow selective decrement in false recognition for the items studied with the verbal elaborators. Demanding recollection of the verbal elaborators (or perceptually specific information that may have been encoded under the guidance of the elaborators) for all items before designating them as "old" is not feasible because only half of the studied items were studied with verbal elaborators and so can be expected to yield such information during recollection; an equal

---

[4]We tested 20 younger adults in the randomly intermixed version. For these subjects, there was a nearly significant overall effect of the encoding condition, with baseline-corrected false recognition for many-exemplar lures in the verbal elaborator condition (.23) lower than in the liking rating con-trol condition (.32), $F(1, 19) = 4.02$, $MSE = .02$, $p = .06$. However, this effect was entirely driven by the 12 younger adults who did not report that they generated their own elaborations for the control items, means of .25 and .41 for verbal elaborator and liking rating conditions, respectively, $F(1, 11) = 14.07$, $MSE = .01$, $p = .003$. Participants who reported that they generated their own elaborations for the control items showed no effect of the encoding condition, means of .20 and .18 respectively, $F(1, 7) < 1$; $F(1, 18) = 4.42$, $MSE = .02$, $p = .05$ for the condition × self-reported strategy interaction. Note that, both across all subjects (.32) and within only those subjects who did not report self-generation of elaborators (.41), the rate of false recognition for the liking rating items is very similar to, or greater than, what was found for liking rating items in the between-subjects design (.33).

number of the studied items do not have such distinctive information, and the items from these two sets are randomly interspersed with one another throughout the test.

The results of this within-subject manipulation are shown in Figure 30.1, with false recognition responses shown in the upper panel and veridical recognition responses shown in the lower panel (data not previously published; we thank Sara Greene for experimental assistance). Both false and veridical responses are shown separately as a function of the *encoding task* (liking rating or verbal elaborators), *age* (older and younger adults), and *category size* (single, where only 1 item from a given object category was shown at study, and large, where 18 items from a given object category were shown at study).

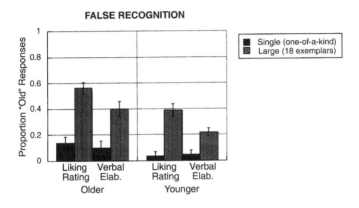

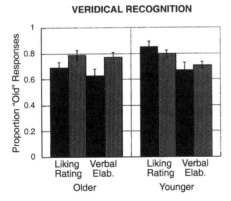

FIGURE 30.1. Proportion of false recognition responses (upper panel) and veridical recognition responses (lower panel) for older and younger adults for pictures encoded with the liking rating task and the verbal elaborator task. Results are shown separately for items where only a single item of a given category was shown at study and for items where a large number of similar exemplars were presented at study. The data have been corrected for baseline differences in false alarms to novel category items. False recognition responses to category items where many exemplars had been presented at study were significantly reduced if items were encoded with the verbal elaborators that emphasized differentiating characteristics of the objects relative to the liking rating comparison task. This reduction in false recognition was observed even though the encoding task was manipulated within subjects and was seen for both older and younger adults.

As is clear from Figure 30.1, and in marked contrast with the earlier findings of Schacter et al. (1999), there was a selective reduction of false recognition for the encoding condition involving distinctive information. The verbal elaborators substantially (and significantly) reduced false recognition responding in both older adults and younger adults: false recognition decreases of 16% and 17%, respectively, compared to the liking rating control condition. In the liking rating control condition, levels of false recognition in both age groups remained at least as high as for the corresponding items in the between-subjects design (baseline-corrected false recognition for liking rating items in within-subjects vs. between-subjects conditions of .56 vs. .53 for older adults, and .39 vs. .33 for younger adults). Furthermore, as also shown in Figure 30.1 (lower panel), this reduction in false recognition was not accompanied, at least for older adults, by a cost in hits for target items; for older adults, hit rates for items that were studied with the verbal elaborators (.88, uncorrected for baseline false alarms) and those studied with the liking rating task (.90) were nearly identical. Younger adults, however, did show a significant decrement in hits for the verbal-elaboration items (.76), relative to the liking rating items (.85), but this reduction was not as great as the reduction in false recognition. An analysis comparing true and false recognition for the large (many-exemplar) categories showed an interaction of item type (target vs. lure) with encoding condition, such that the overall reduction in false alarms (.17) was more than three times as great as the reduction in hits (.05), $F(1, 38)$ = 9.94, MSE = .013, p = .003, with no age × item type × encoding condition interaction, $F <$ 1. Nonetheless, although older adults were able to reduce false recognition responding in the verbal elaborator condition, they continued to show significantly higher levels of false recognition than did younger adults.[5]

Further research will be needed to determine why distinctive information associated with a subset of the studied items could be used successfully to oppose false recognition responding here, in the within-subjects design using categorized pictures but not in the within-subjects version of the converging semantic associates paradigm. (See Table 30.1 for a partial summary of the differing results of these studies.) One possible relevant difference between the two studies is the presence versus absence of temporal blocking during encoding. Whereas items in the distinctive condition of the categorized pictures ex-

---

[5]Because items from the two encoding conditions were presented intermixed with one another on the test, there was only one (common) "baseline" level of false alarms to novel categories, and thus analyses performed on the baseline-corrected scores and on the raw scores will yield identical outcomes with only the absolute levels of responding changed. As has often been observed, older adults also showed higher baseline levels of false alarms (.11) than did younger adults (.05), $F(1, 38)$ = 4.50, MSE = .008, p = .04.

The question of why—even granting that the decrement in hits was smaller than that in false recognition—one should observe decreased hits for large category items at all, particularly in younger adults, is somewhat puzzling. If older adults showed a pattern of decreased false recognition and (more moderately) decreased hits for large category items, this might be attributed to a reduced reliance on general similarity or gist information because other evidence suggests that older adults' apparently "intact" veridical recognition of large category targets may be substantially supported by gist information (see Koutstaal & Schacter, 1997a; Koutstaal et al., 1999, for discussion). In the between-subjects design of Koutstaal et al. (1999, Experiment 2), there was also a reduction in true recognition in the verbal elaborator compared with the liking rating condition, but this reduction was numerically greater in older than younger adults. There, based on signal detection analyses, we suggested that the decrement in hits might have arisen from an overall shift towards more conservative response criteria in the verbal elaborator group. However, the findings from the subsequent within-subject experiment shown in Figure 30.1 clearly suggest that substantial reductions in false recognition and more modest reductions in veridical recognition are observed primarily for categories for which distinctive information was presented.

periment were temporally blocked, the items in the distinctive condition of the semantic associates paradigm were not blocked (i.e., associate lists with, versus without, distinctive line-drawings were distributed throughout the study session). Temporal blocking might have provided an additional cue to allow the selective application of a distinctiveness heuristic in the categorized pictures experiment. However, the findings from our pilot study with younger adults using categorized pictures and randomly intermixed encoding argue against differences in temporal blocking as an explanation. As noted previously, we found that some of the young participants in this pilot study began to generate their own elaborations for the liking task items, thereby invalidating our experimental comparison. However, when we examined the pattern of findings for only those participants who reported that they continued to follow the assigned encoding task, then (in this subset of subjects) we found significantly reduced false recognition for the verbal elaborator lure items compared to the liking rating items (see footnote 4). This finding suggests that temporal blocking was not necessary in order to observe a selective reduction in false recognition for the distinctive condition.

Another possibility that might be explored experimentally concerns the likelihood that participants, at the time of retrieval, could "link" distinctive encoding operations or information with the particular categories for which distinctive information was present. Whereas, for a number of reasons, such linking may have been relatively difficult in the case of the semantic associate lists, it may have been less difficult for the categorized pictures. Indeed, the category names for all of the items, in both the verbal elaborator condition and the control condition, were themselves actually presented during the study phase. Taken together, these outcomes clearly underscore the importance of distinctive encoding in determining rates of false recognition, but also implicate several possible mediating factors that may affect when, and how, such encoding may be used to reduce mistaken recognition.

Recent work has attempted to explore further some of the boundary conditions under which the distinctiveness heuristic may be invoked. One such condition relates to the *diagnosticity* of the distinctive information, that is, the probability that failing to remember distinctive information indicates that the target item is new. For example, in the between-subjects manipulation of the verbal elaborators for the categorized pictures, the distinctive information is completely diagnostic. Because, in this condition, all of the pictures were encoded with verbal elaborators, the presence or absence of memory for the verbal information (or the differentiating features pointed to by the descriptors) is completely predictive of the item's "oldness." However, in the within-subjects manipulation of the same paradigm, verbal elaborators are not completely diagnostic: Because one half of the pictures were encoded with verbal elaborators, and one half with the liking rating task, failure to retrieve associated verbal information might indicate either that an item is new (and so should be rejected) or that the item was studied but not with a verbal elaborator (and thus should not be rejected on these grounds). From the outcomes of the within-subjects manipulation, it is clear that it was not necessary that the distinctive information be entirely diagnostic: Even when only 50% of the pictures were accompanied by distinctive descriptors, participants were still able to reduce false recognition responding. Further, from Table 30.1 it appears that the magnitude of this reduction was at least as great as in the between-subjects design, where all of the pictures were accompanied by distinctive verbal information.

Using a different type of paradigm, Dodson and Schacter (in press) have also shown that individuals may adopt the distinctiveness heuristic under conditions where as few as 50%, or even only 25%, of the items are accompanied, at the time of study, by information that could be expected to be remembered. These studies used a modified version of the

TABLE 30.1. False recognition rates under distinctive and nondistinctive encoding conditions.

Study	Stimulus type	Experimental design	Age group	Baseline-corrected false recognition*		
				Nondistinctive	Distinctive	Reduction
S, I, & R (1999, Expt. 1)[a]	Semantic associates, with vs. without B & W line-drawings	Between subjects	Older	.48	.28	.20
			Younger	.38	.33	.05
S, I, & R (1999, Expt. 2)[a]	Semantic associates, with vs. without B & W line-drawings	Within subjects	Older	.51	.43	.08
			Younger	.30	.31	-.01
K, S, G, & S (1999, Expt. 2)[b]	Categorized pictures, with vs. without verbal elaborators	Between subjects	Older	.53	.45	.08
			Younger	.33	.20	.13
K & S (this volume)	Categorized pictures, with vs. without verbal elaborators	Within subjects	Older	.56	.40	.16
			Younger	.39	.22	.17

* False recognition rates for critical lures (semantic associate paradigm) and large-category exemplars (categorized pictures paradigm) after correction for false alarms to false target control lures and novel category lures respectively.
[a]Results are from Schacter, Israel, and Racine (1999) for conditions where distinctive information was presented at study but not test (i.e., picture + word at study, word only at test).
[b]Results are from Koutstaal, Schacter, Galluccio, and Stofer (1999).

"repetition lag" paradigm used by Jennings and Jacoby (1997). In this paradigm, participants first study a set of words and are then given a recognition test; however, in the recognition test, the new items are repeated. The repeated new items may be repeated at varying lags, with, for example, 4, 12, 24, or 48 intervening items between the initial appearance of a new word and its reappearance. Participants are told to identify as "old" only the studied items: New items, even when they are repeated, are to be classified as "new." The experimental manipulation that allows examination of the role of distinctiveness, and particularly the role of the distinctiveness heuristic, involves varying how the items are studied. In all of the conditions, the items are presented auditorily as words, but, in addition, they are accompanied either by the visual presentation of the word (the non-distinctive condition) or by a line drawing of the word (the distinctive condition). As noted above, Dodson and Schacter found that participants were able to reduce false recognition responses to the repeated new items under conditions where they had studied pictures, even when only 50% or even 25% of the study items were presented as pictures. Critically, in this paradigm, attributing the reduction in false recognition to reliance on a heuristic concerning the ability to retrieve distinctive information is also clearer, inasmuch as it is not possible that participants simply encoded the distinctive categories more effectively (and thus reduced false recognition to related lures within the same category); here, the lure words are unrelated to the words that were studied with the pictorial information.

☐ Dual-Task Performance and False Recognition

As noted above, a key contribution by Fergus Craik has involved work on long-term memory under conditions of dual-task performance or divided attention. This work, partially rooted in Craik's long-standing interest in the notions of reduced cognitive capacity or reduced processing resources as underlying deficits in cognitive aging, has yielded three robust findings: (a) there is a reduction in veridical recognition (a decrease in hits, or an increase in errors of omission) when a secondary task is performed at study (Baddeley et al., 1984; Craik et al., 1996; Mulligan, 1998); (b) with the exception of cases where the materials involved in the memory task and the secondary task tap the same domain (e.g., both involve words, cf. Fernandes & Moscovitch, 2000), there are typically minimal effects on veridical recognition if a secondary task is performed at test (Baddeley et al., 1984; Craik et al., 1996; Iidaka et al., 1999; Naveh-Benjamin et al., 1998; Nyberg et al., 1997), although, particularly in the case of free or cued recall, retrieval may lead to decrements in performance on the secondary task (Anderson et al., 1998; Craik et al., 1996; Naveh-Benjamin et al., 1998); and (c) the pattern of effects found in younger adults working under dual-task conditions (divided attention) often resembles the pattern found in older adults working under single-task conditions (full attention) (Anderson et al., 1998; Craik, 1982; Craik & Byrd, 1982; Whiting & Smith, 1997).

However, another important question one can ask concerns the effects of dual task performance not (as in each of these three findings) on errors of omission, but on errors of *commission*. For example, are similarity-based errors such as those contributing to false recognition, where we may confuse similar-seeming but not previously encountered objects (people, names, pictures, words) with objects that we did, in fact, experience, more likely under dual-task compared to single-task conditions? Here, dual-task conditions during encoding and/or attempted retrieval have been thought to increase the likelihood that participants will rely on a general sense of familiarity, or comparatively broad undifferentiated assessments of the similarity of tested items to previously encountered items, rather than more detailed or specific forms of recollection (e.g., Jacoby, 1991; Jacoby, Toth,

& Yonelinas, 1993), and generally have been found to increase errors of commission. For instance, higher levels of false recognition of semantically related lures have been found under dual-task conditions at study than under a single task (Mandler & Worden, 1973; but also see Seamon, Luo, & Gallo, 1998), and performance of a secondary task at test has been associated with an increased likelihood of misattribution errors (Jacoby, Woloshyn, & Kelley, 1989; Jacoby, 1999b). Indeed, in their paper discussing the role of attentional resources in aging and cognitive deficits, Craik and Byrd (1982) explicitly noted the similarity between the performance of younger adults under conditions of divided attention during learning (Mandler & Worden, 1973) and that of older adults (Rankin & Kausler, 1979), with both of these groups showing an increased tendency to incorrectly endorse synonyms of presented words during recognition testing relative to that shown by younger adults in the absence of dual task requirements. Craik and Byrd argued that these parallel outcomes

> strongly imp[ly] that older people and *divided-attention* subjects do encode something of the meaning of the words learned but that the encoded meaning is less specific and precise. That is, enough of the word's meaning has been encoded to enable the subject to choose that general category at the time of recognition, but not enough to enable him to differentiate between the correct word and a semantically similar distractor item. (pp. 196–197, italics in original)

We recently examined several questions relating to the effects of dual task performance on false recognition (Koutstaal, Schacter, & Brenner, 2001) using the categorized pictures stimuli described earlier. In one condition, we asked if matching older and younger participants on veridical recognition—by asking younger adults but not older adults to perform a secondary task concurrently with the presentation of the pictures—would also lead to an equation of false recognition responding in older and younger adults. More specifically, we asked what effect matching the two age groups on veridical recognition for items where they had encountered only one item of that particular kind—a condition minimally supported by "gist-like" processing or category information and maximally reliant on item-specific processing—had on false recognition of many-exemplar category lures. Would younger adults under these conditions of depressed "item-specific memory" show, as had been found for older adults, high levels of false recognition responding for categories where many similar objects had been studied?

Surprisingly, unlike the typical pattern in the literature, where placing younger individuals under dual task demands has most often yielded outcomes paralleling those found for older adults (e.g., Dywan, Segalowitz, & Webster, 1998; Jacoby, 1999b, Experiment 3; Jennings & Jacoby, 1993; Mäntylä & Bäckman, 1992, Experiment 3; see also Craik, 1982; Craik & Byrd, 1982, for discussion), we found that division of attention during encoding did not simulate the effects of aging for false recognition. Although we were able to closely match the two age groups on level of veridical recognition of one-of-a-kind items, the matched young group did not show a rate of false recognition similar to that of older adults who performed both study and test under single-task conditions. Matching of older and younger adults on one-of-a-kind veridical recognition was especially close when we combined an initial young group who performed the dual task at study only with a further young group who also performed the dual task at study only but in combination with being exposed to the items for a briefer time during study (500 ms rather than 2 seconds).[6]

---

[6]Baseline-corrected one-of-a-kind veridical recognition rates were as follows: younger controls = .77; older adults = .53; younger adults with dual task at study = .61; younger adults with dual task at study and faster presentation rate during study = .38 (average of the latter two younger groups = .50); younger adults with only a faster presentation rate during study and no dual task = .65.

We also did not see rates of false recognition similar to those of the old when, in two further conditions, younger adults were required to perform the secondary task at retrieval, during old/new recognition testing, or at both encoding and retrieval: Decreased resources at retrieval appeared to have a relatively minimal effect on false recognition responses of the young. For older adults, with no secondary task, the baseline-corrected false recognition rate for many-exemplar categories was 43%; for younger adults, also under conditions of no secondary task, similar to the findings from many earlier experiments, the corresponding rate was considerably lower (22%); however, this was also remarkably similar to that found under conditions involving a secondary task at study-only, test-only, and study-and-test, which resulted in false recognition rates of 23%, 24%, and 25%, respectively.

This outcome, showing no effect on false recognition of younger adults under dual task conditions at retrieval, appears to be rather surprising given that recognition (and correct rejections) in this paradigm might be assumed to place considerable demands on "recollection" of item-specific details. Stated in terms of Fergus Craik's framework of environmental support, although recognition tests typically have been construed as placing fewer demands on "self-initiated processing" than free recall, in this paradigm, where numerous similar items have been encountered and the lures may have many shared similarities with the targets, recognition decisions might be thought to require relatively more extensive self-initiated processing (Craik, 1983) than in a typical yes/no recognition test composed of unrelated items, possibly bringing recognition judgments closer to a "source discrimination task." For example, Troyer, Winocur, Craik, and Moscovitch (1999) recently reported greater decrements in secondary-task performance during the retrieval of source information than during retrieval of item information.

The absence of an effect of dual task at test on false recognition also appears to be somewhat surprising given evidence that other forms of (apparently minor) alterations of responding at retrieval have proven to be effective in the opposite direction, that is, decreasing, rather than increasing, false recognition responding by both older and younger adults. For example, using the same categorized pictures paradigm, we found that changing the recognition test format from a simple yes/no decision to a three-pronged, more fine-grained decision, where participants were asked to indicate if the item was "old-and-identical," "new-but-related," or "new-and-unrelated," considerably reduced false recognition among both older and younger adults (Koutstaal et al., 1999, Experiment 1; also see Dodson & Johnson, 1993, showing reduced source monitoring errors in a traditional source memory task given such item-by-item monitoring during testing, and Lindsay & Johnson, 1989, and Zaragoza & Koshmider, 1989, for similar reductions in errors as a function of test format in the misinformation paradigm). If requiring additional scrutiny during retrieval successfully reduces false recognition (and source confusion and misattribution errors), why did making such scrutiny more difficult—through the imposition of the requirement to concurrently perform an attention-demanding secondary task—not increase false recognition? Note that it is not likely that the secondary task that we used was generally ineffective or insufficiently demanding; the task, involving shadowing random digits and monitoring for occurrences of three odd digits in a row, has been used in previous research and, in the present study, led to very clear and significant decrements in veridical recognition among younger adults when imposed at the time of study. Further, it is unlikely that the failure to observe an effect of the dual task at retrieval is a Type II error because this minimal effect of dual task at test on false recognition was observed in two separate conditions, involving the dual task at test-only and at both study-and-test.

Multiple considerations may be relevant here. However, first we would like to outline briefly a further situation where matching older and younger adults on errors of omission did not yield equivalent performance of the two age groups on a form of error of commission. This study entailed a somewhat complex (and slightly diabolical!) "test-priming" procedure, reported recently by Jacoby (1999a). In this paradigm, older and younger participants initially studied lists of related word pairs (e.g., bed sheet, eagle bird, knee bone). Thereafter, their recall for the target words was tested by presenting the first word of each pair, together with a fragment of the second word (e.g., knee b_n_). Additionally, however, during recall, some of the words were preceded by the presentation of a "prime" word that was either *congruent* with the studied word pair (e.g., sheet; bed s_ee_) or incongruent with the studied word pair (e.g., sleep; bed s_ee_). Baseline test items in which no prime word was presented were also included (e.g., &&&&; eagle b__d). Participants were explicitly informed that the prime word would often be misleading and were told that they should be sure to recall the earlier presented target item rather than be misled. Compared with younger adults, older adults much more often incorrectly intruded the incongruent item. Furthermore, this pattern was also found when younger adults were required to perform a dual task during the study phase, thereby depressing their level of correct recall for the baseline test trials to a level equivalent to the older group who performed only the memory encoding task at study.

In both of these paradigms, dual-task demands equated older and younger adults on one type of error, errors of omission, but did not eliminate age differences in a second type of error, errors of commission, involving false recognition and false recall. One possibility is that these age-related differences in errors of commission were found because the retrieval conditions in these two experiments were such as to place particularly stringent demands on the need to strategically oppose not only a very broad "undifferentiated" form of familiarity-based responding, but also relatively specific "target-consistent" features of the lure items. In both the Jacoby (1999a) experiment and the dual-task categorized pictures experiment, multiple features of the lures may have been consistent with participants' memory representations of the studied item. In the Jacoby experiment, the semantic context and some of the orthographic and phonetic information of the (incongruent) lures matched that of the target items. Likewise, in the dual-task picture experiment, in the case of items from large categories, in addition to global sources of familiarity for the categorized lures (e.g., semantic information about the categories), specific perceptual features of the lures, such as color, or overall shape, may have more or less closely "echoed" features of presented target items. Rejection of such similar-seeming lures may have proved especially difficult, with younger adults more often noticing or actively seeking out target-inconsistent features that would allow correct rejection of the lures. This proposal is also consistent with recent evidence reported by Henkel, Johnson, and De Leonardis (1998) from a source monitoring experiment, where older adults showed particular difficulties in discriminating between items that they had imagined versus items that they had actually perceived when the imagined and perceived items were either physically or conceptually similar to one another, for example, a lollipop and a magnifying glass, or a banana and an apple. These age differences in source monitoring errors were found even though older and younger adults had been equated on their level of old/new recognition through using a longer retention interval for the younger adults and were "stimulus specific" in that a similar age-related source monitoring deficit was not found for control items, that is, items where the perceived and imagined items had no particular conceptual or physical similarity with one another.

Nonetheless, although these outcomes underscore the possible particular importance of more stimulus-specific similarities in the lures in contributing to the false recognition performance of older adults, two considerations suggest that age-related differences under these conditions may not entirely or exclusively relate to strategic retrieval monitoring differences in older and younger adults. First, this account might also lead to the expectation that, with dual-task demands imposed at the time of testing, or at both study-and-test, younger adults should also show similarly increased difficulty in successfully rejecting lures. Yet, as the results reported above demonstrated, this outcome was not found. Second, neuropsychological evidence suggests that frontal regions are particularly involved in strategic retrieval and evaluation (e.g., Johnson et al., 1993; Moscovitch, 1994; West, 1996) and older adults' deficits in source monitoring and difficult forms of retrieval have been associated with aging-related declines in frontal lobe functioning (e.g., Johnson et al., 1993; Parkin & Walter, 1992; Schacter, Savage et al., 1996; Spencer & Raz, 1995). However, although, as noted earlier, correlations between measures of frontal functioning and source memory performance have sometimes been found (e.g., Craik et al., 1990; Glisky, Polster, & Routhieaux, 1995; Spencer & Raz, 1994), such correlations have not always emerged (e.g., Schacter, Kaszniak, Kihlstrom, & Valdiserri, 1991; Spencer & Raz, 1994). Furthermore, in the condition of Henkel et al. (1998) where older and younger adults were matched on old/new recognition but showed item-specific deficits in source monitoring, there was no correlation between overall source memory accuracy and a battery of neuropsychological tests measuring frontal function, although there *was* a correlation with measures of temporal lobe-hippocampal function (and both frontal and temporal batteries showed correlations with source accuracy at a longer retention interval).

On the basis of this finding, and also given evidence indicating that (a) in addition to changes in frontal lobe functioning, older adults may also show age-related neuropathology in temporal and hippocampal regions (e.g., Grady et al., 1995; Moscovitch, 1982; Moscovitch & Winocur, 1992; Raz, Millman, & Sarpel, 1990) and (b) older adults may have particular deficits in binding multiple features of an episode with one another (e.g., Chalfonte & Johnson, 1996), Henkel et al. (1998) argued that attributing source memory errors among older adults entirely to frontal lobe functioning would be an over-simplification. Rather, especially under conditions where there is a high level of similarity between studied items, efficient binding processes in medial-temporal regions may be required to prevent confusion. In a review of aging-related patterns of false recall and recognition, we (Schacter, Norman, & Koutstaal, 1998) addressed somewhat similar issues, explicitly noting that, apart from possible age-related differences in specificity of encoding or criterion-setting at retrieval, the high levels of false recognition among older adults for categorically related items might derive from a specific impairment of the hippocampal mechanisms involved in pattern separation and binding (see also Naveh-Benjamin, 2000; and chapter 15 of this volume).

To the extent that (in addition to less stringent retrieval monitoring) older adults *also* show relatively weaker binding of the many features of episodically encountered stimuli, older individuals might be (a) more likely to accept particular lure items because those lures have isolated features that are *consistent* with the studied items, and (b) less likely to reject lures based on the detection of features in the new items that are *inconsistent* with the studied items. Additionally, to the extent that such age differences in the effectiveness of binding and medial-temporal functions might be largely independent of attentional factors relevant during *retrieval*, but possibly more closely "simulated" by a curtailed processing period at study, a further outcome that we observed for younger adults might also follow. Although we found no increase in false recognition among younger adults under dual task conditions at retrieval, we did find a modest and significant increase in false recognition in a condition involving a *faster presentation rate at study*, where pictures were shown for 500 ms rather than 2 seconds.

Finally, more efficient binding may allow an account of why younger adults might prove able to reject categorically-related lures even under conditions of dual-task performance at retrieval. The comparatively rich and detailed nature of the pictures used in the dual task pictures experiment might provide more opportunities for the detection of target-inconsistent information than were present in the previous studies where increased errors of commission were observed under divided attention at test (e.g., errors involving false fame misattribution errors and errors relating to the within-test repetition of lures), and where participants themselves might need to *actively retrieve* or *seek out* contextual information that was not provided in the stimulus itself and that would allow correct rejection of the lure.

More generally, persistent age differences in false recognition of pictures may partially reflect differential emphasis on categorical vs. item-specific information by older and younger adults (cf. discussion in Koutstaal et al., 1999). We are currently exploring this possibility. However, it might be noted that a recent report by Grady, McIntosh, Craik, and colleagues (1999), comparing patterns of brain activation during episodic encoding of pictures versus words in older and younger adults is broadly consistent with the possibility that older adults place stronger emphasis on categorical or lexical information. These researchers reported a stimulus-specific pattern, such that picture encoding was associated with greater activation in extrastriate and medial temporal cortices and word encoding was associated with greater activation in left prefrontal and temporal cortices, but this differential pattern for pictures vs. words was significantly less pronounced for older than for younger adults.

☐ Concluding Comments

We have focused on two streams of research investigating the memory performance of older and younger adults that were previously extensively explored by Fergus Craik with regard to errors of omission, but here are considered in relation to errors of commission. First, taking a cue from a paper by Jacoby and Craik (1979) in which they extended the 1972 levels-of-processing framework so as to emphasize not only the importance of "depth" but also "breadth" of processing and, especially, the role of "distinctiveness" in determining memory performance, we considered the possible role of a "distinctiveness heuristic" in guiding recognition judgments: A strategy whereby individuals come to expect to retrieve distinctive information regarding target items and use the failure to retrieve such information as evidence that items were not previously encountered, thus reducing the probability of mistakenly endorsing nonstudied lure items. Reviewing data from two paradigms, one where distinctive pictorial information (line drawings) was provided in conjunction with associatively related words, and another where distinctive verbal descriptors accompanied detailed pictures of categorically related common objects, we provided evidence that both older and younger adults may adopt such a distinctiveness heuristic—and thereby successfully reduce false recognition responding. However, we also uncovered some puzzles as to the precise conditions under which individuals may fruitfully or successfully adopt this decision strategy. Whereas both age groups were apparently *unable* to use this strategy in the case where, for a given participant, some converging semantic associate word lists were accompanied by distinctive pictorial information and other lists were not, both age groups *were* able to reduce false recognition for categorized pictures under conditions where, for a given participant, some categories of objects were accompanied by distinctive verbal elaborators and others were not. One possible account of these divergent outcomes concerns the ease with which items, at the time of retrieval, could be correctly "tagged" as belonging, or not belonging, to a set of items that should, if they were targets, yield recollection of distinctive information: Such tagging may have been possible for the categorized pictures because explicit category information was provided at study but may have been more difficult for the word associate lists.

Second, we have considered the effects of dual task performance or "divided attention" on errors of commission in older and younger adults. Reflecting on the outcomes of several experimental conditions that varied dual task demands at encoding and/or retrieval in the categorized pictures paradigm, and the results of two further recently reported studies from other labs, using quite different paradigms, we found it necessary to extend our considerations beyond the possible role of frontal factors in contributing to false recognition and source errors in older adults (such contributions also having been indicated by earlier neuropsychological work by Fergus Craik and colleagues, and in work from our own lab involving both functional neuroimaging and intensive study of a frontal lesion patient). In order to accommodate the full range of relevant findings, we suggested that it was also necessary to take into account the effects of aging on hippocampal and medial-temporal processes involved in binding the disparate elements of an episode into a coherent trace (e.g., Chalfonte & Johnson, 1996; Cohen & Eichenbaum, 1993; Grady et al., 1995; Johnson & Chalfonte, 1994; Raz et al., 1990).

Taken together, both manipulations of dual task requirements, and manipulations exploring the availability of and use of distinctiveness information, help to illuminate some of the factors that contribute to memory distortion in older adults. More broadly, the outcomes of our review emphasize the complexity and number of factors that can interplay during both encoding and retrieval in determining the likelihood of "errors of commission" by individuals of either age group.

☐ Acknowledgments

This research was supported by NIA AG08441. We thank Steve Prince for assistance in preparation of the manuscript.

☐ References

Anderson, N. D., Craik, F. I. M., & Naveh-Benjamin, M. (1998). The attentional demands of encoding and retrieval in younger and older adults: 1. Evidence from divided attention costs. *Psychology and Aging, 13*, 405–423.

Bartlett, J. C., Leslie, J. E., Tubbs, A., & Fulton, A. (1989). Aging and memory for pictures of faces. *Psychology and Aging, 4*, 276–283.

Baddeley, A. D., Lewis, V., Eldridge, M., & Thomson, N. (1984). Attention and retrieval from long-term memory. *Journal of Experimental Psychology: General, 13*, 518–540.

Bower, G. H. (1967). A multicomponent view of the memory trace. In K. W. Spence & J. T. Spence (Eds.), *The psychology of learning and motivation: Advances in research and theory* (Vol. 1, pp. 229–325). New York: Academic Press.

Chaiken, S., Lieberman, A., & Eagly, A. H. (1989). Heuristic and systematic information processing within and beyond the persuasion context. In J. S. Uleman & J. A. Bargh (Eds.), *Unintended thought* (pp. 212–252). New York: Guilford Press.

Chalfonte, B. L., & Johnson, M. K. (1996). Feature memory and binding in young and older adults. *Memory & Cognition, 24*, 403–416.

Cohen, G., & Faulkner, D. (1989). Age differences in source forgetting: Effects on reality monitoring and eyewitness testimony. *Psychology and Aging, 4*, 10–17.

Cohen, N. J., & Eichenbaum, H. (1993). *Memory, amnesia, and the hippocampus.* Cambridge, MA: MIT Press.

Craik, F. I. M. (1977). Age differences in human memory. In J. E. Birren & K. W. Schaie (Eds.), *Handbook of the psychology of aging* (pp. 384–420). New York: Van Nostrand Reinhold.

Craik, F. I. M. (1982). Selective changes in encoding as a function of reduced processing capacity. In F. Klix, J. Hoffman, & E. van der Meer (Eds.), *Cognitive research in psychology* (pp. 152–161). Berlin: Deutscher Verlag der Wissenschaffen.

Craik, F. I. M. (1983). On the transfer of information from temporary to permanent memory. *Philosophical Transactions of the Royal Society, London, Series B, 302*, 341–359.

Craik, F. I. M., & Byrd, M. (1982). Aging and cognitive deficits: The role of attentional resources. In F. I. M. Craik & S. Trehub (Eds.), *Aging and cognitive processes* (pp. 191–211). New York: Plenum.

Craik, F. I. M., Govoni, R., Naveh-Benjamin, M., & Anderson, N. D. (1996). The effects of divided attention on encoding and retrieval processes in human memory. *Journal of Experimental Psychology: General, 125*, 159–180.

Craik, F. I. M., & Lockhart, R. S. (1972). Levels of processing: A framework for memory research. *Journal of Verbal Learning and Verbal Behavior, 11*, 671–684.

Craik, F. I. M., & McDowd, J. M. (1987). Age differences in recall and recognition. *Journal of Experimental Psychology: Learning, Memory, and Cognition, 13*, 474–479.

Craik, F. I. M., Morris, L. W., Morris, R. G., & Loewen, E. R. (1990). Relations between source amnesia and frontal lobe functioning in older adults. *Psychology and Aging, 5*, 148–151.

Craik, F. I. M., & Tulving, E. (1975). Depth of processing and the retention of words in episodic memory. *Journal of Experimental Psychology: General, 104*, 268–294.

Curran, T., Schacter, D. L., Norman, K. A., & Galluccio, L. (1997). False recognition after a right frontal lobe infarction: Memory for general and specific information. *Neuropsychologia, 25*, 1035–1049.

Deese, J. (1959). On the prediction of occurrence of particular verbal intrusions in immediate recall. *Journal of Experimental Psychology, 58*, 17–22.

Dodson, C. S., & Johnson, M. K. (1993). Rate of false source attributions depends on how questions are asked. *American Journal of Psychology, 106*, 541–557.

Dodson, C. S., & Schacter, D. L. (in press). When false recognition meets metacognition: The distinctiveness heuristic. *Journal of Memory and Language.*

Dywan, J., Segalowitz, S. J., & Webster, L. (1998). Source monitoring: ERP evidence for greater reactivity to nontarget information in older adults. *Brain and Cognition, 36*, 390–430.

Einstein, G. O., & Hunt, R. R. (1980). Levels of processing and organization: Additive effects of individual item and relational processing. *Journal of Experimental Psychology: Human Learning and Memory, 6*, 588–598.

Fernandes, M. A., & Moscovitch, M. (2000). Divided attention and memory: Evidence of substantial interference effects at retrieval and encoding. *Journal of Experimental Psychology: General, 129*, 155–176.

Glisky, E. L., Polster, M. R., & Routhieaux, B. C. (1995). Double dissociation between item and source memory. *Neuropsychology, 9*, 229-235.

Gluck, M. A., & Myers, C. E. (1996). Integrating behavioral and physiological models of hippocampal function. *Hippocampus, 6*, 643–653.

Grady, C. L., McIntosh, A. R., Horwitz, B., Maisog, J. M., Ungerleider, L. G., Mentis, M. J., Pietrini, P., Schapiro, M. B., & Haxby, J. V. (1995). Age-related reductions in human recognition memory due to impaired encoding. *Science, 269*, 218–221.

Grady, C. L., McIntosh, A. R., Rajah, M. N., Beig, S., & Craik, F. I. M. (1999). The effects of age on the neural correlates of episodic encoding. *Cerebral Cortex, 9*, 805–814.

Henkel, L. A., Johnson, M. K., & De Leondardis, D. M. (1998). Aging and source monitoring: Cognitive processes and neuropsychological correlates. *Journal of Experimental Psychology: General, 127*, 251–268.

Iidaka, T., Anderson, N., Kapur, S., Cabeza, R., Okamoto, C., & Craik, F. I. M. (1999). Age-related differences in brain activation during encoding and retrieval under divided attention: A Positron Emission Tomography (PET) study. *Brain and Cognition, 39*, 53–55.

Israel, L., & Schacter, D. L. (1997). Pictorial encoding reduces false recognition of semantic associates. *Psychonomic Bulletin & Review, 4*, 577–581.

Jacoby, L. L. (1991). A process dissociation framework: Separating automatic from intentional uses of memory. *Journal of Memory and Language, 30*, 513–541.

Jacoby, L. L. (1999a). Deceiving the elderly: Effects of accessibility bias in cued-recall performance. *Cognitive Neuropsychology, 16*, 417–436.

Jacoby, L. L. (1999b). Ironic effects of repetition: Measuring age-related differences in memory. *Journal of Experimental Psychology: Learning, Memory, and Cognition, 25*, 3–22.

Jacoby, L. L., & Craik, F. I. M. (1979). Effects of elaboration of processing at encoding and retrieval: Trace distinctiveness and recovery of initial context. In L. S. Cermak & F. I. M. Craik (Eds.), *Levels of processing in human memory* (pp. 1–21). Hillsdale, NJ: Erlbaum.

Jacoby, L. L., Kelley, C. M., & Dywan, J. (1989). Memory attributions. In H. L. Roediger, III, & F. I. M. Craik (Eds.), *Varieties of memory and consciousness: Essays in honour of Endel Tulving* (pp. 391–422). Hillsdale, NJ: Erlbaum.

Jacoby, L. L., Toth, J. P., & Yonelinas, A. P. (1993). Separating conscious and unconscious influences of memory: Measuring recollection. *Journal of Experimental Psychology: General, 122*, 139–154.

Jacoby, L. L., Woloshyn, V., & Kelley, C. (1989). Becoming famous without being recognized: Unconscious influences of memory produced by dividing attention. *Journal of Experimental Psychology: General, 118*, 115–125.

Jennings, J. M., & Jacoby, L. L. (1993). Automatic versus intentional uses of memory: Aging, attention, and control. *Psychology and Aging, 8*, 283–293.

Jennings, J. M., & Jacoby, L. L. (1997). An opposition procedure for detecting age-related deficits in recollection: Telling effects of repetition. *Psychology and Aging, 12*, 352–361.

Johnson, M. K., & Chalfonte, B. L. (1994). Binding complex memories: The role of reactivation and the hippocampus. In D. L. Schacter & E. Tulving (Eds.), *Memory systems 1994* (pp. 311–350). Cambridge, MA: MIT Press.

Johnson, M. K., Hashtroudi, S., & Lindsay, D. S. (1993). Source monitoring. *Psychological Bulletin, 114*, 3–28.

Klein, K., & Saltz, E. (1976). Specifying mechanisms in a levels-of-processing approach to memory. *Journal of Experimental Psychology: Human Learning and Memory, 2*, 671–679.

Koriat, A., & Goldsmith, M. (1996). Memory metaphors and the real-life/laboratory controversy: Correspondence versus storehouse conceptions of memory. *Behavioral and Brain Sciences, 19*, 167–228.

Koriat, A., Goldsmith, M., & Pansky, A. (2000). Toward a psychology of memory accuracy. *Annual Review of Psychology, 51*, 481–537.

Koutstaal, W., & Schacter, D. L. (1997a). Gist-based false recognition of pictures in older and younger adults. *Journal of Memory and Language, 37*, 555–583.

Koutstaal, W., & Schacter, D. L. (1997b). Inaccuracy and inaccessibility in memory retrieval: Contributions from cognitive psychology and neuropsychology. In P. S. Appelbaum, L. A. Uyehara, & M. R. Elin (Eds.), *Trauma and memory: Clinical and legal controversies* (pp. 93–137). New York: Oxford University Press.

Koutstaal, W., Schacter, D. L., & Brenner, C. (2001). Dual task demands and gist-based false recognition of pictures in younger and older adults. *Journal of Memory and Language, 44*, 399–426.

Koutstaal, W., Schacter, D. L., Galluccio, L., & Stofer, K. A. (1999). Reducing gist-based false recognition in older adults: Encoding and retrieval manipulations. *Psychology and Aging, 14*, 220–237.

Lindsay, D. S., & Johnson, M. K. (1989). The eyewitness suggestibility effect and memory for source. *Memory & Cognition, 17*, 349–358.

Law, S., Hawkins, S. A., & Craik, F. I. M. (1998). Repetition-induced belief in the elderly: Rehabilitating age-related memory deficits. *Journal of Consumer Research, 25*, 91–107.

Lockhart, R. S., & Craik, F. I. M. (1990). Levels of processing: A retrospective commentary on a framework for memory research. *Canadian Journal of Psychology, 44*, 87–112.

Lockhart, R. S., Craik, F. I. M., & Jacoby, L. L. (1976). Depth of processing, recognition, and recall. In J. Brown (Ed.), *Recall and recognition* (pp. 75–102). London: Wiley.

Mandler, G., & Worden, P. E. (1973). Semantic processing without permanent storage. *Journal of Experimental Psychology, 100*, 277–283.

Mäntylä, T., & Bäckman, L. (1992). Aging and memory for expected and unexpected objects in real-world settings. *Journal of Experimental Psychology: Learning, Memory, and Cognition*, *18*, 1298–1309.

McClelland, J. L., McNaughton, B. L., & O'Reilly, R. C. (1995). Why there are complementary learning systems in the hippocampus and neocortex: Insights from the successes and failures of connectionist models of learning and memory. *Psychological Review*, *102*, 419–457.

McIntyre, J. S., & Craik, F. I. M. (1987). Age differences in memory for item and source information. *Canadian Journal of Psychology*, *41*, 175–192.

Moscovitch, M. (1982). A neuropsychological approach to perception and memory in normal and pathological aging. In F. I. M. Craik & S. Trehub (Eds.), *Aging and cognitive processes* (pp. 55–78). New York: Plenum.

Moscovitch, M. (1994). Memory and working with memory: Evaluation of a component process model and comparisons with other models. In D. L. Schacter & E. Tulving (Eds.), *Memory systems 1994* (pp. 269–310). Cambridge, MA: MIT Press.

Moscovitch, M. (1995). Recovered consciousness: A hypothesis concerning modularity and episodic memory. *Journal of Clinical and Experimental Neuropsychology*, *17*, 276–290.

Moscovitch, M., & Craik, F. I. M. (1976). Depth of processing, retrieval cues, and uniqueness of encoding as factors in recall. *Journal of Verbal Learning and Verbal Behavior*, *15*, 447–458.

Moscovitch, M., & Winocur, G. (1992). The neuropsychology of memory and aging. In F. I. M. Craik & T. A. Salthouse (Eds.), *The handbook of aging and cognition* (pp. 315–372). Hillsdale, NJ: Erlbaum.

Moscovitch, M., & Winocur, G. (1995). Frontal lobes, memory, and aging. In *Annals of the New York Academy of Science, 769. Structure and functions of the human prefrontal cortex* (pp. 119–150). New York: New York Academy of Sciences.

Mulligan, N. W. (1998). The role of attention during encoding in implicit and explicit memory. *Journal of Experimental Psychology: Learning, Memory, and Cognition*, *24*, 27–47.

Naveh-Benjamin, M. (2000). Adult age differences in memory performance: Tests of an associative deficit hypothesis. *Journal of Experimental Psychology: Learning, Memory, and Cognition*, *26*, 1170–1187.

Naveh-Benjamin, M., Craik, F. I. M., Guez, J., & Dori, H. (1998). Effects of divided attention on encoding and retrieval processes in human memory: Further support for an asymmetry. *Journal of Experimental Psychology: Learning, Memory, and Cognition*, *24*, 1091–1104.

Nelson, D. L. (1979). Remembering pictures and words: Appearance, significance, and name. In L. S. Cermak & F. I. M. Craik, *Levels of processing in human memory* (pp. 45–76). Hillsdale, NJ: Erlbaum.

Nyberg, L., Nilsson, L.-G., Olofsson, U., & Backman, L. (1997). Effects of division of attention during encoding and retrieval on age differences in episodic memory. *Experimental Aging Research*, *23*, 137–143.

O'Reilly, R. C., & McClelland, J. L. (1994). Hippocampal conjunctive encoding, storage, and recall: Avoiding a trade-off. *Hippocampus*, *4*, 661–682.

Parkin, A. J., & Walter, B. M. (1992). Recollective experience, normal aging, and frontal dysfunction. *Psychology and Aging*, *7*, 290–298.

Rankin, J. L., & Kausler, D. H. (1979). Adult age differences in false recognitions. *Journal of Gerontology*, *34*, 58–65.

Raz, N., Millman, D., & Sarpel, G. (1990). Cerebral correlates of cognitive aging: Gray-white matter differentiation in the medial temporal lobes, and fluid versus crystalized abilities. *Psychobiology*, *18*, 475–481.

Roediger, H. L., III. (1996). Memory illusions. *Journal of Memory and Language*, *35*, 76–100.

Roediger, H. L., III, & McDermott, K. B. (1995). Creating false memories: Remembering words not presented in lists. *Journal of Experimental Psychology: Learning, Memory, and Cognition*, *21*, 803–814.

Salthouse, T. A. (1982). *Adult cognition: An experimental psychology of human aging*. New York: Springer-Verlag.

Schacter, D. L. (1999). The seven sins of memory: Insights from psychology and cognitive neuroscience. *American Psychologist*, *54*, 182–203.

Schacter, D. L., Buckner, R. L., Koutstaal, W., Dale, A. M., & Rosen, B. R. (1997). Late onset of anterior prefrontal activity during true and false recognition: An event-related fMRI study. *NeuroImage*, *6*, 259–269.

Schacter, D. L., Curran, T., Galluccio, L., Milberg, W., & Bates, J. (1996). False recognition and the right frontal lobe: A case study. *Neuropsychologia, 34,* 793–808.

Schacter, D. L., Harbluk, J. L., & McLachlan, D. R. (1984). Retrieval without recollection: An experimental analysis of source amnesia. *Journal of Verbal Learning and Verbal Behavior, 23,* 593–611.

Schacter, D. L., Israel, L., & Racine, C. (1999). Suppressing false recognition in younger and older adults: The distinctiveness heuristic. *Journal of Memory and Language, 40,* 1–24.

Schacter, D. L., Kaszniak, A. W., Kihlstrom, J. F., & Valdiserri, M. (1991). The relation between source memory and aging. *Psychology and Aging, 6,* 559–568.

Schacter, D. L., Koutstaal, W., & Norman, K. A. (1997). False memories and aging. *Trends in Cognitive Science, 1,* 229–236.

Schacter, D. L., Norman, K. A., & Koutstaal, W. (1998). The cognitive neuroscience of constructive memory. *Annual Review of Psychology, 49,* 289–318.

Schacter, D. L., Reiman, E., Curran, T., Yun, L. S., Bandy, D., McDermott, K. B., & Roediger, H. L., III (1996). Neuroanatomical correlates of veridical and illusory recognition memory: Evidence from positron emission tomography. *Neuron, 17,* 267–274.

Schacter, D. L., Savage, C. R., Alpert, N. M., Rauch, S. L., & Albert, M. S. (1996). The role of hippocampus and frontal cortex in age-related memory changes: A PET study. *NeuroReport, 7,* 1165–1169.

Seamon, J. G., Luo, C. R., & Gallo, D. A. (1998). Creating false memories of words with or without recognition of list items: Evidence for nonconscious processes. *Psychological Science, 9,* 20–26.

Smith, A. D. (1975). Partial learning and recognition memory in the aged. *International Journal of Aging and Human Development, 6,* 359–365.

Spencer, W. D., & Raz, N. (1994). Memory for facts, source, and context: Can frontal lobe dysfunction explain age-related differences? *Psychology and Aging, 9,* 149–159.

Spencer, W. D., & Raz, N. (1995). Differential effects of aging on memory for content and context: A meta-analysis. *Psychology and Aging, 10,* 527–539.

Stuss, D. T., Craik, F. I. M., Sayer, L., Franchi, D., & Alexander, M. P. (1996). Comparison of older people and patients with frontal lesions: Evidence from word list learning. *Psychology and Aging, 11,* 387–395.

Troyer, A. K., Winocur, G., Craik, F. I. M., & Moscovitch, M. (1999). Source memory and divided attention: Reciprocal costs to primary and secondary tasks. *Neuropsychology, 13,* 467–474.

Underwood, B. J. (1965). False recognition produced by implicit verbal responses. *Journal of Experimental Psychology, 70,* 122–129.

Underwood, B. J. (1969). Attributes of memory. *Psychological Review, 76,* 559–573.

Wallace, W. P., Stewart, M. T., & Malone, C. P. (1995). Recognition memory errors produced by implicit activation of word candidates during the processing of spoken words. *Journal of Memory and Language, 34,* 417–439.

West, R. L. (1996). An application of prefrontal cortex function theory to cognitive aging. *Psychological Bulletin, 120,* 272–292.

White, M. J. (1983). Prominent publications in cognitive psychology. *Memory & Cognition, 11,* 423–427.

Whiting, W. L., & Smith, A. D. (1997). Differential age-related processing limitations in recall and recognition tasks. *Psychology and Aging, 12,* 216–224.

Whittlesea, B. W. A., & Leboe, J. P. (2000). The heuristic basis of remembering and classification: Fluency, generation, and resemblance. *Journal of Experimental Psychology: General, 129,* 84–106.

Zaragoza, M. S., & Koshmider, J. W., III (1989). Misled subjects may know more than their performance implies. *Journal of Experimental Psychology: Learning, Memory, and Cognition, 15,* 246–255.

31

CHAPTER Gordon Winocur

Commentary: Levels of Neuroprocessing

It is entirely fitting that the organizers of this Festschrift included a session that recognizes Gus Craik's contributions to the neurosciences, but there is also a touch of irony in that decision. A desire to unravel the mysteries of the human brain was not always a priority within Gus's intellectual pursuits. Indeed, he would probably be the first to admit that, throughout most of his career, he wasn't too concerned if semantic encoding went on in the left lobe of the frontal cortex or anywhere else in the brain. But when Gus's interests eventually turned to neuropsychology, as they did in the late 1980s, the creative juices began to flow in predictable fashion. The four chapters in this section reflect Gus's contributions in this area and, importantly, how he and his thinking influenced the work of others.

Gus' journey into the world of the brain began when he and Dan McIntyre (McIntyre & Craik, 1987) published a study in which old and young adults were presented with lists of fictitious facts that they had to remember. They also had to remember the source of each fact—whether it was presented auditorially or visually. As expected, old people were worse at recalling the facts, but they also showed considerable source amnesia, a new finding with respect to aging. Gus and Dan didn't make too much of this result as far as brain function was concerned. However, evidence was beginning to appear that source memory problems were related to frontal lobe (FL) impairment (e.g., Janowsky, Shimamura, & Squire, 1989; Schacter, Harbluk, & McLachlan, 1984). Picking up on this observation, Gus, Robin Morris, and others, repeated the McIntyre and Craik study, but this time included neuropsychological tests of FL and medial temporal lobe (MTL) function (Craik, Morris, Morris, & Loewen, 1991). The results revealed a clear dissociation in which source amnesia in old people correlated significantly with performance on FL tests of strategic function. Source memory problems were found to be unrelated to the more straightforward types of memory controlled by the MTL/hippocampal system.

So, Gus discovered the frontal lobes but, in applying neuropsychological testing to the study of cognitive aging, he also hit on a powerful tool for identifying neural correlates of age-related cognitive decline. Following Gus's lead, many of us went on to demonstrate similar relationships between FL impairment and various forms of explicit and implicit memory loss in older adults (e.g., Glisky, Polster, & Routhieux, 1995; Parkin & Walter, 1992; Winocur, Moscovitch, & Stuss, 1996). This approach is reflected clearly in Don Stuss's research which, for many years, was concerned mainly with cognitive impairment in patients with FL damage. In collaboration with Gus, he found similar changes in normal old people (Stuss, Craik, Sayer, Franchi, & Alexander, 1996) and went on to demonstrate further parallels between the two populations (e.g., Levine, Stuss, & Milberg, 1997). In doing so he provided converging behavioral evidence for the prevalence of FL atrophy in normal aging.

One of Stuss's very interesting findings, as reported in his contributions with Binns to this volume, is that age adversely affects cognitive recovery in patients suffering from FL damage as a result of traumatic brain injury (TBI). This is a significant observation that relates to Gus's view that aging is accompanied by a reduction in cognitive resources. Gus has argued convincingly that the cognitive resources most affected in old age are those that control self-initiated, strategic processes—processes that are linked to FL function. Stuss's results showed that older people, because of diminished frontal capacity, are handicapped when required to compensate for additional FL impairment resulting from head injury. As such, they represent an important extension of Gus's research and theoretical formulations.

The frontal cortex is a heterogeneous structure and there is considerable controversy with respect to the distribution and organization of function across the various regions (e.g., Goldman-Rakic, 1987; Petrides, 1995). Related to this general issue, Stuss and Binns present new evidence that frontal functions exhibit different patterns of change in old age. An especially interesting observation is that aspects of free recall typically associated with FL function can hold up quite well. In a test of word-list memory, Stuss and Binns separated secondary memory and subjective organization components and found very little age-related decline on the measure of secondary memory. This was unexpected in light of evidence that recall and retrieval processes decline relatively early in the aging process. Stuss and Binns's findings suggest that some compensatory mechanism, perhaps along the lines that Cheryl Grady has observed in aging brains, may be protecting recall function (see Grady, chapter 27 of this volume). What is particularly interesting is that, whatever form that compensation may take, it does not seem to involve strategic operations. The evidence for this rests in Stuss and Binns's data, which show that long-term free recall remained strong in old age while strategic functions declined.

As Stuss and Binns points out, these findings have important implications for cognitive rehabilitation. In general, attempts to rehabilitate impaired strategic function in brain-impaired populations have met with limited success. Stuss and Binns's evidence suggests that an exclusive emphasis on such functions in rehabilitation may be misplaced. An alternative, and possibly more fruitful, approach may be to identify functions that remain relatively intact and integrate them into a training program that is geared to the development of new and effective cognitive strategies. In fact, this is one of the premises of a new rehabilitation initiative at the Rotman Research Institute that is directed at older adults and TBI patients. The initiative, which includes Gus and a group of Rotman scientists, emphasizes a wide range of lab and real-world skills training, as well as working on performance-related psychosocial factors (Winocur et al, 2000). The protocol has been subjected to pilot testing with encouraging results, so there may yet be some hope for recovering lost strategic functions.

In the mid-1990s Gus was drawn into the neuroimaging orbit, and he became interested in the use of positron emission tomography (PET) to study brain activation patterns associated with encoding and retrieval processes. Grady and Vidailhet, Christensen, Danion, and Kapur describe some of these studies in their chapters in this volume. In showing that the left prefrontal cortex (PFC) is uniquely involved in deep semantic encoding (leaving posterior cortical regions to process at more shallow levels), Gus and his colleagues confirmed a major principle of the levels-of-processing model: that meaningful encoding of new information is a self-generated, strategic function that necessarily requires the most highly developed and cognitively sophisticated part of the brain.

In an important extension of this work, Grady, Craik, and others (e.g., Grady, McIntosh, Rajah, & Craik, 1998) demonstrated reduced frontal activities in the brains of older people engaged in deep semantic encoding tasks. This finding would be predicted by Gus's earlier work showing that old people's poor memory is related to a reduced ability to encode new information at a deep semantic level (Craik & Byrd, 1982). Interestingly, this pattern was detected clearly when words were used as stimuli, but not pictures. Picture memory was not different between old and young groups, and both groups responded similarly to manipulations of encoding depth. In addition, both groups showed similar patterns of activity in several brain regions during elaborative encoding. The only notable difference was that the older adults, but not the young, showed increased hippocampal activity during deep encoding of pictures. It's not clear what the picture–word difference represents, but, in broad terms, it is in line with Stuss and Binn's conclusion that different functions decline at different rates in old age and that some hold up extremely well.

Gus's impact on the neurosciences is not limited to brain function and cognitive aging. In their chapter, Vidailhet et al. describes their research into neural changes with schizophrenia that was clearly influenced by their collaboration with Gus. Vidailhet et al. make the important observation that there is no reference to memory or cognitive deficits in standard diagnoses of schizophrenia. This, despite the fact, that attentional and memory deficits are among the symptoms of schizophrenia and are better predictors of outcome than symptoms related to psychosis. There is clearly work to be done in identifying the nature of the cognitive disorder and Vidailhet et al. have taken a major initiative with respect to memory disturbances. Adopting a levels-of-processing design, he presented pairs of words to schizophrenics and control subjects under deep or shallow conditions and subsequently tested recognition. The main behavioral finding was that recognition memory by schizophrenics was impaired following deep-encoding instructions, and that this was related to a reduction in frontal activity during encoding. While in its early stages, this line of investigation has important implications for characterizing the cognitive profile of schizophrenic patients, distinguishing it from those of other psychotic conditions and, potentially, for treatment.

As part of his long collaboration with Endel Tulving, Gus was involved in the work that led to the highly influential HERA model: the notion of hemispheric asymmetry in which the left PFC specializes in encoding functions, and the right PFC in retrieval functions. In a particularly important contribution to that model, Gus, Tulving, Kapur, and others (Kapur et al., 1995) provided evidence that the role of the right PFC in information retrieval is in *attempting* to recover information, rather than in the success or failure of that effort. That is a significant discovery for several reasons. It confirms the link between PFC and strategic processes that guide purposeful and goal-directed cognitions. In a broader sense, it underscores the usefulness of functional neuroimaging for validating and evaluating behaviorally oriented theories of FL function that are derived from this basic principle. Shallice's (1982) supervisory attentional theory and Baddeley's (1986) central executive model, for example, make clear predictions about the role of PFC in directing cognitive operations and planning behavior. Gus's work has been instrumental in showing that the technology is available for putting these ideas to the test.

Along these lines, there is a growing controversy in the neuroimaging literature regarding the limits of HERA. There is no doubt that frontal asymmetry with respect to encoding and retrieval processes holds up well for relatively simple tasks. On the other hand, there is evidence that, as tasks become more complex or more difficult, both hemispheres become involved, at least in retrieval (Nolde, Johnson, & D'Esposito, 1998; Raye, Johnson, Mitchell, Nolde, & D'Esposito, 2000). It would seem that Gus's techniques for dividing attention and varying processing demands (e.g., Craik & Simon, 1980; Craik, Govoni, Naveh-Benjamin, & Anderson, 1996) are ideally suited to test this idea and to possibly determining the points at which encoding and retrieval processes are no longer lateralized, but require interhemispheric cooperation. And, of course, this type of analysis needs to be done for the aging brain as well as the young adult brain.

It's bad enough that, as we age, we are less likely to remember events that did happen but, as Koutstaal and Schacter remind us in their chapter, older people are also more likely to remember events that didn't happen. It's not clear that older adults commit every one of Koutstaal and Schacter's seven sins of memory (transients, absent-mindedness, blocking, misattribution, suggestibility, bias, and persistence) but they are guilty of enough of them to be extremely prone to memory distortions.

Koutstaal and Schacter describe two paradigms in which older people reliably show more false memories than young adults. One is Roediger and McDermott's (1995) variation of Deese's test in which people study lists of semantically related words and are then asked to recall them or to make judgments about similar words that were not actually in the original list. The second was a clever, categorized-pictures test that Schacter, Koutstaal, Johnson, Gross, and Angell (1997) developed. For this task, subjects were shown a videotape involving a series of related events followed by a recognition memory test in which pictures of events in the series were mixed with events that had not been shown previously. In both cases, older people were more likely than young adults to "remember" seeing items that, in fact, had not been part of the studied material.

Older people's susceptibility to false memories has been attributed, in some cases, to an encoding deficit resulting from failure to process detailed information about studied items (see Koutstaal Schacter, this volume). This interpretation sounds very much like a levels-of-processing deficit, from which, of course, old people are known to suffer. In contrast to young people, who process item-specific and category-related information, older people adopt mainly a category-based strategy in which the emphasis is on general information that is common to all the items studied. As a result, old people are much more likely to mistake a related item that they haven't seen before for one that they had.

In an important contribution to this debate, Schacter and his colleagues showed that, while old people do not typically adopt encoding strategies that protect against false memories, they have not necessarily lost the ability to do so. Schacter's group found that, within the Roediger and McDermott paradigm, presenting old and young adults with lists of semantically-related words, along with pictures representing each word, resulted in a general reduction in false recognition at test. The effect, however, was significantly greater for older adults. Schacter, Koutstaal, and Norman (1997, 1998) argued that the combined encoding helps produce distinctive representations, and contributes to a heuristic processing strategy that can compensate for old people's failure to spontaneously adopt appropriate strategies. While this approach needs to be assessed in other paradigms, there is the potential here to develop techniques that may help older adults monitor their memories more effectively and suppress false memory intrusions.

In determining the neural basis of false memories, it seems reasonable to begin by looking at structures known to be implicated in true memory. In this regard, the MTL is a likely candidate, and, in fact, Koutstaal and Schacter have suggested that the encoding problem from which old people suffer is a result of MTL/hippocampal impairment. There are also reports of high false recognition rates in patients with FL damage resulting from ruptured anterior communicating artery aneurysms (Parkin, Bindschaedler, Harsent, & Metzler, 1996) or right FL infarcts (Schacter, Curran, Galluccio, Milberg, & Bates, 1996). It would appear, then, that FL and MTL abnormalities increase susceptibility to false memories, although the deficits associated with the respective regions may be quite different.

A recent study by Melo, Winocur, and Moscovitch (1999) specifically addresses this issue. The study utilized the Roediger and McDermott paradigm and was conducted on three groups of brain-damaged patients: (a) amnesics with damage to MTL, (b) nonamnesics with FL damage, and (c) amnesics with FL and MTL damage. All subjects were presented auditorially with a series of lists, each made up of semantically related words. Following presentation of the lists, recall and recognition memory were tested. In the recognition tests, studied and nonstudied words were presented visually on a computer screen. The nonstudied words included critical lures that were semantically related to the studied words in each list. For ease of presentation, only the recall data are reported here.

Figure 31.1 represents each group's recall of word lists that were actually studied. As expected, both groups of amnesic patients were impaired on this measure. Figure 31.2 provides the groups' false memory performance by indicating the number of critical lure intrusions that subjects misattributed to the studies list. Both the MTL-amnesic group and the FL-nonamnesic group exhibited more intrusions then their respective control groups, but for different reasons. The MTL-amnesics were unable to learn and recall the specific words in each list, but, because each list was comprised of semantically related words, they were able to encode the broad semantic features, or "gist," of the respective list. By relying exclusively on semantic gist, the MTL-amnesics were more likely to confuse critical lures with closely related list words. By comparison, FL-nonamnesic patients did not have specific memory problems; they were able to remember the list words as well as the semantic gist. Their problem was strategic in nature and likely due to a failure in working with these memories to filter out the target from the critical list (see Moscovitch & Winocur, 1995, for a more detailed account of the working-with-memory hypothesis of FL function).

The FL-MTL amnesics contrasted with other patient groups in exhibiting a reduced number of false recollections. Like the MTL-amnesics, this group had severe memory

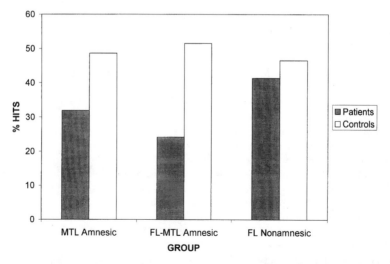

FIGURE 31.1. Percentage of study list words recalled by patient and control groups.

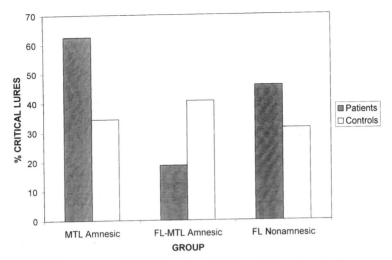

FIGURE 31.2. Percentage of critical lures intruded by patient and control groups

loss, but, because they also suffered FL damage, these patients had trouble extracting the semantic gist from the list or, if they could remember the gist, in using that memory in an effective way. The result was a failure to generate the type of mnemonic information that would support true or false memories.

In general, the performance of Koutstaal and Schacter's older groups most closely resembles that of Melo et al.'s (1999) MTL-amnesic group, but the aging process is extremely variable. In terms of individual differences, it would be extremely interesting to identify a subgroup of older people with relatively good memory, but who display signs of FL dysfunction. Would such a group exhibit increased false memories that are disproportionate to their true memory scores? A similar question could be asked of older people who show signs of combined FL and MTL impairment: Would they exhibit the pattern seen in Melo et al's FL-MTL amnesic group? These intriguing questions invite experimental analysis.

Finally, a comment on prospective memory, a type of memory that received little attention at the Festschrift but which is close to Gus's heart (Craik & Kerr, 1996). We are just beginning to learn about the brain regions that are involved in prospective memory and, once again, it is likely that FL and MTL are implicated.

Prospective memory is remembering to do things in the future. But the "prospective" part of prospective memory is not so much about memory as it is about strategic planning. If we plan to perform specific acts at certain times, we monitor our activities to ensure that we do them. There is also a "retrospective" component, and that's where memory comes in. We have to recall the intentions as well as the actions we want to perform.

On the basis of what is known about brain function, it seems reasonable to assume that the frontal lobes control the strategic planning part of prospective memory, whereas the MTL/hippocampal region is a reasonable candidate for the retrospective component. It follows that damage to either area should produce prospective memory failure, although for different reasons. It is certainly the case that patients with FL or MTL lesions have poor prospective memory, but there have been few attempts to specify the precise nature of their respective impairments.

Part of the problem is in trying to separate the retrospective and prospective components because they are not totally independent of each other. On the other hand, there is some evidence from neuropsychological studies that the two components may be dissociable. For example, Cockburn (1995) has described the prospective memory difficulties of an individual with FL damage but relatively good memory, and an amnesic patient with apparently intact FL function (Cockburn, 1993). On prospective memory tests, the FL patient was able to remember the intended actions but consistently performed them at the wrong time. In contrast, the amnesic patient recognized the sound of a timer as a cue to do something but had little recollection as to the task that he was required to perform.

A similar pattern emerges from a recent comparison of prospective memory in patients with surgically induced damage to the temporal lobes and patients suffering FL impairment as a result of Parkinson's disease or ruptured anterior communicating artery aneurysm (Palmer, 1998). Either type of damage produced deficits in prospective memory, but there was evidence that the mechanisms affected were different in the two populations. This study, which included independent measures of retrospective and prospective components of prospective memory, showed that patients with FL damage were selectively impaired on the prospective test. By comparison, the temporal lobe group, while impaired relative to controls on both measures, performed much worse on the retrospective tests. There is clearly a need for systematic examination of prospective memory in focal-lesioned patients and in young adults using functional neuroimaging techniques. However, available evidence supports the tentative hypothesis that the frontal lobes are necessary for the planning and prospective components that support remembering when, whereas MTL and related structures that support episodic memory are needed to remember what.

☐ Summary

Gus Craik and Bob Lockhart proposed the levels-of-processing model as a framework for relating memory performance to attentional and perceptual processes. As a cognitive construct, it has profoundly influenced the study of learning and memory in young and aged adults, but its impact has extended beyond behavioral processes and beyond these populations. Gus, himself, has shown that the essential features of levels of processing can be adapted to the study of brain mechanisms, and others have followed his lead in using similar paradigms to describe cognitive impairment in brain-damaged patients and in patients with neuropsychiatric disorders. In related theoretical work, Gus formulated a resource model of cognitive function that has shaped thinking and research in the area of cognitive aging. Ideas based on this model are also driving research into the cognitive symptoms of brain-impaired individuals and are being factored into programs of cognitive rehabilitation. Having enjoyed a full career as one of our generation's preeminent cognitive psychologists, Gus Craik has also established himself as a leading behavioral neuroscientist. As he launches the next stage of his career, it is exciting to contemplate that the creative energy that has contributed so much to our understanding of cognitive processes will be directed increasingly to the study of correlated brain function.

☐ Acknowledgments

The preparation of this chapter and some of the research reported therein were supported by grants from the Canadian Institutes for Health Research and the McDonnell Foundation. Thanks to Heather Palmer for having read and commented on an earlier version of the manuscript and to Heidi Roesler for technical assistance.

☐ References

Baddeley, A. D. (1986). *Working memory.* Oxford, England: Clarendon Press.

Cockburn, J. (1993, July). *Dissociations in performance on tests of retrospective and prospective memory after cerebral infarction.* Paper presented at the Europeon Conference of the International Neuropsychological Society, Madiera.

Cockburn, J. (1995). Task interruption in prospective memory: A frontal lobe function? *Cortex, 31,* 87–97.

Craik, F. I. M., & Byrd, M. (1982). Aging and cognitive deficits. The role of attentional resources. In F. I. M. Craik & S. Trehub (Eds.), *Aging and cognitive processes* (pp. 191–211). New York: Plenum Press.

Craik, F. I. M., Govoni, R., Naveh-Benjamin, M., & Anderson, N. D. (1996). The effects of divided attention on encoding and retrieval processes in human memory. *Journal of Experimental Psychology: General, 125,* 159–180.

Craik, F. I. M., & Kerr, S. A. (1996). Prospective memory, aging, and lapses of attention. In M. Brandimonte, G. O. Einstein, & M. A. McDaniel (Eds.), *Prospective memory. Theory and applications* (pp. 227–237). Mahwah, NJ: Erlbaum.

Craik, F. I. M., Morris, L. W., Morris, R. G., & Loewen, E. R. (1990). Relations between source amnesia and frontal lobe functioning in older adults. *Psychology and Aging, 5,* 148–151.

Craik, F. I. M., & Simon, E. (1980). Age differences in memory: The roles of attention and depth of processing. In L. W. Poon (Ed.), *New directions in memory and aging* (pp. 95–112). Hillsdale, NJ: Erlbaum.

Glisky, E. L., Polster, M. R., & Routhieaux, B. C. (1995). Double dissociation between item and source memory. *Psychology and Aging, 9,* 229–235.

Goldman-Rakic, P. S. (1987). Circuitry of primate prefrontal cortex and regulation of behavior by representational memory. In V. B. Mountcastle, F. Plum, & S. R. Geiger (Eds.), *Handbook of physiology. Section 1, The nervous system: Vol. 5. Higher functions of the brain* (pp. 373–417). Bethesda, Maryland: American Psychological Society.

Grady, C. L., McIntosh, A. R., Rajah, M. N., & Craik, F. I. M. (1998). Neural correlates of the episodic encoding of pictures and words. *Proceedings of the National Academy of Science USA, 95,* 2703–2708.

Janowsky, J. S., Shimamura, A. P., & Squire, L. R. (1989). Source memory impairment in patients with frontal lobe lesions. *Neuropsychologia, 27,* 1043–1056.

Kapur, S., Craik, F. I. M., Jones, C., Brown, G. M., Houle, S., & Tulving, E. (1995). Functional role of the prefrontal cortex in retrieval of memories. *NeuroReport, 6,* 1880–1884.

Levine, B., Stuss, D. T., & Milberg, W. P. (1997). Effects of aging on conditional associative learning: Process analyses and comparison with focal frontal lesions. *Neuropsychology, 11,* 367–381.

McIntyre, J. S., & Craik, F. I. M. (1987). Age differences in memory for item and source information. *Canadian Journal of Psychology, 41,* 175–192.

Melo, B., Winocur, G., & Moscovitch, M. (1999). False recall and false recognition: An examination of the effects of selective and combined lesions to the medial temporal lobe/diencephalon and frontal lobe structures. *Cognitive Neuropsychology, 16,* 343–359.

Moscovitch, M., & Winocur, G. (1995). Frontal lobes, memory, and aging. *Annals of the New York Academy of Sciences, 769,* 119–150.

Nolde, S. F., Johnson, M. K., & D'Esposito, M. (1998). Left prefrontal activation during episodic remembering: An event-related fMRI study. *NeuroReport, 9,* 3509–3514.

Palmer, H. P. (1998). *Prospective remembering: A clinical and neuropsychological investigation.* Unpublished Ph.D. dissertation, University of New South Wales, Sydney, Australia.

Parkin, A. J., Bindschaedler, C., Harsent, L., & Metzler, C. (1996). Pathological false alarm rates following damage to the left frontal cortex. *Brain & Cognition, 32,* 14–27.

Parkin, A. J., & Walter, B. M. (1992). Recollective experience, normal aging, and frontal dysfunction. *Psychology and Aging, 7,* 290–298.

Petrides, M. (1995). Functional organization of the human frontal cortex for mnemonic processing. *Annals of the New York Academy of Sciences, 769,* 85–95.

Raye, C. L., Johnson, M. K., Mitchell, K. J., Nolde, S. F., & D'Esposito, M. (2000). fMRI investigations of left and right PFC contributions to episodic remembering. *Psychobiology, 28,* 197–206.

Roediger, H. L., III, & McDermott, K. B. (1995). Creating false memories: Remembering words not presented in lists. *Journal of Experimental Psychology: Learning, Memory, and Cognition, 21,* 803–814.

Schacter, D. L., Curran, T., Galluccio, L., Milberg, W., & Bates, J. (1996). False recognition and the right frontal lobe: A case study. *Neuropsychologia, 34,* 793–808.

Schacter, D. L., Harbluk, J. L., & McLachlan, D. R. (1984). Retrieval without recollection: An experimental analysis of source amnesia. *Journal of Verbal Learning and Verbal Behavior, 23,* 593–611.

Schacter, D. L., Koustaal, W., Johnson, M. K., Gross, M. S., & Angell, K. A. (1997). False recollection induced by photographs: A comparison of older and younger adults. *Psychology and Aging, 12,* 203–215.

Shallice, T. (1982). Specific impairments of planning. *Phil. Trans. R. Soc. Lond. B, 298,* 199–209.

Stuss, D. T., Craik, F. I. M., Sayer, L., Franchi, D., & Alexander, M. P. (1996). Comparison of older people and patients with frontal lesions: Evidence from word list learning. *Psychology and Aging, 11,* 387–395.

Winocur, G., Moscovitch, M., & Stuss, D. T. (1996). Explicit and implicit memory in the elderly: Evidence for double dissociation involving medial temporal- and frontal-lobe functions. *Neuropscychology, 10,* 57–65.

Winocur, G., Palmer, H., Stuss, D. T., Alexander, M. P., Craik, F. I. M., Levine, B., Moscovitch, M., & Robertson, I. H. (2000). Cognitive rehabilitation in clinical neuropsychology. *Brain and Cognition, 42,* 120–123.

AUTHOR INDEX

A

Abbruzzese, M., 352, 356
Abello, B., 85, 97
Abrahams, J.P., 253, 261
Abrams, L., 319, 320
Abrams, R., 352, 360
Ach, N., 132
Acker, J.D., 275, 346
Ackerman, B.P., 137, 147, 195, 207
Adams, P.A., 10, 26, 28, 46
Addington, D., 352, 356
Addington, J., 352, 356
Adolfsson, R., 263, 320
Albert, M.S., 262, 365, 383
Albertson, S.A., 317, 320
Alejano, A., 85, 96
Aleman, A., 352, 355, 356
Alexander, M.P., 134, 180, 192, 334, 335, 336, 337, 341, 342, 344, 345, 346, 347, 385, 392
Allan, K., 130, 132
Alloway, T.M., 25, 45, 189, 190
Almkvist, O., 223, 331
Alpert, N.M., 358, 365, 383
Alsop, D.C., 158, 332
Alvarez, P., 198, 205
Alvir, J.M., 357
Amado, I., 359
Amador, X., 353, 357
American Psychiatric Association, 348
Anats, 182
Andeerson-Brown, C., 181, 191
Andersen, P., 27
Anderson, C.M.B., 195, 205, 209, 213, 223, 226, 232
Anderson, J.A., 26, 106
Anderson, J.R., 29, 30, 32, 45, 161, 166, 200, 205, 288, 292, 295
Anderson, M.C., 244, 251

Anderson, Nicole D., 111, 122, 132, 133, 135, 145, 146, 157, 182, 188, 189, 194, 197, 203, 204, 205, 206, 208–225, 227, 228, 232, 245, 251, 261, 267, 274, 279, 285, 286, 287, 289, 295, 327, 331, 363, 373, 379, 380, 387, 391
Andersson, J., 223, 331
Andersson, R., 263
Andrassy, J.M., 287, 296
Andreasen, N.C., 349, 354, 355, 357, 358, 359
Anes, M.D., 351, 360
Angell, K.A., 387, 392
Antal, A., 359
Antonelli, J.R.S., 287, 297
Appelbaum, P.S., 381
Arbuckle, T.Y., 45
Arenberg, D., 146, 331
Arndt, S., 349, 355, 358, 359
Arnsten, A.F.T., 336, 342, 344
Atkinson, R.C., 39, 45, 222, 223
Atlas, S., 158, 332
Attig, M.S., 288, 297

B

Baars, B.J., 120, 121
Babcock, R.L., 149, 160, 293, 297
Bäckman, L., 211, 223, 253, 255, 257, 261, 262, 263, 264, 267, 274, 320, 325, 327, 331, 363, 374, 381, 382
Baddeley, Alan D., 32, 44, 45, 51, 65, 106, 107, 111–123, 112, 132, 148, 150, 152, 158, 161, 162, 163, 164, 166, 179, 182, 186, 189, 194, 205, 209, 213, 214, 219, 221, 223, 261, 295, 359, 363, 373, 379, 386, 391
Bagoczky, N., 359
Baker, J.R., 27
Balaban, M.T., 67
Ballard, D., 328, 332
Balota, D.A., 286, 295

Baltes, P.B., 153, 158, 253, 263, 300, 313, 314
Bandera, R., 118, 123
Bandettini, P.A., 25
Bandy, D., 134, 383
Bank, L., 259, 262
Bannatyne, P.A., 353, 360
Bargh, J.A., 379
Bark, N., 359
Barker, W.J., 353, 357
Barnekow-Bergkvist, M., 263
Barnes, C.L., 336, 345
Barnes, L., 86, 87, 97
Baron, A., 240, 252, 350
Baron, J.C., 357
Barreau, S., 125, 132
Barrow, S., 349, 357
Bartlett, Frederic C., 8, 24, 247, 251
Bartlett, J.C., 364, 379
Bartz, W.H., 240, 251
Bates, J.A., 357, 364, 383, 388, 392
Battig, W.F., 37, 38, 46
Bauman, E., 353, 357
Beavis, Z., 77, 80
Beckett, L.A., 262
Beckwith, B.E., 255, 261
Beekhuis, M.E., 353, 360
Beerten, A., 288, 295
Begg, I., 32, 45
Beig, S., 328, 332, 380
Bekerian, D.A., 125, 133
Belcher, J.D., 256, 263
Bell, B., 253, 261
Bell, L., 357
Bell, M.D., 355, 357
Bench, C., 133
Benedek, G., 359
Benjamin, Aaron S., 237–239
Bennett, J., 159
Bennett, P.J., 314, 345
Bennington-Davis, M., 255, 264
Benson, D.F., 336, 340, 346
Benton, A.L., 268, 275
Berg, R.A., 259, 261
Berg, S., 263
Berman, K.F., 327, 332, 352, 358
Bermejo, F., 263
Bernik, M., 349, 357
Bernstein, Nikolai A., 49, 50, 53, 57, 65, 68–70
Bertelson, P., 68
Berthet, L., 359
Berzofsky, M., 353, 360
Bichot, N.P., 140, 145
Biessels, G.J., 255, 261
Bigelow, L.B., 358
Bihle, A.M., 57, 65

Bilder, R.M. Jr., 342, 345, 349, 355, 357
Bilger, R.C., 302, 313
Bilik, M., 358
Bindschaedler, C., 388, 391
Binns, Malcolm A., 157, 334–347
Birchmore, D., 159
Bird, A., 257, 263
Birren, J.E., 145, 344, 380
Birtwistle, J., 172, 173, 179, 189, 227, 232
Bjork, E.L., 251, 320
Bjork, R.A., 117, 121, 251, 288, 295, 320, 349, 360
Black, S.E., 190
Blake, R., 300, 314
Blanchard, J.J., 349, 357
Blandard-Fields, F., 296
Blass, J.P., 253, 263
Blaxton, T.A., 41, 45, 56, 58, 66, 72, 80, 87, 97
Blizard, R., 257, 263
Bobrow, D.G., 125, 134, 163, 166
Boies, S.J., 228, 231, 233
Boller, F., 26, 81, 191, 345, 346, 360
Booker, J., 71, 81
Bookheimer, S.Y., 66
Bookstein, F.L., 328, 332
Borchelt, M., 253, 263
Botwinick, J., 336, 344
Boucard, M., 63, 66
Bourassa, D.C., 85, 96
Bourne, L.E. Jr., 40, 46, 209, 224
Bower, G. H., 7, 9, 24, 25, 29, 30, 45, 53, 66, 107, 121, 122, 146, 158, 166, 200, 205, 251, 296, 314, 365, 379
Bowers, D., 57, 66
Bowers, J., 71, 81
Bradley, M.M., 122
Braff, D., 359
Branch, L.G., 253, 261
Brandimonte, M., 391
Brandys, C.E., 346
Bransford, J.D., 32, 40, 42, 45, 46, 52, 72, 81, 88, 89, 91, 92, 96, 105, 107, 208, 223
Brant, L.J., 253, 262
Bravenboer, B., 255, 261
Braver, T.S., 328, 331
Brebion, G., 353, 357
Breier, A., 357
Brenner, C., 374, 381
Brewer, J.B., 19, 25, 188, 189
Bridgeman, B., 53, 66
Briggs, S.D., 275, 346
Broadbent, D.E., 190
Brodbeck, D.R., 52, 66, 72, 73, 80
Brody, J.A., 253, 261
Brooks, Barbara, 4, 51, 53, 56, 57, 77, 78, 80, 101

Brooks, Barbara M., 71–82
Broughton, R., 342, 345
Brown, A.L., 60, 66
Brown, A.S., 72, 80, 266, 274
Brown, G.D.A., 117, 121
Brown, G.M., 67, 133, 206, 224, 345, 358, 359, 391
Brown, J., 8, 25
Brown, J.S., 83, 96
Brown, V., 142, 143, 145, 146
Browne, J., 97
Brownell, H.H., 57, 65
Bruant, A., 353, 357
Bruner, J.S., 112, 122, 247, 251
Bryson, G., 355, 357
Buchanan, R.W., 355, 357
Bucht, G., 263, 320
Buckle, L., 134, 192, 346
Buckner, R.L., 12, 19, 23, 25, 26, 27, 130, 132, 192, 328, 331, 349, 360, 364, 366, 382
Bullemer, P., 241, 252
Bunsey, M., 187, 190
Burgess, N., 67
Burgess, P., 125, 126, 130, 132
Burgess, P.W., 336, 346
Burke, D.M., 317, 319, 320, 325, 331, 333
Burns, H.J., 350, 359
Burns, K.I., 84, 85, 87, 97
Busche, H., 39, 45
Buschke, H., 325, 332
Butler, K.M., 288, 295
Butters, N., 173, 189
Butterworth, R.F., 256, 261
Buus, S., 312, 313
Byrd, M., 135, 137, 146, 148, 150, 157, 158, 164, 166, 195, 205, 250, 251, 286, 295, 325, 326, 327, 331, 363, 373, 374, 380, 386, 391

C

Cabeza, R., 19, 25, 74, 80, 124, 132, 190, 205, 209, 211, 223, 224, 228, 232, 326, 327, 328, 331, 332, 343, 344, 359, 380
Calev, A., 352, 357
Campsall, J., 97
Cantor, J., 266, 275
Caplin, L.J., 136, 147
Capparella, O., 262
Carbonin, P., 262
Carlson, L., 85, 96
Carlson, M., 288, 294, 295
Carmelli, D., 254, 263
Carney, M.W., 255, 261
Carpenter, C.J., 348, 358
Carpenter, P.A., 149, 158, 163, 293, 296, 305, 313

Carpenter, W.T. Jr., 357
Carpentier, A., 25
Carr, C.A., 27
Carr, T.H., 83, 84, 85, 87, 96, 297
Carrier, L.M., 217, 219, 221, 223
Carruth, F.G., 346
Casey, A., 85, 96
Cave, K.R., 140, 141, 142, 145
Cepeda, N.J., 140, 145
Cerella, J., 286, 295, 330, 331
Cermak, L.A., 68, 331
Cermak, L.S., 39, 45, 46, 47, 66, 146, 173, 179, 189, 190, 223, 381, 382
Chaiken, S., 367, 379
Chalfonte, B.L., 200, 201, 205, 206, 377, 379, 381
Challis, B.H., 25, 27, 38, 39, 45, 46, 52, 58, 59, 60, 61, 66, 68, 72, 73, 80, 81, 208, 224, 230, 233
Champagne, S.C., 334, 346
Chan, D., 132
Chao, L.L., 340, 344
Chapman, J.P., 349, 352, 357
Chapman, L.J., 349, 352, 357
Charalambous, A., 83, 96
Cherry, K.E., 150, 158
Chiat, S., 114, 123
Chodzko-Zajko, W.J., 257, 261
Chow, P.C.P., 32, 34, 45
Christensen, Bruce K., 348–361
Christoff, K., 57, 66
Cimino, C.R., 57, 66
Cipolotti, L., 126, 132
Claes, T., 126, 133
Clarke, A.J.B., 71, 81
Cobb, J., 256, 262
Cockburn, J., 390, 391
Cocklin, T., 209, 224
Cofer, Charles N., 8, 25, 26
Coffey, C.E., 267, 274, 329, 331
Cohen, A., 189
Cohen, B.M., 333
Cohen, G., 307, 313, 364, 379
Cohen, J.D., 331
Cohen, J.J., 17, 25
Cohen, N.J., 203, 205, 379
Cohen, R.M., 349, 361
Colcombe, S., 289, 297
Coleman, P.D., 343, 344
Coleman, R.E., 159, 224, 332
Coles, M.G.H., 27
Colombo, P., 189
Colotla, V., 173, 184, 192, 259, 264
Coltheart, M., 121, 166
Connelly, S., 136, 137, 138, 140, 143, 144, 145, 146

Connelly, S.L., 286, 288, 289, 291, 294, 295
Connor, L.T., 158
Conrad, R., 112, 113, 121
Constable, R.T., 23, 25
Conway, A.R.A., 156, 158
Conway, M.A., 350, 357
Cooper, D., 97
Corkin, S., 17, 25, 27
Corwin, J., 242, 249, 252
Costello, 131
Cowan, N., 119, 120, 121, 122, 288, 295
Coyote, K.C., 75, 82
Craik, Fergus I.M., 3–6, 9, 10, 11, 17, 18, 23, 25,
 26, 27, 28, 29, 30, 31, 32, 33, 34, 35, 36, 37, 38,
 40, 41, 42, 43, 44, 45, 46, 47, 48, 49, 51, 52,
 56, 57, 58, 60, 63, 65, 66, 67, 68, 72, 73, 75,
 80, 81, 83, 96, 99, 100, 105, 107, 111, 112, 122,
 124, 132, 133, 134, 135, 137, 145, 146, 147, 148,
 150, 152, 157, 158, 161, 162, 164, 166, 171, 172,
 173, 174, 175, 177, 178, 179, 181, 182, 183, 184,
 188, 189, 190, 191, 192, 194, 195, 196, 197, 204,
 205, 206, 207, 208, 209, 210, 211, 212, 213,
 214, 215, 217, 219, 220, 221, 223, 224, 226, 227,
 228, 230, 232, 233, 237, 238, 239, 240, 245,
 250, 251, 252, 261, 265, 266, 267, 271, 272,
 274, 275, 277, 278, 279, 285, 286, 287, 289,
 293, 294, 295, 296, 297, 299, 309, 312, 313,
 314, 315, 316, 317, 320, 325, 326, 327, 328, 331,
 332, 333, 334, 336, 342, 343, 344, 345, 346,
 347, 349, 350, 354, 356, 357, 358, 359, 360,
 362, 363, 364, 365, 366, 373, 374, 375, 377,
 378, 379, 380, 381, 382, 383, 384, 385, 386,
 387, 389, 391, 392
Crapo, L.M., 253, 262
Cristi, C., 201, 205
Crowder, R.G., 118, 122, 244, 251
Crowe, S., 339, 345
Cummings, J.L., 332
Cunningham, W.R., 336, 347
Curran, H.V., 16, 25, 349, 357
Curran, T., 134, 364, 380, 383, 388, 392
Currie, J.L., 32, 34, 45
Cutaia, M.M., 346

D
D'Agostino, R.B., 256, 262
D'Esposito, M., 152, 153, 158, 266, 275, 327, 328,
 330, 332, 333, 336, 345, 387, 391, 392
d'Ydewalle, G., 68
Dab, S., 126, 133
Dagenbach, D., 297
Dai, H., 312, 313
Dale, A.D., 192
Dale, A.M., 19, 25, 27, 132, 364, 382
Dallas, M., 38, 42, 45, 222, 224

Damon, A., 253, 261
Dancer, A.L., 314
Daneman, Meredyth, 149, 158, 161–167, 293,
 296, 300, 301, 303, 305, 306, 313, 314
Danielson, S.M., 304, 314
Danion, Jean-Marie, 348–361
Darcey, T.M., 27
Davidson, M., 358
Davidson, N.S., 159, 284, 285
Davidson, P.S.R., 268, 274
Davis, H.P., 175, 189
Davis, K.L., 356, 357, 358, 359
Davis, T.L., 266, 274
de Haan, E.H., 352, 356
De le Coste-Lareymondie, M., 57, 67
De Meersman, L., 246, 252
Deacon, T.W., 57, 66
Debner, J.A., 244, 245, 247, 248, 251
Deeg, D.J.H., 260, 262
Deese, James, 8, 26, 364, 380
Degl'Innocenti, A., 267, 274
del Ser, T., 263
DeLeonardis, D.M., 266, 267, 274, 275, 376, 380
Delis, D.C., 359
Della Sala, S., 118, 122, 123
Demb, J.B., 23, 25, 66–67, 203, 207
Dempster, R., 346
Denhiere, G., 96
Denny, L.L., 159, 224, 332
Desgranges, B., 350, 357
Desmond, D.W., 188, 256, 261
Desmond, J.E., 23, 25, 66–67, 134, 189
Detre, J.A., 158, 332
Dettmar, P., 56, 68
Deubel, H., 53, 66
Deutsch, S., 351, 360
Di Scenna, P., 126, 134
Diamond, P.L., 361
Dias, R., 338, 345
Djang, W.T., 274, 331
Dodson, C.S., 273, 274, 371, 373, 375, 380
Dolan, Patrick O., 157, 240–252, 278, 286, 295,
 316
Dolan, R.A., 181, 190
Dolan, R.J., 127, 129, 130, 131, 132, 133, 134,
 187, 189, 191, 205, 223, 224, 333, 351, 358
Donaldson, W., 47, 107, 233
Donchin, E., 23, 27
Doppelt, J.E., 334, 345
Doraiswamy, P.M., 275
Doren, B., 288, 297
Dori, H., 194, 206, 209, 224, 363, 382
Dornhoefer, S., 54, 62, 63, 64, 66, 67, 68
Dornic, S., 45, 121
Dosher, B.A., 201, 205

Doussard-Roosevelt, J.A., 137, 146
Dowin, S., 85, 96
Driver, J., 133
Duchek, J.M., 286, 295
Dudai, Y., 22, 25
Dudley, W.N., 151, 159, 179, 191, 209, 224, 325, 333
Duncan, J., 247, 249, 251
Dunn, J., 256, 263
Dunn, J.C., 43, 45, 81
Dupuis, J.H., 275, 346
Duzel, E., 351, 357
Düzel, E., 81
Dywan, J., 179, 189, 363, 368, 374, 380, 381

E
Eagly, A.H., 367, 379
Earles, J.L., 151, 156, 158, 159, 160, 166, 259, 260, 262, 285
Ebbinghaus, Herman, 7, 25
Eccles, J.C., 18, 26
Eckert, S.L., 361
Edelist, S., 352, 357
Edwards, K.L., 255, 261, 263, 264
Eelen, P., 68
Eichenbaum, H., 203, 205, 379
Einstein, G.O., 365, 380, 391
Eldridge, I.I., 132, 134, 189
Eldridge, M., 106, 107, 179, 194, 205, 209, 223, 379
Elias, M.F., 254, 255, 256, 262, 263
Elin, M.R., 381
Elliott, R., 340, 345
Ellmore, T.M., 327, 332
Emerson, M.J., 320
Emslie, H., 247, 251
Engle, R.W., 156, 158
Erdelyi, R., 359
Ericsson, K.A., 119, 122
Erkelens, D.W., 255, 261
Erngrund, K., 263, 320
Eskes, G.A., 336, 346
Esposito, G., 327, 332
Eustache, F., 350, 357
Evans, D.A., 262
Eysenck, M.W., 32, 44, 45, 51, 66

F
Fabiani, M., 23, 27, 266, 275
Faulkner, D., 364, 379
Faulkner, H.J., 85, 87, 96
Faust, M.E., 136, 143, 144, 147
Feifel, D., 330, 332
Feinstein, A., 352, 357
Ferguson, S., 266, 267, 274

Ferguson, S.A., 275
Fernandes, Myra A., 106, 171–192, 194, 203, 205, 209, 214, 219, 220, 221, 223, 227, 228, 229, 231, 232, 363, 373, 380
Fernandez Calle, P., 263
Feskens, E.J.M., 255, 262
Field, D., 259, 262
Figiel, G.S., 274, 331
Figlozzi, C.M., 66
Filion, D.L., 136, 139, 146
Findlay, J.M., 66
Fink, G.R., 131, 133
Fischer, B., 63, 66
Fischman, A.J., 358
Fish, J., 122
Fisher, R.P., 32, 33, 40, 41, 43, 45, 52, 80, 194, 206, 213, 224
Flashman, L.A., 27
Fleischman, D.A., 318, 320
Fletcher, P.C., 127, 131, 132, 133, 134, 186, 187, 189, 191, 196, 203, 205, 209, 211, 223, 224, 333
Flood, D.G., 343, 344
Fodor, J., 48, 62, 176, 189
Foley, M.A., 247, 252
Folstein, M.G., 255, 262
Folstein, S.E., 255, 262
Forsgren, L., 263
Foster, J.K., 336, 346, 349, 357
Fox, N., 130, 132
Fox, P.T., 134
Fozard, J.L., 146, 253, 262, 331
Frackowiak, R.S.J., 127, 131, 133, 134, 191, 205, 223, 224, 329, 332
Franchi, D., 334, 346, 347, 365, 383, 385, 392
Frankish, C.R., 115, 122
Franks, J.J., 32, 40, 45, 46, 52, 72, 81, 105, 107, 208, 223
Freed, D.M., 17, 25
Freer, C., 247, 251
Freksa, C., 68
Frensch, P.A., 67, 252
Friedman, A., 40, 46, 356
Friedman, D., 266, 275
Friedman, J.I., 357
Friedman, N.P., 320
Fries, J.F., 253, 262
Frieske, D.A., 150, 151, 156, 157, 158, 159, 166, 285
Fristoe, N., 281, 285, 330, 333
Friston, K.J., 133, 329, 332, 354, 357
Frith, C.D., 127, 131, 132, 133, 134, 191, 205, 223, 224, 329, 332, 333
Fukuyama, H., 332
Fulton, A., 364, 379

Furedy, J.J., 56, 68
Fuster, J.M., 336, 345

G

Gabrieli, J.D.E., 19, 23, 25, 56, 57, 66–67, 82, 134, 188, 189, 318, 320
Gaillard, W.D., 66
Gaines, C.L., 159, 166, 285
Gallo, David A., 4, 28–47, 48, 52, 101, 374, 383
Galluccio, L., 364, 367, 372, 380, 381, 383, 388, 392
Ganzevles, P.G., 256, 262
Gardian, D.G., 57, 67
Gardiner, John M., 4, 51, 53, 56, 57, 71–82, 101, 130, 133, 172, 173, 181, 189, 190, 227, 232, 351, 358
Gardner, H., 57, 65
Garry, P.J., 255, 262, 338, 345
Gathercole, Susan E., 113, 114, 115, 116, 121, 122
Gavoni, R., 133
Gavrilescu, D., 194, 195, 197, 204, 206, 210, 214, 215, 219, 224, 227, 232
Gazzaniga, M.S., 26, 190
Gehr, S.E., 301, 314
Geig, T., 357
Geiger, S.R., 391
Gemma, A., 262
George, J., 20, 22, 26
Gerard, L., 293, 296
Gerdt, C., 349, 361
Gershberg, F.B., 127, 133
Geus, B.W.J., 256, 262
Ghaffar, O., 124, 133
Ghaffer, O., 79, 81
Ghoneim, M.M., 16, 25
Giacomoni, F., 358
Gick, M.L., 293, 296
Giersch, A., 361
Giesler, S., 357
Gillespie, G.L., 38, 46
Gilligan, S.G., 53, 66
Gillund, G., 200, 205
Gippenreiter, J.B., 54, 67
Gispen, W.H., 255, 261
Glanzer, M., 117, 122
Glenberg, A.M., 118, 122
Glisky, Elizabeth L., 187, 190, 265–276, 377, 380, 385, 391
Glover, G.H., 19, 23, 25, 66–67, 134, 188, 189
Gluck, M.A., 241, 252, 365, 380
Goff, D., 358
Gold, J.M., 348, 349, 355, 358
Gold, S., 355, 358
Goldberg, E., 57, 67, 342, 345
Goldberg, T.E., 348, 352, 354, 355, 357, 358

Goldman, R.S., 357
Goldman-Rakic, P.S., 336, 345, 385, 391
Goldsmith, M., 133, 247, 252, 362, 381
Goldstein, D., 136, 147
Gollwitzer, P.M., 249, 251
Gonzalez, R.G., 27
Gonzalez-Lima, F., 329, 332
Goodwin, J.M., 255, 262, 338
Goodwin, J.S., 255, 262, 345
Goolkassian, P., 240, 251
Gopher, D., 66, 145, 146, 251, 296
Gorelick, P.B., 254, 257, 262
Gorfein, D.S., 137, 146
Goshen-Gottstein, Y., 177, 191
Gottlob, L.R., 159, 224, 328, 332
Govoni, Richard, 111, 122, 132, 135, 146, 182, 189, 194, 205, 208, 215, 223, 227, 232, 380, 387, 391
Grady, Cheryl L., 133, 223, 314, 325–333, 343, 344, 345, 356, 358, 377, 378, 379, 380, 386, 391
Graf, P., 42, 45, 72, 80, 96, 227, 233
Grafman, J., 191, 345, 346
Grange, D., 351, 358, 359, 360, 361
Gras-Vincendon, A., 351, 358
Grasby, P.M., 124, 133, 134, 191, 205, 223, 224
Green, M.F., 348, 355, 356, 358
Greenberg, S.N., 194, 206, 213, 224
Gregg, V., 22, 25
Greig, T., 355, 357
Greiner, L.H., 256, 263
Gretz, A.L., 122
Griffith, D., 194, 205, 206, 213, 223, 224
Gronlund, S.D., 201, 205
Gross, M.S., 387, 392
Grossman, M., 158, 332
Guerin, S.J., 27
Guez, Jonathan, 194, 197, 206, 209, 210, 214, 219, 221, 222, 224, 231, 232, 363, 382
Guez, J., 206
Guimaraes, A.R., 27
Gundy, M., 189
Gunning, F.M., 275, 346
Gur, R.C., 360
Gur, R.E., 360
Gutierrez-Rivas, H., 82
Guynn, M.J., 13, 15, 25, 187, 190
Guzman, C., 255, 263
Guzman, D.A., 255, 263

H

Haaland, K.Y., 338, 345
Habib, R., 20, 21, 22, 23, 25, 27, 134, 332, 359
Hafter, E.R., 312, 314

Hagendorf, H., 158, 232, 239, 274, 285, 295, 320, 331, 344
Hagner, T., 81
Hale, S., 286, 297
Hall, J., 116, 122
Hall-Gutchess, A., 156, 157, 159
Halligan, P.W., 133
Hamann, S.B., 58, 67
Hambrick, D.Z., 281, 285, 300, 314
Hamer, L., 346
Hamm, V.P., 288, 296, 297
Hammer, M., 259, 262
Hammernik, R.P., 314
Hammersley, R.H., 125, 133
Hammond, J., 68
Hammond, S., 359
Hamstra, S., 301, 314
Hancock, H.E., 283, 285, 300, 314
Harbluk, J.L., 175, 191, 266, 275, 364, 383, 384, 392
Hardenberg, J., 346
Harris, M.J., 359
Harrison, G., 132
Harsent, L., 388, 391
Hart, R.P., 268, 274
Hartley, A.A., 158, 159, 286, 288, 296, 332, 333
Hartman, D.E., 256, 262
Hartman, M., 288, 292, 296
Harvey, P.D., 356, 358, 359, 360
Hasher, Lynn, 135, 136, 137, 138, 140, 143, 144, 145, 146, 147, 152, 155, 158, 159, 160, 165, 166, 195, 205, 222, 224, 246, 249, 251, 286–297, 307, 314, 316, 330, 333
Hashtroudi, S., 247, 252, 265, 266, 267, 274, 275, 362, 381
Hassing, L., 255, 262
Hatano, G., 346
Hawk, T.C., 159, 224, 332
Hawkins, K.A., 352, 355, 358, 364
Hawkins, S.A., 250, 252, 381
Haxby, J.V., 124, 133, 328, 332, 380
Hay, J.F., 244, 245, 250, 251, 355, 358
Hazleton, B.C., 361
Head, D., 275, 346
Head, H., 50, 67
Healy, M., 317, 318, 320
Heaton, R.K., 359
Heckers, S., 349, 354, 358
Hedden, Trey, 107, 148–160, 161
Hegarty, M., 231, 232
Hegele, R.A., 256, 264
Heilmann, K.M., 57, 66
Heinrich, J., 81
Heinrichs, R.W., 349, 355, 358
Heinze, H.-J, 81, 351, 357

Heller, D., 67
Henderson, D., 314
Henderson, J.M., 288, 295
Henkel, L.A., 266, 267, 274, 376, 377, 380
Henson, R.N.A., 129, 130, 131, 132, 133, 181, 186, 190, 351, 358
Herbert, L.E., 257, 262
Heron, A., 112, 122, 237
Herranz, A., 263
Herscovitch, J., 342, 345
Hertel, P., 358
Hertzog, C., 151, 159, 286, 296, 358
Hess, T.M., 296
Hetland, M., 259, 262
Hier, C.M., 287, 296
Hijman, R., 352, 356
Hill, R.D., 255, 257, 262
Hinton, G.E., 26
Hirshman, E., 241, 251
Hitch, Graham J., 106, 107, 113, 117, 118, 121, 148, 158, 162, 163, 166
Hoblyn, J., 358
Hockley, W.E., 201, 205
Hodges, J.R., 16, 25
Hof, P.R., 343, 345
Hoffman, J.M., 267, 332, 380
Hoffmann, J., 68, 133, 205, 223
Hoffmann, J.M., 275
Hökfelt, B., 27
Holland, P.W., 273, 274
Hollingshead, A., 316, 320
Holloszy, J.O., 261
Holloway, R.L., 57, 67
Holmgren, S., 263
Holstein, C., 357
Holyoak, K.J., 191
Hong, J., 346
Hooker, K., 259, 262
Horwitz, B., 133, 329, 332, 380
Houle, S., 22, 23, 27, 57, 67, 68, 124, 133, 134, 206, 211, 223, 224, 228, 233, 327, 331, 332, 336, 344, 345, 347, 350, 358, 359, 360, 391
Howanitz, E., 358
Howard, D.V., 243, 251
Howard, J.H., 243, 251
Howard, S., 68
Howerter, A., 320
Hsiao, A.T., 231, 233
Hughlings-Jackson, John, 49
Hull, A.G., 112, 121
Hull, C.L., 348, 358
Hulme, C., 114, 117, 121, 123
Hultsch, D.F., 259, 262, 325, 332
Humphrey, D.G., 136, 146, 287, 296
Humphrey, G., 125, 133

Humphreys, G.W., 63, 66
Humphreys, M.S., 201, 206
Hunt, R.R., 365, 380
Huron, C., 352, 353, 358
Hvalby, O., 27
Hyde, T.S., 11, 26, 31, 33, 34, 38, 40, 45
Hyman, R., 359

I
Iidaka, T., 132, 188, 205, 209, 223, 224, 228, 232, 363, 373, 380
Imbs, J.L., 361
Incalzi, R.A., 255, 262
Incisa della Rocchetta, A., 127, 133
Irion, A.L., 26
Israel, L., 366, 372, 380, 383
Izukawa, D., 346

J
Jacoby, Larry L., 32, 38, 40, 41, 42, 43, 45, 46, 72, 78, 79, 80, 81, 82, 87, 96, 129, 133, 151, 157, 158, 179, 189, 212, 220, 221, 222, 224, 240–252, 278, 283, 285, 316, 318, 320, 351, 355, 358, 362, 363, 365, 366, 368, 373, 374, 376, 378, 381
James, William, 99, 111, 122
Janka, Z., 359
Janowsky, J.S., 266, 275, 384, 391
Jarvik, L., 259, 262
Java, R.I., 71, 75, 80, 81, 351, 358
Jeannerod, 53
Jeffrey, K.J., 67
Jelicic, M., 75, 81, 260, 262, 349, 357
Jenkins, J.J., 10–11, 26, 31, 33, 34, 38, 40, 42, 45, 47
Jennings, J.M., 150, 151, 152, 157, 158, 177, 189, 223, 286, 295, 331, 344, 355, 358, 373, 374, 381
Jennings, J.R., 27
Jennings, P.J., 27
Jeste, D.V., 359
Jimenez, F.J., 263
Joffe, R.T., 255, 262
Johansson, H., 263
Johnson, M.K., 124, 134, 200, 201, 205, 206, 247, 252, 265, 266, 267, 273, 274, 275, 358, 362, 363, 368, 375, 376, 377, 379, 380, 381, 387, 391, 392
Johnson, R., 247, 251
Johnson, S.C., 27
Johnson-Selfridge, M.T., 355, 361
Johnston, J.D., 11, 26
Johnston, W.A., 194, 206, 213, 224
Johnstone, E.C., 356, 359

Jolles, J., 355, 359
Jonas, D., 289, 296
Jones, C., 358, 391
Jones, E.M., 266, 274
Jonides, J., 120, 123, 153, 155, 158, 159, 160, 194, 206, 327, 330, 331, 332, 333
Jonker, C., 260, 262
Joordens, S., 145, 146
Joreskog, K.G., 152, 159
Josephs, O., 129, 133, 181, 190, 351, 358
Juola, A.F., 222, 223

K
Kahn, R.S., 352, 356
Kahneman, D., 208, 213, 224, 230, 232
Kalmijin, S., 255, 262
Kaminska, Z., 77, 80
Kane, J.M., 155, 357
Kane, M.J., 136, 137, 138, 139, 144, 145, 146, 159, 288, 293, 295, 296
Kanwisher, N., 137, 146
Kapelle, A.C., 255, 261
Kaplan, E., 355, 357
Kapur, N., 119, 123
Kapur, Shitji, 22, 27, 57, 66, 67, 68, 124, 132, 133, 134, 196, 205, 206, 209, 211, 223, 224, 228, 232, 233, 331, 332, 336, 344, 345, 347, 348–361, 380, 386, 391
Karlsson, S., 263, 320
Kaszniak, A.W., 266, 275, 377, 383
Kates, J.H., 337, 346
Katsumi, Y., 332
Katz, D.I., 253, 335, 345
Katz, S., 261
Katz, W.A., 45
Kauffmann-Muller, F., 361
Kausler, D.H., 155, 159, 259, 263, 286, 296, 364, 382
Kazes, M., 351, 359
Keane, M.M., 82
Keane, M.T., 51, 66
Kelemen, O., 359
Kelley, C.M., 212, 224, 247, 252, 363, 368, 374, 381
Kelley, W.H., 12, 25
Kellogg, R.T., 209, 224
Kelso, J.A.S., 107
Kennard, C., 53, 67
Kennedy, A., 67
Kennedy, G, 359
Kennison, R.F., 317, 319, 320
Keri, S., 351, 359
Kerr, B., 208, 213, 224
Kerr, S.A., 261, 287, 295, 389, 391

Kershner, J.R., 349, 359
Kesselman, M., 353, 360
Kester, D.B., 178, 181, 196, 360
Kester, J.D., 111, 122, 189, 205
Kidder, D.P., 151, 157, 159
Kihlstrom, J.F., 266, 275, 377, 383
Kim, M., 140, 145
Kimura, J., 332
Kincaid, D., 156, 159
King, J.W., 62, 67
Kinsbourne, M., 20, 21, 22, 26
Kintsch, W., 87, 96, 97, 119, 122, 155, 159
Kirchhoff, B.A., 23, 26
Kirkby, B.S., 327, 332
Kirkpatrick, B., 357
Kirsner, K., 43, 45, 81, 83, 84, 85, 97
Klein, K., 365, 381
Klemm, T., 56, 68
Klix, F., 68, 158, 205, 223, 232, 239, 274, 285, 295, 320, 331, 344, 380
Kniepeman, K., 253, 261
Knight, R.T., 23, 26, 191, 198, 206, 340, 344
Knowlton, B.J., 181, 190, 241, 252
Koeppe, R.A., 158, 159, 332, 333
Koh, S.D., 348, 349, 352, 353, 354, 359
Kohen, D., 83, 97
Kohonen, T., 23, 26
Kolers, Paul A., 32, 41, 42, 43, 44, 46, 208, 224, 230, 232
Koriat, A., 66, 133, 145, 146, 247, 251, 252, 296, 362, 381
Kormi-Nouri, R., 20, 21, 26
Koshmider, J.W. III, 375, 383
Kounious, J., 266, 275
Koutstaal, Wilma, 23, 25, 26, 27, 126, 130, 132, 192, 278, 328, 331, 350, 360, 362–383, 387, 392
Kowalchuk, D., 301, 314
Krabbendam, L., 355, 359
Kramer, A.F., 136, 143, 146, 287, 296
Kramer, L., 189
Krames, L., 25, 45
Krantz, D.H., 223
Kraus, T.A., 122
Krishnan, K.R.R., 275
Kroll, N.E.A., 20, 27, 198, 206
Kromhout, D., 255, 262
Kruesi, E., 35, 39, 40, 46
Kuck, J., 359
Kugelmass, S., 352, 357
Kuhn, Thomas, 10
Kutas, M., 62, 67
Kwentus, J.A., 268, 274
Kwong-See, S., 167, 301, 307, 314

L
La Voie, D., 317, 318, 320
LaBerge, D., 142, 143, 145, 146
Lader, M., 349, 357
Lafleche, G., 335, 345
Lafronza, V.N., 179, 191, 209, 224
Lagae, C., 288, 295
Lalonde, F., 180, 190
Lamb, M., 301, 314
Land, C., 187, 190, 191
Lang, P., 67
Langstrom, B., 331
Längström, B., 223
Lantenschlager, G., 284, 285
Larish, J.F., 136, 146
Larsson, M., 253, 261
LaRue, A., 254, 259, 262, 263
Launer, L.J., 255, 262, 263
Lautenschlager, G., 159, 166, 285
Lavie, N., 137, 144, 146
Law, S., 250, 252, 364, 381
Lawrie, S.M., 356, 359
Le Breck, D.B., 240, 252
Lean, D.S., 38, 46
Lease, J., 328, 332
Leboe, J.P., 368, 383
LeDoux, J.E., 187, 191
Leech, E.E., 340, 347
Lees Haley, P.R., 256, 263
Lehtio, P., 23, 26
Leino, E.V., 259, 262
Leirer, V.O., 287, 296
Leont'ev, Alexei N., 49, 50, 53, 67
Lepage, M., 79, 81, 124, 125, 127, 130, 133
Lerer, B., 352, 357
Leslie, J.E., 364, 379
Leventhal, E., 159
Leventhal, H., 159
Levin, J.M., 333
Levine, B., 190, 336, 337, 338, 345, 346, 385, 391, 392
Levitt, A.J., 255, 262
Levy, Betty Ann, 4, 83–98, 100, 113, 121
Lewandowsky, S., 81, 205
Lewis, D.J., 187, 190
Lewis, G., 257, 263
Lewis, M., 256, 262
Lewis, V.J., 106, 107, 118, 121, 132, 179, 189, 194, 205, 209, 223, 379
Lezak, M.D., 255, 264
Lhermitte, F., 173, 190, 249, 252
Li, K.Z.H., 135, 147, 261, 286, 287, 289, 295, 296, 297, 309, 314
Liddle, P.F., 329, 332, 345

Lieberman, A., 367, 379
Lieberman, J.A., 357
Light, Leah L., 152, 159, 315–322, 325, 331, 333
Lindenberger, U., 153, 158, 253, 263, 300, 313, 314
Lindenmayer, J.P., 356, 359
Lindgaard, G., 68
Lindsay, D.S., 246, 247, 252, 265, 275, 362, 375, 381
Lindsley, D.B., 19, 27, 56, 67
Lineweaver, T.T., 286, 296
Lister, R., 191
Ljungquist, B., 259, 263
Lockhart, Robert S., 3–6, 10, 11, 25, 28, 29, 30, 32, 34, 35, 40, 42, 43, 44, 45, 46, 48, 49, 51, 63, 66, 67, 72, 80, 81, 83, 96, 99–102, 105, 107, 112, 122, 135, 146, 161, 162, 166, 171, 173, 189, 226, 232, 240, 251, 299, 312, 313, 325, 328, 331, 349, 350, 354, 357, 359, 362, 365, 366, 380, 381
Loewen, E.R., 189, 266, 274, 334, 345, 364, 380, 384, 391
Loftus, E.F., 22, 26, 350, 359
Loftus, G.R., 22, 26
Logan, G.D., 136, 146
Logie, R.H., 118, 121, 122, 163, 166
Loken, W.J., 275, 346
Longman, D.J.A., 121
Lorenceau, J., 63, 66
Lowinger, R., 359
Luce, R.D., 223
Lund, C.E., 359
Luo, C.R., 374, 383
Luria, A.R., 173, 190
Luria, Alexander R., 49, 57, 67
Lustig, Cindy, 286–297, 316
Lyskov, E., 263
Lysynchuk, L., 85, 97

M
Maas, L.C., 333
MacDonald, P.A., 145, 146, 231, 232
Macdonald, R., 345
Mace, W., 61, 68
Macht, M.L., 325, 332
Mack, C., 180, 190
MacKay, D.G., 319, 320
MacLean, Paul, 49
MacLeod, Colin M., 84, 97, 226–233
Madden, D.J., 153, 159, 211, 224, 267, 275, 327, 328, 330, 332
Maddox, G.L., 296
Madigan, S.A., 11, 27, 309, 314
Magata, Y., 332
Mahurin, R.K., 361
Maisog, J.M., 133, 332, 380

Malaspina, D., 353, 357
Malone, C.P., 383
Malone, M.A., 349, 359
Mamourian, A., 27
Mandler, G., 38, 42, 45, 46, 72, 80, 127, 130, 133, 190, 212, 222, 224, 374, 381
Mangels, J.A., 241, 252, 327, 331
Mangun, G.R., 351, 357
Mann, A., 257, 263
Mäntylä, T., 374, 381
Maril, A., 23, 26, 27, 192
Marklund, P., 263
Markowitsch, H.J., 16, 22, 23, 26, 27, 124, 134
Marra, C., 262
Marsh, Elizabeth J., 157, 240–252, 278, 316
Marshall, J.C., 133
Marshuetz, C., 153, 158, 159, 332, 333
Martello, J., 349, 361
Martin, A., 180, 190
Martin, D.W., 194, 206, 213, 224
Martin, Edwin, 9, 24, 26, 86, 87
Martin, L., 97
Martin, M., 157, 159
Martin, O.S.M., 45
Masani, P.A., 237, 239
Masson, M.E.J., 87, 97
Mathews, R.C., 38, 46
May, C.P., 137, 145, 146, 155, 159, 287, 288, 289, 290, 291, 292, 295, 296
Mayes, A.R., 16, 26
Mayhorn, C., 151, 159
Maylor, E.A., 137, 144, 146, 320
Mayzner, M.S., 28, 29, 32, 47
McAllister, T.W., 27
McCabe, L., 309, 314
McCall, A.L., 263
McCarthy, R., 130, 134
McClain, L., 353, 359
McClelland, J.L., 67, 365, 382
McCormack, M.K., 256, 262
McDaniel, M.A., 40, 41, 43, 46, 187, 190, 391
McDermott, K.B., 13, 15, 21, 26, 43, 46, 73, 81, 134, 247, 252, 349, 360, 364, 383, 387, 392
McDowd, Joan M., 107, 135–147, 161, 213, 219, 223, 278, 279, 285, 288, 296, 325, 331, 363, 380
McElree, B.D., 247, 251, 252
McEvoy, C., 358
McGaugh, J.L., 198, 206
McGeoch, J.A., 26
McGlynn, S.M., 75, 76, 81
McGuire, C.L., 286, 296
McGurk, S.R., 348, 355, 359
McGuthry, K.E., 281, 285
McHugh, P.R., 262

McIntosh, Anthony R., 20, 25, 132, 181, 190, 205, 223, 314, 323–324, 328, 329, 331, 332, 342, 344, 345, 354, 359, 378, 380, 386, 391
McIntyre, J.S., 175, 190, 266, 275, 334, 345, 364, 382, 384, 391
McKenna, P.J., 340, 348, 355, 359
McKenna, P.S, 345
McKoon, G., 247, 252
McLachlan, D.R., 175, 191, 266, 275, 364, 383, 384, 392
McNaughton, B.L., 365, 382
McQuain, J., 275, 346
Mearns, J., 256, 263
Mednick, S.A., 290, 296
Meinz, E.J., 156, 160, 300, 314
Mello, N.K., 333
Melo, B., 133, 176, 191, 353, 359, 388, 389, 391
Melton, Arthur, 8, 9, 24, 172, 190
Melton, Arthur W., 26
Menard, W.E., 287, 296
Mendelson, J.H., 333
Mentis, M.J., 332, 380
Merikle, P., 293, 296
Mervis, C.B., 161, 167
Metcalfe, J., 23, 26, 198, 206
Metter, E.J., 253, 262
Metzler, C., 388, 391
Mewaldt, S.P., 16, 25
Meyer, J.S., 256, 257, 263, 346
Miall, 53
Michel, L., 351, 359
Mikels, J.A., 153, 159
Milberg, W.P., 338, 345, 364, 383, 385, 388, 391, 392
Miller, A., 159, 333
Miller, A.L., 361
Miller, B.L., 332
Miller, D.G., 350, 359
Miller, G.A., 29, 46, 112, 113, 120, 122
Miller, L.M.S., 287, 297
Miller, R.R., 187, 190
Millman, D., 377, 382
Milner, B., 16, 17, 23, 26, 127, 133
Milone, F., 213, 225
Minkoff, S., 87, 97
Mione, F., 224
Misanin, J.R., 187, 190
Mishkin, M., 57, 67
Mitchell, D.B., 72, 80
Mitchell, K.J., 387, 392
Miyake, A., 121, 152, 160, 166, 231, 232, 318, 320
Moe, S.M., 255, 263
Moeser, S.D., 35, 41, 46
Mohamed, S., 349, 355, 359
Mohs, R.C., 358

Molander, B., 259, 263
Molina, J.A., 256, 263
Monti, L.A., 82
Morais, J., 126, 133
More, K.A., 257, 261
Moreines, J., 173, 189
Moriarty, P.J., 359
Moritz, C.H., 27
Moroz, T.M., 66, 181, 190
Morrell, R.W., 150, 151, 156, 157, 159, 325, 333
Morris, C.D., 32, 40, 41, 43, 45, 46, 52, 72, 81, 105, 107, 208, 223
Morris, L.W., 175, 189, 266, 274, 334, 345, 364, 380, 384, 391
Morris, R.G., 175, 189, 266, 274, 293, 296, 334, 345, 364, 380, 384, 391
Morrison, J., 343, 344
Morrison, J.H., 345
Morrissey, J., 203, 207
Morrow, D.G., 287, 296
Mortel, K.F., 257, 263, 346
Mortimer, A.M., 359
Morton, J., 125, 132, 133
Moscovitch, Morris, 32, 33, 40, 43, 44, 46, 57, 66, 68, 75, 81, 106, 124, 126, 133, 134, 171–192, 194, 203, 205, 206, 209, 211, 214, 219, 220, 221, 223, 224, 227, 228, 229, 231, 232, 233, 329, 332, 334, 336, 341, 342, 345, 347, 350, 353, 359, 360, 363, 365, 373, 375, 377, 380, 382, 383, 385, 388, 391, 392
Moulton, R.J., 346
Mountcastle, V.B., 391
Mozley, L.H., 360
Mozley, P.D., 360
Mulligan, N.W., 199, 206, 212, 222, 224, 373, 382
Multhaup, K.S., 292, 296
Murdock, Bennet B. Jr., 17, 26, 194, 201, 206, 209, 212, 224, 226, 227, 232
Murphy, D.L., 349, 361
Murphy, D.R., 165, 167, 301, 309, 310, 311, 312, 314
Murphy, K.J., 346
Murphy, M.D., 325, 333
Murray, D.J., 353, 357
Murre, J.M.J., 126, 134
Musgrave, B.S., 8, 26
Muzzolon, R., 262
Myers, C.E., 365, 380
Myerson, J., 286, 297

N
Nadel, L., 126, 134, 187, 191
Nader, K., 187, 191
Nagahama, Y., 327, 332

Nairne, J.S., 27
Naumann, E., 56, 67
Naveh-Benjamin, Moshe, 106, 111, 122, 132, 133, 135, 146, 174, 178, 182, 189, 193–207, 208, 209, 210, 214, 215, 219, 220, 221, 222, 223, 224, 227, 228, 231, 232, 266, 271, 272, 275, 278, 279, 285, 289, 295, 320, 363, 373, 377, 379, 380, 382, 387, 391
Neale, J.M., 349, 357
Neath, I., 27
Neely, J.H., 244, 251
Negron, A.E., 359
Neill, W.T., 137, 146
Nelson, D.L., 32, 44, 365, 382
Nelson, R.F., 334, 335, 345, 346
Nelson, T.O., 32, 44, 46, 318, 320
Neumann, E., 136, 147
Nevin, J.A., 287, 297
Newberg, W.M., 266, 276
Newson, M., 306, 314
Nicholls, A., 83, 97
Nilsson, Lars-Göran, 20, 21, 26, 133, 253–264, 315, 320, 332, 363, 382
Nissen, M.J., 241, 252
Nolan, K.A., 253, 263
Nolde, S.F., 124, 134, 266, 273, 275, 387, 391, 392
Noll, D.C., 331
Nopoulos, P., 355, 358
Nordberg, A., 223, 331
Norman, D.A., 125, 126, 134, 163, 166
Norman, K.A., 350, 360, 363, 364, 377, 380, 383, 387
Nowlin, B., 352, 357
Nuechterlein, K.H., 356, 358
Nuetzel, M.J., 302, 313
Nyberg, E., 124, 133, 176
Nyberg, L., 19, 25, 79, 81, 132, 191, 223, 257, 262, 263, 320, 327, 328, 331, 332, 344, 350, 359, 363, 373, 382
Nyberg, S.E., 293, 297
Nyquist, L., 259, 263
Nystrom, L.E., 331

O
O'Carroll, R.E., 356, 359
O'Connor, M., 266, 275
O'Craven, K.M., 25
O'Kane, G., 286, 297
O'Keefe, J., 67
O'Leary, D.S., 349, 354, 355, 357, 358, 359
O'Reilly, R.C., 365, 382
Ohriner, S., 355, 361
Ohta, N., 20, 26
Oja, E., 23, 26
Okada, N., 346

Okamoto, C., 380
Oliphant, G.W., 84, 97
Olofsson, U., 363, 382
Ortuno, B., 263
Oseas-Kreger, D.M., 136, 146
Oszunar, Y., 25

P
Packer, J.S., 23, 27
Packman, J.L., 37, 38, 46
Paik, M., 256, 261
Palmer, B.W., 349, 359
Palmer, H.P., 390, 391, 392
Palmore, E.B., 253, 263
Palumbo, C.L., 134, 192, 346
Pandya, D.N., 336, 345
Pannasch, S., 54, 62, 63, 66, 67, 68
Pansky, A., 362, 381
Papagno, C., 113, 114, 121, 122
Pappadopulos, E., 357
Papsidero, J.A., 253, 261
Paradiso, S., 354, 357
Parashos, I.A., 274, 331
Pardo, L.V., 130, 134
Parella, M., 358
Park, Denise C., 107, 148–160, 161, 164, 166, 179, 191, 209, 214, 220, 221, 224, 284, 285, 318, 320, 325, 333
Park, J., 137, 146
Parker, E.S., 198, 207
Parkin, A.J., 181, 190, 191, 377, 382, 385, 388, 391
Parrella, M., 359
Pashler, H., 140, 141, 142, 145, 217, 219, 221, 223, 224, 226, 229, 232, 233
Pashler, H.E., 191
Patkau, J.E., 113, 123
Patterson, L.J., 274, 331
Paulsen, J.S., 349, 354, 359
Paulsen, O., 27
Payne, D.G., 38, 46
Peaker, S.M., 115, 116, 122
Pearlson, 354
Pedroza, M.J., 319, 320
Pelchat, G., 340, 347
Penpeci, C., 314, 345
Perfect, T.J., 181, 191, 320
Perlmutter, M., 259, 263
Perlstein, W.M., 62, 67
Perretta, J., 194, 197, 204, 206, 209, 210, 214, 219, 220, 224, 227, 232
Perry, W., 359
Persson, J., 359
Peterkin, I., 255, 263
Peters, A., 344
Petersen, S.E., 25, 130, 134

Peterson, L.R., 8, 12, 26
Peterson, M.J., 8, 26
Peterson, R.A., 349, 352, 353, 354, 359
Petrides, M., 336, 342, 345, 385, 391
Peynircioglu, Z.F., 117, 123
Phillips, L.W., 28, 46
Pichora-Fuller, M.K., 165, 166, 299, 300, 301, 303, 304, 305, 312, 314
Pickering, S.J., 115, 116, 122
Picton, T.W., 334, 340, 345, 346, 347
Picus, I., 355, 359
Pierce, T.W., 254, 255, 262, 263
Pietrini, P., 332, 380
Pinto, A. da C., 117, 122
Pliner, P., 25, 45, 189, 190
Pliskin, N.H., 358
Plude, D.J., 137, 146
Plum, F., 391
Podd, M.H., 352, 358
Podrecka, 130
Pogue, J., 134, 192, 346
Poirier, M.F., 359
Poldrack, R.A., 134
Polk, T.A., 153, 159
Polster, M.R., 16, 26, 187, 190, 267, 274, 377, 380, 385, 391
Pomplun, M., 53, 63, 67, 68
Poon, L.W., 146, 286, 297, 331, 391
Popper, K.R., 18, 26
Posner, M.I., 45, 130, 134, 228, 231, 233
Postle, B.R., 328, 332, 336, 345
Postman, L., 10, 26, 28, 35, 39, 40, 46, 48, 112, 122
Powelson, J.A., 57, 65
Pribram, K.H., 190
Prince, M., 257, 263
Provenzale, J.M., 159, 224, 332
Prull, M.W., 318, 319, 320
Ptak, R., 125, 134
Pugh, K., 25
Puglisi, J.T., 151, 159, 325, 333
Putnam, K.M., 356, 360
Pylyshyn, Z.W., 61, 67
Pynte, J., 67

R

Raajimakers, J.G., 125, 134
Rabbitt, P.M.A., 45, 121, 286, 297
Rabinowitz, J.C., 137, 147, 195, 207, 325, 333
Rabinowitz, W.M., 302, 313
Racine, C., 366, 372, 383
Raddach, R., 67
Radvansky, G.A., 155, 160, 288, 293, 296, 297
Ragland, J.D., 358
Rah, S.K.-Y., 231, 233
Rahhal, T.A., 289, 291, 294, 296, 297

Raichle, M.E., 25, 130, 134
Rajah, M.N., 314, 328, 332, 345, 380, 386, 391
Rames, L., 190
Ramponi, Christina, 4, 51, 53, 56, 57, 71–82, 101
Ramsay, D.S., 256, 262
Ramus, S.J., 241, 252
Randolph, C., 348, 358
Raney, Gary E., 83, 87, 88, 89, 95, 96, 97
Rankin, J.L., 364, 382
Rapoport, S.I., 133, 332
Rashotte, C.A., 83, 97
Ratcliff, R., 201, 205, 247, 252
Rauch, S.L., 358, 365, 383
Raye, C.L., 124, 134, 247, 252, 387, 392
Rayner, K., 83, 97
Raz, N., 192, 265, 266, 267, 275, 329, 333, 336, 337, 342, 346, 377, 382, 383
Reber, A.S., 231, 233
Reder, L.M., 32, 45
Reiman, E., 134, 364, 366, 383
Reineck, R., 331
Reingold, E., 62, 63, 67, 72, 78, 81, 82
Reinick, R., 223
Reinitz, M.T., 203, 207
Reiter, G., 357
Renshaw, P.F., 333
Requin, J., 68
Resnick, R.J., 159
Resnick, S.M., 360
Reuter-Lorenz, P.A., 153, 158, 159, 327, 332, 333
Rhee, S.H., 281, 285, 330, 333
Riccio, D.C., 187, 190
Richardson-Klavehn, Alan, 4, 51, 53, 56, 57, 71–82, 101, 349, 351, 358, 360
Riddle, M.C., 255, 264
Riegler, G.L., 43, 46, 52, 67, 74, 81
Rieser, H., 63, 68
Ritter, W., 266, 275
Rizzio, L., 352, 353
Rizzo, L., 357, 358, 360
Robbins, M.A., 254, 262
Robbins, T.W., 338, 340, 345
Robert, M., 68
Robert, P., 358, 359
Roberts, A.C., 338, 345
Roberts, B.R., 136, 147
Robertson, B.A., 325, 333
Robertson, I.H., 392
Robins-Wahlin, T.-B., 253, 264
Robinson, D., 357
Roediger, Henry L. III, 4, 13, 15, 21, 25, 26, 27, 28–47, 48, 52, 53, 67, 72, 73, 74, 81, 87, 97, 100, 101, 190, 208, 224, 229, 230, 232, 233, 247, 252, 274, 295, 349, 350, 360, 362, 363, 364, 381, 382, 383, 387, 392

Rogers, R.L., 256, 257, 263, 346
Rohmer, J.-G., 352, 360
Rohrbaugh, J.W., 19, 27, 56, 67
Romanao, J., 189
Romanov, V.J., 54, 67
Rosch, E., 161, 167
Rose, C.L., 253, 261
Rose, R., 345
Rosen, B.R., 23, 25, 27, 130, 132, 192, 328, 331, 364, 382
Rosner, B., 262
Ross, B.M., 66
Ross, M.H., 327, 333
Rosse, R.B., 351, 360
Rossi, J.P., 96
Rotte, M., 26, 27, 132, 192
Routhieaux, B.C., 187, 190, 267, 274, 377, 380, 385, 391
Rozensky, R.H., 159
Rubin, S.R., 187, 190, 268, 274
Rudge, P., 132
Rugg, M.D., 19, 26, 129, 132, 133, 181, 190, 328, 333, 351, 358
Rumbaugh, D.M., 66
Rund, B.R., 355, 360
Russell, H.H., 356, 359
Russell, P.N., 353, 360
Ryan, E.B., 307, 314
Rypma, B., 135, 146, 327, 330, 333, 336, 345
Rzeczkowski, C., 302, 313

S
Sabourin, M., 68
Sadek, J.R., 359
Sahakian, B.J., 340, 345
Sainz, M.J., 263
Salerno, J.A., 332
Salthouse, Timothy A., 146, 147, 149, 151, 152, 156, 159, 164, 167, 189, 191, 232, 259, 260, 262, 263, 275, 277–285, 286, 290, 293, 295, 296, 297, 300, 301, 314, 315, 320, 330, 333, 334, 344, 345, 346, 347, 363, 382
Saltz, E., 365, 381
Saltzman, I.J., 10, 26
Salvi, R.J., 314
Samuels, S.J., 83, 97
Sanders, R.E., 325, 333
Sandner, G., 351, 359
Sandstead, H.H., 255, 263
Sanquist, T.F., 19, 27, 56, 67
Sara, S.J., 187, 191
Sarpel, G., 377, 382
Saults, J.S., 259, 263
Savage, C.R., 358, 365, 377, 383

Savoy, R.L., 25
Sayer, L., 134, 192, 334, 346, 365, 383, 385, 392
Saykin, A.J., 23, 27, 349, 352, 354, 360
Scahill, R., 132
Scarone, S., 352, 356
Schacter, Daniel L., 21, 23, 25, 26, 27, 58, 68, 71, 75, 76, 81, 126, 130, 132, 134, 175, 191, 192, 206, 266, 275, 328, 331, 349, 350, 351, 358, 360, 362–383, 384, 387, 388, 392
Schafe, G.E., 187, 191
Schaie, K.W., 145, 259, 262, 336, 344, 346, 380
Schank, R.C., 126, 134
Schapiro, M.B., 332, 380
Scharf, B., 312, 313
Scherr, P.A., 262
Schizophrenic Society of Canada, 348
Schlauch, R.S., 312, 314
Schlenoff, D.H., 62, 67
Schloerscheidt, A.M., 333
Schmitt, F.A., 325, 333
Schneider, B.S., 166
Schneider, Bruce A., 165, 167, 298–314
Schneider, E.L., 253, 261
Schnider, A., 125, 134
Schnorr, J., 39, 45
Schonfield, D., 325, 333
Schooler, C., 136, 143, 144, 147
Schott, B., 81
Schultz, J.N.R., 254, 262
Schulz, L.S., 13, 27
Schwartz, B.L., 351, 352, 360
Schwartz, D.J., 358
Schwartz, M.F., 191, 345
Schwartz, M.L., 346
Schwartz, S., 359
Schwarz, N., 159
Schweikert, R., 117, 122
Seamon, J.G., 38, 46, 374, 383
Seergobin, K.N., 145, 146
Segalowitz, S.J., 374, 380
Sekuler, A.B., 314, 342, 345
Sekuler, R., 300, 314, 345
Selfridge, J.A., 113, 122
Seltzer, J.C., 355, 361
Sengco, J.A., 204, 207
Senkfor, A.J., 266, 273, 275, 276
Shah, P., 121, 152, 160, 166, 231, 232
Shah, S., 359
Shallice, Tim, 113, 114, 118, 123, 124–134, 157, 161, 163, 181, 182, 187, 189, 190, 191, 205, 209, 211, 223, 224, 268, 275, 336, 340, 346, 351, 358, 386, 392
Shammi, P., 57, 67, 337, 346
Shane, B., 255, 263

Shannon, C.E., 112, 123
Sharif, Z., 353, 357
Sharma, T., 356, 360
Sharps, M.J., 287, 297
Shaw, R.E., 61, 68
Shaw, R.J., 135, 146, 151, 160, 288, 296, 318, 320
Shaw, T.G., 256, 263, 336, 346
Shibasaki, H., 332
Shiffrin, R.M., 125, 134, 201, 205
Shifren, K., 156, 160
Shimamura, A.P., 127, 133, 266, 270, 273, 274, 275, 384, 391
Shin, R.K., 158, 332
Shisler, R.J., 156, 158
Shtasel, D.L., 360
Sichel, J.P., 358
Siddle, D.A.T., 23, 27
Siegel, L., 349, 359
Siegler, I.C., 259, 262
Signoret, J.L., 173, 190
Simolke, N., 189
Simon, E., 135, 146, 325, 331, 387, 391
Simons, R.F., 62, 67
Simonson, D.C., 255, 264
Sinden, M., 190
Singer, L., 358
Singh, A., 317, 320
Skoog, I., 254, 263
Skoulding, B.A., 121
Slamecka, Norman J., 125, 134, 227, 233
Small, B.J., 253, 261, 262, 264
Smirnov, A.A., 49, 67
Smirnov, S.D., 54, 67
Smith, A.D., 145, 147, 151, 158, 159, 160, 166, 179, 191, 209, 224, 284, 285, 325, 333, 363, 364, 373, 383
Smith, E.E., 120, 123, 153, 158, 159, 160, 331, 332, 333
Smith, G.A., 286, 297
Smith, J.F., 353, 360
Smith, L.B., 107
Smith, M.J., 353, 357
Smith, M.L., 337, 346
Smith, P.K., 159, 284, 285
Snodgrass, J.G., 192, 242, 249, 252, 266, 275
Snow, W.G., 346
Snowdon, D.A., 256, 263
Snowling, M., 114, 123
Soady, S.A.R., 274, 331
Söderfjell, S., 259, 263
Söderlund, Hedvig, 253–264, 315
Sokolov, E.N., 23, 27, 62, 67
Solso, R.L., 45
Sommers, M.S., 301, 304, 314

Sparling, M., 27
Spearman, C., 279, 285
Spencer, D.D., 25, 377
Spencer, W.D., 180, 192, 265, 266, 275, 383
Speranza, F., 165, 167, 304, 305, 314
Spinnler, H., 26, 81, 118, 123, 191, 360
Spohn, H.E., 354, 360
Sprague, S.M., 255, 263
Spreen, O., 268, 275
Sprenger, A., 62, 68
Springer, A.D., 187, 190
Spritzer, C.E., 274, 331
Squire, L.R., 16, 23, 27, 181, 190, 198, 205, 233, 241, 252, 266, 275, 384, 391
Srinivas, K., 72, 81
Stadler, M.A., 52, 53, 67, 252
Stadler, M.L., 43, 46, 67, 74, 81
Stafiniak, P., 360
Stampe, D., 62, 63, 67
Starr, J.M., 254, 257, 263
Steen, B., 259, 263
Stein, B.S., 40, 41, 43, 45, 47, 208, 223
Steinhagen-Thiessen, E., 253, 263
Stern, C.E., 23, 26, 27, 256
Stern, Y., 261
Stethem, L.L., 340, 347
Stevens, J., 132
Stevenson, J.A., 122
Stewart, M.T., 383
Stiel, S., 68
Stijnen, T., 255, 262
Stine, E.L., 160
Stine-Morrow, E.A.L., 287, 297
Stip, E., 354, 360
Stofer, K.A., 367, 372, 381
Stokstad, E.L.R., 255, 263
Stoltzfus, E.R., 135, 136, 138, 146, 147
Stone, M.V., 66–67
Strauss, M.E., 354, 357, 360
Stuart, G.A., 121
Stuss, Donald T., 19, 27, 50, 57, 66, 67, 68, 126, 127, 131, 134, 157, 180, 190, 191, 192, 255, 263, 334–347, 351, 361, 365, 383, 385, 391, 392
Suengas, A.G., 247, 252
Sugiura, R.B., 27
Sullivan, M.P., 136, 143, 144, 147
Sullivan, R.J., 274, 331
Suppes, P., 223
Suprenant, A.M., 27
Suzuki, W.A., 57, 67
Swan, G.E., 254, 263
Swanson, J.M., 148, 158, 164, 166
Swash, M., 67
Syndulko, K., 19, 27, 56, 67

Szekeres, G., 359
Szymanski, K.F., 231, 233

T
Talairach, J., 134
Tamlyn, D., 359
Tanabe, H., 346
Tanaka, J.W., 204, 207
Tardif, T., 163, 166, 230, 233
Tarter, R.E., 255, 261, 263, 264
Tatemichi, T.K., 256, 261
Taylor, J.O., 262
Taylor, J.R., 268, 274
Taylor, M.A., 352, 360
Taylor, S.F., 153, 159
Taylor, T.J., 126, 134
Temporini, H., 356, 357
Tenpenny, P.L., 83, 97
Terry, K.M., 137, 146
Thelen, E., 107
Theodore, W.H., 66
Therriault, D., 87, 97
Thompson, L.W., 146, 331
Thompson, N., 106, 107
Thomson, D.M., 208, 224, 273, 276
Thomson, N., 132, 179, 189, 194, 205, 209, 223, 379
Thornton, A.E., 275, 346
Thorpe, L.A., 38, 46
Tipper, S.P., 147, 347
Tkachuk, M.J., 122
Tonev, Simon T., 182, 194, 204, 206, 209, 210, 214, 219, 220, 224, 227, 232, 286–297, 316
Torgeson, J.K., 83, 97
Torrey, E.F., 358
Toshio, I., 67
Toth, J.P., 72, 78, 81, 82, 190, 243, 251, 283, 285, 347, 373, 381
Tournoux, P., 134
Trainham, T.N., 247, 251
Traupmann, K.L., 353, 360
Trehub, S., 146, 158, 190, 192, 205, 251, 252, 295, 331, 380, 382, 391
Treisman, A., 53, 68
Tresselt, M.E., 28, 29, 32, 47
Trevarthen, Colin, 53, 63, 68
Trott, C.T., 266, 267, 273, 275
Troyer, Angela K., 106, 171–192, 203, 214, 227, 228, 229, 231, 255, 263, 363, 375, 383
Trumbo, D., 213, 224
Tsaung, M.T., 355, 360
Tubbs, A., 364, 379
Tucker, D.M., 255, 261
Tuholski, S.W., 156, 158
Tully, C.L., 256, 263

Tulving, Endel, 4, 6–27, 29, 30, 31, 32, 33, 34, 35, 37, 40, 42, 43, 44, 45, 47, 50, 52, 56, 57, 58, 60, 66, 67, 68, 71, 79, 81, 82, 99, 100, 101, 105, 107, 111, 112, 113, 119, 122, 123, 124, 130, 133, 134, 135, 146, 161, 163, 166, 167, 173, 184, 189, 190, 192, 198, 205, 206, 208, 211, 223, 224, 228, 229, 233, 259, 264, 273, 274, 276, 295, 325, 331, 332, 333, 336, 337, 344, 345, 346, 350, 351, 357, 358, 359, 360, 361, 380, 381, 382, 386, 391
Tun, P.A., 286, 297
Turkington, T.G., 159, 224, 332
Turvey, M.T., 61, 68, 105–107

U
U'ren, R.C., 255, 264
Uhl, 130
Uleman, J.S., 379
Ulivi, M.S., 136, 147
Umilta, C., 176, 191
Underwood, B.J., 200, 207, 364, 365, 383
Underwood, G.F., 81
Unema, P., 54, 62, 63, 66, 67, 68
Ungerleider, L.G., 133, 332, 380
Uyehara, L.A., 381

V
Vaidya, C.J., 25, 66–67, 75, 82
Valdes, L.A., 137, 146
Valdiserri, M., 266, 275, 377, 383
Valentine, T., 114, 122
Vallar, G., 113, 114, 118, 121, 122, 123
van Boxtel, M.P.J., 256, 257, 263, 264
Van Der Linden, M., 288, 295, 352, 360, 361
Van der Meer, E., 68, 133, 205, 223, 380
van Dijk, T.A., 87, 95, 97
Van Dusseldorp, G., 189
van Harten, P.N., 355, 359
Van Horn, J.D., 327, 332
Van Petten, C., 266, 273, 275, 276
van Thiel, D.H., 255, 261, 263, 264
Vanderwart, M., 192
Vargha-Khadem, F., 57, 67
Vedantham, V., 27
Velichkovsky, Boris M., 4, 12, 25, 27, 38, 45, 48–70, 73, 80, 100
Velligan, D.I., 356, 361
Verfaellie, M., 57, 66, 351, 360
Verhaeghen, P., 149, 160, 246, 252, 344, 347
Vidailhet, Pierre, 348–361
Villanueva, C., 263
Vincent, A., 56, 68
Vinokur, G., 66
Virostek, S., 38, 46
Volke, H.-J., 56, 68

Vranes, L.F., 338, 345
Vriezen, E.R., 177, 191, 337, 346

W
Wade, E., 319, 320
Wade, J.B., 268, 274
Wager, T.D., 320
Wagner, A.D., 19, 23, 25, 26, 27, 66–67, 124, 130, 132, 134, 186, 188, 192, 328, 331
Wagner, E., 332
Wagstaff, D., 194, 213, 286, 297
Wagstaff, R.R., 206, 224
Wahlin, Ä., 253, 255, 261, 262, 264
Waldemar, G., 267, 276
Walden, C.C., 256, 264
Waldstein, S.R., 254, 257, 264
Walker, R., 66
Walla, P., 333
Wallace, W.L., 334, 345
Wallace, W.P., 383
Walsh, D.A., 31, 47
Walsh, K.K., 325, 333
Walter, B.M., 191, 377, 382, 385, 391
Warrington, E.K., 17, 27, 113, 118, 123
Waterhouse, C., 97
Watkins, Michael J., 3–5, 12, 27, 44, 117, 123, 288, 297
Watkins, O.C., 288, 297
Watts, F.N., 261, 295
Weaver, J., 27, 112
Weaver, W., 123
Webb, M.C., 274, 331
Weber, H., 63, 66
Webster, L., 374, 380
Wechsler, D., 268, 276, 347
Weinberger, D.R., 348, 352, 354, 357, 358
Weinberger, N.M., 233
Weingartner, H., 191, 349, 357, 361
Weingartner, H.S., 198, 207
Weiskrantz, L., 17, 27, 166
Weldon, M.S., 39, 43, 46, 47, 52, 67, 72, 74, 75, 81, 82, 208, 224, 230, 233
West, M.J., 343, 347
West, R.L., 177, 192, 329, 333, 334, 347, 377, 383
Westerveld, M., 25
Whalley, L.J., 254, 257, 263
Wheeler, M.A., 19, 27, 50, 57, 68, 337, 347, 350, 351, 352, 355, 361
White, L., 336, 358, 359
White, L.R., 256, 262
White, M.J., 383
White, N., 347
Whiting, W.L., 151, 160, 363, 373, 383
Whitten, W.B., 117, 121
Whittlesea, B.W.A., 368, 383

Whitty, C.W.M., 26
Widing, M., 263, 320
Widom, B., 255, 264
Wiggs, O.I., 180, 190
Wilding, E.L., 130, 132
Wilkins, A., 130, 134
Wilkinson, W.E., 274, 331
Willard, D., 359
Willard-Schroeder, D., 358
Williams, P., 247, 251
Williams, R.B., 181, 191
Willott, J.F., 302, 314
Wilson, A.A., 67, 133, 206, 224, 359
Wilson, B.A., 114, 118, 119, 121, 123, 261, 295
Wilson, C., 97
Wilson, D.F., 357
Winblad, B., 255, 262, 263, 320, 331
Windblad, B., 223
Wingfield, A., 160, 286, 297, 307, 314
Winocur, Gordon, 174, 175, 176, 180, 181, 182, 188, 191, 192, 229, 232, 246, 252, 329, 332, 334, 341, 342, 345, 347, 375, 377, 382, 383, 384–392
Wittgenstein, L., 161, 167
Witzki, A.H., 320
Woerner, M.G., 357
Wolf, E.S., 198, 206, 256
Woloshyn, V., 212, 224, 374, 381
Woodard, J.L., 283, 285
Woodruff, 180
Worden, P.E., 212, 224, 374, 381
Worobey, J., 256, 262
Worthley, J.S., 319, 320
Wynn, V., 118, 122

Y
Yamauchi, H., 332
Yonelinas, A.P., 78, 81, 222, 224, 243, 251, 351, 357, 374, 381
Yun, L.S., 134, 383
Yurgelun-Todd, D.A., 333

Z
Zacks, Rose T., 135, 136, 138, 145, 146, 147, 155, 158, 160, 165, 166, 195, 205, 222, 224, 246, 249, 251, 286–297, 307, 314, 316, 330, 333
Zakzanis, K.K., 349, 355, 358
Zalewski, C., 355, 361
Zangemeister, W.H., 68
Zangwill, O.L., 26
Zaragoza, M.S., 375, 383
Zarella, K., 361
Zarella, M.M., 82
Zarrella, S., 355, 361
Zechmeister, E.B., 293, 297

Zefiro, Th. A., 66
Zhao, Z., 19, 25, 188, 189
Zinchenko, P.I., 49, 68

Zipursky, R.B., 345
Zisook. S., 359
Zwahr, M., 156, 157, 158, 159, 160, 166, 285

SUBJECT INDEX

A

Absent-mindedness, 387
Abstract transfer
  text processing and, 87
Access function of inhibition
  aging and, 288
  deficiency of, 289–291
Accessibility bias, 243
Acoustic analysis, 37. *See also* phonemic
  analysis
Acoustic
  coding, 113
  similarity, 113
Affordances, Gibson's, 52
Age-related memory deficits
  global changes underlying, 237
  health factors and, 238
Age-related variance, 316
  cognitive changes and, 238, 280–284
  self-initiated processing and, 284
  speed of processing and, 152
  working memory and, 149–151
Aging. *See also* cognitive aging
  awareness and control in, 246–247
  bias and, 250
  component process model of memory and,
    177–178
  criterion differences in, 240
  decline in frontal lobe function and, 267
  general theory of, 105
  gradual decline in cognitive function with,
    334–336
  inhibitory function in, 135–142
  integration of content and context at
    encoding and, 271–273
  source memory and, 266
Alcohol
  decreased cognitive performance due to, 256

Aluminum
  decreased cognitive performance due to,
    256
Ambient fixations, 63
Ambient vision, 53
Amnesia
  anterograde, 16–18
  Korsakoff
    levels of processing and, 173
    release-from-PI testing and, 179
  medial temporal and frontal lobe damage
    and, 388–389
  retrograde, 13–15
  source, 384
  working memory and, 118
Association, 7
Associative deficit hypothesis, 200–204,
  227–228
Associative memory
  divided attention and, 201–203
Associative processing
  impairment of due to divided attention,
    200–204
Associative theory of recognition, 29
Associative-cue-dependence, 176, 179
Attention, 107
  inhibitory constraints and, 288
  mechanisms of levels of processing in,
    142–144
Attentional control system, 120
  bottleneck model of retrieval and, 221–222
Attentional landscapes filtering, 63
Attentional requirements
  influence on encoding *vs.* retrieval of, 226
Attentional resources, 164. *See also* processing
  resources
  division of attention and limited, 195
  reduction in due to aging, 148

Auditory processing
  age-related declines in, 165
Aufforderungen, 52
Automatic-nonstrategic processing, 227
  effects of divided attention at encoding
    mediated by, 198–200
Autonoetic consciousness, 50, 71, 79, 350–351
  impairment in schizophrenic patients of,
    352–353

B
Benzodiazepines
  effect on encoding of, 16–18
Bernstein's neurophysiological mechanisms,
  50, 68–70
Betula Study on memory, health and aging,
  257–260, 315
Bias, 238, 387
  accessibility, 243
  accessibility vs. Stroop, 249
  aging and, 250
  aware vs. unaware forms of, 242–243
  two-high-threshold model and, 243, 249
Bias effects
  implicit learning as a source of, 241–243
  in perception, 247–248
Binding
  age-related changes in, 377–378
Blocking, 387
Blood cholesterol
  cognitive function and, 255–256
Blood pressure
  relationship to cognition of, 254–255
Bottleneck model of retrieval and concurrent
    processing, 217–222
Bradyphrenia, 335
Brain activity
  divided attention and, 209–212
  implicit memory tests and, 175–176
  levels of processing and, 56–57
  reductions of due to aging, 327–328
  retrieval processes and, 126–129
  schizophrenia and, 354
Brain physiology
  encoding and, 18–20
  novelty assessment and, 23
Bransford effect, 93
Byproduct theory of trace formation, 10–12
  empirical difficulties for, 13–20
  novelty and, 22

C
Cancer
  impaired cognitive function due to, 255

Cardiovascular reactions
  levels of processing effects and, 56
Category exemplar production
  self-initiated processing demands of, 318–319
Central executive, 113, 117, 120, 162–163
  domain-general, 152
Central processes
  bottleneck model of retrieval and, 217–222
Cerebral white matter lesions
  cognitive function and, 254
Checking process
  right dorsolateral region involvement in, 131
Cobalt
  cognitive impairment due to deficiencies of,
    255
Cognition
  general theory of, 105
Cognitive aging. See also aging
  age-related effects in, 284
  Betula Study on health and, 257–260
  capacity-based explanations for declines
    seen in, 293
  considerations of perceptual and cognitive
    processing as part of, 309
  effects on memory of, 363
  encoding and retrieval in, 211
  frontal lobe function and, 229, 336–337
  global hypothesis for gradual decline in,
    334–336
  inhibitory-decline hypothesis of, 165
  investigative approaches to, 277–278
  levels-of-processing approach to, 299–301
  loss of inhibitory control and, 238
  neuroimaging studies of, 329–330
  neuropsychological testing in, 384
  reduction of brain activity and, 180–181
  self-initiated processing hypothesis and,
    279–280
  sensory aging and, 300
  speed-of-processing view of, 151–152
Cognitive aging theories, 135, 148
Cognitive gerontology, 286
Cognitive load on perception hypothesis, 300
Cognitive neuroscience of memory, 9
Cognitive processing
  effects of aging on, 299
Cognitive psychology, 298
  connection with neuropsychology, 8
Cognitive resource in aging, 153
Cognitive resource theory, 178
Cognitive resources
  environmental support and, 177–178
Cognitive speed
  age differences in inhibitory access control
    and, 290

Common-cause hypothesis, 300
Competition for resources
    divided attention and, 183–187, 230
Component process model, 176–178, 219–220,
    229
    competition for representations or
        structures and, 183–187
    divided attention and the, 185
    release-from-PI test and, 179
Comprehension
    perceptual stress and, 309
    vs. memory, 309–311
Computation span, 149
Computer metaphor, 48
Conceptual priming, 74–78
    effects of divided attention on, 212
Conceptual structures, 50
    brain activity measurements and, 56
Conceptual vs. perceptual processing, 58
Concurrent processing
    bottleneck model of retrieval and, 217–222
    shared-time model of memory and, 215–217
Confabulatory disorders, 126
    frontal lesions and, 176
Congruous encoding, 33
Conscious awareness, 120
Conscious recollection, 350
Consolidation, 18, 198–199
Constant ratio rule, 118
Constructive memory, 15
Content
    distinguishing from context, 265
Context effects, 8
Context memory deficit
    frontal lobe function and, 271
Criterion differences in aging, 240
Cued recall, 8, 33, 40
    self-initiated processing, 319
    speed of processing/working memory and, 152

D
Decision, 8
Deep fixations, 63
Deese-Roediger-McDermott paradigm. See
    DRM paradigm
Degrees of stimulus elaboration, 34
Delayed memory, 8
Deletion function of inhibition
    aging and, 288
    poor self-initiated processing and, 292–294
Dementia
    alcoholism and, 256
Depth
    levels-of-processing framework and, 33, 100,
        365

retention as a function of, 10
Depth of analysis
    trace persistence as a function of, 28
Depth of processing, 29
Descriptions, formulation of, 125
Determining tendencies, 125
Diabetes
    relationship to cognitive performance of,
        255
Differential bias, 243
Differential responses, 28
Differentiation of resource
    in working memory, 153
Directed episodic memory retrieval, 126
Discriminability, 242
    two-high-threshold model and, 243, 249
Dissociations, 238
Distinctiveness heuristic, 367–373, 387
Distractibility
    age related studies of, 340
Distraction
    deficient access control in aging and, 289–
        290
Distractor effect, 62
Divided attention
    at encoding, 193-207, 227–228
    at retrieval, 228–230
    bottleneck model of retrieval and, 218–222
    brain activity and, 209–212
    competition for resources or memory and,
        183–187, 230
    deficient access control in aging and, 289
    effects on memory of, 178–188, 193-207, 363
    evidence concerning the neurological basis
        of, 187–188
    false recognition and, 373–378
    frontal lobe function and, 271–273
    habit vs. recollection in studies of, 245–246
    impaired associative processing, 200-203
    impaired automatic-nonstrategic processing
        and, 198–200
    impaired strategic-effortful encoding and,
        195–198
    memory and, 193–194, 230–231
Domain-specific models, 48, 50–51
Dorsolateral prefrontal cortex
    encoding in the, 187–188
    reduced activity in due to aging, 327
DRM paradigm, 15, 388
Dual-task paradigm, 324
    effects of on errors of omission, 376
Dual-task performance. See also divided
    attention
    effects of on errors of commission, 373–374
Dwell time, 54

E

Early selection
  tendency of old adults toward, 137, 144, 247
Ecphoric information, 12–13
Ecphory, 12–13, 100, 229
  medial temporal association of, 183
Elaborations of the traces, 52
Elaborative processing, 55, 76
Encoding, 105–107, 350
  age-related changes in episodic memory
    related to, 325
  attentional control of, 212–213
  attentional demands of, 213
  brain activity and, 56–57, 385–386
  congruous, 33
  definition of, 12
  degraded perceptual representation and,
    310
  differentiation of perceptual analysis and, 13
  dissociation with perception, 24
  distinctiveness, false recognition and, 365–
    373
  divided attention at, 193–207, 227–228
  effects of age on, 326
  effects of divided attention on, 178–188,
    193–207, 209–212, 230–231
    underlying mechanisms of, 194–204
  frontal lobe involvement in difficult or
    nonroutine operations of, 268–270
  frontal lobe involvement in integration of
    content and context at, 271–273
  functional brain measures of, 18–20
  impairment of in patients with schizophre-
    nia, 353
  intention, 52
  intentional, 35, 59
  interrupted, 13–15
  introduction of concept of, 8
  left frontal involvement in, 125, 127, 228,
    326–327, 328–329
  nature of episodic, 213–214
  novelty hypothesis for, 20–23
  psychopharmacology of, 16–18
  rates of, 8
  realization, 52
  relationship to memory tests and, 52
  rhyme, 72
  self-referential, 53
  semantic, 53
  shared-time model of memory and, 215–217
  spread of, 43
  testing conditions and, 40
  visual, 54
  vs. retrieval, 208

Encoding conditions
  functions of performance dependent upon,
    58
Encoding specificity, 8, 40, 52, 101
Encoding tasks
  Craik-Tulving type, 38–39
  intentional learning instructions and, 35
Encoding/retrieval interactions, 8
Engram, 12. See also memory trace
  novelty/encoding hypothesis resulting in, 23
Environmental support, 343
  aging and, 287, 316
  cognitive aging and, 150, 177–178
  deficient access control and negation of,
    289–291
  reduction of errors of commission due to,
    363
  self-initiated processing and, 317–318, 375
Episodic buffer, 117, 118–120, 162–163
Episodic interpretation, 95
Episodic memory, 79, 350
  age-related changes in, 325
  autonoetic consciousness and, 71
  differentiating aspects of, 317
  directed retrieval of, 126
  distinction between semantic memory and,
    29, 228
  functional imaging of, 124
  impairment of in patients with schizophre-
    nia, 352
  performance components of, 203
  relevance of exploring in schizophrenia,
    355–356
  retrieval conditions of, 129, 163
  use of organization in, 127
Episodic remembering, 101
Episodic transfer
  text processing and, 87
Equivalent perceptual stress, 301
ERPs, 19. See also event-related potentials
Errors of commission
  distinctiveness of, 365–373
  effects of dual-task performance on, 373–
    374
Errors of omission vs. errors of commission,
  364
Event-related potentials, 19, 56, 62
Event-related potentials experiment, 19
Evoked coherences analysis of EEG, 56
Executive functions
  deficits of in schizophrenia, 349
  deterioration of with aging, 337
Expertise, 42
Explicit memory tests, 43, 51, 350

impaired performance of schizophrenic
    patients on, 351–352
Eye movement studies, 53–56

F
Fact memory
    lack of correlation with source memory,
        266–267
False recognition
    age-related increases in, 364, 387 (*See also*
        false remembering)
    distinctiveness at encoding and, 367–373
    dual-task performance and, 373–378
    encoding and, 365–366
False remembering, 15, 240
Famous names paradigm, 77
Fan effects
    inhibitory deficits in aging and, 292–293
Feature selection
    age differences in, 138–142
FeatureGate model of attention, 140–142
Feeling of familiarity, 350
Fixation, 62–63
    encoding and length of, 53–54
    text processing and, 88
fMRI, 18–20
Focal content, 265–266
Focal fixations, 63
Focal vision, 53
Focus of attention
    text processing and, 85
Folic acid
    memory disorders due to deficiencies of,
        255
Free recall, 8, 33, 38–40, 51, 59–60
    divided attention and, 180, 194
    increase in with level of processing, 31
    meaningful processing and, 39
    memory costs of, 220
    retrieval processes in, 29
    self-initiated processing and, 319
    speed of processing/working memory and,
        152
Frequency, 8
Frontal control processes
    evaluation of retrieved information by, 270
Frontal heterogeneity, 336, 342
Frontal lesions
    effects on memory of, 176
Frontal lobe damage
    cognitive recovery in patients suffering
        from, 385
    false recognition and, 364
    neuropsychological studies of, 323

Frontal lobe function
    age related changes in, 341–342, 377
    aging and the decline in, 267
    deterioration of with aging, 229
    neuropsychological tests use to determine, 268
    proactive inhibition and impaired, 173
Frontal lobe theory of aging, 329
Frontal lobes
    involvement of in difficult or nonroutine
        encoding operations, 268–270
    involvement of in difficult retrieval
        processes, 270–271
    involvement of in integration of content and
        context at encoding, 271–273
    memory processes in, 176
    source memory and, 266–267
    voluntary control of attention and the, 178
Full scale IQ
    gradual decline in, 334
Functional incapacity, 253
Functional magnetic resonance imaging. *See*
        fMRI
Functional neuroimaging, 18–20, 23, 318. *See
    also* neuroimaging
    cognitive aging theories and, 329–330
    study of age-related changes in memory by,
        325–326

G
GAPS, 12–13
    novelty hypothesis of encoding and, 22
Garden path experiments
    deletion function of inhibition and, 292
General abstract processing system. *See* GAPS
General cognition
    memory trace as a byproduct of, 100
Gibson's affordances, 52
Global incoherence, 56
Goal neglect, 249
Graphemic analysis, 32, 37, 60. *See also* visual
        analysis
Guessing, 243, 351. *See also* bias

H
Habit
    divided attention and, 245–246
    reliance on in the absence of recollection, 244
Habit-recollection model, 249
Health
    Betula Study on memory and, 257–260
    common and multidimensional definitions
        of, 253
    laboratory indices of, 255–256
    objective ratings of, 259–260

Health (*continued*)
  subjective ratings of, 259
Hemisphere encoding and retrieval asymmetry. *See* HERA
HERA, 124–125, 228, 386–387
  right frontal cortex activation in, 130
Heterarchy, 61
Hierarchical analyses, 48, 51, 60
Hippocampus
  encoding in the, 178, 377
  indexing function of, 126
Hypermnesia, 38
Hypertension
  decreased cognitive function and, 254
Hypoglycemia
  brain damage from, 255

I
Identification, 53
Identity suppression, 137–142
Immediate memory, 8
Immediate serial recall, 113
Impaired strategic-effortful encoding
  divided attention and, 195–198
Implicit learning, 117
  bias effect and, 241–243
Implicit memory, 9
Implicit memory tests, 43, 51, 350
  brain activity and, 175–176
  normal performance of schizophrenic
    patients on, 351
Incidental learning, 106
  recency effect and, 117
Incidental learning instructions, 33–34, 197–198
Incidental *vs.* intentional memory, 71
Information degradation
  cognitive performance and, 301–302
Information processing, 8
  age-related slowing of, 330
Information theory, 112
Information-degradation hypothesis, 300, 309
Inhibition deficit *vs.* recollection deficit
  proactive interference as cause of, 246–247
Inhibitory control
  aging and, 286–287, 330
Inhibitory function
  aging and, 135–142, 155–156, 238–239, 287–288
  description of, 288
Inhibitory-decline hypothesis of cognitive
    aging, 165
Integrated model of text representation, 87
Integrated sensory and cognitive system,
    implications of, 312–313

Integration model of encoding, 58
Intentional encoding, 35, 59
Intentional learning, 106
Intentional learning instructions, 33–34, 366
Intentional *vs.* incidental memory, 71
Interference effects
  in aging, 155–156, 244–246, 327
  Stroop, 156, 246
Interrupted encoding, 13–15
Intoxication
  decreased cognitive performance due to, 256
IQ
  gradual decline in over time, 334
Item memory, 239
  divided attention and, 201–203
  lack of correlation with source memory,
    266–267
  same/different effect for, 316

J
Jacoby process dissociation framework, 129,
    243, 316, 318

K
Kidney failure
  impaired cognitive function due to, 255
Knowing
  vs. remembering, 71, 130, 351
Korsakoff's syndrome
  proactive inhibition and, 173, 179

L
Language acquisition
  phonological loop and, 113–115
Language habits
  impact of working memory on, 115
Language-based redundancy, 112–113
Late correction strategies, 247
Late selection
  tendency of young adults toward, 137, 144
Lead
  decreased cognitive performance due to,
    256
Learning instructions, 33
Left prefrontal cortex
  cognitive functions of the elderly in the, 327
  encoding processes in, 228
Levels of processing, 8, 10, 28–32, 44, 48, 111
  amnesia and, 173
  brain activity and, 56–57
  circularity in definition of, 51, 100
  cognitive aging and, 299–301, 387
  deep, 37
  differential influence of on memory testing,
    53

effect, 43
effect of divided attention on, 212
effects of on memory, 328–329
errors of commission and, 362
evolutionary growth and, 57
explorations of schizophrenia using, 354
eye movement studies and, 53–56
in selective attention, 137–142
incidental tests and, 77
integration of sensation and cognition in, 312–313
involuntary effects of, 72
left frontal involvement in encoding and, 124
limitations of, 24
mechanisms of in attention, 142–144
perceptual priming and, 74
proposal, 3
retrieval and, 71–72
shallow, 37, 38
Lexical analysis, 32, 43. *See also* phonemic analysis
Lexical processing, 73–74, 76
Limited resource model of aging, 287
Limited time mechanism, 151
Liver failure
impaired cognitive function due to, 255
Localization, 53
Localization of function, 19
Location-based suppression, 137–142
Long-term memory, 8. *See also* secondary memory
dual-task performance and, 373
functional imaging of, 163
interaction of with working memory, 115, 162
priming in, 119
semantic coding and, 113
speed of processing/working memory and, 152
Long-term working memory, 119

M
Macro approach to differences in cognitive aging, 278
Magnetic resonance imaging, functional. *See* fMRI
Manganese
decreased cognitive performance due to, 256
Material-specific interference
retrieval processes and, 186–187
Meaning, 53
Meaning-centered episodic transfer
importance for reading fluency, 85–86
Meaningful analysis. *See also* semantic analysis
Medial temporal lobe/hippocampal impairment
age related changes and, 387–388

Medial temporal lobes
age-related changes in, 341–342
associative-cue-dependence of the, 176
levels of processing and, 173–174
role in component process model of, 229
Medication effects
episodic memory deficits in schizophrenic patients and, 354–355
Medication-taking behavior
environmental contexts and, 157
Memory
"headings" of records of, 125
attribute approach to, 365
automatic influence of, 245
component process model of, 176–178
distortions of, 324
divided attention and, 193–194, 230–231
divided attention and competition for, 183–187
effects of divided attention on, 178–188
effects of normal cognitive aging on, 363
history of science of, 7–10
impairment of in schizophrenia, 348–349
intentional *vs.* incidental, 71
multicomponent view of, 365
recognition, 38
shared-time model of, 215–217
storage component of, 118
theoretical framework for exploring, 349–351
vs. comprehension, 309–311
Memory accuracy
knowing *vs.* guessing, 247
Memory awareness, 79
Memory judgments, 8
Memory performance
modulations in task emphasis and, 212–213
Memory representation
in text processing, 92–95
Memory retrieval
secondary task responses and, 219, 221–222
Memory tests
objective measures of health and relationship to performance on, 259–260
relationship to encoding of, 52
used in Betula Study of health and memory, 258–259
Memory traces, 8–9, 100
as a byproduct of perceptual analysis, 10
competing, 118
definition of, 365
divided attention and recovery of, 183 (*See also* ecphory)
ecphoric potential as an affordance of, 101
novelty/encoding hypothesis resulting in, 23
Memory verification, 126

Mental energy, 150, 164, 279. *See also* working memory
Metacognition, 50
Metacognitive coordinations, 50, 57
Metacognitive encoding
  brain activity and, 57
Metacognitive processing, 53
  incidental, 59
Metaphysics, 8
Micro approach to differences in cognitive aging, 277–278
Misattribution, 387
  source confusions and, 363–365
Modified cue recall
  divided attention and, 220
Motor speed measures
  retention of with age, 342
Multiple memory systems, 9

N
Negative priming, 135–142
  aging and, 165
Neocortical representational systems
  competition effect and, 184
Neuroimaging, 9, 162, 385. *See also* functional neuroimaging
  changes in aging seen by, 267
  divided attention and, 187–188, 209–212
  levels of processing manipulation and, 328–329
  neuroanatomic abnormalities in schizophrenia seen with, 351, 354
  studies of memory and aging with, 323
Neurological dysfunction
  interaction between age and, 335
Neurophysiological mechanisms, Bernstein's, 50, 68–70
Neuropsychology
  connection with cognitive psychology, 8
New Look movement in perception, 247
No trials
  levels of processing in, 52
Node structure theory, 319
Noetic awareness, 350
Norman-Bobrow theory of retrieval specification and verification, 132
Novelty assessment, 22, 101
Novelty detection, 22
Novelty encoding hypothesis, 20–23

O
Obesity
  as a lifestyle factor affecting overall health, 256–257
Object actions, 50

Obstructive pulmonary disease
  impaired cognitive function due to, 255
Older adults. *See* aging; cognitive aging
Optomotor behavior analysis, 63
Organization, 8
Orienting questions, 33
Orienting tasks, 10–11
  effect of under reversed conditions, 35
  effect on tests of, 40–43
  manipulation of, 37–40
  nonsemantic, 39–40
  shallow, 34–35

P
Paired-association, 8, 128
Paleokinetic regulations, 50
Parkinson's disease
  bradyphrenia in, 335
Perception
  bias effects in, 247–248
  dissociation with encoding, 24
  influence of redundancy on, 112
Perceptive encoding
  brain activity and, 56
Perceptual analysis, 11, 42
  differentiation of encoding and, 13
  memory trace as a byproduct of, 10, 29
  orienting tasks and, 43
Perceptual deficits
  in aging, 165–166, 238, 300
Perceptual implicit tests of memory. *See also* implicit memory tests
  component process model and, 176–177
Perceptual load
  aging and, 144
Perceptual priming, 73–74
  effects of divided attention on, 212
Perceptual processing, 165
  effects of aging on, 299
  sensory and cognitive psychology and, 298
Perceptual record of experience, 43
Perceptual registration of information
  effects of divided attention on, 199
Perceptual representation system, 350
Perceptual stress
  connected discourse and, 306–309
  use of context and, 302–306
Perceptual traces, 8
Perceptual *vs.* conceptual processing, 58
Perceptual-cognitive processing
  memory trace as a byproduct of, 100
Persistence, 10, 387
Personal sense, 53
Pesticides
  decreased cognitive performance due to, 256

PET, 18–20
Phonemic analysis, 29–30, 32, 37
Phonological analysis, 60. *See also* phonemic
    analysis
    divided attention and, 186
Phonological coding, 113
Phonological deficit hypothesis, 114
Phonological long-term memory, 115
Phonological loop, 113, 162
Phonological short-term memory
    vocabulary acquisition and, 115–117
Physical activity
    relationship to cognitive function of, 257
Picture processing, 63
Pleasantness rating
    effect on recall of, 33–34
Positron emission tomography. *See* PET
Posterior neocortex
    implicit memory tests and, 175
    perceptual modules in, 176
Posterior-anterior gradient
    levels of processing and the, 57
Prefrontal activation, 51
Prefrontal cortex
    differential utilization of, 327
Presentation rates
    effect on recall of, 33–35
Primary memory, 8, 112. *See also* short-term
    memory
    proactive inhibition and, 173
Priming, 9, 21, 42
    age effects seen in tests of, 317
    conceptual, 74–78
    perceptual, 73–74
    working memory and, 118
Proactive inhibition, 171–172
    Korsakoff amnesia and, 173
Proactive interference, 248
    as an accessibility bias effect, 244–246
    fan effects as basis for, 293
Procedural memory, 350
Process dissociation equations, 247–248
Process dissociation framework, 129, 243, 316,
    318
Processing
    concurrent
        bottleneck model of retrieval and, 217–
        222
        shared-time model of memory and, 215–
        217
    divided attention and reduced time of, 194
    impaired associative, 200–204
    relation to storage functions of, 162
    role of memory in, 83
Processing resources

progressive loss of, 154
    reduction in due to aging, 148, 326–328, 363
Prospective memory, 151
    brain activity and, 389–390
Psychopharmacology of encoding, 16–18

Q
Questions
    cueing power of, 40

R
Raney model of text processing, 87–95
Rapid forgetting, 17
Rate of learning
    divided attention and, 180
Reading fluency
    benefits of rereading on, 83–86
Reading span, 149
Recall, 8, 33
    aging effects seen in tests of, 317
    impairment of in patients with schizophre-
        nia, 352
Recency
    effect, 117, 162
    judgments, 8
Recognition memory, 38, 51, 60
    aging effects seen in tests of, 317
    divided attention and, 181, 220
    impairment of in patients with schizophre-
        nia, 352, 386
    increase in with level of processing, 31
    veridical, 374
Recollection deficit *vs.* inhibition deficit
    proactive interference as cause of, 246–247
Record of experience, 43
Redintegration, 117
Redundancy effect, 112
Release-from-PI, 173–174. *See also* proactive
    inhibition
    component process model and, 179
Relevance effect, 62
Remembering, 100
    episodic memory system and, 79
    self-initiated processing and, 287
    vs. knowing, 71, 130, 351
REMO, 124
    limitations of, 125
Repetition effect, 83–84, 364
    mediation of, 86
Replacement model of encoding, 58
Resource demands
    influence of encoding *vs.* retrieval of, 226
Response bias, 78–79
Response integration, 8
Response latency measures, 78

Restraint function of inhibition
  aging and, 288
Retrieval, 8, 52, 105–107
  attentional control of, 212–213
  attentional demands of, 213
  bottleneck model of, 217–222
  brain activity and, 57, 385–386
  effects of divided attention on, 178–188,
    209–212, 228–230, 230–231
  episodic, 350
  frontal lobe involvement in search and
    decision process at, 273
  functional imaging of, 126
  impairment of in patients with schizophre-
    nia, 353
  material-specific interference effects and,
    186–187
  obligatory nature of episodic, 213–214
  reduction in adequacy of due to age-related
    changes in episodic memory, 325
  right frontal involvement in, 126–129, 228,
    326, 386
  role of frontal lobes in difficult processes of,
    270–271
  shared-time model of memory and, 215–217
  vs. encoding, 208
Retrieval conditions, 33
Retrieval cues, 40
Retrieval intentionality criterion, 71–72
  conceptual processing and, 77
  response bias confound in, 78
Retrieval mode. *See* REMO
Retrieval processes, 29, 101–102
  determination of the release of proactive
    inhibition by, 172
Retrieval specification and verification
  Norman-Bobrow theory of, 132
Retrieval volition, 51, 71
  brain activity measures of, 79
  subjective reports of, 78
Retroactive interference, 155–156
Retrograde amnesia, 13–15
Rhyme recognition test, 40, 72
Right prefrontal cortex
  checking processes in, 130–131
  retrieval processes in, 126, 163–164, 228

S
Schizophrenia
  clinical relevance of episodic memory
    defects in, 355–356
  cognitive deficits and memory impairment
    in, 348–349, 385
  episodic memory dysfunction in, 324, 351–
    352

functional mechanisms underlying explicit
    memory impairment in, 352–354
Secondary memory, 8. *See also* long-term
    memory
  release from proactive inhibition and, 173
Secondary task costs, 213, 217
  memory retrieval and, 219, 221–222
Selective attention
  age differences in, 144
  levels of processing in, 137–142
Self-initiated processing, 238, 279–280, 375
  age-related variance and, 284, 287, 385
Self-initiated processing hypothesis, 315–319
Self-referential encoding, 53
  brain activity and, 57
Semantic analysis, 30, 32, 37, 60
Semantic encoding, 53, 113
  brain activity and, 56
Semantic memory, 350
  distinction between episodic memory and,
    29, 228
  divided attention and, 180
  not noetic consciousness and, 71
Semantic processing, 35, 41–42, 102
Semantic similarity, 113
Sensory deprivation hypothesis, 300
Sensory function
  effects of age-related loss in, 300
Sensory psychology, 298
Sensory-cognitive system, 317
  implications of an integrated, 312–313
Serial learning, 8
Serial position effects, study of, 309–311
Serial recall
  immediate, 113
Shallow fixations, 63
Shallow orienting tasks, 34–35
Shared-time model of memory, 215–217
Short-term memory, 8. *See also* primary
    memory
  acoustic and semantic coding in, 113
Signal-detection theory, 240
Simultaneity mechanism, 151
Situation model for text processing, 87–95
Slowing
  deficient access control and, 289
Smoking
  relationship to cognitive function of, 257
Somatic morbidity, 253
Source memory, 156, 239
  aging and, 266
  definition of, 265–266
  divided attention and, 180
  frontal lobe damage and, 175, 266, 273, 316
  frontal lobe impairment and, 384

Source misattributions
   age-related increases in, 363–365
Spatial field, 50
Spatial memory
   speed of processing/working memory and,
      152
Spearman, Charles, 277, 279
Speed-of-processing
   cognitive aging and, 151–152, 164
Spread of encoding, 43
Storage, 8, 118
   hippocampus as critical system for, 126
   relation to processing functions of, 162
   temporary, 120
Strategic elaboration, 196
Strategic functions
   rehabilitation efforts to recover lost, 385
Strategic processes
   impairment of in patients with schizophre-
      nia, 353
Strategic-effortful processing, 227
   impaired encoding due to decrease in, 195–
      198
Stratification paradigm, 48
Strengthened associations, 9
Stroop interference effects, 156, 246, 249
Structural equation modeling, 152
Suggestibility, 387
Symbolic coordinations, 50
Synergies, 50

T
Task emphasis
   memory performance and modulations in,
      212–213
Task switching, 249
TBR, 8
Temporal blocking
   distinctiveness, false recognition and,
      371
Temporary storage, 120
Testing conditions
   encoding and, 40
Text processing
   repetition effect in, 83
Text representation
   integrated model of, 87
Thalamo-pallidar system, 50
Theory of mind, 57
Thyroid disease
   impaired cognitive function due to, 255
To-be-learned, 8
To-be-remembered. See TBR
Top-down processes
   age-related differences in, 312–313

Trace formation, 13
   byproduct theory of, 10–12
   constructive memory and, 15
Trace persistence, 10, 28
Trail Making Test
   profiling age related changes with, 338–339
Transfer effects
   in text processing, 86
Transfer-appropriate processing, 40–41, 43, 48,
      52, 74, 100, 101–102, 230
Transients, 387
Truth effect, 364
Tulving's theory. See GAPS
Two-high-threshold theory, 240, 243, 249

V
Vascular dementia, 254
Vascular diseases
   decreased cognitive function and, 254
Ventrolateral prefrontal cortex
   memory functions and the, 187–188
Verbal intellectual functioning
   retention of with age, 342
Verbal learning, 7, 42
Verbal working memory
   domain-specificity of across life-span, 153
Veridical recognition, 374
Verification process
   right dorsolateral region involvement in, 131
Vertical integration, 58, 61
Vesanic dementia, 356
Vigilance operations
   right dorsolateral region involvement in, 130
Visual analysis, 29–30, 32, 35, 37
Visual processing
   age-related declines in, 165
Visual search, 53–54
Visuospatial sketchpad, 113, 118, 162
Visuospatial working memory
   domain-specificity of across life-span, 153
Vitamin B$_{12}$
   memory disorders due to deficiencies of,
      255
Vitamin deficiencies
   impaired cognitive function due to, 255
Vocabulary
   phonological short term memory and
      acquisition of, 115–117
Voluntary contamination hypothesis, 75

W
Wernicke-Korsakow encephalopathy
   alcoholism and, 256
White matter lesions
   cognitive function and, 254

Wisconsin Card Sorting Test
   profiling age related changes with, 338
Word association
   involuntary elaborative effects in, 74–78
Word recognition
   repetition effect in, 83
Word-centered transfer
   reading fluency and, 86
Word-stem completion
   involuntary lexical effects in, 73–74
Working memory, 106, 111, 350
   aging and inhibitory function in, 155–156
   as an individual differences variable, 149–
      151
   deficient access control in aging and, 289–
      291
   definition of, 148–149
   domain-specificity of across life-span, 153
   impact of aging on, 286–287

   implications of in age-related declines, 156–157
   inhibition functions and, 288
   interaction of with long-term memory, 115,
      118, 162
   perceptual stress and, 305
   proactive interference and, 293
   recency effect and, 118
   role of in long-term phonological learning,
      113
Wundt, Wilhelm, 277

Y
Yes trials
   levels of processing in, 52

Z
Zinc
   cognitive impairment due to deficiencies of,
      255

A. Young: FA-Enc vs FA-Ret.

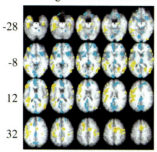

B. Old: FA-Enc. vs. FA-Ret.

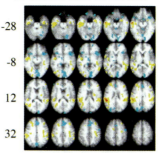

C. Young: FA-Enc vs DA-Enc.

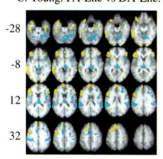

D. Old: FA-Enc. vs. DA-Enc.

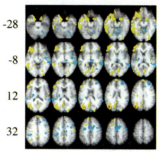

E. FA-Ret. vs. DA-Ret.

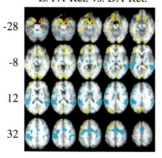

COLOR PLATE I (FIGURE 16.1). Panels A and B show images from full attention conditions for younger and older adults, respectively. Regions that were more active during encoding than retrieval are shown in yellow, and regions that were more active during retrieval than encoding are shown in blue. Panels C and D show images from the encoding conditions, for younger and older adults, respectively. Regions that were more active during full than divided attention encoding are shown in yellow, and regions that were more active in divided than full attention encoding are shown in blue. Panel E shows images from the retrieval conditions for both age groups combined (see text). Regions that were more active during full than divided attention retrieval are shown in yellow, and regions that were more active in divided than full attention are shown in blue. The PET data are superimposed on standard MR images, plotted from $z = -28$ to $z = +48$ mm relative to the AC-PC line, in 4 mm increments. Numbers to the left of each row are the z value of the leftmost image in each row. The left side of each image represents the left side of the brain. From N. D. Anderson et al. (2000).

Pictures

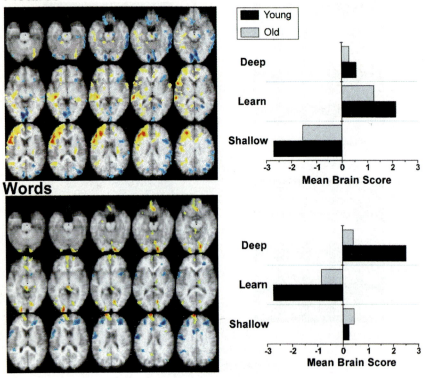

COLOR PLATE II (FIGURE 27.1). Areas of differential blood flow during picture and word encoding carried out using three different strategies (Grady et al., 1999). Areas are shown on magnetic resonance imaging (MRI) templates. Levels relative to the intercommissural line are from −28 mm (top left of images) to +40 mm (bottom right of images). Regions shown in yellow/red have increased activity in those conditions where the mean brain scores (shown in graphs on the right of the figure) are positive. Regions shown in blue have increased activity in those conditions where the mean brain scores are negative. Thus, during both deep picture and deep word encoding, activity was increased in the yellow/red areas seen in the images.